THE

Ocean Sailing

Yacht

VOLUME II

Books by Donald M. Street, Jr.

YACHTING GUIDE TO THE GRENADINES
THE OCEAN SAILING YACHT VOLUME I
A CRUISING GUIDE TO THE LESSER ANTILLES
THE OCEAN SAILING YACHT VOLUME II

THE
OCEAN SAILING YACHT

VOLUME II

by Donald M. Street, Jr.

Drawings by Bruce Bingham

W · W · NORTON & COMPANY
NEW YORK · LONDON

FIRST EDITION

ISBN 0 393 03209 4

1 2 3 4 5 6 7 8 9 0

DEDICATION

In various editorials in *Sail* magazine, Keith Taylor has congratulated the Pardeys, the Roths, the Knights, and the Streets for sailing to the places others dream about, and making their livelihood in the process.

What he has not said is that special praise should go to my wife, Trich. The other wives can accompany their husbands at sea, but Trich must spend much of her time as a captain's widow, taking care of our three children while waiting for the return of *Iolaire* from far places. Those who like my writing should not thank me, but rather my wife, whose patience, understanding, and sacrifices have made it possible for me to spend so much time at sea—gathering the experiences, learning the lessons, that provide material for my books and articles.

Therefore, to Trich, my beautiful wife who so often stays ashore with the family when she would rather be at sea with me, I dedicate this book.

Contents

DRAWINGS

10 CONTENTS

12 CONTENTS

14 CONTENTS

PHOTOS

ACKNOWLEDGMENTS

LIKE Volume I of *The Ocean Sailing Yacht,* this volume would not have seen the light of day without the encouragement of Eric P. Swenson, of W. W. Norton. Bruce Bingham not only did the superb drawings but also served as technical editor, correcting errors and obtaining clarification from me in areas where the information appeared incomplete or hazy. Esther Jacobson again took a disorganized manuscript and reorganized it completely . . . an extremely tough job well done.

Robert Kress, of Michigan Wheel, deserves special credit for drawing up the tables on engines, reduction gears, and propeller sizes; and my thanks go to Jim Wetherald, of Westerbeke, for supplying the information that enabled me to compare the costs of standard engine/propeller installations and those with adjustable-pitch propellers. I am grateful also to Lew Bell, who has provided an expert presentation of methods of soundproofing the engine and engine room. Hugh Merewether was of tremendous help with the discussion of the Ampair wind generator and the Aquair combination wind and water generator. The incomparable library of Jay Paris yielded all sorts of useful items, notably articles published before World War II on propeller drag, and information on the galvanic series of metals.

William Loos, of Loos and Company, Bill Bradley and Harry Spencer, of Spencer Rigging, and Allan MacDonald, of MacDonald Yacht Rigging, all provided much valuable information for the rigging section. As in Volume I, Jon Repke, of Power Products, made substantial contributions to the electrical, mechanical, and refrigeration sections, and this time his assistant, George Stapleton, also helped considerably.

Although Francis Kinney did not personally aid in the preparation of this book, I owe him a great deal. His revision of *Skene's Elements of Yacht Design* provided much of the background material, especially in engineering, for both volumes of *The Ocean Sailing Yacht.* "Skene" should be on every yachtsman's bookshelf.

Thanks should also go to my typists. Ann Glenn, of the trimaran *Rebel,* did a magnificent job of transcribing my early tapes. She had to contend with bad tapes, broken-down tape recorders, and an author she could not contact, but she finally won out. Anne Hammick, Jacqui Dearden, and Gil Hayter, who typed up the manuscript in its later stages, worked under trying circumstances aboard *Iolaire.* And I must acknowledge my debt to my wife, Trich, for her patience as I worked my way through the manuscript, often disappearing into the publisher's office when I should have been at home helping her take care of the family, including three active young children.

Finally, I must pay tribute to *Iolaire*. Celebrating her seventieth birthday, we raced 1,300 miles in three weeks (participating in the fiftieth-anniversary Fastnet Race, followed by the La Rochelle, La Trinité, Benodet, and Solent races), and sailed a total of twelve thousand miles in seven months, continuing my education in maintaining and sailing a good boat.

PREFACE

THE COMMENTS I made in the Preface to Volume I of *The Ocean Sailing Yacht* remain valid. Indeed, the last two paragraphs of that Preface—repeated at the end of this one—are the most important in the entire book. I hope every reader will take them to heart.

Some people may get the impression, in view of my remarks about racing in this volume, that I am against all racing. Nothing could be further from the truth. *Iolaire* and I cross every starting line we can get to, in the cruising division. I am totally uninterested in Grand Prix, ton-level racing, in competition requiring the "skinned-out" yacht. Like thousands of other cruising yachtsmen who love to race, I am searching for a rule that will handicap boats effectively, so that any boat that is well equipped, well skippered, well crewed, and well sailed will stand a chance, whether she is an old C.C.A. cruiser/racer, a converted 8-meter, or a gaff-rigged schooner. Let's hope the rule makers soon come up with a system that will develop good cruising boats capable of racing, instead of the fantastic racing machines developed under the present I.O.R. setup—vessels that only an insane masochist would use for cruising.

Good old boats, like good wine, improve with age. Witness the fact that *Iolaire,* built in 1905, is still going strong; we not only cruise in her but also frequently race, with some success. Her hull is little changed from its original form, though her rig, interior, and deck layout have been vastly altered. An old hull, refitted in the light of modern practice, may give many years of wonderful cruising and occasional racing at a cost that is minimal when compared to the price of a brand-new fiber-glass boat. Furthermore, many a new fiber-glass boat is not designed for serious cruising, but rather is designed to be tied up to a marina each night. Sometimes such a boat can be altered and made into a proper cruising boat.

A final point to remember is that if you sit down and study this book and then insist that everything recommended here be installed on your boat before you set out, you will never go cruising. All life is a compromise, and boats are a tremendous compromise—what is gained in one direction is lost in another. Of course you will wish to make your boat as perfect as possible for the cruising you plan to do, bearing in mind the limitations of the boat, your own time, and your finances, but the essential thing is to get moving. To go cruising is far more important than to spend a lifetime equipping the perfect boat.

J. P. Morgan said, "Young man, if you have to ask how much it costs to keep a yacht, you cannot afford to have one." To this I would have replied, "Mr. Morgan, if I had to wait till I could afford a yacht, I would probably die of a heart attack first, or be too old to enjoy her. I believe I shall buy the yacht, enjoy her, and then figure out how I can support her."

THE

Ocean Sailing

Yacht

VOLUME II

The abbreviation *OSY*-I refers to Volume
I of *The Ocean Sailing Yacht,* by Donald
Street, published by W. W. Norton &
Company, Inc., in 1973.

I

≈≈≈≈≈≈≈≈≈≈≈≈≈≈≈≈≈≈≈

Construction

An ocean sailing yacht can be constructed of wood, steel, aluminum, various combinations of fiber glass and other substances, ferro-cement, almost anything; good proper construction, whatever the materials, is long-lasting. However, every type of construction has its advantages and disadvantages. The yachtsman must decide which is best for him, taking into account the cruising to be done, the materials available, the skills of the builder, the skills of the owner, the money available. Dreaming of an absolutely perfect boat, and trying to build one, often results in building no boat at all.

One would think we were in an age of built-in obsolescence—many yachtsmen are buying boats as they formerly bought cars, changing them every two years. Doing this in an attempt to obtain the ideal ocean sailing yacht is ridiculous. Just to shake down a yacht takes twenty-four to thirty-six months of continuous sailing and living on board, or from five to eight seasons of four to six months each.

Despite what some salesmen of fiber-glass boats suggest when comparing fiber-glass construction with other types of construction, a properly built wooden boat will last practically forever. Given good maintenance and careful handling, she can be passed from one generation to the next. It is amazing to see the number of boats, literally hundreds, that were built before 1905 and are still going strong. Among the more notable are *Dolly Varden,* built in 1872 and still afloat today; *Nell,* a fifty-five-foot ketch, built by William Fife of Fairlie in 1887 and sailing today in good shape and without the aid of an engine; *Vagrant,* a little plank-on-edge cutter, built in 1885 and still to be seen sailing around Dublin Bay; *Paz,* a thirty-five-foot yawl, designed and built by George Lawley in 1888 and still sailing on the

Chesapeake; and *Playmate,* built in Littletown, New Zealand, in 1888 and racing and occasionally winning even today. In addition, there are a number of iron Dutch boeiers dating back to the turn of the century or earlier, but of course it is uncertain whether they were built as yachts, or were originally commercial boats and were later converted into yachts. As we finish this volume, we are collecting material for the next book, on classic yachts built in 1905 or earlier that are still going strong. Any information on this subject that readers can supply will be appreciated.

My own *Iolaire* was built in 1905 by the Harris brothers of Row-hedge, England, and has been described by John Leather, historian for the area, as "a cheap boat built on spec": she was not designed by the builders from a half model or on the stocks, by eye, but rather was simply laid off full size on the mold-loft floor, and then built. She was bronze-fastened to the rail cap but unfortunately iron-fastened across the deck (the reason her deck now looks like a parquet floor!), and the frame futtocks were joined by iron pins. This use of iron has cost me a tremendous amount of money and time over the years. However, *Iolaire* at seventy-two is still going strong; she celebrated her seventieth birthday by sailing twelve thousand miles in seven months, racing 1,300 miles in twenty-two days, beating all the way up the Thames River to St. Katharine's dock in London, and visiting her birthplace on the Colne River at Rowhedge—all without the aid of an engine.

One's ideas on the ideal yacht are bound to be ever-changing, as each new experience broadens one's outlook. Despite a lifetime of sailing, by the time *Iolaire*'s seventieth-birthday cruise was half over, I had altered my views on my dream boat.

I formerly thought that the ideal cruising boat which I would build to replace my dear old *Iolaire,* were I to win the Irish Sweepstakes and have unlimited money, would have the same hull—the forefoot cut away slightly more, but only slightly. She would have twelve inches more beam, for added stability and interior room. The construction would be of aluminum, and the consequent reduction in weight would allow me to increase the ratio of ballast to displacement (one of her problems is that she has too much wood and not enough lead); also, the aluminum construction would give me an additional eight inches of interior space. Her stability would also be increased by integral tanks, which because of her shape, would have a capacity of probably four hundred gallons; she would be a real cruising boat that could afford water for showers. Admittedly, there would be the danger of making her so stiff that the motion would be bothersome, but it is easy enough to reduce stability.

However, while racing in Europe, I heard the noise made by aluminum boats, and discussed with their crews the problems of aluminum—the fact, for example, that it is hot in the tropics and cold in northern climates. As a result, I began to think that wood would be preferable to aluminum for my ideal replacement of *Iolaire*. There were other reasons too for my change of heart, among them the fact that because so many yards have stopped building wooden boats, the stocks of aged wood in England, Scotland, and Ireland were better in 1975 than they were five years before. And some yards were still interested in building in wood.

In addition to wood construction, *Iolaire II* would have six inches or a foot more beam, four inches more freeboard, steam-bent frames, and bronze floors, the latter making possible big water tanks in the bilge which would contribute to stability. There would be heavy bronze chain plates tied to diagonal strapping, the keel being joined to the structure not only by normal internal floors but by external bronze straps at every fourth frame (Drawing 1). The lead ballast keel would be used also as the structural keel, so that the wooden keel could be eliminated, as in Herreshoff's *Nereia*. This method of construction goes back a long way; it did not originate with L. Francis Herreshoff—rather, he inherited it from his father, who was pretty well retired by 1928!

The rudder would have an almost vertical trailing edge, placing the widest part of the blade way down low. The deck would be of ⅜-inch plywood, covered, at a minimum, by ¾-inch teak bedded in bitumastic, and clamps and shelves would be replaced by plywood gussets or hanging knees tying each deck beam onto the frame head. The bulwarks would be bolted into oversized sheer strakes.

These changes would preserve all the advantages of wood construc-

1. *Iolaire II*'s chain plates tied to diagonal strapping, and external bronze straps joining keel to structure at every fourth frame.

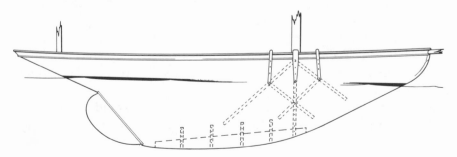

tion, while resulting in a vessel more modern and more thoughtfully built than *Iolaire,* with an increase in the ratio of ballast to displacement—and hence in her stiffness and in her windward-going ability—along with considerably more interior space.

However, although I still feel that *for me* the ideal offshore cruising boat is a modernized *Iolaire,* I am firmly convinced that for longshore work in the waters of the Lesser Antilles, the Bahamas, the east coast of the United States, or Europe, a true, *simple* Freedom 40 (as discussed in the section on cat ketches in Chapter III) is the cruising man's dream boat.

The conclusions about returning to wood were reached in the light of investigations done regarding the proposed construction of an ocean sailing yacht for Joe Huggins. He chartered *Iolaire* for a week in order to sail with me and pick my brains concerning the design for a proper ocean sailing yacht. We discussed in great detail the possibility of adapting existing stock designs, and finally concluded that in view of the costs involved, he would be better off starting from scratch and building a vessel suited to his specific needs. Since Joe is 6 feet 4 inches tall, and Marcia, his wife, is 6 feet tall, a normal boat, with no more than 6 feet 2 inches of headroom, would not fit the bill. Also, he and Marcia wanted a boat that would really sail—not an I.O.R. racing machine, but one that could still beat to windward, that could take them wherever they wished without their having to wait for the wind to blow in the right direction. He commissioned Jay Paris as designer and myself as consultant. The result was the fifty-four-foot *Lone Star.*

The hull is designed along the classic Herreshoff lines, which we decided to try and preserve even though for our purposes *Mobjack* was a little too small, *Bounty* and *Tioga* were a little too large, and the freeboard in both designs was too low. However, since Joe and Marcia desired a large after cabin, we decided to bridge straight across the boat, back aft of a midship cockpit, where the bulwarks are quite high.

The profile is pure Herreshoff. The midship section was originally patterned after that of Herreshoff's *Nereia,* but was later changed in an effort to minimize displacement, and is now halfway between that of *Nereia* and that of *Bounty.*

The rig is like *Iolaire*'s: double-headsail, with a fair-sized main and a short mizzen. Technically, *Lone Star* is a ketch, since the mizzen is inside the after end of the waterline, but it is so short that she is practically a yawl.

It was decided from the beginning that the boat would have a fully feathering, fully reversible, adjustable-pitch propeller, as Joe did not want to be perpetually burdened with unnecessary drag. Also, she was to have an inboard rudder with a trim tab, as described in Chapter II.

In my role as consultant, I collected notes for many months, and then gave them to Morgan MacDonald III for incorporation in a preliminary design. When this preliminary design arrived, I was still investigating the various methods of construction. Sailing from Glandore, Ireland, to the Canaries I had plenty of time to think about the problems, and once in the Canaries I assembled my notes and dictated a tape to Joe Huggins describing the advantages and disadvantages of the different methods of construction, as I saw them. My conclusions are summarized in the following pages.

CONSTRUCTION RULES

As has been oft said, a good boat can be built out of practically any material known to man, provided she is correctly designed and well engineered. With today's new materials, the engineering problems, including collation of the strengths of the materials, are difficult because the designers and builders have had so little time to work them out.

Whether a boat is to be made of wood, fiber glass, steel, cement, or what-have-you, the type of use that is anticipated should be taken into account in the design. A vessel that is never going to leave Long Island Sound need not be as strong as one that will be going around Cape Horn. A cruising boat must, as I have stated a thousand times, be a compromise. Strong construction is necessary, but there is a limit; a boat should not be so strong that there is not enough room for adequate ballast. At the same time, no boat should be so light that while there is plenty of room for ballast, she is stiffer than a church and likely to suffer structurally.

Various rules exist which can serve as guides to successful construction. The owner or prospective owner of a boat already built may examine the construction in the light of these rules and determine whether the vessel is either weak or overconstructed.

WOOD CONSTRUCTION

There are three well-known sets of rules for wood construction—Lloyd's, Herreshoff's, and Nevins'. Lloyd's rules, published by Lloyd's Register of Shipping, deal with the construction of wooden yachts of all sizes likely to be considered. The older editions of these rules also cover the construction of composite yachts—those with wooden decks, planking, and backbones, but steel (or iron) framing.

Herreshoff's rules are also frequently used, and reading them carefully is a most interesting experience. They were formulated by Nathanael G. Herreshoff—the "wizard of Bristol"—and published in 1928 at the request of the New York Yacht Club. They were put together in the twilight of Herreshoff's career, and reflect views he had been developing since 1878. Early editions of these rules are now collector's items, but their text can be found in Francis S. Kinney's revision of Norman L. Skene's *Elements of Yacht Design.*

It should be remembered when reading Herreshoff's rules that they are based on the assumption that extremely good woods, and superb craftsmen, will be available. Also, as suggested by the very light scientific construction these rules call for, they were largely used for racing yachts. Not unexpectedly, in view of Herreshoff's interest in the universal rule, they appear to have been significantly influenced by the standards for the universal-rule boats. However, I think that if one could check with people who knew Captain Nat in the last years of his life, they would state that the rules were regarded as general guides, not absolute prescriptions. In the design of cruising yachts the scantlings were undoubtedly increased slightly because the ballast-to-displacement ratio was not all that important, but longevity was. The rules obviously worked well, even though they called for fairly light construction; if one were to go through *Lloyd's Register of American Yachts,* one would immediately realize that of the yachts still afloat that date back to the years before World War I, between two-thirds and three-quarters were built by Herreshoff.

Nevins' rules are quite similar to Herreshoff's, but simpler to use. They were developed in the 1920's and 1930's by the Henry B. Nevins yard, which was largely staffed by refugees from the Herreshoff Manufacturing Company. Once again, the assumption is that supremely good craftsmen and extremely good materials are available.

When the various rules are compared, it should be noted that Lloyd's rules call for the use of much larger masses of material to hold the boat together, and little or no diagonal strapping, whereas Herreshoff's and Nevins' rules rely heavily on diagonal strapping, which evidently contributed considerably to the strength of the vessel. Exactly why the strapping was put on the way it was (Drawing 2) remains slightly a mystery; I have not found any engineers who have been able to come up with the answer. Many designers that I have talked to would recommend strapping a wooden boat as shown in Drawing 3.

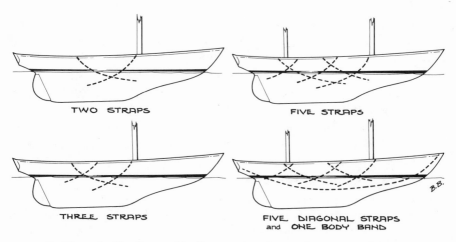

2. Herreshoff's diagonal hull strapping for various mast placements.

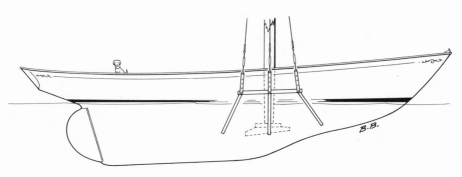

3. Simple strapping as recommended by most designers today.

Diagonal strapping on the deck of a boat is expensive, but the deck will maintain strength and watertightness. If plywood decking is used, the strapping can be dispensed with.

There is one problem with diagonal strapping: once the strapping was secured to the framing, how did Herreshoff secure the plank to the frame at the point where a plank and a diagonal strap crossed? If a hole were drilled through the bronze, the screw would be slack in the planking; if a clear hole were not drilled in the diagonal strap, the screw would not penetrate it. I would appreciate hearing from anyone who knows how this problem was solved.

Between the frames, the diagonal strapping was secured to the planking with screws from the inside out; that is no problem, and is easily understood.

Another construction feature shown in Skene is the body band. This was probably installed in long-ended universal-rule boats, and in their predecessors which were even more long-ended. The "banana effect" is nothing new in yachting; Herreshoff had trouble with this effect at the turn of the century on some of his boats, which were literally bent by the strain of the staysail stay and the backstays leading to the stern. Sometimes the effect was mitigated by running a huge, heavy wire from a turnbuckle at the stemhead fitting down through sheaves bolted to the floors underneath the cabin sole and all the way back by the rudderpost to the stern. The wire was set up tight on a turnbuckle.

A close reading of Herreshoff's rules also makes it apparent that another long-standing construction practice is the use of the ballast keel as a structural keel. As was pointed out earlier, this has been done off and on for the past seventy years. The method bears a lot more investigating, as it eliminates the necessity of trying to find a really large seasoned block of timber.

STEEL CONSTRUCTION

Construction rules for all sizes of steel yachts are available from Lloyd's Register of Shipping. On this side of the ocean, the American Bureau of Shipping puts out rules for steel construction, but they are not really applicable to modern yachts, since they have to do with much larger vessels.

ALUMINUM CONSTRUCTION

Lloyd's has issued a set of rules for aluminum construction, but to the best of my knowledge nothing comparable has been developed on this side of the ocean. The designers and builders just work from their past experience.

FIBER-GLASS CONSTRUCTION

Lloyd's has formulated rules for fiber-glass construction, but there is disagreement among designers and builders as to whether these rules lead to optimum results. In this country, no rules concerning fiber-glass construction for small yachts are available, though the American Bureau of Shipping has issued a set of rules for larger vessels. It is alleged that if the American Bureau of Shipping rules are analyzed, they are seen to be definitely not in agreement with Lloyd's. Which set of rules is best is a subject of much debate.

FERRO-CEMENT CONSTRUCTION

Both Lloyd's and the American Bureau of Shipping are trying to formulate rules for ferro-cement construction, but as yet they have not done so.

WOOD

There has recently been a resurgence of interest in the building of wooden boats. This is reflected, for example, in the development of the apprenticeship programs run by the Museum of Maritime America, in Mystic, Connecticut, the Marine Museum, in Bath, Maine, and the Mariners Museum, in Newport News, Virginia, and is also indicated by the increasing popularity of that wonderful magazine *WoodenBoat*.

Wood construction has many advantages. To begin with, we have thousands of years of experience behind us. A well-built wooden boat will last an amazingly long time. A traditional wooden boat can be repaired anywhere in the world. On an uninhabited island in the Pacific, a palm tree can be cut down and sawn into planks if necessary, for use temporarily, until a good yard is reached. Deck leaks on a soundly constructed boat are relatively few, and are traceable and pluggable. Also, water from leaks in the hull runs down into the bilge and is pumped out, and that's that!

As a material, wood has many desirable properties. It is a very good insulator; a wooden boat is easy to keep warm in winter and cool in summer. Further, wood is a good deadener of sound. Slamming into a head sea, an aluminum or fiber-glass boat can be very noisy if not adequately insulated; on a wooden boat the noise level can usually be considerably lower. Wood has great aesthetic appeal. Certainly, nothing is more beautiful than *Aleph*—the sister ship of the original *Ondine*—built by Abeking and Rasmussen in 1952. Today, lying in English Harbour with her varnish work immaculate, she looks as if she came out of the builder's yard last year. Admittedly, keeping her covered with that much varnish is expensive. But the owner possesses an *objet d'art* that also sails like a witch.

In recent years, wood construction has developed a bad name because of the admittedly high maintenance costs it often entails. However, one should not compare apples and oranges—the maintenance expenses for a wooden boat that is twenty, thirty, or forty years old as against the corresponding expenses for a steel, ferro-cement, fiber-glass, or aluminum boat that is brand new. For two *new boats,* one of wood and the other, say, of fiber glass, the maintenance costs for the engine and electrical and electronic equipment (50 percent of the total maintenance bill for the average cruising boat), and for plumbing, sails, and running rigging, will be exactly alike. Below-deck and on-deck costs will be more or less the same, depending, in the case of a fiberglass boat, on how much wood has been used. Only with respect to maintenance of the topside and the bottom will the costs differ.

Topside maintenance will of course be more expensive for a wooden boat, which will have to be painted once a year, than for a fiber-glass boat, whose original gel coat should last four or five years. However, keeping the gel coat in good shape will require cleaning, polishing, and so on. The total expenditure of time, energy, and money on this job may be as high as 50 percent of the maintenance costs for the topside of a new wooden boat. For new steel and aluminum boats, the topside maintenance costs may sometimes be as high as those for wooden boats.

Bottom painting is necessary for boats of all types once or twice a year, depending on the circumstances. During the first ten years the cost of bottom maintenance for a wooden boat should be about equal to that for a boat made of another material. It is much easier to get antifouling paint to stick to a wooden bottom than to a nonwooden one. On both steel and aluminum boats, anticorrosive paints and barrier coats must be applied before the antifouling paint. Fiberglass and ferro-cement hulls need no barrier coats, but do require special painting procedures (the paint manufacturer can be consulted for details). The difficulty of getting paint to adhere to these two materials is shown by the fact that boats built of fiber glass or ferro-cement frequently exhibit great bare patches when hauled.

Modern bottom paints have reduced the terror of the teredo to a minimum. On *Iolaire* and other well-maintained wooden boats, I have seen few problems with teredo damage. Bottom paints have improved greatly in the last twenty years. When I first came to the tropics in *Iolaire,* it was necessary to haul three times a year to keep a clean bottom. As the years went by and bottom paints improved, hauling became a twice-a-year proposition; then it was done every nine months, and now, with International Bottomkote, we haul once a year.

As a vessel grows older, the maintenance bill increases. On a wooden boat seams will need recaulking, bolts will have to be removed or tightened up, and so on. A fiber-glass boat may develop problems with blisters on the bottom. If comparisons are made between the maintenance costs for boats of similar age, instead of between those for old wooden boats and for new boats of other materials, it will be seen that the wooden boats' reputation for having excessive maintenance costs is highly undeserved.

Like maintenance costs, the costs of new wood construction turn out to be somewhat lower than might have been expected. The yards building in wood today are relatively small. They are not supporting high-priced buildings, big front-office staffs, and salesmen. They are not spending large sums on advertising, or giving brokers and distributors as much as 20 to 40 percent of the total cost of a boat. At this writing, if the construction is kept simple, the cost of a wooden boat can be held to about $2.20 per displacement pound in England, Ireland, and Scotland. In Down East Maine, and in Nova Scotia, the cost will be about $3.50 to $4.00 per displacement pound. Some of the old-time managers who used to build in wood and are now putting out production fiber-glass boats will admit—when backed into a corner—that they can probably build a wooden boat (especially "one off") for less than a fiber-glass boat.

Furthermore, the assumption that there is a shortage of men capable of working in wood does not hold water. So many yards have discontinued wooden-boat construction that the few left have available a pool of labor to call upon, consisting of those who have stopped working and those who are at other yards, building, say, with fiber glass but ready to quit at once given the chance because they like working with wood.

The older yards still building wooden boats are likely to have shipwrights and senior men who are in their late fifties or early sixties. Many of these people started working at the age of twelve or fourteen, undistracted by T.V., motorcycles, and the like. In their youth their only interest was in building boats, and today they still have pride in workmanship and in the finished product. They are a different breed of men from those in the labor force of the fiber-glass-boat manufacturer.

Of course, there are some disadvantages to wood. For one thing, if the boat is to have a long, trouble-free life, the construction must be excellent. Very strict specifications must be drawn up, governing the selection of the wood, seasoning, rot prevention (both by the application of wood preservatives and by proper ventilation of the completed boat), the choice of materials for fastenings, and—of course—the actual construction of the vessel. Bad wooden boats are unbelievably bad; good wooden boats are wonderful. Unfortunately, the young designers coming along today are usually interested only in fiber glass, aluminum, or esoteric methods of using wood. For this reason, the person intending to build in wood must seek out a designer who really knows the material—not just the new methods but the old traditional ways of doing things. There is no substitute for experience in the design and construction of a wooden boat.

Furthermore, even among the traditional wooden-boat designers there are some who do not adhere to the time-proven rules, so that although they design good-looking, fast boats, their methods of construction leave much to be desired. The little schooners of the Chester area in Nova Scotia, for instance, are famous—or rather infamous—in that exactly what holds the keel onto the rest of the boat seems to be a great mystery. Anyone who owns a Nova Scotia schooner (and some Maine schooners are weak in the same respect) would be well advised to read the section on outside bronze floors later in this chapter, and install outside straps to keep the ballast keel, wooden keel, and frames firmly together.

Another of the major problems in building in wood today is the difficulty in obtaining seasoned timber. However, with patience, it is generally possible to take advantage of a long lead time. Between the day one first thinks about having one's dream boat designed and built, and the day the keel is finally laid, as much as two or three years may have passed. This has been the case with *Lone Star;* the preliminary conception—displacement, sail area, accommodation, and the like—was developed in April, 1975, but the keel is not being laid until January, 1978. If the timber is purchased as soon as the decision to build has been made, and if it is at once picked up from the warehouse and delivered to the builder, you are home free. First of all, timber that is even halfway decently aged when first purchased, will be well aged three years later. Second, costs are going up so rapidly that the money spent is as good as money in the bank. If at the end of three years you decide not to build your boat, good, well-aged, air-dried timber will have gone up in value so much that you will most likely be able to sell it at a profit.

However, one should not build in wood unless one really loves wood. Love of wood is just as important as technical knowledge and skill. Few people would say that working with fiber glass, steel, or aluminum is aesthetically pleasing, but working among nice, clean, fresh-smelling wood shavings is a deeply satisfying experience.

TYPES OF WOOD CONSTRUCTION

Composite

This type of construction—consisting of wooden hulls with steel framing, clamps, and deck beams, and steel girders supporting the stem, stern, keel, and horn timber—is very rarely seen today, but was popular between the wars. A boat built in this manner, if she is well constructed originally and well maintained, apparently will last almost forever. The clipper ship *Cutty Sark,* now on permanent exhibit in Greenwich, England, is of composite construction, with teak planking secured to iron frames, and it is believed that she is in such condition that with a good refit she might possibly even sail again. Similarly, the hull survey reports for *Eilean,* a seventy-two-foot ketch designed and built by Fife, and for *Zigeuner,* a fifty-five-foot yawl designed and built by Robertson, indicate the durability that can sometimes be attained in composite boats under proper conditions. However, if leaks are allowed to start, dead water may lie in the bilge and the boats can deteriorite very rapidly.

Few, if any, yards employ the composite method today. George McGruer stated in 1975 that he felt it would still be possible to build a boat in this manner, but did not know how the costs would compare with those for conventional wood construction.

Cold Molding

Large cold-molded hulls have been with us since World War II, having been pioneered by A. E. "Bill" Luders in his Luders 24's (basically small 6-meters) and his beautiful little Luders 16's. The ultimate in cold molding is probably found at Souter's of Cowes. This method of construction—in which the hull is built up out of thin strips of wood laminated to the desired thickness and molded into shape—produces a light, strong, rigid vessel. It is a somewhat expensive method, and should be undertaken only by an extremely good yard, since proper quality control is essential.

There are some disadvantages. For one thing, though a hole knocked in the side of the hull can be fixed, the process is troublesome and expensive. Also, delamination has been known to occur, and this is most difficult to repair. By the same token, some insurance underwriters dislike this type of hull because if there is damage to some part of it, and the owner insists on a repair that gives "new for old," he may have to get practically a whole new hull, and will expect reimbursement accordingly.

Epoxy Saturation

In the newest method of wooden-boat construction, epoxy is used first to saturate layers of wood and then to laminate them, so that the whole structure is basically a single epoxy unit. The result is an extremely beautiful, light, rigid hull, as seen in *Golden Daisy,* Dr. Gerry Murphy's 1975 Canada's Cup winner. The method appears to be superb, but of course it has not been around as long as conventional wood construction. To find how it will stand the test of time, one can only gaze into a crystal ball.

Strip Planking

Strip planking is a very old method of construction; indeed, it was used for some of the boats now in the Museum of Maritime America, in Mystic, which were built in the last century. The method enjoyed a resurgence of popularity in the 1950's and early 1960's, in two adaptations. In one of these, the procedure was to strip-plank the hull and fiber-glass the outside, leaving the inside to be coated with paint, wood preservative, or what-have-you. In the other, the procedure was to strip-plank the hull and then seal it inside and out with Dynel cloth and resin. The first of these procedures seems to produce a fair amount of rot; the second seems to produce massive amounts. However, saturating the planks in epoxy before they are used appears to eliminate this problem.

Sheet Plywood Covered with Fiber Glass

Construction of sheet plywood covered with fiber glass may be suitable for light racing dinghies or for rowing dinghies, but it should not be considered for an ocean sailing yacht unless budgetary limitations make it the best practical alternative. One class of ocean sailing yacht built by this method in the 1950's developed a bad reputation for rot in the Lesser Antilles, and some owners took heavy losses. Almost invariably, the widespread rot under the fiber glass makes extensive—and expensive—repairs necessary.

FRAMES

Grown Wood Frames

Grown wood frames are made from natural crooks, which are seldom seen today. However, obtaining them is not impossible, and if you are building your own boat, or having a small yard build her, it may be desirable to do so. Grown wood frames are tremendously strong and are especially suitable for the aft sections of the boat, where steam bending is very difficult. While your dream boat is still in the planning stage, if you drive through the New England countryside some fall day, you will find the ideal timber for keels, knees, frames, and the like —Herreshoff's beloved pasture-grown white oak. Buy the tree as it stands in the pasture, and have the farmer fell it. In this day and age, it is relatively easy to cut it with a chain saw into pieces that can be loaded into a truck. A couple of weekends' work, and the aid of the farmer's tractor, may be needed for grubbing out the stump. Cart the whole thing home and store it, and natural crooks are available for building your vessel.

In years gone by, grown and sawn frames were merely pinned together—a source of weakness, especially if the pins were made of iron. Today, the frames are not only screwed and/or pinned together but also joined with an epoxy glue, and are therefore much stronger than formerly. This was aptly demonstrated when *Daru* was wrecked; her sawn frames, glued together, were infinitely stronger than anyone could have expected.

Sawn Frames

If the services of a really good mold loftsman are available, building with sawn frames does have a great advantage. When the thirty-eight-foot ketch *Daru,* and her sister ships, were built, the loftsman not only laid out the frames but determined the bevel of each frame and marked the timber accordingly, every foot or so. Then a long arm was bolted to the band-saw table, and when the frames were being cut, the table was tilted to follow the markings for the bevels. As a result, when the frames were set up, only a little trimming of the bevel was required to fair them up to receive the planking. Ron Smith estimates that this precutting of the bevels saved a hundred hours of labor.

Steam-Bent Wood Frames

The steam-bent frame (known as a "timber" to our British cousins) is more commonly used on the east coast of the United States than on the west coast and in England, where grown or sawn frames are often used. Because the grain runs the full length of the frame, a steam-bent frame is infinitely stronger than one which is grown or sawn. Nevins' rules for the construction of wooden yachts specify that sawn or grown frames should have a sectional area 50 percent greater than that listed in the tables for steam-bent frames with an equivalent function. Lloyd's rules for the construction of wooden yachts make no direct comparisons of the sizes required for the various types of frame. However, examination of the Lloyd's formula for frame sizes, and of the tables provided, indicates that basically Lloyd's rules require grown frames to be 40 percent heavier than steam-bent frames for similar vessels with similar frame spacing. Nathanael Herreshoff had such a low opinion of sawn frames that he never even mentioned them in his rules for the construction of wooden yachts. It might also be noted that the men at the Herreshoff Manufacturing Company were so good at steam bending that they steam bent frames of much larger size than practically any other yard in the world.

The inexperienced person who attempts steam bending may come to a lot of grief unless he remembers certain fundamentals. *Green* oak should be used. The general rule of thumb in deciding the duration of steaming is thirty minutes per square inch of section. A frame steamed too long becomes brittle. One must work fast and use plenty of clamps.

Bending frames of up to 1½ by 1½ inches is not very difficult, but for those above that size expert supervision is necessary. One way to keep the process manageable when a larger frame is needed is to make it of two smaller frames bent on the flat and laid one on top of the other, with the fastening penetration both layers of wood. For *Lone Star,* 2½-by-1¼-inch frames are being made in this manner.

The method was used back in the late 1940's by the Purdy Boat Company for the seventy-foot motor sailer *Sorrento.* Her frames consist of two layers bent on the flat and secured with through bolts and screws, and even today they show no sign of problems.

There seems to be no limit to the size of frame that can be steam bent, given the time, money, skill, and energy. John Gardner, of the Museum of Maritime America, in Mystic, points out that in 1876 a full-rigged ship of 1,500 tons, *The New Era,* built of wood in the United States, had steam-bent frames that were 24 by 24 inches at the heel, 18 by 18 inches at the head, and about 30 feet long. How they were bent no one knows, but they certainly were.

Similarly, the men who worked at Herreshoff, Lawley, and Luders during World War II tell unbelievable stories of how eighty-three-footers for the U.S. Coast Guard, and nonmagnetic mine sweepers, were framed by a gang of experts in incredibly short times despite the large size of the steam-bent frames that were required.

FLOORS

Wooden Floors

In the average American yacht the wooden floor is a straight timber fitted across the keel and secured with three bolts per frame (Drawing

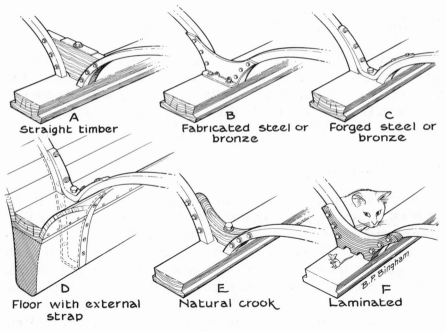

4. Keel floors.

4A). Since the floors are quite deep, installation of water tanks underneath the cabin sole is rather difficult.

In old British vessels, natural crooks were usually used for wooden floors (Drawing 4E). Today, these are not obtainable commercially, but as has been pointed out, it may be possible for the individual to buy a suitable tree out in the country and cut it up. (Another alternative, when natural crooks are not available, is to use laminated floors, as shown in Drawing 4F). Floors made of natural crooks or laminates are infinitely stronger than floors of straight timber, since the grain is continuous from arm to arm. Also, the arms can be extended up the frames, giving additional support to the frames.

By contrast, in most vessels of Nova Scotian construction, the heel of the frame is boxed into the keel and secured with a single fastening, and a few floors are placed haphazardly on the keel, without being attached to the frames. Eventually, the fastening in the heel of the frame works loose, the keel is attached to the rest of the boat by the garboard only, and leaks result. As a result, surveyors are very suspicious of boats built in this manner.

Steel Floors

Many boats have floors that are fabricated of steel and have flanges, or angles, for use in bolting them to the keel and/or frames (Drawing 4B). If these floors are well galvanized, with zincs being used, and if the bilge is kept dry and all bolts piercing the planking and framing are well plugged on the outside, they will last a very long time. The floors of the classic Fife boats built in the 1920's and 1930's are still doing fine. However, if water is allowed to accumulate in the bilge, or any electrolysis develops, deterioration will be incredibly fast.

Forged-Steel Floors

What are usually referred to as forged-iron floors are generally made not of iron, but of a type of low-carbon steel, less strong than modern steel, but much more corrosion resistant. They are strap floors forged of solid blocks of metal, without angles, and laid across the keel and inside the frames (Drawing 4C). Since they are bolted through the frames and the planking, they can be easily removed; indeed, the common practice has been to pull the floors out of the deepest part of the bilge every twenty years or so, and use them as patterns for their own replacements.

An advantage of these floors is that they take up no room in the bilge, so water tanks can be dropped in on top of them. A disadvantage is that they must be checked across the throat every few years, since they do tend to corrode there.

Bronze Floors

Bronze floors are sometimes cast in the same shape as the forged-steel floors (Drawing 4C), and at other times are made in strap and angle form, like the fabricated steel floors (Drawing 4B).

Bronze floors are very strong, and under proper conditions can be expected to outlive the boat. However, electrolysis may occur when several different types of bronze are present. Therefore, the same type of bronze should be used for floors, keel bolts, floor-timber bolts, and so on. Indeed, if possible, all the bronze should be purchased from the same foundry, so that there will be no variation in the alloy.

Outside Bronze Floors

Through the years, I have noticed on many a boat bronze straps extending from the lead keel up over the wooden keel and bolted through the frames (Drawing 4D). These are generally said to have been installed after the boat was constructed, to add strength and to stop the keel from wiggling and keep the garboard seam tight when the boat is heeled down going to weather. As a quick look at Drawing 5A

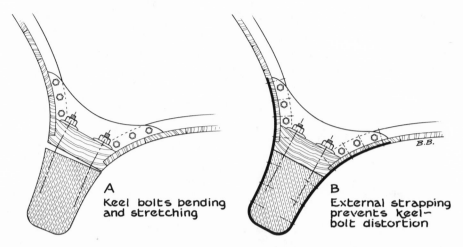

A
Keel bolts bending
and stretching

B
External strapping
prevents keel-
bolt distortion

5. Keel-bolt distortion and its cure.

will make clear, in this situation the keel bolts do have a tendency to bend, and no matter how infinitesimal this bending is, the windward garboard seam does try to open. The problem is largely eliminated when outside strap floors are installed (Drawing 5B). Indeed, Herreshoff's rules specify floors of this type for original construction. If more yacht designers read these rules and acted accordingly, there would be far fewer wooden boats troubled with leaking garboards.

Installation of outside strap floors on an older wooden boat is relatively simple. Depending on the size of the boat, they will be from ⅛ inch up to perhaps ¼ inch thick. Those which are no more than 3/16 inch thick are relatively simple to bend and to replace. Secured to the lead keel with screws, and bolted through the frames, these straps will strengthen any boat. They will be especially effective in the frames under the mast step, where, if ⅛-inch straps are used, they can be carried right down under the stem and up the other side and bolted into place; separation of the keel from the garboard will then be virtually impossible.

BACKBONES

As L. Francis Herreshoff has pointed out, obtaining a wide piece of oak, well seasoned, for a keel is difficult; hence, people frequently use teak or some other comparable hardwood. In some areas, pitch pine and good Oregon pine (also called Douglas fir) have been used with success. In his own designs (see *The Common Sense of Yacht Design*) he sometimes solved the problem by dispensing with a wooden keel altogether, adding antimony to the lead when casting the keel. The lead keel fastened to the garboard with bronze screws (the floors being attached to the keel with lag screws or bolts) has withstood the test of time. Old-fashioned long-keel designs, such as those of Herreshoff's own *Nereia* and *Araminta,* are admirably suited for this method, which did not originate with L. Francis Herreshoff but rather with his father, Nathanael.

Stopwaters

Stopwaters (*OSY*-I, Drawing 1) frequently cause leaks in older boats. What most people forget, even good carpenters, is that a stopwater should be installed in the rabbet at each stem scarf, and every stopwater should be covered by the plank edges. After many years of fighting stem leaks in the stopwater area, I have come to the conclusion that when such a leak starts, if one cannot really stop it immediately by tightening the stem bolts, one had best not waste time on temporary measures such as trying to put in another stopwater outside the planking edge, or through the planking. Instead, the planks on each side that cover the stem scarf and stopwater should be removed, the scarf bolts driven out, and the seam and joint carefully cleaned, to remove the caulking in the planks and the dirt in the joint that make it impossible to really tighten up the stem scarf and stopwater. Then the stopwater is knocked out, new bolts are installed, the whole shebang is cinched tight back together again, and a new stopwater and new planks are installed.

CEILINGS

In the wooden commercial vessel of traditional design, the ceiling consisted of inside planking firmly spiked to the frames and forming an integral portion of the structure. A boat with a hole knocked in her outside planking might literally float on her tightly caulked ceiling. However, in the dead air spaces between the inner and outer planking, rot frequently commenced. To prevent this, the area above the shelf and clamp might be blocked off with wooden salt boxes that had holes drilled in their bottoms; rock salt dropped into the boxes would run down the side of the hull. In a large vessel, as much as a ton or so of rock salt would periodically be packed into the salt boxes.

In traditional yachts, the ceiling—as specified by both Herreshoff's and Nevins' rules—was installed from the depth of the bilge right up to within one plank of the sheer strake. An air space left up above was supposed to make it possible for air to circulate behind the ceiling. Closely fitted (normally of tongue-and-groove construction) and firmly fastened to the frames, the ceiling formed an integral part of the vessel—in effect, a partial girder. Belt frames were installed on top of it at certain points to strengthen the boat, and bulkheads with interior joiner work were then attached to the ceiling.

At first glance, this arrangement may appear satisfactory; however, ventilation behind the ceiling was poor at best, and in many instances, eventually the frames were completely rotted out, so that the vessel was held together just by the shelf clamp, bilge stringer, and caulked planking. Once a boat that is ceiled in this manner begins to go, the only way to repair it is to tear out the whole interior—an undertaking so expensive that it is seldom worth while.

Another problem is that although under Herreshoff's and Nevins' rules the ceiling had to be firmly secured to the frames, most builders tended instead to attach it with galvanized-iron nails, which in time disintegrated. The ceiling thus contributed nothing to the strength of the boat. Further, since the bulkheads could be attached only to the ceiling, not to the frames, they had little structural role; they were hardly more than partitions which tended to slide around, and the passageways slowly became trapezoidal as the bulkheads slipped down toward the bilge (Drawing 6).

As a young boy, I spent a tremendous amount of time hanging around the old Purdy Boat Company, in Port Washington, Long Island. They built yachts of superb quality. I remember once asking Milt Purdy the reason for ceiling a boat. His reply was short and to the

6. Bulkhead sliding toward bilge.

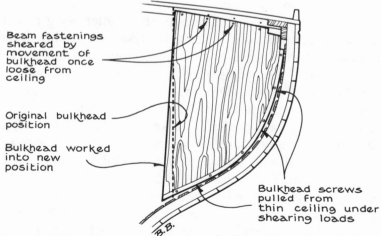

Beam fastenings sheared by movement of bulkhead once loose from ceiling

Original bulkhead position

Bulkhead worked into new position

Bulkhead screws pulled from thin ceiling under shearing loads

point: "The only reason to put a ceiling in a boat is to hide bad work-manship." Poorly fitted planks, cracked frames, could be covered by the ceiling.

At the end of World War II, good waterproof plywood became available, and builders began more and more to stop installing ceilings. When the ceiling is dispensed with, the interior of the boat is more ventilated and the bulkheads can be bolted directly to frames. On a well-built boat, the interior planking and frames are not ugly, but rather can be seen as a work of art.

To prevent people, clothes, or what-have-you from leaning against the frames of the boat or lying on the planking, which will be damp if there is a leak, ⅜-by-1½-inch strips of mahogany or teak can be secured to the inside faces of the frames. If oval-head screws are used, these strips can be easily moved.

KNEES

Knees are supporting members consisting of two arms set at an angle one to the other. They are placed at various points of stress—around the mast partners, at the ends of the cabin, in the corners of the cockpit —to keep the boat from working or straining. Knees installed in the vertical plane are known as hanging knees; those in the horizontal plane are known as lodging knees (Drawing 7A).

In years gone by, natural crooks were used for knees. Hackmatack was considered the best wood for this purpose. If hackmatack was not available, oak was frequently used. The roots of the oak were believed to make knees vastly superior to those from other parts of the tree.

To provide the necessary strength and support, a knee must be perfectly fitted to the timbers. A grown knee, therefore, must be supremely well seasoned. If it shrinks and changes shape after being bolted into place, it becomes almost useless; only the fastening passing through it continues to furnish support. For this reason, grown knees are seldom used in boats today. Instead, if wooden knees are desired, they may be made of laminated wood (Drawing 7B), and glued, screwed, and bolted into place. Sometimes plywood gussets are used.

Metal is also a suitable material for knees. Indeed, the best knees— and the most expensive—are fabricated of bronze (Drawing 7D). Bolted and screwed with bronze to the wooden structural members, they will last for the life of the boat and then some. Galvanized knees can be forged by a blacksmith of heavy wrought iron or mild steel, and then galvanized (Drawing 7C), or can be built up—fabricated from mild steel, and then galvanized. The forged mild-steel knees appear to

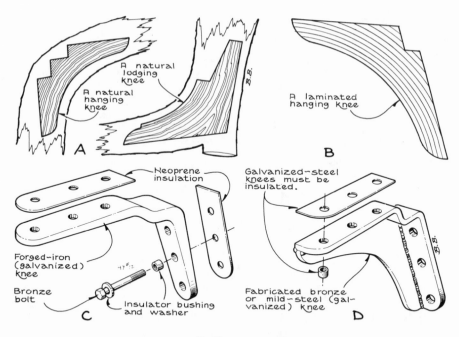

A natural
lodging
knee

A natural
hanging
knee

A

A laminated
hanging knee

B

Neoprene
insulation

Galvanized-steel
knees must be
insulated.

Forged-iron
(galvanized)
knee

Bronze
bolt

Insulator bushing
and washer

C

Fabricated bronze
or mild-steel (gal-
vanized) knee

D

7. Knees.

last just about forever. The fabricated ones are less durable, but are considerably lighter and easier to make; good blacksmiths capable of forging knees are few and far between.

Many builders secure iron knees to the timbers with iron bolts. However, experience has shown that bronze bolts are preferable. Each bolt should be insulated from the iron by a Tufnol bushing and a Tufnol washer under the head of the nut (Drawing 7C). Furthermore, an iron or galvanized-steel knee must be well separated from the adjacent wood. One or two layers of heavy canvas should be used, or neoprene or sheet rubber (perhaps from an old inner tube); in addition, there should be some type of bitumastic (a good antirot agent) between the canvas and the iron, or a layer of Thiokol between the rubber and the iron. Since an iron knee should be kept dry, any leaks in the area must be eliminated. An iron knee should *not* be bonded to any other metal by an electrolysis bonding strap (see the section on electrolysis in Chapter XIII).

Breasthooks

The breasthook (Drawing 8) is the knee holding together all the timbers forming the bow—stem, covering board, sheer strake, shelf,

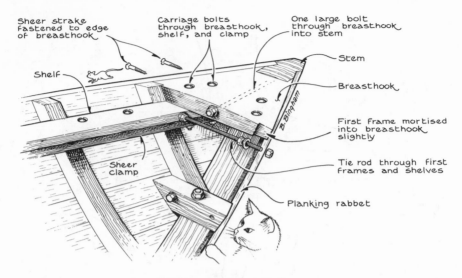

Sheer strake
fastened to edge
of breasthook

Carriage bolts
through breasthook,
shelf, and clamp

One large bolt
through breasthook
into stem

Shelf

Stem

Breasthook

First frame mortised
into breasthook
slightly

Sheer
clamp

Tie rod through first
frames and shelves

Planking rabbet

8. Breasthook installation.

and the like. It may be a heavy grown knee, or it may be made of laminated wood, bronze, or iron.

When an older wooden boat is being purchased, the construction and installation of the breasthook should be carefully checked. It is not uncommon to see the top two or three planks sprung away from the stem because of overloading on the stem caused by an inadequate breasthook.

Correspondingly, when a new boat is being built, the breasthook must be properly installed. In a boat constructed according to the rules for a modern rig, the compression on the head stay tends to have a shortening effect (sometimes referred to as the "banana effect"); the breasthook helps prevent this in wooden boats.

SHELVES AND CLAMPS

Shelves and clamps should be firmly bolted to the frames and deck beams (*OSY*-I, Drawing 3). Also, the bolts that are used should be made of good bronze. All too frequently, builders decide to save a little money by substituting bolts of galvanized iron, on the assumption that with a tight deck, water will not get through. This may be true during the first ten years of the boat's life, but eventually, the seam between the deck and the covering board begins to leak, water reaches the shelf and clamp bolts, and they corrode, starting rot under the deck beams, and all sorts of other problems.

This is one of the troubles with my beloved *Iolaire*. The deck beams are fastened to the shelf with iron rods. Over the years, I have scarfed and/or sistered the outboard end of every deck beam in the boat; this job would have been unnecessary if the builder had used bronze bolts.

Knees as a Substitute for Shelves and Clamps

If shelves and clamps are eliminated, a tremendous amount of space under the covering board becomes available for bookshelves, small lockers, and the like. One wonders about the longitudinal rigidity of a boat in which this has been done. However, according to Herreshoff's rules, shelves and clamps can be dispensed with if there is a knee joining every frame and deck beam, and an oversized sheer strake. The first large universal-rule boat constructed in this manner was *Vayou,* a seventy-five-footer. Built in 1904, she is still sailing along, with her original sheer. I myself first saw knees at every deck beam used instead of shelves and clamps in Sven Hansen's *Anitra,* a forty-eight-foot ocean racer designed by Sparkman and Stephens and built by Oscar Plym in Sweden in 1959. In 1976 she still held her shape perfectly, and there was no sign of leaking between the covering board and the sheer strake. Thus it does appear that although construction of this type is possibly a little lighter than the normal shelf-and-clamp variety, if properly done it is a very effective method of tying a boat together.

BULWARKS

In years gone by, the bulwarks of cruising yachts ranged in height from eight to twenty-four inches; on some large yachts they were as high as three feet. They were supported by stanchions passing through the covering board and bolted to the frame heads (Drawing 9A).

9A. Bulwarks supported by stanchions bolted to frame heads.

9B. The "devil seam."

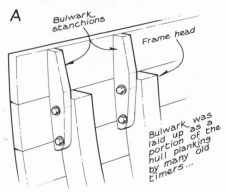

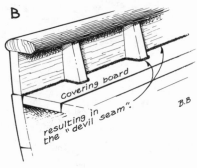

Sheer clamp and beam shelf not shown, for clarity

These stanchions have always caused trouble. The outermost seam on deck, between the covering board and the bulwarks was called the "devil" (Drawing 9B); it of course passed around the wooden stanchions. "The devil to pay" is an old seamen's expression referring to the practice of "paying" (or filling) this seam with molten pitch. The complete expression is "cold pitch and the devil to pay."

To minimize the trouble at this seam—notably, the formation of rot in the area of contact with the stanchions—on properly constructed yachts the bottom plank of the bulwarks was only screwed to the stanchions, the screwheads then being plugged. (On commercial boats, the bulwarks might instead be lightly spiked to the stanchions.) Further, the seam between this bottom plank and the covering board was left either uncaulked or with a small space showing (Drawing 10A). It was then relatively simple to pull this bottom plank off every three years or so, clean out around the base of the stanchion, harden down the caulking, repay the seam around the stanchion head, and then fit the plank back into place.

Today, a much more common method of supporting the bulwarks on yachts is to spike them down through the covering board into the sheer strake. When this type of construction is used, the seam between the covering board and the sheer strake is not caulked; instead, one or two strands of cotton are laid down on the sheer strake, and the covering board is placed on top of it and fastened to the deck beam. Then the bulwarks are spiked down through the covering board and into the sheer strake.

The problem with this method is that the fastenings hold well only in

10A. Bulwarks screwed to frame stanchions.

10B. Bulwarks bolted or drifted into sheer strake.

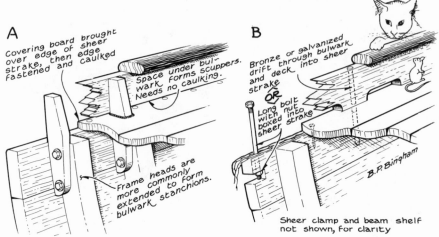

A

Covering board brought over edge of sheer strake, then edge fastened and caulked

Space under bulwark forms scuppers. Needs no caulking.

Frame heads are more commonly extended to form bulwark stanchions.

B

Bronze or galvanized drift through bulwark and deck into sheer strake

OR

Long bolt with nut into boxed sheer strake

B.P.Bingham

Sheer clamp and beam shelf not shown, for clarity

shear, not in tension. As the years go by, the covering board works slightly loose from the sheer strake, and a leak commences. Usually the seam is then caulked, but this process merely forces the covering board away from the sheer strake, thereby initiating a vicious cycle of more leaks, more caulking, more leaks, more caulking. Probably what should be done when the leak first develops is to refasten the bulwarks either with extremely long bolts or with bronze drifts on which the portion that will reach into the sheer strake is threaded, somewhat like the end of a grip-fast nail.

If the sheer strake is thick enough, and skilled carpentry is available, it is best to drill a hole horizontally into the sheer strake, drill a hole in the vertical plane to match up with the first hole, drive a bolt down, place a nut on the end of the bolt, cinch the nut up tight, and plug the hole (Drawing 10B). On large boats with heavy bulwarks and 1½-inch or 1¾-inch planking, this method of securing the bulwarks is fairly standard. A good workman may be able to use this method even with ⅞-inch planking.

The late Laurent Giles found a way to make securing the bulwarks easier on comparatively small boats. He would specify an oversized sheer strake. For example, a boat with ¾-inch planking would have a 1-inch sheer strake. This strengthened the hull at the point where it needed strength, and also gave him the necessary meat for fastening the bulwarks by the nut-and-bolt method.

High bulwarks usually have lifeline stanchions tied into them (*OSY*-I, Drawing 106), and any strain on the stanchions is transferred to the bulwarks, which will flex and work loose if secured only with bolts of relatively small diameter. Therefore, braces should be placed adjacent to each stanchion, or the stanchion base should also form the bulwark brace (Drawing 11). Because the inevitable flare in the bulwarks

11. **Reinforcing bulwarks to withstand the bending strains of the lifeline stanchions.**

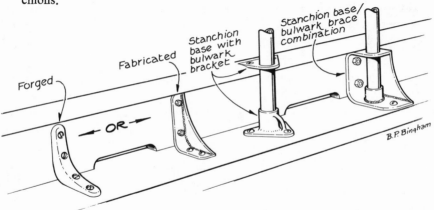

causes variation in the angle of junction with the deck, the braces cannot all be identical, but generally three patterns will suffice for an entire boat. A casting which does not fit exactly may be shimmed into place with a piece of wood, or it may be laid on an anvil and given a couple of good whacks with a large copper hammer, which will change the angle by 10 or 15 degrees. The slight bend which results is acceptable in a heavy casting with strength to spare.

SKYLIGHTS AND HATCHES

There are a number of ways of attaching units such as skylights and hatches to the deck. The method favored by Herreshoff and popular today with many designers is to lay up the deck with planks or plywood, cover this with canvas or fiber glass, then fasten the hatch, skylight, or other structure directly on top of the deck. The canvas or fiber glass is then turned upward on the inboard side of the hatch or skylight to form a water sill. This arrangement (Drawing 12A) is very simple and extremely watertight, but it does not provide a caulking seam. If the canvas or fiber glass cracks, leaks may develop along the joint. The only remedy in this event is to pack the exposed corner with polysulfide and cover it with a molding, in the manner shown in Drawing 12E.

Another relatively simple method, employed by some fine yards, is to plank the deck and lay down a very thick margin plank which has been rabbeted to receive the skylight or hatch (Drawing 12B). The results are attractive, and an excellent seam is provided, which is caulked with cotton and polysulfide. It remains watertight for a long time, and is easy to maintain.

A method somewhat less satisfactory—and rarely seen—is to lay up the deck with planks or plywood in the normal manner but extend the margin plank only partially onto the carlin. This arrangement (Drawing 12C) provides a rabbet to receive the deck structure, which is set onto a heavy layer of bedding compound or polysulfide atop the carlin. The seam between the hatch or skylight and the margin plank is then caulked with cotton and polysulfide. The flaw in this type of construction is that it provides two possible passages through which water may eventually leak; therefore, the margin plank must be bedded to the carlin at the time of its installation. If leaks do occur, the type of bedding and protective molding shown in Drawing 12E may be used to remedy the situation.

A construction method which requires very accurate craftsmanship, and is therefore employed only by the very finest yacht yards, does

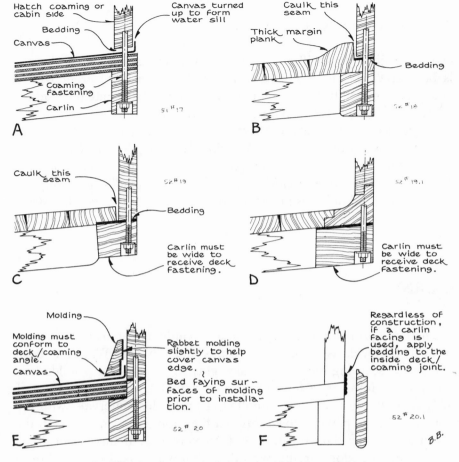

A

Hatch coaming or cabin side
Bedding
Canvas
Coaming Fastening
Carlin
Canvas turned up to form water sill
51 #17

B

Caulk this seam
Thick margin plank
Bedding
52 #18

C

Caulk this seam
Bedding
Carlin must be wide to receive deck fastening.
52 #19

D

Carlin must be wide to receive deck fastening.
52 #19.1

E

Molding
Molding must conform to deck/coaming angle.
Canvas
Rabbet molding slightly to help cover canvas edge.
Bed faying surfaces of molding prior to installation.
52 #20

F

Regardless of construction, if a carlin facing is used, apply bedding to the inside deck/coaming joint.
52 #20.1
B.B.

12. Securing hatch, skylight, or cabin side to deck.

not use a margin plank. Instead, a large ledge timber, rabbeted on two edges, is placed on top of the carlin before the deck planking is laid (Drawing 12D). When the planking and hatch frame are attached to this ledge timber, shallow half-lap joints are formed which are difficult to caulk. Glue is generally used for the hatch joint, while bedding compound is employed for the deck joint. Rarely, on very large boats, a light strand of cotton may be forced into the deck joint. This type of construction should be avoided. An extremely high level of craftsmanship is required, and even at best the number and complexity of the joints may tend to limit their strength, and they are likely to work and leak in a short time.

Another method to be avoided is one that is sometimes used on workboats and on yachts built by amateurs. The hatch, skylight, or other structure is attached directly to the carlin atop a layer of bedding compound or polysulfide, and the planking is extended to the edge of the coaming. Canvas or fiber glass is then laid over the deck and brought a short distance up the side of the coaming. Eventually, the canvas or fiber glass will crack and begin to leak at the point where it is bent upward. Therefore, builders usually cover this corner with a heavy coating of bedding compound or polysulfide, and then add a protective molding as a backup seal (Drawing 12E).

Regardless of the method of attachment, the inner side of the joint must be finished off with a plank facing (Drawing 12F). The joint is first heavily covered with bedding compound or polysulfide; then the facing is screwed into position. This not only provides an additional watertight seal, but lends an attractive finish to the inside of the structure.

CABINS

There are probably as many methods of building cabins and securing them to the deck as there are designers and builders. What has been said about securing hatches and skylights to the deck also holds true for cabins. However, a few rules do exist that always apply. First of all, the cabin must be through-bolted at fairly close intervals, with the bolts (or drifts) passing down through the cabin sides and through the carlin and set up tightly with nuts (Drawing 13). If this is not done, a weak area develops, in line with the cabin windows. Literally dozens of boats have had their cabins fracture along this line in heavy weather, but have survived. How many missing boats have sunk for this reason no one knows.

Sid Mashford points out that since the bolts pass all the way down through the cabin sides, it is imperative that the nuts on their bottom

13. Securing cabin trunk—recommended placement of through bolts or rods.

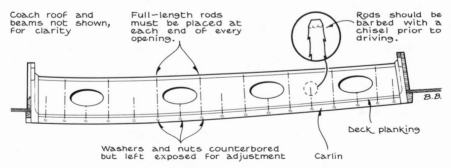

Coach roof and beams not shown, for clarity

Full-length rods must be placed at each end of every opening.

Rods should be barbed with a chisel prior to driving.

B.B.

Deck planking

Washers and nuts counterbored but left exposed for adjustment

Carlin

ends be accessible. For five or six years after a boat has been built, these nuts must be tightened at least once or twice a year. The reason for this procedure is that as the wood ages, it will try to shrink, and if it cannot do so because it is firmly held by the long bronze bolts, the cabin side will fracture along the grain. This was pointed out to me in the spring of 1976; it explains why one sees so many well-built boats with longitudinal cracks in their cabin sides.

Unless plywood is used for the cabin top, the beams should be dovetailed into the cabin sides (Drawing 14), to make a very rigid structure, which cannot spring. If the beams are dispensed with and a molded top is used, it should be secured with a cleat that is glued and screwed to the cabin sides, so that the bearing surface is increased. Also, whatever type of construction is employed, the lower the cabin sides can be kept, the stronger the whole will be.

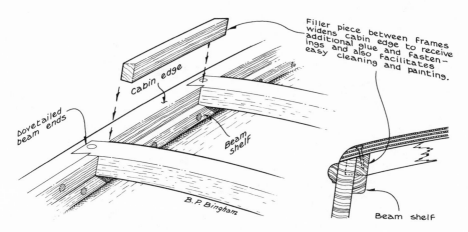

14. Attachment of cabin beams to cabin sides.

If the cabin is very long, its top should be supported at various points by hanging knees of laminated wood or bronze. Additional support should be provided, wherever possible, by heavy plywood bulkheads that have been made an integral part of the structure of the boat, being securely fastened to the frames, deck beams, cabin carlins, or cabin sides by screws, bolts, glue, and the like, not just shoved into place with a few finishing nails. Further, the shelf should be held to the cabin carlin by tie rods, and the deck beams should be dovetailed

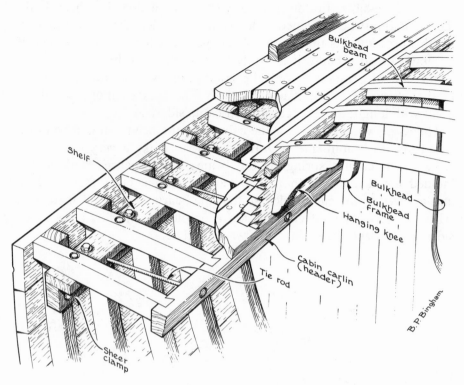

15. Structural elements of a long cabin trunk.

or firmly secured into the carlin, to minimize the chance of the deck working or (in the case of a caulked deck) spreading (Drawing 15).

BOWSPRIT BITTS AND SAMSON POSTS

Bowsprit bitts cause a tremendous amount of trouble. In some vessels the bitts are bolted to two deck beams and supported by iron struts (Drawing 16). This arrangement may be adequate, provided the boat has a gaff rig; since such a rig is basically held by the staysail stay which leads to the stemhead, the thrust aft is reduced. With a Marconi rig, the amount of thrust directed aft on the bowsprit is far greater. Unfortunately, when I replaced the bitts on *Iolaire,* I retained this type of installation despite the fact that the previous owners had changed her to a Marconi rig, and thereafter, until modifications could be made, the thrust developed against the bitts caused them to wriggle slightly—not visibly, but enough so that periodically the forward four feet of the foredeck had to be recaulked.

One way to avoid this sort of difficulty is to have the partners of the

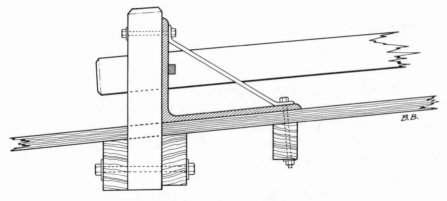

16. *Iolaire*'s original bowsprit bitts.

bitts or samson post securely bolted to heavy deck beams which are firmly fastened to the shelves and clamps. Bitts are then passed down through the deck and bolted to a heavy floor which in turn is bolted to the stem timber. A samson post can be installed in this manner, or can be stepped directly into the stem timber (Drawing 17). This problem is further discussed in the section on bowsprit support in Chapter IV.

17. Structural elements of bowsprit samson post or bitts.

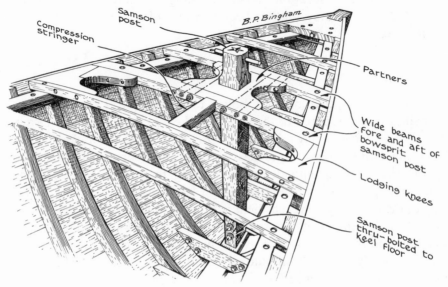

FASTENINGS

Screws

Galvanized-iron screws must be securely plugged, not just covered with glazing, because they will last only if completely protected from water. On a boat fastened with iron screws, those in the lower planks, deep down in the bilge, are usually the first to go; the bilge water works between the frames and the planking, destroying the threads of the screw ends.

On all screws, the fine, sharp edges deteriorate first; hence, when the planks of a boat are spiked to the frame with galvanized-iron nails, and the hood-ends are fastened with screws of the same material, the nails will last longer and give less trouble than the screws.

Silicon bronze, known under the trade name Everdur, appears to be the best material for screws; it is strong, highly corrosion resistant, and not too difficult to machine.

Aluminum-bronze screws, available in England, are tremendously strong. They are probably preferable to silicon-bronze screws when aluminum-bronze bolts, plates, straps, and the like are being used.

Monel makes excellent fastenings, but it is tremendously expensive, and although itself inert, it may cause other metals nearby to deteriorate.

Stainless-steel screws were thought to be excellent in the years immediately after World War II; however, surveyors are now finding problems with deterioration. When the plug is removed, though the head of the screw may look perfect, the end often turns out to have lost its threads.

Keel Bolts

On many boats, the floors are bolted to the structural keel, and then the ballast keel is secured to the structural keel by hanger bolts (Drawing 18A)—"coach screws" to our British cousins—or keel bolts (Drawing 18B) which do not pass through the floors. The latter type of construction frequently leaves something to be desired; when the bolts holding the floors to the structural keel corrode and must be replaced, the only way to reach them is to remove the ballast keel, which must then be refitted at the end of the operation—an expensive and time-consuming procedure. To avoid this difficulty, most designers and builders specify that bolts should extend through both the ballast keel and the floors (Drawing 18C).

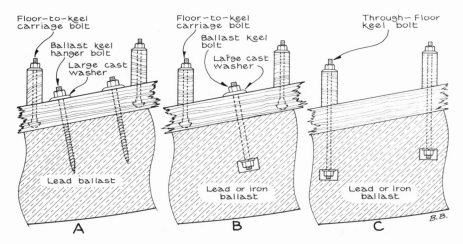

18. Securing the ballast keel.

Keel bolts have caused tremendous amounts of trouble because water eventually reaches them and gives rise to deterioration; the number of keels that have literally fallen off is unbelievable. Therefore, on any boat more than ten years old, the keel bolts should be checked. This can be done by removing them for examination, which is sometimes difficult and frequently costly.

If they are to be checked in this manner, the keel bolts to be removed should be those that are hardest to reach, since the last person to do the job almost certainly settled for those more easily accessible. When they are knocked out for inspection, some of the keel bolts come out in bits and pieces; those are obviously to be rejected. The ones that emerge intact and appear to be in good condition require further testing. The standard method is to lay the keel bolt over two blocks of wood and hit it with a sledge hammer; if it bends easily or cracks, it should be replaced.

In England, one step ahead of America in this respect, an alternative method for checking keel bolts is available. They can be X-rayed. The procedure is not cheap, but it is cheaper than removing the bolts for inspection—or having the keel fall off. The service is performed by X-Ray Marine (for address, see Appendix) for a flat charge per boat. People wanting this done notify the company in the fall, a schedule is set up, and the boats are visited and X-rayed during the winter.

KEEL-BOLT MATERIALS: *Bronze* is the material most commonly used for keel bolts on good yachts. Given a lead keel, bronze or wooden floors, and no trouble with electrolysis, these bronze keel bolts will be good for twenty or thirty years. Given a bad case of electrolysis, they may fall out in a year.

Monel keel bolts practically never cause trouble, since Monel is so inert that it doesn't deteriorate at all; however, as has been mentioned, other metals in the vicinity may deteriorate.

Stainless-steel keel bolts are to be avoided at all costs, since stainless steel corrodes and pits badly when placed where it cannot be reached by oxygen.

Iron keel bolts are routinely used on boats with iron keels. The fact that both ends of such bolts may appear to be in good condition means absolutely nothing, since deterioration occurs most extensively at the place where the iron and wood join, the bolt becoming wasp-waisted. Therefore, at least once in six years, iron keel bolts should be either removed for inspection or examined by X ray.

Center-Line Structural Fastenings

Even on a well-maintained yacht, the assembly bolts or driftpins holding the deadwood together are frequently forgotten. For example, *Lord Jim,* a seventy-two-foot gaff schooner, which had undergone numerous repairs, was thought to be in excellent shape when she went aground off Mustique, but it turned out that the deadwood was only loosely tied together; all the iron driftpins holding the deadwood, keel, and rudderpost were completely corroded, and in some cases they had almost disappeared. Luckily, although she pounded thirty-six hours on her deadwood, the planks weren't sprung. She had been refastened, and the whole deadwood section was held together just by the hood and plank fastenings. To avoid situations of this type, all center-line driftpins or bolts should be checked in the same fashion as keel bolts are checked.

STEM SCARF JOINTS

The stem scarf joint, where the two sections of the stem come together and the stem meets the forward end of the keel, is among the largest causes of trouble on wooden boats. In the original construction, the several parts forming this joint are fastened together with heavy bolts, the stopwater is drilled through the rabbet to prevent water from running laterally along the scarf, and the planking is put on. Thus, the stopwater is *underneath* the planking and cannot be seen.

As time passes, the strain caused by the head stay pulling the stem up, while the mast is trying to drive itself through the bottom of the boat, results in a leak at the stem scarf joint. The first remedy, of course, is to tighten the bolts; the second is to remove and inspect the bolts, if the least suspicion about them exists, and replace them as necessary. Frequently, though both ends of the bolts look perfect, the water running along the stem scarf may have caused bad deterioration at the center, so that they are wasp-waisted and must be discarded. The next step in dealing with a leaky stem scarf joint is to wait until the boat is really dried out, in the winter, remove the old bolts, install bolts of a larger size, and cinch them up good and tight.

At this point, if the leak continues, another stopwater is usually installed, either through the planking (which is possible but difficult, because it involves going directly across the stem scarf) or immediately outside the planking (which is easier, but much less satisfactory). On many boats, *Iolaire* included, people continue to attack the problem in this manner until the stem finally begins to look like Swiss cheese.

A better remedy does exist, which I finally used on *Iolaire*. Had I adopted it when I first purchased her, I would have saved myself time and energy both in working on the boat and in pumping the bilge. As noted in the discussion of stopwaters, the recommended procedure is to remove the planking on either side of the stem scarf joint, knock out the bolts, clean out the joint, install oversized bolts, cinch the whole thing up tight, and only then, replace the stopwater and the two planks. Once this has been done, there should be no problem for another twenty years. If desired, further reinforcement can be obtained through the installation of outside strap floors, as described earlier in this chapter.

WORM PROTECTION FOR WOODEN HULLS

With modern bottom paints, the teredo, that old bugaboo, causes little difficulty. *Iolaire,* using International Bottomkote tropical formula, hauls only once a year. However, certain areas of the world have odd problems of their own. For example, in the seas around Cape Town, South Africa, dwells a teredo that will go through any bottom paint and some copper sheathing, and allegedly even attacks fiber glass. In the supposedly safe brackish rivers around Miami and Fort Lauderdale, a putty worm is found which, though it does not go into the planking, will eat up every bit of cotton caulking in the bottom of a boat that has been allowed to sit unprotected. Similarly, the Englishman has his gribble. So when entering unfamiliar waters, it is a good idea to check with local yachtsmen and commercial fishermen, to be forewarned.

Remedying Worm Damage

Several ways of remedying worm damage are mentioned in *OSY*-I (Ch. I). A new method which is being used with increasing frequency, is to dry out the boat completely and then, with the aid of a grease gun, pump epoxy resin into the affected areas. To do this, one first secures a ½-inch lag bolt and drills a hole the length of it. Next, a grease fitting is placed on the head of the bolt (Drawing 19). A ⅜- or ⁷⁄₁₆-inch hole is drilled in the affected area, the lag bolt is inserted, and epoxy resin is pumped into the hole through the lag bolt, with the aid of the grease gun. One of the various seam compounds made with Thiokol or some other polysulfide can also be used in this manner to stop the leaks caused by worm damage.

19. Hollow lag bolt with a grease fitting, used to force epoxy into a worm-damaged area.

If the boat cannot be completely dried out, the same method may still be employed, but the substance pumped in should be either fungicidal bedding compound or a mixture of equal parts of white lead and tallow.

STEEL

Since steel is readily available world-wide, and many yards are experienced in working with it, one can get a hull built at a competitive price at a commercial yard. The hull can then be transferred to a yacht yard for completion; or one can hire a couple of woodworkers, an electrician, a machinist, and a mechanic to complete the job; or one can finish it off oneself. In any event the total cost will be infinitely less than it would be for a hull built in a yacht yard, with the yacht yard's large overhead.

Steel today is immensely strong; the weight of a modern steel hull is considerably less than that of a comparable hull built ten or fifteen years ago. Integral tanks can be built into the hull, giving tremendous fuel and water capacity. The interior space available is infinitely better than that of a wooden hull of comparable size. And with modern steel, the corrosion problem has been vastly reduced.

However, the steel hull does have various disadvantages. A good ballast-to-displacement ratio is difficult to get with a steel hull of less than sixty-five feet. Rust, if it is extensive, may cause structural damage to the vessel, and even if it has not reached that stage it ruins the appearance. The avoidance of rust requires tremendous amounts of expensive maintenance, and may nevertheless turn out to be not altogether possible. Hulls frequently rust from the inside out: the rust begins in spaces—behind lockers, under heads, under engines and battery boxes, and the like—that cannot be reached. Also, the rail cap on a yacht is invariably made of wood, and a wooden deck is laid over the steel; achieving a seal between the wood and the steel which permits no rust or staining to come out from under the wood is at best extremely difficult.

Steel hulls tend to be noisy at sea; and more important, they are hot in a hot climate and cold in a cold one. This problem may be partially alleviated by the use of insulation, but although the living areas can be insulated, the lazaret, forepeak, bilge, and the like are left uninsulated, and cold air leaking out of these compartments makes the boat very difficult to heat.

ALUMINUM

At the time this volume is being written, aluminum construction is less expensive in the top yards than wood. As each year goes by, more and more yards are learning to handle aluminum—to the point where even shrimpers and tugboats are being built of it. (In some areas, boats are being built of aluminum alloy so highly corrosion resistant that they are left unpainted.) As in the case of the steel boat, the yachtsman today is not forced to have the work done at an expensive yacht yard, but can have his boat constructed at a commercial yard, and then finished off by his own crew or at a small, inexpensive yacht yard.

With aluminum construction, tanks can be integral, giving large fuel and water capacity and contributing to stability. And aluminum is light. In all but the smallest sizes, an ocean cruising yacht built of aluminum can be at least as light as her wooden counterpart. Consequently, a very good ballast-to-displacement ratio can be attained. The strength of aluminum is considerable. In a small steel boat, if an attempt is made to keep the weight down, the plating may be susceptible to dishing or denting, but with aluminum, plating can be strong enough so that this is not likely to occur. *Gulvain,* designed by Laurent Giles and his partners and built in 1949, is still in good shape and sailing today. She was constructed of riveted rather than welded aluminum.

Furthermore, there is no rust problem. And if corrosion does occur, the resulting aluminum oxide is white and in no way as unsightly as the red streaks from a steel hull.

Aluminum does have some disadvantages. In an out-of-the-way area it may not be too easy to repair, and like steel it is hot in summer and cold in winter. Also, it is noisy. I think what put me off aluminum was my experience in the 1975 racing circuit in Europe. Sailing in the Solent in preparation for the start of the Fastnet, every time aluminum boats tacked it sounded as if machine guns were firing. When they dropped off a wave they sounded like gigantic kettledrums. Subsequent talking to some of the crews revealed that on many of the boats in heavy weather, it was so noisy belowdecks that sleeping was very difficult. Not too hot a situation on a cruising boat.

There is always the horrible specter of electrolysis on aluminum boats. Aluminum is a much more active metal than steel. There should be no problem if everything is correctly done, with insulation wherever necessary, and stern tubes, deck fittings, and the like made of the proper alloys. However, if anyone subsequently goofs on the wiring, serious trouble with electrolysis may develop in a very short time.

FIBER GLASS

There are many types of fiber-glass construction, and as the years go by new ones come to the fore, each being described as the answer to all the problems connected with this material. Everything on a boat is a compromise. Each type of construction is a compromise. Some are better than others, but nobody has managed to eliminate all the problems connected with any one method or material, and fiber glass is no exception.

STRAIGHT FIBER GLASS

In the earliest type of fiber-glass construction, which is still probably the most popular, fiber-glass roving and mat saturated with resin are laid into a mold. Once the mold has been built, at some expense, it is used for the shaping of numerous hulls, so the method is not suitable for a "one-off" boat. Whether the resulting vessel is good, bad, or indifferent, depends on the design and the builder.

Many early boats of this type—for instance, the original Bounties, which like the DC-3's were constructed before too much was known about the material being used—were drastically overbuilt; they are still around and holding together quite nicely. They cannot compete as racing boats against the modern ocean racer, because they just have too much glass and not enough lead, but they are certainly extremely good cruising boats and club racing boats.

As time goes by, boats are becoming lighter and lighter, because of the influence of the racing rule. Many of the new boats of straight fiber-glass construction are literally eggshell thin, and have an alarming tendency to come apart in heavy weather. For examples of this happening I would suggest writing to Victor Jorgensen of *The Telltale Compass* (which is completely honest, as it has no advertising) requesting that he forward the issues containing accounts of boats coming apart (for address, see Appendix).

One major problem with fiber-glass construction is that although the designer may draw up a set of specs providing for a boat with adequate strength, as time goes by the squeeze is put on the production manager of the concern building the boat. The materials required are extremely expensive, and labor costs are always going up. Hence, at times corners are cut: the full amount of fiber glass, resin, and the like specified by the designer is not used, and the finished hull is therefore weak. Unfortunately, it is difficult, if not impossible, for the layman to ascertain whether a completed boat fulfills the designer's original specifications. So it's a good idea to hire your own independent surveyor to follow your hull through the production line from the first lay-up of the gel coat right through to the completion. Doing this may seem expensive, but in the long run it will undoubtedly result in substantial savings; and you will be in a position to reject the boat if construction is not in accordance with the designer's specs.

Another disadvantage of straight fiber glass is that, like steel and aluminum, it is hot in summer and cold in winter.

BALSA CORE

In their search for a method of building a light, rigid hull that would be warmer in winter and cooler in summer than the straight fiberglass type, builders began experimenting with squares of balsa wood placed to form a core between two layers of molded fiber glass. The result was indeed a light, rigid, solid hull and deck, with fairly good insulation. Unfortunately, however, it was discovered that in time water penetrated the fiber glass and was absorbed by the balsa core. This made the boat heavier than originally designed. Furthermore, the water-soaked balsa core soon rotted. For this reason, many vessels are now built of solid fiber glass up to the waterline, with the balsa core used for the topside, deck, and cabin. This is an excellent means of construction, but with a few drawbacks. How durable the balsa wood will be, no one knows, since the method hasn't been used long enough. And when sailing in cold-water areas, from the waterline down you have a very cold boat.

AIREX FOAM

There are various advantages to the combination of fiber glass and Airex foam (expanded PVC). Construction is relatively simple. A mold is built, Airex foam is laid over it, and fiber glass is laid over the foam; then the hull is turned over, and the interior is fiber-glassed. The result is a hull that is light, rigid, and strong, and that is in effect insulated like an icebox or refrigerator. Thus the problem of heat in summer and cold in winter is eliminated. Also, the price is low enough to make production of "one-off" hulls possible. This method would seem to be the answer to the yachtsman's prayers. However, the grinding and fairing of the laid-up fiber glass to produce a good yacht-type finish is a long, tedious, miserable job. Also, individuals drilling holes in the interior lining of the hull to attach lashing eyes for sea boots, small fittings, or the like may suddenly discover water coming out of the holes, to the point where they think they have drilled right through to the sea. Checking proves this to be not so. Evidently, what happens is that water leaks in through microscopic holes in the outer hull. Airex foam, according to engineering reports, cannot absorb water, but it does sometimes break loose from the fiber glass, and then there is room for an appreciable amount of water to enter, filling the minute voids between the inner and outer hulls. How long this water can remain inside without causing serious delamination problems is not known. And so far, no method has been discovered for removing it.

C-FLEX

C-Flex is a fiber-glass material which makes it possible to construct a hull without the use of a mold. It is a planking material consisting of plastic reinforced with fiber glass and rods, alternating with unsaturated fiber-glass roving bound together by lightweight fiber-glass cloth. It has the desirable ability to bend sideways as well as lengthwise, which eliminates many of the problems of fitting usually associated with planking through compound curves. Construction takes place over a light framework to be removed after completion. The final bulkheads may be prefabricated and used as part of the construction framework.

FOAM CORE

In this method of construction, which was used for the Carib 41's and also for some boats in Europe, polyurethane foam is poured between two fiber-glass hulls. In Sweden, in a variation on this method, the two hulls were held apart by curlicues of fiber glass (*OSY*-I, Drawing 4). At first, this type of construction appeared to be wonderful, but unfortunately, it has not stood the test of time. According to reports from Sweden, the two layers of the hull break loose from the foam, leaving a soft mush inside. The same thing has happened to the Carib 41's; they are taking on water, and how much longer they can go on is problematical. However, it must be admitted that at the end of seven years of very hard use (and to a large extent abuse) in the bareboat charter trade in the Caribbean, the Carib 41's are still going. Since they sail for twenty-five to thirty weeks a year—so that their seven years of use is probably comparable to twenty or thirty years of use in the United States—one may well stop and wonder. Perhaps the idea is good, but the details have yet to be properly worked out.

DISADVANTAGES OF FIBER GLASS

Like every other material, fiber glass has its disadvantages—some inherent, some induced. For one thing, designers and builders still have a great deal to learn about the limitations of fiber glass. It has only been around for about thirty years, whereas experience in wood reaches back through the centuries. Until recently, the type of government specifications applicable to steel and aluminum construction did not exist for fiber glass. However, this situation is changing; fiber glass is becoming one of the most thoroughly studied and tested materials in boating history.

Even the builder with a sound knowledge of the material may be forced by the racing rules to construct boats that are far under the acceptable offshore scantlings. After all, a light boat is a fast boat. But it may be left to the buyer to realize that a boat designed for racing

and limited onshore cruising simply is not an ocean sailing yacht—
while the advertisements and salesmen try to convince him otherwise.

Builders may also ignore proven engineering principles simply to
accelerate production and cut costs. They are constantly striving to
find an easier way to build a boat, and may turn their backs on the
designers' recommendations for fear of being priced out of the market.
For example, they may try to economize in the amount of fiber glass
and resin used in the hull and deck. I would say offhand that perhaps
70 percent of all the boats called cruisers are actually 30 percent below
the scantlings acceptable for continual offshore voyaging. A boat actually suitable for family use in relatively protected waters may be presented and sold as an ocean sailing yacht. To be sure, many sailors
have made repeated successful long-range voyages in skimpily constructed stock boats, but unknown numbers have been turned back or
even swallowed by the ocean.

It would be interesting to see what would happen to the layout and
structural design of fiber-glass boats if the manufacturers' executives,
advertising managers, and corporation controllers spent some real
ocean time aboard their products. I believe they would wish to turn
out a new type of boat—a noncompromise ocean sailer—if only sufficient buyers could be found able to pay the substantially higher price
that would be necessary.

The effects of skimping in construction came home to me on one
recent delivery trip: I decided that I finally knew the reason a boy
scout should learn how to tie a sheepshank—namely, to tighten the
rigging of a fiber-glass boat going to windward. Although we tightened
up the rigging twice between Morehead City and St. Thomas, when we
sailed into St. Thomas the lee rigging was completely dead slack; you
could almost have tied an overhand knot in it. Once again, we thought
the rigging needed tightening, but we discovered as we powered alongside the gas dock that once the sails were off the boat, everything was
bar tight. The slackness had been just the result of the hull flexing. One
expects a phenomenon of this sort on a racing boat when hydraulic
backstay tensioners are put in. They set tension on the backstay of ten,
fifteen, or twenty thousand pounds, and something has to give. In what
is often referred to as the "banana effect," as the head stay tightens,
the boat bends, and the lifelines go slack. But the vessel that we were
delivering was just a "cruising boat," and there was no hydraulic backstay tensioner—just a very limber hull.

It is possible to err in the other direction. Some fiber-glass boats on
the market today are advertised as "superbly strong," and are indeed
massively constructed. However, they are built with so much fiber

glass that there is little room for ballast. The ratio of ballast to displacement drops way down, so although the boat may be tremendously strong, she will not stand on her feet going to windward. Fortunately, these overbuilt, underballasted, tender, slow, and cumbersome monsters are not the norm. There is an expression among the real cruising people that appropriately expresses the problem: "Sail the world . . . one way!"

The person interested in purchasing or building a fiber-glass yacht should seek out unbiased information. The results of some very reliable boat tests have been published in *The Telltale Compass,* which is not influenced by advertisers, and copies of these are available. It is also a good idea to hire a competent surveyor to make certain that the hull being purchased conforms to, or exceeds, the designer's original specifications. The surveyor can also monitor the construction of the interior, the installation of machinery, and the execution of many details, thereby protecting the purchaser's safety as well as his financial interests. If the builder finds some pretext for objecting to the presence of the surveyor, he should be rejected in favor of someone willing to be more cooperative.

Even a strong, well-constructed fiber-glass hull may be subject to certain maintenance problems.* For example, in the Caribbean there is a strange disease affecting many fiber-glass boats; frequently, when they are hauled, blisters are found on the bottom, which if pricked produce a liquid that is *not* water. Exactly what the liquid is I do not know, as there has been no opportunity for me to have it chemically analyzed. However, more important than the identity of the liquid is the fact that inside the blister are soft, broken-down fiber-glass fibers. In one case, I cut out the blister and was an eighth of an inch into the hull before the surveyor made me stop. This particular boat must have had a hundred blisters. The fiber-glass people are continually blaming this condition on "poor construction" or "bad lay-up of the first layer inside the gel coat." However, surveyors in the Caribbean report that these bottom blisters are found on boats of many different ages, produced by many different manufacturers. I saw one Bounty yawl built on the west coast back in the 1960's on which the blisters only appeared in 1976.

The cause of these blisters is still unknown. The sole common denominator among the affected boats—aside from the fact that they are all made of fiber glass—seems to be that they have been in the water continuously for four or five years, without being hauled out and al-

* An entertaining footnote on this subject was a spoof, run in *Yachting Monthly* and *Sail* magazine, which described a "polyestermite" which dines on fiber glass. It is reported that a number of panicky readers took it seriously.

lowed to dry for five or six months. *Yachting Monthly* for December, 1976, had an excellent article on this problem, which—it appears—will get much worse as time goes by.

Another problem with fiber-glass hulls is that if the bottom paint is not applied in exactly the right way, getting it to stick is very difficult. Frequently, when the boat is originally built, the wax is not completely removed from the bottom; then the paint soon falls off, unless it has been prepared with care according to the manufacturer's recommendations. Even years later, the bottom paint may crack and flake to the point where it must be completely removed. This occurs far more frequently with a fiber-glass hull than with one made of wood.

In addition, the owner of a fiber-glass boat may find himself confronted with little nagging problems which, though they do not concern serious structural deficiencies, may drive him crazy over a period of years. But then, almost every boat owner suffers from these in one way or another.

Sometimes, the top and bottom halves of the vessel are joined together so loosely that the seam leaks like a sieve, and may even come apart in places. Almost all fiber-glass boats, after a few years, have leaks at the hull–deck joints, varying from minor drips to waterfalls. Leaking around the frames of the portlights is close to universal.

A disadvantage of balsa-core and foam-core decks is that when one desires to install an extra fitting, one must check the builder's plan to find out if there is a core of wood or fiber glass at the appropriate place. If not, a hole must be cut on the underside of the deck, the balsa or foam core removed, a block of wood fiber-glassed into place, and the inner layer of the deck re-fiber-glassed before the fitting can be bolted down. As a result, mounting a winch or a pad eye may be far more expensive than it would be on a wooden, steel, or aluminum boat. But without these precautions the hardware may eventually loosen and leak, or the installation may fail completely.

In an effort to achieve beauty, all too many of the boats are furnished with a molded headliner. This is great for the vessel's appearance, but from a practical standpoint it may be a complete disaster. Water from a hidden leak in the deck may run back and forth across the headliner to the opposite end of the boat, possibly in the process shorting out half the electrical system. A leak may be in the bow, but water finally finds its way into the quarter berth back aft. One friend told me that on a trip to Bermuda and back again in a thirty-nine-foot ocean racer, water from the headliner shorted out electronic gear worth approximately ten thousand dollars.

When I discussed this subject with Jack Sutphen, he said, "Hell, there's a simple solution. As soon as you get the boat, just take a saber saw and cut the whole headliner into little pieces and throw it over-side; it doesn't look good, but you sure as hell can find your deck leaks, and the water won't run around inside your headliner." A solution, but rather a drastic and unaesthetic one.

On most stock boats, interiors are molded as a single unit and dropped into place. Since these rarely have drain holes, water from deck leaks, and spray down below from the hatches, may end up on shelves, in lockers, and so on. Slamming to windward, you may sud-denly discover that the beautiful handy ledge along the cabin side, upon which you have placed your tape recorder, tape, camera, spare film, or whatever, has a lot of water in it.

You might open the settee locker to get out some canned goods and find several inches of rusty water sloshing around in it. The only way to get rid of this water is to remove all the cans, bail out the locker with a paper cup, and sponge down the interior. The final solution may be the installation of small-diameter scuppers of plastic tubing, which will drain water from the captive compartments into the bilge.

By contrast, in a wooden boat, whatever water finds its way in— through hatches, deck leaks, an open portlight, or what-have-you— soon runs down through everything into the bilge automatically.

FERRO-CEMENT

One problem with ferro-cement construction is that achieving a good ballast-to-displacement ratio is very difficult (though not impossible). Hence, ferro-cement should be used only where massive hull weight, with relatively little fixed ballast, is required—for motor sailers, for example, or for replicas of traditional types such as coastal schooners and fishing trawlers and draggers. The difficulty of obtaining seasoned timbers of the size necessary for building boats such as the schooners *Harvey Gamage, Bill of Rights,* and *Shenandoah,* and the resultant problems that they tend to have with rot as years go by, suggest that ferro-cement might be suitable for boats of this type, provided, of course that the construction was really well done. There are some very fine builders, doing excellent jobs with this material. Indeed, one occa-sionally sees a ferro-cement hull so beautifully built and finished, so smooth and fair, that one thinks it must be an extremely good fiber-glass hull. However, a tremendous number of those in the field are nothing but charlatans, making outlandish claims of how easily and cheaply cement boats can be built.

The top experts feel that while there are advantages to cement construction, a really well constructed cement boat will be no less expensive than a really well constructed steel boat.

It must be remembered, also, that the cost of the hull represents less than one-quarter of the total cost of a boat. The outlay for rigging, interior, wiring, engine, sails, and so on will be about the same no matter what materials is used in the construction; indeed, most experts feel that building the interior is actually more difficult and expensive in a cement boat than in a wooden boat. Since the hull represents only one-quarter of the total cost, even if the cement hull were 50 percent cheaper than a comparable hull of another material, the actual saving would be merely one-half of one-quarter of the total cost—*just 12* or *13 percent!!*

II

~~~~~~~~~~~~~~~~~~~~~~~~~~~~~~~~

Cruising Hulls

APPEARANCE

The ocean sailing yacht is a cruising boat, and as L. Francis Herreshoff said, should be designed to the rule of the sea, not to a rating rule created by mathematicians. Since the cruising man is not concerned with any rating rule, there is no reason why his boat should not be beautiful.

Of course, ideas of beauty and proportion do change with the times. In 1955, when I first saw *Iolaire,* she was considered a good-looking but high-freeboard boat, with her thirty-two inches of freeboard amidships on forty-four feet of overall length. Today, we often discover that her freeboard is lower than that of boats ten feet shorter.

However, despite the present popularity of high-freeboard boats, in my view none are more beautiful than the yachts designed in the 1930's by L. Francis Herreshoff, and between the mid-1930's and the early 1960's by Sparkman and Stephens and Philip Rhodes, with extremely low freeboard. I think too many modern cruising boats have excessively high freeboard that is not offset by functional advantages. Most important is the fact that high freeboard is very detrimental to windward performance, especially in light airs.

This problem is compounded when a boat has a raised-deck aftcabin poop, for—particularly in heavy airs—this creates unnecessary weather helm. On many of the vessels built in this manner, the poops recall those of old Spanish galleons—in their proportions and also in their effects. The Spanish galleons carried a very small mizzen because the high poop essentially acted as a sail, forcing the bow into the wind to the point where practically no mizzen was required. Similarly, on some after-cabin ketches with a high poop, there is vast windage aft (apparently not anticipated by some designers), which produces the extreme weather helm.

CLASSIC STYLE

In the 1975 Fastnet Race, when *Iolaire,* much to everyone's amazement, led Class I across the starting line and enjoyed her moment of glory (until the fleet caught up and charged on by), we looked out to weather and saw the Solent covered with sails. Modern ocean racers sprinted to windward in welters of spray, with a great air of purpose. However, one boat stood out with sparkling beauty as she thrashed her way to windward, keeping up quite well with the biggest and newest of the ocean racers and charging on through the smaller ones. This was the lovely old *Latifa,* possibly Fife's crowning creation—a seventy-two-foot yawl with every curve in perfect harmony. There she was, with her big mainsail, great huge jib topsail, genoa staysail, and mizzen, eating out to windward with the best of them (and undoubtedly taking a horrible beating under the I.O.R. rule)—a boat which, forty years after launching, is still considered one of the finest appearing in the world. She not only goes like hell but looks good doing it—and that's my idea of real class.

Some of the beautiful older boats, built either to no rule or to the very old R.O.R.C. or C.C.A. rules and kept in excellent condition, may not do well under the I.O.R. rule, but in straight size-for-size boat-speed racing may still be competitive against their modern counterparts of similar size. The real dividend, which can't be matched by the modern racers, is that these older boats are unquestionably better sea boats, with far more of the built-in comforts.

I have often wondered why more cruising-boat designers do not reflect the conceptions of L. Francis Herreshoff, Sparkman and Stephens, John Alden, Philip Rhodes, William Fife, Alfred Mylne, Robert Clark, and Charles Nicholson, perhaps using one of their hulls as a basic point of departure, and I am glad to see that a trend in this direction has developed recently. It would certainly be possible to modernize the rig and power plant, raise the freeboard slightly while maintaining the same sheer line, reduce the height of the bulwarks, and raise the deck to give more interior accommodation, while still preserving the incomparably beautiful lines and excellent sailing qualities of these old designers' best boats. The result in each instance would be a classically beautiful yacht that would sail well and would provide the interior accommodation most yachtsmen insist upon today.

The individual who wishes to own a yacht of this type may find that his best bet is not to have a new one designed and built, but rather to pick up one of the old beauties secondhand. At this writing, a new Nicholson 70, Ocean 71, or Swan 65 costs about $550,000. By contrast, a big old wooden seventy-footer in superb condition can be bought for $100,000, and even if the owner then spends $50,000 to bring her completely up to snuff—modernizing the rig, electronics, electrical system, refrigeration, and so on—he still has put only $150,000 into the boat. The remaining $400,000, invested to yield 10 percent, will give him $40,000 per year to pay for the supposed extra maintenance required by a wooden boat. And since the maintenance costs for a *really good* wooden boat will be nowhere near $40,000 more than those for her modern sister, the person who invests *wisely* in a beautiful old yacht will be well ahead of the game.

The same situation also exists, to a degree, with respect to smaller boats. A superbly built fifteen- or twenty-year-old wooden fifty-footer can sometimes be had for $30,000, whereas a modern aluminum or fiber-glass fifty-footer is likely to run to $120,000 or $150,000. The difference in price leaves an awful lot of money available for maintenance.

STABILITY

As I have often observed, life is a compromise, especially when it comes to boats. My experience in racing *Iolaire* is a case in point. Despite a long, straight keel, seven feet of draft, and very heavy displacement, when reaching and running she will stay right smack up with fast modern ocean racers of comparable size. In fact, as long as there is not too much windward work, she frequently beats them. However, like many of the other older cruising and racing boats, poor *Iolaire* just has too much wood and not enough lead. Thus, when going to windward, she, and others like her, may be down to reefed main and No. 3 genoa, while the modern ocean racer stands up like a church under No. 2 genoa and full main, and therefore moves much faster.

DIRECTIONAL STABILITY

As each year goes by, it seems that keels get shorter and shorter and steering becomes harder and harder; steering some of the modern ocean racers is like trying to walk on the edge of a knife. Watching some of the older ocean racers or cruising boats going downwind with spin-

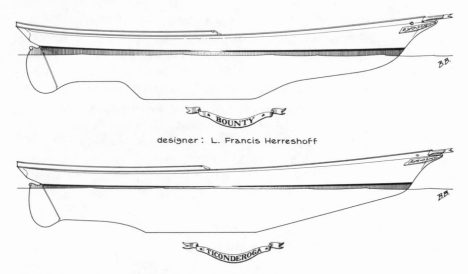

designer : L. Francis Herreshoff

20. Underwater profiles of *Bounty* and *Ticonderoga,* showing the distinct cut-out between keel and rudder which enhanced rudder efficiency.

nakers up, in the same area as modern ocean racers, one can see astounding differences in their handling qualities.

The cruising boat needs a keel long enough so that she can be easily kept on course. On the other hand, too long a keel will make the boat very slow in turning. This problem was recognized many years ago; Herreshoff, on *Ticonderoga* and *Bounty* (Drawing 20) had both ends of the keel cut out, to reduce the amount of wetted surface and to shorten the turning radius as well.

STEERING

TILLER STEERING

As the years go by, I become more and more convinced that a tiller provides the easiest means of steering a boat. At present, of course, there are size limitations, a forty-five-foot boat probably being the largest that can comfortably be steered by a tiller attached directly to the rudder. However, the possibilities offered by installation of a trim tab on the rudder have not been really well investigated. The more I discuss the subject with engineers and boatbuilders, the more I am convinced that it would be practical to install a trim tab on the trailing edge of the rudder, with linkage through a system of bell cranks or control cable. The boat could then be steered by means of a six-inch tiller controlling the trim tab instead of an eight-foot tiller controlling the rudder (Drawing 21). With an outboard rudder, putting in this system would be dead simple. Why have I not installed it on *Iolaire?* There is only one reason—lack of money. For further discussion of trim tabs, see the sections on rudders, later in this chapter.

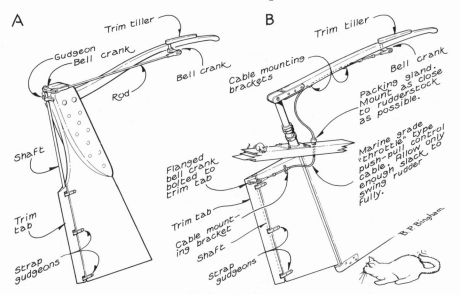

21. Rudder with trim tabs: A, outboard; B, inboard.

WHEEL STEERING

Worm Steering Gear

One limitation of worm steering gear (often called Edson gear) has recently been pointed out to me. Mounting it on a fiber-glass boat is very difficult, if not almost impossible, because the fiber-glass hull flexes just enough to cause the close tolerances on the worm gear to grip, bind, and sometimes freeze up.

In vessels that are equipped with this type of gear, the one infrequent cause of trouble is its unbelievable reliability. Because it fails so seldom, the need to carry emergency steering may often be overlooked. However, with Edson gear, the helm must be close to the rudderhead and thus well aft, in a very exposed position, subject to damage in heavy weather. On *Eleuthera* and *Ticonderoga,* for example, waves coming aboard have slammed the helmsman into and through the steering wheel. In each case, the wheel was largely demolished, and no emergency tiller steering was available. The crews showed tremendous ingenuity in rigging up a new steering wheel of vise-grip pliers, pipe wrenches, sail battens, tape, string—the works. However, a reliance on improvisation is hardly wise; instead, some form of tiller steering should be prepared, so that if the wheel fails, a pin may be pulled, the Edson gear disconnected, and the emergency tiller installed.

Geared Quadrant Steering

Geared quadrant steering has pretty much disappeared from the yachting scene. I have sailed only one boat equipped with this type of system—the old *Zigeuner*—and I found it absolutely superb, having a feel exactly like that of a tiller. Furthermore, with straight-drive rack-and-pinion gearing (Drawing 22), there is practically nothing that can

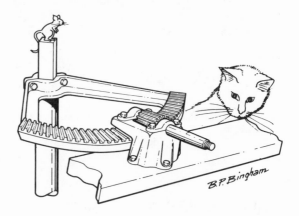

22. Geared quadrant steering.

go wrong. Edson is now manufacturing this excellent steering gear, so perhaps it will soon be seen more often.

Hydraulic Steering

Despite its lack of feel, hydraulic steering is becoming increasingly popular; in my opinion, however, it should be avoided if possible in a cruising boat. So far, I have delivered to the United States three boats equipped with hydraulic steering, and in each case the seals let go early in the trip, and the emergency steering gear had to be used thereafter. These seals evidently do not stand up well in the tropics, and needless to say, they fail only when the system is in use—that is, when the vessel is at sea. Draining a hydraulic steering system, dismantling it, replacing the seals, and reassembling it while at sea, is not the easiest thing in the world to do. Fortunately, however, when hydraulic steering does fail, if it is properly designed one need only pull one pin to disconnect the entire system, so that the emergency tiller can be installed. When *Atlantica*'s hydraulic steering gave way, the emergency tiller worked so well that we never did try to fix the hydraulic system, even though a voyage of two thousand miles remained.

It is possible to prevent trouble with hydraulic steering. If the system is torn down once a year, everything is polished and checked, and the seals are replaced, it will probably stand up satisfactorily. And under certain circumstances, hydraulic steering does have advantages. For one thing, with a properly designed system, even a very small person, or a twelve- or fourteen-year-old child, can handle the helm of a forty-five- or fifty-foot boat for hours without requiring relief.

Also, the system is well worth considering for boats with a center cockpit fairly far forward and the rudderpost well aft. In this situation, installation of most types of steering requires running cable long distances, over sheaves, around many corners, and around the quadrant. All too often, this is imperfectly done: some leads are not precisely lined up, some blocks are not quite properly bolted in, and a failure results. It is much easier to run a couple of hydraulic hoses from the steering position, around corners as necessary, and back to the rudderhead.

Loss of Steering

Almost every boat with wheel steering that is over five years old has lost her steering at some time or other.

Rudder failures are caused not only by cables breaking, but also— all too frequently—by quadrants letting go. Apparently some foundries occasionally cast a rudder quadrant out of Cheddar cheese instead of good bronze. Therefore, the rudder quadrant should be carefully examined for cracks at regular intervals, perhaps by the same methods used to spot-check swage fittings.

In view of the likelihood of failure, the boat with wheel steering must have emergency steering that will function satisfactorily under all normal conditions. Although some emergency systems are more than acceptable, many of the standard designs produced by the stock builders are grossly deficient. Redesigning them sometimes requires major alterations to the boat.

The only way to really test a boat's emergency steering is to try it out in a wind of at least 15 knots—running dead downwind, jibing back and forth four or five times, tacking, reaching, and beating. A trial of this sort will make obvious any inadequacies.

A preliminary test, useful if the procedure just mentioned is not practicable, begins with taking the boat out under power, with the emergency tiller in place, revving up the engine absolutely full bore, and trying to slam the tiller hard right and hard left. If the boat responds satisfactorily, the next step is to back down full, get her going as fast as possible in reverse, and then give her half right, half left rudder, five or six times. If she doesn't pass these tests—back to the drawing board.

Loss of steering resulting from loss of the rudder is discussed in *OSY*-I (Ch. XX).

HELM LOCKS

There are many types of helm locks, plain and fancy, and a good number of them fail to fulfill the two most important requirements— that they permit fine adjustment, and that they be easily engaged and disengaged.

The simplest lock of all consists of a piece of line tied around the tiller and secured elsewhere, to the weather sheet winch, for example. The problem with this arrangement is that it may put tremendous strain on the tiller when the boat is dropping off a wave, possibly causing either the tiller or the rudderhead casting to break. On *Iolaire,* we have a way to prevent this from happening; a short length of heavy shock cord is fastened to the weather coaming, and then some line is attached to the shock cord and secured to the tiller by a towboat hitch (for details on the towboat hitch, see the section on securing lines in Chapter V). The shock cord provides enough give to take the bending strain off the tiller. When the helm has been steadied, a light piece of shock cord is looped over a lee sheet winch and then over the tiller. Quite fine adjustment is possible with this method, and disengagement is easy.

On a boat with the type of tiller that pivots in the vertical plane, a tiller comb can be used to lock the helm (Drawing 23A). This too can be engaged or disengaged instantly, and it permits fairly fine adjustment, provided some care is taken. However, because the tiller is firmly held, and there is no provision for absorbing shock, the tiller and rudderhead are subject to severe strain.

Similarly, some boats have as a helm lock a beam across the cockpit with holes for the belaying pins (Drawing 23B). Once again, the

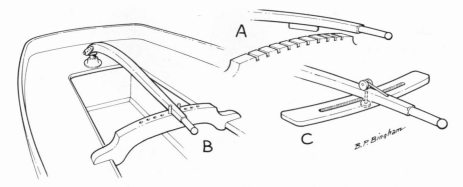

23. Tiller locks: A, comb; B, movable belaying pins; C, *Dorade*'s eccentric cam and slotted beam.

method is effective and simple, but may result in strain on the tiller and rudderhead.

An arrangement that worked well on the original *Dorade* consists of an eccentric cam mounted on a bolt which passes through the tiller and also through a curved plate or beam with a slot in it (Drawing 23C). This makes possible very fine adjustment, and can be quickly and easily engaged and disengaged.

With wheel steering, the problem is simpler, since most steering stands are equipped with a helm lock. It usually consists of a jaw lined with brake-band material, which fits around a sleeve firmly secured to the helm shaft. The jaw is generally closed by twisting a screw handle. In a few systems, an eccentric cam is used. This may be preferred by some sailors.

RUDDERS

SEPARATE RUDDERS

In the late 1950's and early 1960's, in the attempt to increase boat speed in light airs, the keel of the ocean racer was made shorter and shorter, and the rudder was separated from the keel. This type of design was advantageous to the racer for two reasons. First, when the aspect ratio of keel and rudder is raised, their lifting powers are increased considerably, resulting in a corresponding reduction in wetted surface. It is wetted surface that is the primary cause of drag at lower speeds. Second, moving a rudder away from the center of lateral resistance increases its steering leverage; a smaller rudder can therefore be used to achieve the same steering force, resulting in a further reduction in wetted surface and more light-air speed.

Though advantageous to racing, however, these design changes are detrimental to cruising. Concentrating the underbody area of a boat, giving her a short, deep keel instead of a long, shallower profile, can be compared to cutting off the ends of a tightrope walker's balancing pole. The shorter the pole, the more frequent and rapid its movements must be to equal the balancing effects of a longer pole. By the same token, the boat in which the fore and aft areas of the underbody are relatively small will tend to change direction (primarily as a result of wave action) more often and more quickly, and the helmsman's responses will have to be correspondingly frequent and quick. In rough seas, which have more of a tendency to change the heading of the boat with each wave, he may be worked to death—and all but the very best helmsmen oversteer anyway. So the cruising man suffers, as does his steering gear, autopilot, self-steering vane!

Today, some keels are so short that steering is like trying to balance something on the point of a pin. This state of affairs may possibly be satisfactory on a racing boat, but it is certainly not acceptable on the ocean sailing yacht.

To a limited extent, the design of the rudder may help to rectify the situation. A rudder in the aftermost position does restore a little of the directional stability it has stolen from the hull. A skeg, especially a large one, replaces a substantial portion of the "balancing pole," but it will by no means provide the directional stability attained with a longer-keeled hull.

Many free-standing spade rudders are partially balanced (the rudderpost is located about 25 percent aft of the leading edge), and the result is relief of the torque loads of the rudderpost, the strains on the steering gear, and the pressures on the wheel or tiller which the helmsman has to fight. A partially balanced rudder is consequently easier to handle and less prone to failure than a nonbalanced, free-standing spade rudder. Both, however, are very likely to develop bent stocks because their lower ends are unsupported.

Most spade rudders and many rudders mounted on skegs are designed with the top of the rudderpost raked forward. I have never heard even an attempt at an explanation for this type of design, although one high-ranking naval architect said, "It looks fast, and that helps sell boats!" John H. Hughes, in "Rake and Rudder Power" in

Yachting World, January, 1976, reprinted in *Sail,* May, 1976, presented a very strong case for having the top of the rudderpost raked aft even when the rudder is hung back aft on a skeg. He condemned the rudderpost with the top raked forward as totally unsatisfactory. The nature of the problem is indicated in the graph accompanying his article (Drawing 24). Although Hughes stated that he would be interested in finding out the reason for raking the top of a rudderpost forward, few, if any, letters defending this type of installation have appeared in *Yachting World* or *Sail.* The conventional profile, with the

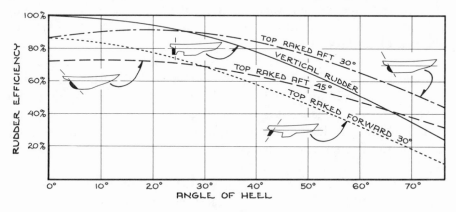

24. Effect on rudder efficiency of rake of rudderpost.

top raked aft, seems to be the best. Perhaps the rudderpost mounted in this position could be combined with the skeg to give extremely good steering in all conditions.

A separate rudder may be desirable, provided it is combined with a keel of adequate length. Although Herreshoff did not mount the rudder on a separate skeg in *Bounty* and *Ticonderoga,* he did place it all the way aft. Furthermore, as Drawing 20 makes evident, there was a distinct cutout between the ballast keel and the rudder.

Bounty and *Ticonderoga* are regarded as greyhounds on a reach or a run, but their windward-going performance is not too good. One wonders whether this weakness is fundamentally caused by their lack of draft, or is a result of their old-fashioned ketch rig. Perhaps if the rigging were improved, and if a rudder mounted according to Herreshoff's basic idea were combined with a modern shorter keel (a compromise between the high-aspect-ratio I.O.R. keel and a long cruising-boat keel), the result might be an extremely fast, weatherly cruising yacht.

OUTBOARD RUDDERS—TRIM TABS

Outboard rudders hung on the stern of a double-ender or a transom-sterned boat have much to recommend them to the cruising yachtsman. They are easy and cheap to construct. They can be made incredibly strong. They are dead simple and almost foolproof, as there is no bronze rudderstock that must pass through a stuffing box, or large wooden rudderstock that must come up through a large wooden rudder trunk, where worms can feast. Their great advantage is that they may be easily removed when hauling, and in many cases they may be shipped or unshipped while the vessel is afloat, which at times greatly simplifies rudder repair. (However, some—for instance, the Westsail outboard rudders—are usually installed in such a fashion that they cannot be removed unless the boat is hauled, so they lose this important advantage.) And finally, it is very easy to rig a vane self-steering gear to an outboard rudder, since the trim tab can be secured to the after edge of the rudder and is easily supported, as was shown in Drawing 21.

Kaiser, the builder of *Gale Force,* provides a trim tab on the trailing edge of the outboard rudder as standard equipment. Why all builders do not follow his example is almost incomprehensible, since the installation is relatively simple to make, especially during the original construction. The only understandable deterrent seems to be the slight added cost. The great advantage of the trim tab is that with a simple bell-crank arm it can be adjusted so that there is neutral helm, and hence the tiller load is minimized. A small person can then handle a big rudder, or one can install one of the small electric autopilots with low amperage drain—the Autohelm, for instance—which can run off the wind vane or the compass. Or the autopilot can be rigged directly to the trim tab, as was done on *Coryphaena* (mentioned in *OSY*-I, Ch. XVII), which had a very small electric self-steering gear encased in a plastic box about the size of a shoe box and secured to the rudder-head. Because this self-steering gear first activated the trim tab, instead of having to drive a whole rudder, its amperage drain was very low; indeed, a 250-ampere truck battery supplied enough power for a voyage across the Atlantic.

The connection of the trim tab by means of a simple linkage to a wind vane mounted on the rudderhead (Drawing 25) is infinitely cheaper than the use of an Aries or similar vane gear, and though perhaps not quite so effective, the method does work. Frank Casper (Cruising Club of America, Blue Water Medal winner, 1969) has

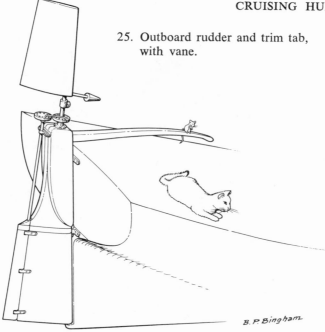

25. Outboard rudder and trim tab, with vane.

sailed the thirty-two-foot double-ender *Elsie* probably a hundred thousand miles under this rig (see *OSY*-I, Drawing 204).

When examining an outboard rudder, one should make sure that both the rudder itself and its fittings have been properly designed.

INBOARD RUDDERS—TRIM TABS

Installing a trim tab on an outboard rudder is duck soup. However, on a boat with an inboard rudder, mounting a trim tab and designing and building a linkage so that it can be operated from on deck is difficult—though not impossible.

Bill Tellier, on his fifty-three-foot Camper and Nicholsons cutter *North by East,* built back in the middle 1960's, had a trim tab on his inboard rudder, connected up through the rudderstock to a linkage that went back to a wind vane mounted on the stern pulpit. He reported that the whole affair worked excellently except that people either stepped on or tripped over the bronze-rod linkage running across the stern deck. This problem was solved by covering it with a teak box.

F. George du Pont's *Waupi,* designed by Francis S. Kinney, of Sparkman and Stephens, and built in 1965 by Derecktor, is another of the few boats having an inboard rudder with a trim tab. This can be activated from the forward end of the tiller; by twisting what looks like a motorcycle grip, the helmsman can adjust the trim tab for neutral helm.

The great advantage of this type of trim tab is that when the trim tab is adjusted to neutral helm, a small child, wife, or small electric, minimal-drain tiller autopilot can handle the steering on even a fairly large boat. On *Waupi* the system works so well that when the racing rules changed so that *Waupi* took a penalty for having the adjustable trim tab—and the designers tried to get Du Pont to remove the trim tab to reduce the rating—he and his crew decided they liked it so much they would keep it and pay the penalty.

It is to be hoped that in years to come, more designers and builders will experiment with the trim tab on the inboard rudder rigged up through the rudderstock. I have wanted one on *Iolaire* for the last fifteen years and only the lack of time and money has held me back from installing it.

BALLAST KEELS

Although their view may be regarded as rank heresy, a few experienced seamen are firmly convinced that the ballast keels of cruising yachts should be as short as is physically possible, to keep the ends of the boat as light as possible. If a vessel has a fairly long keel, it can be protected when grounding by a sheet-copper worm shoe fitted at each end of the ballast keel (Drawing 26). Even when exposed to worms, greenheart will last for many years. And when the time does come to replace the worm shoe, the keel bolts do not have to be disturbed; one need only pull the copper tacks.

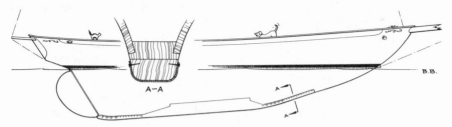

26. Copper worm shoe on boat with long keel and short ballast keel.

Admittedly, in ocean racers a short ballast keel frequently produces a motion so quick as to be distinctly uncomfortable. But this happens because all the weight is concentrated amidships when racing, and the racing crew is always trying to keep it that way. In the cruising boat, however, weight naturally spreads out: very soon there may be a dinghy hanging in davits over the stern; a lazaret full of spearfishing gear, lines, scuba tanks, weight belts, swim fins, coal pots; a forecastle loaded with anchor lines, tools, what-have-you; and in addition, a windlass on deck and chain in the chain locker. In short, since weight in the ends of a cruising boat builds up very rapidly, even long-keel boats, such as copies of *Bounty* and *Ticonderoga,* could probably be improved by having the weight of the keel concentrated amidships. If necessary, the keel could be deepened a few inches as well.

STERNS

In a modern racing boat, the form the stern may take is heavily influenced by the I.O.R. rule. On a cruising boat, especially one with an aft cabin, the stern is usually designed to provide the greatest possible amount of interior space. But other considerations should be taken into account as well; like everything else on a boat, the stern represents a compromise. All sorts of sterns, if judiciously designed, can be perfectly seaworthy; many factors will be involved in the process of choosing among them.

TRANSOM STERNS

The seaworthiness of the well-designed transom stern is demonstrated by the performance of boats with sterns of this type. Among those with enviable reputations in this respect are the Vertues, designed by Laurent Giles, and the vessels with Wanderer-type hulls (similar to the Vertues in design), of which easily 150 or 200 have been built. The Falmouth Quay punts too are extremely seaworthy boats which have transom sterns. Usually, the transom stern is only slightly immersed when sailing, and therefore causes very little extra drag. The Micia-class vessels designed by Illingworth and Primrose in the early 1960's were transom-sterned, and were extremely successful both as ocean racers and as cruising boats; so were the Rustlers designed by Kim Holman. Indeed, the latter were fast enough to win their class R.O.R.C. points and class championship, and yet were superb for cruising.

The transom stern has numerous advantages. First of all, it is infinitely easier and cheaper to build than sterns of other types. Second, it is always accompanied by an outboard rudder; this sort of rudder is

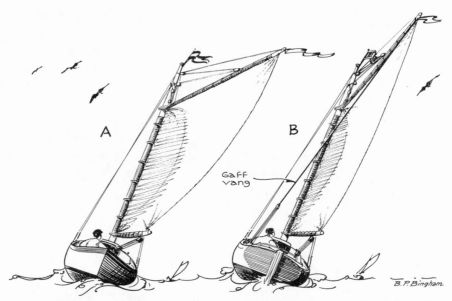

27. Feasibility of vanging the gaff: the gaff vang can be used on the wide-quartered, transom-sterned boat (B), but not on the narrow-quartered double-ender (A).

simple to construct and to repair, and as was pointed out earlier in this chapter, with very little difficulty, a trim tab and self-steering gear can be mounted directly on it. A homemade self-steering gear such as Frank Casper has made for *Elsie* is both cheap and effective. A further advantage of the transom-sterned boat is that because the transom is relatively wide, there is plenty of room aft for a decent cockpit, and for a good spread to a permanent double backstay or running backstays. On a gaff-rigged boat, the width of the stern makes available a decent angle for vanging the gaff to windward. Doing this on a double-ended boat is practically impossible (Drawing 27).

DOUBLE-ENDER STERNS

Double-enders certainly have a wonderful reputation for seaworthiness. The Norwegian lifeboats designed by Colin Archer are among the most seaworthy boats known, but they are not fast. Since their job is to stand by as rescue boats for the fishing fleet, they have been designed to weather the worst of the winter gales; in light airs or flat calm, they are complete dogs. In contrast, some fine-sterned double-enders—not Colin Archers—are designed to be fast.

Whatever their speed, double-enders do have various disadvantages. From a cruising standpoint, first and foremost is the fact that room on deck aft is very restricted, so cockpit space is markedly reduced. Second, on a gaff-rigged double-ender, it is difficult to rig a vang properly

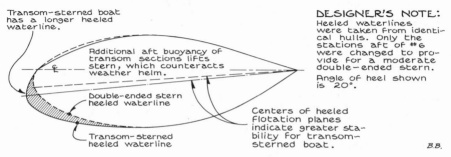

Transom-sterned boat
has a longer heeled
waterline.

Additional aft buoyancy of
transom sections lifts
stern, which counteracts
weather helm.

Double-ended stern
heeled waterline

Transom-sterned
heeled waterline

DESIGNER'S NOTE:
Heeled waterlines
were taken from identi-
cal hulls. Only the
stations aft of #6
were changed to pro-
vide for a moderate
double-ended stern.
Angle of heel shown
is 20°.

Centers of heeled
flotation planes
indicate greater sta-
bility for transom-
sterned boat.

B.B.

28. A double-ender usually develops more weather helm when heeled than her transom-sterned sister.

to the stern. In addition, because of the more gently curved waterline aft when heeled, double-enders usually have extreme weather helm when well heeled down going to windward (Drawing 28). In comparison with transom-sterned boats, they are expensive to construct. And—once again—it must be remembered that while the Colin Archers, intended for rescue work, are seaworthy enough to plug along in the face of a gale, they cannot be expected to move fast in light air.

CANOE STERNS

Some canoe sterns are very short, snubbed, and rounded, but as designed by Fife in *Latifa* and L. Francis Herreshoff in *Istalena* and *Mitena,* they are among the most beautiful sterns imaginable (Photo 1). Their great advantages are that they are strong, there are no right-angled corners to be built and reinforced, and they present no square surfaces to a following sea, by which it can push the vessel around and make steering difficult.

1. Canoe stern. TOM MCCUE

On a short-ended boat, the canoe stern has the same disadvantage as the double-ended stern—the restriction of deck space back aft—but on a really large boat, of sixty feet or more, space in the extreme stern is not at a premium; also, especially if the boat is long-ended, the canoe stern provides an excellent place to attach the mizzen backstay—and a most beautiful profile.

COUNTER STERNS

Counter sterns have been standard on yachts from time immemorial. They come in all sizes and shapes, ranging from the incomparably beautiful sterns of Herreshoff's *Ticonderoga* (Photo 2) and *Bounty,* and the graceful ones found on the schooners (basically copied from the old Gloucester fishermen) designed by Alden before World War II, through the small, lovely counter sterns on vessels of the late 1930's and 1940's by such designers as Rhodes and Sparkman and Stephens, to the boxlike versions found on many modern yachts.

All of them carry the deck line at a decent width all the way aft, and have some place where a permanent backstay can be attached. Because of the width provided, it is usually possible to set up a vang to the weather quarter, on gaff-rigged boats. On larger yachts, room may be available for stern davits from which to swing a dinghy. In general,

2. *Counter stern,* Ticonderoga. TOM MCCUE

except in the smaller boats, where a transom stern is more popular, most yachtsmen prefer the counter stern.

One of the great difficulties with counter sterns, especially the truly beautiful ones of the sort designed by Herreshoff and Alden, is that they are subject to rot. There are two reasons for this problem. For one thing, ventilation in a counter stern is inherently inadequate. At the same time, because of the graceful curves in an Alden or Herreshoff stern, large blocks of timber must be used for various corner pieces. If these blocks are not perfectly fitted and perfectly seasoned, cracks and voids develop which can easily fill with fresh water, the great cause of rot in the superstructure of yachts.

Therefore, if a boat with this type of stern is under consideration, a knowledgeable individual should be found who will not only examine the stern carefully from the outside but also penetrate back under the cockpit and go over the entire structure with a fine-toothed comb. Once the boat is purchased, two big ventilators (not mushroom ventilators) standing twelve inches high should be installed immediately, one in each corner of the stern, to assure a really good flow of air (see the section on ventilation in Chapter X). An ideal model for this type of situation is the ventilator supplied by Manhattan Marine (for address, see Appendix), which will prevent normal rain from driving down below (Drawing 29). At the moorings, these ventilators may be left either facing forward, or—in bad weather—facing aft; in both cases, air will pass from aft forward, and the area of the transom and lazaret will be completely ventilated. Further, they provide nice big handholds, and enable one to throw large quantities of rock salt into the stern to prevent rot.

At sea, except on very calm days, the ventilators will generally have to be removed and their intake holes covered with screwed-down plates. However, when sailing in the tropics, it may be best to leave them in place to get extra air through the boat; in normal weather, the amount of salt water that will penetrate belowdecks through the ventilators is relatively small, and can be taken care of by the bilge pumps.

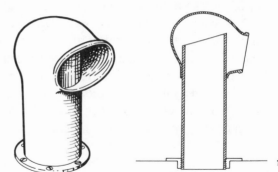

29. Manhattan Marine ventilator.

MULTI-HULLS

In *OSY*-I (Ch. II), I made my distaste for the multi-hull as an off-shore cruising yacht well known. Many experienced multi-hull advocates maintain that I am adopting this attitude arbitrarily; they point out that I have had little experience in sailing multi-hulls generally and no experience in sailing them offshore. But though my personal acquaintanceship with multi-hulls has been limited, I have had the opportunity to learn a good deal about them: I have been in the marine-insurance business for a number of years; I have been around yachts all my life; and I have lived for the past twenty years in the West Indies, where I have met an unbelievable number of long-distance cruising yachtsmen.

To be sure, some amazing passages have been completed on multi-hulls with remarkably little difficulty. Alain Colas' trip in his trimaran *Maneureva,* formerly *Pen Duick V,* from England to Sydney in eighty-four days, and then back to England in eighty-seven days, established a record for a sailing vessel which will probably not be beaten in our lifetime. Similarly, the late Jurgen Wagner in *World Cat,* a forty-foot ketch-rigged Rudy Choy cat, sailed around the world in eighteen months with little difficulty and no rig failures. The Glenns have cruised two-thirds of the way around the world in the past nine years aboard *Rebel,* a home-built, sloop-rigged Piver trimaran, and have had few problems. They report that *Rebel* has done all they have asked of her.

However, there is another side to the coin. Most of the early trans-pacific races for multi-hulls were notable for the small number of finishers as compared to the number of starters. Similarly, the breakdown rate has been rather large in the various multi-hull races to Bermuda, and tremendous in the single-handed transatlantic races, although multi-hulls pretty well cleaned house in 1972 and 1976. And in the 1974 Round Britain race for two-man crews, one of the multi-hulls capsized despite the presence on board of an experienced crew.

Dick Newick's trimarans are among the best, if not *the* best, of their kind—simple, strong, light, with a low sail plan. Over the years—more than twenty, since Dick constructed his first catamaran, *Aye-Aye,* in Christiansted—Newick multi-hulls have built up a remarkable record for speed and safety. Three of the Val-class Newick trimarans entered the 1976 Singlehanded Race, and one of them, *Third Turtle* (Mike Birch), won her class and finished second, only hours behind Eric

Tabarly's ocean racer *Pen Duick VI,* * while the other two finished very near the top in both corrected and elapsed time.

But even Newick's multi-hulls have had their share of mishaps. His *Aye-Aye,* after eighteen years of successfully carrying little old ladies back and forth between Christiansted and Buck Island, finally managed a 180-degree capsize, luckily with only a couple of people on board, between St. Thomas and St. Croix. She was spotted by a passing aircraft and towed in upside down, minus her rig, but no lives were lost and the hull itself was not badly damaged. Similarly, *Cheers,* off to leeward of Guadeloupe on her original qualifying run for the Singlehanded Transatlantic Race, was caught aback and flipped over, luckily only onto her side. She lay at a 90-degree angle of heel, with her float up in the air and the completely unflappable Tom Follett sitting there scratching his head and trying to figure out what to do. Luckily, the sea was comparatively calm, a freighter happened along, and with the aid of the freighter's crane the boat was righted. Tom waved his thank you and sailed off to finish the qualifying run, cross the Atlantic, and do spectacularly well in the Singlehanded Race. But he was lucky on this occasion—someone was looking after him.

Phil Weld, in another Newick-designed trimaran, was not quite so lucky. He was roaring along toward England for the start of the 1976 Singlehanded Race in his *Gulf Streamer,* which had already twice crossed the Atlantic and had weathered the edge of a hurricane (see *Yachting World,* August, 1976, and *Sail,* August, 1976), but she flipped, and he spent five days on an upside-down hull before being rescued by a freighter. The superb construction of the Newick trimarans, incidentally, is indicated by the fact that months after *Gulf Streamer* capsized, she was found by a Russian trawler floating upside down, relatively intact. The trawler towed her back to the factory ship, which took her out of the water and back to Russia. Whether Phil Weld will ever be able to get his trimaran out from behind the Iron Curtain remains in doubt.

Also en route to start the Singlehanded Transatlantic Race, a Val trimaran flipped, floated around upside down, and was picked up by a freighter intact and carted back to shore. The owner of this vessel, demonstrating complete common sense, then decided to go cruising instead of racing single-handed across the Atlantic.

* In my view, and that of many other people, Birch's trimaran finished second, not Colas' great monster *Club Méditerranée,* which stopped at St. John's, Newfoundland, to receive aid and then restarted, and therefore cannot be considered a finisher in a single-handed race. Even in a normal fully crewed race, if one accepts outside aid one is disqualified and should withdraw.

The wisdom of his decision was emphasized for me by a conversation I had with Dick Newick in September, 1976. While Trich and I were taking our second honeymoon on a Stone Horse (a great little cruising boat), we stopped off at Vineyard Haven to see Dick and another old friend, Dave Dana. Dick talked me into going sailing with him in *Third Turtle,* the Val trimaran that had done so well in the Singlehanded Transatlantic. She is a great little sailing machine. We took off on a cold, miserable, wet day, with the wind blowing about 25 knots. We carried a No. 2 jib and full main, as I remember, and tore along almost hard on the wind, clocking certainly 12 or 13 knots, maybe in surges hitting 16. It was a thrilling experience. But as I sailed the boat, Dick kept cautioning me, "Watch the lee hull, watch the lee hull. Don't let it bury." Finally, after about twenty minutes of this, I asked Dick what would happen if the hull buried. "Oh," replied Dick, "we'd flip." At that point I stated that I thought anyone fool enough to race one of these things across the Atlantic could not be in his right mind. The multi-hull is great for racing around buoys, but no way would you get this man offshore in one!

It cannot be denied that the loss of life at sea on multi-hulls has been horrendous. Two of the leading designers, Arthur Piver and Hedley Nichols, went down with their own boats, and in one period of eighteen months, seventeen people were killed in the waters between Australia and New Zealand. No one really knows the total number lost in multi-hulls over the years.

A catamaran or trimaran is completely unforgiving. If you roar along under spinnaker in a well-designed mono-hull, you can take a knockdown, lay her on her side, and know that she'll skid along and eventually—when the sheets are eased or break, or the kite shreds—come back up. There are numerous stories of mono-hulls that have rolled 360 degrees. Back in the 1930's, this was done by *Sanjeford,* a forty-five-foot Colin Archer lifeboat, then owned by Earling Tambs, and by the thirty-two-foot schooner *Cimba,* which capsized between New York and Bermuda. *Doubloon* did it twice in the Gulf Stream; *Tzu Hang,* when owned by Miles Smeeton, capsized twice in the Roaring Forties (pitchpoling on at least one of these occasions). *Damien,* sailed by two Frenchmen—Jerome Poncet and Gerard Janichon—did it off Cape Horn and still managed to get to the Falkland Islands; and most recently *Sorcery,* a sixty-foot ocean racer, flipped 360 degrees and survived. In short, although not all of the numerous mono-hulls that have capsized have come back up, many have. But no one has ever heard of a single multi-hull that has capsized 180 degrees and come back up unaided. They have ultimate stability when they are up-side down.

Admittedly, some trimarans have shown that if they do capsize 180 degrees the hulls will stick together, so that one can literally live aboard the wreck waiting to be rescued. Possibly the crew of a good multi-hull has a better chance of surviving in these circumstances than the crew of a mono-hull. But the chances that such an upset will occur in the first place appear to be infinitely less for the mono-hull than for the multi-hull.

A look at the stability curves of a catamaran and a trimaran as com-pared with the curves of mono-hulls (Drawing 30) makes clear the reason for this situation. The deep-keel boat and the keel/centerboarder maintain the ability to recover regardless of the angle of heel—even when upside down. The curves of the catamaran and trimaran are wonderful at low angles of heel, but drop off sharply as the critical point is approached. Literally hundreds of mono-hulls have been knocked flat to 90 degrees or slightly beyond and have come up with relatively little damage. Thousands of mono-hulls have taken 70-degree knockdowns and have come back up with nothing worse than a bad scare to the crew. But a catamaran or trimaran has little or no chance of recovering from even a 50-degree knockdown. If sea and wind conditions give her a large angle of heel, a dangerous situation can easily develop. And this is most likely to occur just when the weather hull is flying and the crew is in seventh heaven with elation at a fabu-lously fast passage. Thus *Golden Cockerel,* with a full crew on board and an experienced skipper in the person of Bill Howell, managed to dump upside down right in the middle of the Solent, with numerous senior members of Lloyd's Underwriters watching the finish of the

30. Stability curves of catamaran, trimaran, deep-keel yacht, and keel/center-boarder, showing inability of multi-hulls to right themselves after capsizing.

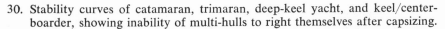
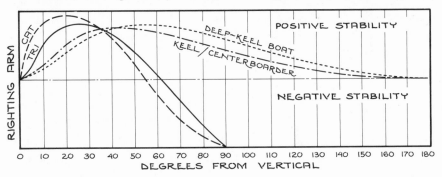

race. Needless to say, the insurance rates on multi-hulls went up immediately.

The multi-hull is more vulnerable than the mono-hull not only because it lacks the ability to recover after capsizing, but also because to be fast, it must be light. Where a forty-five-foot cruising mono-hull will surge along at a maximum of probably 8 or 9 knots, protected against collision with floating objects by 1¼-inch or 1½-inch planking and heavy frames, or by ⅛ inch or more of steel plating, ¼ inch of aluminum, or a substantial thickness of fiber glass (heavy fiber glass on a cruising boat as against superlight fiber glass on a racing machine), a forty-five-foot multi-hull may do 16 or 17 knots and have nothing between it and the sea but extremely light fiber glass, ⅜-inch plywood covered with fiber glass, or fiber glass and foam.

In my two decades on *Iolaire,* we have collided with floating objects at night on three separate occasions. Once, a gouge ¼ inch deep and fourteen feet long was left in *Iolaire*'s 1½-inch pitch-pine bottom planking. In another case, we hit something so hard that some of the copper sheathing was stripped off the deadwood. The third time, we were not going very fast when we struck the obstacle; the boat first stopped dead and then moved forward slowly, and we could hear whatever-it-was bumping along the keel as we slid over it. What would have happened if we had been in a lightly constructed multi-hull in any of these situations is something I do not like to think about.

A look at the circumstances under which the different kinds of vessels are designed and built, and at the types of crews they have, will suggest further reasons for the high casualty rate among multi-hulls. Of the mono-hulls cruising in the Caribbean, two-thirds are professionally designed and built and in good condition; one-sixth are home built and absolutely first class, as good as those professionally built; the remaining one-sixth are either overage or poorly designed and built by amateurs. Of the crews, roughly 50 percent are excellent sailors who really know what they are doing; 30 percent are good sailors who still lack experience but have their heads screwed on right and are eventually going to join the ranks of the excellent sailors; 10 percent are none too good; and the final 10 percent are disaster cases—accidents looking for some place to happen.

By contrast, of the multi-hulls, only about one-third are professionally designed and built; one-sixth are professionally designed and home built, with professional-quality construction; one-sixth are professionally designed and home built, with construction of indifferent quality; the remaining one-third are really dreadful: built to a known design but unsoundly constructed, poorly designed by the owner, or designed by a second-rate so-called naval architect. There is almost as much con artistry connected with the designing of multi-hulls as there is in the selling of ferro-cement boats; unfortunately, some of the worst multi-hull designers happen to be the best salesmen, so though their designs are poor, they turn up everywhere.

A look at the crews on multi-hulls also reveals an appalling situation. Most seamen who live in the Lesser Antilles would regard no more than 10 percent of the multi-hull crews they have met as really experienced sailors, with sufficient previous offshore experience in mono-hulls. About 40 percent are basically good sailors who gained their experience in small boats, became enthusiastic about multi-hulls because building a vessel of this type appeared to be a cheap, quick way to obtain a boat capable of making extended passages offshore, obviously intend to become really good seamen—and in many cases will do so. The law of the sea is survival of the fittest, especially in the case of multi-hulls—make one critical mistake and you're in very serious trouble, possibly losing your boat or your life; a mono-hull invariably gives a second chance. But fully 50 percent of the people cruising on multi-hulls are running a very high risk of fatal disaster; one wonders how they've gotten as far as they have without doing themselves in. It has been said that the Lord protects fools and drunks—perhaps we should add "and well-intentioned but inexperienced multi-hull sailors."

One has to look very hard to find a yachtsman who has had a great deal of experience in offshore sailing and racing, with thirty or forty thousand miles at sea in mono-hulls under his belt, and has then swung to multi-hulls, has sailed in them for long periods of time, and continues to race and cruise in them.

To be sure, one must admit that many mono-hull sailors race in multi-hulls, especially under the wide-open single-handed racing rules. Under these rules the mono-hulls and multi-hulls race together. As each year goes by, the competition gets greater. Ocean racing, especially single-handed ocean racing, has been likened to skating along the knife edge of disaster. In the early days of single-handed ocean racing, that knife edge was fairly dull, but as time has passed it has been sharpened, until finally it is like a straight razor, being honed ever sharper, and disaster is but a hair's breadth away. Indeed, the high casualty figures make one wonder about the advisability of long single-handed ocean races, or for that matter, of any single-handed ocean races—or even long single-handed passages, since one can't stay awake twenty-four hours a day.

In the 1976 OSTAR Race, 224 boats started, 139 finished within the time limit, 65 retired, 11 were sunk and/or abandoned (with two skippers still listed as missing), and 9 finished after the time limit. In addition, the casualties include the boats (their exact number unknown) that were lost on their qualifying cruise. Also unknown is the number of those that filed the entrance fee and then did not start, in many cases because of problems encountered on the qualifying cruise.

In competitions such as the OSTAR, multi-hulls, with their spectacular speed as demonstrated by the trimaran *Third Turtle,* are of course very popular. But looking at these figures one can easily see why most experienced yachtsmen have a rather low opinion of multi-hulls generally, and why many members of Lloyd's Underwriters in particular have a very dim view of insuring multi-hulls for offshore voyages. It is worthy of note that at this writing, we find Tom Follett, certainly one of the more experienced multi-hull sailors still with us, sitting up in Nova Scotia having a "lead mine" (a mono-hull with an extremely heavy lead keel) built for cruising!

Certainly, one of the most exciting things in the world is to go tearing around the buoys in a racing multi-hull. And a multi-hull can also prove its worth for cruising—in an area with miles and miles of water three feet deep, or indeed in any sheltered area where the shore can be easily reached in a life raft. Many experienced multi-hull sailors today have a trapdoor in the wing section underneath the life raft so that they can launch it even if the boat is completely upside down—not a bad idea, but it says little for their confidence in their own craft.

Finally, for the last five years I have continually asked offshore multi-hull enthusiasts to name five experienced offshore cruisers with a fair amount of offshore racing under their belts who have switched permanently from mono-hulls to multi-hulls. At this point, I have yet to locate a single person with those qualifications, much less five. Now that I have asked this question in the book I will probably discover many, but so far, trying to find one has been like looking for a needle in a haystack.

III

≈≈≈≈≈≈≈≈≈≈≈≈≈≈≈≈≈≈≈≈≈

Cruising Rigs

YAWLS

Most modern so-called cruiser/racers are sloops or cutters, and the great majority of these, if they are to be used for cruising, would benefit from being made into yawls. Because they are primarily intended for racing, these boats generally have a boom so short that a small mizzen could be dropped into place with no alteration of the sail plan other than the installation of chain plates, a mast step, and the like. Even in light to moderate weather, and especially in sloppy conditions, the addition of the mizzen would give these boats weather helm to hold their heads up, though the sail would probably be doused if a strong breeze developed.

A skipper accustomed to handling yawls tends to send the mizzen up and down like a Yo-Yo. If a well-made genoa is in place it will take a good hatful of wind when it blows up, and then the easiest way to achieve balance is to reef the main and set the mizzen. When the wind moderates and the vessel is off the wind, setting the mizzen staysail is less trouble than shaking out the reef. When it blows up harder again, down comes the mizzen staysail. Off the wind, in the average forty-foot yawl, the mizzen staysail will have an area of about 250 square feet, and setting it and taking it down will therefore be easier than changing from the No. 3 to the No. 1 genoa, as one would have to do to maintain speed on a boat rigged as a sloop or cutter.

On a run or broad reach, of course, the mizzen must be taken down. Going to windward, when the wind increases, a switch to a smaller headsail may first be necessary; once the working jib has been set and the main has been reefed, undoubtedly the mizzen will be dropped. If more wind develops, the main can be doused, the storm trysail set, and the mizzen either left down or reset, depending on whether or not the boat has weather helm.

The flexibility of the yawl, especially the double-headsail-rigged yawl, is made evident in the routine followed with *Iolaire*. In the Lesser Antilles, the usual rig is No. 1 jib, genoa staysail, full main, and mizzen. As soon as it begins to blow up to any extent, a reef is tied into the main. If the wind increases further, the jib is rolled up, the mizzen is doused, and the boat balances well with the staysail and reefed main. If it blows up still harder, usually the main is doused and the staysail and mizzen are sufficient. Going dead to windward, the main is doused and the storm trysail is hoisted and used in conjunction with the genoa staysail and mizzen. In storm conditions, she will heave to with the mizzen sheeted flat, three feet of jib rolled out to weather, and the helm lashed halfway down. She will ride just like a duck about five points off the wind, making relatively little leeway, with the decks dry.

On many a modern sloop or cutter, great difficulties are experienced when anchoring. As soon as sail is doused, way is lost, and when the anchor is dropped, the bow may fall off, turning the boat 180 degrees back downwind. Once the anchor is set, the boat often tacks around it, taking up a huge amount of room in a restricted area. In contrast, with a yawl one can sail into the anchorage, douse the headsails to obtain clear vision forward, ease the mizzen sheet, and then back the mizzen as needed—in this operation using the mizzen much as one would use a headsail except that the directions are reversed, so that, for example, the mizzen is backed to starboard to make the bow go to starboard. Even a long-keeled boat can be made to tack instantly by backing the mizzen. When ready to anchor, one heads into the wind, douses the main, backs the mizzen to take way off the boat, and drops the hook. Then, by placing the helm amidships and backing the mizzen to port and starboard to pick up sternway, one can still keep the bow into the wind to set the anchor. Finally, the mizzen is sheeted in flat, and the boat will lie quietly head to wind. Not only that, but the mizzenmast makes rigging the awning a simple proposition.

The mizzen can be invaluable when the vessel is to back into a slip or Mediterranean mooring. The mizzen is backed, the anchor line is slacked—and the process of getting into a slip or mooring stern to is often easier under sail than under power.

The yawl comes into her own even more when picking up the anchor under sail. On a sloop or cutter, when the anchor is to be sailed out, first the mainsail is hoisted, and then a headsail. The headsail is backed to throw the boat's head off, and is then sheeted. Next a series of short tacks brings the vessel up over the anchor. During this operation the crew on the foredeck may well be attacked by the headsail and headsail sheets, and/or chased around the foredeck by the staysail club. However, on a yawl, the headsail is either hoisted in stops or left on deck in the bag; a roller-furling headsail is left rolled up. The mizzen and main are hoisted and sheeted flat. Then the mizzen is backed hard to port or starboard, the anchor line is slacked fifteen or twenty feet, and the bow falls off; next, the mainsail fills, and the mizzen is allowed to flop loosely as the boat gathers way. Once the yawl has worked well out to one side of the anchor, the mizzen is backed hard to windward, and she tacks and sails off in the other direction. Three or four tacks bring her up over her anchor, the line is snubbed up tight, and the anchor is broken out by the weight of the vessel. During this whole operation the anchor crew will probably be standing calmly on the foredeck drinking beer, instead of dodging headsail sheets. When the foredeck crew reports, "Anchor broken out," the mizzen is backed to throw the bow off onto the desired tack.

The boat may then fall off on either starboard or port tack and sail away. If anchored in the midst of a fleet, the skipper may instead decide to back the mizzen alternately to port and to starboard and back out through the entire fleet. One frequently sees well-handled yawls backed a full quarter of a mile through a fleet of moored boats. In other circumstances, a 180-degree turn may be desired. To accomplish this, once again the mizzen is first alternately backed to port and to starboard, until plenty of sternway has been achieved. Then, with a light lashing line, the main boom is tied off center, onto what is to become the weather side; the helm is put down on the opposite side; and the boat starts backing her stern to windward. The person backing the mizzen should hold the mizzen boom only about 10 degrees to windward of the center line. At this point the leeches of the main and mizzen become the luffs, and the luffs become the leeches.

With care, a well-handled boat can be backed to windward for a very considerable distance. Whether a medium-sized cruising boat can actually be made to tack while going backward is still a moot point, but by this method one can certainly sail a yawl backward to windward. When the boat has pivoted as desired, the lashing line on the main is slipped, the main and mizzen are allowed to run, and off she goes downwind.

Coming alongside or leaving a dock without the aid of an engine is not all that difficult in a yawl. Variations in circumstances demand corresponding changes in the handling of the sails, and the presence of the mizzen makes available all sorts of combinations, to be used as needed. Even when *Iolaire* had an engine, we seldom employed it for coming alongside or leaving a dock, and in the six years since it has been removed we have had no difficulty in this respect, managing perfectly well by sail alone not only in the West Indies, but also in the ports of Bermuda, the United States, Canada, England, Ireland, and France—all areas where the trades are notable by their absence and the tidal currents are notable for their strength.

Many people wonder why I recommend a yawl rather than a ketch. A properly rigged yawl will do all the things a ketch can do—at least as well, and in many instances much better. On a ketch, the mainmast has been moved forward to provide room enough for the mizzen, and thus both mainsail and fore-triangle are smaller than on a yawl of similar size. As a result, the ketch is not as fast as a yawl broad off or to windward in light or moderate breezes (because the extra headsail area is missed and the rig usually has a lower aspect ratio). When a ketch is running wing and wing, the mizzen is sometimes doused because it may be of little use, and the mizzen staysail is often doused because it may blanket the main. About the only time a ketch may be slightly faster than a yawl is when the wind is on the quarter or the beam, so that a big mizzen staysail can be used. In addition, the mizzen on a ketch is in many cases too large to be backed easily. Also, except in midship-cockpit boats, on most ketches the mizzen is in exactly the wrong place—in the middle of the cockpit, where it is in everybody's way.

For rigging an awning, the yawl is almost unbeatable; only a midship-cockpit ketch can be regarded as superior in this respect. On the latter, the awning can be rigged easily and efficiently between the masts to shade most of the deck, including the most essential portion—the cockpit. On an aft-cockpit ketch, an awning can easily be rigged between the masts, but it will give neither shade nor any other protection to the cockpit. On a yawl, however, the awning covers almost all of the deck, including the cockpit. If it is correctly designed (see *OSY*-I, Ch. VII), it will fit the boat to perfection, be easy to rig, and remain firm and not flap even in a squall.

Finally, the mizzen masthead on a yawl is an excellent place for the whip antenna of the radiotelephone, high enough for decent reception, yet not necessitating insulators in the standing rigging, which many experienced yachtsmen object to. It is also a perfect location for a small windcharger, which can produce all the electricity required by a well-thought-out ocean cruising yacht (for a description of our experience with this device on *Iolaire,* see Chapter XIII).

Admittedly, the yawl rig is of dubious value to boats of under thirty feet, although it should be remembered that the Falmouth Quay punt, a superbly handy little vessel, has a mizzen stuck back on the very tip of the stern. And once sixty feet is reached, the mainsail on a yawl becomes so big that it is hard to handle, while the mizzen has also grown so much that it is difficult to back; at this point, switching to a ketch rig is probably advisable. However, there is no doubt in my mind that for vessels of from thirty-five to fifty-five feet, the yawl rig is best.

Unfortunately, today the rating advantage given to a yawl in racing is just not enough. The individual eager for victories must have a sloop, cutter, or rule-beating ketch. The good cruising yawl which can also race—the excellent cruiser/racer of the old C.C.A. rule—has been killed off by the I.O.R. rating rule.

KETCHES

The owners of ketches have frequently objected strongly to the views presented in *OSY*-I (Ch. III). In general, these views still seem valid to me, but I will grant that the advantages of the midship cockpit on ketches were not sufficiently emphasized. The most important point is that a midship cockpit eliminates some of the worst disadvantages of the ketch—in particular, it saves the helmsman from getting cross-eyed looking around the mizzen. Further, as has been mentioned, when a sloop, cutter, or yawl reaches a length of sixty feet or over, the mainsail does tend to get rather big; a ketch rig then makes possible a mainsail of more manageable size.

Advances in technology and sailing technique have brought about much rethinking concerning the design of ketch rigs. Under the racing rule, the price is high if there is a substantial distance between main and mizzen masts. But now designers have learned how to take advantage of this distance when going to weather by shortening the main boom, making it possible to set a "mizzen genoa." In effect, this means that a modern I.O.R. ketch can use some type of mizzen staysail on virtually every point of sail—something which was formerly impossible. The separation between main and mizzen is now sizable and sometimes extreme, as in the newest *Ondine* and *Equation,* designed to carry such mizzen genoas.

These ocean racers have proved that ketches will go to windward, but their rigs tend to be so esoteric that they are grossly impractical for cruising. Exactly how the mizzenmast on the new *Ondine* is stayed is not obvious, and the fact that it remains in the boat without three or four

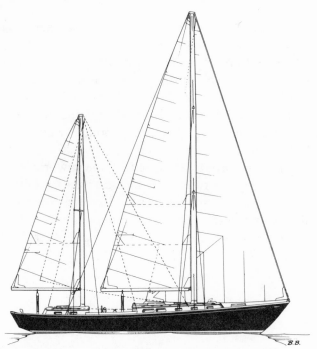

31. Ocean-racing ketch rig modified for cruising.

men pulling strings in different directions is a marvel. Possibly a more conservative version of the modern ocean-racing ketch rig might prove practical for a long, narrow cruising boat (Drawing 31).

Indeed, many seamen think that the sailing performance of most ketches, especially the older ones, would be vastly improved if the main boom, and in many cases also the mizzen boom were shortened. Mizzen backstays could then be rigged, and larger headsails could be installed, with little or no loss of drive in the sail plan. The result would be not the tall, narrow ribbons of the new ocean-racing rig, but something falling between that and the long, low—practically leg-o-mutton —rig of the older ketches.

WISHBONE KETCHES

The wishbone ketch was first popularized by the late Fritz Fenger. The advantages and disadvantages of this rig are discussed in *OSY*-I (Ch. III). Val Schaeffer sails the eighty-five-foot motor-sailing wishbone ketch *Camelot* with few problems, although he has an extremely small crew. In his opinion, the difficulties encountered in hoisting and in lowering the big main wishbone sail, which have given this type of boat a bad name, can be eliminated by proper handling.

When hoisting or lowering the main wishbone sail, one must come around so that the wind is slightly forward of the beam, and the sail is luffing. Dousing sail is greatly facilitated if there is a downhaul brail line. The brail line is secured to the sail on the starboard side slightly below the miter, then threaded through eyes on the side of the sail down to the clew, back through the clew to the opposite side of the sail, then through a small block secured to the luff rope of the sail, and on down to the deck. When dousing, the sail is eased until it is luffing, the course being altered if necessary to achieve this. Then the halyard is thrown off, the brail line is manned, and down comes the sail, to be stowed on the track, in its bag.

When hoisting, the brail line is cast off, the sail is taken out of its bag, and hoisting begins; the wishbone is eased and of course adjusted so that the sail continues luffing until fully raised and out-hauled.

Val also feels that all of the staysail booms should be chopped up as fuel to cook steaks. By using loose-footed staysails of various sizes, he has increased *Camelot*'s performance immeasurably. However, because she was not originally designed for loose-footed staysails, there is continuous trouble with sheet leads interfering with deckhands, ventilators, lower shrouds, and the like.

It would be interesting to see what sort of rig could be put on a big wishbone ketch if one started from scratch and planned everything out, using various sizes of main staysail and of genoa staysail in the fore-triangle. *Camelot*'s present rig is as shown at left in Drawing 32. Were Val to have an unlimited budget, he might give her a new rig, as shown at right in the drawing.

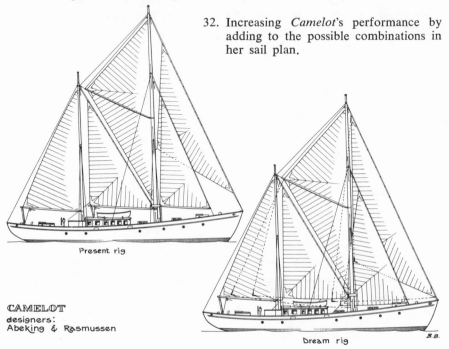

32. Increasing *Camelot*'s performance by adding to the possible combinations in her sail plan.

Present rig

CAMELOT
designers:
Abeking & Rasmussen

Dream rig

B.B.

CATBOAT VARIATIONS

CAT KETCHES

Cat ketches have been quite popular among longshore commercial fishermen off various parts of the northeast coast of the United States— Kingston lobster boats were cat ketches, and so were many of the New Haven sharpies. Dr. Jerry Milgram found a big loophole in the I.O.R. rule, which he exploited with his odd-looking but very fast cat ketch, *Cascade*. He claims that this was not only a great rule-beating rig at the time of its conception, but also an excellent, easily handled rig for cruising. The rules have since been amended to penalize this kind of rig, and *Cascade* has been slightly modified, but the original idea has lost none of its validity. Few are convinced that a cat-ketch rig is suitable for ocean cruising, but perhaps it will indeed prove to be fine for longshore cruising, when used with various sizes of mizzen staysail.

Gary Hoyt, in his Freedom 40, has come up with a most esoteric, strange-looking, and hard-to-comprehend rig (Drawing 33A) which in practice has turned out to be absolutely superb. Once the sails are up they are dead easy to handle—this is a real cruising man's rig—and the boat is extremely fast. Whether anyone would want to take her across the Atlantic, or from the United States to the Islands in the late fall, with the danger of a winter gale, seems doubtful, but certainly for cruising in Europe, in the Lesser Antilles, or in exposed waters along the east coast of the United States, she would be hard to beat.

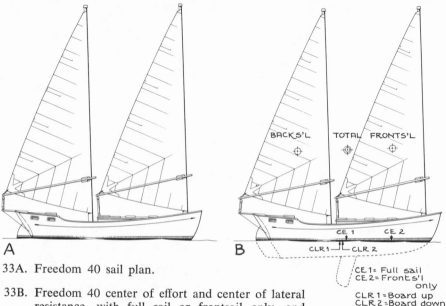

A

B

BACKS'L   TOTAL   FRONTS'L

CE 1   CE 2

CLR1   CLR 2

CE 1 = Full sail
CE 2 = Fronts'l only
CLR 1 = Board up
CLR 2 = Board down

33A. Freedom 40 sail plan.

33B. Freedom 40 center of effort and center of lateral resistance, with full sail or frontsail only, and centerboard up or down.

The boat has a cat-ketch rig, with double-luffed sails that wrap all the way around the masts and are rigged to wishbones. This is placed on top of a hull, designed by Halsey Herreshoff, which has a long keel profile, being 40 feet LOA and 35 feet LWL, with 12 feet of beam and 3½ feet of draft. The rig spreads about 760 square feet on two 45-foot masts; the vessel is regarded as a ketch only because the after mast is a few inches shorter than the forward one. Indeed, since the crew members tend to disagree about whether she's a schooner or a ketch, and to speak of the sails as the foresail and main or the main and mizzen, depending upon which view they support, we found it desirable, when sailing her, to refer to the sails as the "frontsail" and "backsail." That way, there could be no confusion.

Once the sails are set, one has literally nothing to do—just two sheets to trim, a board to adjust, and a boat to steer. To tack, one just puts the helm down and the vessel is off on the other tack, with nothing else to be done.

Tacking to windward, while all the other crews are killing themselves cranking genoas, the hardest work for the Freedom 40's crew is opening beer cans for the skipper. Going downwind, they do have to work once in a while, setting and trimming a mizzen staysail or occasionally playing the sheets a little. (In racing, the great advantage of a ketch over a schooner is that the penalty for a ketch's mizzen staysail is far more equitable than that for a schooner's fisherman staysail, and a ketch can point much higher to boot.)

How is a cat ketch shortened down? On Milgram's *Cascade,* normal jiffy reefing is used on both sails, but on the Freedom 40, one drops the backsail and sails on. Looking at the hull profile and noting the relative positions of the center of effort (CE) and the center of lateral resistance (CLR) as shown in Drawing 33B, one might conclude that the boat would have tremendous lee helm and be most difficult to handle once the backsail was dropped. At least, that's what we all thought until we sailed her. In fact, nothing could be further from the truth; she will tack, jibe, run, and beat under the frontsail alone.

If the frontsail alone is not quite enough, one can put up a small backsail (trysail), on the after mast (Drawing 34A), sheet it in, and be off once more. On the other hand, if it blows too hard even for the frontsail alone, this can be taken down, and a small frontsail and small backsail can be used instead. In still heavier weather, one can heave to under the backsail alone, or take down the backsail and run like hell for home under the small frontsail! With the centerboard all the way up, she still keeps up with a Morgan 41 with a big genoa. Incidentally,

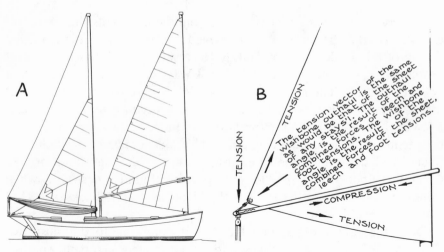

34A. Freedom 40 with frontsail plus small backsail.

34B. Wishbone angle eliminates need for a vang.

with the board up, the Freedom 40 draws only 3½ feet, so a tremendous amount of otherwise inaccessible cruising ground is opened up.

If she is really flat becalmed, the dinghy can be thrown overside to serve as a yawl boat (push boat); with two small Seagulls or one large one clamped to the dinghy's stern, she will do 4 or 5 knots—enough to get everyone home for cocktail time. The prototype Freedom 40 also carried a pair of sweeps, which one used while standing in the cockpit. These worked well but did require a lot of muscle.

Many people insist that the Freedom 40 cannot possibly go to windward because she has no jib or genoa, but her performance proves otherwise. The double-luffed sails wrapping around completely unstayed masts function as beautiful airfoils, undisturbed by masts or rigging. The wishbone sets down at an angle (Drawing 34B), so that it acts much like a boom vang. When the sheets are eased, the sail swings out on a flat plane, there being very little tendency for the clew to rise or for the sail to twist. Thus the sail develops unbelievable forward drive on a reach or run. When the Freedom 40 sailed in the 1976 and 1977 Antigua Sailing Weeks on closed courses, to windward she kept up with a Pearson 41, while off the wind she hung tight onto the Swan 44's.

A great advantage of the cat ketch with unstayed mast is that she can be handled in restricted waters, and when sailing alongside or leaving a dock, with minimal difficulty. If the sheets are freed, the sails will be able to run out fully and luff even when the wind is on—or aft of—the beam. Since there are no shrouds to interfere, the sails will just

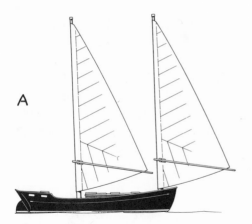

A

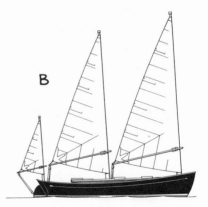

B

35A. Freedom 40 with sails streaming forward of abeam.

35B. Freedom 40 with third mast.

pivot on around until they are streaming right downwind (Drawing 35A). I would say that in restricted waters a cat ketch is much easier to handle than a conventional sloop, and is even easier to handle than a ketch or yawl. I wonder if perhaps the addition of a tiny mizzen, which would turn her into a three-masted schooner of the type sometimes known as a "Cape Horn" (and what would the Grand Prix boys do in *this* case!) would provide the ultimate in sail handling in restricted waters (Drawing 35B).

However, everything is a compromise; with the mizzen in place, the self-steering gear could not be mounted on the outboard rudder. One possible alternative might be to have a mizzen so small that it could be removed for offshore work and replaced with the vane of the self-steering gear. But perhaps we're getting too esoteric altogether.

The Freedom 40 is refreshing and practical in design, and it is interesting to speculate on how it will develop over the next five to ten years. In any event, there are likely to be a good many unemployed winch grinders, since they're not needed on this boat. Also, the mother and father with five small children may be dissatisfied, because there are so few strings for the children to play with.

The Freedom 40 which we sailed was the prototype, and some small details had not then been altogether worked out. I have now spent eight days sailing her (on two separate occasions a year apart), seven of those days without the owner present, and I believe that once fully refined, she will be one of the finest cruising boats in existence. One possible improvement might be the use of modern fiber-glass masts strengthened with carbon fiber. I only hope that the boat will soon be perfected and available, and that she will be bought by people who love to sail and will not ruin her by installing a lot of machinery, so that they spend a disproportionate amount of time alongside the dock caring for the equipment, instead of out on the water sailing.

The Freedom 40 is an odd-looking boat, but having sailed her for eight days, watched her race in Antigua Week 1976, and raced against her in Antigua Week 1977 (she beat *Iolaire* on both elapsed and corrected time), I am convinced that for coastwise work, hers is certainly the ideal cruising rig.

CAT SCHOONERS

The Block Island boat, a cat schooner with an overlapping foresail and unstayed masts, is seldom seen today, but this rather strange rig does work, and is much faster and more close-winded than one might expect. Possibly, as in the cat ketch, the sailing performance is enhanced by the absence of rigging. Augie Hollen has built a copy of the old Block Island boat *Roaring Bessie,* 32 feet LOA, 29 feet LWL, 12 feet of beam, and 5 feet of draft. The lines came from the *Rudder Sailboat Plan Book* (Rudder Publishing Company). In her he has sailed up and down the Caribbean at great speed, shocking the owners of modern cruising and racing yachts, who cannot believe that a boat will go to windward without a genoa. Augie's does require some sail handling, since every time he tacks, his loose-footed lug foresail must be trimmed like a genoa. I have not sailed in this boat myself, but he reports that when it blows up, he merely reefs his main somewhat, hangs onto his foresail until hell freezes over, and then finally reefs both sails down gradually. Again, one should think twice about taking this type of boat across the Atlantic, but certainly for longshore ocean cruising it bears investigation, especially if the new fiber-glass masts strengthened with carbon fiber could be used.

THE GAFF RIG

Many people have taken me to task for the views on the gaff rig which I presented in *OSY*-I (Ch. III). One of these people spent an hour extolling the virtues of the gaff-rigged schooner, making points with which I had to agree. However, when I observed that to take advantage of these virtues a man should have a wife who loves to sail, and three big, teen-age sons, he stated that this was his exact situation.

Only a few superb seamen maintain that a boat of this kind is suitable for shorthanded cruising.

I must admit, however, that after writing the book, I was on the receiving end of a little poetic justice. All my life I have been trying to achieve two hundred miles a day under sail, and on several occasions I have come pretty close. On *Arabella*'s fast transatlantic crossing, and on a number of fast passages on *Antilles,* we averaged over 190 miles every day. Indeed, some people have said, "Don, you have an overactive conscience. You should just do your navigation with a thick pencil, and you'd achieve your two hundred miles."

In 1973 I was asked to deliver *Atlantica*—a forty-five-foot Nova Scotia-built gaff-rigged schooner—from Grenada up to Halifax. The voyage turned out to be the finest long passage I've ever made. Toward the end, I finally attained my two hundred miles in one day—200.5 miles noon to noon, as measured by celestial observation rather than by log (noon sights crossed with longitude lines, course 010° magnetic, no surface currents, just south of Halifax). I was not the navigator—in fact, the navigator would not announce the day's run until he had cross-checked it by means of an afternoon sun line! On succeeding days, we covered 180, 200.5, and 160 miles, proving that a well-sailed gaff-rigged schooner, on a reach or a run, can certainly pick up her skirts and trot.

The whole time, we were going dead downwind, wing and wing, with foresail, main, main topsail, and sometimes fisherman staysail—flying. The boat was easy to handle—everything set perfectly, and we went like a train—but I shudder to think of what would have happened if anyone had fallen overside, for we had a tremendous amount of string about the place: the main boom was held forward with a preventer and vanged down; the main gaff was held off the lee shrouds by a vang led aft to the weather quarter and set up with a four-part block and tackle; a preventer from the tip of the main gaff was led forward to the bow; and similarly, the foreboom was held forward by a preventer and held down by a vang, and the fore gaff was held forward by a preventer and vanged to the hounds of the mainmast.

Since making the trip on *Atlantica*—covering two thousand miles in 13½ sailing days—I have been firmly convinced that gaff-rigged schooners, and gaff rigs in general, are vastly underrated. Frequently, the problem is that people just do not understand the vessel and know how to rig her correctly. Much can be learned by reading the cruising and racing books written around the turn of the century.

Certain types of boat unquestionably lend themselves to the gaff rig. For example, the little short-ended boat with a plumb stem and an

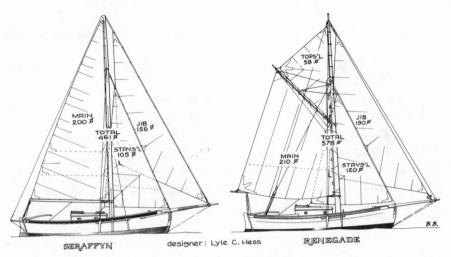

36. Rig comparison, short-ended boats—the gaff-rigged vessel generally carries greater sail area than her Marconi-rigged sister.

almost plumb transom practically demands it unless one has a bowsprit. To accommodate a Marconi rig, the mast has to go up so high that the sail area needed to move the hull properly in all weather conditions may not be obtainable (Drawing 36). The Pardeys, of *Seraffyn,* will probably object to my views, as their boat is Marconi-rigged. However, with a gaff rig accompanied by a roller-furling jib or a jib set on a traveler (*OSY*-I, Drawing 68) 578 square feet of sail can be spread on an overall length of twenty-six feet (as opposed to 461 square feet with the Marconi rig). When increasing wind makes it necessary to shorten down, dousing the topsail and taking in the jib reduces the sail area to a more manageable level.

On a small boat, all the complicated gear of a fidded topmast, or a long pole waving in the breezes once the topsail has been doused, can be avoided by the use of the kind of rig found on *Curlew,* a Falmouth Quay punt built in 1898 which has been sailed for many years and many miles by Tim and Pauline Carr. In their rig, which they state works extremely well, a light, grooved dinghy spar functions as a very long jackyard on the luff of the topsail. The jackyard with the sail attached is hoisted to the masthead; then the topsail is sheeted to the gaff end, and the topsail tack hauled down. Because this jackyard is slotted, the topsail, once down, may be taken off and stowed below, while the jackyard itself is lashed along the cabin top. By contrast, the old-fashioned method of lacing the topsail to the jackyard left one with the problem of where to stow it. It should be remembered, however, that a topsail is worth while only if it provides at least one-third the area of the mainsail.

Most important, on gaff-rigged boats, is the elimination of gaff sag.

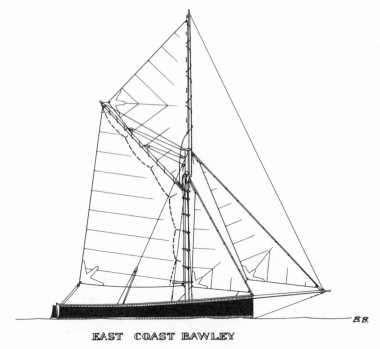

EAST COAST BAWLEY

37. On a gaff-rigged boat, the use of brails can quicken furling for the short-handed sailor.

This can be accomplished by placing a vang at the end of the gaff and a tackle on the vang, and leading the vang to the weather quarter. This arrangement of course does not lend itself to a double-ended boat, on which there is not a sufficient breadth at the weather quarter, but adequate breadth is obtainable on a short, squat, wide-sterned boat (Drawing 27, Ch. II) such as the Quay punt or the inshore bawley.

For inshore work, many gaff-rig enthusiasts like the old bawley rig used along the east coast of England (Drawing 37), with a loose-footed mainsail that can be brailed up against the mast when not in use, a standing gaff, and an extremely large topsail. This rig makes it possible to work one's way through a crowded anchorage by brailing up the mainsail, stowing the staysail, and sailing under the large topsail and the jib. Thus one can see where one is going, and the topsail, being up high, catches the lightest of zephyrs. If the jib is fitted with roller-furling gear, it can of course be doused in an instant, and then all that is really needed is a tiny mizzen perched on the stern, probably unstayed, which will enable the vessel to stream comfortably downwind once moored.

The Vertues, designed by Laurent Giles, were originally gaff-rigged, but later the Marconi rig was adopted (Drawing 38). The Marconi-rigged Vertues are certainly much better to windward, but probably not much—if at all—better off the wind. Further, almost all of them have engines, for use in very light airs. I wonder how a Marconi-rigged

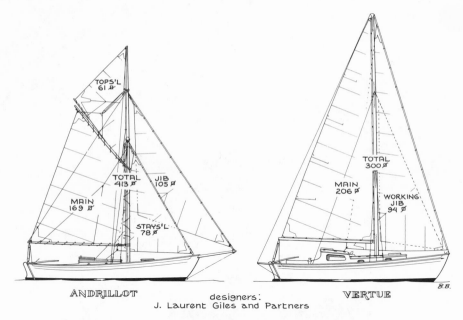

ANDRILLOT

designers:
J. Laurent Giles and Partners

VERTUE

38. Although *Vertue* was an "advancement" over the older *Andrillot*, she carried considerably less sail.

Vertue would do in light or moderate airs, even going to windward, against her gaff-rigged sister *Andrillot,* the latter of course having more top-hamper and less stability, but also much more sail area.

Fifteen years ago, the gaff rigs on the Dublin Bay 24's were replaced by Marconi rigs with aluminum spars, apparently because of trouble in finding crews willing to cope with the double-jackyard topsails—magnificent sails, tremendously picturesque, but evidently beasts to handle, except for those who really understand them. It was then discovered that in most conditions the boat that had kept the old gaff rig could beat her modern Marconi-rigged sister—genoa, aluminum mast, and all—around the normal triangular course. One wonders.

PLUMB MASTS VERSUS RAKED MASTS

Sharply raked masts are seldom seen on modern racing or cruising boats, for two reasons. With raked masts it is not possible to take advantage of the full fore-triangle area, as charged by most measurement rules. Also, there is some sacrifice of windward performance. However, from the cruising standpoint, raked masts do have a few very definite advantages. With a sharply raked mast, the shrouds can be led aft and then also act as backstays (Drawing 39). The greater the forward pressure on the mast, the tighter the shrouds become, and the more

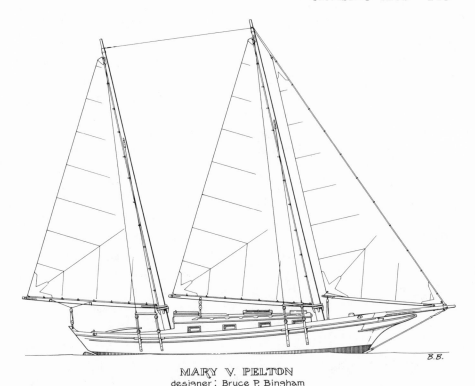

MARY V. PELTON
designer: Bruce P. Bingham

39. Radically raked masts with shrouds acting as backstays.

effective they are as backstays. Further, on schooners, ketches, and yawls, a sharply raked mast frequently brings the halyard directly over the stowage position of the dinghy. Thus the dinghy can be picked up in a sling, spun upright in the air, swung outboard, and dropped straight into the water. When the same operation is performed with a plumb mast, the dinghy or launch, which on larger boats can be quite heavy, must be held aft to prevent it from swinging forward while in the air.

Another advantage of the sharply raked mast, which few people realize, is that when the boat jibes, it does so less violently; the jibing sail begins to slow down after crossing the center line and floats gently out onto the new tack. In effect, gravity tends to hold the boom amidships, and the result is a kind of cushioning as the boom regains the strain of the sheet. A final advantage, on boats using square sails, is that because the shrouds can be led well aft, and the spreaders raked well aft—or in the case of a beamy boat, possibly dispensed with—the handling of square sails is much simpler.

The great disadvantage of the raked mast is that in light airs, off the wind, the boom will tend to swing in to amidships. Therefore, it must be held out by fore guys or preventers.

RIG ALLOWANCES

The present rig allowances in the I.O.R. rule have resulted in a complete bastardization of the cruising yacht. The vast majority of the boats designed under the I.O.R. rule are cutters; yawls are noticeable by their absence, and the ketch which could be cruised or raced with a fair degree of success, given good gear and good handling, has disappeared completely. The ketches still found (Drawing 40A) are in effect two sloops, one following the other. The mizzenmast is just slightly shorter than the main, in some cases only inches shorter. However, the complicated nature of the rigging needed to keep the mizzenmast upright and straight makes such a vessel totally impractical for cruising unless she is always sailed with an army on board. The ultimate in rule-beating was the original rig of the cat ketch *Cascade* (Drawing 40B), with two sails of almost equal size; being a ketch, *Cascade* was not penalized as highly for her mizzen triangle area as she would have been for the area between the masts if she were classified as a cat schooner.

40. Two extremes of the ketch rig as influenced by the I.O.R. racing rule, neither suitable for cruising: A, typical I.O.R. ketch; B, the cat ketch *Cascade*.

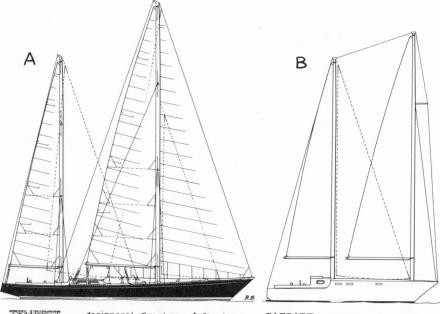

TEMPEST   designers: Sparkman & Stephens   CASCADE   designer: Jerry Milgram

The gaff schooner *Lord Jim,* although sailed by Joel Byreley, has never done well in racing because the penalty for her between-the-masts area is a high impost under the I.O.R. rule, while under the old C.C.A. rule, and in the Storm Trysail rule, which gave her the better deal, the schooner could be competitive, given the right conditions. Ed Raymond, who certainly has had a lifetime of experience in handicapping boats (though not in rating them) feels that for genuine competition the between-the-masts factor should be reduced by 15 percent for a staysail schooner and by 20 percent for a gaff schooner—possibly a little more if a lot of windward work is anticipated.

Normally, a gaff schooner can do well when racing only if the sheets can be eased much of the time: that is, with the wind forward of abeam, permitting slightly eased sheets, or on the quarter, making possible total use of the sail area. Dead to windward, the rig is just too inefficient—a fact which is not specifically taken into account by most measurement rules; and dead downwind, the sail area cannot be fully utilized. A few staysail schooners have raced successfully. For example, at various times in her career, *Bounding Home,* a Sweisguth design, distinguished herself in longshore races on the east coast of the United States. And *Niña,* under the command of the late Commodore DeCoursey Fales, aided by the famous professional yachting skipper Captain Teddy Thorsten, did well up through the middle 1960's. The Bermuda Race, in which they won Class A and placed overall, was a great swan song for the three—the Commodore, the Captain, and *Niña.* Luckily, the Commodore passed on to the sailors' Valhalla before the arrival of the I.O.R. rule, which would not have been equitable for *Niña.*

Cruising boats should be given a fair shake in the ratings, so that they have the opportunity to race competitively. As a matter of fact, this opportunity may have already arrived: the P.H.R.F. handicapping system, very popular with west-coast cruising people, is now sweeping the country. At this writing, it has just been instituted on Long Island Sound. Also, a new performance handicapping system (M.R.H.) has been accepted by the American I.O.R. Technical Committee and will be applied to special cruising classes at Block Island Week this year. Only time will tell how truly fair these systems are, but I have to give the racing-rule boys a lot of credit for recognizing an agonizing problem and trying to solve it. Under these rules, every schooner or ketch should be qualified to race around the buoys and in moderately serious club events as well as offshore; a capable skipper and crew, sailing a cruising boat with a proper rig and good sails, should have a chance to hit the winning column, or at least to cross the starting line feeling that with a few lucky breaks they may emerge near the top, instead of knowing at the outset that they will be Tail-End Charlie.

IV

~~~~~~~~~~~~~~~~~~~~~~~~~~~~~~~~~

Spars and Standing Rigging

SPARS

MATERIALS

Wood

In this day and age, the wooden spar is rapidly becoming as extinct as the carrier pigeon. Living in the tropics, and viewing the matter from the insurance standpoint, I couldn't be more pleased. Wooden masts in the tropics have a great potential for developing rot, coming unglued, and falling down at very inopportune times.

However, many boats do still have wooden spars, and when a replacement is necessary, the owner often wants another wooden spar, to preserve the appearance of the boat. Similarly, those who are now building traditional wooden boats generally want traditional wooden spars for them.

But obtaining wooden spars today is becoming a time-consuming and expensive proposition. To begin with, almost no good spruce or fir can be found, so yards are switching to Oregon pine (also called Douglas fir). This is available in long lengths, and if it is of good quality, is perfectly acceptable. Another difficulty arises because the craftsmen capable of making the round or the beautiful oval wooden spars that were used for yachts in the 1930's, 1940's, and early 1950's, are fast becoming scarce. One by one, the yards that built these spars, with their wonderful woodworking equipment and assortment of bits for routing the inside and rounding the outside of the spar, are going out of business. People are instead building box-section spars, as popularized by L. Francis Herreshoff, for which lumber in the more commonly available sizes may be used. Correctly proportioned box-section spars may not be as beautiful as the oval-shaped ones, but they are certainly less expensive and less difficult to construct.

In my view, the best place to turn to for large wooden spars is Holland, where there are two firms (for addresses, see Appendix) which specialize in them. These firms can make oval-shaped spars, but seem to concentrate on the box-section type. We have found their services invaluable on occasions when one of the larger charter yachts in the West Indies has lost her rig and needed spars in a hurry. At a time when wooden spars are extremely expensive in the United States, and only slightly less so in England, Scotland, and Ireland, these companies make them economically and well, and with unbelievable rapidity. One of the firms, Van der Nuit, built the mast for the sixty-eight-foot ketch *Pride of Cockaigne* in a remarkably short time, and completed the spar for the sixty-seven-foot schooner *Shearwater* within ten days of receipt of the order.

Furthermore, they will make spars of absolutely any size, being among the apparently few firms left in the world that are still equipped to build really large spars. *Janeen,* a 116-foot Herreshoff schooner which is rigged as a staysail schooner, with a mainmast so tall it just barely fits under Brooklyn Bridge, had a new mast made by Van der Nuit at a most reasonable price.

However, although they work quickly and make a beautiful and economical spar, the spreaders which they provide tend to rot out in the tropics very rapidly. Also, many feel that the design of their spreader and mast fittings could be improved. Therefore, it is recommended that the person ordering spars from one of these firms have the spreaders made of fir, not heavy ash, and supply his own drawings for the mast fittings. The latter should be basically copied from the superb designs produced in the late 1940's and 1950's by Sparkman and Stephens, Rhodes, and L. Francis Herreshoff, and fabricated in bronze. Shroud attachments probably hit their highest stage of development in this era.

For any wooden spar built in this day and age, a resorcinol or epoxy glue should definitely be used. The old casein glue, although water-resistant, is definitely not waterproof, and in the tropics, with poor maintenance, very soon weakens critically.

Aluminum

Aluminum spars are becoming more and more popular each year. Most people fail to recognize their real limitations. Corrosion, especially in the tropics, is a much greater problem than most spar manu-facturers located in temperate climates realize, or are willing to admit, despite the information continually being fed back to them. On any yacht with stainless-steel fittings pop-riveted to the mast, if the fittings down around the base are removed after five or six years in the tropics, a case of massive corrosion, possibly even a vast hole, will probably be revealed under the stainless-steel or aluminum plate. The only way to prevent electrolysis between the mast and a fitting is to make sure that the fitting—whether mounted on a wooden pad, a stainless-steel pad, an aluminum pad, or what-have-you—is well insulated from the mast by a layer of polysulfide seam compound, a good, thick rubber gasket, and then more polysulfide seam compound.

The wooden winch pad is a potential source of massive and danger-ous corrosion, for unless the pad is perfectly fitted to the mast, and a rubber gasket with a really heavy layer of polysulfide seam compound on each side is inserted between the pad and the mast, water will work its way under the pad. Similarly, care should be taken that there are no places where the mast touches wooden joiner work belowdecks, since corrosion is very likely to develop there.

Trouble is also caused by handhole covers and by the numerous openings in the mast required when there are internal halyards. These of course allow large quantities of water to get in, and unless there is a large drain hole at the bottom that is checked weekly, the water may collect, reaching as high as the lowest halyard hole. This causes cor-rosion inside the mast, and impairs the stability of the boat.

Finally, if an aluminum spar is to last for a really long time, espe-cially in the tropics, it should be anodized and painted with two-unit epoxy paint. Older spars that have become corroded should be sanded down to the bare metal; next, an etching primer, and then the two-unit epoxy paint, should be applied, in accordance with the manufacturer's directions for painting aluminum.

ALUMINUM SPARS—HANDHOLE COVERS: If handholes are cut in the mast, the covers should fit outside of them and should be firmly at-tached with numerous screws, so that the structural integrity of the mast is not affected.

When *Iolaire*'s mast arrived from Sparlight eleven years ago, I was unhappy with the British flush handhole cover, which was similar to the one shown in *OSY*-I, Drawing 28, except that it was held in place by only four screws. This arrangement has many disadvantages, the foremost being the fact that the hole is small; in this instance, my left hand was the only one on board that could fit into it. Second, of course,

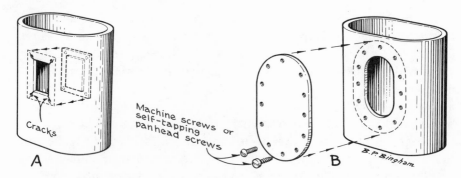

41. *Iolaire*'s handhole cover: A, original, with cracks in mast radiating from screw holes; B, replacement.

if this type of handhole cover is dropped, it is likely to fall inside the mast, so that the mast must be lifted in order to retrieve it.

Further, I wondered about the weakening effect of this installation on the mast. However, I assumed that Sparlight, having had vast experience, knew a lot more about this subject that I did. But in November, 1976, while working on the winches around the base of the mast, we discovered small cracks radiating from the screw holes for the handhole cover (Drawing 41A). Careful examination revealed that the mast was sheared a third of the way around its circumference. Since we had on board an extra section of spar, we were able to cut from part of this a large cover to fit outside the handhole, overlapping the edges by approximately two inches. This was secured to the mast with twelve ¼-inch stainless-steel screws, and the structural integrity of the mast appears to have been reestablished (Drawing 41B).

ALUMINUM SPARS—EXTRA MATERIAL: When ordering an aluminum spar, or buying a boat which already has one, the individual who expects to do extensive cruising, especially in out-of-the-way areas, should obtain and store on board an extra section of from three to six feet long (depending on the size of the boat) having the same extrusion as the spar. This extra section can be used for a butt plate, if the spar is lost and bits and pieces retrieved; for reinforcing handhole covers; for a plate on the spar at the point where corrosion under a winch has resulted in a hole; and for reinforcing any other portion of the spar that appears weak or corroded.

Fiber Glass

The fiber-glass masts first successfully built by Oscar Plym, in Sweden, and now obtainable there from Ocean Boats (for address, see

Appendix) have stood the test of time, have no corrosion problems, and are comparable to aluminum masts in weight and price. More yachtsmen and designers should investigate them, especially for use on the Freedom 40, where the masts are completely unstayed.

Kevlar

Dave Dana is experimenting with masts made of Kevlar. Perhaps this will turn out to be the material we have been seeking for light, non-corroding spars.

SHROUD ANCHORAGES

The masthead on an older mast, with wires spliced around it, frequently looks like a rat's nest. The masses of wire, difficult to work on and not particularly strong, make it a real disaster area. But with some careful planning, the more modern tang rig can be substituted for the wires spliced around the mast. Using the instructions found in Francis S. Kinney's revision of *Skene's Elements of Yacht Design,* the average person can perform the calculations needed to determine what bolts and screws will provide adequate support for the shrouds and stays. For the person not too good at calculating, the "by guess and by God" method is to find a wooden mast on a boat similar to one's own—preferably with mast tangs designed by Sparkman and Stephens (Drawing 42) or Philip Rhodes or (for box-section spars) by L. Francis Herreshoff (Drawing 43)—use wire of the same size, and copy the design of the mast tangs. Herreshoff's basic fittings are good, but do require machining and special bolts. Many riggers recommend that instead of the bronze rods with gun-stock bolts at each end, bronze pipe with drilled and cottered nuts should be used to attach the tangs. Because this pipe is hollow, it saves weight.

Most tangs should be secured to wooden spars by *roundheaded* wood screws—well staggered, so that no two of them lie on the same line of the grain. I always wondered why roundheaded wood screws were invariably used on good mast-tang installations; finally, a good engineer explained to me that when a flatheaded screw is used, the mast tang must be countersunk at each screw, and since the metal thickness in the immediate vicinity of each screw is thereby reduced by about 66 percent, the possibility arises that the tang may actually tear along the edges of its screw holes. Further, the reduction of the tang's bearing surfaces against the screws, because of the countersinking, causes the edges of the screw holes to act as shearing blades when the tang is

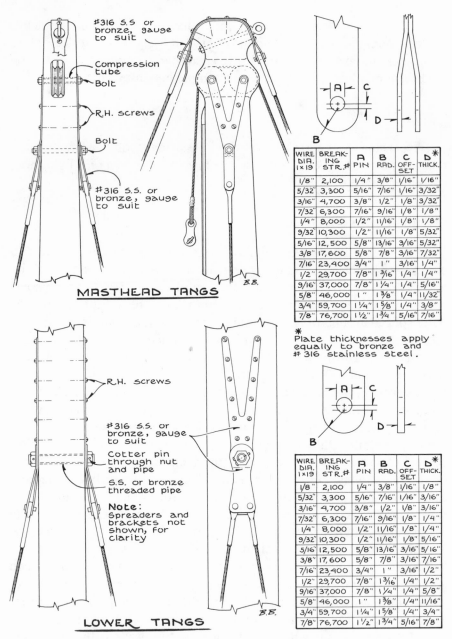

MASTHEAD TANGS

WIRE DIA. 1×19	BREAK-ING STR.#	A PIN	B RAD.	C OFF-SET	D* THICK.
1/8"	2,100	1/4"	3/8"	1/16"	1/16"
5/32"	3,300	5/16"	7/16"	1/16"	3/32"
3/16"	4,700	3/8"	1/2"	1/8"	3/32"
7/32"	6,300	7/16"	9/16"	1/8"	1/8"
1/4"	8,000	1/2"	11/16"	1/8"	1/8"
9/32"	10,300	1/2"	11/16"	1/8"	5/32"
5/16"	12,500	5/8"	13/16"	3/16"	5/32"
3/8"	17,600	5/8"	7/8"	3/16"	7/32"
7/16"	23,400	3/4"	1"	3/16"	1/4"
1/2"	29,700	7/8"	1 3/16"	1/4"	1/4"
9/16"	37,000	7/8"	1 1/4"	1/4"	5/16"
5/8"	46,000	1"	1 3/8"	1/4"	11/32"
3/4"	59,700	1 1/4"	1 5/8"	1/4"	3/8"
7/8"	76,700	1 1/2"	1 3/4"	5/16"	7/16"

* Plate thicknesses apply equally to bronze and #316 stainless steel.

LOWER TANGS

WIRE DIA. 1×19	BREAK-ING STR.#	A PIN	B RAD.	C OFF-SET	D* THICK.
1/8"	2,100	1/4"	3/8"	1/16"	1/8"
5/32"	3,300	5/16"	7/16"	1/16"	3/16"
3/16"	4,700	3/8"	1/2"	1/8"	3/16"
7/32"	6,300	7/16"	9/16"	1/8"	1/4"
1/4"	8,000	1/2"	11/16"	1/8"	1/4"
9/32"	10,300	1/2"	11/16"	1/8"	5/16"
5/16"	12,500	5/8"	13/16"	3/16"	5/16"
3/8"	17,600	5/8"	7/8"	3/16"	7/16"
7/16"	23,400	3/4"	1"	3/16"	1/2"
1/2"	29,700	7/8"	1 3/16"	1/4"	1/2"
9/16"	37,000	7/8"	1 1/4"	1/4"	5/8"
5/8"	46,000	1"	1 3/8"	1/4"	11/16"
3/4"	59,700	1 1/4"	1 5/8"	1/4"	3/4"
7/8"	76,700	1 1/2"	1 3/4"	5/16"	7/8"

42. Sparkman and Stephens tangs for wooden masts.

under high tension; they can actually cut the heads of the screws completely off if there is the slightest vertical movement. Also, because the downward movement of the edges of the tang's countersunk holes against the angled sides of the screwheads has a wedgelike effect,

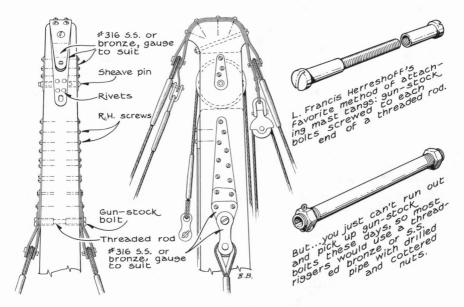

Sheave pin

#316 S.S. or bronze, gauge to suit

Rivets

R.H. screws

Gun-stock bolt

Threaded rod

#316 S.S. or bronze, gauge to suit

L. Francis Herreshoff's favorite method of attaching mast tangs: gun-stock bolts screwed to each end of a threaded rod.

But...you just can't run out and pick up gun-stock bolts these days, so most riggers would use a threaded bronze or S.S. pipe with drilled and cottered nuts.

43. L. Francis Herreshoff tangs for wooden masts.

the screws may be forced out of the mast if their heads aren't broken off first. In addition, the screwheads themselves exert a wedgelike effect, and can actually cause the screw holes in the tang to grow gradually larger, until there is hardly any metal remaining. Though this process takes years, the ultimate effect should not be forgotten.

Tang Materials—Stainless Steel

Some knowledgeable individuals believe that stainless steel should not be used aloft for masthead fittings, tang materials, tang fittings, and the like because of the danger of failure through undetected fatigue, and recommend mild steel instead. However, if mild steel is used, one must remember that it has a much lower strength (P.S.I.) than, say, No. 316 stainless steel, so a considerable increase in metal thicknesses is required. When this is calculated, an additional factor of 15 percent should be added to compensate for the weakening effect that hot-dip galvanizing has on mild steel.

If stainless steel is used, a bottle of Spotcheck testing liquid should be kept on hand (for source, see Appendix). The standard method of checking steel for minute fracture lines is to paint this light-blue liquid on the fitting; the minutest hairline crack, not visible to the naked eye, is then sharply defined as a dark-blue line.

MASTHEAD DESIGN

Most designers would recommend altering the old-fashioned mast-head to a modern shape (Drawing 44A). With the aid of an electric planer and a good carpenter, in an amazingly short time one can re-build the masthead so that it is neater, lighter, and stronger than be-fore, with room for the extra fittings, spare halyards and stays, and the like which the offshore sailing man may wish to place aloft.

The top of the mast should be shaped to serve as a crane for the permanent backstay. The topping lift should have its own separate tangs and clevis pin. The forward face of the mast should have a crane to carry the head-stay tangs. If needed, a block of wood is usually in-serted to fill out the mast to the correct angle, thus allowing a fair lead for the head stay.

Even on a cruising boat which is not to be raced at all, installation of a bail or eye for the spinnaker-halyard block is well worth while. This is quite simple to do while the spar is being built; later on, addi-tion of the bail or eye would be difficult and expensive, since removal of the spar would be required. Most commonly, a silicon bronze eye bolt is used for the attachment of the spinnaker-halyard block. Passing through the forestay/backstay tangs and completely through the mast-head, this eye bolt also serves as the forestay/backstay tang bolt.

44. The modern wooden masthead (A) is a vast improvement in windage, weight, and strength over its old-fashioned predecessors (B and C).

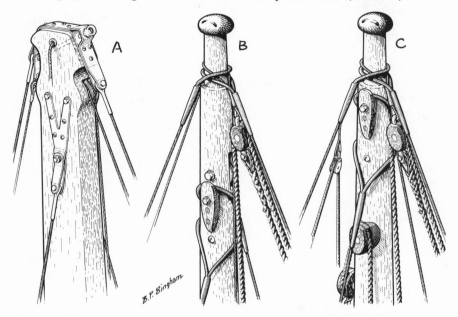

The shroud tangs are usually completely separate from the forestay/ backstay tangs, and they always bend away from the mast below the halyard sheave box, which is the mast's weak spot, so that the shroud side forces will not be applied above this point. Occasionally, the shroud tangs are extended above the sheave box and over the masthead (where they are brazed or riveted to the forestay/backstay tangs), and then down the opposite side of the mast, but even then, they must not bend away from the mast until they are a safe distance below the sheave box.

With the advent of stainless steel, many yards have started making a welded cap plate that fits on top of the mast and has two separate cranes for the spinnaker halyard. In this installation, again, the shroud tangs should be carried below the sheave box before being bent outward to receive the shroud terminals. A fitting of this type is always slightly suspect, since one does not know the ability of the welder who made it. A welded fitting, especially aloft, should be inspected for cracks periodically, with the blue liquid Spotcheck previously described.

Mastheads for Aluminum Spars

The design of mastheads for aluminum spars becomes increasingly refined as time goes by and more and more yards become familiar with the art of welding and tapering aluminum masts. Frequently, the entire masthead fitting is welded up of aluminum, so that the electrolysis problems caused by using dissimilar metals are eliminated. The welds should of course be examined periodically for cracks, with Spotcheck.

Some people prefer mild-steel fittings on aluminum spars, because mild steel can easily be welded by practically any welding shop, so they can be repaired just about anywhere in the world. Also, there is less of an electrolysis corrosion problem with mild steel and aluminum than with stainless steel and aluminum. On the debit side, mild-steel fittings are certainly not as strong as properly designed stainless fittings, and must be galvanized or painted.

Stainless-steel masthead fittings on aluminum spars, like those on wooden spars, must be carefully inspected periodically with Spotcheck. Also, they must be well insulated from the aluminum; otherwise, massive corrosion problems are inevitable.

MAST BOOTS

One of the most aggravating things in the world when slogging along to windward feeling miserable, with spray flying everywhere, is to have water pouring belowdecks through an improperly secured mast boot.

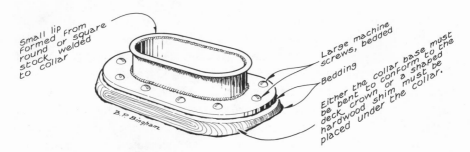

Small lip from formed or square round welded stock to collar

Large machine screws, bedded

Bedding

Either the collar base must be bent to conform to the deck crown or a shaped hardwood shim must be placed under the collar.

B. P. Bingham

45. Metal deck plate for mast boot.

Avoiding this problem requires the use of a bronze, stainless-steel, or aluminum plate with a lip (Drawing 45), watertight and firmly fixed to the deck. The mast boot should be secured tightly around the mast with a good, marlin lashing that is then waterproofed with three or four coats of a mixture of equal parts of varnish and linseed oil. The boot is next folded down around the lip of the plate and secured again with the marlin lashing, which is then waterproofed as before.

In years gone by, the mast boot was normally made of canvas, and was waterproofed after being put into place. Exactly how the mast boot for an oval mast of, say, thirty inches in circumference was made to fit down over a deck plate which because of wedges (wooden or rubber) had a circumference of, say, thirty-six inches or more, is beyond me. I have never been able to get any sailmaker who knows the answer to let me in on the secret.

Some manufacturers of aluminum spars supply a neoprene mast boot that can be fitted tightly over the spar, secured by a hose clamp, and then folded down over the mast-partner coaming and secured by another hose clamp. However, this boot seems to be made of relatively thin neoprene, which deteriorates very fast in the tropics even if protected from sunlight by a canvas or Dacron cover. Furthermore, it can only be installed or removed when the mast is out of the boat, so replacement is difficult if a boat is likely to be in commission twelve months of the year. One solution to this problem is to install three or four of the boots before the mast is put into the boat. Then, when a boot deteriorates, the mast chocks are removed, the old boot is cut away, the next boot is slipped up in its place and secured, and the chocks are reinstalled.

We discovered a few months ago that a satisfactory mast boot for *Iolaire* can be made from an old rubber inner tube. It is cut to shape, wrapped around the mast very carefully, with a six-inch overlap, secured tightly to the mast by a hose clamp, and then folded down and secured with another hose clamp. An arrangement of this sort is absolutely watertight, provided the joint in the rubber is placed aft of the mast partner, facing aft. My mate Selwyn Nimblette, from Grenada, did this job so carefully that since then we have not had a drop of water belowdecks from around the mast.

MAST FITTINGS, METAL WINCH TABLES

The mounting of mast fittings, notably metal winch tables, is frequently very inadequate. Not only are they poorly insulated from the mast, so that corrosion is bound to occur (as described earlier in this chapter), but often the winches are machine-screwed to the tables and the tables simply pop-riveted to the mast with six or eight aluminum pop rivets. The shear loading strength of aluminum pop rivets is variable; with halyard tension that may be in the region of 4,000 pounds, the result is sometimes a negligible margin of safety. No wonder so many winches go flying up the mast during heavy weather.

Where pop rivets are used, they should definitely be of stainless steel, not aluminum. But most riggers will agree that all fittings on the mast, with the exception of the sail track, should instead be secured with stainless-steel machine screws. Merely pop-riveting winch pads, cleats, or the like to the spar may be cheap and economical for the manufacturer, but if the boat is to be sailed in the tropics, or must be in commission twelve months of the year, the outcome will inevitably be massive problems at some time in the future.

STEPS ON THE MAST, RATLINES

As each year goes by, more and more boats are seen with steps going up the mast. Experienced seamen have various opinions about them.

It is universally agreed that on a gaff-rigged cruising boat of any size, if there are topmasts, steps or ratlines going up the masts are essential, to facilitate handling of the topsails. They enable someone to go aloft to clear any fouls in the topsails, or—where the topsails are permanently set on hoops along the topmast—to furl the topsails.

On a modern Marconi-rigged boat, steps or ratlines up the mast to the lower spreaders are often useful. For example, Hank Taft requested that I rig ratlines for him on *Taio Hae* when he was preparing for a winter of cruising the Caribbean. He pointed out that he would have to spend a lot of time sitting in the lower spreaders doing eyeball navigation, and that although he was in pretty good physical shape and could outpull me on a line and outcrank me on a winch, there was no way he could hoist his 230 pounds to the spreaders with speed and alacrity. Hence, he wanted the ratlines.

However, some Marconi-rigged boats have steps going all the way to the masthead, and one wonders whether these are really worth while. First and foremost, their very presence may be what makes it necessary to go up the mast frequently, since halyards and sails tend to foul the steps. Second, if a boat is thoughtfully rigged with spare halyards, one seldom has to go up the masthead while at sea; usually, when a halyard is fouled or breaks, the spare can be used. Furthermore, the individual who does climb the masthead finds himself standing there hanging on; to get his hands free for working, he must first securely lash himself into place. The single-handed sailor may have no alternative. For him, steps to the masthead are possibly desirable, but most other seamen would rather be hoisted aloft in a boatswain's chair, which leaves both hands free. Hence, one really should give careful thought to the advantages and disadvantages of steps or ratlines to the masthead, before going to the expense of installing them.

Ratline Installation

Modern ratlines (Drawing 46) are usually made of ash or oak, and securely seized into place with marlin, which is then made waterproof with a mixture of equal parts of varnish and linseed oil. If the ratline lashings are regularly painted with this mixture, they will last practically forever.

Lashing directly to galvanized rigging will work well. However, lashing directly to stainless-steel rigging, whether with marlin or with wire, is not practical. The ratlines soon begin to slip, with the result that the

46. Ratlines served to shrouds.

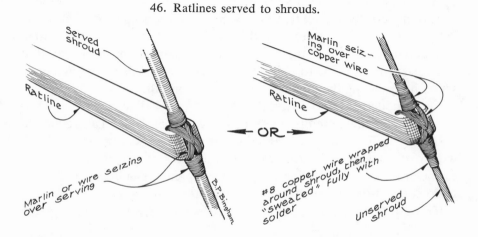

footing they supply feels insecure, and the boat looks bad. My prime recommendation is to first serve the shrouds completely, from top to bottom, then paint them with three or four coats of the mixture of varnish and linseed oil, and only then secure the ratlines to the shrouds, over the servings. One may also seize the ratlines with wire and then sweat them with solder; this procedure will definitely prevent them from slipping down the shrouds.

On some modern Marconi-rigged boats that spend the summers up north and the winters in the Caribbean, it may be desired to have ratlines up only while in the tropics. Someone on *Antilles* dreamed up an excellent installation to fill this need. Two extra lower shrouds, of $\frac{3}{16}$-inch stainless-steel wire, were secured by shackles to a plate hanging from the lower-shroud tang and to adapter plates to the lower-shroud turnbuckles. The ratlines were then installed with turnbuckles to adjust the tension, and were secured to the auxiliary stays. When the boat headed north, the whole installation was unshackled, coiled up, and stowed below. I copied the same arrangement on *Taio Hae,* and it has been used satisfactorily on other boats as well.

REACHING STRUTS

Though not essential for the cruising boat that carries spinnakers, a reaching strut is a very useful item of gear. Few cruising boats will carry the spinnaker pole hard up against the head stay except in the very lightest of airs, and on a close reach, but even for the pole just approaching the head stay, the load is immeasurably reduced by use of the reaching strut.

Also, the reaching strut can make an excellent boat boom for keeping the dinghy alongside, where it is less likely to be stolen on a dark night, and at the same time preventing it from continually banging against the boat. If the reaching strut is too short to be an effective boat boom when it is pivoted from the mast, two extra fittings can be screwed into the bulwarks; attached here, the reaching strut should be long enough to extend to the dinghy. If it is still too short, one can try using the spinnaker pole.

BOOMS AND BOOM ATTACHMENTS
Attachments

The best end fitting for a wooden boom consists of a bronze cap that fits over the entire end of the boom; it is easily held in place by one or two rivets or screws.

The bails carrying the mainsheet blocks should extend around as much of the boom as possible. If the boom is hollow, a solid block of wood should be inserted into it wherever a bail is to be secured, and the bail should then be attached by at least three bolts, to spread the load, or—better still, in most cases—by bronze rivets passing all the way through the boom. The advantage of these is that they can be ground down flush.

OUTHAUL TRACK: The outhaul track should be made of a heavy bronze, so that it is considerably heavier than the sail track. If the out-haul track is so long that the last slide will be over it, a large slide that will fit the outhaul track should be installed on the sail; the other slides of course fit the track of the boom.

It is essential that the outhaul track be bolted right straight through the boom, as screws hold well in shear, not in tension. Under sail, the major load on the outhaul is vertical rather than horizontal.

The outhaul fitting should have a jaw wide enough to accept the rather thick clew cringle of a cruising sail. The pin should be lined up so that the foot of the sail maintains a straight line, without a rise or dip at the outhaul.

GOOSENECKS: The plates joining the end of a wooden boom to the gooseneck slider—or, with a fixed gooseneck, to a point on the after face of the mast—should spread the load over a fairly large area of the boom, and should be secured to it by rivets or screws. The gooseneck should be designed so that the boom is free to rotate around its own axis; otherwise, the very great twisting strain which exists when sheets are eased may very well splinter the boom. This is one respect in which the great L. Francis Herreshoff fell down. Many of the goosenecks he designed do not permit the boom to rotate around its own axis, and there have consequently been numerous boom failures on Herreshoff boats.

The jaw on the gooseneck, like that of the outhaul fitting, should be wide enough to accept the tack cringle. The hole in the gooseneck jaw should be slightly above the top of the boom, so that the foot of the sail leads into the gooseneck without a rise or dip. Similarly, it should be positioned so that the luff rope leads vertically down the after face of the mast.

Roller-reefing booms usually have a setback (called a "cut back," "knock back," or "rub back") from the after face of the mast to make room for the roller-reefing gear (Drawing 47A). The rub-back dimension must be given to the sailmaker when sails are ordered. The bot-

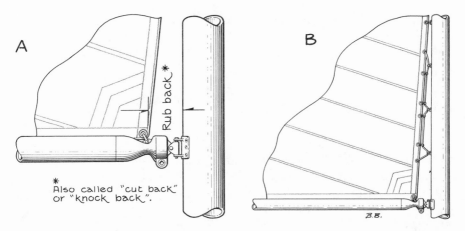

47. Roller reefing: A, rub back; B, jack line to keep the luff tight when the sail is full set.

tom six to eight feet of the luff of the sail can best be secured by a jack line that can be adjusted or disconnected as the sail is reefed (Drawing 47B).

Aluminum Booms

The fittings for an aluminum boom are basically the same as those for a wooden one. Bails are usually secured to the boom by machine screws or pop rivets, instead of rivets or bolts. Since a boom receives plenty of salt spray, and corrosion is inevitable, a gasket and insulating compound should be used under every fitting.

The great advantage of the aluminum boom is that the outhaul, topping lift, reefing lines, Cunningham lines, and the like can all be easily led inside, so that there are no exposed lines to chafe or foul. When, in addition, sheet stoppers and innovator winches are installed, the result is a nice, clean—though expensive—boom.

Jib and staysail clubs are discussed in the section on club jibs and club staysails in Chapter VI.

BOWSPRITS

In years gone by, when every yacht had a bowsprit, most seamen and designers understood this spar—its problems, its idiosyncracies, and its rigging. Because it was understood, it did not cause quite as much trouble as one might have expected. Today, few yachtsmen really understand the bowsprit, and innumerable difficulties are encountered on the yacht that has one.

The various types of bowsprit include the old-fashioned, the fixed, and the A-frame.

Old-Fashioned Bowsprits

Especially on the old British boats, the bowsprit (Drawing 48) was in reality a great, long pole offset to one side of the stem and sticking out a mile in front of the vessel; it could be retracted when entering a harbor or in very heavy weather. The bowsprit carried only the jib, which could be set·at any point along it with the aid of a traveler, and the jib topsail, which was set to the end of the bowsprit in light airs. The rig was actually held in the boat by a staysail stay set to the stem-head. This was the most essential stay in the entire boat. In very light weather, large headsails were set, but in heavy weather the bowsprit

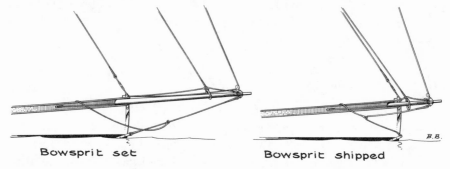

Bowsprit set   Bowsprit shipped

48. Old-fashioned British bowsprit with traveler.

was used only to set relatively small headsails. Thus the strains were not too great and the topmast stay, jibstay, and bobstay could be set up with tackles.

This long, running bowsprit was not the widow-maker one might have expected it to be, since in heavy weather people seldom actually walked out on it. The jib, mounted on a traveler, was handled from the deck (*OSY*-I, Drawing 68); the jib topsail was set up only in very light airs, when there was little danger of going overside.

Fixed Bowsprits

The fixed bowsprit was more rightfully known as a widow-maker, because crews were continually having to go out onto the end of it in heavy weather to muzzle the jib or jib topsail. Safety harnesses were

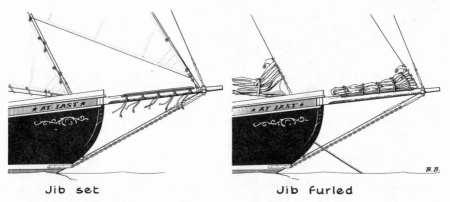

Jib set   Jib furled

49. Old-fashioned bowsprit with lash-down rails.

unheard of, and only in the worst weather would a seaman even dream of wrapping a line around his waist.

The standard fixed bowsprit (Drawing 49) usually had wooden handrails along its top, with lanyards to lash a stowed jib. The topmast stay came to a turnbuckle at the end of the bowsprit. The jibstay came over a roller at the end of the bowsprit, and was secured and adjusted beneath it with a turnbuckle. The roller was used so that when the jib was doused it did not have to be removed from the stay. Instead—as shown in the drawing—it was hauled down tight to the end of the bowsprit (which could not have been done if there had been a turnbuckle at the base of the jibstay), and the clew was hauled back tight; then a good, snug furl was thrown in the jib, the leech and foot were rolled in toward the miter, and the lanyards rove through the handrails were taken up over the sail, crossed, and knotted tightly. If the lanyards were closely spaced, the jib was held to the bowsprit so firmly that it would last through a hurricane.

The jib topsail did have to be unhanked and stowed below, but in the days of cotton sails, this was strictly a light-weather sail, taken off before the end of the bowsprit started dipping into the water.

A-frame Bowsprits

Attaching a pulpit to the end of a bowsprit is costly and difficult—*Iolaire*'s pulpit shakes and shimmies like an old belly dancer. For this reason, many designers have switched from the conventional bowsprit to the A-frame (*OSY*-I, Photo 82), which with anchor roller, pulpit, and so on forms a single unit. This is an excellent though expensive installation. It must be carefully designed, for if the A-frame is too light it will tend to spread under load, decreasing in length and thereby slackening the head stay.

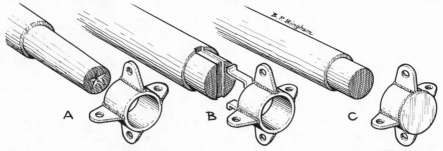

50. Crance irons: A, ring style; B, with strap to keep it from sliding aft; C, cap style.

Crance Irons

The crance iron, which is placed at the end of the bowsprit and takes the head stay, bowsprit shrouds, and bobstays, must be carefully made. All too often it is just a ring set on the end of the bowsprit (Drawing 50A). With modern rigs, the ring tends to splinter the wood and slide aft along the bowsprit. A strap can be fitted to prevent this (Drawing 50B), but though this design is generally successful, sometimes the strap is pushed down into the wood until the lips no longer hold and the crance iron moves aft. For this reason, the best design consists of a cap which fits over the entire end of the bowsprit and cannot possibly slip aft (Drawing 50C). Needless to say, one must remove this cap from time to time to make sure there is no rot starting beneath it.

Roller-Furling-Jib Installation

If a roller-furling jib is carried on the end of the bowsprit, the roller-furling drum should be mounted about eighteen inches aft of the head stay, possibly even farther away on large boats, a little closer on small ones. Unless there is a decent separation between the roller-furling drum and the head stay, when the jib is being rolled up off the wind, its luff will try to roll around the head stay. Also, if the separation between

51. Double bobstays, with the inner taking the strain of the roller-furling jib, and the outer taking the strain of the forestay.

drum and head stay is not adequate, when a light jib is left hanked onto the stay, the drum will bear against the bag and make it most difficult to roll and unroll the jib. The fitting for the roller-furling jib should not put unsupported strains on the bowsprit; hence, there should be double bobstays, with the inner one meeting a crance iron directly under the roller-furling drum (Drawing 51).

Bobstays

The bobstay on the bowsprit must be much stronger than the head stay, the exact strength depending on the rig. Three rigs frequently seen are the gaff rig, with the staysail stay basically supporting the mast (Drawing 52A); the Marconi rig, again with the staysail stay basically supporting the mast (Drawing 52B); and the modern Marconi rig, with a staysail stay that can be disconnected, and the whole load carried on the head stay (Drawing 52C). In the modern Marconi rig, the entire installation is supported by the bobstay, and in view of the loads involved, as will be shown in Drawing 56, many seamen feel that with this type of rig there should be a double bobstay. Further, if the outer bobstay can be of a fixed length, with the tension adjusted by moving the bowsprit (as will be described shortly, in the section on bowsprit support), a turnbuckle can be dispensed with, and the removal of this weak link from the rigging "chain" eliminates one source of trouble.

52. Fore-and-aft mast support: A, gaff rig with topmast; B, Marconi cutter or double-headsail Marconi sloop; C, Marconi sloop with removable staysail stay.

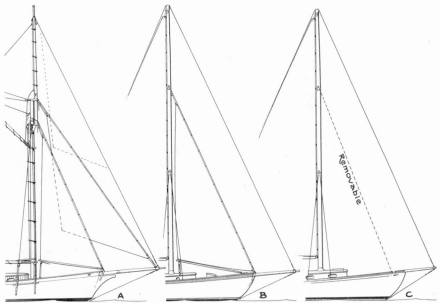

The bobstay should be of 1 by 19 wire, with Norseman or Sta-Lok fittings, which may be taken apart and inspected to ensure that they are in good shape. Chain should not be used for the bobstay, because size for size and weight for weight it is much weaker than wire (see Appendix, Table VI). Also, under extreme loads, chain links tend to flatten, and the chain stretches. Solid rod, which is sometimes used for the bobstay, has the disadvantage that, like rod rigging, it usually works perfectly and then gives way all of a sudden; 1 by 19 wire, however, generally provides a warning, in that one or two strands will go before the whole wire does.

Dolphin Strikers

If the angle between the bobstay and the bowsprit is very small, a dolphin striker will be needed, particularly on a boat with a long bowsprit (Drawing 53A). When this is installed, angles x and y, as shown in the drawing, must be equal; otherwise, the dolphin striker will tend

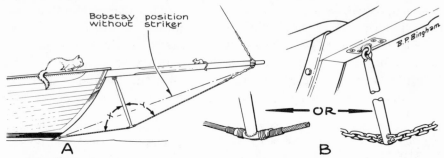

53. Dolphin striker: A, effect on bobstay angle; B, methods of securing to bobstay.

to slide forward or aft. The dolphin striker should be free to pivot athwartships; if it cannot pivot in this manner, when the bobstay lies across the anchor line or hits the dock, the dolphin striker may be torn right out. The old-fashioned dolphin striker—with a forging of two eyes, one inside the other—can pivot in this manner, and is satisfactory even today. To prevent movement fore and aft, the dolphin striker should be firmly secured to the bobstay with heavy seizing wire (but must periodically be checked under the seizing); in some cases, the bobstay is actually shackled to the dolphin striker (Drawing 53B).

Bowsprit Shrouds, Bowsprit Webbing

Bowsprit shrouds support the bowsprit athwartships. The modern short bowsprit does not place too great a load on the bowsprit shrouds, which can therefore be led directly to the hull (Drawing 54A). However, where the bowsprit is long, struts (called "whiskers") for the bowsprit shrouds become necessary (Drawing 54B). Like the dolphin striker, these struts must be allowed to pivot—in this case, in the vertical plane, so that they will not become bent when people stand on the bowsprit shrouds. At the same time, they must be well served to the shrouds, so that they will not slip fore and aft.

54. Bowsprit shrouds: A, led directly to hull; B, with struts (whiskers).

The bowsprit shrouds should be large enough in diameter to enable one to walk barefoot on them without ruining one's feet, and are therefore usually made of 1 by 19 wire of at least ¼ inch in diameter.

To allow for sail dousing on the bowsprit, most boats carry a bowsprit webbing (Photo 3). On *Ticonderoga,* Dacron webbing and lan-

3. Bowsprit webbing. TOM MCCUE.

4. Ticonderoga's *bowsprit webbing.* TOM MCCUE

yards are run from the bowsprit shrouds up to the lifelines on the bow pulpit, practically making a cocoon (Photo 4). A sail can then be dropped directly into the webbing, furled, and secured to the bowsprit, with no danger of its going overside. The one disadvantage of this rig is that although it simplifies sail handling, it complicates anchor handling.

Bowsprit Support—Inner End

In the days of the gaff rig, the bowsprit support provided by struts and by bitts bolted to the deck beams was more than enough. However, with a modern rig, the bitts supporting the bowsprit should be not only securely bolted to the deck beams but also extended all the way to the stem timber and bolted to a floor. Two methods for supporting the thrust aft on the bowsprit bitts or samson post are shown in Drawing 55. Unfortunately, when I replaced *Iolaire's* bowsprit bitts seventeen years ago, I kept to the original design, not stopping to realize that with a modern rig the thrust aft on the bowsprit would be much greater than it was originally. *Iolaire's* bitts should be designed to take a load of over 29,000 pounds (Drawing 56), and the bobstay should take a load of 28,000 pounds, which—as has been mentioned—necessitates ½-inch 1 by 19 wire, or a double bobstay.

Bowsprit support is often supplied by one massive samson post, a tenon being cut on the bowsprit to fit into it. Another method is to pass the bowsprit between two bitts and support it with an iron or

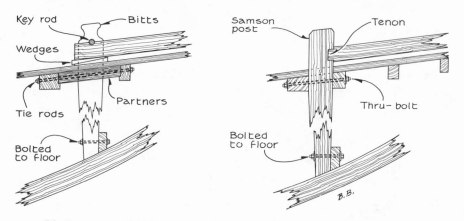

55. Recommended installations for bowsprit bitts and samson post.

56. Load diagram, *Iolaire*'s bowsprit and stays.

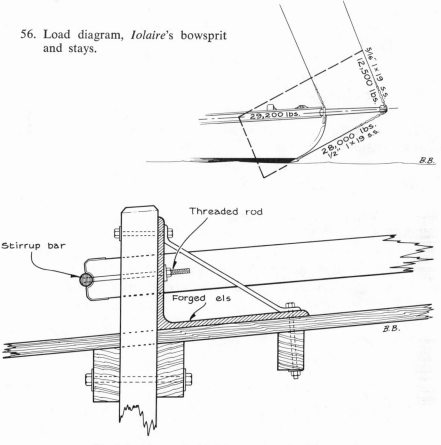

57. *Iolaire*'s method of bowsprit adjustment.

bronze bar. A third method (Drawing 57), which is now used on *Iolaire,* is to pass the bowsprit between the bitts and support its inner end with a heavy stirrup bar. Two threaded rods with nuts on their outboard ends pass through the bitts. To keep the stirrup bar from split-

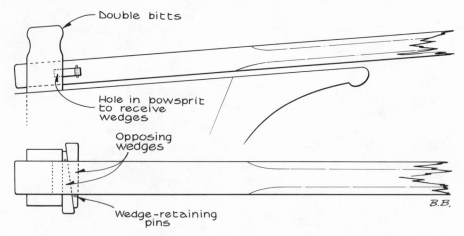

58. L. Francis Herreshoff's method of bowsprit adjustment.

ting the bowsprit, the inboard end is protected by a metal strap. The bowsprit can be jacked in and out to tighten or loosen the bobstay as circumstances demand, and a turnbuckle—a potential weak link—can therefore be dispensed with.

L. Francis Herreshoff advocates the use of two wedges to move the bowsprit in and out (Drawing 58). This is a crude and simple method, with which it is very difficult to get a fine adjustment, or to secure sufficient pressure.

Installing Bowsprits on Existing Boats

If a bowsprit is to be added to an existing boat, one should check carefully on the possibility of installing an offset bowsprit, as was done years ago, especially on English boats. When a bowsprit crosses the stemhead, the latter must be protected with a cap to prevent rainwater from soaking into the end grain of the wood and causing rot. But the offset bowsprit pierces only the bulwark, so recutting of the stem is not necessary. Also, in many cases it leaves a clearer foredeck than the conventional type, and is easier to rig and unrig.

SHROUDS AND STAYS

SHROUD ANGLE

If spreaders are too narrow, tremendous compression strains are built up in the boat and on the spar; the minimum angle between the mast and the shroud or stay should be 7 degrees, and anything more than that is all to the good insofar as decreasing the strain on the rig is concerned. However, as I have so often stated, everything is a compromise. If the spreaders are made very wide, the compression strain will be reduced, but so also will the windward-going capability of the boat, because flattening the genoa will no longer be possible.

The windward-going capability of the average bareboat in the Caribbean is often alleged to be the same as that of a loaded sand barge. How much of the difficulty can be attributed to hull design and how much to bad rigging is problematical. One popular stock ketch suffers from great beam, heavy displacement, and insufficient draft, as well as too wide spreaders—these boats are licked before they start. By contrast, the Carib 41's have a hull design which enables them to reach and run like absolute bandits—as has been demonstrated many times in weekend regattas in Bequia, and in the race from St. Vincent to Petit St. Vincent—and they even go to windward fairly well, but once they come hard on the wind they leave a little to be desired. Having observed them from other boats, and having talked to good sailors who have sailed on them, I gather that the difficulty is directly caused by the fact that the spreaders are about as wide as the boat (fourteen feet of beam for an overall length of forty-one feet), and the shrouds going to the side of the boat make sheeting the headsail properly practically impossible.

When I was working with Caribbean Sailing Yachts, I personally drew up the specifications for the Carib 41, and I brought together CSY and Alan Gurney, who then, with great rapidity, designed the Carib 41. When the Carib 41 preliminary design was sent to me, I recommended some sixty-odd changes; Alan Gurney accepted forty-odd of these, but many of them were scrapped after I was fired. The most important of my suggestions was that the shrouds be moved inboard a minimum of eighteen inches, and preferably two feet. This change would have increased the cost of the Carib 41, and slightly reduced the deck space, but it would have made her into a boat that would go like the clappers off the wind and also go to windward.

This suggestion was subsequently proved to have been right. After the builders of the Carib 41 went broke, and after a long and involved chain of events, Norrie Hoyt and some friends obtained the mold and built another Carib 41, with the same hull but a slightly different type of construction (to avoid the problems associated with the foam core, as described in Chapter I). They put up a slightly taller mast with narrow spreaders, so that the headsails could be sheeted in flat at the proper angle, and they placed the genoa track well inboard. As a result, although this Carib 41 has a very beamy hull, her genoa does not scoop up water when she is going to windward. And judging from what

I have heard about the runs turned in on long trips, she really barrels along to windward, downwind, and in every other direction.

Accordingly, when rerigging a boat—particularly an older one—and when ordering new sails, one should carefully examine the width of the spreaders. Frequently, chopping the spreaders a little will vastly improve the trim of the headsails. Even the best-formed boats cannot go to windward with wide spreaders that prevent the headsails from being properly sheeted. A badly shaped fat cruising boat or motor sailer, designed more for comfort than for speed, is almost licked by hull shape, especially if she is also hindered by the drag of a big three-bladed propeller. To offset these handicaps, a superb windward-going rig is necessary.

SPREADER WIDTH AND SHROUD PLACEMENT

On older boats with wooden masts, the combination of a large mainsail and small fore-triangle tended to produce a relatively tall, light spar. To reduce compression strains, spreaders were usually considerably wider than the boat, but this width did not particularly create problems, since these vessels did not carry large genoas which overlapped the mast. Further, on older boats, the ratio of length to beam was usually such that the chain plates had to be placed out at the rail.

In contrast, modern racing boats have exceedingly narrow spreaders. Further, the ratio of length to beam is often so great that for the genoa to be sheeted properly, the chain plates must be set well inboard from the rail cap. However, modern aluminum spars can take the compression strains caused by shrouding to such a narrow base. Because the genoa is sheeted to the deck inboard of the rail cap when going to windward, it is inside the bow wave. In older boats, with the genoa sheeting outside the lifelines, the bow wave landed in the middle of the genoa, and switching to a high-cut genoa or a double-headsail rig was therefore necessary much earlier than it is for the modern fiber-glass racing boat under similar circumstances.

However, most modern cruising boats have failed to follow the example of the racing boat, much to the detriment of their windward-going ability. Admittedly, the racing machine with its tall, narrow rig, narrow spreaders, and narrow sheeting base has gone to one extreme—possibly not the right one for cruising. However, the cruising boat has largely gone to the other extreme, and is likely to have not only a wide sheeting base and a wide hull, but chain plates that go right to the rail cap, so that it is impossible to trim the genoa correctly.

If a cruising boat is to go to windward satisfactorily, a double-headsail

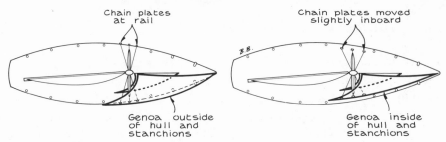

Chain plates at rail

Chain plates moved slightly inboard

Genoa outside of hull and stanchions

Genoa inside of hull and stanchions

59. On some boats it is possible to narrow the shroud base to allow for closer headsail sheeting. A reputable naval architect should be consulted concerning the feasibility of this arrangement.

rig should be strongly considered, one which allows for wide spreaders but has the lower shrouds set far enough inboard for the genoa staysail to be sheeted at the deck inboard of the upper shrouds (*OSY*-I, Drawing 40C).

The jib topsail must also be sheeted inboard. The sheet must pass inside the upper shroud when the vessel is going to windward, but must be moved outside as soon as sheets are eased—a pain in the neck when it is blowing hard. A better arrangement might be to slightly narrow the shroud base (Drawing 59), so that the jib or genoa may be sheeted outside the upper and lower shrouds. Find a reputable naval architect and discuss it with him.

SINGLE- VERSUS DOUBLE-SPREADER RIG

In this day and age, except in the ton racing classes, boats of forty feet or less almost universally have a single-spreader rig. However, on ocean cruising boats of over forty feet, the suitability of this rig is questionable. Admittedly, the single-spreader, double-headsail rig makes it possible to carry a taller, and therefore larger, genoa staysail than can be carried with a double-spreader rig (Drawing 60). However, what is

60. A single-spreader rig (A) can set a larger genoa staysail than a double-spreader rig (B).

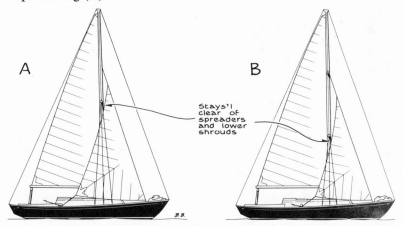

A

B

Stays'l clear of spreaders and lower shrouds

gained in one respect is lost in another: with the single-spreader rig, if the spreader collapses or the upper shroud breaks there is no hope of keeping the mast in the boat. With the double-spreader rig either a spreader or one shroud can be lost and, with luck, the rig can still be saved, since the length of panel left unsupported due to the breakage of the shroud or the collapse of the spreader is reduced.

DIAMOND RIG

The types of diamond rig found in trimarans (Drawing 61A and C) are to be avoided. On mono-hulls, the old-fashioned double-diamond rig (Drawing 61C) is left over, like a bad hangover, from the 1930's. Where a boat still has this rig, most riggers recommend changing it immediately, by one of the methods shown in Drawing 61D; the upper diamond should either be linked to the intermediate shroud by a heavier lower panel, and also linked to the spreader, or it should be brought

61. Modifying diamond rigs for ocean cruising.

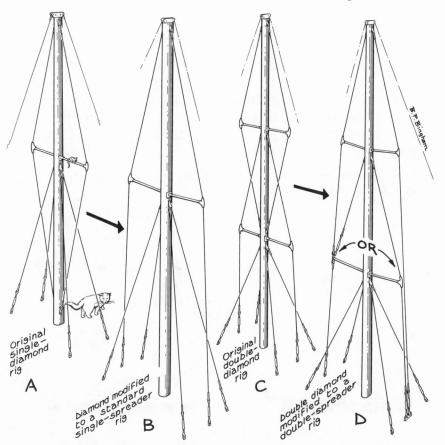

Original single-diamond rig

A

Diamond modified to a standard single-spreader rig

B

Original double-diamond rig

C

OR

Double diamond modified to a double-spreader rig

D

down to the deck on a separate chain plate, the latter arrangement being generally preferred. A recommended modification of the single-diamond rig is shown in Drawing 61B.

The great disadvantage of the diamond rig is that a single shroud supports the upper two-thirds of the mast (from the lower shrouds upward). If this shroud fails, the best helmsman in the world cannot possibly get the boat onto the other tack before most of the mast goes overside. By contrast, if the upper or intermediate shroud lets go on the properly designed two-spreader rig, with an oversized mast, the chance that a capable helmsman will be able to get the vessel onto the other tack and save the mast is quite good.

GROOVED HEAD STAYS

The grooved head stay may be acceptable on ocean racers with big crews, but has no place on the ocean cruising yacht. Like the luff-roped mainsail on a slotted mast, the sail on this type of head stay tries to feed itself overside as it comes out of the groove. The grooved head stay is hard to handle, expensive, and prone to damage, and shipping a replacement to out-of-the-way areas is difficult, if not downright impossible.

SPREADER BASE FITTINGS

On many of the vessels with modern aluminum masts, each spreader base fitting is welded to a plate which is then machine-screwed directly to the mast. I've even seen these plates attached to the mast by pop-riveting. The spreader base fitting is cast in the form of a socket, and the spreader itself is simply a length of aluminum pipe. The spreader is held at a fixed angle both fore and aft and in the vertical plane. Needless to say, the spreader tips must be secured firmly to the shrouds. People should be warned not to walk out toward the end of the spreader, since a bad strain can be thrown onto the base fitting, which is rigidly fixed to the mast. Further, when running dead downwind, the mainsail exerts considerable pressure on the spreader tip, especially on the upper spreader. The spreader in turn exerts considerable leverage on the base plate. As a result of these loads, for which this type of stainless-steel fitting is not really too well designed, cracks are likely to develop at the welds between the socket and the base plate. These fittings should therefore be very carefully checked at regular intervals.

To avoid these difficulties, many seamen prefer the spreader pivoting in the horizontal plane, as then the slack lee rigging allows the spreader to swing a considerable degree forward. Also, when two vessels lock spreaders when coming alongside, or rafting, the chance that a pivoting spreader will swing free is considerable, whereas a fixed spreader will either tear out of the mast or strain the base fitting.

ATTACHING THE SAIL TO THE MAST

GROOVED, OR SLOTTED, SPARS

Slotted spars in combination with a luff rope without slugs are *de rigueur* on racing machines, but from the cruising man's standpoint, although fine on booms, such an arrangement on the mast should be avoided. In a squall, as soon as the mainsail is dropped, it feeds out of the groove and straight overside. Similarly, when a sail must be set during a high wind, one person has to haul the sail up, while a second person feeds it into the groove. Finally, with a slotted spar there is no practical way to furl the sail. The racing man's technique of winding it around the boom is not particularly practical for quick furling in a squall. Where there is a slotted spar, cylindrical slugs should be fitted to the luff rope (Drawing 62). The slot can then be used merely as an oval-shaped sail track, the sail being dropped and left attached to the mast while furled in the normal fashion.

62. Slug for use with luff-rope track and slotted mast.

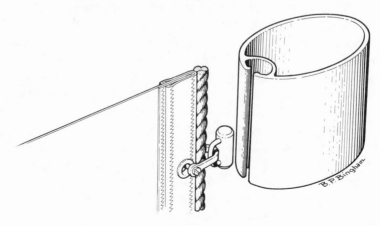

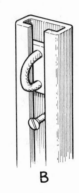
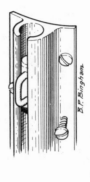
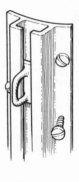

A   B   C

63. One loose screw can prevent a sail from dropping when track fastenings
are in the path of the slides (A and B); a flanged track (C) eliminates the
problem.

SAIL TRACK

Sail track can be either male (with the slides passing around the
track, as is standard on older American wooden masts) or female
(with the slides—known as slugs—passing up inside the track, as found
on European vessels). In both of the traditional types (Drawing 63A
and B), a fastening can work loose and jam the track. However, now
there has been developed a female track with outside flanges for the
fastenings (Drawing 63C); this arrangement makes it impossible for a
loose fastening to jam the track. When track of this type is used, the
fastenings should be doubled up where the head of the single- or double-
reefed mainsail (or large storm trysail) and the head of the reefed
trysail attach to the mast.

RIGGING WIRE

On an ocean sailing yacht, one's life may depend upon the quality
of the rigging. Therefore, one is well advised to seek out the best. Harry
Spencer, of Cowes, Isle of Wight, England, and Allan MacDonald, of
Yacht Haven West, Stamford, Connecticut, are not the only riggers in
the world by a long shot, but they are among the most experienced,
especially in handling the larger sizes of rigging.

For many years MacDonald justly advertised his firm as "Riggers to
the 12's." He proudly boasts that his is probably the best rigging loft in
North America, and when one visits the loft and talks to him and his
crew, one tends to agree. His help in preparing *Iolaire* for her seventieth-

birthday cruise was considerable. He gave us a tremendous amount of rigging; items from his bits-and-pieces box and his "goodies" locker (holding odds and ends that had come off various boats) enabled *Iolaire* to make her twelve-thousand-mile trip with spares for all of her running rigging.

When one visits England and walks into Harry Spencer's establishment, one is astounded. About twenty years ago, Harry started a rigging and towage service in Cowes with, as he said, ten quid and a borrowed launch. He is now without doubt the premier rigger in the world. Downstairs, standing in the middle of the floor, is one of the biggest swaging machines in existence, which can swage wire of larger diameters than can be handled by any of the swaging facilities readily available in the United States. Indeed, Palmer Johnson and other top American yards order their heavy standing rigging from Harry and have it delivered by airfreight. Similarly, nowhere in the United States can one find a comparable assortment of heavy rigging wire. One looks at the coils of ⅝-inch, ¾-inch, ⅞-inch, and even 1-inch, 1 by 19 stainless wire stacked on the floor, and one realizes that Harry is entitled to call himself "Rigger to the World."

MacDonald's and Spencer's are without doubt among the top organizations to which one can turn to have a modern yacht rigged. But until recently it has been difficult to find anyone qualified to do traditional rigging—on a replica of a classic yacht, or on an old yacht being restored—since the men who know how to do this rigging are generally old and retired. However, there has appeared on the scene a new group—the St. Margaret's Rigging gang, headed by Nicholas S. Benton. I first ran into this group abroad *Western Union,* an old schooner in the midst of restoration, for which they were providing the rig of a late-nineteenth-century coastal schooner. *Western Union* is distinctive; she was built in Key West, Florida, about sixty years ago, and until Castro took over Cuba maintained the cable between Cuba and Key West under sail!

The St. Margaret's Rigging gang does superb, old-style, traditional work—all the more remarkable because the members of the group are quite young. They have evidently studied the old rigging manuals, and have learned to do this beautiful rigging through historical research, instead of having old-timers show them how.

The only true test of rigging is five or six years of use at sea—relaxing, waiting, doing a bit of worrying, and preparing as best one can for whatever may come. This is what we try to do on *Iolaire*. She has a double-headsail rig, with a head stay, a staysail, two roller-furling luff wires, and double upper backstays. A running backstay can be set up in heavy weather when needed, and there are double lower shrouds, as well as intermediate shrouds, and an oversized spar. We figure that if a shroud or stay goes, with any luck, we should be able to keep the mast in the boat and rig another shroud or stay, even at sea. For this purpose we carry a length of $\frac{5}{16}$-inch 1 by 19 wire with a Norseman in one end and another ready for installation in the other end if necessary. And sooner or later, we are likely to need these spares, for with wire end fittings, the question is not, Which is the best? but, Which is the least bad? as all are prone to failure.

WIRE CONSTRUCTION

1 by 19 Stainless-Steel Wire

If properly installed and of the correct size, good 1 by 19 wire should last for many years. On *Iolaire,* we tested one of our $\frac{5}{16}$-inch 1 by 19 lower shrouds in the rigging loft of Harry Spencer, of Spencer Rigging. The results are listed in the Appendix (Table IX). This shroud's terminals were bronze sockets filled with zinc. It was tested to 10,000 pounds, and its ultimate breaking strength was 12,500 pounds. The wire had been in use for thirteen years—all in the tropics, on a boat that sailed about three thousand miles a year, mostly in heavy weather. Despite its durability, however, wire of this type should be carefully checked at regular intervals.

Rod Rigging

Rod rigging has a very variable reputation. It has become increasingly popular for racing, and today, a few manufacturers can justifiably claim that they have not had a single failure with it. However, they are referring to the experience on top-notch ocean racers, where the rigging is continually checked, and replaced upon the slightest suspicion of anything less than perfection. By contrast, a cruising yacht, in an out-of-the-way area, has no adequate facilities for checking the rod rigging. Furthermore, if the rigging is suspicious, or fails in some remote part of the world, there may be no way for the manufacturer to ship the replacement—perhaps a fifty-foot rod that will only coil into a ten- or twelve-foot circle. And sooner or later, a replacement will be necessary, for rod rigging is of questionable reliability: not only has it frequently failed under tension, causing rigs to go overside, but it has been known to fail on the lee side, while under no strain whatsoever. Talking to various ocean-racing people, I gather that it usually fails at the upper end, where there is no toggle, so perhaps the chances of failure can be minimized, for those unfortunate enough to have rod rigging, by the installation of toggles at both ends.

Once the rod breaks, until a new one made to fit can somehow be obtained, one may be forced to use galvanized-iron wire with bulldog clips, bought at the nearest hardware store. Therefore, until the new types of rigging (discussed in the following sections) have proved themselves, the ocean-cruising yachtsman will do better to stick with dear old 1 by 19 stainless.

K-Kore Rigging

K-Kore is a new type of experimental rigging, produced by Loos and Company. It looks like 1 by 19—that is, the outer layer consists of eleven stainless-steel strands—but the whole core is made of Kevlar. This rigging was given to us to test on *Iolaire,* but unfortunately arrived just before we took off across the Atlantic on her seventieth-birthday cruise. We finally mounted it at Plymouth, just before leaving on our way back across the Atlantic.

In the Appendix (Table IX) are the results of a test, made before installation, on two lower shrouds; these were stretched under tension by Bill Bradley of Spencer Rigging, to show the amount of stretch at the various loadings. The results were particularly gratifying in that they verified that the K-Kore rigging was strong, and also that our old 1 by 19 rigging with cast-bronze sockets, zinc filled, was still in good shape.

By switching to K-Kore wire, we basically saved thirty-five pounds aloft. The $\frac{5}{16}$-inch wire gave us a 20-percent increase in rigging strength with a 30-percent saving in weight. Technically, we could have kept the same strength and saved more weight by using wire of a smaller diameter, but we decided to make haste slowly. The end terminals still have us worried, because they're swaged on, with a layer of epoxy placed on the wire before the terminal is installed. We are now experimenting with Castlok epoxy fittings for the K-Kore rigging. These have stood up to the tests on the rigging-loft floor, but how they will stand up through the years of actual use remains to be seen. As for the K-Kore rigging itself, it lasted for over ten thousand miles, apparently doing fine, but three days of heavy sailing in the 1977 British Virgin Islands regatta stranded almost all of this rigging. The Kevlar core held, but the stainless wire let go!

Parafil

Parafil rigging, consisting of a PVC pipe filled with Kevlar and having a terminal at each end, has been used experimentally on *Great Britain III*. It is the newest thing in rigging—so new that it cannot as yet be evaluated. It is extremely light, and light but strong rigging is most desirable for the average cruising boat, which needs everything possible that will improve windward-going performance, which is always the weak point. Despite what many say to the contrary, a cruising boat must go well to windward, as one spends a tremendous amount of time doing it, willingly or unwillingly.

WIRE END FITTINGS

Splicing

Splicing is an excellent method of terminating wire ends; however, the splice is no better than the man who makes it. Good riggers can throw in a splice so fast you can hardly see it, and it will hold tremendous loads, but many poor splices are made and then concealed with serving. Further, especially with stainless steel, pounding the splice too hard with a mallet, in the attempt to flatten it and make it look good, may work harden the material, aging it and causing it to fail prematurely.

The yachtsman who insists that splicing is the only proper and safe way to end a wire should remember that *Lively Lady,* going around the world, had to abort her nonstop trip from Australia to England and swing up to New Zealand to have much of her rigging replaced, because many of the splices in her standing rigging started to let go—yet these were comparatively new.

Solid thimbles, which are by far the best for any wire splice that is going to carry a heavy load, are today practically impossible to find; however, welding a rolled-metal thimble closed across the throat (Drawing 64) will increase its strength and minimize the chance of its distorting under load.

Soft-lay galvanized wire is infinitely easier to splice than hard-lay

Weld here

64. Strengthening a rigging
    thimble.

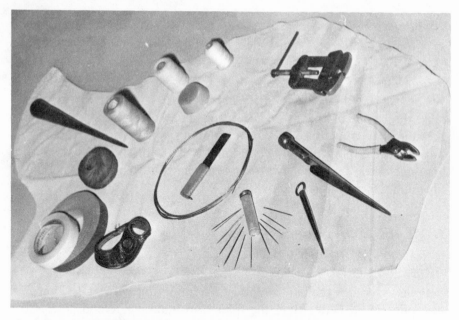

5. Splicing vise made by Herman Melin, and materials for basic sail mainten-ance. PAUL WOLINER.

stainless-steel wire, but though the galvanized wire of thirty or forty years ago may have lasted for tremendous periods of time, the product available today is evidently totally different, and expecting soft-lay galvanized to last very long, especially in the tropics, is now the height of optimism.

One of the most important prerequisites for good wire splicing is a proper splicing vise, one that will hold the wire tightly around the thimble. The best that I have ever seen for light wire (Photo 5) was made by Herman Melin, the head rigger at Ratsey and Lapthorn, un-fortunately now retired. If enough people contact him through Ratsey's (for address, see Appendix), perhaps he'll go back to making his beautiful spikes and splicing vises, or someone else will pick up the patterns and continue.

Probably the best splicing vise ever made for heavy-duty rigging wire is an old beat-up one used at Spice Island Boatyard, Grenada (Photo 6). This vise, two years younger than God, has had a long and varied history. A vise of this type is available at Durko (for address, see Ap-pendix), and in 1976, at the Annapolis Boat Show, I learned that a similar vise may be obtained from the St. Margaret's Rigging gang (for address, see Appendix). It is also possible to make one's own splicing vise (Drawing 65).

6. *Vise for heavy-duty wire, Spice Island Boatyard.* DAVID MAX

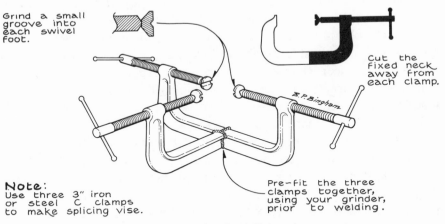

Grind a small
groove into
each swivel
foot.

Cut the
fixed neck
away from
each clamp.

Note:
Use three 3" iron
or steel C clamps
to make splicing vise.

Pre-fit the three
clamps together,
using your grinder,
prior to welding.

65. Homemade wire-splicing vise.

Poured Sockets

The poured-zinc socket is an extremely good fitting. Properly installed, it will be just about as strong as the wire itself. However, it is a bronze casting, and a casting is always suspect. I've had two failures of poured sockets on *Iolaire*, one of them on the last day of the seventieth-birthday cruise. For this reason, bronze sockets should be kept highly polished; then, if cracks develop they are likely to be spotted by the person doing the polishing.

Swage Terminals

Swage terminals should be made only by the big hydraulic tool that rolls each fitting through just twice—in and out. If the tool is too small, the fitting must be run through a number of times, and it is then, in the estimation of many riggers, unfit for use. In the tropics, it sometimes does not last a year.

To the best of my knowledge, in the United States the only heavy-duty machine with the correct dies for swaging wire $\frac{7}{16}$ inch or more in diameter is at Hazard Wire Rope (formerly a division of American Chain and Cable, now part of the Bridon American Corporation), in Wilkes-Barre, Pennsylvania. I am told that delivery on wire and fittings ordered through this concern is likely to take three or four months; the only way to obtain a piece of wire fitting from them in a hurry is to go there in person. A faster method to have large wire swaged is to get in touch with Spencer Rigging (for address, see Appendix), and settle the matter with Harry Spencer or his sidekick Bill Bradley. If a swaging machine of the correct size is just not available, most riggers advise switching to some other type of fitting.

Swage fittings are prone to failure over the years. Infinitesimal cracks appear, usually at the bottom end of the wire. How long the fittings last before developing these cracks depends largely on the use to which they are put; a racing machine with very light rigging that has a safety factor of perhaps 1.5 to 1, or 2 to 1, is likely to suffer from cracked swages long before a cruising boat whose rigging has a safety factor of 3 to 1, or 4 to 1. All swage fittings should be examined periodically with the aid of the blue liquid Spotcheck that machinists use for inspecting crankshafts. Once a fitting is cracked, there is no way of determining how much of its strength it retains. Therefore, it should be immediately replaced.

If a boat is to be used in the tropics, under no circumstances should swage fittings be installed, since they are bound to fail. People from the tropics who report this are often regarded as soft in the head, but any reputable surveyor in the eastern Caribbean, will confirm that swage fittings are so prone to failure in the tropics that they should not be considered for use there at all.

Crimp Fittings—Nicopress

The old Nicopress sleeve fitting is really much better than people give it credit for being. If the wire is an adequate size for the job, and is bent around a slightly oversized thimble, and two sleeves are then carefully crimped on, one above the other, the fitting will last many years.

Iolaire's mizzen rigging was installed in 1962 and only recently began to give up, after fifteen years of very hard usage.

Cone Terminals

In a cone terminal, a wire is slipped through a casing and then spread, a cone is inserted on the core of the wire, and the spread wire and cone are pulled back into the casing. Finally, a stud is screwed into the casing, and crimps the wire around the cone. Major problems with cone terminals still exist. For one thing, a fitting for $\frac{7}{16}$-inch wire is not made; the next size after 10 millimeters ($1\frac{3}{32}$ inch) is 12 millimeters ($\frac{1}{2}$ inch); further, although the Norseman catalog shows the 10-millimeter fitting, at times they insist that they do not have it. Since $\frac{7}{16}$ inch is a very common American rigging size, I can't imagine why cone fittings for that size are not made. No wonder these fittings do not sell well in the United States.

Recently, there have been a few instances of the casing exploding. It used to be thought that this could happen only with very small cone fittings (3-millimeter and 4-millimeter), but now there have been reports of explosions with fittings of 8 millimeters ($\frac{5}{16}$ inch). These seem to occur on hard-driving racing boats, probably using fittings one size too small.

NORSEMAN FITTINGS: Norseman end terminals were the first of the cone type that really worked. Earlier fittings of this sort had a cast casing, which tended to explode under heavy loads. The Norseman fitting, which is machined out of solid stainless steel, has had an almost perfect safety record, the few recent instances of explosions notwithstanding. Installation is simple, and can be done on board the boat, whether at sea or in port. The fittings are basically foolproof—but not damn-fool proof. Basically, an eye fitting is stronger than a jaw fitting, and rigging should be designed to use only eye fittings; Norseman jaw fittings leave something to be desired in that a flush screw pin is used, rather than a clevis pin with a cotter key. The jaw may be strong enough, but only the slightest misalignment puts a bad strain on it, causing one side to crack off.

STA-LOK FITTINGS: Designed by Lee Ward, who was formerly with Norseman, the Sta-Lok fitting now produced by Leeward Rigging is similar to the Norseman, and like it, is superb. Indeed, many riggers feel that especially in the larger sizes, the Sta-Lok is easier to use. Sta-Lok fittings are not offered in as wide a range of types as Norseman fittings, but as shown by the tables in the Appendix, they are available for approximately the same sizes of rigging wire.

CASTLOK FITTINGS: Castlok, the newest type of terminal on the market, is similar to Norseman and Sta-Lok, but has a cone fitting filled with epoxy glue. The engineering reports on the Castlok fitting are extremely good, it looks superb, and as has been noted, the fittings of this type may turn out to be ideal for K-Kore rigging; but how they will stand the test of time, no one knows.

One complaint many riggers do have at present is that the instructions do not sufficiently emphasize the importance of making absolutely sure that all oil and grease have been cleaned off the wire prior to the insertion of the epoxy. Also, the fitting is not perfect for use as an on-board spare, because the epoxy filler has a definite shelf life. If the fitting is to be carried as a spare, one must carefully check the expiration date prior to taking off on a long cruise.

Matching End Fittings, Turnbuckle Fittings, and Mast-Tang Fittings

Matching the various fittings can be a massive problem, especially now that England is in the great process of metrification. The standard Norseman eyes match up, in diameter, with nothing on this side of the ocean; one must either install a smaller-sized pin in the turnbuckle, and bush the turnbuckle jaw, or drill out the Norseman eye, which is of course not desirable. One wonders why Norseman and Sta-Lok do not produce their screw-in end fittings with holes of various diameters, or put a little extra meat into the fittings, so that they may be slightly drilled out without being weakened.

There have also been introduced in England some superstrength

Superston turnbuckles, and these have pins whose diameters do not match up with the eyes in American swage fittings. To complicate the matter further, American swage fittings may be had with either a "marine eye" or an "aircraft eye" (the latter listed under the heading "MS-20668 Eye" in Table XIII, Appendix), and each type of eye accepts pins of different diameters.

While having an argument with Norseman at the New York Boat Show many years ago, I received unexpected backing from Alan Gurney, the English naval architect practicing in the United States. He said, "It's so difficult to get everything to match up that I say to hell with Norseman fittings and just use swage fittings with marine eyes, because I know they will all match the American turnbuckles. If I go to Norseman on standing rigging, I have to put in a full day's labor drawing up the specifications to alter the turnbuckles' designs to the Norseman eyes, or vice versa."

Because of these problems in matching, when rerigging is necessary one must check the catalog carefully (see also the rigging information in the Appendix) to make sure that everything ordered will fit together—and sometimes, apparently, it just can't be done.

IN-LINE RADIO INSULATORS

Although radiomen love in-line radio insulators, riggers hate them. As I have often stated, all terminal fittings are bad, though some are worse than others; the number of joints in wire rigging should be kept at an absolute minimum. In-line insulators may prove perfect when tested, but over the years they have built up a reputation for failure, and when they go, they usually take the whole rig with them. Without the rig, there is of course no antenna, no radio. Accordingly, use of the standing rigging as a radio antenna should be avoided, if at all possible.

V

Running Rigging

WINCHES

Winches have become very esoteric; one can spend almost as much money on winches as on all the rest of the boat. Not only two-speed but also three-speed winches are now frequently seen.

One thing which should be checked when a winch is to be purchased is the power ratio (mechanical advantage) provided at each speed. Some two-speed winches have ratios of 8 to 1 and 96 to 1. The gap between these is too great: at 8 to 1, a winch is not powerful enough to do much work; at 96 to 1, it will sheet in a sail of any size, but only very slowly. Many seamen feel that two-speed winches should have no more than a triple power jump, and possibly just a double one—with ratios, for example, of 8 to 1 and 24 to 1, or of 16 to 1 (approximately that of an old geared winch) and 32 to 1 or 48 to 1.

We have noticed, when racing old *Iolaire* against modern competition, that our 18-to-1 and 22-to-1 winches seem to sheet her headsails almost as fast as the modern two-speed models; we just have to put two big men on the handle and horse the sail in. Some of our competition does have the option—which we lack—of putting a smaller man on the handle and turning at low speed, to bring the sail in more easily but also much more slowly.

From the cruising standpoint, it is most important that the diameter of the winch drum be large enough to enable a relatively small person to tail up adequately with four or five turns. The most powerful winch in the world is useless if the diameter of the drum is too small to make tailing up relatively easy. When short tacking to windward, my six-year-old son can tail up to sheet the genoa staysail with five turns on an old, large-diameter 22-to-1 Nevins, but he cannot tail up on the more powerful but small-diameter Barient 22's we have recently installed! (We obtained these by chance. They were mounted on the cabin top of a boat being trucked across the country; when they missed clearing a bridge by half an inch, the drums were scored and the winch mountings were torn right out of the cabin top, leaving two gaping holes. We bought the winches for fifty dollars each—it's an ill wind that blows no one any good!)

The self-tailing winch originally brought out by the Woolsey paint company (how did they get into the winch business?), and since then copied and improved by all the other winch companies, certainly has a place on the cruising boat. At present, with a No. 1 jib and staysail at least three or four people are required to tack *Iolaire*. If we had self-tailing winches, two people could do the job!

Everyone disagrees about which is the best winch—Barient, Barlow, Lewmar, Gibb, Enkes . . . Since most boats are equipped with winches of just one make, there is no chance to compare the various makes under the same circumstances. A good way to run comparative tests on winches would be to mount models from all the major manufacturers on one boat, use them for a year of hard cruising and/or racing—like *Iolaire*'s seventieth-birthday cruise—and compare their performance. Ian Nichols of Barient and I discussed this idea just before the start of the 1975 Fastnet Race. He agreed with me, and stated that if other manufacturers were willing to do the same, the next time *Iolaire* undertook a long cruise, he would arrange for a Barient winch to be placed on board for evaluation.

In this day and age, winch systems are getting extremely elaborate. As Peter "Turkey Legs" Vandersloot points out, on some of the modern ocean racers two guys stand at a central pedestal driving position while a third guy throws gears, and the winches from one end of the boat to the other turn, sometimes causing confusion because the right drum turns at the wrong time. Another objection to this arrangement is that the mechanical linkage becomes so complicated, with so many gears and bearings, that the friction loss between the driving position and the drum is considerable. This too was discussed with Ian Nichols before the 1975 Fastnet Race, and he pointed out that no matter how good the gearing is, every right-angle bevel drive increases friction by about 10 percent. Thus, three right-angle bevel drives in the drive system mean a friction loss of 30 percent. One wonders how much is gained by use of the remote drive, with a friction loss like this.

Further, a winch drive-gear system must be as carefully aligned as that of an engine. In this respect, the modern, lightly constructed ocean racer, especially if made of fiber glass, has the same problem as did the long, narrow, light, high-speed powerboats of the 1930's—the hull flexes considerably. Consequently, a winch system which is in perfect alignment when the boat is moored may be out of alignment when she is sheeted hard down, slamming to windward, and the resulting friction will then cause huge power losses and throw great strain on the boat.

The final objection to fancy cross-linked and remote-drive winch systems, from the standpoint of the cruising yachtsman, is that the money would probably be better spent on food and other equipment. For the price of a fancy winch system the average forty-footer could probably go cruising for a year to eighteen months.

It is true that in years gone by most cruising yachts, and indeed many racing yachts, were drastically underwinched, and therefore difficult to sail when shorthanded. However, today many racing boats and some cruising boats are ridiculously overwinched; tremendous amounts of money are spent on gilding the lily with fancy winches that are not essential.

There is one silver lining to this dark cloud. As racing yachts get more and more competitive, and their owners are more and more likely to install new, elaborate winches, the old but perfectly good winches that are being replaced become available for sale. In looking for used winches, therefore, one should check yards which have a large number of ocean racers stored, or rigging lofts which specialize in rewinching boats.

TOP ACTION VERSUS BOTTOM ACTION

For handling large sails and heaving in long lengths of line with fairly heavy loads, one must unquestionably have either a top-action winch or a bottom-action winch with a good, powerful remote drive. Both of these, needless to say, are expensive. However, even on comparatively large boats, there are many applications for conventional bottom-action winches.

The halyards on headsails of up to 300 square feet can well be handled by a bottom-action winch, since most of the heaving on the halyards is done with no load. Either the person hauling or the tailer can crank in without having to wait for all the turns to be thrown on the winch. To be sure, with the bottom-action winch one cannot get a full swing, but if the helmsman, the man on the sheet, and the man hauling on the halyard cooperate, there should be only a foot or two to take up under tension.

Similarly, for headsails of up to 150, or possibly 200, square feet, the bottom-action winch is very convenient if there is a good powerful crew; one can heave in on the slack on the sheet with a single turn, and throw on extra turns, and then either the heaver or the tailer can crank down on the winch without first having to look around, find a handle, and insert it. Indeed, on many boats it is possible to leave the winch handle permanently in place.

Another advantage of the bottom-action winch, not often considered, is that when it is used as a sheet winch, a cleat can be dispensed with. Instead of being led to the cleat, the sheet may be passed three times underneath the handle and around the drum. It may not look secure, but it will hold. This has been our standard method of securing the main and staysail sheets for the past twenty years.

A bottom-action winch may also be used on occasion as a switching winch. For example, the process of switching the genoa staysail from inside to outside sheet leads involves taking up the slack in a hurry and cranking down only a foot or so, and is considered by many sailors to be easier with a bottom-action than a top-action winch. Similarly, the boom vang is heaved in by hand, and only the last six inches need be set up with a winch. By the same token, a bottom-action winch mounted on the boom, with the handle permanently in place, is extremely useful for heaving down on the reefing clew when reducing sail, or for taking up on the topping lift on large boats.

Therefore, before condemning the bottom-action winch, one should carefully check the size of one's boat, the size of the sails, the way the boat is handled, and the cost differential between top- and bottom-action winches.

LINE TENSIONERS

Nicro/Fico has developed a really ingenious rig, referred to as a Line Tensioner (Drawing 66), which can replace a three- or four-part tackle or a small winch. Because Line Tensioners are removable, one

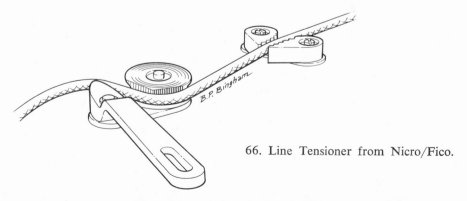

66. Line Tensioner from Nicro/Fico.

or two can be employed in four or five different places. They can be used, among other things, for outhaul adjustment, clew reef-cringle tensioning, topping-lift adjustment (on large boats only), and down-haul and Cunningham adjustment.

MOUNTING WINCHES

The normal, old-fashioned method of mounting a winch was to bolt it to a wooden block spread across several deck beams (*OSY*-I, Draw-ing 59). However, in this day and age, with both good carpenters and good wood expensive and difficult to find, and in the light of more modern thinking on the whole subject, this method is no longer pre-ferred.

Winch bases fabricated out of bronze or stainless steel (*OSY*-I, Photo 62) may seem expensive, but in the long run they frequently prove cheaper. The bolts through the deck and the backing block underneath the deck are relatively short, and easy to install, and the winch is secured to the winch base by short machine screws and nuts (Drawing 67A). Consequently, the total cost of fabricating and bolting down the metal winch base compares favorably with the cost of fabricating a huge wooden block and obtaining half a dozen ⅜-inch bronze bolts, twelve or eighteen inches long, which require, in addition, skilled drill-ing (Drawing 67B).

Ease in removing the winch from the pad is essential, as on some winches—the Barient 22 for instance—it is impossible to get at one of the sets of ratchets without removing the winch from the pad and driving out the shaft for the set of gears and ratchets with a punch.

67. Simple winch bases for wooden cockpit coamings.

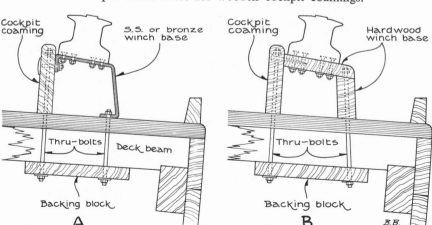

On boats with high but strongly mounted cockpit coamings, like *Iolaire,* a relatively cheap, easily fabricated winch pad, combining metal and a block of wood, may be used. An angle is welded to a bronze plate, cut to the shape of the winch, and is bolted to the cockpit coaming, and the outer edge of the plate is secured with two long bolts down through a pad fastened under the deck beams. Correctly made, this installation is neat, simple, and strong. However, it is suitable only for boats with cockpit coamings well secured to the deck.

Occasionally, one sees winches secured to metal brackets which are just bolted to the coamings, having no connection to the deck. This arrangement is inadvisable except for very small winches mounted on very heavy coamings.

BLOCKS

In years gone by, almost all blocks were of the wooden-shelled type made by Merriman, Nevins, Abeking and Rasmussen, Dauphine of Lunenburg, and others (Photo 7). Then, for a time, these blocks fell

7. Wooden-shelled block with anchor trip hook.
MERRIMAN

into disrepute, being heavy and crude, and requiring regular varnishing. However, today many seamen feel that there is much to be said for them, especially since a few of the new superlight blocks do not always fulfill their manufacturers' claims. The catalogs specify tremendous load-carrying capacities for these new blocks, but these figures are often very optimistic, and based on the performance of factory-fresh hardware under optimum conditions. All too often, when sailing on a racing machine, we have ended up breaking the snap shackles on the blocks, as well as on the ends of halyards, on boom-vang tackles, and the like.

The old Merriman blocks seem to survive very well (except for the really old ones with iron straps, manufactured before World War II). I have some big Merriman snatch blocks that are at least twenty-five or thirty years old and are still going strong. If anything does break, the company is very good about sending replacement parts. Also, if the wooden shell falls apart, a local carpenter can make new cheek pieces.

In recent years, Merriman has been almost the only supplier of these traditional blocks, and they have become very expensive. However, all is not lost. The Dauphine family has been making blocks for well over a hundred years in Lunenburg, Nova Scotia. At one point the Dauphines had a huge shop, and supplied the Nova Scotia fishing fleet. Now, in a relatively small shop, they produce beautiful blocks at a very reasonable price. However, as they freely admit, because the strength of the cast-bronze straps is suspect, the blocks should not be used where they will be required to take a heavy load—as turning blocks or halyard blocks, for example.

Now, in the United States two different small companies—Troy and Sailors Art—are making blocks with stainless-steel straps at a reasonable price (for addresses, see Appendix). I really hope they can continue to maintain their excellent quality while keeping their attractive prices.

A word of warning about rubber-shelled blocks—in the tropics, they should be put out on deck only when the vessel is actually sailing. If they are left perpetually in the sun, in eighteen months or two years the rubber shell will deteriorate to the point where it is of no practical use.

TACKLES

Many a modern yachtsman has become so enamored of winches that he has almost forgotten that tackles exist, despite the fact that there are now available superb blocks for making up tackles. A most useful piece of equipment is a three- or four-part tackle with a snap shackle at each end, and a cam cleat built into one of the blocks. It can be of service, for example, when a sheet lead needs to be switched: a rope strop with an eye splice in the end is thrown around a line, the tackle is put on the strop (Photo 8), a strain is taken, and the sheet lead is moved. Furthermore, by placing a tackle on a tackle, and having a couple of big guys heave on it, tremendous power can be developed.

8. *Tackle on rope strop.* LAURENCE LE GUAY

SHEETS

On racing boats, the mainsheet is now generally led to a full-width traveler, with a slider on rollers that has its own tackle, allowing it to be adjusted to windward or to leeward. The tail of the tackle may be taken to a winch on larger boats. The tackle is absolutely necessary on the real hot racing machine because occasionally the mainsheet is actually led to the windward side when sailing to weather. But such an arrangement is not essential on a cruising boat, because mainsail twist can be removed by the use of a boom vang.

9. *Guard above winch, for sheets.* LANDS' END

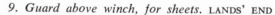

However, one thing that can be very useful on the modern cruising boat is a guard above the winch (Photo 9), through which the mainsheet is led. One person can then heave on the mainsheet and another around the winch with no danger of a riding turn developing, as is all too common with the usual system of leading directly to the winch.

HALYARDS

INTERNAL HALYARDS

More and more, internal halyards are considered essential on the modern ocean racing boat. However, I don't advise them on the cruising yacht, especially if the halyard exits are designed in such a way that several sharp turns are required. These simply add friction; as a result, extra power to hoist sails—perhaps even an extra man—will be necessary. Further, if a halyard breaks, although it is possible to fish a new halyard down through the mast, doing so may take all day.

However, all is a compromise. On the standard cruising-boat mast with all halyards external, the windage is considerable, and certainly does not help the vessel's performance going to windward, which is when a cruising boat most needs help. Therefore, some of the halyards which are not used all the time for hauling sails could well be placed inside the mast. For instance, on *Iolaire,* which has double roller-furling headsails, I intend to transfer the halyards for the roller-furling jib and roller-furling staysail to the inside of the mast. This can be done, in my view, because the roller-furling headsails are still rolled at the time they are hauled up, and do not need to be set in a hurry; hence the added friction is not too important.

I am also considering having the main halyard placed inside the mast, since the main-halyard winch is powerful enough to handle the added friction, and no one is needed to tail. But I would keep my other halyards and topping lifts external.

EXTERNAL HALYARDS

One practice that dates back to the days of the racing boat with all halyards external could well be followed on cruising boats today. Halyards not used regularly, such as spare jib halyards, spinnaker halyards, and the like, are best kept coiled in a line locker, with only a light

⅛-inch Dacron messenger aloft in their place. The result will be considerably less windage and weight aloft—a standard ¼-inch wire halyard with a ½-inch rope tail on a fifty-foot mast weighs twelve pounds —and also a reduction in wear and tear on the halyards. Each halyard of course should have a rat tail with an eye splice in it at the end, which can be secured to the messenger by means of a double sheet bend and a piece of tape. We found this arrangement most satisfactory on *Iolaire*'s seventieth-birthday cruise.

SHEAVES

In old-fashioned rigs which had all halyards external, the jib halyard, instead of being taken off a crane on the face of the mast, was often run straight through the mast from forward to aft, coming down the port side of the mast to a winch. The main halyard too was run through the mast, coming down the starboard side to a winch. In the old days, this setup required two very large sheaves (Drawing 68A), as it was imperative that the main-halyard sheave protrude beyond the mast fore and aft, so that from the after edge of the sheave there was a straight lead to the head of the sail, and from the forward edge the halyard led clear and would not wear a groove in the forward face of the mast. Similarly, the jib-halyard sheave had to protrude from the forward face of the mast. Even on small boats the main-halyard sheave had to be almost six inches in diameter, and some of the largest boats required as much as a twelve-inch sheave, a massive, expensive piece of brassware. However, someone always builds a better mousetrap. Now, almost universally, tandem sheaves are used for the main halyard, and these can be much smaller, because the wire is making two small 90-degree turns, instead of one large 180-degree turn (Drawing 68B).

68. A single pair of sheaves (A) requires a very large hole cut through the wooden masthead, which weakens it severely; a tandem pair of sheaves (B) requires a much smaller hole.

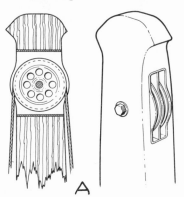
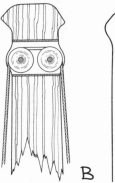
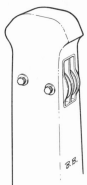

A   B

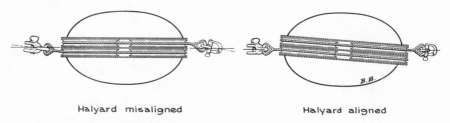

Halyard misaligned   Halyard aligned

69. Cocking the sheave box for proper halyard alignment.

Further, a number of years ago, in order to eliminate the extra jib-halyard blocks cluttering the forward face of the mast, good designers and spar builders developed a sheave box having a pair of tandem sheaves placed side by side, with the main halyard moving from aft forward, the jib halyard passing from forward aft, and the sheave box cocked so that the respective halyards ended up on the center line on their respective sides of the mast (Drawing 69). Some designers then went one step further, and placed three sets of tandem sheaves through the mast—the main-halyard sheaves in the center, the jib-halyard sheaves on the port side, and sheaves for a spare messenger on the starboard side (Drawing 70). If the main halyard broke, a spare halyard could be attached to the messenger and rigged from aft forward, to serve as a spare main halyard; if the jib halyard broke, the messenger could haul the spare halyard through from forward aft, to serve as a spare jib halyard. One could also rig a spare genoa halyard in place for hoisting headsails rapidly or for hoisting one headsail on a light jackstay for poor man's twins.

On boats with a three-fourths or seven-eighths rig and only the main halyard going through the masthead, there were two commonly used methods for rigging a spare main halyard or a line to hoist a man aloft without the main halyard. Some designers and spar builders used a flag-halyard block large and strong enough to take a ½-inch line. Given

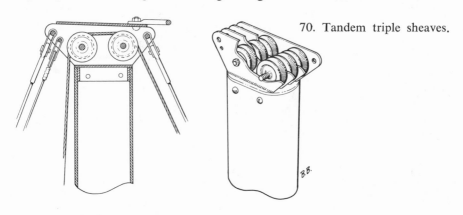

70. Tandem triple sheaves.

a rat tail with an eye splice, this line could be threaded through the block, using the flag halyard as a messenger. Other designers provided a copper tube of large diameter, well flared at the ends, passing athwartships through the mast. With a light flag halyard again serving as a messenger, a line with a block secured to it (and a halyard threaded through the block) was led through the copper tube and then hauled in until the block two-blocked at the masthead. The line through the block functioned as a halyard to hoist a man aloft.

With respect to a modern installation, it must be remembered that in the course of time, an aluminum sheave tends to wear and become thin, and the halyard is then likely to jump the sheave. Unfortunately, some manufacturers are extremely slow in supplying spares. It took me eighteen months to get a new sheave. Machining one out of solid stock may not be practical, in an out-of-the-way area like the Lesser Antilles, because of the impossibility of finding a piece of aluminum sufficiently large and thick to be suitable for a sheave of—say—3½ inches in diameter. Accordingly, especially if using an arrangement like that shown in Drawing 70, with a total of six sheaves in the mast, one would be wise to order two spare sheaves when ordering the mast.

Halyard sheaves in the mast are best lubricated by means of a graphite bushing or oil-impregnated brass bearing, which will last practically for the life of the boat.

Sheave Boxes

With a wooden mast, if the problem of wire halyard jumping the sheave is to be avoided, an actual sheave box welded of bronze or stainless-steel plate (Drawing 71) should be made, and installed in a slot cut in the mast. Merely lining the slot with copper is a perfect way to invite a jammed halyard. The sheaves and sheave-box tolerances must be very carefully matched, allowing a minimum of clearance. Otherwise the halyard, especially when one gets down to ⅛-inch wire, can easily jump the sheaves and become jammed between them and the sides of the box.

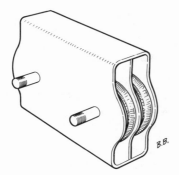

71. Typical sheave box.

SPINNAKER HALYARDS

I have been taken to task for not dealing at all with spinnakers in *OSY*-I. In truth, they do have a place on the ocean cruising yacht. Further, even the individual who does not plan to use spinnakers may find it worth while to install the fittings on the mast. There is always the possibility that at some future date one may change one's mind. Besides, having the spinnaker-halyard fittings aloft means that blocks can be shackled on and light messengers installed, so that spare halyards are available for emergency use.

Even prestretched Terylene or Dacron will stretch, especially when under heavy load—as in a spinnaker halyard. A situation which is often encountered begins with the spinnaker halyard stretching as it is heaved up tight under load and almost two-blocked at the masthead. This arrangement works perfectly until the guy is tripped loose, and the load comes off the halyard; as the halyard contracts, the splice is promptly pulled right into the block, jamming so tightly that often only the entire crew pulling down on the spinnaker can get it out again. To prevent this difficulty, on many boats the spinnaker halyard is secured with a bowline to the halyard shackle. The bowline is moused with serving. Where the spinnaker halyard is already spliced and the boat's owner or skipper is loath to have it cut off, an overhand knot can be tied eight inches back from the spinnaker-halyard shackle. This knot will prevent the splice from pulling into the block and jamming.

Most experts seem to prefer rope to wire for spinnaker halyards. They point out that the wire chafes on a long passage and may have to be cut and then spliced or Nicropressed. Further, because the spinnaker halyard is always hauled by hand except for the last few feet, wire just will not do. Most spinnaker halyards are double-ended (with shackles on both ends for use on port or starboard tacks) so wire-to-rope splices are out of the question. Often, when the halyard begins to show chafe in one area, it may be overhauled.

On long passages, the spinnaker should be hoisted on two halyards. There have been tremendous advances in recent years in the installation of spinnaker-halyard blocks. Probably the best method is to set out two blocks on cranes (Drawing 72A), well ahead of the mast, in a Y. The strain is then taken on the lee halyard, which should consequently lead clear of everything, the weather halyard just hanging slack and secured in case the lee halyard chafes and breaks. When one prepares to jibe, the strain is taken on the weather halyard; then the spinnaker is jibed, and the former lee halyard, now the weather halyard, is slacked and secured.

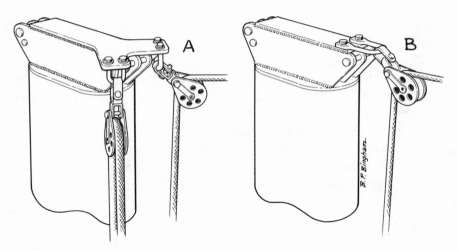

72. Spinnaker-halyard blocks: A, twin swivel blocks on Y-shaped crane; B, single block shackled to bail.

Some people prefer a single fully swiveling spinnaker-halyard block, secured to a U-shaped bail (Drawing 72B). This is the arrangement most commonly supplied by the manufacturers of aluminum masts, and it seems to have passed the test of time.

On a racing boat, spinnaker halyards are usually internal. On the ocean cruising yacht, most experienced seamen prefer external halyards, since with them there is much less friction when the sail is hauled aloft. Also, only the external halyards can be made double-ended. As with other external halyards, the use of a light messenger will substantially reduce weight and windage and at the same time prevent the halyard from deteriorating in the sun and chafing the mast 365 days of the year. This point cannot be overemphasized.

JIB SECURED TO BOWSPRIT TRAVELER

As I mentioned when describing this arrangement in *OSY*-I (Ch. V), I have not been enthusiastic about securing the jib to a bowsprit traveler. This feeling is shared by others, some of whom have told me they dislike it because they feel that it cannot eliminate the sag in the luff of the jib. However, most of them have tried it with a Marconi rig. Sag in the luff of the jib is not as serious on a gaff-rigged boat. The little Falmouth Quay punt *Curlew,* built in 1898 and beautifully sailed by Tim and Pauline Carr, has this arrangement. They feel that it works perfectly, and would have no other. Having watched *Curlew* sail, I have revised my opinion. It should be noted also that if sag *is* experienced, a good sailmaker—provided he is told about the problem—can cut the luff in a way that takes this fully into account, so that the sail will set perfectly.

The traveler passing around the bowsprit should be a large bronze or iron hoop, well leathered, and oiled so that sliding is easy. The halyard and the luff wire of the sail, and the halyard and tack blocks, must be oversized, to minimize stretching under load. A winch to set the whole rig up is absolutely essential.

The great advantage of this rig is that it makes it possible to set a jib without going out on the bowsprit, which is difficult on a boat like *Curlew,* with an eight-foot bowsprit and no pulpit or netting.

GUYS AND VANGS

GAFF RIG

Guys and vangs on the gaff rig will be discussed together, because what is a guy on one point of sail frequently becomes a vang on the other, just as the spinnaker sheet and guy exchange roles on every jibe.

The first major problem with the gaff rig is, of course, hoisting the gaff to the top of the mast. The second major problem is controlling gaff sag while under sail. Even when going to windward, there is usually a substantial sag to leeward by the gaff which puts excessive twist in the sail, so the lower portion of the sail must be overtrimmed or boom-vanged very heavily to enable the upper portion to draw. Similarly, as the sheet is eased on the sail, the gaff begins to fall off at a much greater rate than the boom, once again making it necessary to overtrim the lower portion of the sail or tighten the boom vang excessively. For this reason, gaff-rigged boats have a reputation for often carrying heavy weather helm when on a beam reach.

These difficulties can be eliminated by setting up a line from the end of the gaff to the weather quarter (Drawing 73A). This vang takes considerable strain—on the forty-five-foot gaff-rigged schooner *Atlantica,* even with a four-part tackle attached to the vang, two of us were needed to heave it up tight and secure it around the cleat. Therefore, the vang should be run through a block and then taken to the weather-sheet winch, or if necessary, a special winch should be installed. We discovered on *Atlantica* that by putting a vang on the main boom, and by holding the gaff vang, or easing it very slowly in comparison with the easing of the mainsheet, we could take most of the twist out of the

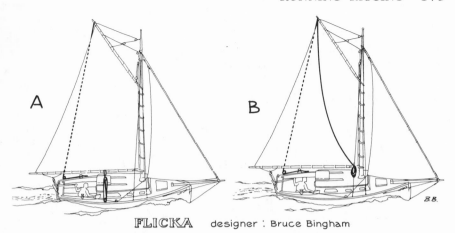

FLICKA   designer : Bruce Bingham

73. Gaff vang: A, led to weather quarter; B, in stowed position.

mainsail. This eased the weather helm entirely, making her a completely different boat, and a joy to steer on a reach.

The steering gear had packed up on the first day of the trip, and yet we had no trouble steering the whole two thousand miles with the emergency tiller as long as we were careful in trimming the gaff vang. If the gaff vang was too slack, weather helm immediately built up, and the sheet trimmers received a loud howl from the helmsman as the tiller tried to pull his arms out of their sockets.

Many experienced seamen feel that on a gaff-rigged sloop or cutter there should be two vangs, each secured to the end of the gaff, extending down opposite sides of the sail and of such length that they may be tied off at the tack of the sail (Drawing 73B). If the weather vang is taken aft, a tackle or a line leading to a winch may be snapped into it and adjusted as necessary. When broad off, the lee one can be passed outside the rigging, then run forward and secured to prevent the gaff from accidentally jibing, or from bouncing around in a seaway. When rigged in this manner it is called a "guy" or a "preventer." The wider the stern, the better the angle will be on the weather vang when going to windward—narrow-sterned boats have trouble vanging the gaff to windward.

On gaff ketches, and on the gaff foresail on schooners, a vang (A in Drawing 74) can lead from the end of the gaff to the mizzen or main, and then down the forward face of the mast to a small winch or tackle; a single vang (B in Drawing 74)—again made up to the correct length to reach to the tack, for ease of stowing—can be secured to the gaff of the after sail. As on the sloop or cutter, when broad off, this vang can be passed outside the lee rigging and secured forward

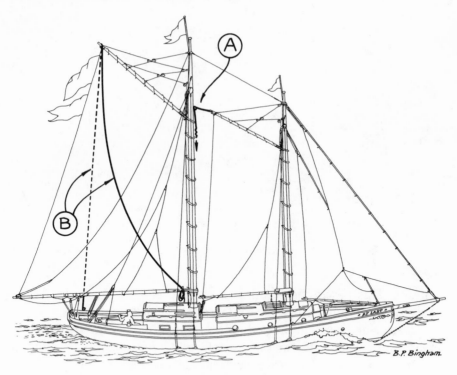

AT LAST
designer: R. McGilvray

74A. Vang/guy from forward gaff to after mast (mizzen on gaff ketch, main on gaff schooner). B. Single vang/guy on after sail.

to keep the gaff from jibing or jumping around in a seaway, and it is then known as a guy or preventer. Similarly, when a boom vang is led forward to prevent jibing, it is referred to as a guy or preventer.

VANGS

Much argument has been raised by my contention, in *OSY*-I (Drawing 69), that the vang should lead out at a 45-degree angle for optimum leverage. I was first made aware of this point by Cutty Mason's book *Ocean Racing;* herewith are the diagrams demonstrating it (Drawing 75). It should have been made clear that this principle applies only when the boat is running dead downwind or on a full broad reach. As the boom is sheeted inboard, the advantages of the angling diminish very rapidly. At the point where the boat is beam reaching, there is no longer any advantage and the vang should be led straight downward, as far aft on the boom as possible.

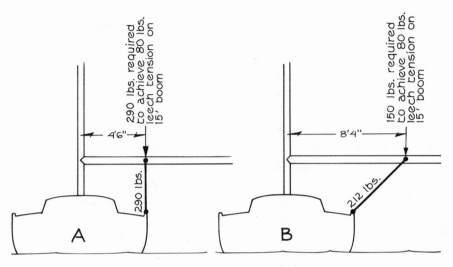

75. Leading the vang outboard at a 45-degree angle.

MAIN-BOOM FITTINGS

MAINSHEET RIG

On an ocean racer, or on a vessel of one of the ton classes, a center mainsheet rigged to a full-width traveler is desirable because it makes possible some control of the amount of twist in the sail, as required by the specific conditions, while increasing boom bend in heavy air; thus it assures excellent control of the sail shape. However, center-mainsheet rigging should be discouraged on the ocean sailing yacht. When sheeting from the middle of the boom, the sheeting lever is so short that the mainsheet rig even on comparatively small mainsails will be six or sometimes even eight parts leading to a winch. This may be great for the block and winch manufacturers, but it will be awfully hard for your small wife to trim. It also fills up the cockpit with a lot of extra line when sailing to weather.

To prove the point to yourself, take out a sailing surfboard with the midship sheeting arrangement. Sail hard on the wind, sheet down flat, and then ease the sheet and trim it in a number of times, to ascertain how much strain is needed to flatten the mainsail. Then sail back to the dock, rerig the sheet to the very end of the boom, cut the number of purchase parts in half, and go for another sail. You will discover that although leading in over the stern is a little awkward, trimming is infinitely easier, and much less purchase is required.

I first became aware of this situation when I was a boy growing up in Manhasset Bay, during World War II. In those years, anything that walked was a crew—so I was a crew, though quite a small one. I soon discovered, on the Atlantic-class thirty-foot day racers, that the boats with the mainsheet leading along the boom down to the forward part of the cockpit were impossible for me to trim. However, those with mainsheets led in over the stern were no serious problem even for a little guy like me. Therefore, the mainsheet on the cruising boat should be led from the boom end unless doing so is absolutely impossible.

A main traveler used with sheeting to the end of the boom can—admittedly—add immeasurably to the control of twist in the sail, thus increasing the power of the sail and helping to tune the amount of helm. However, some cruising sailors, myself among them, would rather use a double-ended mainsheet with twin lower blocks. On large boats, the ends are led to a small winch on each side; on small boats, to a cleat on one side and a small winch on the other.

An advantage of the double-ended mainsheet is that it may be eased back and forth so that no single segment is continually under use. A double-ended mainsheet will last almost forever.

OUTHAULS

Outhauls are extremely varied in design. The simplest is a pad eye screwed and/or bolted to the boom, with a lashing line going through the clew cringle of the sail. At the other extreme are the elaborate screw-type devices with remote control found on many of the new aluminum booms.

An adjustable outhaul should be set up so that it is easily reached and adjusted when the boom is eased all the way out. This can be done on the aluminum boom by running tackles, wires, rods, and so on internally through the boom to a convenient control point. However, the most normal method on both aluminum and wooden booms is to have a wire fixed to one side of the boom end pass around the outhaul, down through a cheek block on the opposite side of the boom, and then along the boom (preferably through a fairlead or a copper or plastic tube secured to the boom) to the outhaul tackle (Drawing 76). The purchase and size of the tackle will depend on the size of the sail. Indeed, on a small boat with a ten-foot boom, 2-to-1 purchase may well be sufficient, so that an outhaul tackle is not necessary. Booms of the larger sizes will require a two-, three-, or four-part tackle. The tackle attached to the outhaul wire can be made up of a cheek block and a

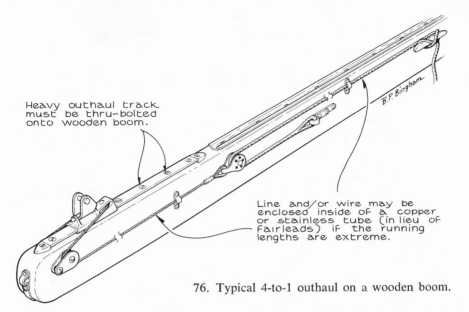

Heavy outhaul track must be thru-bolted onto wooden boom.

Line and/or wire may be enclosed inside of a copper or stainless tube (in lieu of fairleads) if the running lengths are extreme.

76. Typical 4-to-1 outhaul on a wooden boom.

running block with a sail slide on its back to prevent the tackle from twisting and sagging when slack.

A new style recently introduced on some racing boats is to have a fixed outhaul fitting. The foot of the sail is pulled out to approximately the correct tension, and is secured. Any further adjustment of the tension on the foot is done by means of a Cunningham tackle attached to the foot near the tack of the sail. The tackle is either heaved tight by hand or led to a small winch.

REEFING GEAR

SLAB REEFING

Roller reefing is rapidly becoming as dead as the dodo; reefing methods on most boats have taken a full circle and arrived back where they started—at slab reefing.

If there is any area in which the ocean racer should be admired and copied, reefing is certainly it. In particular, slab reefing—one of the most popular methods used by racers today—has been raised to an absolute art. Racing crews can reef faster than you can bat an eye, often keeping every stitch of sail up until the very last safe instant. Their proficiency, of course, is partly due to the fact that they practice until they can reef with their eyes closed. It is also due to recent advances in hardware design.

In slab reefing, the reefing tack may be just lashed to the boom with a piece of extra line, or held to the boom with a lanyard snap-shackled to the reefing-tack cringle. This kind of lashing takes valuable time, and results in a rather sloppy reef. A popular alternative is to splice a reefing-tack line into a strong pad eye on the port side of the mast or boom, near the gooseneck, and then pass the line through the reefing-tack cringle and down to a cleat on the starboard side. This line remains in position—left slack—when the sail is fully hoisted; when reefing is necessary, the line is drawn up tightly and secured, to hold the reefing tack in its correct position once it has been lowered.

An even faster method of securing the reefing tack is to use a reefing-tack hook. This makes it unnecessary to spend time lashing, or tying knots, or tightening lines; one need only lower the sail and place the reefing-tack cringle on the hook. The reefing-tack hook may take several forms. It can be made from a cut shackle and fastened to the gooseneck with a bolt that replaces the gooseneck clevis pin. A look at almost any ocean racer will show how it's done.

In slab reefing, the clew outhaul must be very carefully positioned. Usually it is led from a pad eye on one side of the boom, up through the reefing-clew cringle of the sail, down to a cheek block on the opposite side of the boom, then forward to a small winch on the boom. I like a bottom-action winch because the handle is always there and it doesn't get in the way when one is throwing turns onto the drum. An adjustable topping lift is necessary for the efficient use of this rig.

The actual reefing is quite simple. Ease the mainsheet, take up the boom on the adjustable topping lift, and slack the halyard to a position which has been predetermined and marked. Then snap in, hook, or lash down the reefing-tack cringle. Next, crank in the reefing-clew line until the reefing clew is two-blocked, and secure the line. Crank up hard on the halyard (or take down on the downhaul, if you have a sliding gooseneck) to tension the luff of the sail. Then roll up the bunt of the sail and tie up the reef points securely, slack off the topping lift, and resheet. (If the sail doesn't have reef-point lines, it will be necessary to lace up the bunt with a long line.) The whole operation can be completed by an experienced seaman in three or four minutes.

JIFFY REEFING

Jiffy reefing is an improvement on slab reefing. A 7 by 19 wire is secured to the reefing-clew and reefing-tack cringles, and run through an envelope sewn on the sail in the reef position (Drawing 77). Since the sailmaker may be unable to perfectly match the slightly stretchable

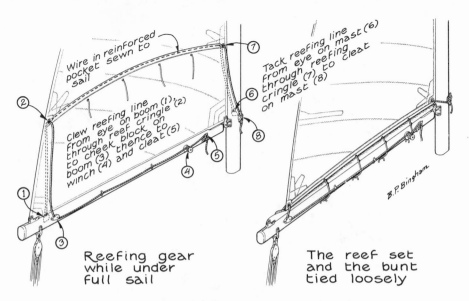

Reefing gear
while under
full sail

The reef set
and the bunt
tied loosely

Wire in reinforced
pocket sewn to
sail

Clew reefing line on boom (1)(2)
From eye on boom on
through reef cringle
to cheek block on
boom (3) thence to
winch (4) and cleat (5)

Tack reefing line on mast (6)
From eye on reefing
through (7) to cleat
cringle (7)(8)
on mast

B.P.Bingham

77. Jiffy reefing, with wire sewn into the sail.

Dacron sailcloth with unstretchable wire, it is a good idea to have him install a lashing line from the eye in the wire to the reefing-tack cringle, to make possible slight adjustments from time to time. Below the wire envelope, small grommets—with or without reef points—are secured to the sail, the first one being about eighteen inches forward of the reefing clew. The total number of grommets needed will depend on the length of the boom—three ought to be plenty for a twelve-foot boom, and four for an eighteen-foot boom.

By and large, the reefing procedures are like those of normal slab reefing; the reefing-tack line and the reefing-tack hook described in reference to slab reefing can be used for jiffy reefing as well. The important difference between the two methods is that in slab reefing the reef points actually help support the foot of the sail, while in jiffy reefing the wire assumes all of the foot tension. The only thing the reef points (or lacing line) do is prevent the bunt of the sail from flopping around in an unseamanlike fashion. Hence, it is not necessary to tie up the bunt until the reefed sail has been sheeted and the boat is under way again.

Having used roller reefing, slab reefing with points (and with lacing lines and hooks), and jiffy reefing, the crew of *Iolaire* is firmly convinced that jiffy reefing is the quickest and safest method for both racing and cruising boats.

When jiffy reefing or slab reefing is installed, location of the clew hardware on the boom is critical. If placement is too far inboard, the foot of the sail will end up too slack; if too far outboard, the clew will not be held down firmly enough against the boom, and will there-

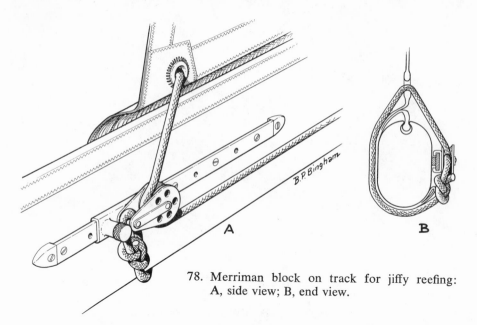

78. Merriman block on track for jiffy reefing: A, side view; B, end view.

fore tend to ride up, resulting in a poorly setting sail. Once the hardware is fastened, its position becomes fixed. However, Merriman has developed a cheek block with an eye on it, that slides on a piece of track secured to the side of the boom (Drawing 78A). The reefing-clew line is tied to the eye on the block, led underneath the boom, up through the reefing clew cringle, down through the block, then forward to the small winch. The block is then adjusted to the correct location on the track while the sail is in the reefed position. Once set properly, it rarely has to be moved.

One might expect that the block would be torn right off the track or the track off the spar. However, as shown by the end view of the boom (Drawing 78B), the downward pull on the tied end of the reefing-clew line is nearly the same as the upward pull on the line passing through the block. Hence, the two forces almost balance each other, and the strain on the track is minimized.

SECURING LINES

Normally, line is secured to a cleat. In the days of linen and manila line, half hitches were never used on small boats and were generally not used on larger boats (except, possibly, with halyards) because if the line shrank, the half hitch might be absolutely irremovable. Now, in the Dacron and nylon age, most good seamen will agree that a half hitch is acceptable when finishing off the line to a cleat (Drawing 79A). The most popular method still is to finish off with a simple round turn

A
B

79. Securing line to cleat: A, finishing with a half hitch; B, finishing with a round turn.

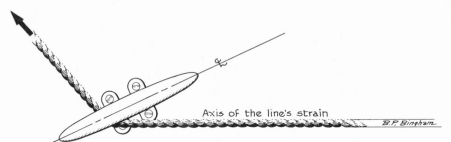

Axis of the line's strain

80. A cleat should be cocked slightly from the axis of the line's strain.

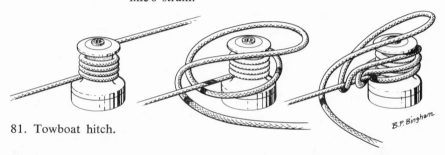

81. Towboat hitch.

(Drawing 79B). In addition, all cleats should be cocked from the line of pull whenever possible (Drawing 80). Cleats are discussed in Chapter VII.

At times, however, the necessity for cleats must be minimized. For instance, since *Iolaire*'s maximum beam is only 10½ feet, and her cockpit is roughly six feet wide at the section of the boat where the hull is narrowing down, there is little space between the bulwarks and the cockpit coamings for cleats. In circumstances of this sort, line may be secured directly to the bottom-action winches, as described earlier in the chapter.

If line is to be secured directly to a top-action winch, a towboat hitch can be used (Drawing 81). This involves taking five turns around the winch, then passing a bight of the line underneath the standing part, back over the top of the winch, back under the standing part, over the top of the winch, back under the standing part, and then over the winch. The process sounds and looks complicated, but it takes no more time than cleating, and enables one to save the space that would have been occupied by the cleat.

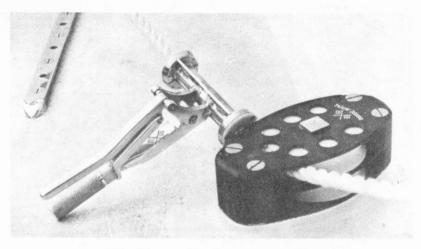

10. "Line grabber." PALMER JOHNSON

STOPPERS

The traditional stopper is a length of line eye-spliced at one end and pig-tailed at the other. It is used when one wishes to maintain tension on a line which is being transferred from one winch to another, or is being removed from a winch needed for a different line. The eye of the stopper is placed on a nearby cleat, and the other end is tied to the line with a rolling hitch. This method is adequate when the line on which tension is to be maintained is made of manila or laid Dacron, but when it is made of braided Dacron or any type of nylon, a stopper tied to it in this manner will slip. To prevent this from happening, after the rolling hitch has been completed, the pigtail is simply wrapped spirally five or six times around the line and finished off with a clove hitch. The stopper will then hold any strain the line is given.

Several types of mechanical stopper are now available. A most interesting and useful piece of gear, developed for ocean racing, is the "line grabber" (Photo 10), which is in effect a pipe wrench used to grip a rope. The stopper is clamped on a line, a tail is secured to the stopper, and the tail is then taken to a winch and heaved up tight, or is tied off on a cleat; then the line is slacked off, transferred to the desired position and resecured, and the line grabber is removed.

This is not really a new idea. The mainsheet rigs of some of the old "J" boats included a six-part mainsheet onto which was clamped a mechanical line stopper (like the one shown in the photo). This took a

11. Fixed line stoppers. SCHAEFER MARINE

six-part tackle which was led up the deck either to a winch or to fifteen or twenty men; either way, tremendous power could be developed.

FIXED LINE STOPPERS

Another device first developed for the ocean racer is the fixed line stopper (Photo 11). Fastened to the mast or cabin top, this stopper can be used to tie off a halyard, a boom vang, or the like, which can then be removed from the winch, freeing it for other purposes. Another type of line stopper, installed in the quarter blocks of many racing boats, makes it possible to tie off the sheet under load, again leaving the winch free for other use. Most fixed line stoppers are available in models for either vertical or horizontal mounting.

The installation of fixed line stoppers makes it possible for one winch to do a number of jobs. For instance, the spinnaker halyard, spinnaker-pole topping lifts, and spinnaker-pole inner-end lift, or the halyards and topping lifts of the various running sails, can be led through the stoppers; and if properly placed, three or four stoppers can then be serviced by one winch.

Similarly, on the smaller ocean sailing yachts, if the halyards, down-hauls, reefing lines, and the like are all brought back along the cabin

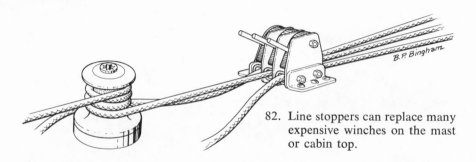

B. P. Bingham

82. Line stoppers can replace many expensive winches on the mast or cabin top.

top through vertically rather than horizontally mounted stoppers (Drawing 82), they will emerge so close together that one winch can handle four or five lines. This installation will take up much less room and cost much less money than would the equivalent number of winches and individual cleats.

LAZY JACKS

In the days of canvas sails that would soak up 50 percent of their weight in water, and were difficult to furl when dry and impossible to furl when wet, lazy jacks were common on cruising boats and were even seen on some racing boats. Today, they are seldom found except on traditional or gaff-rigged vessels.

There are probably as many variations in the rigging of lazy jacks as there are seamen, but basically they are rigged as shown in Drawing 83A. A great disadvantage of lazy jacks is of course their tendency to chafe the seams of the sails. For this reason, some people rig them so that they may be disconnected on long passages. However, if this is done, when the sails are to be doused, they must first be trimmed in, and the lazy jacks then reconnected.

For years, it was alleged that one disadvantage of roller reefing was that it made rigging lazy jacks impossible. However, on the seventy-foot schooner *Veleda,* Mike McMillan has rigged lazy jacks which work extremely well, and she has roller reefing, with the old-fashioned outer end fittings, and with topping lifts which lead approximately two-thirds of the way up the mast and then down again to a tackle. He has led lines (three to a side) from one topping lift, down under the boom, and up the other side to the other topping lift (Drawing 83B). To be sure, one does have to make certain that the lee topping lift is slack, so that the chafe on the mainsail is minimal. But the presence of the lazy

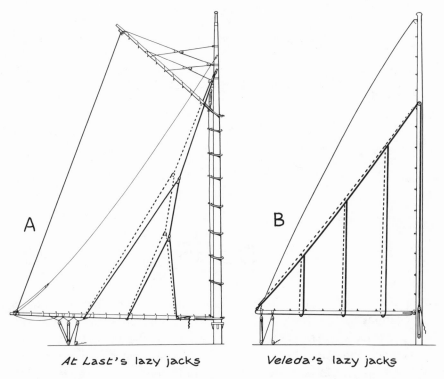

A   *At Last*'s lazy jacks   *Veleda*'s lazy jacks

83. Lazy jacks: A, *At Last*'s conventional gaff system; B, *Veleda*'s topping-lift system.

jacks means that even with a small crew, a big sail may be handled; when the halyard is cast off, the sail falls right between the topping lifts, flaking down fairly well without the aid of five men standing on cabin tops, ladders, or what-have-you.

VI

~~~~~~~~~~~~~~~~~~~~~~~~~~~~~

Sails

Being connected with the sail-making business as an agent for Cheong Lee Sailmakers of Hong Kong, and being located in an inaccessible area—the Lesser Antilles—I find that one of the most frustrating of the problems continually arising is the absence, on board the average yacht cruising from one end of the world to the other, of a copy of the sail plan.

Just as a cruising yacht should always have on board the repair manuals for all of her equipment, for reference when anything breaks down, so there should be available a sail and rigging plan. But the proper sail plan is frequently out of date. As years go by and new sails are ordered, a good sailmaker will recommend changes to the rig; when these are made, the plan should be altered accordingly. This is usually not done. When measuring for sails and cross-checking against the sail plan, I seldom find that the actual measurements agree with the plan. But when the time comes to order new sails, the job is greatly facilitated if the actual sail plan is on board. Indeed, changes may be difficult to comprehend and to carry out correctly if the sail plan is not available.

All information that affects the making of the sail should be carefully recorded. For example, attached to the sail plan should be a detailed list of specifications—the rub-back (knock-back or cut-back) dimension, if any, at the tack; the jaw dimensions for the tack and outhaul fittings; the distance from the tack of the genoa to the first hank; and so on. Otherwise, the sailmaker may, among other things, supply a genoa with a lower snap located so that it lines up with the middle of a turnbuckle.

A set of typical specifications (such as one might use in ordering sails), with accompanying comments, will be found in the Appendix.

CHOOSING A SAILMAKER

Sailmakers vary in the extreme, ranging from those who are superb, and produce perfect sails, to those who turn out sacks that look as if they were made by Omar the Tentmaker. Even among good sailmakers there are some basic differences in philosophy which the cruising yachtsman ignores at his peril. For example, the sailmaker who speaks of his cruising sails as being cheaper than his racing sails should be avoided absolutely. There is no way that a good cruising sail can be made more cheaply than a racing sail of comparable size. A cruising sail should be at least one weight of cloth heavier than the racing sail, since for cruising, reliability and strength are more important than lightness, and the tack and clew should be much more heavily reinforced. Consequently, more material and more hand labor are required. Frequently, the cruising sails from a good loft are cheaper than the racing sails because they are cut by an apprentice, who may or may not have achieved competence. Some internationally famous lofts, widely recognized for their perfectly setting racing sails, are known by cruising yachtsmen to put out cruising sails which are unbelievably poor in cut and workmanship.

The best sailmaker for your boat is the one who will come aboard, have a beer, discuss your sail problems, and perhaps even go out with you for an afternoon sail. Since he is then not operating merely on the basis of a sail plan and a stack of correspondence, he is more apt to take a personal interest in the sails, to check on all the dimensions, the location of the sheet leads, the performance of the boat under various circumstances, and consequently to make better sails for you.

In some areas of the world, competent sailmakers are difficult or impossible to find. In the Lesser Antilles, for example, the few good sailmakers are so busy that for all intents and purposes they are unavailable. In a situation of this sort, sails must be ordered from afar, and hence the sailmaker cannot inspect the boat in person. However, it may be possible to find a sailmaker with a responsible agent in the area who will come on board, measure the boat, and discuss the sails, sail plan, and rigging, instead of merely writing down and forwarding the order, and who has proved that he stands behind his sails and is willing to rectify the errors that must inevitably crop up from time to time, even with the best of workmanship. This is the kind of service, for example, that I myself supply in the Caribbean in my capacity as agent for the Hong Kong sailmaker Cheong Lee. As a result, Cheong Lee sails made according to my specifications, and identifiable by the red eagle—*Iolaire*'s emblem—at the tack, seldom require repairs, and have an excellent reputation. By inquiring locally, one may be able to find in almost any area an agent who works in this manner.

REINFORCING NEW SAILS

CRINGLE REINFORCEMENT

All too often the death of a beautiful, well-cut sail is caused by inadequate reinforcement of the head, tack, and clew cringles, or of the reef cringles. In an extreme case, the clew cringle begins to distort, becomes egg-shaped, and pulls the hand stitching through the cloth. In years gone by, in order to reinforce a head, tack, or clew cringle, after the bronze ring was sewn into the sail, the sailmaker would seize it to smaller cringles, also sewn into the sail (Drawing 84). This arrangement was strong but bulky, and when used on headsails, had a tendency to catch in the rigging during tacking. It was very difficult to get the tension in the extra seizing exactly even, so that the threads or wire lay down flat.

Some sailmakers now reinforce the cringle by sewing some Dacron tape to the sail, passing it through the cringle, and sewing it to the other side of the sail (Drawing 85). Some really good sailmakers then further reinforce this arrangement by hand stitching with heavy waxed Dacron twine through both sides of the sail and the tape, making it all but impossible for the cringle to move. This should be done not only on all clew cringles, but also on the head and tack seizing cringles on all headsails (Drawing 86A), to reduce the likelihood of their tearing out.

The thimbles at the ends of the luff wire should be either solid or of rolled stainless steel, welded across the throat (Drawing 86B). Further, they should be outside the sail (Drawing 86A), because replacing a broken luff wire in then much easier, and readjustment of the tension

Holes are punched through the clew patch (1); bronze rings are placed in the holes (2) and secured by alternating long and short hand stitches with sail twine (3 and 4); brass cringles are "riveted" through each hole to protect the stitching (5); the clew corner is cut or burned to final shape (6); the small cringles are connected to the large cringle with seizing wire (7); the clew rat tail is sewn to the sail (8); and the clew corner and rat tail are finally protected by a strip of rawhide hand stitched to the sail (9).

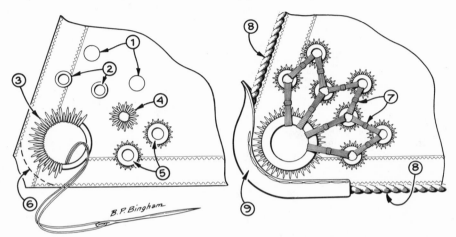

84. Old-fashioned clew-cringle reinforcement.

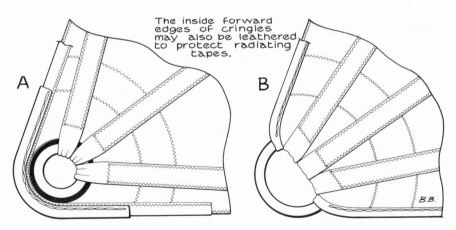

85. Modern clews use either a hydraulically pressed stainless-steel barbed thimble (A) or a heavy stainless-steel D ring (B). In addition the cringle of the cruising sail should be reinforced with radiating Dacron tape.

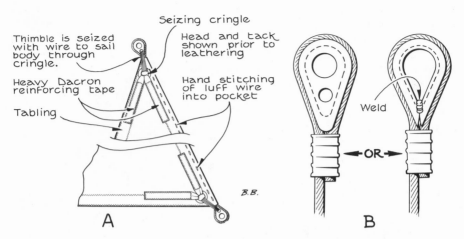

Seizing cringle

Thimble is seized with wire to sail body through cringle.

Head and tack shown prior to leathering

Heavy Dacron reinforcing tape

Hand stitching of luff wire into pocket

Tabling

Weld

B.B.

A

OR

B

86. An excellent method of reinforcing the headsail head and tack is to seize the luff-wire thimbles to seizing cringles that are set into the patches of sail and reinforced with radiating Dacron tape (A). The thimbles should be solid castings or rolled stainless steel welded at the throat (B).

between the luff wire and the sail—if it should be necessary—becomes a relatively simple operation.

Finally, the reefing-clew cringle should be at least as strong and as heavily reinforced as the main clew cringle—and preferably, even stronger—for reefing is likely to be done when it is blowing very hard, so although the sail is reduced in size, the strain will probably be greater than that on the full-main clew.

PRESSED CRINGLES

The newest thing in sailmaking is a cringle, used at the clew and tack in headsails and mainsails, that is set into place under tremendous hydraulic pressure. At first glance one would expect this type of cringle to be weak, but any sailmaker who has run tests on it will affirm that it is as strong as, or stronger than, one made with the traditional sewn-in ring. However, what will happen in the long run is still unknown. In some cases, although the ring is made of stainless steel, the thimble that presses through it is made of aluminum, and how this will stand up over the years, lying salt-soaked in damp lazarets, has yet to be seen. Many people feel that the aluminum will eventually dissolve; already we know that on boats that continually sail in the deep tropics, the pressed clew cringle falls apart from corrosion in a year or so. However, some pressed cringles do have stainless-steel thimbles. They are worth insisting upon.

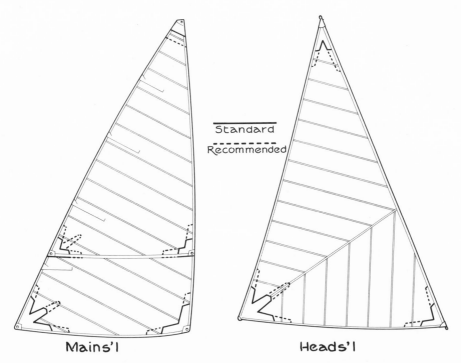

Standard

Recommended

Mains'l   Heads'l

87. Normal sail-reinforcing patches (*solid line*) are usually inadequate for extended, rugged cruising. To increase sail life, they should be enlarged (*broken line*).

CORNER REINFORCEMENT PATCHES

The reinforcement patches to which the cringles are sewn should be really large, the exact size depending upon the size of the sail: a small mizzen of fifty square feet will have patches only two or three feet long; on a boat of sixty or seventy feet, the arms of the patches will be at least six feet long; and on a ninety-foot yawl like *Gitana,* they may reach twelve or fifteen feet.

The ending of the reinforcement patch is frequently not considered. I have often seen reinforcement patches ending several inches below a seam, as indicated by the solid lines in Drawing 87, but it is better for them to be carried up, when laid out on the floor, to six or eight inches above the seam, as indicated by the broken lines in the drawing. This is especially important on headsails, since frequently a headsail is laid out in such a manner that if the patches are not extended onto the next panel, the load on the seam from the clew is actually doubled.

Some sailmakers reinforce the leech of a sail in the area of a reefing patch with a length of Dacron webbing. This does tend to distribute the leech tension over a considerable distance, but it creates a stress-concentration point at the ends of the webbing that could become the start of a tear. It is better for the tensions on the sail to be dissipated into the body of the sail more gradually. I therefore recommend the use of a tapered, three-strand rat tail instead of webbing, as this will stretch a little under stress. The closer the stresses are to the tapered ends, the more readily will they blend into the body of the sail.

TABLING

Tabling is the doubling of cloth that reinforces the three sides of the sail. On cheaper sails without a large degree of roach, the leech is just turned over and stitched, to form the tabling. On more expensive sails, when the sail is laid out, the excess cloth is cut off and is folded to form the tabling, which is then sewn back on (Drawing 88). Sailmakers occasionally lay the tabling so that its seams match up with the seams in the sail body, but many seamen feel that this is a mistake in that the seams in the tabling and the seams in the panel of the sail are likely to give way at the same time. If the tabling is placed as shown in the drawing, so that the seams do not coincide with those joining the panels, a stronger sail is produced, since the seams in the sail are then supported by the tabling cloth, and vice versa.

88. The strongest, most distortion-resistant tabling is cut to the predetermined finish curves from the excess at the edges of the sail being made. It is then sewn to the sail body with the seams offset from those on the sail proper, to eliminate weak points.

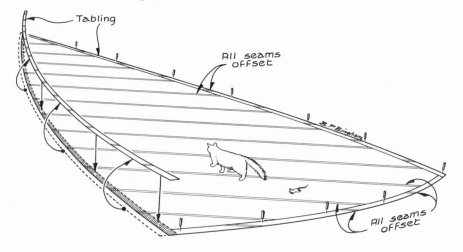

CHAFE PROTECTION

Chafe Patches

Chafe patches should of course be installed wherever the sail will be chafing against the spreaders, stays, shrouds, or what-have-you. However, trying to plot out the exact location for chafe patches from the sail plan is all but impossible. One alternative is to use oversized chafe patches, which are likely to cover the necessary areas simply because they are so large. A better approach is to lay out the old sail on the floor, find the chafe spots, draw an exact picture of the sail, showing their location, and send it to the sailmaker.

If this cannot be done—because the boat is new, for example, or because the rig has been changed—the sails should be ordered without chafe patches, used for a number of weeks, until the chafe spots develop, and then returned to the sailmaker for the installation of the chafe patches where necessary.

Seam Chafe Prevention

If chafe on the seams from spreader tips, backstays, and the like is anticipated, instead of putting the large patches on the sails for protection, it is much simpler to sew on, over the seams, strips of Dacron slightly wider than the seams themselves. Rip-stop nylon tape, split in half, is also excellent for this purpose (Drawing 89). Then the chafing strips must wear out completely before the stitching of the seams is exposed to possible damage.

89. Rip-stop tape sewn over the spinnaker seam (A) and foot edge (B) as chafe protection.

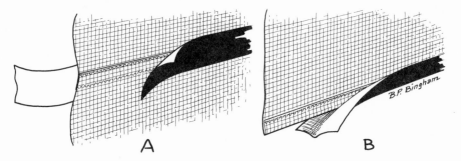

A   B

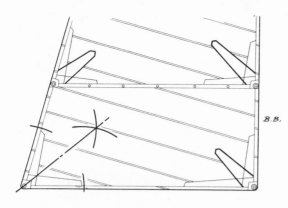

B.B.

90. Additional reinforcement may be added to a sail in the form of patches which bisect the angle at each corner.

REINFORCING EXISTING SAILS

If the reinforcements on an existing sail are not adequate, they can be strengthened. It is relatively simple to open up, say, the leech tabling and reinforcement patch, slip a layer of Dacron underneath them (if the sail is new, the same weight of Dacron as the sail; if the sail is old, one weight lighter), and extend the leech reinforcement to join the reefing-clew cringle reinforcement. Also, the reinforcement patch along the foot of the sail may be extended, and a patch may be placed diagonally up the sail, bisecting the angle between the foot and the leech (Drawing 90); the tack and head of the sail can be similarly reinforced as well.

The cringles themselves should also be reinforced if they have been merely sewn into the sail. The procedure is to remove the inner thimble with a cold chisel or grinder, and sew one, two, or three Dacron-tape reinforcements (the number depending on the size of the sail) around the ring and up the sail, tacking them into place with machine stitching, and reinforcing them with hand stitching. A new thimble is then installed.

When sails get old, they almost always split from the leech inward. To prevent this situation, and thereby immeasurably increase the life of a sail, the leech tabling may be opened, and a new tabling slipped underneath, as described in the following section.

RESTITCHING SAILS

Restitching a sail is more complicated than most people realize; indeed, especially where a large sail is involved, restitching is harder than making a new one. When a sail is being made, it is laid out on the floor and the panels are "struck up"—numbered, and fed through the sewing machine in consecutive order. The stitcher is therefore dragging only one thirty-six-inch panel through the machine at a time. The portion of the sail already stitched up lies outside the machine, on the floor. However, getting to the middle of a large mainsail or genoa that needs restitching is a three-man proposition: the bulk of the sail must be rolled tightly, to fit under the arm of the machine, and one person must push the sail through while another pulls and the third person sews. No wonder sailmakers charge so much to do a really good job of restitching a large sail!

A few sailmakers do have special machines with extra-long arms to allow the bunt of the sail to pass through the machine. However, these are not found in the average loft.

When restitching sails, or arranging to have them restitched, one should remember that, as has been mentioned, they almost invariably tear from the leech in, not from the luff out. Therefore, on large mains, mizzens, and headsails, the last ten feet of the leech should be triple stitched, or if necessary, quadruple stitched. A genoa or genoa staysail should be restitched inward from the leech to a point a few feet forward of the place where the upper shroud chafes the sail when tacking (Drawing 91). Further, miter-cut sails should be resewn four, five, or even ten feet up from the foot—depending on the size of the sail and the capacity of the machine available.

91. Seams (*dark lines*) in genoa and genoa staysail which should receive extra rows of stitching.

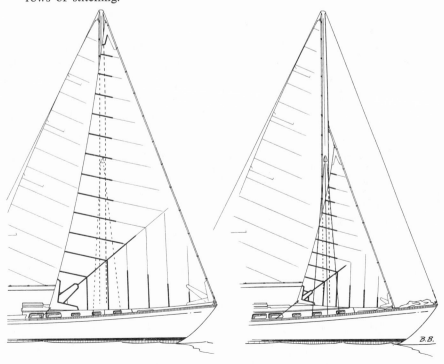

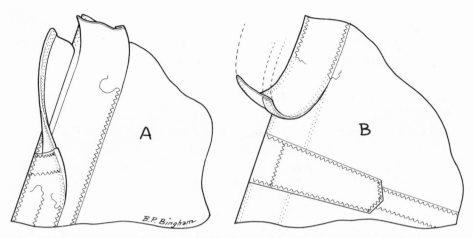

92. Reinforcing an old sail: A, adding a new tabling under the original; B, adding a wedge at the leech end of each seam.

Restitching in from the leech is complicated by the fact that the leech line passes through the tabling; if each seam is sewn leech to luff, there will no longer be space for the line.

There are three solutions to this problem. The first, which is best but expensive, is to remove the leech tabling, restitch each seam, restitch the leech tabling, and then sew the tabling back onto the sail. This is a job which should be done only by a very experienced sailmaker.

The second method, which is also expensive but if properly done will increase the life of the sail considerably, is to open up the tabling, restitch the seams, and then slip in a piece of Dacron 2 to 2½ inches wide—basically a new tabling—inner edge bare, outer edge folded over. The sail is then restitched, an extra row of stitching being placed on the tabling (Drawing 92A). This new tabling can be one or two weights of cloth lighter than that of the original sail, so that it will stretch into place and the sail edges will not curl.

The third solution is to pull the leech line out of the sail, restitch the seams completely, then take Dacron tape of a suitable width and stitch it up the sail over the tabling, with the leech line inside the Dacron tape. This is not the most desirable method, but it will work, and the Dacron tape will strengthen the leech of the sail.

If the leech seems particularly weak, a reinforcement wedge should be sewn at each seam (Drawing 92B) its length depending of course on the size of the sail.

The job of checking sails for chafe, tears, and seams requiring restitching should not be left to the sailmaker. He is a very busy man, and cannot afford to spend two days going over the sails inch by inch and marking them for repairs. Rather, take the sails out onto a nice, cool, open area, such as a basketball court or a lawn, spread them out, and have the whole crew go over them with a fine-toothed comb. The work that needs to be done should be immediately recorded in a notebook, a typical entry being something like the following: *"Genoa*—stitch third seam down from head, 2′ in; chafe patch 6′ aft of patch, chafe patch dimensions as follows: . . ." Then, along with the sails, the sailmaker can be presented with the notebook, specifying exactly where the sails need to be restitched, strengthened, furnished with chafe patches, and so on. The result will be an easier job for the sailmaker, and a reduced bill; and after the sails have been returned, the notebook can be used as a checklist when they are examined to make sure that all the work has been done.

Restitching Spinnakers

As they grow old, spinnakers should be center stitched, just as a general policy. All too often, when spinnakers go it is because the thread has weakened, though the material may still be in fairly good shape. Where the spinnaker chafes on the head stay, the foot and leeches should be not only restitched but also reinforced, by means of some rip-stop tape split up the middle, stitched on over the restitched seams, and also stitched into place *outside* the original seams (Drawing 89). The seams will be reinforced, and the stitching will be protected from further chafe in that a full layer of nylon will have to be torn off or chafed through before the head stay can again begin to abrade the stitching.

SAIL REPAIR

The ocean sailing yacht should have on board enough equipment to repair all the sails and, in fact, probably restitch most of them completely. A full sail-making kit should be carried, with spare cloth of various weights, grommets, thimbles, grommet tools—the entire works —since in many parts of the world sailmakers are not available.

The standard old household, hand-powered Singer sewing machine will chew its way very nicely through two layers of 8-ounce Dacron. Even though it may not provide a "zigzag" stitch, it is perfectly acceptable. Many good sailmakers insist that straight stitching is better on Dacron than zigzag; in any event, both types are obviously accept-able. Now, a new hand-powered zigzag machine is available from a company in England (see Appendix). The hand-powered machines will not go through the heavy corner patches of an 8-ounce sail, but the stitching required for these patches can be done by hand.

Ocean sailing yachts large enough to require sails of 10½-ounce (or heavier) fabric are large enough to carry a regular industrial sail-maker's sewing machine. It need not be kept assembled at all times. A standard machine of this type, on its table, with the legs removed, can be packed into a box 36 inches long, 12 inches wide, 12 inches high, which should be easily stowable on a large yacht. The big machine will pay for itself ten times over, for sails which are kept in good condition, and restitched regularly, seldom have to be taken to the sailmaker for extensive repairs. The sail-making gear can also be used to make awnings, cushion covers—even clothes, in an emergency!

Enough could be said on sail repair to fill a book. Indeed, on the whole subject of sails, the yachtsman is well advised to buy *Sails* and *The Care and Repair of Sails,* two books by Jeremy Howard-Williams, which are extremely thorough. But one trick not shown in any book on sail repair, which Val Schaeffer of *Camelot* and Mike McMillan of *Veleda* swear by, is the use of contact cement. If you have an old sail that is falling apart and that tears whenever you try to stitch it, find some other material of similar age, cut out a patch, smear the sail and the patch with contact cement, and slap the two together. The re-paired sail may look like hell, but it will last for an amazingly long time. Not very nautical, but extremely practical.

MAINSAILS

There is little to add to what was said about mainsails in *OSY*-I (Ch. VI) except to reemphasize the usefulness of Cunningham holes on cruising sails. Some cruising boats have grossly inadequate outhaul tackles, and the main-halyard winch or tackle may be very much on the small side. The best solution, of course, is to install a more suitable winch or tackle. But a luff Cunningham is invaluable for making small adjustments in the luff tension, since it is easier to tighten by pulling down than by hauling up.

On the subject of reef points, I personally do not advocate the in-stallation of more than one row unless the reefs are very small, say, only four or five feet apart. A modern I.O.R. mainsail with a 3-to-1 aspect ratio loses a comparatively small proportion of its area when only single-reefed. If the low-aspect-ratio mainsail (2.5 to 1 or less) needs to be double-reefed, it probably should not be up. The weakest part of the sail, which has been continuously exposed to the wind and sun, is then in use. And if it is blowing hard enough to necessitate a double-reefed main, it may be blowing hard enough to demolish the sail if a seam should open or a cringle begin to pull. So you may be risking the loss of the mainsail or the expense of a large repair bill. Also, there may not always be a sailmaker handy.

If a large storm trysail—the same size as the double-reefed main— is hoisted when it is blowing hard, the mainsail will not be over- strained by being set double-reefed. The trysail is so seldom used that there is little chance of its being damaged even in a high wind. On *Iolaire,* although we have retired several mainsails when they have be- come too old, in twenty-one years of sailing we have never had a main completely demolished, or even seriously torn by the wind, because whenever it is blowing really hard, we use an oversized storm trysail instead of double-reefing the main.

HEADSAILS

DOUBLE-HEADSAIL RIG

Many seamen advocate the double-headsail rig for cruising boats larger than about thirty-five feet and racing boats larger than about forty-five feet. Admittedly, when one becomes involved with Illing- worth and Primrose's highly refined double-headsail rig (*OSY*-I, Draw- ing 89), one can get overloaded with sails, but on a cruising boat, a simpler version can involve far fewer sails than on a racing boat, and yet provide a great degree of flexibility for almost all weather condi- tions.

Most of those experienced with the double-headsail rig will generally agree with the selection of sails shown in Drawing 93. The high-cut No. 1 genoa (*G1*) can be sheeted to the end of the main boom for reaching, and is used in conjunction with the genoa staysail in the lightest of airs. The No. 1 jib (*J1*) is the normal working headsail, used in conjunction with the genoa staysail. The No. 2 jib (*J2*) is a heavy sail to be used at 15 knots and over, in conjunction with the genoa staysail. (This sail should be of the same length in the luff as the staysail, so that if necessary it can serve as an emergency replacement.)

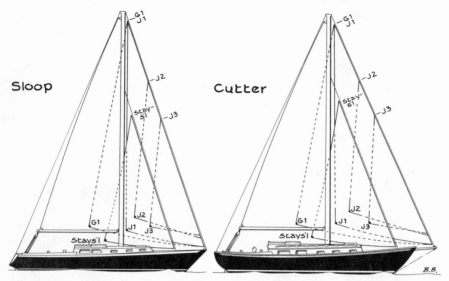

93. Recommended sail inventory for double-headsail rigs, sloop and cutter.

The No. 3 jib (*J3*) can be used in conjunction with the working staysail in heavy weather, and in absolute gale conditions can be set on the staysail stay as a storm staysail.

The normal cruising boat would set either one of two staysails—the genoa staysail or the working staysail—the latter being used only in heavy weather or in conditions where a tremendous amount of short tacking is done and the crew does not want to bother with tacking the genoa staysail. However, on *Iolaire* we also have a light reaching genoa staysail with 30 percent more area than the genoa staysail. When the wind eases off, the first thing done is to set the light genoa staysail, rather than the hard-to-handle No. 1 genoa.

The great advantage of this rig is its flexibility. In the lightest of airs, the genoa and the light reaching genoa staysail can be used, providing tremendous area. As the breeze increases, the genoa can be removed, and the boat will continue under mainsail and light genoa staysail without slowing too significantly before the No. 1 jib is set. When it begins to blow harder, the light genoa staysail is replaced by the smaller genoa staysail. If the wind continues to increase, the main should next be reefed. After this, the No. 1 jib should be doused, so the boat continues under reefed main and genoa staysail while the No. 2 jib is being hoisted. If the wind increases still further, the No. 2 jib should be replaced by the No. 3 jib, which, being used mainly in fairly heavy weather, can be of very heavy cloth and is practically a storm jib. If the weather unfortunately deteriorates still more, the working staysail should be substituted for the genoa staysail. The sails to be used beyond this point, when actual storm conditions develop, are discussed later in the chapter. Once the weather eases, the sequence can of course be reversed, with the headsails being switched in easy stages, so that the vessel is never sailing bald-headed, hobby-horsing in a seaway.

For a boat with a bowsprit, the double-headsail rig has another great advantage. On such a boat, a genoa, except a very high-cut one, could be troublesome when sailing in a heavy chop or when heeling excessively, since the bow wave coming up well aft of the tack of the sail will probably be scooped up by the foot. Even boats without bowsprits often have this trouble with low-cut genoas. However, this problem does not exist with a low-cut, deck-sweeping genoa staysail, since its tack is usually inboard of the stem and clear of the bow wave. Yet the combination of this genoa staysail and a high-cut No. 1 jib will provide about the same area as a 135- or 140-percent I.O.R. genoa set alone.

On large cruising boats, of sixty-five feet and over, the double-headsail rig is practically essential. The genoa on boats in this size range is a massive thing—simply to hoist it or even to move the sail bags takes the whole crew—and it is correspondingly difficult to stow. Indeed, the cruising boat with a single-headsail rig will require three or four headsails of various sizes which present a stowage problem. With the double-headsail rig, the No. 1 jib and genoa staysail, together giving almost as much area as the 150-percent genoa, are much easier to stow, being two smaller units instead of a single, larger one. On very large boats, a light reaching genoa staysail can provide additional sail area which may satisfy all but the hottest racing enthusiasts.

It should further be noted that on boats with club staysails and big No. 1 jibs, a light reaching genoa staysail set with a No. 1 jib is preferable to just one big genoa. In light airs, the club staysail can be dropped and stowed, and the light genoa staysail tacked down to leeward and hanked onto the stay. Admittedly, the last three to four feet of the staysail on a small boat, or six to eight feet on a larger boat, will have to be freestanding, without hanks. This portion will stand up adequately if the sail is winched up tight, however, since it is used only in light airs. Sail area, and performance, will be greatly enhanced, without the necessity of struggling with a large, unwieldy genoa.

High-Cut Jibs

There are some difficulties with the high-cut jib used with the double-headsail rig. First and foremost, the high-cut jib must be sheeted well aft, and when the sheet is thrown off to tack, it thrashes around wildly. Anyone in its way can be seriously injured. I have seen tough racing

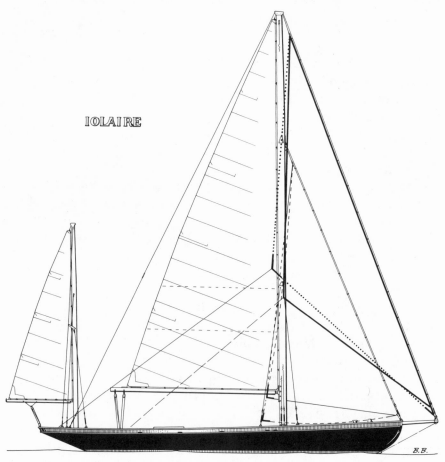

IOLAIRE

94. *Iolaire's* high-cut No. 1 racing jib (*dotted line*), compared to her No. 1 low-cut cruising jib (*solid line*).

crews laid out cold when hit across the head; my wife picked up a broken rib; and another friend broke a bone in the back of his hand. All these injuries were inflicted by the $\frac{9}{16}$-inch Dacron sheet from a 350-square-foot high-cut jib, on boats of forty-five or fifty feet. Such a long sheet actually acts like a bullwhip. The longer it is, the more devastating its power. Further, because the sheet is usually led so far aft, the angle of the sheeting base from the tack is reduced, and if a boat does not have an extremely efficient underbody or is excessively heavy, the effect of strapping her in so tightly when going to weather is simply to increase leeway. Also, since the high-cut sail has a higher center of effort than a lower-cut sail of the same area, the boat's stability is somewhat reduced.

Accordingly, the clew location of a high-cut jib involves a compromise between efficiency and safety. For example, *Iolaire's* high-cut No. 1 jib for racing (dotted outline in Drawing 94) is a tremendously effective sail, but because the sheet leads all the way to the quarter it must be handled with great care. The No. 1 jib used for cruising (solid outline in Drawing 94), which is still considerably high-cut, has a sheet which leads farther forward, and therefore does not tend to sweep the entire deck at every tack.

The other great problem with the high-cut jib is that as soon as the boom is eased any distance, the jib sheet leads underneath the boom, thereby causing tremendous chafe on the boom. The very simplest method I've seen for eliminating this chafe on small cruisers is to firmly fasten a substantial stainless-steel or hardwood hook to the underside of the boom facing outboard. The hook should be no farther inboard from the end of the boom than one-third of its length. When the sheets are eased, the jib or reacher sheet is pushed outboard with a boathook and maneuvered into the hook on the boom. This arrangement not only solves the boom chafe problem but improves the width of the sheet base as well. However, the hook will chafe the line quickly, so one must keep an eye on it, and overhaul the sheet occasionally.

Another method of solving this problem is to take the weather jib sheet all the way around the outside of the weather rigging, around the staysail stay, and back outside the lee rigging, and then reeve it through a snatch block on the boom, and thence forward to a winch. Doing this is of course rather a long and tedious project.

I have found my own solution (Drawing 95). The first step is to

95. Rigging a tag line to reduce boom chafe and improve the transverse sheet lead when reaching.

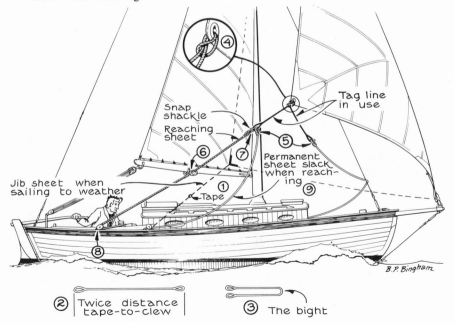

mark one of the jib sheets with a tape at the point that is about three feet forward of the block when the jib is sheeted down flat (1). Next, eye splices are made at both ends of a separate tag line which is twice the distance from the clew to the tape mark (2); this line is then doubled (3), the bight is passed through the clew cringle of the jib, both splices are brought back through the bight (4), and the line is heaved tight. The jib sheets having been disconnected from the clew of the sail, each is now attached to one of the eyes of the tag line, with a bowline knot (5). Next, a reaching jib sheet is reeved permanently through a swivel block underneath the end of the main boom (6), and secured to a cleat near the gooseneck.

When the boom is eased far enough forward to begin to foul the jib sheet, it is a simple matter to reach out, secure the reaching jib sheet to the tag line by means of a snap shackle (7), and reeve the tail of the reaching sheet through a snatch block on the rail (8) and to a convenient winch. Then the strain can be taken on the reaching sheet leading to the end of the main boom, and the normal jib sheet can be eased off (9). This arrangement sounds complicated, but in actuality it is quite simple—infinitely easier than dragging the weather sheet all the way around the boat.

CLUB JIBS AND STAYSAILS

In the Lesser Antilles we have formed a group which is doing everything possible to remove the jib and staysail clubs from boats, cut them into little pieces, and use them as fuel for a nice, big barbecue. I think the jib club is really superfluous on a proper ocean sailing yacht or—indeed—on any sailing yacht.

The presence of a club results in drastic limitation of the staysail area. Depending on the height of the lower spreader and the placement of the lower shrouds, a genoa staysail (Drawing 96C) may be as much as 65 percent larger than a club staysail (Drawing 96A). Admittedly, the genoa staysail, although a real puller, is more difficult to handle, but on *Iolaire* a genoa staysail of 230 square feet can be handled in most weathers, even when short tacking, by my six-year-old son and ninety-pound wife, with the aid of a big winch.

Also, without the club, a sail can be much more effectively shaped. Although the loose-footed staysail in Drawing 96B has only 20 percent more area than the club staysail shown in the drawing, it has tremendously greater drive because it assumes a more efficient airfoil shape throughout its length. The portion that overlaps the mainsail creates a very desirable "slot" effect, which increases the power of the

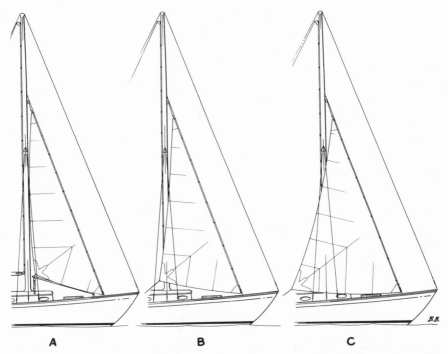

96A. Club staysail. B. Loose-footed overlapping staysail. C. Genoa staysail.

mainsail. The sheet lead can be exact, so that the whole sail is pulling. Further, the overlap is small enough so that on swinging from one tack to the other only very short sheets need to be handled, and only a couple of cranks on the winch are needed to trim the sail in absolutely flat. Even a fourteen-year-old can take care of a staysail of this shape on any boat except the largest.

The one advantage of the club jib or staysail is that when sailing in close quarters, one need not trim the sail on each tack. However, this may also be a disadvantage, for unless someone is forward with a tag line to hold the club to leeward while the boat tacks, or a tag line is rigged back to the cockpit, there is no possibility of backing the sail to help the boat around, if caught by a backwind while tacking. But because of all the friction in the blocks, easing the sail in light to moderate airs is sometimes impossible, unless someone runs forward to help it.

All too often, the sheets on club staysails are rigged entirely wrong— an indication of the sailing ignorance of some of the stock yacht manufacturers. In some cases, the sheets are led directly to the center of the deck or cabin, as shown at left in Drawing 97; more often, the lower sheet block is replaced by two individual blocks, but the resultant sheet tension still leads to the center of the boat. And although the club jib or staysail is self-tending when tacking, the clew immediately rises up,

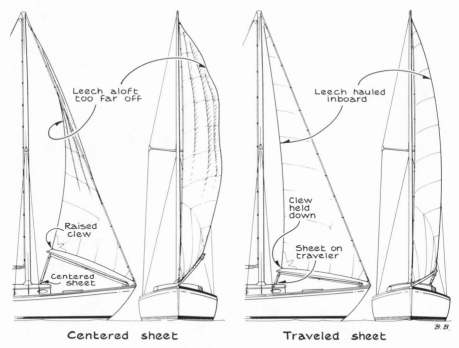

Centered sheet   Traveled sheet

97. Club staysail when reaching: sheeted to center line and sheeted to a wide traveler.

allowing the head of the sail to sag off to leeward and begin to flog. With little or nothing to hold the bow of the boat away from the wind, weather helm builds up drastically, so the sail is of very little use as a driving sail when rigged this way. The situation may be corrected by rigging a boom vang to hold down the boom, but of course the sail is then no longer self-tending.

The sheet should always be led to a horse or sliding traveler which extends, if not the full width of the deck, certainly the full width of the cabin top, so that the sheet almost always leads straight down, as shown at right in Drawing 97. Further, the hauling part of the sheet must always be led forward along the boom, through a turning block at the gooseneck or gooseneck pedestal, then back down the deck to the cockpit. So much friction is built up with this rig that it is sometimes difficult to sheet a club staysail.

Further, because of the aft rake of the stay, the club always has the natural tendency caused by gravity to swing inboard to the center line (the same problem that a boom has with a sharply raked mast). In very light winds, a preventer is usually necessary to keep the club staysail outboard when reaching or running. On small boats, this preventer can usually be made up of heavy shock cord, so that it doesn't have to be readjusted with every slight change in trim. When a club staysail is blanketed by the main while running or broad reaching, it will almost always swing inboard, sometimes with considerable violence, and can take its toll on the hardware or even injure an unsuspecting crewman. Under these circumstances, and when the foredeck must be clear of the swinging club during the approach to an anchorage, it would be best to hook the end of the club into its lift and forget it.

One other important point: club staysails are very often not properly attached to the stay. Except under certain conditions (described later), there should always be a jack line on a club staysail. Otherwise, it may be difficult to drop sail fully.

Despite all our dreams, the hours spent in port living on the boat outnumber by 10 or 20 to 1 the hours spent actually under sail. And when the boat is at anchor or in port, the staysail club usually leads right down the middle of the foredeck. On large boats, one must duck under it; on small boats, one must climb over it. Either way, it's a pain in the neck. The problem can be easily solved by seizing the club lift to a shroud rather than running a topping lift to the mast, as this will hold the club off center, near the side of the boat.

A club jib or staysail is fairly expensive. By the time the necessary deck fittings, travelers, club, tack fitting, and so on have been obtained, anywhere from three hundred dollars on the smallest boats up to thousands on the larger boats may have been spent.

In fact, a good sailor can manage very well without the club. On a moderate-sized boat, a loose-footed staysail (Drawing 96B) is relatively easy to sheet on either tack. When short tacking up a harbor with, say, three people aboard, a forty-footer should be quite easy to handle if she is rigged correctly. The helmsman should be within reach of the genoa sheet to throw it off as the boat comes around; on small boats, he should also be able to handle the sheeting of the staysail, especially if the boat has been set up with self-tailing winches. The other two men on board can then be solely concerned with taking in the jib sheet. If the boat is over forty feet, a four-man crew is necessary to handle her while she tacks; when she is working her way up to an anchorage, the jib can be doused and she can sail up under staysail and main if shorthanded.

I have talked four yachtsmen into removing their staysail clubs and temporarily leaving their staysails loose-footed, and *not one* has reinstalled the club.

And now, having soundly condemned the supposedly self-tending club jib and staysail, I must emphasize again that if one rigs this type of sail correctly, it can be quite nice. On some of the small day racers—

Stars, Etchells 22's, 5.5's—loose-footed nonoverlapping jibs have been successfully rigged to circular tracks, so that they are self-tending. One wonders if these sheeting systems might also be suitable for the cruising boat.

Having spent eight days sailing the Freedom 40, and twelve days watching her race (all too often from astern), I am tremendously impressed with the ability of the self-tending wishbone to handle the sail at all points of sailing with little or no twist. There is no reason why a staysail could not be rigged with such a wishbone. It would eliminate the problem of twist when the sheet is eased. However, there would still be the problem of the wishbone swinging inboard, since it would be canted downward pretty severely. Sidney Herreshoff installed half wishbones on some of the boats produced by the Herreshoff Manufacturing Company just prior to World War II. Fritz Fenger was a great advocate of them; his wishbone ketches had wishbones on the main trysail, the main staysail, and also the mizzen staysail. Blue Bradfield had this rig on *D'Vara,* a small ketch on which he and his wife sailed halfway around the world, and they were very happy with it. So perhaps it would be worth while for those who want a self-tending headsail to try some experimentation along these lines.

Club-Staysail Topping Lifts

The topping lifts for staysail clubs need not be as complicated as those for main or mizzen booms. Except on a large boat, it is usually sufficient to have a wire lift of fixed length leading down to a light lashing line that is adjusted so that the topping lift is slack when the staysail is sheeted in flat. When sail is lowered, it is best to secure the staysail club off to one side, by tying it off to the lower shroud or snapping it to a wire lift seized to a shroud, to keep the foredeck as clear as possible.

Large boats rig club-staysail topping lifts similar to those for their main booms, but smaller (see *OSY*-I, Ch. V).

Loose-footed Club Staysails

The staysail need not be attached to the club along its entire length; it can set well if attached only at the outhaul and the tack. If this is done, a strong outhaul fitting must be designed, as all the strain will be concentrated at the clew outhaul instead of being distributed all along the foot. Also, pad eyes should be installed on the deck, so that the staysail may be removed from the club and sheeted to the deck loose-footed.

There are many advantages to rigging the staysail in this fashion. The man who wants his staysail self-tacking when in tidal waters may not want to use the staysail club out at sea, and will prefer not having to climb over it when trying to switch to other sails. If the staysail is loose-footed on the club, downwind the outhaul can be cast off and the sail used loose-footed, with the club lashed down on deck; for the offshore portion of a trip, the club can be removed and stowed below.

Years ago, *Antilles* had a club-footed working jib which was used while sailing near the Virgin Islands. However, when she took long offshore passages the club was usually removed and she was sailed with a loose-footed jib. Having sailed offshore both with and without the club jib, most of the crew preferred to take off the club for offshore passages, and finally it was permanently removed.

Club Jack Lines

By and large, a sail on which the foot and luff do not meet at a right angle—i.e., a club jib or staysail or a main or mizzen set on a sharply raked spar—should have a jack line. On a club jib or staysail a jack line can be avoided by use of a fisherman-style rig (*OSY*-I, Photo 25). To douse the sail not rigged in this fashion, either the outhaul must be slacked or a jack line must be installed, because as shown in Drawing 98, distance *AB* is much shorter than distance *AC,* so the jib or staysail snaps cannot possibly move down the stay unless the sail is allowed to sag back away from the stay or the clew is allowed to move forward.

As shown in the drawing, the jack line should be adjusted so that it is tight when the sail is hauled up tight on the halyard; there should be no sagging from the lowest fixed hank down to the tack—i.e., in the area of the jack line—if the halyard tension and the jack-line tension are correct. The jack line is laced through eyes secured to the luff of the sail (*OSY*-I, Photo 53) in the same way that a jack line is secured to the roller-furling mainsail, and is then passed through the eye in a special jib hank obtainable from Merriman and several other manufacturers, as shown at the center in Photo 12. If this special hank is not available, a small grommet can be seized to a standard jib snap, as shown at right in Photo 12.

To determine the length of the jack line on the luff of the sail, take out the sail plan, and using as a radius the distance from the tack to the

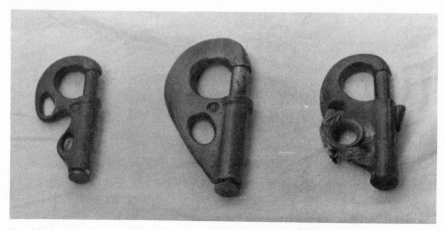

12. *Jib hanks:* left, *standard;* center, *for jack line;* right, *standard with grommet.* DAVID MAX.

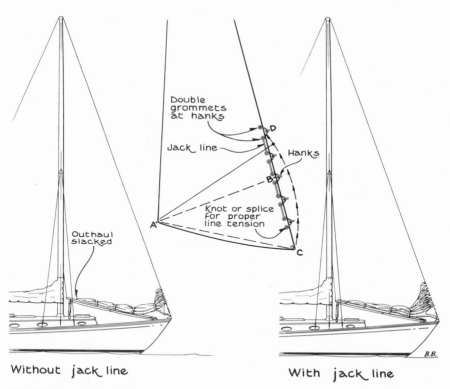

Double
grommets
at hanks

Jack line

Hanks

Knot or splice
for proper
line tension

Outhaul
slacked

Without jack line

With jack line

98. Club staysail without a jack line cannot be dropped fully unless its outhaul
is eased first; club staysail with a jack line will not hang up when dropped.

clew (*AC* in Drawing 98), swing an arc to the luff (at *D*). The jack line should extend up the luff of the sail to the point intersected by this radius. A rough rule of thumb, useful if the sail plan is not available, is to measure the foot of the staysail and extend the jack line the same distance up the luff.

Goosenecks for Jib Clubs

Most seamen will agree that the jib or staysail club should pivot about a point a short distance aft of the stay rather than on the stay itself. Use of the staysail or head-stay turnbuckle for this purpose (*OSY*-I, Photo 23) is not a good idea, since no matter how carefully engineered, this arrangement puts a side load on the turnbuckle, and increases the chances of its failing; also, disconnecting the staysail stay in light airs to give a clear foredeck is made very difficult. If the jib club pivots from a pedestal gooseneck or fisherman style (*OSY*-I, Photos 24–25), a staysail-stay release lever (*OSY*-I, Photos 50–51) can be installed. Then the sail may be dropped and disconnected from the staysail stay, and the stay released from the release lever and tied aft.

Club Jibs and Staysails in Light Airs

Expecting a club jib or staysail to perform at all in light airs, especially on a reach, is pretty optimistic; the club is just so heavy that it will hang amidships or near amidships, unless a preventer is used, and the result will be absolutely no drive. Instead, one should use a light reaching genoa staysail, sheeted outside the shrouds and overlapping the mast by 20 to 25 percent of the base of the fore-triangle (Drawing 96C).

When the club jib or staysail is dropped, the light genoa staysail may be hanked on above it, the bottom five feet or so (depending on the size of the boat) being allowed to stand free without snaps, and then hoisted. In conjunction with a high-cut No. 1 jib, this will give the same sail area as a 150-percent genoa.

The light reaching genoa staysail is particularly valuable on a really large boat—sixty-five feet or more in length—when one does not want to wrestle with a large genoa and may not have the gear to handle one. Since it is to be used only in light airs on a reach, it can be made of fairly light Dacron, and will be easy to handle and easy to stow.

ROLLER-FURLING HEADSAILS

Though I dislike roller *reefing,* I am a great advocate of roller *furling.* Roller-furling headsails have become tremendously popular in the last few years, but the idea is not new; in my library I have some books printed prior to the turn of the century showing roller-furling headsails on inshore cruising boats. However, now that roller furling is all the rage, many people adopt it, as they do so many fads, without analyzing their particular needs and problems, and they end up with something that doesn't work quite right. The great fad today in yachting refrigeration is holding plates; people assume that one can just stick a couple in any corner of the boat and have a refrigerator and/or freezer—but it doesn't work that way! Similarly, slapping some roller-furling gear on a jib and hauling it up produces an arrangement which in all likelihood will either fail completely or give very unsatisfactory performance.

Not only has the average yachtsman given little thought to the problems encountered with roller-furling headsails, but the situation has been further complicated by the fact that the figures and recommendations presented in the fittings catalogs are usually geared for weekend sailing, not ocean cruising. Numerous companies make roller-furling gear, and all are very optimistic about the size sail their product will hold. Gear is recommended for a specified sail area, but no distinction is made between light genoas to be used for going to windward, heavy working jibs and jib topsails, and light downwind sails. In point of fact, a jib topsail of 340 square feet which is going to be used in winds of up to 20 knots needs the exact same size of gear as a genoa of 650 square feet which will be used in light and moderate winds. The same gear may also be adequate for a sail of 850 or 1,000 square feet which is only going to be used downwind. However, the catalogs do not recognize this situation. The unsuspecting yachtsman may look at the catalog, choose gear rated for 600 square feet, hang a jib of 450 square feet on it, and suddenly find himself with busted shackles, exploded blocks, or broken halyards.

The basic strength of the roller-furling gear is extremely important. The gear itself should be of the largest size practical. This is essential, because a roller-furling headsail is held only at the three corners, and hence the sail, and particularly the luff, receives no support whatsoever from the head stay. I myself have always believed that the head stay should be dead slack, particularly when sailing to weather. The entire strain is then taken on the roller-furling luff wire, with the head stay being there only to hold the rig in the boat if the roller-furling gear should fail. Some may not fully share my opinion, but I have had excellent results with this arrangement.

The person who intends to set up his roller-furling headsail with a very tight luff, as I do, must make sure that certain important conditions are fulfilled. For one thing, it is essential that the sailmaker be advised that this arrangement is being adopted. He will then tailor the sail shape for a minimum of luff sag; otherwise, when the sail is up, the luff will be too flat and the draft too far aft. It is also essential that the gear used be extremely strong and of the highest quality. Since the luff of the jib will take the entire loading of the head stay, the luff wire of the jib, and the roller-furling gear, must have the same ultimate breaking strength as the head stay. When choosing roller-furling gear, you should check the diameter of your head stay, look up the breaking strength of the wire in Table VI, in the Appendix, and select gear that will withstand the same strain.

Unfortunately, most of the strength figures for roller-furling gear in the catalogs are at least somewhat optimistic, apparently because in addition to assuming that most buyers will use the equipment only for onshore or day sailing, the manufacturers generally assume that the luff wire will be kept slack. Hence, the catalog figures are not reliable guides to the selection of gear substantial enough for the ocean sailing yacht.

One way to make sure that the gear is actually strong enough is to buy directly from the manufacturer instead of from a dealer, general distributor, or marine-hardware store. You can then describe your particular situation to the people in the engineering department, and question them about the actual strength of the equipment, instead of depending simply on catalog recommendations made in terms of sail area. Also, you may find that the manufacturer is willing—for a slight additional charge—to have the hardware independently certified as capable of carrying a specified load. It is almost routine for quality concerns to provide this kind of certification to builders and designers, and the manufacturer may welcome it because it demonstrates that he has supplied equipment of the strength specified—so any failures will be the result of your error in judging your requirements, not of flaws in his product. Should the manufacturer refuse to obtain independent certification, you would be well advised—for the sake of your own peace of mind at sea—to take your business elsewhere.

If for some reason you cannot deal directly with a manufacturer, you will have to base your purchase on the information supplied in the catalog. But be sure that you receive a guarantee of the listed strength, and then test the equipment for yourself. Start by obtaining a short piece of wire with 80 percent of the breaking strength of the head stay. This wire, having a known breaking strength, serves as the measuring stick. Put proper terminals on it, shackle it to the roller-furling gear under consideration, and connect up the gear—with halyard blocks and halyard wire of the size you plan to use on your boat—to a tree, telephone pole, dead man, or what-have-you. Next, place a chain block on the other end of the roller-furling gear, and crank up the chain block until the wire breaks. If the gear or halyard blocks fail before the wire breaks, go back and request gear of a larger size.

It is more than likely that gear selected in accordance with the manufacturer's recommendations will fail this test. A quick inspection of typical gear will reveal the reason for this failure. If the clevis pin at the upper end of the head stay has a diameter of ½ inch, how can a roller-furling gear held to the stemhead or bobstay fitting by a ⅜-inch pin be expected to be of the same strength as the head stay? (See Table VI for the shearing strengths of pins and the breaking strengths of shackles.) It is doubtful whether there is, on the market today, any roller-furling gear advertised for a 500-square-foot jib which is in fact strong enough to carry a 500-square-foot *windward-going jib* on a ⅜-inch, 1 by 19 wire, with an adequate safety factor. Much of the gear on the market today is running on a minimal margin of safety.

The difficulty is compounded by the fact, which many people forget, that wire stretches, and that the 7 by 19 wire used for halyards stretches much more than the 1 by 19 used for head stays. As shown in Table VI, a ¼-inch 1 by 19 head stay has a breaking strength of 8,000 pounds, a ⁵⁄₁₆-inch 1 by 19 head stay has a breaking strength of 12,500 pounds, and a ⅜-inch 1 by 19 head stay has a breaking strength of 17,600 pounds. Looking at the strength table, one should immediately realize the complete impossibility of installing a single-part 7 by 19 halyard of the same breaking strength as the head stay. The halyard would be much too large, and the masthead sheave would be immense. At the same time, as indicated by Table X, the stretch would be considerable. Obviously, the solution is to go to a two-part halyard (Drawing 99A), since the loading will then be halved. Even a three-part halyard (Drawing 99B) is sometimes used, on very large boats only. For a head stay of ¼-inch 1 by 19 wire, a two-part halyard should be of ³⁄₁₆-inch 7 by 19 wire; if the head stay is of ⁵⁄₁₆-inch 1 by 19, the halyard should be of ¼-inch 7 by 19; and if the head stay is of ⅜-inch 1 by 19, the halyard should be of ⁹⁄₃₂-inch 7 by 19. These are *bare minimum sizes*—for a halyard with approximately the same breaking strength as the head stay. If one wishes to eliminate stretch and minimize fatigue, halyard wire one size larger should be used in each instance.

Also important is the size of the blocks. As indicated in Drawing 99, with a two-part halyard the load on the running block (*A*) is double the

The luff wire of a roller-furling headsail must have the same strength as the head stay. The running blocks (A and B) should have the same breaking strength as the head stay and luff wire. Stated another way: block A must have twice the breaking strength of the halyard; block B must have three times the breaking strength of the halyard.

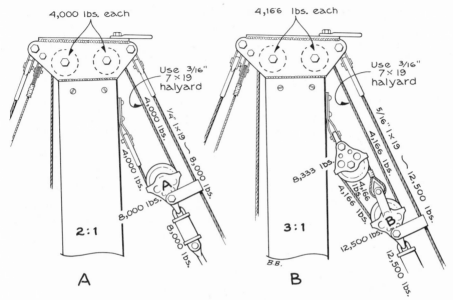

99. Roller-furling-jib halyard: A, two-part; B, three-part.

load on the halyard wire—because of the 180-degree turn—so the breaking strength of the block should be double that of the halyard, and equal to that of the head stay; for a ¼-inch 1 by 19 head stay the block should have a breaking strength of 8,000 pounds; for a ⁵⁄₁₆-inch head stay the block should have a breaking strength of 12,500 pounds; and for a ⅜-inch head stay the block should be really large and heavy, with a breaking strength of 17,600 pounds. With a three-part halyard, the running block (*B*) must have a breaking strength three times that of the halyard, and again equal to that of the head stay.

The safe working load for the roller-furling gear as a whole will be a percentage of the ultimate breaking strength. Once this strength has been calculated, the result can be checked by the late Nathanael Herreshoff's method—testing to destruction. In general racing practice, the safe load is considered to be 50 percent of the breaking strength. Sometimes, in an effort to save weight in hot racing machines, a load of 75 percent of the ultimate breaking strength is regarded as acceptable. But then, it has been stated that ocean racing is skating on the knife edge of disaster; and some designers and competitors hone the knife edge very sharp.

Iolaire has double roller-furling gear—a roller-furling jib and a roller-furling staysail—and we have been extremely happy with the installation. When asked if it always works perfectly, I reply, "Hell no—does a hanked-on jib always work perfectly?" I have had occasional trouble with the roller-furling gear, but I have also had plenty of trouble with hanked-on headsails. All in all, I'll take the properly designed roller-furling gear.

We originally started installing the roller-furling gear on *Iolaire* about fifteen years ago, and it took us a full two years to work the bugs out of the system. Halyards, shackles, blocks—even the gear itself—exploded. And have you ever had a jib streaming from the masthead with a ten-pound roller-furling gear firmly attached to the tack, periodically sweeping down across the foredeck and attempting to kill anyone up there trying to muzzle the jib? At one point we declared *Iolaire*'s foredeck a hard-hat area whenever the wind reached more than 15 knots.

We now have a 340-square-foot roller-furling jib topsail; we started with a No. 3 genoa of 450 square feet, a sail given to me by Percy Chubb in return for navigating *Antilles* up to the United States one spring. The crew of *Antilles* did not like the roller-furling three-quarters genoa because they could not get the luff to stand straight enough, but this sail gave us yeoman service for many years before it died. After exploding various gears of unknown manufacture and origin, we finally ended up with the standard Merriman roller-furling gear: a drum 6 inches in diameter is supported by ½-inch pins. Also, the halyard block is attached to the top swivel by a ½-inch pin, and the strapped block sheave is supported by a ½-inch pin. The halyard passes through the mast over two sheaves and down to a winch. It is made of ¼-inch 7 by 19 wire, and has had to be changed once or twice, but has presented no special problems and has withstood the test of time. To avoid having a huge pile of line at the foot of the mast—since with a fifty-foot luff, a two-part halyard requires a hundred feet of line—we spliced the ¼-inch wire into a fifteen-foot length of ½-inch line, and then spliced a ⅜-inch tail into that.

I do not really believe that this size of roller-furling gear has the same breaking strength as the 5⁄16-inch 1 by 19 luff wire of the jib; indeed, I have a strong suspicion that the gear is probably operating at 75 percent of the ultimate breaking strength in heavy weather, which is not good. And with the *Antilles* genoa, the safety factor was almost nonexistent! But the next size larger gear is massive, with a drum 10 inches in diameter, supported by ⅝-inch pins, and it costs a veritable fortune. An intermediate size would certainly be welcome. (On our 230-square-foot genoa staysail, however, gear of the same size does have an adequate safety factor, and it has given yeoman service.)

I have never been able to find anyone who has tested this Merriman gear to destruction, but ours has stood a fifteen-year test. With the passage of time, the holes in the jaws have become ever so slightly egg-shaped. We regularly check the bearings, since evidently the extreme loads tend to flatten them, making the gear hard to roll up. Furthermore, when bearings are made of steel—as they almost always are in gear of this sort—no matter how well packed or well sealed they are, eventually salt water gets in and corrodes them, which certainly must increase the friction when the gear is rolled up. Hence, it is a good idea always to carry spare bearings for the roller-furling gear, as we do, and to change bearings frequently.

I have not tried any of the roller-furling gear that has come onto the market recently. Some of it looks good, but the manufacturers appear unwilling to state in their catalogs the ultimate breaking strength of the equipment. Two firms, insisting that their gear was adequate, gave me swivels, which Loos and Company tested to destruction for me. Both exploded at considerably below 12,500 pounds.

Once gear of the proper strength has been obtained, care should be taken to install and use it to the best possible advantage. For example, on *Iolaire* we have been able, with the two-part 7 by 19 halyard— essential for a roller-furling jib with a 1 by 19 luff wire—to reduce sag to an acceptable level, as is evident in Photo 13, taken during the 1975 Fastnet Race, which shows *Iolaire*'s roller-furling jib in use. It must be realized that *Iolaire* is in her seventies; on a newer, stronger boat, the halyard could be set up even tighter and sag eliminated still further; however, the more sag is eliminated, the more load is thrown onto the luff wire and the roller-furling gear, which may easily explode if over-loaded. We obtain adequate halyard tension by leading the two-part halyard to an 18-to-1 winch, but if adequate tension cannot be achieved with the winch available, an easy alternate method is to run dead down-wind and crank up while the whole rig is leaning a little forward. Once on the wind, the halyard tension will be more than adequate.

When a two-part halyard is used, if the block is not kept from spinning, the halyard will get wrapped around itself, and hoisting the sail will be impossible. The standard method of solving this problem is to attach the halyard block to the head stay by a metal plate or double hooks; another method, which allows more flexibility, is to attach the block temporarily to the head stay, prior to hoisting, with three strands

13. Iolaire *racing, with roller-furling jib.* BEKEN OF COWES

of light marlin. The block cannot spin while the sail is being hoisted, and once the sail is up, the marlin breaks. When this method is used, if—for example—a three-quarters genoa or a high-cut jib has been hoisted on the roller-furling halyard, and the wind lightens, the No. 1 genoa can be hanked onto the head stay, a spare halyard attached, and the No. 1 genoa hauled up behind the roller-furling jib. The latter may be either rolled up and left aloft, or dropped, as circumstances demand. Similarly, if it starts to blow too hard for the roller-furling jib, the No. 3 jib can be hanked onto the head stay and hoisted on a spare halyard, and the roller-furling jib again rolled up, to be left aloft or taken down as circumstances demand. In both of these cases, hoisting the new sail is dead simple, since it is hauled up to leeward of the roller-furling sail, but the roller-furling halyard must be slightly slackened to place some tension on the head stay. Similarly, when these procedures are reversed, the sail is doused in the lee of the roller-furling headsail. These operations are of course impossible if the block for the roller-furling jib is secured to the head stay by a metal plate or hooks.

A roller-furling jib can be rolled up either head to wind or with the wind on the quarter, so that it is partially blanketed by the mainsail. The advantage of the latter method is that when the vessel is running off, the apparent wind across the deck is lessened, making it much easier to roll up the jib. However, a careful eye must be kept on the jib, since unless some tension is kept on the sheet, the flogging sail does tend to try to pick up the slack head stay.

It is virtually impossible to roll up a headsail while running dead downwind, as it will blow out forward and promptly wrap itself around the head stay, jamming everything up well and truly. The only solution then is to roll the thing out and try again, either head to wind or with the wind on the quarter.

When an attempt is made to roll up the jib while running broad off, the sail will try to wrap itself around the head stay. This tendency can be minimized by putting a substantial separation between the luff of the roller-furling jib and the head stay; the exact distance will depend on the size of the boat: nine inches on a thirty-footer, eighteen inches on a forty-five footer, two feet or more on a larger yacht.

Also, a bagged sail is frequently hanked onto the head stay and tied to the pulpit. Without this separation between the roller-furling gear and the head stay, the roller-furling sail tends to foul and bind on the bagged sail, and is therefore very hard to roll up.

Another problem is that when the sail is being rolled up, the shackle or pins in its tack often try to catch on other lines on the foredeck. The solution is to slip a short length of PVC pipe over the foot of the roller-

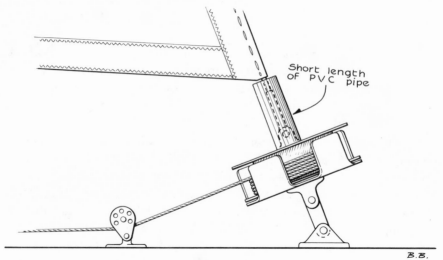

100. **PVC** pipe at tack of roller-furling headsail.

furling headsail, secure the sail to the roller-furling gear, and then drop the pipe down over the fittings (Drawing 100).

There is a size limitation on roller-furling headsails. Manufacturers and salesmen will demonstrate at the boat shows how easy it is to roll the sail in and out, and doing so is indeed dead simple in light airs with perfectly operating gear; however, once the gear gets a little old, if one is caught in a squall, with a wind of perhaps 35 or 40 knots, a lot of muscle power, frequently backed up by a winch, will be needed to roll up even a 340-square-foot jib. If something jams or goes wrong (like the wire-to-rope splice pulling out, as happened to us once) it is entirely possible to flog the clew out of a perfectly good sail before it can be fully rolled up. To be sure, a light genoa considerably larger than 340 square feet can be set on roller-furling gear, but only if one remembers to roll it up in good time before a squall hits.

Roller-Furling Luffs

ROLLER-FURLING LUFF WIRES: For the ocean cruising yacht, a roller-furling headsail set on a 1 by 19 wire is by far the most practical, though it may not be the most efficient. The sail need not be set all the time; it can be dropped, and even with a 5/16-inch luff wire, a 340-square-foot jib of 8-ounce Dacron can be coiled up into a round bag twenty-four inches in diameter and twelve inches high—easily handled, easily stowed, and easily shipped to any part of the world. Further, because the sail is set on its own roller-furling gear, with the head stay separate, other sails can be hanked onto the head stay, as has been mentioned. On *Iolaire* our options are further increased because we have a roller-furling genoa staysail as well as a roller-furling jib. We can put big genoas and No. 3 jibs on the head stay, and similarly, in light airs we can set a huge, hanked-on, light reaching genoa staysail on the staysail stay, and in very heavy weather, we can hank a small heavy-weather staysail onto the staysail stay and drop the roller-furling genoa staysail. This degree of flexibility cannot be achieved with the various other roller-furling rigs.

ROD ROLLER-FURLING HEAD STAYS: The rod-luff sail may be fine in Long Island Sound, but for offshore or long-distance cruising, forget it. One is committed to one sail sewn onto a rod which is fixed in place, with no chance of taking it down at sea. And when it is taken down, it cannot be coiled into a circle less than six or seven feet in diameter. How one stows a bundle of this size in the average yacht beggars the imagination. Further, shipment of such a bulky item to a remote part of the globe will involve great difficulty and expense.

GROOVED ROLLER-FURLING HEAD STAYS: Popularized by Stearn, Hood, and a few others, the grooved roller-furling head stay is certainly the most efficient roller-furling gear available today. It results in minimal sag, and sails can be changed as desired, since any size of headsail can be fitted on the same grooved gear. However, there is one very great disadvantage for the ocean-cruising yachtsman. Although a job like rolling up a No. 1 genoa can be performed by one or two men with ease, other procedures are more difficult unless one has a big crew. For instance, if the No. 1 genoa is to be removed and replaced with the No. 3 jib, the halyard must be dropped, and the sail then feeds down the luff-groove and probably overside, forming a great big sea anchor held at three corners only. Once this has been retrieved from the sea and stuffed down below, the replacement sail is brought up on deck, and is secured—again—only by the three corners, while one tries to feed it into the luff-groove and hoist it without losing it overboard. Operations of this sort are easy with three or four good men on the foredeck, but not with only a couple of people. I wonder if the use of sail slugs fastened to the luff might solve this problem. Indeed, even a racing boat fitted with a grooved head stay might carry several headsails fitted with slugs, so that when not competing, the skipper and his family could raise and lower cruising canvas with ease.

The other problem is that if the headfoil is damaged in an out-of-the-way area, shipment of a replacement may be just about impossible. That it can be damaged is demonstrated by the experience, in English Harbour, Antigua, of a very nice modern cruiser/racer with a headfoil.

Somehow or other, through mishandling, the stay apparently developed a 720-degree twist in the seventy-foot headfoil. Needless to say, the owner became more than a little worried, and he finally got the designer himself to come down. Exactly what the latter did no one quite knows; he spent a long time going up and down the mast and finally reduced the twist from 720 degrees to a mere 180 degrees, but one wonders what effect all this had on the strength of the foil. If a replacement foil had been necessary, it would probably have been easier to sail the boat up to the United States than to get shipment down to Antigua.

Roller Twins

Roller twins—jenny twins—as popularized by Wright Britton, of Britton of Southport, have much to be said for them. Most people who have installed them swear by them, and certainly in view of the amount of time Wright and his wife have spent at sea in *Delight,* and the areas in which they sail, it seems evident that he is not a man who would push a piece of gear which did not work or in which he did not have complete faith.

Basically, this system consists of two Dacron or nylon sails, varying in size from 120 percent to 150 percent of the base of the fore-triangle, secured to a single roller-furling wire and rolled around it by Britton's superb roller-furling gear. With both clews secured together, these sails may be used as a jenny; or they may be rolled up, unshackled, and then individually shackled to the spinnaker/whisker poles stowed vertically on a long track up the forward face of the mast. After having been shackled to the poles, the sails are rolled out, and at the same time, the slider carrying both poles is pulled down, winging out the sails.

This is a good gear, and it certainly does work, but needless to say there are disadvantages. Although the twins can be used clewed together as a genoa or reacher, they are obviously not cut for windward-going ability. Further, the two long poles stowed vertically on the mast certainly do not help the stability of the boat, or the windage when going to windward. Also, when the wind is on the quarter, with the weather jenny twin pulled way forward and the lee jenny twin swung aft, there comes a time when the lee pole must be disconnected and its sail sheeted to the end of the main boom or back to the deck. Then, what is to be done with the pole, which is already shackled into the carriage with the other pole?

Furthermore, this gear is expensive, and many seamen who have experimented with poor man's twins have concluded that dollar for dollar, they are a better investment. Basically, the only extra equipment needed to make poor man's twins work is one becket block with a swivel, plus some ⅛-inch or ³⁄₁₆-inch 1 by 19 wire approximately the length of the head stay.

Roller-Furling Drums

CLOSED DRUMS: With a closed drum, there is a space limitation—the number of turns that can be accommodated depends on the diameter of the drum and the diameter of the line and/or wire. On the old Merriman gear, the drum was designed for wire with a rope tail, and the tail splice which was therefore required was the weak point in a system which had adequate capacity and in other respects worked well. If the jib was being rolled up in heavy weather and the tail splice pulled out, one could easily flog the clew out of the sail before anyone managed to grab the wire in his bare hands, take it around the winch, and roll up the jib.

The Britton system has a closed drum, but it is large enough for ⁵⁄₁₆-inch or ⅜-inch line, with a breaking strength of 1,800 or 2,600 pounds, to be rolled up inside the drum.

One disadvantage of all types of closed drum is that if the sail is rolled out quickly, unless a little strain is kept on the roller-furling line, it may take a riding turn inside the drum; this is most difficult to clear. A second disadvantage results from the fact that in varying wind conditions the sail rolls up at varying degrees of tightness and thus uses different amounts of line. Consequently, even if initially there is enough line on the drum so that when the sail is rolled up, five or six turns of the sheet may be taken around it, after a week or so at sea one suddenly finds oneself at two in the morning with all the line off the roller-furling drum and two feet of clew still blowing in the gale. With a low-cut jib this is no major problem; one reaches up, undoes the sheets, and passes the clew around the rest of the sail as many times as necessary. However, with a high-cut jib and the clew fifteen feet in the air, one is foxed.

OPEN DRUMS: The problem of running out of line before the sail is completely rolled up is unlikely to occur with open drums, since they are very large in diameter, and usually accommodate plenty of ⁵⁄₁₆-inch or ⅜-inch line. However, with open drums, if the guides are not perfectly made it is all too easy for the line to drop off while the sail is being unrolled. If the wind is blowing hard this is a disaster, since rolling up the sail by hand—which is the only way to clear the foul—is then impossible.

GROOVED DRUM, ENDLESS LINE: The latest type of roller-furling gear (Photo 14), with a grooved drum and an endless line, was invented by Wright Britton, who probably has more sea-going experience than any other living cruising yachtsman. I first saw this gear at the 1976 Annapolis Boat Show, and had many discussions with Wright over its disadvantages and advantages. In the end, he lent me his two-year-old gear from *Delight,* so that I could try it for myself.

At the start, there were some teething problems with it. The shackles did not match up with the tack and head fittings on my roller-furling jib, with the fittings on my bowsprit, or with my halyard block; adapter plates had to be made. Further, we first tried using the gear with a non-endless line, and the line tended to jump off the drum and wrap itself around the base of the fitting, resulting in complete disaster. Wright was called on the telephone, and on his advice an endless line was spliced up and passed through a snatch block in the port quarter. We had one or two more foul-ups while we adjusted the endless line's tension in accordance with Wright's directions—so that when it was picked up it could be raised barely as high as the lifeline stanchion (that is, about twenty-four inches). On *Delight,* Wright ran his line to a spare genoa-sheet eye-slide car and adjusted the tension by moving the car

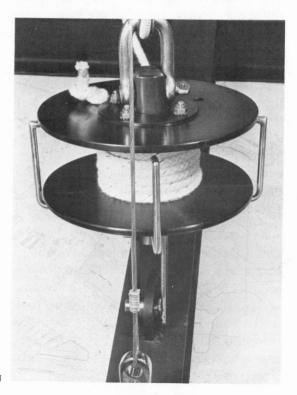

14. Brittton roller-furling gear. WRIGHT BRITTON

on the genoa track. In our case, we put a lashing line from a pad eye to a snatch block, and as the endless line stretched through use, we slowly took up on the lashing line and moved the snatch block farther aft. We had the disadvantage that the snatch-block swivel tended to twist, carrying the roller-furling line around itself and thereby building up the friction on the line. Therefore, we checked the snatch block every day. Now we have fixed the swivel, and all is well.

If I were installing this gear again, I would run the endless line through a sliding cheek block of the type used for jiffy reefing. A short length of track could be mounted on the deck inside the bulwarks, or at some other convenient spot, and the block could be slid aft on the track to adjust the tension. Being mounted on a track, the block would not be able to swivel and throw a twist on the line.

The one problem with this rig is that installation does require someone to do a long splice. This should be a perfectly simple operation for a competent yachtsman, but we were amazed to discover how few have actually mastered it!

The rig really does work. We installed it in January, 1977, and after a shakedown cruise of a couple of days, we undertook a typical *Iolaire* hard-driving sail: we cruised from Grenada to Trinidad, raced back to Grenada, raced on the south coast of Grenada, then made a 420-mile jump to St. Thomas, and completed a ten-hour dead beat to windward on a 30–35 knot blow to get to Tortola for three days of racing in the British Virgin Islands regatta, the first day, with winds of 30 knots and gusts of up to 40 or 50 knots; next came a 210-mile beat direct to Guadeloupe, followed by participation in the Guadeloupe–Antigua race and Antigua Sailing Week. At the end of four weeks, eleven races, and a thousand miles of hard sailing, we were firmly convinced that this new Britton gear is excellent. One strong person is able to roll up our big jib alone in the worst squalls—even while we are still going to windward, so any alteration of the course is unnecessary. This could be done with no other gear we have tried.

Subsequently, we sailed an additional three thousand miles, and participated in twelve races. I am convinced that the Britton gear is the best roller-furling gear available on the market today. In particular, the endless line with the grooved drum is perfect—one never has the problem of too much or too little line on the drum.

The gear comes in various sizes, from which the selection for a particular vessel should be made in the light of the area of the downwind sails, light-weather genoas, and hard-working jib topsails, and the strength of the head stays, as explained at the beginning of the section on roller-furling headsails.

Roller-Furling-Gear Bearings

For roller-furling gear, *ball* bearings, steel rather than stainless, are generally used, and over the years they tend to corrode and flatten, making it rather hard to roll up the sail. However, the Wright Britton gear has a double set of stainless-steel *needle* bearings. Engineers tell me these are much more likely to absorb thrust without flattening. Also, conventional roller-furling gear generally has only thrust bearings, to take the thrust load, and lacks radial bearings, to take the side load caused by the misalignment of the jib sagging off to leeward. To the best of my knowledge, the Britton gear is the only roller-furling gear that has both thrust and radial bearings. Needless to say, it is expensive, but a gear that will roll up the jib with no foul-ups in the small hours of a cold, rainy morning is worth a little extra money.

LIGHT SAILS

SPINNAKERS

On a cruising boat, the process of setting, trimming, and taking down a spinnaker should be rather different than on a racing boat, because one should take plenty of time—spinnaker handling on a cruising boat should not be done in a hurry.

The spinnaker on a cruising boat should always be set in stops, or in some system similar to stops. The simplest arrangement of this sort requires only a bottomless bucket or bottomless tin can and some rubber bands. The bucket or can should have two inches of diameter for every ten feet in the luff of the spinnaker; the number, length, and thickness of the rubber bands depends on the size of the spinnaker and the amount of wind expected. About ten may be used for a forty-foot luff. The rubber bands are stretched onto the bucket, and the bucket is placed over the head of the spinnaker. The head swivel is then hitched onto the head stay, bow pulpit, or whatever is handy. Next, one person runs down the luff and leech, straightening them; a second follows, sliding the bucket down the sail and feeding the sail carefully through the bucket. Every four feet or so, a rubber band is popped off the bucket onto the sail. The result is a very neatly and quickly stopped spinnaker that is ready to hoist and that may easily be stowed for future use.

Some spinnakers have a full-length zipper on the luff; this Zipper

Turtle was invented by Ike Manchester, of Manchester Yacht Sails. The spinnaker is rolled up tightly from each luff toward the center, and the two sides of the zipper are brought together around the bundle and joined from top to bottom by means of the zipper slide. At the bottom, the sail is secured by stopping twine, a rubber band, or what-have-you. One side of the zipper is slightly longer than the other, and the slide is now brought to the end of this side and removed. When the stop is broken, the sail instantly unzips from foot to head.

An even newer idea, similar to this, is the Spinnaker Sally. I am not quite sure how well it works with a very large spinnaker, but so far, it appears to be foolproof.

On a cruising boat, double sheets and guys—that is, both a guy and a lazy guy, a sheet and a lazy sheet—should always be used for hoisting and setting the spinnaker. However, going to the expense of double shackles is not necessary; both the guy and the lazy guy can be tied with bowlines into the swivel ring on the snap shackle. If the lazy guy is to be removed, in light airs, it is possible to pull in the clew of the spinnaker and disconnect the lazy guy by untying the bowline.

A spinnaker net should always be rigged for use at sea, even in light airs and smooth conditions. A wrapped or hour-glassed spinnaker inevitably surprises you at the most unexpected times. In higher winds or a big swell, a net is essential, so unless one has a permanent automatic spinnaker net rigged with shock cord and sliders between the head stay and the mast (Drawing 101A), some kind of jury rig must be installed. There are several ways of doing this. The results are less than perfect, but appear to be adequate.

On a double-headsail-rigged boat with a roller-furling jib, it is helpful to roll out the clew of the jib about three or four feet, take the sheet outside the upper shrouds, and take a strain on it, securing it to a cleat. If there is no roller-furling jib, you can take a spare halyard, secure the halyard shackle to the head stay, and run a light downhaul from the shackle to whatever is handy. Then secure the staysail-halyard shackle to the spare-halyard shackle. Hoist the spare halyard up the head stay until the staysail halyard is leading downward at an angle of approximately 30 degrees below the horizontal. Secure the downhaul. The result is a poor man's spinnaker net, made without extra gear (Drawing 101B).

An equivalent method can be used on a single-headsail-rigged boat. Since no staysail halyard is available, the procedure is to throw one end of a light line over the lower spreaders, secure the forward end to the spare-halyard shackle, then snap the halyard shackle to the head stay. Attach a downhaul to the halyard, and hoist the halyard up the head

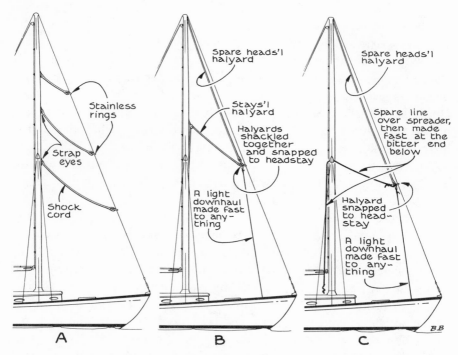

101A. Permanent spinnaker net. B. Staysail halyard used as spinnaker net. C. Poor man's spinnaker net.

stay until the line leading aft to the spreader is at an angle of about 20 degrees above the horizontal. Finally, the downhaul and the line leading down from the spreader are secured. The result, once again, is a poor man's spinnaker net (Drawing 101C).

A method used by John Walsh is simply to hoist the storm jib upside down, and lead the sheet back to the quarter.

On the subject of jibing a spinnaker, so much has been said in the racing books that further discussion here seems unnecessary. In any case, the spinnaker should not be set unless you have at least one—and preferably two—good spinnaker men on board. The points to remember are that the crew should be carefully briefed beforehand, the jibing operation should be slow and easy, and it should be done going from dead downwind to dead downwind, which is much easier than going from a reach to a reach.

Dousing the spinnaker on a cruising boat should be done the easy way, with the spinnaker pulled in tight behind the mainsail while the boat is running almost dead downwind. The lazy guy is first taken in through a snatch block placed close behind the main rigging, and thence led to a spare winch or cleat. The topping lift is slacked to a previously marked position (making it possible to reach the end of the spinnaker pole to trip the tack snap shackle once the pole is in the forward position). Then the after guy is slacked away slowly, with the fore guy being taken up at the same time, until the pole is almost against the head stay. Once the fore guy is snugged up, the foredeck man can reach up and trip the spinnaker tack free of the snap shackle.

At this point, the man on the sheet takes up all the slack he can, secures it, and then begins to gather in the spinnaker. The foredeck man runs aft to the mast and start paying out the halyard, taking care not to allow the spinnaker to get ahead of the man doing the gathering. Using this method, on all but the largest boats the entire spinnaker dousing can be done by four men—one at the helm, one on the after guy, one on the sheet, and one handling the topping lift, fore guy, tack shackle, and halyard. The after-guy man can come forward to help the foredeck man stow the pole and other gear while the sheet man bags the spinnaker. On smaller boats the job can be done by three people, since the helmsman can slack the after guy; the second man can slack the topping lift, take up the fore guy, trip the shackle, and then slack the halyard; and the third man takes up the sheet and gathers in the spinnaker. It is even possible for two people to douse the spinnaker of a small or medium-sized boat, but they must be real pros—cruising at 100 percent of racing efficiency!

Cruising Spinnaker Gear

To ease handling the spinnaker on a large boat, especially in strong winds or when changing from a spinnaker to a genoa (or vice versa), it may be worth while to add a pole after guy and a pole fore guy to the regular spinnaker-control lines (Drawing 102). Rigged in this way, the pole will remain in position even when the spinnaker guy is eased, so the foredeck man will be able to haul the tack of the spinnaker to within his reach with the spinnaker lazy fore guy, without having to adjust the pole position. The foredeck man can then trip the tack snap shackle to douse the spinnaker, and snap in—say—a genoa clew for rigging wing and wing. In this case, once the genoa is raised, the man on the spinnaker-guy winch simply cranks the genoa clew out to the end of the pole, and the boat is off and running again. Similarly, if a spinnaker is to be reset in place of a wung-out genoa, the spinnaker guy (serving as the genoa sheet) is eased, and the foredeck man hauls the clew inboard with the lazy fore guy, trips the snap shackle, drops the genoa, and then sets up the spinnaker with the tack in the snap shackle. When hoisting the spinnaker, the crew simply hauls in on the spinnaker guy and trims the sheet while the foredeck man hoists.

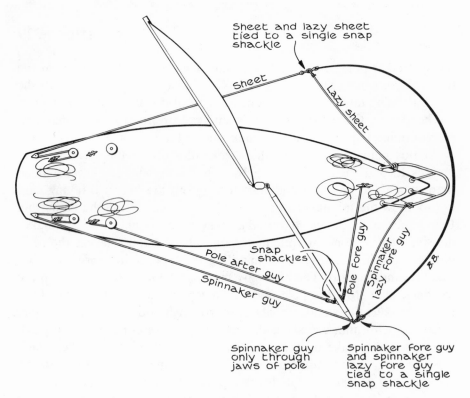

Sheet and lazy sheet
tied to a single snap
shackle

Sheet

Lazy sheet

Pole fore guy

Spinnaker lazy fore guy

Snap shackles

Pole after guy

Spinnaker guy

B.B.

Spinnaker guy
only through
jaws of pole

Spinnaker fore guy
and spinnaker
lazy fore guy
tied to a single
snap shackle

102. Rigging a spinnaker pole with its own fore guy and after guy.

It's really as simple as that.

Saddles on the pulpit, as discussed in the following chapter and shown in Photo 16, also immeasurably simplify the handling of the spinnaker pole on a cruising boat.

Much of the fancy and expensive gear which the racing boys insist on having when they set a spinnaker is not absolutely necessary for cruising. Both guys can be tied into the same snap shackle, so that only two shackles are needed for the guys and sheets. The fore guy does not need a special block lead and winch, but can be led through the mooring cleat forward and secured to it.

The inner end of the pole does not really need a tackle; just a slider, with a plunger which can be dropped into the holes in the spinnaker-pole track, is sufficient. If the pole cannot be moved up as necessary by brute force, the jib halyard can be hitched onto it and cranked up. This procedure will usually move even the stubbornest of poles. If there is difficulty in getting the butt end of the pole to come down, a short length of line can be thrown around it and led down to a spare halyard winch, and it can then be cranked down. Indeed, even the inner-end slider is not essential; the butt end of the pole can simply be fixed into a plate set at a convenient height. This arrangement, admittedly, not as efficient as the ultimate racing rig, is quite sufficient for a cruising boat.

It is worth remembering that light Dacron or nylon sails take up little space and are usually less expensive area for area than other cruising sails; furthermore, second-hand racing spinnakers that are not quite good enough for racing can frequently be picked up at relatively low prices. A tremendous amount of wonderful, quiet, calm sailing can be enjoyed on a vessel under the pull of carefully set and trimmed light-weather sails, and in a fresh breeze one can experience sailing at its very best.

To be sure, a spinnaker should really be set only by someone who understands what he is doing, and should be taken down before it is too late—basically, when the boat reaches a speed 10 or 15 percent below its known hull speed, or when steering begins to get difficult. But given the practice and experience, the correct gear, and some understanding of the gear, playing around with light sails in light airs becomes fun rather than work.

MIZZEN STAYSAILS

As stated in *OSY*-I, mizzen staysails on ketches and yawls are great cruising sails. Many people forget that on the average ketch the mizzen staysail is of the same areas as, or slightly larger than, the mainsail; on a yawl it is one-half to two-thirds the area of the main. Hence, for downwind passage making, a wonderful rig for ketches and yawls consists of the No. 2 genoa set to windward on a pole, the No. 1 genoa sheeted to the end of the main boom (which is squared off, with the mainsail furled), and the mizzen staysail set over the main boom and tacked to the weather rigging and sheeted to the end of the mizzen boom, which is also squared off. This rig provides ample sail area, yet reduces the chafe problem to a minimum; also, an awning—very welcome in the tropics—can be set under the mizzen staysail.

A mizzen staysail used on a reach will be limited in size by the distance from the tack point to the end of the mizzen boom, and its luff length will be limited by the distance from the tack point to the mizzen masthead. However, once the wind is on the quarter and the sheets are eased, a much larger mizzen staysail, unlimited by these dimensions, may be set. For example, on *Iolaire* our small mizzen staysail has an area of 320 square feet, whereas our large mizzen staysail, used on broad reaches, has an area of 450 square feet—40 percent greater (Drawing 103); actually, it is the same size as the mainsail. Off the wind, there is no substitute for sail area to make a boat go.

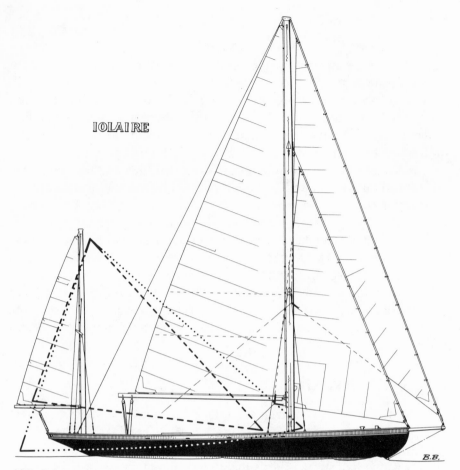

IOLAIRE

103. *Iolaire*'s small mizzen staysail (*broken line*) and large mizzen staysail
(*dotted line*).

FISHERMAN STAYSAILS

I have sailed on schooners very seldom, and on those occasions when
I did so, we had trouble with the fisherman staysail. Therefore, I wrote
to Ed Raymond, of Hathaway, Reiser and Raymond, for information
on this subject. His reply—brief, clear, and to the point—is reproduced
verbatim.

6-1-77

Hi Don,

I am sorry that I have been unable to respond earlier to your
questions about fisherman staysails.

My ex-partner Alden Reiser claimed that the first sail that he
worked on was a fisherman. He was at that time about twelve years
old and in Nova Scotia; that would have been about 1890.

I do not know the origin of this type of sail. A few pictures taken before the turn of the century show small standard fisherman stay-sails set on yachts. The large queen type appears only in pictures taken after about 1910. Most of the early pictures show the standard gaff topsail or club topsail. These were brutes to handle and often required sending a man aloft. They often took complete charge when carried slightly too long. The use of the fisherman staysail probably reached its zenith in the 1928–32 era, when the staysail schooner became popular, and the sail only lost its popularity when schooners lost theirs.

Sails of the fisherman type must be set and trimmed with judgment, like most other sails. Since the advent of synthetics, they are made with stretch luffs and heads to give draft and shape control not previously possible.

Hoisting and lowering must be done with the peak halyard and the sheets completely free, so that the sail floats like a flag. This procedure takes all the fight out of the sail and makes it easy and safe to handle. If set over a gaff foresail, the sail must be lowered and rehoisted when the vessel is tacking. This is not necessary even with a queen size on a staysail-rigged schooner.

Sheeting is usually to the main boom, though sometimes to the deck, well aft. My experience racing them indicates that the boom is preferable. Trimming differs from that for other sails in that the peak halyard is used as a second sheet; it must be slacked when reaching and running in order to prevent severe distortions, and should be adjusted to the conditions and feel of the sail.

I have always been impressed with the speeds most schooners could obtain when all of their sails were properly set. They do not point high, so sail them very fast and the results prove quite satisfactory. In my years of handicapping I found that schooners in general needed a rig factor which tended to lower their ratings from 15 to 20 percent (staysail and gaff). Their worst point of sailing is dead downwind, where they just cannot apply their sail area.

There is nothing more that occurs to me—except to wish you a Happy New Year, and good sailing.

ED

TOPSAILS

For the detailed information on topsails in *OSY*-I (Ch. VI) I was indebted to Roger Fothergill of *Tern IV*. Since then, I have sailed two thousand miles on a gaff-rigged schooner with her topsails set continually, so I have had more than a little time to contemplate the matter of topsails. Helpful suggestions and ideas on the subject have also been given to me by Tim and Pauline Carr of *Curlew,* who have had a good deal of experience with topsails. Hence, there are a few additional comments to be made on this subject.

Most people are scared stiff of messing with topsails, but in actuality, once a little experience has been gained, they are not that difficult to handle. They are certainly worth while in that they do increase the sail area, and—more important—they increase it high up, where the wind is found in light weather. Time after time, one hears of gaff-rigged boats ghosting along when their more modern sisters are flat becalmed, and the only thing drawing is the topsail, high in the air.

If a topsail is to be used at all, it should be of decent size. In days gone by, on the old English cutters, the area of the topsail was frequently as much as one-third that of the mainsail. However, the topsail should be slightly smaller than the area to be filled, as otherwise it is very difficult to get the sheet lead exactly right. On *Atlantica,* on a reach, when we allowed the gaff peak to sag slightly to put draft into the mainsail, the topsail set beautifully. But on the wind, if we peaked the gaff up to make the mainsail set perfectly, the topsail set poorly; and if we dropped the peak of the gaff slightly to make the topsail set

104. Topsails: A, thimble-headed; B, jackyard at mast only; C, double jackyard; D, on hoops to topmast, with furling brails.

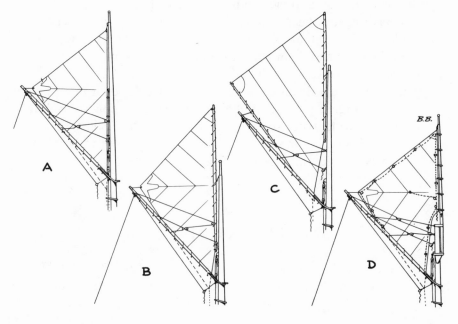

properly, then the mainsail set poorly. Had the topsail been slightly smaller, we would not have had this problem.

Curlew has a jackyard topsail which enhances her light-air performance. Originally, the sail was laced to the old yard, but Tim and Pauline then obtained a grooved spar to use as a yard. They report complete success with this, as the tension along the yard can be adjusted before the sail is hoisted. When the topsail is to be stowed for a long period, sliding it out of the grooved spar is much easier than unlacing it would be.

Various topsails are shown in Drawing 104. If I were to own a gaff-rigged boat, I would have a thimble-headed topsail for average sea conditions, and a double-jackyard topsail, with light aluminum or fiberglass grooved spars as the yards, for light-weather work.

Information on setting a topsail "coaster," or "fisherman," style—that is, permanently aloft on hoops, furled from deck level—can be found in Howard I. Chapelle's excellent book *The American Fishing Schooners.*

STORM SAILS

As I have often stated, I feel very strongly that the storm trysail should be the same size as the double-reefed main, so that it can be used instead of the mainsail in heavy weather. If the storm trysail is correctly rigged—that is, stowed on a spur track—hoisting requires no more effort than does double-reefing a main. Being more sturdily reinforced and less weakened by wear, the storm trysail has a much better chance than the double-reefed main of avoiding damage when it is blowing hard. Further, double-reefing a mainsail usually moves the leech so far inboard that the boom is inadequately supported, especially on older boats with low-aspect-ratio sails and heavy wooden booms. Drawing 105 illustrates the most accepted sequence for shortening down on an ocean cruiser: a double-reefed main and a staysail (*A*); a large storm trysail and staysail for the same boat (*B*); and a reefed storm trysail and a storm staysail, which has about two-thirds the area of a normal staysail (*C*).

On double-headsail-rigged boats, the No. 3 jib should be interchangeable with the storm staysail: if there is enough room, both of these should be carried, so that if one tears, the other is already in use; if space is limited, they can simply be interchanged, as required by circumstances.

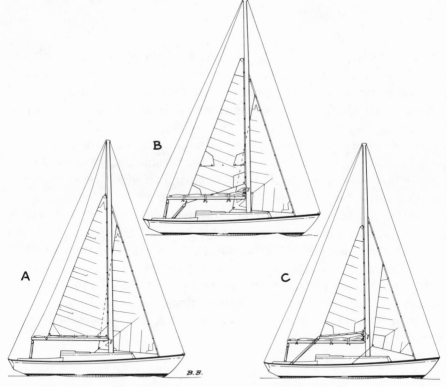

105. Shortening down for heavy weather: A, reefed mainsail and heavy staysail; B, storm trysail and heavy staysail; C, reefed storm trysail and storm staysail.

A storm sail must be heavily reinforced. Most sailmakers disapprove of roping all three sides, because a baggy sail usually results; however, a storm sail should always have extra-heavy tape reinforcement on the foot and leech. Also, its slides or hanks should be spaced at two-thirds of the distance specified for the mainsail of the same boat. On more than one boat, the slides have been suddenly stripped from the track, so that the storm trysail was left secured only at the head, tack, and clew, almost impossible to douse, and the gear was severely strained.

SETTING THE STORM TRYSAIL

Sheeting

A storm trysail should have good large cringles at all corners. Some people sheet a storm trysail like a genoa—with one line through a snatch block to a winch—but many feel that this arrangement is risky in that it is too easy to lose control of the sheet, which is then almost impossible to retrieve in very heavy weather. For this reason, experienced yachtsmen often prefer to have two three-part tackles, one to each pad eye set about halfway between the center line of the boat and

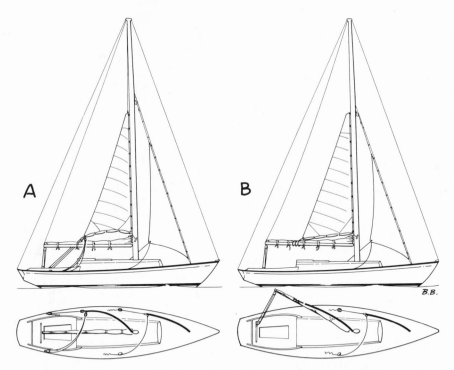

106. Sheeting storm trysail when off the wind: A, sheeting to deck or rail cap hauls clew too far inboard; B, sheeting to the boom reduces the curve in the clew, eliminating excess weather helm.

the rail cap. If this is not possible because the pad eyes are too far out-board, once the trysail has been sheeted, the weather sheet can be set up to haul the clew to windward in the same way that the mainsail traveler is hauled to windward by a tackle on the larger racing boats.

This arrangement, in which the storm trysail is sheeted with tackles to the deck, is the one normally used when going to windward. How-ever, as the wind comes abeam or aft of the beam, the sail sheeted in this manner takes a very poor shape; the leech just curves back into the boat and provides little drive (Drawing 106A), and the result may be a considerable increase in weather helm. Therefore, when the sheets are to be eased, the better method is to top up the boom with the topping lift until it reaches the level of the clew of the storm trysail, lash the clew of the storm trysail securely to the boom with rolling hitches (or better yet, use special fittings, installed for this purpose), and then slack off the topping lift until the boom is hanging on the trysail (Drawing 106B). Then the mainsheet can be taken up, the trysail sheet slacked off, and the boom eased out, with a boom vang to hold it down. The trysail will hold an efficient shape, without a flapping leech, and will maintain drive even on a reach or a run. If the trysail is short-footed, a slight tension on the topping lift will ease the strain on the leech and thus reduce the chance of its splitting.

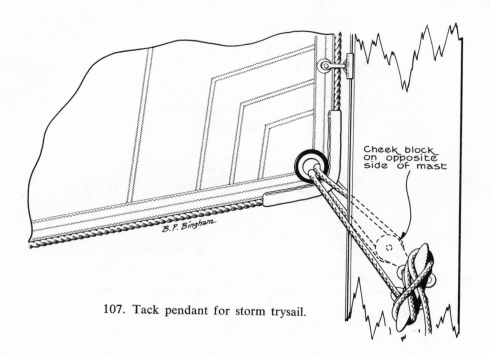

Cheek block
on opposite
side of mast

B.P. Bingham

107. Tack pendant for storm trysail.

Luff Tension

At the tack of the storm trysail should be a large cringle with a pendant spliced to it. To set up, reeve the tack pendant through a snatch block or open cheek block set on the mast, or through the hole in the base of a mast cleat, lead it back up through the cringle, then lead it down to a cleat (Drawing 107). On small boats, a three-part purchase should be sufficient, but on larger boats the three-part purchase should then be led to a winch. The correct angle of lead for the sheet can be obtained by moving the trysail up or down the mast—hoisting the trysail has the same effect as moving the sheet lead forward.

REEFING THE STORM TRYSAIL

To reef the storm trysail one must unshackle the weather sheet from the clew cringle (only screw shackles should be used for the trysail), stand up on the main boom, shackle the weather tackle to the reefing-clew cringle, reeve a spare tackle through the reefing-tack cringle, and then take up on the weather sheet and the tack tackle. Hauling simultaneously on the two enables one to lower the sail with a minimum of flogging. Once the trysail is in the proper reefed position, one can switch the lee sheet to the reefing-clew cringle and harden up while easing the weather sheet. The bunt of the sail may then be tied up by means of reef points. If the reef is so deep that one cannot reach the reefing-clew cringle when standing on the main boom, pendants must be spliced into the reefing-clew cringle and secured to the leech of the sail by a light line which can be broken when desired. The sheet tackles can then be shackled to the pendants and sheeted as described earlier.

SWEDISH STORM TRYSAILS

In Scandinavia, the so-called "Swedish mainsail" has been popular for many years. Photographs of it, and discussions of its virtues, appear in books written by Uffa Fox prior to World War II. Basically, this is a narrow mainsail cut with a very hollow roach (Drawing 108A). In the days of canvas sails, obtaining a strong enough leech was most difficult, and this sail therefore had a wire leech line. However, now that Dacron, with its greater strength, is in use, the sail should be much easier to cut.

To set this sail easily one must have a separate switch track and also a track along the boom, so that the sail can be bent on the boom and then on the switch track prior to hoisting. With roller reefing, the second track or slot can be placed on the underside of the boom, and the boom can then be rotated 180 degrees when the sail is to be hoisted.

This type of storm trysail is largely unknown outside Scandinavia, but those who have used it are very enthusiastic about its employment to reduce mainsail area.

108A. Swedish mainsail. B. Gaff trysail.

GAFF TRYSAILS

Normally, a storm trysail is three-sided, but many gaff-rigged boats have such short masts that hoisting a three-cornered sail with sufficient area to be effective is hardly possible. Further, a number of people who are very experienced with the gaff-rigged cutter have told me that on this boat, with its long bowsprit and excessive windage forward, the Marconi trysail just does not work successfully, because the center of effort is much too far forward; they maintain that a gaff trysail should be used on a gaff-rigged cutter (Drawing 108B).

The gaff trysail is usually set loose-footed. On smaller boats, the try-sail gaff—which is about two-thirds the length of the regular gaff—is short enough to be easily handled, and can be left permanently bent onto the sail; on larger boats, the trysail and the gaff can be stowed separately, and the gaff bent on before use.

To set a storm trysail on a gaff, the mainsail is dropped and well secured, and the halyards are removed from the gaff and secured to the trysail gaff, which is fastened to the mast by a strop with parrel balls. The sail is secured to the mast with a lacing line at the luff, or with strops with parrel balls. Then the trysail may be hoisted, with the gaff carefully controlled by vangs to the peak. Alternatively, the trysail may be hoisted in stops, and then the sail broken out.

Among the old sketches of *Iolaire* are some showing that the late R. H. "Bobby" Sommerset used a gaff trysail on her. When the wind moderated, before switching to the regular mainsail, he would set a small topsail above the gaff trysail, thus giving it a long leading edge. If the wind increased again, dousing the topsail was much easier than switching back from reefed main to storm trysail. The trysail gaff was short enough to swing inside the topmast backstay, and the latter could thus be left permanently set up.

STORM HEADSAILS

Storm headsails must have very heavy hanks, preferably either Merri-man heavy-weather jib hanks (*OSY*-I, Photo 55) or Abeking and Rasmussen staysail hanks (*OSY*-I, Photo 56), which cannot flog open. There must be a heavy wire luff, and pendants at the head and tack of such length that the halyard splice is on the winch when the sail is hoisted. Hanks should be placed at the top and bottom of the head pendant, since otherwise the halyard shackle may wrap itself around the stay as the boat pitches and rolls. Sheets should be knotted into the sail or secured with screw shackles; snap shackles—unless of the

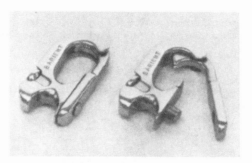

15. Barient snap shackle. BARIENT

new Barient type (Photo 15)—may flog open. Even these have been known to open under severe flogging.

Instead of being folded, a heavy-weather headsail should be stopped with strong rubber bands. If this has been done, one can hank the sail onto the stay, hoist it, set up the halyard really tight, make everything secure around the mast, and when all is ready, go aft and sheet the sail. Thus, the hoisting and sheeting becomes a one-man rather than a three-man job, and the sheet doesn't flog around trying to kill somebody.

VII

~~~~~~~~~~~~~~~~~~~~~~~~~~~~~~~

Deck Layout

COCKPIT SIZE AND DRAINING ABILITY

On a yacht that is only going to cruise Long Island Sound or other sheltered waters, the cockpit need not be as watertight as the cockpit on an offshore yacht. However, all too many supposedly offshore cruising and racing yachts have oversized cockpits, improperly drained and insufficiently watertight. According to the I.O.R., the maximum volume of the cockpit, below the lowest coaming, should not exceed 6 percent of the boat's waterline length times beam times freeboard aft (6% L × B × FA). The height of the cockpit sole above the load waterline should be at least 2 percent of the waterline length (2% L above LWL).

Many think this rule is honored rather in the breach than in the observance. Further, most seamen feel that before a boat is used for serious offshore cruising, the cockpit should be tested. This can be done by taking the emergency bilge pump from the yard and filling the cockpit to the top. One can then observe, first, whether the cockpit is watertight; second, whether it is small enough so that when it is full of water, its sole stays above the vessel's waterline; and third, whether it drains in a reasonable time. Exactly what constitutes a reasonable time is up to the individual skipper; most seamen would say that a cockpit that cannot drain itself in five minutes is not very well designed, and is probably unacceptable for serious offshore work, though it may be adequate for alongshore sailing.

FANNY BARS (CROQUET HOOPS)

What to call the U-shaped devices frequently placed alongside the mast on modern ocean racers, to support those who are cranking the halyard winches, is beyond me. I have heard people refer to them as "fanny bars" and as "croquet hoops." On a large or beamy boat with a halyard mounted on the mast, they are certainly worth while. However, they should be installed carefully. I have heard crews complain bitterly that their boats' fanny bars were not properly placed. It is most discouraging to spend time and money mounting equipment and then find it not doing its job.

WINCH-HANDLE HOLDERS

Various beautifully molded PVC winch-handle holders are sold, which match particular winch handles perfectly. However, these are costly, and one can instead make a holder out of PVC pipe of the correct diameter to allow the winch handle to drop inside (Drawing 109). The pipe is screwed to the mast—a stainless-steel machine screw being used for an aluminum mast, a self-tapping screw for a fiber-glass mast, or a wood screw for a wooden mast. One need only drill on one side of the pipe a hole of the correct size for the screw, and on the opposite side a hole large enough to allow a screwdriver to reach the screw. The result is not fancy, but the savings may be great enough to pay for an extra winch, if enough of the holders are made.

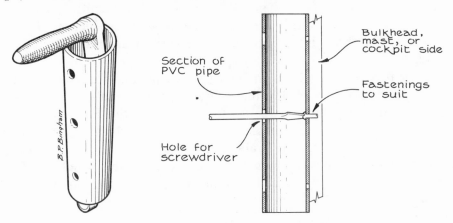

109. Winch-handle holder made of PVC pipe.

CLEATS

Cleats have changed drastically through the ages; describing them all would require a complete book.

Few experienced seamen would deny that the best general all-around cleat has long been the hollow-cast Herreshoff type (*OSY*-I, Drawing

103). In determining size, the general rule of thumb is that there should be 1 inch of cleat length for every ⅛ inch of line diameter.

Admittedly, the modern cam cleat has many uses on boats, and it certainly has amazing holding power. However, in general it is regarded as suitable only for light strains on small lines that are not critical to safety; it is not appropriate for general installation on the ocean sailing yacht because one may inadvertently knock a line out of such a cleat.

Now there is another type of cleat available for consideration, the Clamcleat. Judging from the reports of some users—notably Bruce Bingham, who races his thirty-six-foot schooner *At Last* very successfully in a regular schooner circuit and against modern cruiser/racers—this is suitable for use throughout the boat.

Bruce and Kate Burke have been sailing *At Last* for several years and many thousands of miles without any other help, except for an occasional yank on a line by Sabrina, the Labrador retriever. You can imagine that they really have their hands full, especially when one of them is below. The boat was originally equipped with Herreshoff-type cleats for sheets, downhauls, outhauls, topping lifts, backstays, and reefing gear, but they found that when short tacking, reefing, or maneuvering in tight quarters, they wasted valuable time undoing lines or making them fast. They then switched over almost entirely to cam cleats, but soon realized that some of the larger lines, such as sheets, tended to slip through the cam cleats when wet or under a tremendous load.

Now they use the new aluminum Clamcleats, and they report that in these the security of any line—large or small, wet or dry—is so positive that they have no desire to go back to the Herreshoff-type cleat. Further, Bruce says that sheeting is so fast, and small line adjustments are so quick, that it is almost like having two extra people on board. However, he would not recommend Clamcleats for halyard, because the angle of their attachment is not advantageous for this use.

GALLOWS FRAMES

Every cruising man should consider a gallows frame. Sometimes they are crude and ugly; sometimes they are beautiful and expensive.

In years gone by, making a gallows frame (*OSY*-I, Photo 72) was very simple since the frame fittings and base fittings could be ordered from Merriman Brothers. However, when the company became Merriman Holbrook many of the old products—these fittings among them —were discontinued.

Now the situation is changing once again. The demand for these fittings caused by my reference to them in *OSY*-I has caused Pat Black to decide to put them back into production. Merriman Holbrook has borrowed the base and end fittings from me to use as patterns, and the cruising man can now buy the necessary aluminum or bronze fittings off the shelf. This hardware produces a really good gallows frame.

SHROUD ROLLERS

On boats with overlapping headsails, and even on boats with high-cut jibs that don't overlap the mast, shroud rollers—which help the sheets to feed around the shrouds—are useful. However, many of the commercial rollers cost a fortune. Making one's own out of wood is time-consuming, and wooden rollers are difficult to maintain.

The simplest solution is to use PVC pipe. Before the terminal fitting is placed on the wire, slip over the shroud a washer, a six-foot piece of PVC pipe, and another washer (this will allow the rigging to be end for ended if desired). Then the terminal fitting can be installed. The washer adjacent to the terminal fitting should be of such size that it will spin freely on top of the fitting, and it should be large enough in diameter to support the pipe. For some sizes of wire and some terminal fittings, two or three washers staggered in size may be needed (Drawing 110A).

110. Shroud-roller installations: A, on new rigging before terminals are in place; B, on existing rigging, with terminals in place.

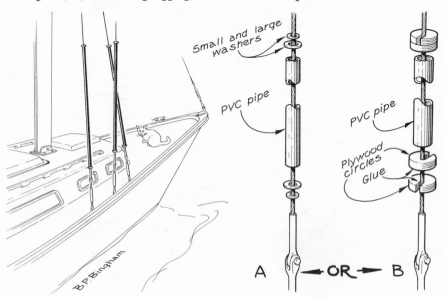

If the terminal fittings are already on the rigging wire, all is not lost. Buy PVC pipe wide enough to slip over the fittings, and then cut from plywood (¼ inch to ⅜ inch thick) a series of circles slightly larger in diameter than the pipe. Drill a hole the diameter of the rigging wire through the center of each circle, and cut a slot from the outside edge of the circle to the center, so that it may be placed over the wire. Slip the pipe over the terminal fitting and wire; then position two of the wooden circles at each end of the pipe. With their slots facing in opposite directions, join each two circles with epoxy glue (Drawing 110B). Sand, and paint or varnish, and—presto—shroud rollers for a quarter of the cost of those sold commercially. The PVC shroud rollers on *Iolaire* lasted about ten years before they had to be replaced.

PULPITS

Pulpits come in all sizes and shapes, but most of them lack one thing which many yachtsmen feel is a great asset—chocks, or saddles, for the spinnaker/whisker pole (Photo 16). The forward end of the pole can be placed in a saddle, the topping-lift after guy and fore guy attached, and the fore guy set up just hand-tight. The pole will then stay in the saddle unattended while the foredeck man attaches the inner end to the spinnaker-pole mast fitting. As a result, one man can handle a fairly large spinnaker pole, although normally two men are required

16. Wishbone's *bow pulpit, showing spinnaker-pole saddle.* A. C. LEONARD

because until the pole is completely rigged, the forward end slides around the foredeck or the top of the pulpit. The saddle is, in effect, almost an extra foredeck man.

AWNINGS

What was said concerning awnings in *OSY*-I (Ch. VII) essentially still stands today. However, Vivatex, which I recommended for awnings, is becoming harder and harder to get, and I must admit that eventually it rots out in the sun. Dacron and nylon are still useless as awning materials, but some of the new acrylic fibers that look and feel like canvas make excellent awnings; they are relatively immune to sunburn, and appear to be extremely long-lasting.

As for side curtains, I still dislike them, because they add bulk to the awning and prevent one from seeing out while standing under it. However, some experienced yachtsmen have pointed out to me that with the protection of side curtains that extend to within two or three feet of the deck and are secured to the lifelines, one can sit and eat on deck even in a hard rainsquall. How delightful! This will be the case only if there is also a foredeck awning or a forward curtain. Otherwise, rain will blow in under the forward end of the awning and get everything soaking wet whether there are side curtains or not. Therefore, if side curtains are installed to keep the deck dry, a foredeck awning must be installed as well.

Awnings can make wonderful rain catchers when the boat is lying at anchor. Even in places where the climate is relatively dry, like St. Thomas, at the northern end of the Lesser Antilles, or the Gulf of California in Mexico, enough rain can usually be gathered off the awning to take care of ordinary water needs. Once an awning has been installed, it should be checked after a rain to see where water seems to gather. In each such place, one can cut a hole and sew in a canvas funnel fitted with a hose-to-hose coupling and a hose clamp. Another method is to cut a hole in the awning, reinforce it with a heavy patch and grommet, and then install a nylon through-hull fitting through the grommet. A hose attached to the funnel or through-hull fitting can be run from there down to the water tank (Drawing 111). The hose must be at least ½ inch in inside diameter, ¾ inch is even better. Small hose tends to become air-bound for some reason. This arrangement will probably solve the problem of taking on water, and will provide much better water than one is likely to get from the shoreside supply in very dry areas.

Incidentally, one advantage of a roller-reefing boom for the cruising

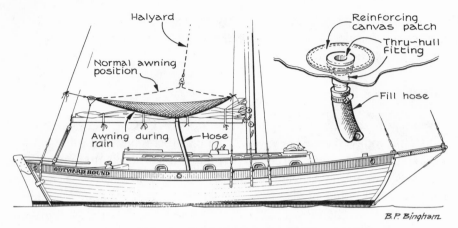

111. Awning used as rain catcher.

yachtsman is that it can be used to gather water. If a rainsquall is encountered when sailing, one need only roll one turn in the boom on the roller-reefing gear, *rolling the sail to leeward,* and top up the main boom on the topping lift (no cruising boat should be sailing with a nonadjustable topping lift). Water will come pouring off the sail, and running forward to the gooseneck in a veritable cascade. Once the salt has washed off the sail, which takes only a few minutes, the hose and funnel can be lashed underneath the gooseneck, and the water tank will be filled in a very short time.

For the discussion of ventilators and hatches, see Chapter X.

BOARDING LADDERS (ACCOMMODATION LADDERS)

When yachts were very large, and crews dressed in white uniforms welcomed the owner and his guests, the boarding ladder was used as a stairway from the tender or dinghy to the deck of the mother ship. It was commonly called an "accommodation ladder" (Photo 17). It was often fashioned with rope-mat stair treads, fancy rope works, and even a carving of the vessel's name. In construction it was a work of art, and its maintenance required a craftsman's hand. But if the yacht sailed off and began to heel, and the crew had forgotten to stow the ladder, it would begin to drag alongside, and inevitably it tore the fittings from the rail cap, destroying itself at the same time.

A further problem was that in a swell, dinghies and launches would fetch up underneath the boarding platform, and capsize or flood. Also, this type of ladder was extremely difficult to stow.

17. Old boarding ladder of the type used on a 65- or 70-foot boat.
TOM MCCUE

Today, with higher freeboards, it may be almost impossible to retrieve a man overboard without the aid of a ladder, unless one attaches a halyard to him and cranks him up out of the water. Boarding ladders should be considered essential even for climbing on board from the dinghy. They are now usually made of light alloy or plastic, in a variety of different designs. Some are good, some poor, some unbelievably bad.

The ladder I recommend is shown in Photo 18 (for supplier, see Appendix). It folds up like an accordion, tight and small. *Iolaire*'s,

18. Modern folding boarding ladder: left, *open;* right, *collapsed.* GAIL ANDERSON

which is a full six feet long, can be stored in an 11-by-4-by-12-inch space.

As purchased, the ladder is normally too short; it should extend at least two, and preferably three, feet below the waterline, for the convenience of swimmers. The legs that are supplied inevitably bend or break, so when assembling the ladder, it is best not to install them, but rather to secure to it, just at the waterline, a fender six inches in diameter. This will not break, and will hold the ladder far enough from the boat so that it does not scratch the hull.

Admittedly, being made of aluminum and stainless steel, this ladder does not last forever, but our general experience—using the boat twelve months of the year in the hardest conditions—is that it can last about three years. Since deterioration is gradual, one does not have to assemble a whole new long ladder every three years. Instead, one can buy a new ladder and use it in bits and pieces to repair the old one, as needed.

VIII

Anchors and Anchoring

TYPES OF ANCHOR

FISHERMAN ANCHORS

As stated in *OSY*-I, the fisherman anchor has been much maligned. People still do not really understand the difference between the old-fashioned fisherman, or yachtsman, and such fisherman-type anchors as the Nicholson and the Herreshoff. All three are shown in Drawing 112.

As the drawing shows, the flukes on the yachtsman form right angles with the arms. This anchor is not too good, since the flukes tend to foul, are fairly blunt, and do not have sufficient area to really hold.

112. Anchors with folding stocks.

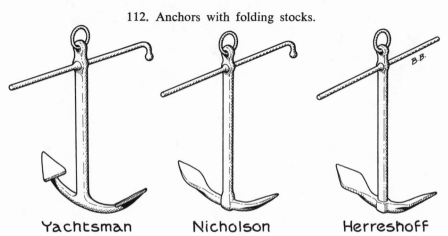

Yachtsman   Nicholson   Herreshoff

The Nicholson is what many refer to as a rock pick—great in rock, although not very good in mud or sand because it lacks fluke area. Historically, this anchor is the seaman's old reliable. One would have to look very hard to find better and more experienced seamen than those of the Royal National Life-boat Institution. On all of their boats the biggest storm anchor, which they use when they are anchoring on a lee shore while slacking away to drift down on a wreck, or when they are otherwise relying on the anchor rather than the engine, is an old faithful Nicholson.

Herreshoff Anchors

The Herreshoff, designed by the late "Captain Nat" Herreshoff, is beloved by most traditional yachtsmen, who regard it as superior to the types of anchor shown in Drawing 113: the plow (of which the CQR is the best-known example); the lightweight (for example, the Danforth); the patented Northill, which has become almost extinct; and the navy, or stockless, anchor, found only aboard ships and very large motor yachts.

I believe the Herreshoff would be even more popular if yachtsmen really examined the differences between the various types of fisherman anchor. The Nicholson has relatively narrow flukes; the standard

113. Some of the anchors popular with cruising yachtsmen.

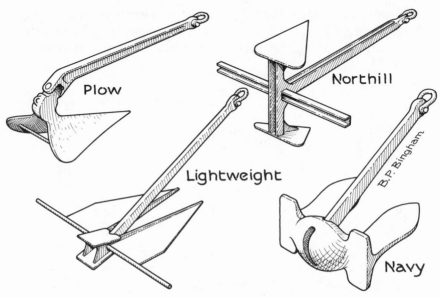

yachtsman has large, essentially triangular flukes; the Herreshoff has diamond-shaped flukes. The great advantage of these diamond-shaped flukes is that when riding around in a calm or swinging in a tide, the anchor line will exhibit relatively little tendency to foul and lift the anchor out. Further, the diamond-shaped flukes have much more area than the flukes of the normal yachtsman.

The Herreshoff anchor is well loved not only for its holding power but also because it can be separated into three pieces—the stock, the crown, and the shank—so that even a forty-four-foot boat like *Iolaire* can stow a 150-pound anchor of this type in the forepeak.

A great advantage of the Herreshoff-type anchor is that once it is dug in, the scope can be shortened down considerably and the anchor will still hold. When ready to leave, if anchored in hard sand, we regularly sail directly up over the anchor and snub up at a short stay; twenty tons of boat stops. We then sit and wait for a couple of minutes while the anchor works its way out of the sand. We always sail the anchor out, and we find that our fifty-pound Herreshoff copy with line but no chain, hung from the bowsprit, is infinitely easier to handle than a lighter anchor with chain. A thirty-five-pound CQR with twelve feet of chain has a total weight of forty-seven pounds; if we used this combination we would have to go out on the bowsprit to ease the shackle and knot over the chocks, which is not necessary with the Herreshoff secured directly to line.

Coral cutting the line has never been a problem because we sail in an area of clear water, and can usually pick an anchoring spot free of coral. When there is any doubt, one should dive overside with a face mask and snorkel. If I were sailing elsewhere, I would change my anchoring techniques as necessary. For example, I might shackle two or more fathoms of chain to the anchor, as circumstances demanded.

Obtaining a Herreshoff-type anchor is becoming increasingly difficult. At one time, a three-piece galvanized-steel anchor very close to the original was made by Nevins. Abroad, Abeking and Rasmussen produced a very similar anchor—almost an exact copy. Also, for many years Wilcox-Crittenden made an anchor that had the same shape, but could not be disassembled. It is this anchor, which has tremendous holding power, that has been our old faithful on *Iolaire* for too many years to count.

With this anchor we have dragged so seldom that it is hard to remember the occasions on which we have done so, except of course for a few times when some idiot has come in and picked up our tripping-line buoy thinking it was a mooring buoy, pulled the anchor out of the bottom, and dropped it back into the water without a by-your-leave!

Unfortunately, production of this model has been discontinued. A few years ago when I called Wilcox-Crittenden to get one, I was told that it was being sold out. I purchased a fifty-pound anchor for thirty-five dollars. A few months later, when I wanted to buy another, I learned there had been a run on it—at a time which coincided with the publication of *OSY-I*!

Later, I discovered that C. E. Beckman (for address, see Appendix) had some Herreshoff-type anchors. Again a run started on them, and finally Peter Duff, who wanted to be sure that future owners of his wonderful little Stone Horses would have a good Herreshoff-type anchor, bought the sixty remaining twenty-five-pound copies! At the present rate of Stone Horse production these will last for perhaps two years. The only concern actually making the Herreshoff anchor today is Paul Luke (for address, see Appendix).

The various anchor manufacturers publish their own versions of charts of holding power, each showing that the particular anchor in question has greater holding power than all the others. I myself take these claims rather lightly; I would rather trust my own experience. Since your circumstances and experience, your particular boat and cruising grounds, may be very different from mine, you must judge for yourself. A great number of notable yachtsmen have endorsed the Danforth lightweight, and I have heard some amazing stories about this anchor. Some people who are widely known and respected in world cruising will use no anchor except a plow, such as the CQR. However, I will stand by my guns in defense of the Herreshoff. The price of this anchor is high, but I emphatically believe it is worth it.

PLOW ANCHORS

Every type of anchor has some distinct advantages and some disadvantages. Among the advantages of the plow is the fact that it is one of the most easily stowed anchors available. If a boat has a bowsprit, this anchor is usually housed up snugly against the roller on the bowsprit. On a knockabout, the roller is most commonly built into a heavy steel fabricated extension, to prevent the anchor from making contact with the hull. In either case, dropping anchor is only a matter of paying out the chain and rode. Stowed in this fashion, the plow need never be taken on deck, where it might snag sheets or sails or become a dangerous obstacle underfoot. Its holding power in sand and mud seems quite impressive, and I have heard that it makes a very good rock hook.

It is reported to have difficulty in penetrating kelp or grassy bottoms, but is better in this respect than the lightweight—as popularized by Danforth, for example. The Pardeys, of *Seraffyn,* and the famous Hiscocks, of the *Wanderers*, use plow anchors almost exclusively, so they may be worth serious consideration.

LIGHTWEIGHT ANCHORS

The lightweight anchor made popular by Danforth has tremendous holding power in sand and mud. However, as mentioned, it has more difficulty than the plow in penetrating grass and kelp, and it should not be used on rocky or coral bottoms because it lacks the ability to hook in as does the Herreshoff, the yachtsman, the Nicholson, or even the plow. A further disadvantage of the lightweight is the fact that dropping it while the boat is moving in excess of 3 knots is almost futile, because the flukes tend to be raised by the passing water, so that the anchor returns to the surface; it may actually plane along the tops of the waves even if attached to a substantial length of chain. Also, when stowed, this anchor adds clutter to the foredeck or cabin top, and may snag on lines or sail. Many coastal sailors whose cruising grounds have mud or sand bottoms prefer the Danforth because in these circumstances its holding power is high in relation to its weight. However, in view of the various disadvantages, my recommendation would be to use the lightweight only as a small kedge, or as an emergency secondary anchor.

I'm afraid I'm a pessimist—a "belt and braces [suspenders]" man. I regard anchors from the point of view not of which is the best, but rather of which is least bad. This attitude is exemplified by my choice of anchors for *Iolaire*. In addition to our standard operating anchor (the fifty-pound Herreshoff copy), we carry a thirty-five-pound Danforth with twelve feet of chain, a thirty-five-pound CQR with twelve feet of chain, and—stowed in the bilge, as life insurance—a three-piece, 150-pound Nevins (very similar to a Herreshoff) with ninety feet of ½-inch chain. As anchor warps, we carry a three-hundred-foot length of ⅝-inch nylon, and two 150-foot lengths of ⅝-inch nylon, along with the usual dock lines that can be pressed into service as emergency warps, and, of course, spinnaker sheets and guys of ½-inch Samson braid, which is amply strong as back-up anchor line.

ANCHOR-RODE MATERIALS— CHAIN

Unfortunately, few people really understood what was meant by the unusual chain shackle described in *OSY*-I (Ch. VIII). It is a shackle with an oval-shaped clevis pin held in place by a hardwood peg (Drawing 114); to open the shackle, one merely hits the end of the clevis pin with a punch and hammer, shearing the wooden peg. It provides for the rapid slipping of the chain.

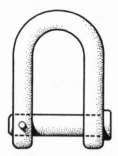 

114. Quick-release chain shackle.

The bitter end of the anchor chain should be securely fastened belowdecks to the heel of the mast or to a pad eye bolted to the keel or floor timber. The normal method of securing the end is with a screw shackle, but when an emergency arises and the chain must be slipped, chances are that the shackle is frozen and time is lost hacksawing through the chain. A better way to secure the end of the chain and still make sure that the chain can be slipped in a hurry is to use line for this purpose. The bitter end of the chain should indeed be fastened to a pad eye or to the heel of the mast—somewhere belowdecks—very securely, *but* this should be done by means of a piece of ½-inch line long enough to allow the bitter end of the chain to be brought up on deck. The line can then be cut with a knife in a matter of seconds, making it unnecessary to fight a frozen screw shackle in the depths of the chain locker.

When anchoring with chain, one should remember that although sliding a weight down the anchor rode is great in theory, it is at times difficult in practice. Have you ever tried to connect the horseshoe to a fifty-pound pig of lead and then tip the whole lot over the side at two in the morning when it is blowing like hell and the bow is plunging? Of course, each case is different, but having damn near drowned on a couple of occasions rigging slider, sling, ballast, and so on, we usually prefer a second anchor.

When we use this method, the two anchors are not placed on the same chain; to do this would require a little more faith in chain than is justified. The late Jack Carstarphen, who had previously been completely sold on chain, became unenamored of it on his 1959 cruise from Miami to St. Thomas in the old *Shellback*. During this cruise he frequently had to anchor in shallow water, chop, and high wind. Several times, the chain broke when he fetched back on it. Similarly, just the other day, in moderate conditions, one of the Ocean 71's broke her chain while picking up the anchor. The chain appeared to be in perfect condition. When I lost *Iolaire* in 1957, both the anchor and chain held, but the shackle broke!

Therefore, do not keep all your eggs in one basket. If several anchors are needed, put them out on separate lines, in a V forward.

If the vessel starts snubbing up on the chain, something must be done, since the shock load can have a number of consequences—it may break the anchor loose, break the chain, or tear the chain stopper, cleats, windlass, bitts, what-have-you, out of the deck; in any event the result is a disastrous accident. One way of dealing with this situation is to veer enough chain so that the weight of the chain keeps the vessel from snubbing; another, is to secure a nylon line to the chain (preferably with a chain hook, though a rolling hitch can be used), slack out a length of chain greater than that of the nylon line, and then resecure the chain. Enough nylon should be used to allow a fair degree of stretch; nylon will stretch up to 50 percent before breaking. One will then be riding on the nylon line, which—acting like a big rubber band —serves as a snubber. If the nylon should break, the vessel will snub up on the chain and another nylon shock absorber can be rigged.

Even when protected from shock, chain definitely does not last forever. If used continually, going in and out over the bow roller, the galvanizing and the metal can wear considerably. In certain areas of the world, chain can be regalvanized, but before having this done, one should check with local yachtsmen to be absolutely sure that the people undertaking the operation are competent.

When chain is ordered, the windlass wildcat (gypsy) should be sent to the manufacturer to make certain that the new chain fits exactly. Similarly, if the boat's chain is in good shape, and a new anchor windlass is being ordered, a foot or so of the chain should be sent to the windlass manufacturer to ensure a perfect match. Also, every windlass or capstan should have a chain stripper to knock the chain free of the wildcat (Drawing 115). Otherwise, any slightly worn section of the chain will tend to jam in the wildcat, to everyone's disgust. A chain stripper is seldom built into a small yacht windlass, but one can be fabricated by a good welder.

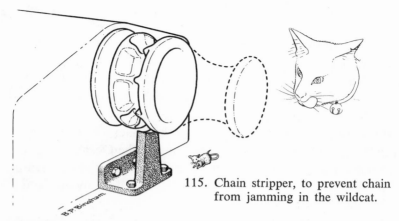

115. Chain stripper, to prevent chain
from jamming in the wildcat.

OVERSIZED LINKS

At each end of the twelve-foot length of chain that is secured to a Danforth or CQR anchor, there should be an oversized link. Without such a link, it will be necessary to use a shackle with substantially less breaking strength than that of the chain; ⅜-inch chain, in the absence of an oversized link, can accommodate only a 5⁄16-inch shackle. The oversized link is also desirable because it enables one to tie the anchor line directly into the chain instead of screwing the 5⁄16-inch shackle into the chain, joining a larger shackle onto the 5⁄16-inch shackle, and then tying in the line.

Chain should always be ordered in fifteen-fathom lengths, with over-sized links at both ends. The lengths should then be joined by Simpson Lawrence chain shackles (Drawing 114; see also *OSY*-I, Photo 90), which can be easily removed. There are several reasons for this procedure.

First and foremost, the outer end of the chain tends to wear and rust well before the inner end, and this arrangement makes it possible to throw away the outer shot (ninety feet), or send it for regalvanizing, without having to discard or send the entire chain.

Second, when anchoring in very deep water, one does not want to have 150 feet of chain hanging straight down, since its weight is considerable. When lengths are joined by shackles, one can separate the first shot from the remainder of the chain, secure a line to it, and anchor with a combination of chain and line.

Third, though most boats normally anchor with chain on one side and line on the other, in some areas one may wish to put both anchors down with chain. If the chain consists of fifteen-fathom shots, with oversized links and proper chain shackles, it is easy to veer an anchor on one shot of chain, disconnect the chain and put a line on it, put the other anchor on the other shot of chain, veer that, and thus have chain on both anchors. Doing this is of course impossible if the chain consists of one single length, and is difficult if the shots are connected by screw shackles.

CHAIN WASHING

A boat large enough to necessitate always anchoring with chain should also be large enough to have a high-pressure water system on deck, so that the chain can be hosed down as it comes on board, instead of being laboriously scrubbed off link by link. When chain is not well washed, a boat begins to smell like a poorly maintained fishing boat rather than a yacht.

If a T-valve is installed, the high-pressure water system can also be used as an emergency bilge pump. However, it is extremely important to have an interlock on the three-way valve; this makes it impossible to cross connect the overboard intake line with the bilge line, which would cause the boat to flood rapidly.

CHAIN STOWAGE

The chain locker of a wooden boat should be lined, since the chain should not be allowed to lie against the planking of the vessel, or to touch the bronze floor-timber bolts. Contact with these bolts frequently causes local electrolysis, so that although the chain appears to be in good shape, every once in a while one may discover a link that has been lying against a bronze bolt and has corroded.

Every chain locker should be well ventilated, so the chain can dry out instead of lying in dampness, corroding. Also, the locker should have really large limber holes; then, periodically, all the chain can be veered and the locker scrubbed out completely.

ANCHOR STOWAGE AND HANDLING

HAWSEPIPES

In years gone by, almost every large yacht had the anchor chain led through a hawsepipe. A good design may make it possible for the anchor itself to be stowed in the hawsepipe, but the length of the hawsepipe must be slightly greater than that of the stock of the largest anchor to be stowed in it. Otherwise, the stock will project above the deck and give a foul lead to the anchor windlass or capstan.

There are disadvantages to hawsepipes. They should not be used with line, since line will tend to chafe within the pipe and the pipe may be too long to be provided throughout with adequate chafing gear. Second, as indicated by the old seamen's expression "Mind your hawsepipes" (which appears in Conrad's stories), they may cause serious trouble. Rumor has it that some ships have even been lost because of cracked hawsepipes; they are of large diameter, they have no sea cocks, and if they crack, it is almost impossible to repair them to keep the water from pouring in through the crack during heavy weather.

In the days when most large yachts had hawsepipes, the anchor was taken up on deck during long offshore passages, and the chain was disconnected, pulled through the hawsepipe, and sent below. A plug with a hook was secured over the outer end of the hawsehole; then a lanyard was hooked to a block and tackle and led up through the hawsepipe, and the plug was cinched firmly into place. If this arrangement is adopted, the plug should fit well, having an adequate, almost waterproof, gasket on its inside face. Then, if the hawsepipe cracks, the plug can be inserted and cinched up tight, and concrete can be mixed up and poured down the pipe, to solidify and block the leak.

Lightweight Anchors Stowed in Hawsepipes

In the estimation of many experienced seamen, the ideal rig for the honest cruising boat of over fifty-five feet is a cast lightweight stowed in a hawsepipe (*OSY*-I, Photo 87) and raised by a really good electric or hydraulic windlass (preferably the latter, since it usually has a reliable back-up hand gear). To prevent a lightweight (such as a Danforth) from chewing up the planking under its tips when it is stowed, brass or stainless-steel chafe plates (Drawing 116) are usually installed. These chafe plates should be as small as possible—just large enough to take the chafe of the anchor in the stowed position. They should be well bedded in bitumastic (oil/kerosene-based tar) to prevent rot from forming underneath. Admittedly, the new polysulfide bedding compounds are wonderful in that they retain their elasticity forever. However, they are probably not as good as old-fashioned bitumastic for preventing rot. In addition, every three years the chafe plates should be removed, the wood underneath checked for rot, and the plates rebedded and reinstalled. Failure to do this inevitably results in a large repair bill for the replacement of rotten planking under the plates.

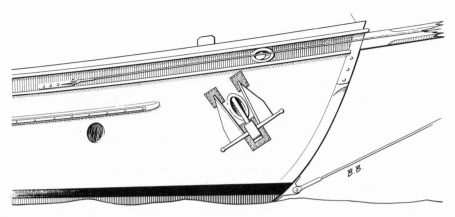

116. Anchor chafe plates on bow.

ANCHOR WINDLASSES AND CAPSTANS

Anchor windlasses and capstans are sometimes electric, but as Larry Pardey points out, electricity, copper, and salt water produce green gunge. Expecting an electric motor to operate faithfully year after year right up forward, in the wettest part of the boat, is really the height of optimism; indeed, it is amazing that electric windlasses perform as reliably as they do—a great tribute to the sealing effect of an O ring.

On larger boats, hydraulic windlasses are quite popular. A hydraulic pump is belted off the main engine, and hydraulic piping (in the old days, it was rigid copper pipe, hard to install; nowadays, high-pressure reinforced hose can be used) brings the oil forward to a hydraulic motor attached to the anchor windlass. The result is an excellent, powerful, and practically foolproof method of handling the anchor. Unfortunately, hydraulic windlasses of this sort are really only suitable for boats of at least fifty-five feet.

However, on the forty-foot yacht *Pedlar,* a Buchanan-designed cutter, I spotted a wonderful *small* hydraulic windlass, suitable for boats as small as thirty-five feet and—the owner reports—powerful enough for boats of up to fifty or fifty-five feet. This windlass has been on his foredeck for twelve years and has given absolutely no trouble (except for difficulty in matching the chain to the wildcat; but I noticed that there was no chain stripper, so possibly that was the cause). The windlass is made by PNP Marine, also the manufacturers of hydraulic adjustable-pitch propellers (for address, see Appendix). On *Pedlar,* this windlass is powered by a hydraulic pump belted off the main engine, but it could probably also be powered off a hydraulic propulsion system, though an expensive valving operation would be required.

Location of the Anchor Windlass or Capstan

As time passes, the anchor windlass or capstan and the chain stowage seem to move farther and farther forward. Admittedly, the ocean cruising yacht is not attempting to be an ocean racer; still, there is no point in building in unnecessary disadvantages. Piling anchor windlass, chain, and so on into the eyes of the boat is detrimental to windward performance. It should be noted that a boat's tendency to pitch increases dramatically as weight is moved away from the center of buoyancy. More technically, the moment of inertia (the plunging moment) varies with the *square* of the distance between the center of buoyancy and the center of gravity of the weight in question. Hence, many feel that the anchor windlass should be as far aft as is practicable. The deck may be protected by a sacrificial strip of wood secured to it, or by removable wooden troughs in which the chains run while the anchors are being raised.

A Combination Anchor Windlass and Sheet Winch

Many yachtsmen, especially those with racing boats which do some cruising, do not want to clutter up the foredeck with a big anchor windlass which they seldom need. However, at certain times in certain areas they do use chain and require something more than a sheet winch to handle it. If a wildcat were cast into the bottom of the drum on a spinnaker fore-guy winch mounted on the foredeck, the winch could also be used to handle the anchor chain (Drawing 117).

The chain would come up over the chain roller and through a chain stopper around the winch, to a swiveling removable navel chain pipe (*OSY*-I, Drawing 126). To take in the chain, one would merely crank the winch. To veer the chain, one would put on the stopper, pull up

117. Winch drum modified for use as capstan.

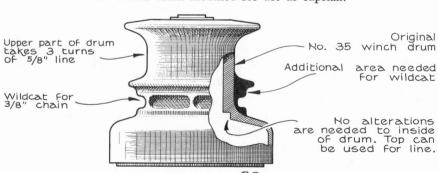

Upper part of drum
takes 3 turns
of 5/8" line

Original
No. 35 winch drum

Additional area needed
for wildcat

Wildcat for
3/8" chain

No alterations
are needed to inside
of drum. Top can
be used for line.

B.B.

extra chain from belowdecks, drop the chain off the winch, swivel the navel pipe to the correct leads, lift the stopper, and allow more chain to run off.

I have discussed this idea with numerous winch manufacturers, and some of them were interested, and thought that it might be worth working on. The one disadvantage would be, of course, that only three turns of ⅝-inch line could be taken around the winch when heaving up the anchor line, but three turns would probably be enough. With ½-inch fore guys, there would still be enough room on the drum for four or five turns, which would be sufficient.

ANCHORING

As more and more people take up yachting and long-distance cruising, anchorages become increasingly crowded. At the same time, the anchoring technique of the average yachtsman has become worse and worse, to the point where it is almost nonexistent.

ANCHORING PROBLEMS

Anchoring problems may be caused by poor holding, by a bottom fouled with waterlogged timber or other miscellaneous junk that can get over the fluke of an anchor and prevent it from digging in, by extreme depth, or by a number of other things that cannot be blamed on the yachtsman and his equipment. However, all too often, when an anchor drags, the yachtsman is responsible.

The most common cause of anchor failure is that the purchaser started at the wrong end of the scale—he asked, "How light an anchor can I use?" rather than, "What is the heaviest anchor that can be handled, in view of the capacities of the crew and of the gear?" Many boats attempt to anchor with what experienced yachtsmen refer to as a "watch charm"—a fourteen-pound high-tensile Danforth with ten feet of chain. This combination of anchor and chain is just too light, and the anchor will probably bounce over the bottom. If it does finally dig in, it will hold against tremendous strain, but getting it to dig in is much too difficult.

No boat should use a Danforth of less than twenty-eight pounds. With twelve feet of chain the total weight will still be only forty-seven pounds. A yachtsman incapable of handling forty-seven pounds of anchor and chain would be better off in his bath chair, reading about sailing instead of trying to do it. Many people contend that a twenty-eight-pound Danforth is too large to stow, but as shown in *OSY*-I (Photo 102), the stocks of a Danforth can be made removable, and it can then be stowed in a minimum of space.

When a CQR is used, expecting anything which weighs less than twenty-five pounds to hold right away is somewhat optimistic. Even with my beloved Herreshoff (which all too many people refer to as a yachtsman, as noted earlier in this chapter), a weight of twenty-five pounds is the absolute minimum, and thirty-five pounds is preferable.

Another source of trouble in getting a Danforth to hold is that people tend to forget that because of the fluke area this anchor can water-ski to the surface when the vessel is moving at 3 knots or more. In certain harbors, such as Road Town, in Tortola, which is exposed to the east, some people come blithely downwind—either sailing, or under power with their sails furled—and put the engine in neutral, but because of the 15- or 18-knot trade wind behind them, don't slow down noticeably. Then they heave over the Danforth and about sixty feet of line. Occasionally it does dig in, the boat spins round, and by pure luck they are there. More often, as the anchor line snubs up, the anchor gives one or two bounces on the bottom, and because the boat is still doing about 4 knots, water-skis to the surface. This can really spell trouble.

The other favorite procedure is to come sailing into the harbor, power up to the anchorage, drop the anchor (giving it plenty of scope), cleat it down, and wander back aft. Then the wind catches the bow of the boat and swings it off, and the boat swings around beam to the wind and then dead downwind and sails off, snubbing up hard on the anchor, which bounces across the bottom instead of digging in.

To anchor correctly, one should bring the boat head to wind, or head to tide (in areas where she is likely to be tide-rode rather than wind-rode), drop the anchor, and let the boat fall back downwind or down tide while the anchor line is slowly paid out, with some strain being taken on it, to allow the anchor to work its way to the bottom. Give the poor anchor a chance!

TRIPPING LINES

Many seamen feel that a tripping line should always be secured to the crown of the anchor to simplify clearing it if it is fouled, or if someone fouls it. Frequently, when your boat is lying stern to, another boat's anchor will be laid across yours; if your anchor is buoyed, it is then possible to drop the inner end of the line and pick up the anchor on the tripping line. However, of late in the Islands numerous yachtsmen have reported having trouble with their tripping lines, in that other sailors have picked up tripping-line buoys under the impression that they were mooring buoys—and having tripped the anchors, have then redropped them without having enough sense to warn those concerned about what happened. Suddenly, a boat that was properly anchored is whistling down through the mooring area with wind and tide, like an express train. For this reason it is recommended that you paint on the tripping buoy the words "Danger! High Explosives!"

One other method of avoiding this problem is to adjust the length of the tripping line so that the buoy is about ten feet beneath the surface. If the anchor is fouled you can dive down, grab the tripping line, and tie another line onto it, but since the buoy is submerged, no one can pick it up or inadvertently run over it and get the line around his propeller.

When a tripping line is used, it must be remembered that a submerged buoy is trying to float the anchor. If a one-gallon bottle, which has eight pounds of buoyancy, is attached to a fourteen-pound high-tensile Danforth, the anchor will barely sink, much less hold. Therefore, a small pick-up buoy should be used instead.

Another possibility is to dispense with the buoy entirely. The tripping line is then attached to the crown of the anchor and fed back toward the boat. This method is complicated in that both anchor and tripping line must be hauled in when the anchor is picked up. It is employed in some areas because in a strong tide the buoy will disappear, being towed under by the tide, and the tripping line will then be useless. Also to be noted is the fact that in areas of strong tide and much floating debris, a large accumulation of weeds and the like around the tripping line can quite easily trip the anchor.

KEDGING OFF

As mentioned in the next chapter, every yacht should be able to run out an anchor to kedge off. With modern sheet winches, once one or two anchors are properly set, the power that can be obtained is infinitely superior to that which an engine is likely to develop, as the following figures indicate.

A standard 4-108, swinging a three-bladed propeller at 3,000 shaft rpm, with a direct drive, develops 638 pounds of thrust *when the boat is moving*. With a 2-to-1 reduction gear at 1,500 shaft rpm, the engine still develops only 815 pounds of thrust *when the boat is moving*. When the boat is sitting still, either tied up or anchored out, the amount of thrust developed is considerably less. However, if the boys put their backs into it, a 40-to-1 sheet winch with two men cranking can easily develop 3,000 pounds of line pull. Clearly, an anchor and winch is the route to go when trying to get unstuck.

If the anchor line is taken to the anchor windlass, or to the sheet winch, and the boat still fails to move but the anchor does not come home, the anchor line should be slacked, and a bowline tied in it well ahead of the boat. From this bowline, sheets should be led to the various sheet winches. A moderate-sized cruising yacht may have four two-speed cockpit winches with a mechanical advantage of 40-to-1. Since each winch should easily develop 3,000 pounds of line pull, the total for all four winches will be 12,000 pounds. If that won't move the boat, nothing will.

Modern ocean racers usually have so many winches around the cockpit that if lines are led to all the winches, the boat can literally pick herself up out of the water—like the man who's so strong he can reach around, grab himself at the back of the neck, and lift himself off the ground.

IX

~~~~~~~~~~~~~~~~~~~~~~~~~~~~~~~~

Dinghies

DESIGN

A good dinghy is absolutely essential for the cruising yacht, since the real cruising yachtsman is likely to find himself in areas where there are no marinas, docks, launch services, or what-have you. No one ever has—or for that matter, ever will—come up with a design for the perfect dinghy. However, through the years some very good dinghies have been built. Unfortunately, many of the best are no longer available. The late Uffa Fox's Duckling, built by Fairey Marine, with its rounded bow looked somewhat like a bathtub, but was a superb dinghy. Although only ten feet long, it would carry six people in calm water; it went well with a low-powered outboard, rowed extremely well when empty, and rowed satisfactorily when loaded. It also sailed well with a minimum rig and a single leeboard, and towed without problems in all weathers. This dinghy was hard to beat—but it is no longer manufactured.

Back in 1904, Herreshoff designed a dinghy (Drawing 118), a copy of which was built recently at Mystic Seaport. Even this model is not perfect; the design does not show bilge skids or a skid on the keel. The yachtsman who carried a dinghy like this probably had as crew two huge Norwegians who never slid the dinghy onto anything, but instead picked it up and carried it like a toy. However, adding skids, on a modern version, would be quite easy. It was carvel-built, with planking ¼ inch thick and with ½-inch-square frames on 6-inch centers. The length was 11 feet 6 inches, and the beam, 48 inches—a practical size for a forty-five-foot yacht, but probably too large for most boats used for cruising today. Because of the rounded stern, the dinghy was doubt-

The Herreshoff dinghy is a superb example of a fine yacht tender, but it is too large for storage aboard a boat of less than forty-five feet. A good loftsman could doubtless build one to a smaller scale.

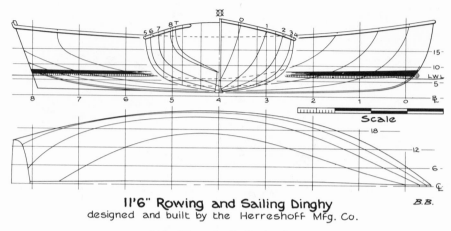

11'6" Rowing and Sailing Dinghy
designed and built by the Herreshoff Mfg. Co.

B.B.

118. Herreshoff dinghy lines.

less harder to row than it would have been with a heart-shaped stern, but it probably carried its load just as well. Indeed, especially in this respect it was a great dinghy. It weighed 120 pounds, and with 600 pounds on board, it still showed 11½ inches of freeboard; with 900 pounds, 10 inches of freeboard.

In the opinion of many, the Ned Williams dinghy is the finest-rowing yacht dinghy to be found. Ned Williams died at ninety-eight; his son, who is in his late seventies, is still alive but has retired. The dinghy, which was built in Cowes, Isle of Wight, can be recognized at a distance by the distinctive shape of the stern. The dinghy is of superior construction: even the last frame, with a bend across the keel that is greater than a right angle, is bent in one piece, without a single break. An eleven-footer with a beam of 44 inches and a depth of 19 inches will easily carry six people in calm water. It weighs 140 pounds, rows like a dream, and tows well. Like the Herreshoff dinghy, the Ned Williams dinghy and its close relative, the Lawley (Drawing 119), are probably too large for most modern cruising boats, but they could be scaled down nicely to usable size.

In the near future, dinghy design is probably going to retrogress tremendously, because of the rules recently formulated by the U.S. Coast Guard regarding the carrying capacity of dinghies. As John

The Lawley dinghy, with lines similar to those of the Ned Williams dinghy, is the epitome of a sweet and practical tender. The size may be judiciously changed as necessary.

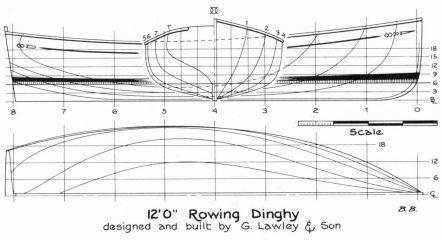

12'0" Rowing Dinghy
designed and built by G. Lawley & Son

119. Lawley dinghy lines.

Gardner, small-boat curator at the Museum of Maritime America, in Mystic, has pointed out in numerous articles, the specifications conceived by the Coast Guard will produce a square box that will neither row, power, nor do anything but float nicely in a flat, calm pond. The rule is based on the erroneous concept that the basically good dinghy is one with tremendous initial stability; in reality, one judges a dinghy by its ultimate, not its initial, stability.

A case in point is the Gloucester dory, designed to carry two men and a ton or more of fish, which is certified by the Coast Guard for two persons. If one stands on the rail, on a good Gloucester dory, the rail will go down and almost touch the water, but the dinghy still will not capsize.

Similarly, the Saints dinghy (Photo 19; Drawing 120), which was designed for fishing, has very little initial stability but tremendous ultimate stability. When one first steps into this dinghy, one feels as if it is about to capsize, but because of the shape, like the Gloucester dory it picks up tremendous stability as it heels over. Thus I, weighing 125 pounds, can stand on the gunwale of my 13-foot Saints dinghy with both hands in my pockets, and the dinghy will not capsize. Of course, the Coast Guard would probably certify it as safe to carry only one person.

The Saints dinghy, characterized by a high dead rise and soft bilges, is extremely stable, easily towed, and delightful to row.

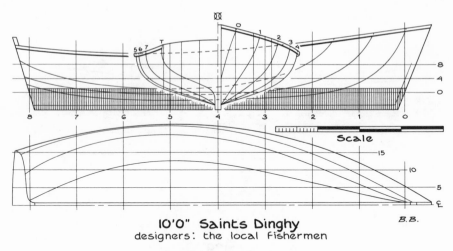

10'0" Saints Dinghy
designers: the local fishermen

B.B.

120. Saints dinghy lines.

One encouraging facet of the dinghy scene is the workshop held at Mystic Seaport every spring. This includes a row-by of dinghies, and a discussion on dinghy design, construction, and the like; it serves as a clearinghouse for information on dinghies. Anyone seriously interested in a good working dinghy should write to John Gardner, Assistant Curator for Small-Craft Studies, Museum of Maritime America, Mystic, Connecticut 06355, for information on design, builders, material suppliers, and so on.

SIZE

One should carry as large a dinghy as is humanly possible. The minimum useful dinghy is a six-foot pram, and that has a practical carrying capacity of only about 300 pounds, possibly 400–450 pounds in calm water. A properly designed stemhead (pointed-bow) dinghy nine feet long should carry 600 pounds adequately in calm water; a twelve-footer, 900 pounds.

SAINTS DINGHIES

The Saints dinghy is undoubtedly one of the finest dinghies in the world. It is referred to in the Lesser Antilles as a Saints boat because yachtsmen often encounter it in the vicinity of Les Saintes (islands off

19. Saints dinghy. ANNE HAMMICK

Guadeloupe), but a few yachtsmen who have visited Marie Galante
have found it to be even more common there. It is basically a beach
fishing boat—designed to be launched from a beach, to be rowed or
sailed out to windward, and to heave to out of the Atlantic swell, with
one man sitting in the eyes of the boat, holding its head to wind, while
his mates hand line off the stern. Once the fish are caught, the men sail
back to their island, skid up onto the beach, and store the dinghy for
the night.

The Saints dinghy has a very high dead rise and slack bilges, is very
narrow at the waterline, and has a beautiful heart-shaped stern. Because it is narrow at the waterline and yet wide at the sheer, it is easily
driven. It is so wide at the rail that one can without difficulty swing ten-
foot oars, and make the boat fly. With a light load—say, five or six
hundred pounds on a thirteen-footer, the stern is out of the water. As
the load increases, needless to say the rowing performance suffers, but
the load capacity of the thirteen-footer is somewhere around 1,200 to
1,400 pounds—so it is certainly a fabulous dinghy. Its disadvantage is
that having been built for commercial fishing, it is quite heavy, and
since the minimum practical length is thirteen feet, it is suitable only
for a fairly large yacht, which can pick it up on slings or davits and
stow it right side up. I wonder what sort of dinghy could be made of
fiber glass and foam if one could use as a model a good Saints dinghy
twelve feet long.

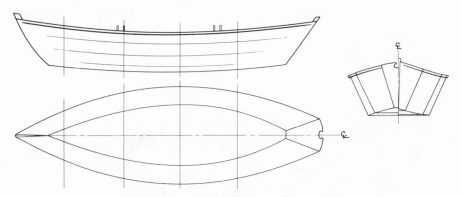

121. An easily built, minimum dory for fun and character; this model should not be considered practical at a length of less than eleven feet.

GLOUCESTER DORIES

Like the Saints dinghy, the Gloucester dory has a lack of initial stability, which one must get used to, but plenty of ultimate stability. It is a superb dinghy, one that rows well, carries weight well, and is cheap and easy to build, but—again like the Saints dinghy—it is hard to stow, since it will only stow well right side up. However, when several are carried, one can yank out the seats and stow the dories one on top of the other. Big fishing schooners frequently carry two stacks of dories, with six in each stack.

It used to be generally thought that these dories could not be shorter than sixteen feet; usually they were slightly longer. When H. G. Phillipps, of *Voyager*, showed up in Lunenburg with a design for an eleven-foot dory having a beam of thirty-one inches at the bottom and forty-four inches at the rail (Drawing 121), the builders looked at him askance. Indeed, at first they refused to take on the job, saying the dory would be too small, too cranky, totally useless, and no damn good. Only after much persuasion did they build one, which turned out so well that Phillipps ordered another. Furthermore, after the builders had tried it, they began to knock out this model for other people, on a semistock basis.

Dinghies of this size and shape are especially suitable for *Voyager*, because she is a beautiful old gaff-rigged schooner and carries dinghies in true fisherman's fashion; they are picked up with lifts from the tips of the fore and main spreaders, swung inboard, and dropped onto the waterway where they nest one inside the other. A great thing about the schooner rig is that it does make dinghy handling dead simple—the method used on *Voyager* is picturesque and practical.

FLAT-BOTTOMED DINGHIES

While practical for rowing around harbors, flat-bottomed dinghies in general do not make satisfactory yacht tenders. By and large, only those that are fairly heavy are any good, and the heaviness normally makes them unsuitable if they are to be taken up on deck. Also, handling qualities are usually sacrificed to ease of building, and the result is the type of design that is not popular for yacht tenders.

PRAMS

Building a stemhead (pointed-bow) dinghy shorter than nine feet that has a decent shape is almost impossible with wood. In this size, a wooden dinghy must either be round-bowed like a Duckling or dhow-bowed like the Dyer Dhow, or else take the form of a pram. With fiber glass, construction is much simpler.

The pram—a dinghy with a transom at each end—has been popular in Europe for many years. Our fine little, less-than-minimum dinghy (Photo 20), six feet long, with 42 inches of beam and 18 inches of depth, is a good load carrier. It goes well with two big adults aboard (with three, if a fast outboard comes by one is in for a swim), and is

20. Iolaire's pram. TOM MCCUE

wonderful with three small children. (Incidentally, Ed White, in the Fort Lauderdale area, is molding a 6½-foot fiber-glass pram with almost exactly the dimensions of *Iolaire*'s pram.)

The ubiquitous Sabot pram (see *OSY*-I, Photo 108) makes an extremely good minimal tender for a small yacht. A dinghy of this type with a folding or removable transom can serve as a spray dodger for the main companionway (Drawing 122). If stowed in this manner, the dinghy can be of greater length than could otherwise be accommodated. Unfortunately, however, the removable transom does discourage the use of an outboard motor.

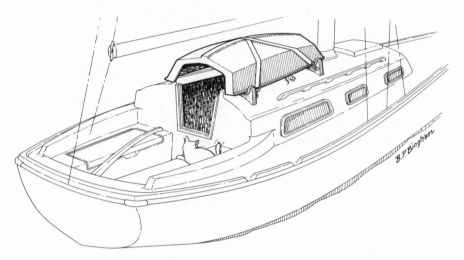

122. A dinghy with a folding or removable transom may be stowed so as to serve as an effective spray dodger.

A lapstrake, or clinker-built, pram is much easier to build than most people realize. If the material is handy, a pram can be knocked out by a good carpenter with an apprentice helping (to buck the rivets) in a couple of days. Construction of a pram also makes a good winter project for a father and his small sons. A backbone pattern is set up, the midship section is cut and secured in place, and the bow and stern transoms are cut and secured to the frame and keel batten. Next, planking is cut, spiled, and secured in place with copper nails. Then the pram is turned over, and some of the steam-bent frames are popped into place. Since steam bending oak or Canadian rock elm takes thirty minutes per square inch of section, only ten to fifteen minutes will be required to steam bend frames of ⅜ or ½ square inches. It should be remembered (something I didn't know and learnt the hard way) that if a frame is oversteamed, it gets brittle and can break. The remaining frames are sprung into place and riveted, and the gunwale, the seat risers, and the rest follow.

INFLATABLES

Inflatable dinghies are rapidly taking the yachting public by storm. However, the view expressed in *OSY*-I (Ch. IX) still holds: an inflatable dinghy that is used twelve months of the year, especially in the tropics, has a life expectancy of approximately two years, so depreciation (and therefore relative cost) is high. For example, at this writing the selling price of an Avon Redstart is $500, FOB England, so the depreciation on a two-year basis is $250 per year. Of course, an inflatable used only in the summer in northern waters may last eight, ten, or more years if given good care.

For the person doing a lot of skin diving, especially with tanks, an inflatable dinghy is an absolute must. Trying to get in and out of a rigid dinghy while encumbered with weight belts, tanks, spear gun, and the like is at best a very difficult operation and a good way to crack some ribs. One method of achieving the best of both worlds is to carry a good large rigid dinghy, for general use, and also a smaller rubber dinghy, deflated, and stored either inside the large dinghy or below-decks. Then one can go to the diving area in the larger dinghy, with the rubber dinghy in tow, to be used for the actual diving.

Although the rubber dinghy with wooden floorboards is fast and stable, and has great load-carrying capacity, a model *without wooden floorboards* is to be preferred. For one thing, the job of assembling a dinghy that has floorboards is difficult and tedious. Furthermore, on most dinghies, the floorboards are made not of teak plywood, but of mahogany plywood, which must be varnished or painted and is therefore very slippery and very difficult to maintain. Where teak plywood is used, it would be a great improvement to just paint the edges and a one-inch border around the edges with epoxy paint, which will keep the water from penetrating the plywood, but leave the rest of the floorboards bare wood.

Many people owe their lives to the fact that when their boat sank, the rubber dinghy made a fairly good life raft. However, in recent years a number of people have lost their lives in the Caribbean because their outboard quit and their oars were so short that they were unable to row the inflatable dinghy—so they just drifted off toward Central America, a thousand miles to leeward. For safety's sake, a rubber dinghy must be equipped with oars of the proper length, as discussed later in this chapter.

THE NEED FOR GOOD RIGID DINGHIES

Few really experienced seamen will deny that a rigid dinghy is absolutely essential on the ocean cruising yacht, not only for the convenience and pleasure it affords but also for the sake of safety. As noted in the section on kedging off at the end of Chapter VIII, if the anchors can be run out, the modern racers, with their powerful winches, can almost drag themselves across dry land. Yet how many boats have been lost because they have gone aground and have not had an adequate dinghy on which an anchor could be rowed out to windward?

The R.O.R.C. racing rule is correct in principle in requiring every yacht to carry a tender capable of laying an anchor, so that kedging off will be possible in case of grounding. Practically speaking, however, the regulation is just about meaningless, since it does not specify the size of the anchor to be used or the conditions under which carrying it out should be possible. For example, the rule could require that the dinghy be capable of rowing an anchor out when a 15-knot, or better a 20-knot, breeze is blowing.

In the summer of 1975, a number of ocean racers were carrying little one-man inflatable dinghies to fulfill the requirement. A dinghy of this type would hardly float the anchor and twelve feet of chain, let alone the anchor line and a man to do the rowing. With all of these crammed inside the dinghy, there would be no hope of ever rowing out to windward in any sort of breeze.

When we arrived in Cowes for the Fastnet Race that summer, we saw a number of boats lying aground on their sides, left by the falling tide. They had run aground, did not come off immediately, could not be poled off with spinnaker poles, and not having decent dinghies with which anchors could be run out, they could not be winched off. Hence, when the tide went out, they lay down flat in the mud, one of them with her keel bent substantially out of shape.

Most of these boats were stranded until the tide came in. The situation probably could have been avoided if they had had really good dinghies and could have thrown over one or two anchors and run numerous lines out to them. And yet some seamen say rigid dinghies are not necessary!

Many people feel that in most cases, when kedging off is to be done, someone on board should feed the line to the person rowing out the anchor. Admittedly, the drag of the line through the water can be considerable, but this procedure is much safer than carrying a big coil of line in the dinghy. Many a man has drowned, or narrowly escaped drowning, because he either capsized the dinghy or caught his foot in the coil of line as he dropped the anchor overboard. Further, there is nothing more frustrating than dropping an anchor, rowing back to the boat, and discovering that the anchor has been put down thirty feet too far from the boat and the anchor line won't reach.

MATERIALS

Wood

TRADITIONAL CARVEL-PLANKED CONSTRUCTION: Until recently, in southeast Maine and in Nova Scotia, beautiful little rowing dinghies used for fishing were still being made with carvel-planked (smooth-planked) construction. Exactly why this type of construction persisted so long in those areas I don't know, and I will leave the question to the experts. The problem with a carvel-built dinghy is that keeping it in good shape is very difficult, and when it dries out or works, the planks must be refastened or recaulked. Weight for weight, it is doubtful whether a carvel-built dinghy can be as strong as a lapstrake dinghy, or one built of fiber glass for that matter.

TRADITIONAL LAPSTRAKE (CLINKER-BUILT) CONSTRUCTION: The lapstrake method of construction is definitely not dead. The greatest advantage of a dinghy with this type of wood construction is that when it gets old and begins to leak, if one only has time, patience, and a small boy to help, one can tighten the rivets, stop the leaks, and give the dinghy many more years of life. One should be very careful, however, not to overtighten the rivets and thereby split the framing or planking.

About 1969, I bought at a very good price a secondhand lapstrake dinghy of uncertain age. It was spruce-planked and copper-riveted, and had been built by Ned Williams, of Cowes, Isle of Wight. Everyone thought it was comparatively new, though it must have been at least fifteen or twenty years old. When it unfortunately went adrift, after five years of use, it still looked like a new toy. Admittedly, it did require a good deal of maintenance, but not that much more than a fiber-glass dinghy, and in cost (especially as compared to that of a rubber dinghy, which would have lasted only two years), we were way ahead.

Although Ned Williams has died, and his son is no longer building lapstrake dinghies, good small dinghies of similar shape can still be obtained in England or Ireland. In shopping for such a dinghy, shipyards should be avoided, since their prices are high. By contrast, a small builder, perhaps working in his own backyard, at this writing typically charges, in U.S. terms, thirty to thirty-five dollars per foot of dinghy length for a fully finished, fully equipped dinghy—varnished, with oars, oarlocks, the works. Compare these prices to those asked for standard fiber-glass dinghies, and one wonders. In the United States, too, if one noses around, one can find people who are still willing to build a lapstrake dinghy and charge a reasonable amount—comparable to what one would pay for a fiber-glass dinghy.

Further, it should be noted that the cost of finishing a beautiful lapstrake dinghy contributes substantially to the price. A few small boatyards that specialize in building fine wooden dinghies are happy to sell them unfinished (needing paint and varnish) or semifinished (needing oarlocks, floorboards, thwarts, and the like) at considerably reduced prices. Because the situation is ever-changing, no names and addresses are being specified here. However, Jonathan Wilson, of *WoodenBoat* (for address, see Appendix), and John Gardner, at the Museum of Maritime American in Mystic, Connecticut, are certainly able to recommend various small boatyards that build wooden dinghies.

As anyone can see by visiting the Thousand Islands Museum, in Clayton, New York, or any antique-boat show, or by attending the small-craft workshop at Mystic Seaport, a well-designed, well-built, and well-cared-for wooden dinghy can last a very long time, giving a tremendous amount of pleasure and immeasurable pride.

Glass-Reinforced Plywood

Although some boatbuilders advise very strongly against building a large boat of wood covered with fiber glass, few disagree that sheet-plywood dinghies reinforced with fiber glass, especially fiber-glass tape, can be light, strong, and long-lasting. George ("Porgy") Rapier, of St. George's, Grenada, for many years built the Sabot over a form. He used light sheet plywood held together by fiber-glass tape. These boats were unbelievably light, and Porgy, who was a skilled carpenter, could knock them out in an unbelievably short time.

When this method is used, putting together the backbone and frame is half the problem, but if four or five people who want dinghies of this type pitch in, once they are started they can pop them out at a very rapid rate. This type of dinghy is usually built with a plank keel. Sheet plywood is glued and fastened to the keel, chine, seat riser, and gunwale. There is no framing at all, the midship section being held in place by the center thwart. All corners are reinforced with fiber-glass tape.

21. Good fiber-glass dinghies.

Fiber Glass

Properly designed fiber-glass dinghies (Photo 21) are excellent. They are few and far between, but they can be found. Most boat owners seem to have forgotten a few facts. For one thing, fiber glass is not very resistant to abrasion; hence, sliding a dinghy up on the beach chafes the bottom at a rapid rate, and frequent reinforcement of the fiber glass may be necessary. Only a few builders correctly attach iroko, teak, or oak skids, further protected by half-oval brass strips, to take the chafe. Second, most builders (Jarvis Newman, of Cape Cod, and Dyer are among the notable exceptions) fail to recognize the necessity for an adequate wooden gunwale around the edge of the dinghy, to which a fender may be readily secured. Where the manufacturer does not provide a wooden gunwale, one can usually be installed—epoxy-glued to the fiber-glass shell and secured with copper rivets or bronze screws (Drawing 123). A canvas-covered rubber fender is then secured to the gunwale with copper tacks, as described later in this chapter.

STRAIGHT FIBER GLASS: The most common type of dinghy con-

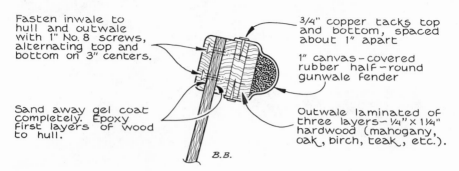

Fasten inwale to hull and outwale with 1" No. 8 screws, alternating top and bottom on 3" centers.

3/4" copper tacks top and bottom, spaced about 1" apart

1" canvas – covered rubber half – round gunwale fender

Sand away gel coat completely. Epoxy first layers of wood to hull.

Outwale laminated of three layers– 1/4" x 1 1/4" hardwood (mahogany, oak, birch, teak, etc.).

B.B.

123. Recommended gunwale construction for fiber-glass dinghy.

struction is straight fiber glass. Careful design is necessary if a dinghy built in this way is to stand any rough usage and still be light enough to carry up the beach, hoist on board, and what-have-you. For years, there was a complete dearth of decent fiber-glass dinghies. Most of those on the market were throwaway models—poorly designed, poorly constructed, with inadequate oars and oarlocks. Gradually, during the last few years, a handful of manufacturers, in most cases fairly small boat shops, have begun to build some really superb fiber-glass dinghies, that row well, tow well, sail well—and operate very nicely with a small outboard. (Of course, the outboard must be of the right size. On a rowing dinghy with a beautiful heart-shaped stern, a 5- or 10-h.p. outboard, even at half throttle, pushes the boat too fast—it just digs a hole and sits in it. A correctly shaped rowing dinghy will operate adequately even in high wind conditions with almost any of the very minimal outboards on the market today.)

Unfortunately, because of the new and completely unrealistic regulations instituted by the U.S. Coast Guard concerning reserve buoyancy requirements of boats, many of these builders are either going, or will go, out of business. The Coast Guard just will not let them build a properly designed dinghy—all in the name of progress.

A great advantage of the fiber-glass dinghy is the fact that one can often buy the bare shell from the molder and finish it oneself. With sufficient time and effort—and attention to the advice in this chapter— one can end up with a truly practical, long-lasting fiber-glass dinghy. It should especially be noted that any straight fiber-glass dinghy *must* be provided with buoyancy. Otherwise, if it capsizes, it will sink. And in the process, one might just as well provide it with enough buoyancy so that it can serve as a back-up lifeboat, as described later in this chapter.

FOAM PLANK: This method of building boats, in which strips of foam are fiber-glassed into place inside a molded hull, is quite old, but it has been used for dinghies only recently. Paul Johnson, of *Venus*, has employed it in constructing his two-sectioned double-ender, and is most enthusiastic, reporting that the result is a light, rigid hull with built-in flotation.

CONSTRUCTION DETAILS

SEATS

Rowing Positions

Our Ned Williams dinghy was wonderful for rowing because there were two possible positions. With three people on board, it balanced beautifully if one person sat in the bow and one in the stern, while the rower sat on the center thwart. With only two people in the dinghy, the rower sat on the forward thwart, and all was still in balance. Unfortunately, the dinghy should have been a little longer; when two people were rowing, the person sitting forward tended to bang his knuckles on the back of the person on the center thwart. An additional four to six inches of separation between the thwarts, which were thirty-six inches center to center, would have eliminated this problem.

Our present lapstrake dinghy is not a particularly good one. Among the problems is the fact that the forward thwart is too far forward, where the boat is so narrow one cannot swing a decent pair of oars. The dinghy rows fine with three people on board, but is very difficult to row with only two. We need a new dinghy!

In a small pram, moving one's weight a few inches forward or aft changes the trim drastically. Also, it is impossible to row from the forward position in a small pram; the act of pulling the oar depresses the bow, and the weight of the person pulling the oar farther depresses the bow, so the pram may ship water and then an impromptu swim may result in short order. Therefore, on a pram of six or seven feet, a fore-and-aft rowing bench (Drawing 124) may be preferable to a thwart. If, in addition, a small foredeck is installed, the dinghy will be much less likely to swamp in a head sea. With a fore-and-aft bench, the middle of one's bottom is eighteen inches forward of the oarlocks when one person is rowing; with two people on board, the oarsman slides a little farther forward. Rowing is not quite so comfortable then, but it is possible; if one wants to be a real pro, one can install a second

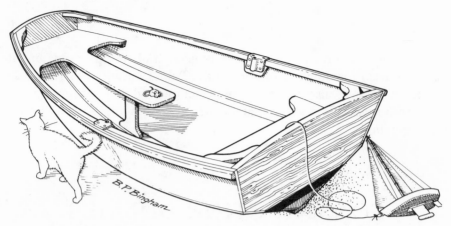

124. On a small dinghy, a fore-and-aft seat may be more practical than a thwart.

set of oarlocks, about eight inches forward of the usual oarlock position.

Critical Measurements

The height of the seats will frequently be determined by the use of the boat; when the hold is shallow, the seats will often have to be higher than desired to leave room underneath for fish, beer, ballast, or the like. For a yacht dinghy to row well and be comfortable for the oarsman, the seats should be approximately twelve inches above the floorboards and seven inches below the gunwale. Hence, the yacht dinghy should have a depth of nineteen inches from the gunwale to the floorboards. The total depth from the gunwale to the keel can be substantially greater than this, since some designs—that of the Saints dinghy, for example—allow for a considerable bilge below the floorboards. However, a dinghy with these dimensions may be larger than most yachts can conveniently carry.

The distance between the seats is also critical. In a dinghy of average size, with a forty-two-inch beam and seven-foot oars, the two rowing positions should be about forty inches apart, if possible. Otherwise, the forward rower will continually poke the after rower in the middle of the back. When two people row, if the oars are short, each person should use his own set; if the oars are long, each person should swing one oar. The person rowing on the starboard side of the boat should sit on the port side, and vice versa.

Seat Construction

On dinghy hulls of very light wood or thin fiber glass, there is a hard spot at the point of contact with the seat. Squeezing the dinghy be-

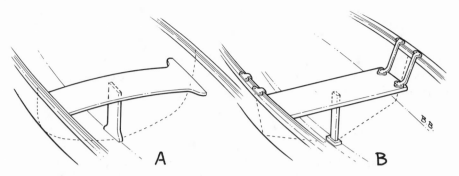

A   B

125. Types of seat installation which eliminate the hard spot caused by contact of hull with thwart: pilot-gig thwart (A) bends when hull is subjected to an impact; Dyer thwart (B) is not connected to hull sides but
instead joined to gunwale by means of bronze brackets.

tween two boats, or banging hard against the side, may easily result
in a hole going all the way through at this spot. Turning the dinghy
over can also put a bad strain on this area.

To eliminate this problem, the very lightly constructed pilot gigs
of the southwest coast of Ireland, the Scilly Isles, and southwest England, have curved seats (Drawing 125A), each with a center post
underneath to support the weight of the rower. When one of these
gigs bangs a ship while coming alongside, the seat springs up, allowing
the whole hull to flex. The Dyer dinghy now has a similar seat (Drawing 125B). A light center support is provided, and the seat is tied
into the gunwale by bronze brackets which allow a good deal of flexing
and thus eliminate the hard spot in the side of the boat. If one cannot
obtain the brackets from Dyer, one can improvise by bending brass or
stainless-steel pipe, flattening the ends, and bolting it to the seat and
the gunwale.

On some boats, like our lapstrake dinghy, the center and after seats
are removable, to allow stowage of a smaller dinghy inside, as shown
later in this chapter.

Finish

The oarsman's seat should be left bare, since otherwise, when he
pulls hard on the oars, he may slide right off and end up on the bottom
of the dinghy. Throughout the world, on the small boats which fishermen still row, the seats are left bare. Also, in areas where the dinghy
is fancily painted and kept like a yacht, although the seat may be
painted, the center section, where one sits, will be left unpainted.
Manufacturers should stop installing seats of varnished mahogany in
their dinghies, and use bare teak instead. Their excuse for not doing
so is that teak is expensive. But if the cost of putting four good coats

of varnish on the mahogany, and sanding between coats, is taken into account, mahogany seats are seen to be at least as expensive as those made of bare teak.

FLOORBOARDS

Like seats, floorboards should not be varnished, but instead should be made of thin teak or other wood that can be left bare. John Gardner, of the Mystic museum, reports that in the old days chestnut was used for dinghy floorboards, because it did not have to be painted and was not turned dark by salt water. Painting and varnishing seats and floorboards is a dead loss, yet some builders persist in equipping dinghies with seats varnished to a high gloss, and with slick, varnished mahogany floorboards—very difficult to maintain and keep looking good, and sneaky traps to catch the unwary and throw them to the bottom when they step aboard. Among the most perfect nonskid surfaces is the one made by God—teak. It is so easy to install teak seats and teak floorboards, which merely need to be scrubbed. They would certainly be worth the small additional expense.

Securing Floorboards

On the modern fiber-glass dinghy, securing the floorboards is usually pretty simple; one just cuts strips of ⅛-inch or ³⁄₁₆-inch teak, fits them into place, and fastens them to the inside bottom of the dinghy wih epoxy glue.

On a wooden dinghy, the bottom of the boat is divided into five sections. I recommend the following method for fastening floorboards: The center floorboard is secured on top of the keel, over U-shaped fittings which are a drive fit into the keel (Drawing 126A). Or it may be set over bronze eyes threaded into, or bolted through, the keel (Drawing 126B). The fittings or eyes protrude through slots cut into the center floorboard, which is then held in place by tapered wooden wedges

126. Effective methods of securing the center dinghy floorboard.

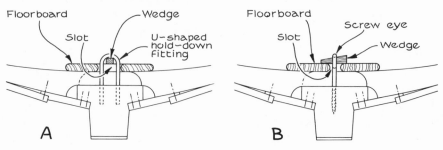

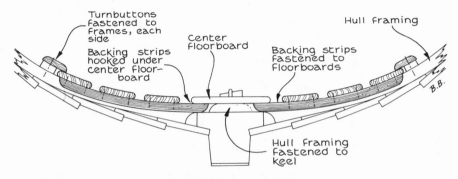

127. Recommended method of installing dinghy floorboards.

driven into these fittings or eyes. The remaining floorboards are divided into four sections, each consisting of three floorboards, ¼ inch thick, to which three backing strips are secured by copper rivets or bronze screws. The backing strips should extend inboard of the floorboards, to latch underneath the center floorboard. The thickness of the backing strips should be the same as, or slightly less than, that of the frames, so that the load of someone walking on the floorboards is taken by the frames rather than the planking. When the floorboards have been shoved into place, they are secured by turnbuttons, one on each outboard edge (Drawing 127).

FOOT BRACES

I think every dinghy should have a foot brace of some sort. This can increase the oarsman's pulling power amazingly. Sometimes, an oarsman can brace himself by jamming his little toes against the frames on the side of the dinghy; other times, when the dinghy is of suitable length, he may be able to use the after thwart as a brace. However, it is preferable to install a foot brace that is adjustable, for use by anyone, of any height (Drawing 128).

128. An adjustable foot brace will increase one's rowing power amazingly.

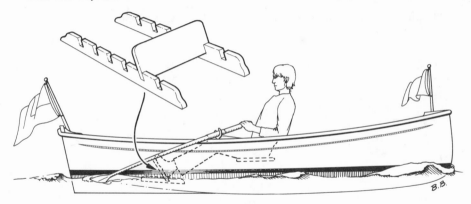

FENDERS (RUB GUARDS)

Every dinghy should have a really good, soft, nonstaining rub
strake, properly secured so that it does not come off every two weeks.
The expenditure for this fender is more than counterbalanced by the
resulting reduction in time devoted to sanding, painting, and repairing
dings and dangs on the topsides.

On sharp-stemmed dinghies, providing an adequate fender for the
stem is extremely difficult. I fought this problem for the better part of
my life, and finally the late Jack Carstarphen, of *Maverick,* showed me
a solution. Find an old, punctured, discarded fender, the type with an
eye in each end. Then cut an end off, put a small split in its bottom
edge, and firmly screw the thing over the stemhead. The result is a big,
soft fender that will not damage the mother ship, even if it gets caught
under the overhanging stern.

On most fiber-glass dinghies, securing a fender so that it will stay
on is almost impossible. However, a few manufacturers install an inner
and outer wooden gunwale secured with glue and copper rivets or
bronze screws through the fiber-glass shell, similar to the one shown in
Drawing 123. When this gunwale is provided, a half-round or three-
quarter-round canvas-covered gunwale guard may be purchased, secured at the bow of the boat, then stretched down both sides under
tension, and fastened to the wooden gunwale by copper tacks one inch
apart. A fender that is installed in this fashion will remain in place for
years.

Two cautions must be observed. First, the copper tacks must be
tested with a magnet, to make sure that they are not just copperplated.
Second, on many dinghies a three-quarter-round fender tends to lift
the oar out of the oarlock; if a check of the oarlocks indicates that
this would occur, a half-round fender should be chosen (Drawing 129).

129. The dinghy gunwale fender may interfere with rowing unless properly
    chosen and installed.

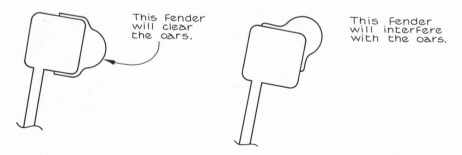

This fender
will clear
the oars.

This fender
will interfere
with the oars.

TRINKA 10

designer: Bruce Bingham

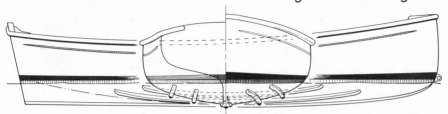

130. Dinghy skids along the keel and bilges not only prevent extreme bottom chafe, but add immeasurably to the strength of the boat. They must be through-bolted to make possible periodic replacement, and well bedded to ensure watertightness.

SKIDS

One of the major problems with fiber-glass dinghies is that, almost without exception, good keel and bilge skids are not provided. Fiber glass does not like chafe; sliding a dinghy up over the edge of a dock, or along a shingle beach, is a great way to ruin it, unless it is equipped with good skids. Even sliding a dinghy on a sand beach rapidly wears off the gel coat along the keel and the bilges. Water penetration starts, followed by delamination and all sorts of other difficulties. The fiber-glass dinghy requires skids not only on the center of the bottom but also on both bilges (Drawing 130). The skids should be made of replaceable wood, covered with half-oval bronze or stainless steel. They should be at least one inch deep on the bilges and one inch deep on the keel. A dinghy thus equipped can be slid over comparatively rough ground without the risk of chafe on the bilges or of holes punched in the bottom by rocks.

DRAIN PLUGS

Every dinghy should be provided with two drain plugs. One should be installed near the center line amidships, for use when the dinghy is being scrubbed down as it sits on deck on skids, or on the dock. Water may be splashed into the dinghy, and when the plug is removed, the water will drain out. Similarly, rain water can be drained from a dinghy left sitting on the dock.

The second drain plug should be installed in the stern, as close to the center line of the transom as possible. When a dinghy is pulled up on a beach, all the water runs to the stern. If the dinghy must be tipped on its side for draining, the hull is strained, since all the weight rests on the middle part of the gunwale; also, invariably large quantities of sand end up inside the dinghy, and on a shingle beach, the topsides get chewed up. However, if there is a drain plug in the stern, the dinghy can easily be drained while remaining upright. Similarly, while it is on the beach, one can throw a few buckets of water into it, and wash all the sand and mud and fish scales out through the stern. Furthermore, with the stern drain opened the dinghy will bail itself while being towed, but of course one must then remember to close the drain.

The standard dinghy plug—the plastic affair built for the racing dinghy—is cheap, and easy to install, but rather small. Cleaning out the dinghy will be easier if the stern plug is 1 inch or 1½ inches in diameter, but finding a plug of this size is most difficult.

TOWING EYES

Every dinghy should have a good towing eye secured well down in the bow, close to the waterline. The towing eye must be through-bolted, and the painter should be well secured to it, in such a manner that it will not chafe. For example, it may be tied in by a bowline with a bight (two turns through the eye) or a fisherman's bend. In any case, the end of the knot should be moused, since otherwise it may come undone when the dinghy is bouncing around; indeed, I lost my beautiful lapstrake Ned Williams dinghy on the south coast of Anguilla when the knot (which apparently had been secured, and had been in the line for weeks) came undone one night; the dinghy promptly took off for Panama.

Situations of this sort can be avoided by splicing the painter into the bow eye (with a substantial thimble to eliminate chafe), but what one gains in one way, one may lose in another. Indeed, the fact that a dinghy painter was spliced into the bow eye almost caused the end of my sailing career fifteen years ago. We had decided to go spearfishing, and had proceeded to a good spot between Petit Martinique and Petit St. Vincent. We tied our collapsible four-pronged Swedish anchor onto a twenty-foot line, which was then tied onto a fifty-foot dinghy painter, to give us plenty of scope and good holding. When we tossed the anchor over, it held, and all was well.

One of the party stayed in the dinghy taking photographs, while two of us went spearfishing. After about fifteen minutes, my companion decided the current was too strong for fishing, so he swam back to the dinghy and climbed in. Just then, I shot a beautiful five-pound red snapper, which was obviously going to make a good dinner. But as I headed for the dinghy, I spotted a rather large shark, that started circling, and I decided that he'd better have the red snapper, rather than me. I dopped the fish off the end of the spear, and while the shark swam down and gobbled it up, I started swimming hard. But the current had increased, and I found myself having great difficulty in swimming back to the dinghy. I yelled to my two companions to pull up the anchor and come and get me in the dinghy. They started pulling up the anchor, but a couple of minutes later, they still hadn't reached me, so I yelled again for them to pull up the anchor and get moving. They screamed back that they couldn't. The anchor was fouled on some coral. The trouble was, the knot securing the dinghy anchor to the painter was still fifteen feet under water, and neither of my friends could dive well enough to reach and untie it. They could not undo the painter at the bow of the dinghy because it was spliced in. And they could not cut the line because neither of them had a knife (no seaman should go anywhere without a knife in his pocket). The shark was now appearing much more interested. I dropped my spear gun, covered the last few yards in an Olympic-type sprint, took hold of the stern of the dinghy, and rolled in, with the shark not very far behind. *Moral:* Everyone should always carry a knife, and one wonders about splicing the painter into the bow of the dinghy.

BUOYANCY

Most dinghies are drastically lacking in buoyancy when swamped. For example, fiber-glass dinghies (unless they are of foam-plank construction or have integral flotation tanks) will sink like a stone. For this reason most of them have foam buoyancy blocks secured under the seats; but in many cases, the blocks are far too small.

For safety's sake, every dinghy should be so buoyant that even when it is fully swamped, one person can climb on board and bail it out. (The U.S. Coast Guard standard is even higher.) Wooden dinghies, which do float, seldom float high enough to permit bailing in this manner. Additional buoyancy can be provided in a number of ways. Styrofoam blocks can be secured under the seats. Inflatable dinghy buoyancy bags, like those carried in racing dinghies, can be secured under or along the seats. A final method is to secure the yacht's air-filled fenders with shock cord inside the dinghy. This serves a dual purpose, since it provides stowage space for the fenders, which would otherwise be taking up space in the lazaret, and also provides enough buoyancy to float a swamped dinghy. When the fenders are needed—because the boat is alongside the dock—the dinghy will not be needed, so the fenders can be removed from the dinghy and used on the yacht. When the dinghy is needed, the yacht will be away from the dock and will obviously not need the fenders, so they can be secured in the dinghy.

A rigid dinghy with added buoyancy, such as that provided by a yacht's fenders, serves as a good back-up life raft. The need for such a backup is made apparent by experiences like those of the Robertson family, set adrift when whales sank their boat, who survived for about three weeks in their dinghy after their life raft gave way. This dinghy was of rigid construction. If it had had adequate flotation, obtained by one of the methods just described, the long incredible journey certainly would have been a lot less nerve-racking. And Maurice and Maralyn Bailey, who spent 117 days adrift after their boat sank, would have had great difficulty in surviving if they had not had a back-up dinghy—in their case, like their life raft, inflatable.

OARS

The oars available today are not only expensive but also in many instances rather poorly designed. All too frequently, the makers overlook the fact that although an oar made of a heavy wood like oak or ash lasts forever, it functions very badly unless it is trimmed down to minimum dimensions.

MATERIALS

Spruce

Spruce is commonly used for oars because it is light and tough. It does have a disadvantage in that a spruce oar must be larger in diameter than an ash oar. On a windy day, spruce oars, being light, may practically blow out of the oarlocks when feathered. Also, spruce is very prone to rot, so it is not at all uncommon for spruce oars, as they get old, to break at the oarlocks as a result of rot under the chafing leather.

Ash

Ash oars are by far the best available for general use. Ash is tough and springy. Although the wood is heavy, a correctly proportioned ash oar will weigh little more than a spruce oar, because its dimensions can be much smaller than those of the spruce oar. I had one pair of seven-foot French oars that were incredibly long-lasting. (In the end, one of them was stolen.) They had been picked up in Martinique in an emergency about fifteen years ago. They were good oars, but so heavy that they were practically impossible to swing. We trimmed them down three or four times, and the final result was a pair of oars light enough for even my ninety-pound wife and my small daughter to use.

Sassafras

Sassafras is a light, tough wood—heavier than spruce, much less prone to rot, and excellent for oars. But one has to be a real lover of wood, and a detective, to find any today. Oars made of sassafras should have dimensions slightly larger than those specified for oars of oak or ash in the following section.

SHAPE AND SIZE

Basically, an oar shaft should be so tapered—especially if made of oak or ash—that when one holds the loom in one hand, places the other hand midway down the oar, touches the blade to the deck, and leans, there is some flexing. An oar that does not flex is too heavy, and will be hard to swing and lacking in power at the end of the stroke.

The type of tapering that is desirable for oars made of a heavy wood is illustrated by the final dimensions of the oars from Martinique which we cut down: the shaft 1½ inches in diameter, tapering to 1⅛ inches before the blade; the blade 4½ inches wide and 24 inches long, tapering in thickness from 1⅛ inches down to ⅜ of an inch.

Length

One reason most people use outboards in this day and age is that rowing a yacht dinghy is sometimes almost impossible. In many cases, the difficulty is the fault of a badly shaped, badly made dinghy with poor oarlocks. But even with a good dinghy rowing is a problem if—as often occurs—the oars are the wrong length. On the other hand, any old barge box can be rowed in smooth water, given a decent set of oars. Even on the little inflatable, which has a deserved reputation of being very hard to row, the rowing can be vastly improved by use of a pair of good oars of the correct length.

When oars are too short, the oarsman finds it difficult to get them

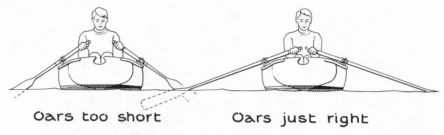

Oars too short   Oars just right

131. Effect of oar length on rowing angle.

down into the water, and his strokes develop little power (Drawing 131). Throughout the world, boatbuilders, old fishermen, old yacht skippers, all mention the same approximate figure for the length of an oar: it should be twice the beam of the boat plus 6 inches. This means that the smallest rubber dinghies should be rowed with eight-foot oars, the larger ones with ten- or twelve-foot oars. Perhaps if the correct oars were used, the reputation of rubber dinghies as being difficult to row would disappear or at least diminish.

Few dinghies of any type on the market today have oars of anywhere near the proper size. Most dinghies, no matter what their length, have a beam of at least 40 inches, and therefore would require oars of at least 86 inches (i.e., over seven feet); a 44-inch-wide dinghy requires oars of 94 inches (almost eight feet). Even the smallest dinghy, with a beam of 36 inches, requires oars over six feet long. In other words, the oars for a short, fat dinghy may be the same length as, or possibly longer than, the dinghy itself. These are desirable even though, unfortunately, they will be too long to be stowed inside the boat.

The inexperienced individual will immediately say, "Well, I cannot swing an oar that is six, seven, or eight feet long," but that is an absolutely ridiculous assumption, as shown by our personal experience. Our kids have all learned to row the little six-foot pram. Our son was first taught at the age of five, with four-foot oars, but though he is deaf, and at that time did not talk well, within a few weeks of learning to row he made it known that he wanted the six-foot oars. And he was able to use them.

The oars on our larger dinghy are of a length—eight feet—which many people maintain is too hard to handle. However, my wife Trich, who is only 5 feet 2 inches tall and weighs between ninety and ninety-five pounds soaking wet, happily rows with these oars. In calm water, even my son can manage them, though with some difficulty. Similarly, when I had a thirteen-foot Saints dinghy, with a beam at the rail of five feet, one person could easily swing a pair of ten-foot oars, and when my wife and I rowed together, each with one oar, sitting on alternate seats, we had no trouble swinging twelve-foot oars, although neither of us is a large individual. We could make the dinghy fly just about as fast as if we had a 4-h.p. outboard.

So, measure the beam of your dinghy at the rowing thwart. Measure your oars. Remember the rough rule of thumb: the length of the oars should be twice the beam of the dinghy, plus 6 inches. And one last observation—dinghies with two rowing positions should have two pairs of oars, since the forward thwart is shorter than the main thwart and therefore requires oars that are slightly shorter.

Blade Size

The correct size of an oar blade is determined by the use to which the oar will be put. The scull, as the oar for a racing shell is called, has a long, light, spoon-shaped blade, with its end of large size (Drawing 132), to provide maximum forward motion in proportion to the amount of effort expended. Similarly, the oars for Adirondack guide boats, which are used on sheltered lakes and streams, have large blades. In areas where the waters are rougher, the blades are correspondingly smaller, the ultimate example being those of the oars on the curraghs of the west coast of Ireland, which are rowed out to sea in exposed areas continually swept with westerly gales. There, while rowing in a head sea, the oarsman does not wish to feather, since the effect of a wave, or the wind, hitting the blade may be to throw the oar out of the oarlock. The curragh oars have long, narrow blades. The fisherman of the Lesser Antilles, who rows into high easterly winds and swell, has the same problem, and although the West Indian has never seen a curragh oar, he has developed a similar one—long and narrow, and used without feathering.

In blade width, the average oar for a yacht dinghy should be somewhere between the curragh oar and the shell oar.

132. Sculls—oars styled like those used for racing shells—can increase rowing power by as much as 25 percent through the reduction of stalling, but are suitable only for calm waters.

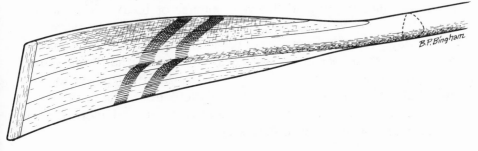

133. Herringbone stitch is recommended for sewing an effective and lasting leather onto the oar.

CHAFE PREVENTION

The standard, traditional method of preventing chafe on an oar is to cover the section in contact with the oarlock with leather. The leather is soaked in water for two or three hours, and placed on the oar while wet. One method of attaching the leather is to tack it into place; when it dries, it shrinks up tight, and it lasts for many years. However, there is no doubt that the copper tacks weaken the oar, and allow water to penetrate, causing the oar to rot and eventually break. For this reason, many people prefer to sew the leather onto the oar with a herringbone stitch (Drawing 133). Regardless of whether the leather is tacked or sewn, it is important that the seam be lined up with the vertical edge of the blade. Then, when the oar is in use, the stitching will face upward; the leather will chafe on its forward, bottom, and after faces, but not on the top face, where the seam is.

Recently, plastic sleeves of various diameters have come onto the market. These are slid over the oar and jammed into place. People also use fiber-glass tape for chafe protection, as we did at one point simply because we could not find leather or plastic. A disadvantage of both the plastic sleeve and the fiber glass is that when one pulls hard, the oar protected with one of these tends to ride up in the oarlock, so the chance of its jumping out of the oarlock is greater than it would be if leather were used.

Tip Chafe Prevention

On a well-made, well-balanced oar, the tip is relatively thin and therefore rather fragile and likely to splinter or break when the oar is used as a pole to push off the beach, rocks, or what-have-you. In the old days, beautifully made copper chafe tips, which were secured to the oar with copper tacks, were available in most hardware stores. Today, these tips are practically unobtainable, so people cover the last few inches of the oar with fiber-glass or Dynel tape secured with epoxy. As the tape wears away, it can be sanded down, and more can be added, secured with epoxy, as necessary.

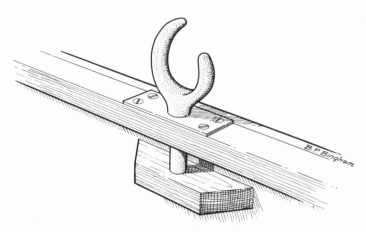

134. The typical British oarlock is likely to hold the oar securely even when rowing is done in heavy chop. Its installation is very strong.

OARLOCKS

When a seven- or eight-foot oar is swung, especially if the oarsman's feet are well placed on an adjustable brace, a tremendous amount of strain is placed on the oarlock. An oarlock of the standard American type may pull right out after a few months of hard rowing. Therefore, I recommend that oarlocks of the British type (Drawing 134) be purchased, or if necessary, custom-made. Here, the load on the oarlock is taken not only on the gunwale but on the lower block, which can be securely riveted to the sheer strake of a wooden boat (or fiber-glassed to a fiber-glass boat) and also lapped over the frame (on a fiber-glass dinghy, the block may also be bolted to the shell).

The exact distance between the after edge of the rower's seat and the pivot point of the oarlock is rather critical. I have found a distance of eleven inches to be almost universal on well-designed dinghies.

SAILING

SAILING RIGS

A sailing rig for a dinghy is not essential, but it is a wonderful addition, and will make life much more pleasurable, especially if there are small fry in the crew. The rig should be simple and easily repairable. After all, sailing a dinghy is not done to win the Olympics, but just to change the pace and have some fun. I think the sprit rig (Drawing 135),

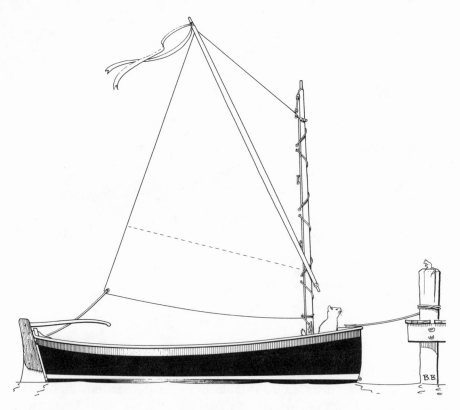

135. The sprit rig is quickly set up, and is easy to handle and convenient to stow.

with or without boom, is one of the best and simplest for the small sailing dinghy. If it is to be used by two small fry, one can mount the mast a little farther aft, and set a genoa jib or genoa staysail, as used by West Indian fishermen. This provides one more string to pull, so both mariners are kept busy. A great advantage of this rig is that all the spars will store inside the boat. Some Marconi-rigged dinghies, such as the Trinka, are designed with masts that separate in the middle, so that, again, the mast and boom can be stored inside the boat.

A sailing dinghy does not necessarily need a centerboard or daggerboard. A single leeboard on one side of the dinghy, as described in *OSY*-I (Ch. IX), is more than sufficient.

A wonderful description of a sailing rig for a small dinghy that is so simple that in a single day one can do everything required (including the making of the sail) is to be found in an article by Des Sleightholme in *Yachting Monthly* for October, 1973.

Recently, an unusual new rig for sailing dinghies that may be very useful has come onto the market (for supplier, see Appendix). Invented by Lauri Katailer, from Finland, this rig just clamps onto the stern of the dinghy like an outboard (Drawing 136). The mast, the

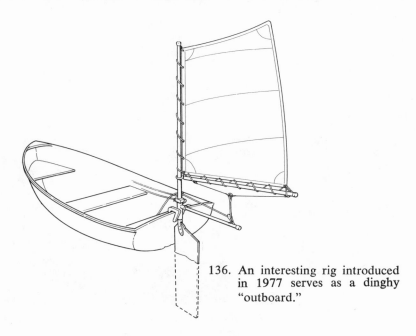

136. An interesting rig introduced in 1977 serves as a dinghy "outboard."

sail (a four-sided spritsail), the combination centerboard and rudder, and the bumpkin are all part of a single unit, which can be fastened to any dinghy. It has been tested on the small pram, the moderate-sized stemhead dinghy, and even on the rubber dinghy with a wooden stern to take an outboard. The numerous English yachtsmen who have tried it have all come back, scratching their heads, to report that while not thoroughly efficient, it does work. This rig can be stored in a box not much larger than an outboard, and it can be used on any dinghy that has a fairly rigid transom. With no holes to drill, no centerboard box to construct, no leeboard to mount, it may be a giant step forward.

SAILING SURFBOARDS

The individual seeking higher performance than is obtainable with the spirit rig on a dinghy, had best consider switching to one of the sailing surfboards—the Sunfish, Windsurfer, Minifish, Sailfish, or Hobie 10. It must be borne in mind, however, that a boat of this type is not a substitute for a tender. In my opinion, the best sailing board for use with the average sailboat, is the Hobie 10. The Sunfish (Photo 22) and similar models certainly provide superior performance, but they have definite disadvantages. Stowing something thirteen or fourteen feet long is very difficult on a sailboat of average size, and even on the large motor sailers, stowing boards such as the Sunfish may be a problem, necessitating special racks, hold-downs, and the like. On smaller boats they really get in the way. Also, getting them up onto the beach may be a little difficult unless there are two strong people. However, the Hobie 10, being ten feet long and forty-two inches wide at the stern,

22. *Sunfish.* LARRY METZLER

can be stowed inside an eleven-foot dinghy. On *Iolaire,* we place it inside a dinghy which is kept right side up; but I am sure that if we put our minds to it, and built a new dinghy and rack, we could carry both the Hobie 10 and the dinghy upside down over the skylight, on center. On a larger boat that carries a Boston Whaler, the Hobie 10 can be dropped inside the Whaler and secured there while the latter is being towed (Drawing 137). A fifteen-foot Whaler should not mind the additional weight—ninety pounds—while towing.

Indeed, this Hobie is so light, at ninety pounds fully rigged, that two fairly light individuals—such as Trich and myself, or one of us and Dory (our thirteen-year-old daughter)—can pick it up and carry it to the beach with no trouble at all. Obviously, it is not a good weight carrier. It's a single-hander for one heavy person, but with two light-weights aboard (children or small adults) when the wind is blowing the sailing can be exciting. Unfortunately, this wonderful boat is no longer in production. Let us hope that someone will again produce a sailing surfboard of this type in the very near future.

Another excellent sailing board for the young and active is the Windsurfer. If the yacht is large enough to carry two of these, the younger members of the crew can race themselves to exhaustion.

137. A small surfboard-type sailing dinghy, such as the Hobie 10, can often be stowed inside a larger dinghy with a removable thwart.

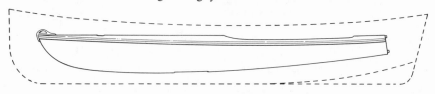

OUTBOARDS

There is a good deal of disagreement about the selection of an out-board, but a few facts should be remembered. If a light dinghy, rigid or inflatable, must go fast—to tow a water skier, for example—a complicated, high-speed, high-rpm American-type outboard is necessary. However, if one has a small dinghy just to chug around in, or to use as a yawl boat or towboat for a yacht which has no engine, or when the yacht engine is not working, one should find an outboard with a large, slow-turning propeller, which will provide maximum thrust.

The difference in thrust between a small, fast-turning propeller and a large, slow-turning one is well illustrated by an experience that Chet Hewitt had in St. Thomas about twenty years ago. He owned a little Tortola sloop which was powered in flat calm by a standard 10-h.p. high-rpm Johnson attached to a removable A-frame on the side of the boat. When the Johnson died, he somehow obtained a 4-h.p. Seagull Century Plus (with reduction gear) for his weekend cruise. All was well until the wind died as he was coming into St. Thomas harbor. He mounted the Seagull in place of the Johnson, and started the engine —and it folded up the A-frame bracket like an accordion.

THE DINGHY AS TOWBOAT OR
YAWL BOAT (PUSH BOAT)

Selecting an Outboard

The amount of thrust necessary to push a boat in calm water is much less than people realize. For example, to push a boat at $.7\sqrt{LWL}$ requires only 5 pounds of thrust per ton; *Iolaire,* with a displacement of roughly twenty tons and a waterline length of thirty-five feet, needs only 100 pounds of thrust to do about 4 knots, and a sailboat of 25 to 27 feet LWL, displacing perhaps ten tons, needs only 50 pounds of thrust to do 3½ knots. Needless to say, as indicated by the chart (Drawing 138), considerably more thrust is required for higher speeds.

That maximum thrust is supplied by a big, slow-turning propeller is apparent from the accompanying table. (More comprehensive test figures, for a variety of engines, are presented in Chapter XIV.) As the table indicates, a really big propeller with a high reduction gear ratio is what is wanted for an outboard which is to be mounted on the stern of a dinghy used as a yawl boat, or on a bracket on the mother ship.

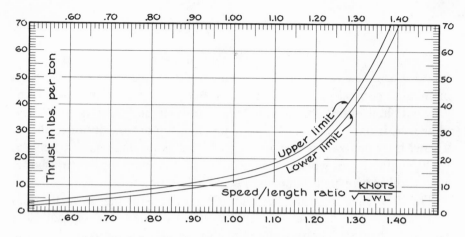

138. Relationship between thrust required and speed.

Here is where the Seagulls, with their big propellers, come into their own. All of the Seagulls are relatively slow-turning and have plenty of torque. The medium-sized Seagull has a 3.5-to-1 reduction, and swings a propeller with a 9-inch diameter and 8-inch pitch, producing between 65 and 75 pounds of thrust. The large Seagull—the Century Plus—which has a 4-to-1 reduction (but no reverse gear) and a propeller with an 11-inch diameter and 10-inch pitch, produces upward of 75 pounds of thrust, enough to push the average-sized auxiliary. Indeed, it will push *Iolaire* along very nicely in calm water at about 3 knots.

However, being a belt and braces man, I prefer to have two small Seagulls, in the hope that if one fails, the other will run. Also, the two small Seagulls are much easier to handle than one big one. In calm water, with these two Seagulls mounted on the stern, our dinghy—secured alongside *Iolaire*—will push her very nicely at 3 knots.

Another advantage of the dear old faithful Seagull is its simplicity. Having a single cylinder and very few moving parts, it will continue to chug along no matter what. If it does stop running, it can usually be fixed with a hammer, a screwdriver, one or two wrenches, a cold chisel, and a piece of sandpaper. Furthermore, there is available through Clymer Publications (for address, see Appendix) one of the best outboard manuals I have ever seen. With its aid one should be able to keep a Seagull operating just about forever.

In addition, satisfactory trade-in arrangements can be made if desired. In 1975 we sent two Seagulls back to the manufacturers. One of these, they insisted had been under water for at least six months (in

8-h.p. Outboard, at 5,000 RPM

REDUCTION GEAR RATIO	SHAFT RPM	PROPELLER DIAMETER AND PITCH, IN INCHES	CALCULATED STATIC THRUST, IN POUNDS
5:1	1,000	17 x 10	287
4.5:1	1,100	16 x 9	278
4:1	1,250	15 x 8	268
3.5:1	1,429	14 x 7	257
3:1	1,667	13 x 6	244
2.5:1	2,000	10 x 7	208
2.5:1	2,000	8 x 9	166

truth, it had been under water intermittently, but not continuously), but it actually ran sometimes. The other ran regularly, if I used the correct curse words. For thirty pounds (about fifty dollars) apiece and the trade-in of the old Seagulls, we received two completely rebuilt engines, for all intents and purposes brand new—a really great deal.

The one major difficulty with the Seagull is one which occurs mostly in the tropics. It contains a number of small screws made of cadmium-plated steel which tend to freeze up. When that happens they must be drilled out to disassemble the engine. Tropical yachtsmen would jump at the chance to acquire a special kit, even at the cost of a few dollars, that would supply the correct stainless screws to replace the cadmium-plated ones.

When I discussed this matter with Seagull representatives at the London Boat Show, they promised to look into it and let me know. However, though I have sent two letters to them with a parts list showing exactly what screws are needed, I still have not been able to get hold of the required parts. In their absence, one solution to this problem is to pull out the offending screws once a month, pack them in grease, and then shove them back in. They will then be relatively easy to remove when the engine needs repair.

Until recently, there was no small outboard with a big propeller on the American market. Even today, an examination of the thrust produced by the various propeller and reduction-gear options available makes it obvious that the outboard manufacturers have not pushed the problem to its logical conclusion. It should be noted that the drag which may be expected with a larger propeller is unimportant in an outboard for a dinghy because when the dinghy is being towed, the outboard is in the "up" position, and hence there is no propeller drag. Increasing the reduction gear ratio and the propeller size would not appreciably change either weight or handling characteristics.

The American manufacturers have just begun to build a type of engine specifically intended to push small sailboats: they now offer a "sailors'" series, with improved thrust at lower speeds (5–6 knots). Although this is a high-rpm engine, it does have a reduction gear, so it turns a large propeller at a relatively low shaft rpm. This American outboard, and the foreign copies of it, have two to four cylinders, complicated carburetors, and a self-rewinding self-start—they are very well engineered. Since they operate on a gas–oil mixture of 25 to 1 or 50 to 1, there is a considerable saving in oil purchases, and in the long run their fuel costs are lower than those of the Seagull. However, more work needs to be done. For one thing, any propeller that exhausts through its hub, as some of these models do, will have very poor thrust in reverse! Also, because these engines are much more complicated than the Seagull, they are much more expensive to repair, and because of the generous use in them of metals that do not stand up well in salt water, they reach the end of their life much sooner.

Securing a Dinghy Used as a Yawl Boat

A dinghy that is to serve as a yawl boat had best be secured on the quarter. A few fenders should be placed between the dinghy and the yacht. The dinghy should be strapped firmly alongside; use of the winches will probably be required to tighten the bow and stern lines holding the dinghy as nearly parallel as possible to the mother ship. A spring line should be rigged from the inside of the bow of the dinghy to the stern of the mother ship; also, if reverse is to be used, a spring line should be rigged forward from the stern of the dinghy to the cockpit winch (Drawing 139). A couple of spare sails thrown into the bow of the dinghy will provide a little weight, so that it does not bounce around too much. Keeping the dinghy level in this manner will maximize the thrust from the engine.

Since the noise of the outboard will prevent people from hearing

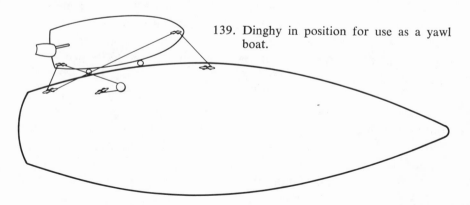

139. Dinghy in position for use as a yawl boat.

23. Iolaire's *outboard stowage.* DAVID MAX

one another, the following signals are very useful: one finger up means "Go forward"; two fingers, "Go into neutral"; three fingers, "Reverse"; a thumb up, "Speed up"; a thumb down, "Slow down"; and an index finger across the throat, "Cut it off."

OUTBOARD STOWAGE

If the outboard is stowed in such a position that fuel will not spill out of the tank, and if it can be periodically run even though not placed in the water, starting problems will be minimized. An outboard stowed below, in the lazaret or anywhere else, probably won't start after two or three weeks at sea. Dampness will have penetrated the ignition; the carburetor will be gummed up with old fuel. If it is stowed upside down, the cylinder may be frozen into place by water spilling into it from the water jacket, and all sorts of things happen. Therefore, if possible, the outboard should be mounted on the stern pulpit (Photo 23). Then, every three or four days someone can run it for a few seconds. The fuel will be sucked out of the carburetor, the carburetor jet will be kept clear, the ignition wire will be dried out, and in general the engine will be kept in good functioning order. Since we instituted this program on *Iolaire,* we have had little trouble keeping our outboards running reliably, whereas before, we were continually having problems with them.

SECURING

When a yacht is at anchor, the dinghy is normally trailed off the stern, but in this position it is always a problem. Whenever someone wants to get into the dinghy, it is pulled alongside. If it has a poor fender, it bangs up the topsides; even if it has a good fender, it tends to knock and wear the paint. Also, if the mother ship has a long transom, the dinghy gets under it, and bangs the stern whenever there are waves from a passing outboard or powerboat. If the dinghy is kept alongside instead of off the stern, it continually bangs up against the side of the boat, knocking the paint off.

There are two different solutions to this problem. If the boat has a reaching strut, one can just secure the reaching strut into place, tie it to an upper shroud with a sail stop, and pass the dinghy painter through the outboard end of the reaching strut. The dinghy will then lie alongside, a couple of feet away from the boat. Occasionally, if the dinghy is quite large, it may touch the side of the boat, but it won't bang into it. (However, there is the danger of forgetting to duck under the reaching strut, and putting a dent into the aluminum pole with one's head.) If the reaching strut is not quite long enough for this arrangement, a plate-eye fitting identical to the mast fitting for the reaching strut can be fastened to the toe rail of the bulwark. The reaching strut can then be secured to the bulwark, but a topping lift, fore guy, and after guy, instead of just a sail stop to the upper shroud, will have to be rigged and put into place.

The second solution, for the boat that does not have a reaching strut, can be used in waters where there is a reverse tide, and the dinghy and the boat lay in opposite directions. The spinnaker pole can be rigged in place of the reaching strut, and a hauling-out line run through the jaws of the spinnaker pole. The spinnaker pole will be long enough to prevent even the largest dinghy from touching the side of the boat.

In certain areas, dinghy and outboard thievery is a major problem. The only complete solution is to take the dinghy up on deck every night. However, there are partial solutions. One old dodge that I formerly used is to worm a piece of $\frac{1}{16}$-inch stainless-steel wire up inside the dinghy painter. Then, when someone tries to cut the dinghy painter, he ends up with a very dull knife. This method did work for us; on three separate occasions we found the painter cut through to the wire. All we had to do then was put the wire through a new painter.

Another solution is to rig a wire through the painter to an electric bell, so that it rings when the contact is broken. This sounds like a good idea, but it is somewhat like locking the barn door after the horse is stolen; unless you have a shotgun, or another dinghy in which to give chase, you may find yourself just listening to the alarm as the dinghy disappears into the darkness.

A third solution is to padlock a stainless-steel wire to the outboard, run it through the towing eye and on up to the boat, and padlock it to the boat. The difficulty is in remembering to do this every night. On one boat, this technique was used with great success for two years; then one night someone forgot to rig the wire, and sure enough, the dinghy was stolen. Furthermore, even this method does not stop the really persistent thieves. Some have stolen big, massive wire cutters from yachts, and then used them to cut through the chain, wire, or what-have-you securing the dinghy to the boat or the outboard to the dinghy.

It should be remembered that marine insurance does not cover the loss of an outboard or dinghy unless the outboard is locked onto the dinghy with an antitheft device, and the dinghy is marked with the name of the mother yacht. Also, the bigger the outboard, the more likely it is to be stolen, so precautions should be taken accordingly.

Finally, it is noteworthy that the small Seagull can be easily removed and put on board for safety each night, and the small rowing dinghy which will not take a high-powered outboard motor is not very popular with dinghy thieves. The old-fashioned varnished lapstrake dinghy is so uncommon that it is extremely conspicuous, and is therefore seldom stolen.

DINGHY HANDLING

BEACHING

Landing through Surf

When considering whether to land through the surf, one should remember that surf appears much calmer from the seaward than from the landward side. Hence, if the surf appears bad even from the seaward side, one should not attempt to land.

When a landing is to be made through the surf, a dinghy that rows well should be swung around, so that the stern is toward the beach. The oarsman should backwater slowly until the dinghy is just outside the surf line. At that point, someone in the stern, facing forward, should coach him, helping him to get the bow exactly square—i.e., at right angles—to the surf line. Once in that position, the oarsman should slowly back in, staying just outside the breakers, waiting for a lull. And when it comes, he should backwater like mad, riding in on the back of a wave. As soon as the water is shallow enough, those in the stern should jump out, grab the stern, and run the dinghy up on the beach. For this operation, everyone should wear shorts or bell-bottom trousers!

When going in bow first, one should again wait outside the breakers for a lull, then pull like mad, running in on the back of a wave. As the bow touches the beach, those in the stern should hold the stern square to the surf, to keep the dinghy from being swept back by the undertow, and the bow man should jump out and hold the bow. The dinghy is then carried up the beach on the next wave.

To be sure, the Australian surfboat experts plane in on the face of a breaker, but that technique is for the brave and skillful only.

When landing through the surf in an outboard, one must go bow in. Once again, the correct procedure is to lie to just outside the surf line until a lull in the surf is spotted. Then, as with a rowing dinghy, one should go in on the *back* of a wave. The throttle is kept wide open until the dinghy beaches; at that point, the motor should of course be cut immediately. The release holding the motor in the "down" position should have been disconnected previously, to allow it to flip up.

As soon as the dinghy hits the beach, everyone should jump out, holding the bow on the beach and the stern square to the surf, so that the next wave will not swing the boat broadside. When the wave comes, the dinghy should be run higher up. When the beaching has been completed, the stern should be raised and the dinghy pivoted so that it is facing bow out.

Handling on the Beach

If the dinghy is too heavy to be picked up and carried up a sand beach, all is not lost. Slide the dinghy as far up the beach as possible; then raise the bow and slide the oars (or sticks found on the beach) underneath the dinghy, placing them up the beach at three-foot intervals. Kept upright, resting on its center brass skid, the dinghy will then very easily slide up even a steep beach, since the sticks will prevent it from digging into the sand. Finally, pull the stern drain plug to let out the water, raise the stern (even if the dinghy can't be carried, one can usually lift one end), pivot it around on its bow, and it is facing downhill, ready for launching.

Launching through Surf

When a dinghy is to be launched through the surf, it should be pushed down the beach until it is lifted by each incoming wave. Then one person—or in the case of a large dinghy, two—should hop in and get the oars into place; the remainder of the crew should grab the dinghy as soon as it floats, push hard to seaward as long as they can, and then jump in, while the oarsmen heave their guts out. It is in this situation that—in a ten- or twelve-foot dinghy with two expert oarsmen—eight-foot oars really come into their own.

An outboard dinghy that is to be launched through the surf should have a motor with reliable starting. The dinghy is shoved into the water until it is just afloat, the motor is prepared to start, and the crew gets ready to jump in. When a wave comes in, one person pushes the dinghy out far enough so that the motor can be dropped into the "down" position; then it is started and put into gear, everyone piles aboard, the throttle is opened wide—and fingers are crossed. It goes without saying that a dinghy launched off a beach should not under any circumstances be overloaded.

On the east coast of South Africa, where there are no harbors and the Indian Ocean swell comes rolling in, the South Africans insist on going to sea in small open runabouts, launching and landing through the surf. Indeed, launching through the surf is regarded as great sport: there is fabulous sport, fabulous fishing—and also a rather high casualty rate.

HOISTING

The slings that are used to hoist a dinghy, as described in *OSY*-I (Ch. IX), should be quite long, at least three times the length of the dinghy. The operation of inverting the dinghy in the air can be simplified if the boathook, with a chock fitted on it, is used as a spreader. (A yacht's boathook should be approximately the same length as the spinnaker pole.) This arrangement (Drawing 140) enables even a small child to turn the dinghy right side up or upside down.

As mentioned in Chapter III, hoisting the dinghy is easier if a yacht has sharply raked masts, à la *Mary V. Pelton* (Drawing 39), since then the dinghy does not try to run forward, as it tends to do when there are plumb masts.

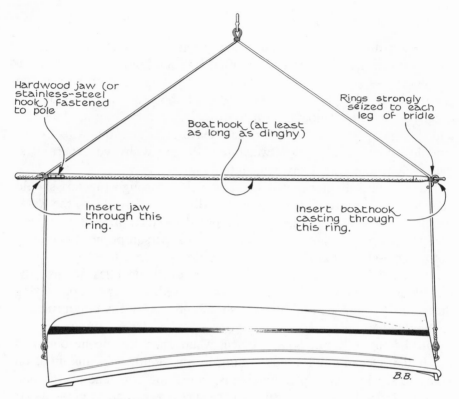

Hardwood jaw (or
stainless-steel
hook) fastened
to pole

Rings strongly
seized to each
leg of bridle

Boathook (at least
as long as dinghy)

Insert jaw
through this
ring.

Insert boathook
casting through
this ring.

B.B.

140. Boathook used as a spreader, to prevent the hoisting bridle from hanging
up on the ends of the dinghy being inverted.

Taking a Dinghy on Deck While Under Way

Often one is towing a dinghy in moderate conditions, and then it
begins to blow up and one desires to take the dinghy aboard, where it
will be safe. Most yachtsmen regard doing this as a major project, but
it should not be too hard on a low-freeboard boat. Even on a high-
freeboard boat, though more difficult, the task is not impossible.

Just how easy this operation could be in years gone by, when boats
had much lower freeboards, I learned on board the old *Lutine,* back in
1955. Brian Stewart and I were on watch while sailing back to England
from the Brittany coast, towing the dinghy. When it began to blow at
about two in the morning, Brian decided that it was time to take the
dinghy on board. I was about to duck below to get some of the off
watch to help, but to my surprise, he said the two of us could do it with
no trouble. He asked me to stand by the jib sheet, while he put the helm
down; *Lutine* tacked, and I resheeted the jib on the new tack, leaving

the genoa staysail sheeted to weather. The helm was lashed, and the mizzen was eased off until half aflutter. The yacht lay floating like a duck, just about rail down. Brian whipped out a pair of pliers, disconnected the lifeline, lifted out three midship stanchions, and had me take the painter of the dinghy forward to the bow. When I had pulled the dinghy forward until it was floating amidships, the painter was tied to the after lower shroud, I came aft, and the two of us slipped the dinghy over the rail cap into the lee scuppers, turned it over, lifted it onto the cabin top, and secured it in place. Then we rerigged the lifeline, resheeted the genoa staysail, and trimmed the mizzen, and off we went, without having had to call anyone up on deck.

When we towed the dinghy on *Iolaire,* we sometimes took it on board in similar fashion. Other times, we would pull the dinghy up alongside, leading the painter all the way forward through the bow chock, pick up the lifting sling of the dinghy and attach it to the spinnaker halyard, yank away on the spinnaker halyard until the dinghy was lifted clear of the lifelines, swing it on in, upend it and lower it to the lee scuppers, turn it upside down, and lash it down. All this was of course done while we lay hove to, with the staysail sheeted back and the mizzen trimmed or luffing as conditions required.

After all, in the days of the old Bristol Channel pilot cutter, once all the pilots had boarded the incoming ships, the boy left alone on the cutter had to load the dinghy single-handed if he did not want to tow it back. He led the dinghy painter well forward to the bowsprit, and secured the topsail halyard to the dinghy, with the boat heeled well over on the port tack. When as much strain as possible had been taken on the topsail halyard, the boat was tacked. As she came upright and fell off on the other tack, the dinghy, lifted by the topsail halyard, rose up into the air, ricocheting off the rail cap, the skylight, and the like. The operation was hard on the boat, and hard on the dinghy—but of course these were heavily built commercial vessels.

Schooners have the easiest method. If lifts are rigged on the fore and main spreaders, and tackles are hitched to the bow and stern of the dinghy, it can be easily lifted out of the water and swung on board. Even if the boat is sailing along at a considerable speed, heaving to is not really necessary when a good crew is aboard.

On the modern boat, with the extremely high freeboard, getting the dinghy on board while under sail is a real problem. But though difficult, it is not impossible. About the only way to do it is to heel the boat way over and then lift the dinghy on a halyard. Removable lifeline stanchions certainly help.

24. Hobie *10 stowed inside dinghy.* ANNE HAMMICK

STOWING

On yachts with a crew of more than four permanently living and cruising on board, it is certainly convenient to have two dinghies. Otherwise, a few crew members are continually being stranded ashore while the main group is on board, unable to hear the poor souls calling for the dinghy—or vice versa. However, with two dinghies, there is a double stowage problem.

One solution to this problem is to have one good rigid dinghy and a smaller rubber dinghy, serving strictly as an emergency backup. Another solution is to carry two rigid dinghies of different sizes, the larger having removable seats. Then one can remove the seats, stow the dinghy upright, and drop the smaller dinghy inside it. This is the method used on *Iolaire,* where our six-foot pram or ten-foot Hobie fits inside our lapstrake dinghy placed upright on chocks alongside the hatches (Photo 24).

A better solution, if the deck layout permits, is to store the smaller dinghy upside down in chocks, then remove the seats from the larger dinghy and store it upside down on top of the smaller one (Drawing 141). This is the method I would like to use on *Iolaire,* but unfortunately, the deck layout cannot be altered, and our small pram, picked up secondhand, does not quite fit inside the larger dinghy. Some day, I may build a small pram that will fit around the hatches and stow under-

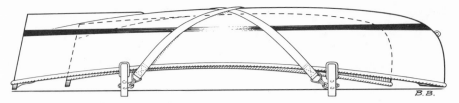

141. Two dingies stowed upside down, one inside the other.

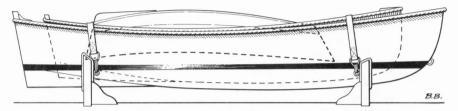

142. Three dinghies stowed in the space of one, as aboard *Escapade*.

neath the larger dinghy, so that we can carry two dinghies in the space now used for one.

The ultimate development of this method was seen in the 1938 Bermuda Race, when one of the large ocean racers carried three dinghies specially built by The Anchorage (Dyer)—a twelve-foot stemhead dinghy, right side up; inside it, a standard Dyer ten-foot dinghy; and upside down on top of these two, a small pram (Drawing 142).

Another solution is the fifteen-foot double-ended dinghy made in Holland that consists of two parts which can be latched together to make one big dinghy, and can be separated for easy stowage (one inside the other in an eight-foot space) or for use as two separate dinghies. The great advantage of this arrangement is that at fifteen feet, the dinghy has tremendous load-carrying capacity—enough so that it could serve as a lifeboat—and it rows and sails well, while the two parts can also be employed individually as circumstances demand.

Paul Johnson, designer of the little wooden gaff ketch *Venus,* and the larger fiber-glass gaff-rigged ketch *Vinus,* has designed for his new boat a foam-plank double-ender with built-in flotation (Photo 25; Drawing 143). It separates into two parts, the larger being 8 feet 6 inches long. The parts stow one inside the other, and can be used separately when necessary. The double-ended dinghy can even be rigged for sailing. It rows beautifully and also serves as his lifeboat. He points out that the boat on which he sailed across the Atlantic, an eighteen-foot Shetland double-ender, was only three feet longer than this double-ended dinghy. He figures he ought to be able to survive in a double-ended dinghy with built-in buoyancy for a fair amount of time.

25. *Paul Johnson's double-ender.* ANNE HAMMICK

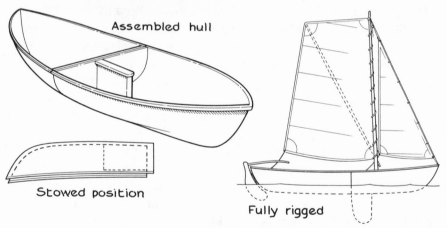

Assembled hull

Stowed position

Fully rigged

143. Paul Johnson's jointed double-ender.

DAVITS

Dinghies were once universally stowed in davits even on comparatively small boats. One photo of *Iolaire* shows her sailing along on a
shy reach with the dinghy hanging outboard in davits (Photo 26).
With the low boom that *Iolaire* carried in those days, exactly how they
got the boom to clear the davits when they eased the sheets is beyond me.

The davits on the older boats were usually mounted in brackets outboard (Drawing 144A), with a strong, though clumsy-looking, mounting. This arrangement must have made coming alongside a dock more

26. Iolaire's *dinghy in davits*. BEKEN OF COWES

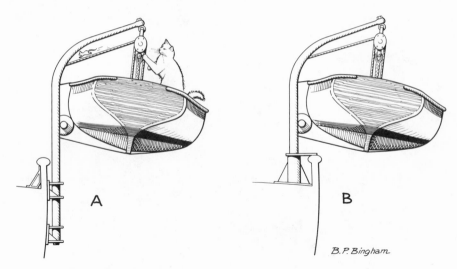

144. Dinghy davit mountings: A, outboard; B, inboard.

than a little interesting, since even with the brackets removed, four large iron studs remained, sticking out to snare anything and everything.

Today, davits are typically mounted inboard of the bulwark (Drawing 144B), setting in a socket in the deck and a bracket in the top of the bulwark. This type of mounting is good as long as the bulwark is firmly secured and has good support braces in the vicinity of the davits.

Davits are now seldom seen on boats much less than sixty to sixty-five feet long. That is unfortunate, for properly designed davits, with a good set of chocks to receive the dinghy, certainly make taking the dinghy on board and stowing it much less of a problem.

Gary Hoyt's Freedom 40 has davits which make taking the eleven-foot dinghy on board absolute duck soup. The dinghy is hoisted on the davits, swung inboard, dropped on the waterway, with the outboard still on its stern, tied down, and all is comparatively well. With a proper set of dinghy chocks bolted into place, this arrangement would be perfect. As it is, it is still good.

If a boat has a stern wide enough to accommodate a dinghy, the davits today are often mounted there. The dinghy is certainly taken aboard with ease when there are stern davits, and—the great advantage —it is always instantly ready to be launched. Also, the dinghy is stowed in an out-of-the-way place, and it provides easy storage for spearfishing equipment, face masks, swim fins, and the like.

However, this rig does have disadvantages. First of all, because the capacity of the davits is limited by the width of the stern, except on a fairly large boat the dinghy cannot be more than eight, or at most nine, feet long. Further, the weight of the davits and the dinghy, right at the end of the boat, inevitably hurts the boat's windward-going ability. Frequently, especially on a boat that carries a couple of big anchors, a heavy bowsprit platform, a heavy pulpit, and the like at the other end, it is the cause of tremendous hobby-horsing, which completely ruins sailing performance. One should remember that, as pointed out with respect to the location of the anchor windlass, the moment of inertia varies with the *square* of the distance between the center of gravity of the weight and the center of buoyancy.

Before deciding whether to install stern davits, one should consider carefully both the boat and the area where she will be sailed. On a really large boat—of seventy or eighty feet—the stern davits sometimes provide a perfect place for a good, light rowing and sailing dinghy; the weight of a light dinghy back aft is not detrimental on a boat that size, and a heavy dinghy, such as a Boston Whaler or Dell Quay dory, can be stowed amidships. On smaller boats, of forty or fifty feet, if stern davits are installed it is best to provide alternative dinghy stowage for use in long passages where the wind is expected to be forward of the beam, or the course is dead to windward.

X

Accommodation

BUNKS

Two types of berths, frequently found, which were not discussed in *OSY*-I are pipe berths and Root berths.

PIPE BERTHS

In the past, the pipe berth had a galvanized-steel frame and a canvas bottom sweated up with a lanyard, with a mattress on top. The version currently popular on racing craft with Spartan accommodations usually has a frame of aluminum pipe. A Dacron bottom, lashed into place, supports the mattress. On a pipe berth, a two-inch polyfoam mattress is adequate; the four-inch mattress required on a wood-bottomed berth is not necessary. The great advantage of a pipe berth is that its angle may be adjusted, by means of chains, lanyards or handy-billies with jam cleats. It can be folded up out of the way when not needed, so there should be two straps with D rings to keep the mattress and bedding in place when it is in the raised position (Drawing 145).

145. Pipe berth with bedding hold-down straps.

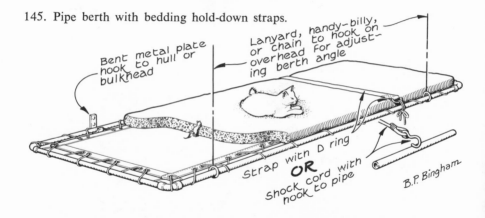

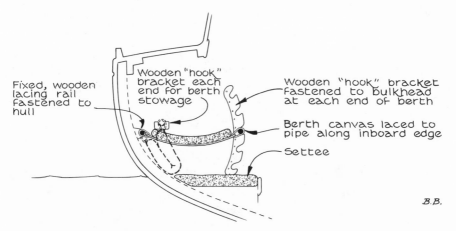

146. Root berth can be adjusted to accommodate any angle of heel, and can be stowed out of the way when not in use.

ROOT BERTHS

The Root berth (Drawing 146) was devised by L. Francis Herreshoff. A length of Dacron is secured on one side to a batten fastened along the hull and on the other side to a piece of aluminum pipe which —depending upon the angle of heel—drops into one of several chocks. Other chocks, on the side of the hull, make it possible for the Root berth to be folded up during the day, in similar fashion to the pipe berth, and when folded, it can form a comfortable backrest for the lower settee in a small boat.

PILOT BERTHS

A curtain that closes off the face of the pilot berth is most useful, giving privacy to the occupant, and allowing him to read at night without having his light disturb anyone. His own sleep is not interrupted during a change in watch, since the closed curtain keeps light out. Finally, on a cold night, a blanket hung on the curtain rod or lanyard will go a long way toward preserving warmth in the bunk.

MATTRESS COVERINGS

The standard covering for mattresses on most boats is vinyl, which is virtually waterproof and easy to keep clean. However, it makes a most uncomfortable surface to sleep on, being slippery, and hot in summer and cold in winter. For this reason, many cruising yachtsmen prefer a Vivatex mattress cover. Though not waterproof, it is water-repellent—and it breathes and is comfortable to sleep on. For additional comfort, a second mattress cover, of a soft, washable material, can be placed over the Vivatex. Admittedly, a cloth cover is harder to keep clean than one made of something like vinyl, but it certainly looks better, and is infinitely more comfortable.

If a vinyl mattress cover is felt to be essential, it should have a zipper around three sides, and the mattress underneath should be covered with Vivatex. Then the top (vinyl) cover can be unzipped and folded back at night, so that one can sleep on the softer cover within. This method of covering mattresses has been standard on United States submarines for the last thirty or forty years.

LEE CANVASES

After fighting lee canvases of all sizes and shapes for many years, we finally came up with one that has worked out as the perfect lee canvas for us aboard *Iolaire* (Drawing 147). The upper pilot berths in our main cabin have good high bunk boards, but the lower bunks are settees and use lee canvases. The bunks are 6 feet 6 inches long, with their forward ends against two lockers that form half bulkheads and their after ends against a bulkhead. We made each of our lee canvases twenty-four inches high—that is, extending twenty inches above a four-inch cushion—and a full six feet long. A length of ⅜-inch Dacron with eyes at both ends is sewn along the top edge, like the luff rope on

147. *Iolaire*'s lee canvas.

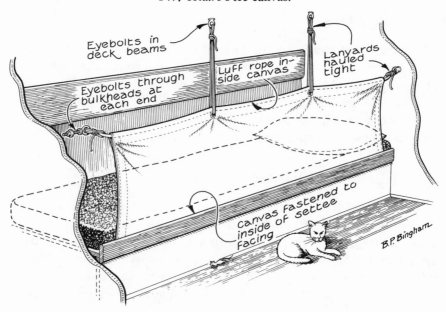

a sail, and short lanyards are spliced into the eyes. Two grommets with long lanyards through them are also set into this edge, at equal intervals. The bottom edge of the lee canvas is secured to the inner edge of the settee facing. The canvas stows underneath the settee cushion when not in use.

When the lee canvas is needed, it is dragged out from under the cushion, and the lines from the two eyes in the luff rope are tied to two eyes securely bolted to the bulkheads, pulled tight, set up as three-part tackles, and secured with rolling hitches. The lanyards from the two grommets are led up to the overhead, secured to eyes in the deck beams, again threaded back and forth as three-part tackles, and secured with rolling hitches. A little bit of work is required to set everything up, but once inside the lee canvas, one can sleep in perfect safety and comfort and never worry, no matter how far over the boat may heel. All those who have used these lee canvases have regarded them as the best they have ever encountered.

SECURING CUSHIONS

Securing cushions, especially settee back cushions, has always been a problem. The common-sense fasteners, snaps, and wooden brackets do work, but they are hard to use. Luckily, today Velcro is on the market, and the problem is solved. One need only attach a strip of Velcro to the back of the settee with epoxy glue, and stitch a matching piece onto the cushion cover. Then, when the cushion is shoved into place, the Velcro holds it there; when the cushion needs to be moved, it is easily yanked free.

Similarly, in years gone by cushion covers were closed by means of knots, zippers, buttons, or clips—all of which gave trouble. Now, with Velcro stitched along both sides of the opening, the cushion cover can be closed with just the pressure of the hand, and yet opened readily when desired.

HEADS

The more technical aspects of heads—sink drains, showers, pumps, sump tanks, and the like—are discussed in Chapter XII, but a few basic matters will be considered here.

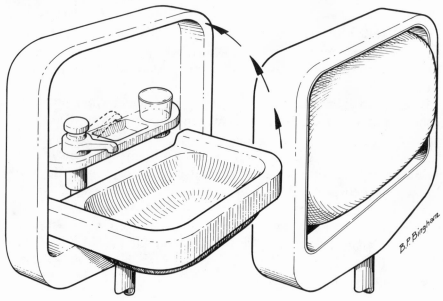

148. Fold-down sink.

SIZE

The size of the head is of course governed largely by the size of the boat and sometimes by the size of the people. At a bare minimum, the head with a fold-down sink (Drawing 148) can be 27 inches wide by 36 inches deep, provided there are no giants in the crew.

For a head having a permanent sideboard with lockers, shelves, sink, and the like, and a sliding door, the minimum dimensions are a width of 36 inches and a depth of 48 inches. These are the measurements of *Iolaire*'s head. This size is adequate for the average person, but anguish for any really large friends, so a width of 40 inches, with the depth of 48 inches, is really preferable.

It should be noted that even the minimum-sized head will be more than adequate if it is situated opposite the hanging locker, and the hanging-locker door and head door may be swung in opposite directions (*OSY*-I, Drawing 142), so that when in use the head occupies almost the entire width of the boat.

The height of the toilet in relation to the sole is also important. There is nothing more uncomfortable than sitting in the head and having one's feet dangle. Because of the curvature of the hull, the toilet will frequently be mounted well above the main part of the cabin sole, but there is no reason why the platform on which it is set should not ex-

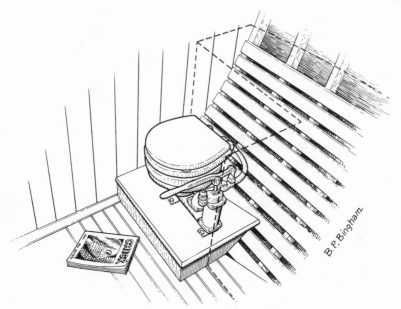

149. When the base of the toilet is too wide for the head sole, installation on a platform is necessary.

tend out far enough to allow one's feet to rest on it (Drawing 149). The head will then be comfortable and practical both for a man standing up and for a man or woman sitting down.

MARINE TOILETS

At best, marine toilets are hard to keep clean and maintain, and there may be hidden problems as well. A toilet may appear to be beautifully designed and built, with a vitreous-china bowl, a solid-bronze or plastic pump, everything first rate—but watch out! Sometimes the bolts securing the bowl to the base or holding the lid and seat in place may be only chrome- or brass-plated steel. It's advisable to check them with a magnet just to be sure. If they are indeed made of steel, they had best be replaced, before they rust, freeze up, or break up. I myself prefer to use bolts of Everdur bronze for the replacements. I have run into a lot of "stainless steel" that is not stainless at all, but only rustless; the result has been ugly streaks that could have been avoided.

ELIMINATING SMELLS

Nothing gets a crew seasick faster, and nothing makes a boat more unattractive, than a smelly head. If the head is well pumped after each use—for at least fifteen strokes, and preferably twenty or twenty-five—

the problem will be minimized. Also, if the sink drains into the head, pumping will be necessary every time the sink is used, so additional water will be flushed through the system and the chance of smells developing will be further reduced. Finally, a shot of Clorox dumped into the head once a day and flushed on through will be helpful. Ammonia should not be used for this purpose.

Even if all of these precautions are taken, when people are living on board it will be necessary to give the entire compartment a good scrubbing, first with salt water and then with fresh water, at least once a week.

HOLDING TANKS

In the matter of sanitation, the yachting industry and the yachting public, both completely disorganized, are being used as whipping boys by politicians. No one wants to seem opposed to conservation, or to protection of the environment, but look at the facts.

The same politicians who are insisting that yachts have purification devices or holding tanks are doing little or nothing to minimize the amount of raw sewage dumped into the sea. New York State legislators have passed a stringent marine antipollution law, yet until mid-1976 they allowed the World Trade Center, with its tens of thousands of occupants, to discharge all sewage, raw, into New York Harbor. Similarly, in many areas the marine pump-out stations themselves either dump raw sewage back into the harbor directly or transfer it to a municipal sewage system which in turn dumps it back into the sea, untreated or semitreated.

Even where proper treatment facilities do exist, difficulties may arise because the number of pump-out stations is so small in relation to the number of yachts needing to use them that obtaining a berth alongside a station, to pump out, may be all but impossible. Furthermore, the average-sized yacht cannot carry a tank large enough to take care of the sewage on a six- or seven-day offshore passage. Therefore, among boats being sailed offshore, most of those with holding tanks have a bypass valve, so that the head can be pumped directly overside at sea (and frequently in port by those who do not like to use their holding tanks or cannot unload them at a pump-out station).

The various purification devices are expensive and of dubious reliability, and take up considerable space. Also, they consume considerable quantities of electricity—to the point where the average auxiliary yacht will frequently suffer flat batteries, while the boat without an engine will require installation of a generator, at considerable expense, to run the head.

Victor Jorgensen, of *The Telltale Compass,* the newsletter which can "tell it as it is" because it carries no advertising, has been trying to investigate the claims of the various manufacturers of the new marine-sanitation units. In general, these manufacturers seem very optimistic about the efficiency, reliability, and low power draw of their systems, but their claims appear not to stand up under test conditions. Unfortunately, no independent laboratory has conducted really extensive tests on marine heads at this time.

Finally, although several states in the U.S., and the Federal Government, have promulgated regulations, none are realistic or enforceable. Changes are inevitable, and it is therefore too early to make useful recommendations other than to sit tight.

MAIN-CABIN TABLES

THE NECESSITY FOR A GIMBALED TABLE

That a gimbaled table is necessary on an ocean sailing yacht is obvious; it is somewhat less obvious that this type of table is necessary also on a cruising boat that anchors every night. The owners of coastal cruising boats are likely to say, "Oh well, we don't have to have a gimbaled table, since we put the anchor down at breakfast time and dinner time." But what about lunch? The poor cook stands there trying to make sandwiches and pass them out, trying to chock bowls of soup in the corners so they won't fall over; there is no place to put anything down. Even the person eating out of a stew bowl, since he uses one hand to hold the bowl and the other to hold the fork or spoon, needs somewhere to set his coffee or beer—for very few of us are lucky enough to have prehensile toes.

Every boat, no matter how small, should have a gimbaled table, even if it is only 1 or 1½ feet square. Though not very large, such a table does provide a place to put things down, making it possible to relax and eat. You can cruise without a gimbaled table—and you can hit yourself over the head with a hammer—but how much more pleasant life becomes when you stop!

CONSTRUCTION

The upright supports for a main-cabin table should extend above the ends of the table. If the supports stop below the ends (Drawing 150A) instead of extending above them (Drawing 150B), the weather leaf will continually rattle against the windward side of the support when the table is allowed to gimbal in a seaway. This can be disturbing to the people trying to sleep in the main cabin.

On some boats, a folding table is used in the main cabin to save space. Such a table should be chosen or constructed with care, since many of those found on stock boats are wonderful finger mashers and nail breakers.

With a little thought and proper engineering, a gimbaled folding table can be designed (Drawing 151). A pipe of large diameter is passed through the bulkhead at the forward end of the main cabin and secured to the bulkhead by means of a large flange, or a rod with a bushing can be fitted through the mast. A heavy leg, well weighted at the bottom, is pivoted over the pipe or rod, and a hinged table top is fastened to this leg. If the cabin is small, a 22-inch top can fold down against the gimbal weight, which is pinned into place when not in use so that it does not swing back and forth; when open, a table top of this size can be supported by a diagonal strap. If more table space is desired, the top may instead be made to fold upward, against the overhead. Since the average main-cabin table is 2½ feet off the cabin sole, if the cabin is 6 feet high, a table 3 feet long can be folded up against the forward bulkhead. The outer end of a top of this length will be very hard to support. Therefore, a folding gimbaled table of this size should be constructed in such a manner that when the top is folded down for use, a machine screw threaded into the table edge drops into a slot in a piece of pipe firmly secured to the cabin sole. This piece of pipe may be left permanently installed, or it may pass through an opening in the cabin sole to a socket underneath. Then, once the table is folded up, the pipe can be removed and stowed in a rack under one of the main-cabin berths.

DINETTES

Recently, the dinette has become increasingly popular on stock boats. This arrangement has obvious advantages, and also great disadvantages.

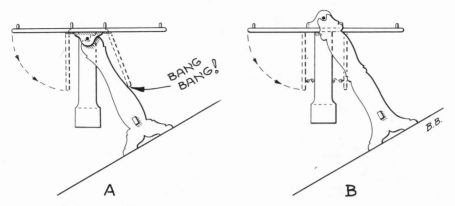

150. Gimbaled table: A, supports stopping below table top; B, supports extending above table top.

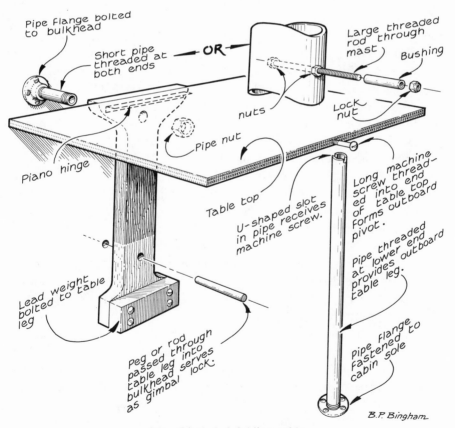

151. Gimbaled folding table.

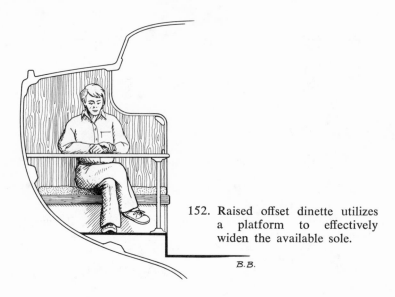

152. Raised offset dinette utilizes
a platform to effectively
widen the available sole.

B.B.

A well-designed dinette can be a boon. Since standing headroom is
not needed, the dinette can be placed to one side, well offset, and
raised above the cabin sole (Drawing 152), leaving a clear passageway
in the main cabin. One can walk through without folding one leaf of
the table, or climbing over people and picking up a few bruises on the
way. Also, for people living on a boat, the dinette provides an area
in addition to the chart table where one can spread out papers and
work undisturbed.

A gimbaled dinette table is not usual, but it is feasible on a large
boat. (Drawing 153). *Flica II* and *Good Hope*, although designed independently, on opposite sides of the Atlantic, have dinette tables
gimbaled in approximately the same manner.

The main disadvantage of having a dinette is that bunk space may
be sacrificed. Most designers do attempt to have the dinette function
also as a double bunk. Fancy arrangements have been devised whereby
the dinette table drops down level with the settee and then a leeboard
is dropped in to form a bunk. However, many yachtsmen feel that
while the dinette is a great place for eating, it is a very poor place for
sleeping. Each time one wishes to eat, the bunk must be disassembled
and the table made up. For a bunk, the location is rather public. Further, unless an adequate bunk board on the inboard side is provided—
and in most cases it is not—the occupants end up in a pile on the lee
side of the bunk; then, on the other tack, they fall out.

Modern interior designers are very clever in designing dinettes.
Frequently, however, what is intriguing in a floating gin palace tied up
at a marina does not work out too well offshore. I must admit that the

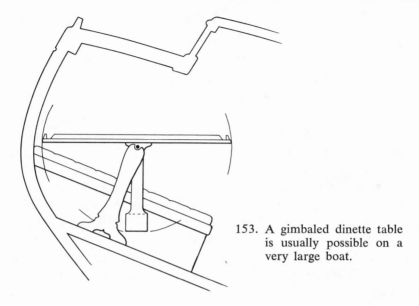

153. A gimbaled dinette table is usually possible on a very large boat.

most intriguing dinette was the one originally designed for *Flying Fifty*. A semicircular table pivoted on a 2-inch chrome-on-brass pole, secured between the cabin sole and the overhead. Ample access to the center of the semicircular settee was obtained by pivoting the table 90 degrees, either fore or aft (Drawing 154). During a cocktail party, of which there were many on *Flying Fifty* in those days, when the large table was not wanted, one merely slid it all the way up against the overhead and slipped a pin through a hole just below it, and presto! the large table was gone and in its place was a small one suitable for cocktails.

154. *Flying Fifty* dinette, with an unusual table arrangement.

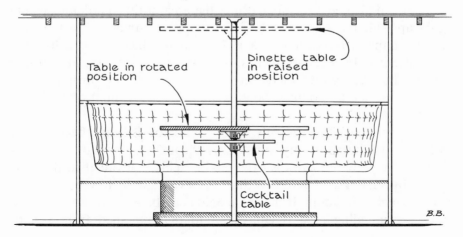

LIGHTS

There should be a few red lights belowdecks, so placed that people coming below do not spoil their night vision. Finding red shields for white lights has been a never-ending problem. For a while, a red bulb dip, which enabled one to convert ordinary light bulbs into red bulbs, as necessary, was available from West Products; let us hope that some-one else will now take over production of this useful item.

Another solution is to install the anti-night-blindness fluorescent light made by REC Specialties (for address, see Appendix). This lamp has a double switch, enabling one to choose white or red light. Al-though the unit is expensive, it would seem well worth while to install one over the chart table, one in the galley, and one in the head—the three places where lights are used at times when night blindness must be avoided.

VENTILATION

A few points about ventilation that were made in *OSY*-I (Ch. VII) deserve repeating. Anyone planning the ventilation of a boat should perform the ribbon test. With the boat either anchored or sailing, a piece of woolen yarn is first placed at a height of three inches above the deck, then at heights of six, twelve, sixteen, and finally eighteen inches. The increasing motion of the yarn as it is raised demonstrates inescap-ably that unless a ventilator is at least twelve—and preferably eighteen—inches high, it is almost not worth installing.

It should also be remembered that the area of the ventilator opening goes up with the square of half the diameter—thus, for a four-inch diameter the cross-section area is 12.5 square inches, for a five-inch diameter it is 19.6 square inches, for a six-inch diameter, 28.2 square inches. In other words, increasing the diameter of the opening by 50 percent, more than doubles the area and thus the amount of air passed below.

However, even a relatively large ventilator is less effective than a hatch. If a hatch twenty-four inches square is opened six inches, an area of 144 square inches is exposed—roughly equivalent to that pro-vided by eleven four-inch ventilators, seven five-inch ventilators, or five six-inch ventilators. If the same hatch can be opened twelve inches, the corresponding area is equivalent to that obtained from twenty-three four-inch, fourteen five-inch, or ten six-inch ventilators. The conclusion is inescapable; although boats should have as many ventilators as possible, the hatches should be so arranged that they can be opened under way in most conditions, because they provide infinitely more air than do ventilators.

Since almost everyone's dream cruise is in the tropics, the requirements of ventilation in the tropics should be kept in mind in the design of the dream boat. For hot weather, every cabin should have at least one ventilator and one hatch; the head should have two ventilators, for intake and exhaust. The hatch location most often overlooked by designers is in the middle of the main cabin, over the table. If a hatch is not provided here, the main cabin becomes hot and uninhabitable, both at sea and in port.

HATCHES

Goiot Two-Way Hatches

The newest Goiot hatch (for supplier, see Appendix) represents one of the greatest recent advances in hatch design (Photo 27). Not only can it be opened two ways—thus providing a feature which seamen and writers have been requesting, mostly in vain, for many years—but it can be opened both fore and aft from belowdecks. Normally, to reverse the direction in which the opening faces, one must go out on deck to pull the pins. The chances are it will be raining!

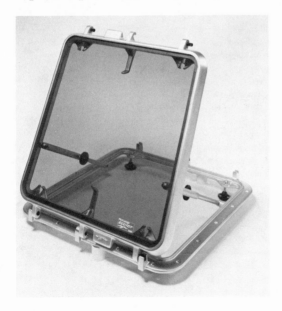

27. Goiot hatch. GOIOT

Griffiths Hatches

Also excellent is the Griffiths hatch (Drawing 112, *OSY*-I), which can be made up with a Lucite top, to provide maximum light below-decks. It has an advantage over the Goiot hatch in that, if it is made square, hinges can be installed on all four sides, so that one can always open it facing downwind when sailing, or to windward when tied up at the dock. However, as we know, everything is a compromise. Whether to choose the Goiot, which opens only two ways but can be switched from belowdecks, or the Griffiths, which is more flexible but requires one to go up on deck to pull the pin, must be decided by the individual yachtsman.

WIND SCOOPS

A wind scoop that works no matter which way the wind is blowing is shown in *OSY*-I, Drawing 148. Also useful is the familiar galley stay-sail—sometimes known as the "dancing nun," among other things (Drawing 155A). Dave Davis, of *Muki,* has invented a Dorade-type wind scoop so designed that plenty of air is pushed below, while rain is excluded by the baffle arrangement (Drawing 155B). This is wonderful for use in the tropics in the rainy season, since extra ventilation is needed below whenever the wind dies down, but ordinary vents must be disconnected every time a rainsquall comes through.

155. Increasing ventilation: A, galley staysail; B, *Muki*'s Dorade-type wind scoop; C, *Muki*'s bunny ears.

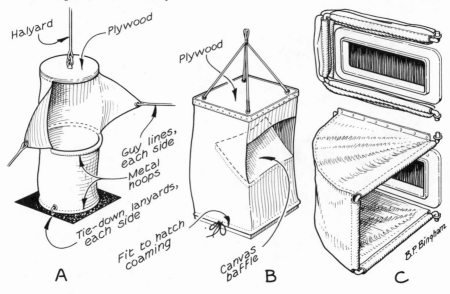

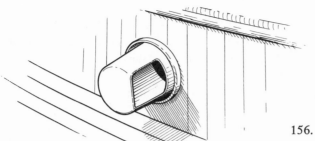

156. Plastic trash can cut
to serve as wind scoop.

Because the after cabin on *Muki* suffers from very poor ventilation, Davis also designed what he calls "bunny ears" (Drawing 155C). Basically, each of these consists of a bronze hoop that pivots, and a canvas scoop that snaps onto the side of the cabin around the port. During short sails, each of the ears can be folded back and secured with a snap, and of course they can be removed when the boat is really out to sea.

On boats with round portholes in the side, getting air belowdecks is frequently a problem. Various expensive methods have been used to scoop air in, but the easiest and cheapest is to obtain a plastic bowl or trash can of the right diameter and cut the forward surface as shown in Drawing 156. When the porthole is open, one merely shoves the plastic can or bowl through it. If it starts to rain, turning this scoop 90 degrees, so that the cutout faces downward, will keep the rain from spraying in.

PORTS

The size and location of ports should be carefully considered. In some cases, they can be dispensed with altogether. For example, they may be unnecessary on a boat where the cabin trunk is so low and the bulwark so high that the only thing visible through a port would be the inside of the bulwark. Admittedly, however, the brightness which ports add to a cabin may make them an asset even in the absence of a view.

Ports should be thoughtfully located, both to preserve the appearance of the boat and to make sure that they are present where they are essential. There should be one in the head, and one in the galley, the latter so arranged that the cook can look out at the scenery while standing at the stove. If the galley is aft and the cabin trunk extends to the cockpit, an oval or rectangular port at least fifteen inches long can be installed between the galley and the cockpit. This can be left open under the dodger in all but the worst weather, giving ventilation to the galley, and enabling the cook to talk to those in the cockpit, and to pass things up from the galley to those on deck without having to send things through the companionway.

Small portlights—those no larger than 15 by 9 inches—seldom need protective covers if made of heavy tempered glass, since they are all but indestructible. Fixed doghouse windows larger than this will need protective covers, as discussed elsewhere.

The relative merits of opening and fixed portlights is a subject of much debate. The opening portlights have several disadvantages. They are expensive, vastly overrated as an aid to ventilation, and very likely to leak. An open portlight will provide excellent ventilation when the boat is moored at a dock, with the wind on the beam, or when she is sailing on a reach, if the spray is not flying too badly. However, when the boat is sitting at anchor and pivoting into the wind, little or no air will pass through the opening unless a wind scoop is installed.

The ocean sailing yacht with opening portlights must carry a full supply of spares. Gaskets deteriorate rapidly in the tropics, and every portlight made seems to have a gasket of a different size. The second most frequent cause of failure in a portlight is the breaking off of the locking lugs by an overenthusiastic crew member trying to tighten it down. Therefore, it is absolutely essential that spare locking wing nuts and locking lugs be carried, as well as the pivot pins for both the lugs and the portlight hinges.

An opening portlight can be a real pain in the neck unless proper precautions are taken. If it is opened when the boat is heeled, the water resting on the lip drops down onto the chart table or bunk, or into the galley (Drawing 157A). The same thing may occur even at anchor on boats with cabin trunks that have tumble home. To eliminate this problem (Drawing 157B), drain holes can be drilled into the frame; also, as a backup, a ledge should be run along the inside of the cabin trunk and extended all the way aft to a piece of ⅜-inch copper tubing which can be epoxied into the wooden trough, and which leads down to the bilge. Thus any water that drips in from a portlight when it is opened, or improperly secured, will end up in the bilge rather than in someone's bunk.

Another problem with opening ports is that the minute rain begins, it pours into the cabin. To minimize the amount of rain that comes in when the boat is at anchor, a small hood may be placed over the portlight (Drawing 157B). This helps, but does not altogether eliminate the difficulty. However, some more thoroughgoing solutions do exist.

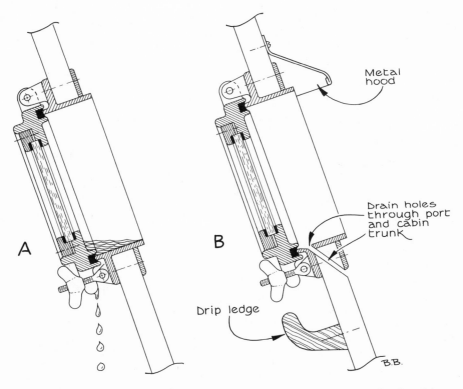

157A. The inevitable port leak. B. Reducing port leakage and eliminating drips.

On one boat—*Sylvia*—I saw an interesting arrangement. When the port was opened, a clear plastic molded unit, angled inboard at 45 degrees, was slipped into a flange attached to the wall just below the port. Any rainwater that came in, drained right out again.

Another design (Drawing 158), seen on *Cherubini,* is a variation of the old Herreshoff portlight. It consists of a flat plate of tempered glass held up by V-shaped brackets and kept in place by wedges supported by the brackets. Drain holes drilled diagonally through the cabin side take care of any leaks. When the port is closed, the plate glass is wedged firmly against the cabin side. When ventilation is desired, the wedges are pulled and then dropped between the glass and the cabin side; the result is an opening of approximately 30 degrees, which admits air but no light spray or rain. In really good weather, when greater ventilation is desired, the plate glass can be removed and slipped into a rack in the overhead.

If this rig is installed, care must be taken that the V-shaped brackets are securely fastened to the side of the cabin; otherwise, they can be knocked out all too easily in heavy weather. Also, they should be of

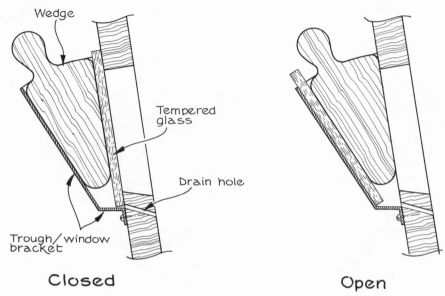

Wedge

Tempered
glass

Drain hole

Trough/window
bracket

Closed   Open

158. Herreshoff-type portlight.

such material (e.g., bronze or stainless) that the flanges supporting the wedges will not bend or break off.

One great advantage of this arrangement is that in heavy weather one can remove the glass and install really heavy emergency shutters with little or no difficulty. Another advantage is that one is not limited to standard stock sizes, but rather can have the ports of any size and dimensions desired.

The best portlight I have seen eliminates all of the problems that have been mentioned. This is the Rainguard portlight (for supplier, see Appendix). It pivots from the bottom to a half-open position. Any rain or dollops of spray that find their way in drain out through holes in the bottom of the frame. For full ventilation, the unit can be lifted out of its pocket and stowed in the overhead. This is a truly great piece of equipment that does not seem to have been really well publicized.

Ports in the hull are usually found only on large boats. Because they are under water for a large portion of the time, they should have an inner metal cover that locks down protectively over the glass plate. Nevertheless, if they are opening rather than fixed ports, they tend to cause a great deal of trouble. If they are improperly secured when going to sea, the result may be a wet bunk. If they are forgotten altogether, the water pouring through the twelve-inch hole may flood the bilge. And if they are simply left open for ventilation, it is always possible that a fast runabout will come by and dump in a bucketful of water.

DOGHOUSE WINDOWS

Large doghouse windows are fine if cruising is to be done in sheltered waters only, but they are not recommended for offshore sailing unless really good storm shutters are provided as well. This fact was brought home to me when I read the story of *Doubloon*'s double capsize. Here was a proven twelve-year-old ocean racer that was rolled completely over. Her doghouse windows were stove in, and she was saved from flooding through the use of emergency shutters made out of floorboards. The crew would have had a much easier time if she had carried real emergency storm shutters.

The best storm shutters are also the most expensive—heavy pieces of 1-inch Plexiglass or ½-inch Lexan secured over the doghouse windows by means of stainless-steel or bronze bolts that either pick up threaded plates recessed into the sides of the doghouse or are extended right through the sides of the doghouse. This arrangement provides ample strength and also allows light to enter. The same installation is also frequently made with ¾-inch plywood instead of Plexiglass. Shutters of this type are strong and cheap, but do leave it rather dark and unattractive down below.

If the windows are not too large, and extremely bad weather and rough seas are not anticipated, emergency shutters can be made, to be installed after disaster has struck—i.e., after a doghouse window has been knocked out. In constructing one of these, the first step is to cut a piece of plywood about two inches larger in every dimension than the doghouse window. Next, 1-by-2-inch cleats are cut, to bridge the gap between the perimeter of the window and the shutter. The cleats and the wooden shutters are drilled to take ⅜-inch or ½-inch carriage bolts with wing nuts on the inside, the exact dimensions depending of course on the size of the window. The emergency shutters should be clearly marked when they are made, with top and bottom, inside and outside, plainly identified. Similarly, the cleats should be carefully numbered and labeled. Then one will be able to assemble the shutters rapidly when they are needed, instead of having to put together a jigsaw puzzle in heavy weather. The disadvantage of this type of rig is that it cannot be installed until after the doghouse window has been smashed.

CABIN HEATING

In *OSY*-I, I firmly condemned the usual kerosene and alcohol cabin heaters on the grounds that although they provided heat, they lacked drying power, and sometimes even seemed to be producing moisture. Since then, it has been pointed out to me that the situation is vastly improved if the kerosene, alcohol, or gas cabin heater is properly vented, and exhausted outboard.

Further, in Europe, there are electrically activated, diesel-fueled hot-air heaters. The fumes are exhausted outboard, power consumption is relatively low, and the heat is more than adequate. We were pleasantly surprised, when on a powerboat on the Shannon River, to find that the hot-air heating system of our boat was excellent, producing hot, dry air. Whether or not it will work under sail, I am not sure, but it certainly worked superbly at anchor. Wright Britton, of *Delight,* has installed a system of this type, and reports that it works well.

Diesel-fueled heaters are usually installed in the engine room, and the hot air is brought fore and aft by means of flexible ducts. On yachts with air conditioners, the same ducts may be used for both heating and air conditioning, being transferred from one unit to the other, as desired. Since the amount of electric power drawn by different heaters varies widely, it is essential to check the rquirements of the unit under consideration against the battery capacity of the boat in which it is to be used.

SOLID-FUEL STOVES

Solid-fuel stoves will burn wood, coal, peat—any solid fuel one can lay one's hands on. The actual choice of fuel will be largely governed by what is available, the climate of the area, and whether the stove is to be used continuously, or merely for a few hours now and then.

Wood

Of course, the best wood for fuel is hardwood, which is difficult to ignite, but burns slowly. Softwood can be lit instantly with a match, but burns quickly. Commercially available firewood will probably be too bulky for the stove; it can be cut with a bench saw into short lengths to fit the firebox, and then split into small pieces. The latter can be done on board the boat with a hatchet and a hammer. Also suitable as fuel are the scraps that can be found in a yard building wooden boats— the offcuts in the woodworking shop near the band saw, for example.

Since wood fires smoke, one must make sure the ventilator is functioning really well when wood is to be used.

Charcoal

Charcoal is a popular fuel, since it is relatively easy to light, burns with little or no smoke, and does not leave too much ash. However, it does burn very rapidly, and it is hard to store in that the normal pressed-charcoal briquettes will disintegrate when wet into unusable powder. They should therefore be packed in plastic bags.

When lighting charcoal, it is best to use paper and wood chips as kindling. Lighter fluid or gasoline should never—repeat, *never*—be used on charcoal that has previously been lit, even if the fire has apparently gone out. There may still be a hot spot, and squirting lighter fluid or gasoline on it will result in a big flare-up, or worse yet, an explosion, which will severely burn anyone in the vicinity.

Coal

Coal comes in all types, ranging from the soft, brown variety only slightly harder than charcoal to good old hard, blue Pennsylvania anthracite. The latter is extremely difficult to obtain and difficult to light (one must start off with wood) but once lit, it burns extremely slowly, with a hot flame, little ash, and little smoke. The effort required to find it is worth making.

Back in 1963, my late wife and I arrived on October 12 at the Maury and Spence boatyard, South Norwalk, Connecticut, to discover *Cantilena* covered with eight inches of snow—a poor beginning we felt, for a delivery trip to St. Thomas.

Jack Maury came along to open up the boat, and asked if he could be of any help to us. I looked at the nice big coal stove and replied, "Yes, please get me a box of wood chips and two fifty-pound sacks of hard anthracite coal."

Jack looked at me and said, "You want charcoal, don't you?"

"Hell no, I want hard blue anthracite." Jack came back ten minutes later with the wood chips, and then forty-five minutes later with the anthracite.

The next morning, he asked if he could charter *Iolaire,* and we made the necessary arrangements. This decision to charter my boat seemed to me rather sudden, since he knew very little about me or the boat. Subsequently, while sailing in the Caribbean, he explained why he had made up his mind so quickly. He said he had seen many delivery skippers pick up boats and all of them wanted different things, often things that were less than essential; because I had attacked the basic problem immediately on arrival, I had impressed him as someone who knew what he was doing—someone he would like to sail with.

Similarly, as noted in *OSY*-I (Ch. X), when Carl Hovgard, head of the Nevins yacht yard, entered *Circe* in the 1955 Transatlantic Race—the first since World War II—and asked Rod Stephens to supervise the preparations, one of the first things Rod did was to tell him to buy a hundred pounds of good hard, blue anthracite coal for the cabin heaters. In Rod's view, this coal, and a board for the emergency head, were the two most important things to be obtained.

Pressed Peat

Pressed peat is not found on the western side of the Atlantic, but it is cheap and readily available in Ireland. It is a very practical fuel, being clean, easy to handle, and easy to light, and it burns slowly, with a good heat; it does, however, leave a fair amount of ash.

SMOKE HEADS

Any heating stove that burns with an open flame must have venting outboard, not only to remove moisture but also to get rid of the fumes. Otherwise, the boat may be uninhabitable because of the smell, and the carbon monoxide that is released may actually kill. Even in the coldest weather, a few ventilators must be left open, to prevent asphyxiation.

Good smoke heads are also needed to prevent back drafts. When these occur, kerosene and alcohol stoves are none too happy, and solid-fuel stoves immediately fill the boat with smoke which in heavy weather is almost impossible to get rid of, and which can make even the toughest crew instantly seasick.

Finding a good smoke head today is most difficult, and making one is a sometime proposition. The old-fashioned Liverpool (*OSY*-I, photo 118; Drawing 151) does work. An emergency variation consists of a straight pipe with a U-shaped piece of metal bent over the top (Drawing 159). If this piece is properly placed, the wind blowing through it will give rise to a Venturi effect. This device does work, but it must be readjusted whenever the course is altered or the sails are trimmed—trim the sails; then trim the smoke head.

The "whirlybird" smoke head (Photo 28) has built up a reputation for reliability in all conditions. It is easily protected by a bracket or hoop, and the stronger the wind, the better it sucks.

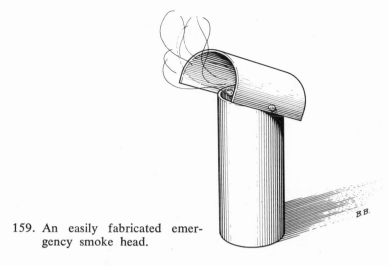

159. An easily fabricated emergency smoke head.

28. *"Whirlybird" smoke head.* PERKO MARINE HARDWARE AND LAMP CO.

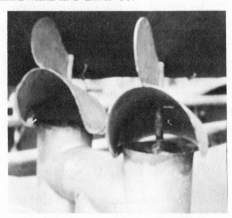

29. Jolie Brise *smoke head.*
GEORGE G. LEE

The most interesting smoke head I have ever seen is the one on *Jolie Brise* (Photo 29). Free-pivoting, with tail feathers, it always points dead downwind. This smoke head has stood the test of time, having been in use on *Jolie Brise* for over forty years, in all weather condition. It is connected to a coal stove which burns twenty-four hours a day. The crew members of *Jolie Brise* have complete faith in this simple unit. Further, an Englishman pointed out to me that in the days of coal stoves and coal fireplaces, units like this were to be found on the roofs of hundreds of thousands of houses in England.

Smoke-Head Blowers

The real professional Down East yachtsman, with a lifetime of experience, may be able to get a blazing fire going in three or four minutes even on a cold, wet, windy night, when the air in the boat is as cold as the outside air, so that there is no natural ventilation through the smoke head. However, for the rest of us, more often than not instead of a warm blaze, the result is a smoldering fire, a smoky cabin, and a semi-asphyxiated crew. Similarly, at sea, when the sails are re-trimmed and the course is altered, we are likely to experience a sudden back draft which blows smoke down into the boat, putting out the fire and driving the entire crew up on deck, coughing and choking.

There is a simple way to solve both these problems: merely mount a 12-volt blower on the back end of the exhaust pipe leading to the smoke head. Then, when the stove is to be lit, turning on the blower creates a good draft immediately. Similarly, at the first sign of a back draft due to an improperly trimmed smoke head, flipping the blower on will restore the proper draft, and the smoke will be sucked out of the boat. In preparing for *Iolaire*'s seventieth-birthday cruise we made the mistake of neglecting to install a blower of this type, and we suffered accordingly. If we had put it in, life would have been much pleasanter. The power drain of such a blower will not be excessive even for boats with minimal power, since normally it will be used only in emergencies, for four or five minutes at a time; if the stove and the smoke head are properly designed, once the fire gets going, the blower will be unnecessary.

EMERGENCY CABIN HEATING

If you are stuck in a cold-weather area with no chance of obtaining a cabin heater, don't give up the ship. Go to the nearest garden-supply house, buy some clay flowerpots (one for each stove burner, plus a couple of spares, as they are fragile), place them upside down over the burners, and leave the stove on continuously. The results will not be as good as those obtained from a cabin heater, but life will be bearable; and amazingly, the heat produced seems dry. If flowerpots are not available, bricks can be used. If worst comes to worst and all else fails, try piling some big rocks on the stove—primitive, but better than nothing.

INSULATION AND CONDENSATION

Because fiber glass is an excellent conductor of heat and cold, fiber-glass boats frequently sweat a great deal. There are various methods of eliminating this condensation. Some people attach scraps of carpeting to the hull with contact cement, but exactly how one keeps this carpeting clean, and dries it out once it is wet, is beyond me. Another method, which does appeal to me, is to obtain squares of cork, as thick as possible, and epoxy glue them to the inside of the hull. Some of the best fiber-glass hulls are teak ceiled, more or less as on a wooden boat. The ceiling is attached to light frames fiber-glassed to the hull, and ample spaces between the ceiling strips allow the hull to breathe. This is the best-looking installation, but it is very expensive.

CABIN SOLES

What materials are most suitable for cabin soles is a subject of much debate. On the old European boats, of even the finest construction, the cabin soles were always very rough and crude, and were kept covered with rugs. However, trying to keep rugs clean and neat on a true cruising boat is, in the estimation of many, one step away from an impossibility. My advice to the crew on a boat whose owner afflicts them with a rug is twofold: spill battery acid on it, or insist that it is mildewed and must be thrown overboard.

TEAK AND HOLLY

The best cabin sole by far is built of teak planks approximately 2 inches wide and ¾ inch thick, with a thin strip of holly glued to one edge of each plank. The holly is just a little thicker than the teak, so it protrudes slightly above the surface when the planking has been laid down. In the areas where the sole is to be permanent (under settees, for example, and under the galley counter), the planks are screwed to the sole beams. The parts of the sole that will be walked upon should be removable, or at least have very large removable sections. These are built to match the permanent sole, the teak and holly being planked onto backing strips.

A varnished teak and holly sole is really beautiful, and because of the holly ridges, it is not slippery. Holly is a very hard wood, and will not wear down noticeably even after a decade of use.

Many stock fiber-glass boats have a sole made of $\frac{1}{16}$-inch teak and holly veneers glued to plywood. A sole of this type is as beautiful as the planked sole, but because it has no ridges it lacks the nonslip quality of the real thing. I have heard of the veneers separating from the plywood in a few cases. For this reason, it is desirable to have the exposed edges of the permanent sole, and all the edges of the removable sections, thoroughly sealed with epoxy to retard the entry of moisture into the plywood.

LIFT-UP RINGS

On many boats, the old standard lift-up rings are bolted to the removable portions of the cabin sole. When these rings are being purchased, they should always be checked with a magnet. All too often, though the ring is made of brass, it is penetrated by a steel pin, which lets go in a year or so.

Another device for lifting a cabin sole is a plate with a key (Drawing 160). This is neater than the lift-up ring in that it is flush with the sole, whereas the ring has a hollow dish which always holds water. In addition, it is stronger and more reliable than the lift-up ring. One or two keys are kept in the cabin, secured in brackets. To raise the sole, one need only insert a key into the plate and then turn it 90 degrees.

If lift-up rings or other devices are not available, a hole one inch in diameter can be drilled into the cabin sole. Then one can place a finger in the hole and pull up the floorboard. If this method is used, the

160. Floorboard lift-up plate with a simple bent-rod key. If the key is lost, a new one can be made quickly.

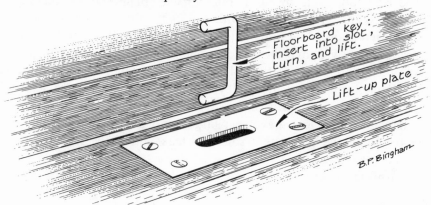

floorboards should be well trimmed to prevent jamming, since the finger is not nearly so strong as a lift-up ring or lift-up tool.

DUSTBOX

One of the beautiful touches found aboard most Sparkman and Stephens custom-built boats is the placement here and there in the cabin sole of small, stainless-steel dustboxes concealed beneath gratings. One can sweep the litter from the cabin sole straight into the dustbox, and then lift out the box and empty it, instead of having to hunt for a dustpan, which always seems to be stowed where it can't be found.

PETS

During the twenty years I have lived in the Lesser Antilles, I have seen an unbelievable variety of pets on visiting yachts, among them parrots, cats, dogs, boa constrictors, an ocelot, an orangutan, monkeys, lizards, and other esoteric creatures. My advice to the single-handed ocean-sailing yachtsman who feels he needs some company is to find a good-looking girl. Failing that, if he decides he needs a pet, he should examine the pet situation as carefully as he would the girl situation, and try to use his head rather than his heart in making a choice.

Parrots are fairly common shipboard pets. They do serve as someone to talk to, but they make a fair amount of mess. Personally, I dislike parrots; it seems that every time I get near one, no matter how friendly it appears, it takes a chunk out of me.

A cat, especially a good ratter, is great on a large ship, since it keeps the rodents under control. However, on a small boat, the smell of the cat is pervasive. It is apparent the minute one steps on board, even before going belowdecks. The cat's sand, sawdust, or what-have-you must be dealt with. And a cat is useless for keeping watch.

For this reason, many yachtsmen prefer dogs as pets on board. A dog that sleeps on deck will make a hell of a racket if anyone tries to cut the dinghy loose or sneak aboard at night, so few thieves will come near a boat if a dog is present. However, a large dog may be expensive to feed in remote areas, frequently as expensive as a person, and takes up almost as much room as a person. In heavy weather, a large dog is in danger of losing its footing and going overside. A small dog takes

30. *Schipperke, or Belgian barge dog.* D. M. STREET, JR.

up little room, consumes little food, and still makes enough noise to scare away a thief. In heavy weather, it can be kept down below or can curl up in the cockpit corner under the dodger, without occupying a lot of room. For these reasons, many yachtsmen feel that the ideal dog for a boat is the Schipperke, or Belgian barge dog (Photo 30). Small, smart, an excellent watchdog, a good swimmer, a good ratter, and a loyal pet who will follow its master like a shadow, this dog is just about ideal.

A yacht that visits foreign shores will encounter various problems with pets. In some areas, pets are not allowed ashore, even to be transported from the boat to the airport for shipment home by airfreight. England, and many of the former British colonies, do not permit animals to enter the country until they have gone through a six-month quarantine period. However, where pets are not allowed on shore, keeping them on board the yacht should not be too difficult.

In any case, the pet's various shots should be kept up-to-date, and papers should be carried to prove that this has been done.

MUSICAL INSTRUMENTS

Although musically inclined crew members may provide great entertainment, their instruments can be a very mixed blessing. Admittedly, I have never seen a full-sized harp or a bass fiddle on shipboard, but there may be two or three guitars, and in that case, a couple of crew members may end up sleeping on deck. A good guitar seems to be much more fragile and prone to damage from dampness than a crew member. Full-sized accordions just take up too much room, and though the wail of bagpipes is wonderful to hear from the foredeck of big *Ti,* few smaller boats can stow the player and the pipes!

It is too bad that those who are musically inclined are not more interested in the old squeeze-box—the concertina—which takes up little space, easily stows in a seabag, and is a traditional instrument of seamen.

Even better, from the skipper's standpoint, is the old hornpipe or its modern equivalent, the harmonica. It is so small it can be kept in one's pocket, even a dunk in the drink doesn't hurt it if it is flushed out with fresh water, and some people are marvels with it. I well remember a couple of very pleasant night watches on the Freedom 40 when watchmate Harvey Loomis entertained us with his mouth organ.

These points are worth discussing in detail, before a trip begins, with the musically inclined members of the crew.

XI

~~~~~~~~~~~~~~~~~~~~~~~~~~~~~~~~~~

Galley

LOCATION

Back aft is not always the proper place for the galley. We have been very happy on *Iolaire* with a forward galley. The main disadvantage of this location—the extra motion—doesn't bother us, as we have all developed strong stomachs; and on our wonderful Heritage stove (the forerunner of the Luke stove), keeping pots from tipping over is no great feat even in the worst weather.

At the same time, the forward location has several advantages. For one thing, no matter how much cooking is done, though the galley and forecastle may get hot, the rest of the boat is not affected. This is important in the tropics. To be sure, *Iolaire* is unusually well ventilated. Not all forward-galley boats can be expected to provide this advantage.

Further, in the days when we did chartering, my crew and I could retire to the forecastle forward of the galley, pull the curtain, and be safe from our charter party. We could cook to our heart's content without being bothered, while the passengers enjoyed their privacy as well.

Similarly, now that we do very little chartering but live on board, my crew has the whole forward portion of the boat completely to himself—the galley, his bunk, a comfortable place to sit and read, a place where his friends can come aboard, enjoy a beer, and listen to the radio without interfering with my family or friends.

Galleys aft may be fine when one is delivering a boat or cruising with one's family and friends—but when living aboard, I'll take the forward galley.

It should be borne in mind, however, that *Iolaire*'s forward galley is practical, despite a boat length of just forty-four feet, only because she is a very heavy-displacement boat and has a very easy motion. I doubt very much that anyone could survive in a forward galley on a modern light-displacement yacht of the same length. By contrast, in the old days of "proper" yachts and "professional" crews, the forward galley could be found, amazingly, even on boats of only thirty-five feet, with the professional crew living in the forecastle and cooking in the galley sometimes with only four feet of headroom. The famous Herreshoff-designed and -built *Dolphin* (sailing since 1914 and still racing) has this arrangement even today. However, on a boat this small a forward galley is really not practical unless the cook has a cast-iron stomach.

In a word, if considering a forward galley, one should take into account the type of sailing to be done and the size and motion of the boat, and one should be very careful to discuss the situation with the cook or cooks, before coming to a decision.

LAYOUT

More and more thought is being given to the galley, and on some boats very esoteric arrangements have been introduced. Some of these work, and some don't.

One of the newest ideas that apparently does work, although it requires a fair amount of space, is to gimbal the entire galley—the stove, the icebox or refrigerator, everything. This was first tried on Tom Watson's *Palawan* and apparently has also worked out well on certain other boats; on hard-bilged centerboarders with rather semicircular sections, it has been possible to gimbal the sideboard and sink as well as the stove, so that there are plenty of places where one can put things down without worrying about their sliding around.

Another problem that has been of continual concern to cooks is that in the galley they are cut off from the rest of the boat, with visibility, and ventilation, none too good. In large part, this feeling of isolation experienced by the cook can be eliminated by careful design.

An example of a good galley is the one being designed for *Lone Star* by Jay Paris, reflecting my ideas and the desires of Marcia Huggins, wife of the owner (Drawing 161). There are certain general requirements for a galley, and each cook also has his own individual preferences. Both must be taken into account in the design for a particular boat.

Basically, one should expect a galley where the cook has room enough to work, and is out of the main lane of traffic. However, some cooks—

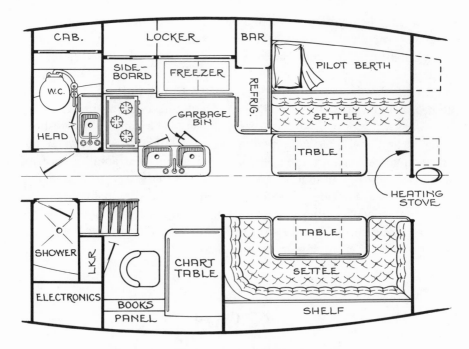

LONE STAR, Main Cabin Plan
designer : J. E. Paris

161. *Lone Star* layout, showing galley.

Marcia among them—do not want to be closed off from the rest of the crew; they prefer to be able to communicate with those in the cockpit and in the main cabin.

Furthermore, the galley should be situated so that people can help the cook without getting in the way, and so that they can reach ice, liquor, soft drinks, and the like without bothering the cook, who has more than enough to do trying to prepare the next meal.

Another essential requirement is that the cook be able to work in the galley in heavy weather without being thrown all over the place. On some boats, straps are provided, which the cook can lean against. Even better is a U-shaped galley with the open end forward or aft; then the cook can place his hip against the lee counter no matter what tack the boat is on.

Further, the arrangements should be such that the cook not be thrown into the stove when it is on the lee side, and that the roast not try to jump out of the oven when it is on the weather side. For this reason, many people advocate a stove mounted athwartships. In the past, however, it was almost impossible to find an athwartship *gimbaled* stove. The advantages gained through the athwarthship mounting were counterbalanced by the difficulty in keeping pots on the stove and food in the pots in the absence of gimbaling. Many cooks claim that in this situation deep pots are the answer, but how does one fry an egg when the stove is heeled 20 degrees?

Recently, people have solved the problem by having athwarthship gimbaled stoves made to order, and now even this is unnecessary, since Paul Luke has come out with a stove of this type. Accordingly, the *Lone Star* stove is gimbaled, and is mounted on the after bulkhead, so that there is less danger that the cook will be thrown against the stove or that the roast will try to jump out of the oven into the cook's lap.

The sideboard, too, is gimbaled. Having sailed many miles on Percy Chubb's *Antilles,* which has this amenity, I know that a gimbaled sideboard is an absolute godsend for the cook. Such jobs as making sandwiches and chopping onions, green peppers, potatoes, and the like are infinitely easier if they can be performed on a gimbaled surface. Otherwise, at a 30-degree angle of heel, the vegetables being chopped are likely to end up on the cabin sole. Further, in heavy weather, getting food from the stove to the table is most difficult. An intermediate resting place, where the food can be set down, makes the job much easier. And if food is being dished out directly from the stove, each person can grab his plate from the gimbaled sideboard and place it on the table.

Two sinks, installed so that they drain on both tacks, make dishwashing easier. Fresh water is provided by a pressure system and also by a foot pump, and salt water is provided by a gravity feed.

The garbage bucket is set out of sight on a gravity-hinged locker door, by means of the arrangement shown later in this chapter.

The 5-cubic-foot refrigerator and 10-cubic-foot freezer have a double system, for complete dependability. The refrigerator is both top opening and side opening to keep the loss of cold at an absolute minimum. When there is a top door only, all too often the food needed is down at the bottom of the refrigerator, and the amount of cold lost as one removes everything to get to it may be considerable. When there is both a top and a side door, the intelligent cook who wants to minimize the amount of cold lost through the side door can periodically pull out the food to be used during the next few days and put it on the shelf accessible through the top of the box. To prevent the crew from using the side door—letting all the cold out, and taking food the cook is reserving for the future—the installation of a lock would probably not be ill advised.

Lone Star has enough stowage space in the galley for a normal two-week supply of food. On longer trips, as is customary, food will be

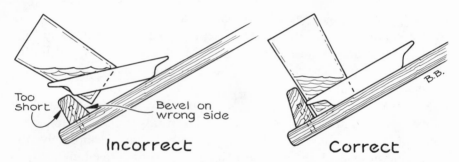

Too short

Bevel on wrong side

Incorrect

Correct

B.B.

162. To be effective, fiddle rails must be properly designed and installed.

stowed not only in the galley, but under the main-cabin bunks and all through the boat. Because friction latches are useless in heavy weather, all locker doors have positive latches; drawers of course have the standard lift-up notches. The sliding doors in the galley are transparent, to eliminate the frustrating and time-consuming job of searching for food, condiments, and the like. A 2½-inch transparent lip in front of all shelving makes the contents easily visible while preventing them from falling out when on the weather side.

The dishes (from Yachting Tableware) have been purchased and sent to the builders, so that properly fitting chocks in which they will not rattle around can be installed in the lockers. Similarly, all pots and pans, cutlery, and other utensils have been purchased and sent to the builders, so that provision can be made for proper stowage in the boat. Removable fiddle rails (Drawing 162) are provided throughout the galley.

A 12-volt electric blower will remove smells from the galley during heavy cooking, but will of course be only intermittently used; the continual exhaust draught will be provided by an exhaust ventilator—the particular model to be chosen after some tests have been performed. Some of the new low-profile exhaust ventilators that have been produced in England appear to give extremely good performance.

Fluorescent lighting is to be installed. The exact location of the lights will be determined by experiment after the boat is completed. On a dark night, a couple of people will stand in the cockpit while others, down below, move the lights around until they have been placed so that they adequately light the galley and belowdecks areas, but do not blind the crew on deck. Further, at least one red light will be provided, so that crew members can go below at night to navigate, make coffee, or what-have-you without losing their night vision.

SINKS

There is always a great debate concerning the best shape for sinks, and no one will ever resolve it. We are most happy with our South Western Marine Factors oval sinks, 8 inches deep and 12 inches fore and aft, two of which fit in a space of 12 by 18 inches. Because these are good and deep, plates are stood in them on their sides; a minimal amount of water is needed, and it does not tend to spill out. Other people prefer large sinks, perhaps 13 inches square, in which plates can be laid down flat. With these, dishwashing is easier but considerably more water is used, so the choice is difficult.

A third view is that of the late Bobby Sommerset. When he purchased a boat, he immediately removed the sink, because he felt it was just a place for storing dirty dishes, and when there was no sink, people would have to put the plates in a bucket, wash them at once, and put them away—a strong-minded man's way of ending the dirty-dish problem.

STOVES

GIMBALING

Gimbaled Versus Nongimbaled Stoves

It is possible to go to sea without a gimbaled stove. One hears stories of *Yankee, Westward,* and similar yachts that have cruised around the world without a gimbaled stove. However, in most of these cases the cook has been an old-time professional, who has spent his life at sea and can cope with the nongimbaled stove. Also, boats like *Yankee* and *Westward* are large heavy-displacement vessels with a slow motion, and they sail at small angles of heel. Trying to cook on a non-gimbaled stove on a modern lively boat is a different matter. Life is just too short. No matter how good the hold-downs for the pots, cooking is difficult, since the food splashes back and forth and tends to spill. Even in port, there may be problems; the wake of a passing powerboat can cause pots to jump off the stove.

I know that Lin Pardey alleges that a nongimbaled stove is perfectly acceptable, but then, she admits in her writing that when she goes to sea, although she is not actively seasick, she loses most of her desire to eat, so she probably spends very little time in the galley.

31. Emergency gimbaled stoves. WEST PRODUCTS

Emergency Gimbaled Stoves

Keeping a crew well-fed and happy practically necessitates a well-fed, happy cook. Keeping a cook happy without a gimbaled stove is just about impossible. Therefore, the boat with a large, fixed, non-gimbaled stove—a coal stove, for example—should also carry at least one emergency gimbaled stove (Photo 31), such as the Sea Swing or a small gimbaled butane-canister camping stove. On small boats, a single unit will suffice; on large boats, two are probably necessary.

Before a cruise, it is absolutely essential to try bolting such a stove into its intended location, to make sure that its placement is convenient. At the same time, one should ascertain that there are some pots that will fit the top of the small stove, and hold-downs that will keep them there.

Given this emergency equipment, one can live moderately happily with a nongimbaled stove even on an ocean sailing yacht.

Design of Gimbaled Stoves

Gimbaled stoves must be correctly ballasted if they are to work well at sea, but unfortunately this is seldom taken care of in their design. The little two-burner Primus slung from overhead gimbals (Drawing 163) will operate quite well with no ballast because even with pots on top of the stove, the center of gravity is far below the pivot point. Still, the addition of five or ten pounds of lead, placed in the base as low as possible, will be an improvement.

The more standard stove with oven (Drawing 164) may be dangerous if unballasted. When the stove has nothing on it, the position of the pivot point (A) and the center of gravity (B) is as shown in the drawing at left. Once two or three big pots full of stew, water, coffee, or the like are placed on the top of the stove, the center of gravity

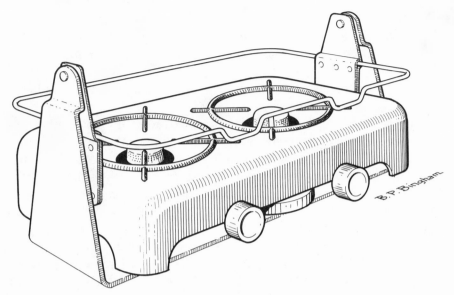

163. Two-burner Primus with overhead gimbals is ideal for the small cruiser with minimal galley space, and can serve as an emergency range for the larger boat.

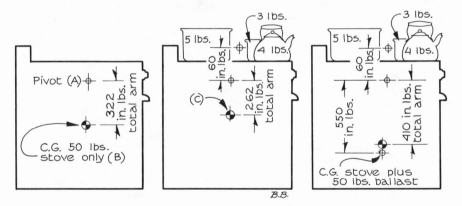

164. The convenience and safety of a standard marine gimbaled stove may be increased considerably by adding ballast, as indicated by the changes in the stability of the stove under various circumstances: unballasted and not in use (*left*); unballasted and in use (*center*): ballasted and in use (*right*).

moves up to somewhere around *C* (in the center drawing), so the stove has reduced stability. If the cook should then happen to lean or fall against the stove, it might capsize all too easily, upsetting the pots, making a mess of the galley, and perhaps badly injuring him.

To operate effectively, therefore, the full-size gimbaled stove should have forty or fifty pounds of ballast down in the very base, as shown in the drawing at right. Whether a stove is adequately ballasted can be determined by leaning on it, with a fair degree of weight. If this cannot be done without spilling the contents of the pots, additional ballast is needed. All too often when delivering a boat we have found that the stove required ballast, and being unable to obtain lead, we have had to stow bricks, rocks, or what-have-you in its bottom.

One of the few properly ballasted models on the market has been the Luke stove. However, as has been stated before, all life is a compromise: what is gained in one direction is often lost in another. The iron base plate in the standard Luke stove provided weight and stability, but it rusted, and had to be periodically chipped with a chipping hammer. The two-inch oven vent which could be added was difficult to cut and expensive to install.

The new Luke stove has an aluminum base plate, which does not rust and is easy to keep clean but provides no stability. One must add thirty or forty pounds of lead—preferably bolted to the outside of the base plate, since (I have been told) lead inside the oven might emit fumes when heated, and these could be absorbed by the food.

The Freedom 40 is equipped with this stove, and when I sailed her we found that though the stove did gain stability from the addition of lead to the base plate, it still oscillated, causing the pots to slide around. Unfortunately, we did not have Paul Luke's excellent hold-downs to keep them over the burners. However, we finally restrained the stove with some light shock cord, as shown in *OSY*-I (Drawing 161), and this dampened the motion beautifully.

In contrast, *Iolaire*'s stove (though mounted forward, while the Freedom 40's stove is mounted amidships, where the motion should be relatively slight) almost never has any problems with oscillation. I wonder if the reason might be that *Iolaire*'s stove is not only heavy (for after all, the Freedom 40 stove was equally heavy once the lead had been added), but equipped with a two-inch vent pipe at the after end. Perhaps this pipe provides enough friction to prevent the oscillation. The Freedom 40's stove does not have this vent pipe, and pivots on two ½-inch stainless-steel bolts, which of course produce little friction that might dampen the motion. Not all change is progress.

SAFETY

Oven-Door Stop

Every stove with an oven should be equipped with a door stop—a stainless-steel wire screwed into the oven door and into the side of the oven in such a manner that when open, the door falls only to the horizontal position. Then the roasting pan can be eased out onto the door when basting is necessary or when the roast is to be served. In heavy weather, moving a turkey directly from the oven to the table is sometimes a tricky proposition. Furthermore, a number of people have been badly burnt because a door hanging straight down hooked onto the cabinet below it when the boat rolled, and everything came flying off the stove. Therefore, if the stove manufacturer has not already provided one, a door stop should be installed.

Fuel Shutoff

No matter what fuel is used, it is absolutely imperative that there be a fuel-line shutoff that is readily accessible even with the stove on fire. Countless bad fires on boats have been caused by the failure to have this type of shutoff.

COAL STOVES

A coal stove can be very desirable for a boat which is to be sailed in cooler areas. It requires a really good smoke head, like the one carried by *Jolie Brise* (see Chapter X), and also a good blower, as described in Chapter X. A coal stove thus equipped can always be made to draw, in any condition of wind and sea.

If the galley is in the forecastle, bulkheaded off from the rest of the boat, a coal stove is extremely useful in that it keeps that area warm and dry. When coming off watch, the crew can hang up soggy, wet sweaters, socks, and the like, out of the way, and know that they will be dry for the next watch, four or five hours later.

The stove should always be mounted so that the doors are athwartships. Otherwise, if the boat drops off a wave, the doors may fly open, and out will come coal, roast, and what-have-you. Since a coal stove is ungimbaled, the pots used must be deep, and the fiddle rail or other device to hold the pots on the stove must be extremely good. I wonder if it would be possible to design a gimbaled coal stove, with a stovepipe forming part of the gimbal.

KEROSENE STOVES—THE PRIMUS

Many of the Primus stoves are not particularly good; they are usually made of enameled steel, which rusts all over the place. However, an excellent kerosene stove is obtainable; undoubtedly the best value in the world for a stove of this type is the Taylor Para-Fin (for address, see Appendix). It is really well built, the English equivalent of the Luke, being constructed of solid-brass plate, either plain or chrome plated, joined by nuts and bolts in such a manner that the entire unit can be taken apart for cleaning. The stove is available in various models, for practically any size of boat: with two burners and a warming grill, with two burners and an oven one can bake in, or with three burners and a two-burner oven. High-quality (but expensive) kerosene stoves are also produced by Shipmate (for address, see Appendix).

The owner of a kerosene stove should remember that if kerosene is unobtainable—and for some strange reason it is getting harder and harder to buy—mineral spirits can be used. This fuel provides a cleaner and hotter flame than does kerosene, but eventually will burn the side out of the burner. Therefore, a remote shutoff, which can be easily reached even with the stove on fire, is important.

ALCOHOL AND GAS STOVES

Alcohol and gas stoves are being discussed together because most manufacturers offer the same stove, with only the burners changed, for use with each of these fuels. Stove alcohol is becoming harder to find, and more expensive, with each passing year. Therefore, although it may be all right as stove fuel for a weekend cruiser, it certainly is not suitable for a boat which will be cruising extensively or will have a crew living on board for months at a time. Where serious cruising is contemplated, the alcohol stove should be converted to kerosene or to bottled gas.

If one really scrutinizes the stove market, and checks with stove owners, one will soon recognize that the best buy today in an alcohol or gas stove is the Luke copy—or perhaps one should say development —of the old Heritage stove. This stove is made of stainless steel, with bronze burners and grates and an aluminum top, and has a really good set of hold-downs to keep the pots in place. Some other stoves may look like the Luke, but they are not as well manufactured and have too many rapidly corroding iron parts, the burners among them. Iron burners may rust out in as little as a year, and corroded iron burners are extremely dangerous. So although these stoves may be cheaper than the Luke, they are probably not worth what they cost in the long run.

We have the ancestor of the Luke stove on *Iolaire;* it is now over twenty-five years old, and still going strong. Periodically, I order new burners or grates from Paul Luke. He reports that ours is the only boat in the world on which stove grates are expendable. But we find that when used twelve months of the year, grates last only about eighteen months. The heat and the scrubbing in salt water cause them to waste away and become so thin that they fall apart.

For many years, I contended that this stove would be close to perfect if it had a grill, so that one could toast bread and broil chicken or barbecue spareribs. After the absence of a grill was mentioned in *OSY*-I, so many people pestered Paul Luke about it that he started to make one, so now the stove has just about everything.

The other possible improvement that I mentioned in *OSY*-I (and my doing so did not at all endear me to Paul Luke) was the installation of a two-inch vent pipe in the stove gimbal, as shown in *OSY*-I, Drawing 154. Without this vent, on hot days in the summer or in the tropics, the fat, soot, and smoke from a roast make the galley, which all too often is located in the main cabin, uninhabitable. Living in Maine, Paul does not encounter the problem of heat in the galley, and he therefore cannot understand the reason for the two-inch vents and swears he is no longer going to install them. It is to be hoped that those ordering stoves from him will not have too much trouble persuading him to change his mind.

Recently, Paul Luke came up with his new model (Drawing 165), an athwartship gimbaled stove with four burners on top, an oven, and a broiler. Once adequate ballasting has been added, it is really perfect, especially since the athwartship mounting means that the turkey will not try to jump out of the oven on one tack. The one improvement I

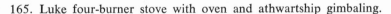

165. Luke four-burner stove with oven and athwartship gimbaling.

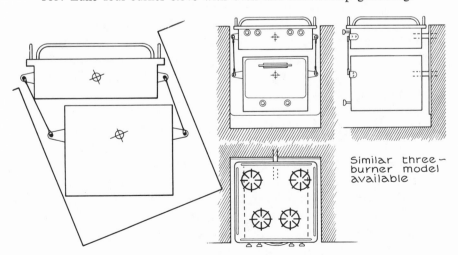

Similar three-
burner model
available

would like to see on this wonderful new stove is, once again, the addition of a vent. This could be accomplished by substituting for the pivot bolt a hollow pipe two or three inches in diameter, connected to a two-inch pipe leading up to the deckhead and exhausting through a smoke head.

Alcohol Stoves—Dangers

Few people realize that vaporized alcohol in an enclosed space, in contact with a hot stove burner or an open flame in the cabin heater or cabin lamp, may explode. This danger is brought home by the account of a horrible alcohol explosion in an article by John G. Patrick in *Sail,* May, 1978.

Bottled Gas

Three different types of bottled gas are available for cooking on board. Since these gases have varying storage requirements, one should be very careful when purchasing gas to select the type suitable for the bottles at hand. Improper storage can lead to disaster.

BUTTA GAS: Butta gas, or calor gas, is rather common in Europe, but is on its way out, since weight for weight propane is a good deal hotter.

COMPRESSED NATURAL GAS (CNG):   Natural gas is used on boats on the west coast of the United States and is beginning to be found on the east coast. It is supposedly safer than other types of gas because it is lighter than air and will not settle in the bilges. It burns with an extremely clean flame. Storage is in steel bottles, weighing thirty-two pounds apiece; because CNG is in a vapor state even when stored, the bottles can be placed in any position, and can be kept in lockers with venting through the top, which is much easier to put in than venting through the bottom.

One disadvantage is the fact that bottled natural gas is still difficult to obtain except on the west coast. Fuller descriptions of the problems involved in using natural gas can be found in *Sail* for October, 1974, and in *The Telltale Compass* (for address, see Appendix).

PROPANE: Propane is the gas most commonly used on board; if the stove has been properly installed and maintained, it is quite safe. The standard old yachting bottle in which propane was formerly stored—

the steel cylinder twenty inches long and ten inches in diameter made by Suburban Propane—is now unobtainable. However, aluminum gas bottles of all sizes and shapes, which can be stowed vertically or horizontally, are available from Worthington Cylinders (for address, see Appendix).

A good idea of how much propane will be required for an offshore journey can be gained from our experience on *Iolaire*. On her seventieth-birthday cruise, with a crew which varied from five to seven cooking two hot meals a day and doing a moderate amount of baking on a stove with three burners on top and two in the oven, twenty pounds of propane lasted about twelve or thirteen days.

FILLING PROPANE AND BUTTA-GAS BOTTLES: The following discussion does not apply to the handling of liquid petroleum (L.P.), which is stored at very high pressure.

At times, filling the gas bottles involves problems. Frequently, bottles are not interchangeable. Some have female fittings; some have male fittings. The plant which supplies the correct bottle may be fifty miles away and reachable only by taxi—an expensive proposition. However, all is not lost; there is an out. When planning to do extensive cruising, one should visit the nearest bottled-gas depot to obtain the necessary parts, and using copper pipe, make up a number of adapters (Drawing 166)—male to male, male to female, and double female. Then one can refill the gas bottles oneself, under all circumstances.

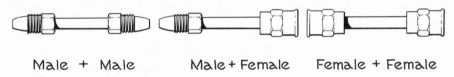

Male + Male   Male + Female   Female + Female

166. Various types of adapters, for refilling gas bottles in all circumstances.

Having picked up a bottle of the correct gas from the local distributor, one need only cross connect it to the empty bottle, setting the bottle to be emptied higher than the one to be filled. In cold weather, one should open the two valves and pour two or three kettlefuls of boiling water over the bottle to be emptied. As the latter warms up, the increased pressure will drive the gas into the bottle to be filled. In the tropics, the bottle to be filled should be placed in a tub, with ice packed around it; then, when boiling water is poured over the bottle to be emptied, the gas will blast on through.

It should be remembered that although butta (calor) gas and propane will both work in the same stove, they are quite different. Butta gas is stored at a much lower pressure than propane. Indeed, the gas bottle used does not have a relief valve. Accordingly, though one can keep butta gas in a propane bottle with no trouble, the reverse should not be done. There have been cases in the tropics where a butta-gas bottle filled with propane was left sitting out in the sun, and the increased pressure caused the valve to blow out. Luckily, the bottle itself did not explode. There was a hell of a racket, but—on these occasions —no one was killed. Do not put propane in a butta-gas bottle.

GAS LINES: Gas lines should be carefully checked at least once a year, especially if they pass behind the woodwork. All too often the copper pipe is buried behind the woodwork so it will not mar the beauty of the cabin. If salt water gets behind the woodwork and corrodes the pipe—out of sight and out of mind—the resulting leak in the gas line is frequently discovered only too late, when an explosion occurs.

GAS-BOTTLE SHUTOFF VALVES: The newest gimmick in gas-bottle shutoff valves is an electronic type, controlled by a switch in the galley, with an indicator light that goes on automatically when the gas is on. This is extremely useful, since it enables one to close the gas-bottle valve without having to go on deck. Such a switch is available from Marinetics (for address, see Appendix).

A variation on this theme is to be found in the installation, also mentioned in *OSY*-I, which we have on *Iolaire* (Drawing 167). A

167. *Iolaire's* through-deck gas shutoff valve.

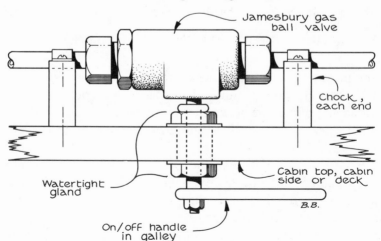

Jamesbury Corporation 90-degree on/off ball-cock valve is mounted upside down on the deck, and attached to a shaft which, coming through a stuffing gland, connects with a handle in the overhead of the galley. If the handle is athwartships, the gas is off; if it lies fore and aft, the gas is on. Any crew member sitting in the galley or main cabin can instantly see if the cook has forgotten to shut the gas, and can turn it off himself. The valve is of bronze, with a stainless-steel ball and Tufnol seals. It was installed roughly twelve years ago and still works perfectly. Once a year, as a test, we disconnect the line, open the gas bottle (which has its own valve), turn off the Jamesbury valve, and put a match to it. So far, there has never been even a flicker of blue flame. Obviously, this is a very good valve.

GALLEY UTENSILS

POTS

One exceedingly useful pot that was not mentioned in *OSY*-I is the pressure cooker.

Every boat should have a pressure cooker. For one thing, when a pressure cooker is used, the time required to prepare many dishes is greatly reduced. For another, food in a pressure cooker will not slop out no matter what the stove does. Even if the cooker jumps right off the stove and lands upside down in the middle of the galley, the lid will stay on. One can just retrieve and replace the pressure weight and slap the cooker back on the burner. A third advantage is that in an emergency anything normally done in an oven—even baking a cake—can be done in a pressure cooker, by a good cook with proper instructions to follow. Accordingly, if one has a pressure cooker, one should be very careful to take along a good pressure-cooker cookbook, or at least a cookbook with a good section on the use of this utensil.

NONSKID PLATES AND CUPS

The nonskid plates and cups sold by Yachting Tableware (for address, see Appendix) are a tremendous boon to the yachtsman. They are better than advertised; they will stick to a Formica, polished, or varnished surface up to about a 30-degree angle of heel. I first came upon them while preparing to deliver from Marblehead to St. Thomas a Morgan Out Island 41 which was without a gimbaled table (how can a seagoing Out Island boat not have a gimbaled table?). We purchased six deep bowls and six mugs, and used nothing else. As long as the bowls or cups were not so full so that the contents spilled out, all was well; never once did they skid off the table.

GARBAGE

For a clean, neat galley, the garbage bucket must be readily accessible, yet out of sight. A very good arrangement is to set the garbage bucket on a shelf mounted near the bottom of a gravity-hinged locker door (Drawing 168). The garbage bucket should be at least 9¼ by 16 by 18 inches—the larger the better. The locker should be as airtight as possible, and the interior should be well sprayed, to discourage cockroaches.

168. Gravity-hinged door for garbage locker.

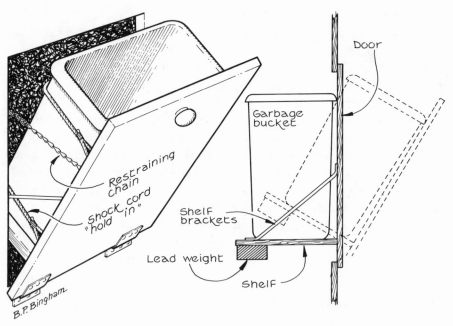

GARBAGE DISPOSAL

Garbage disposal on the ocean sailing yacht is always a problem, and the solution depends on one's location. When the vessel is tied up at a marina in a civilized area of the world, one can simply carry the garbage ashore in a plastic container and leave it in the nearest garbage can.

When cruising along a coast, it may be possible to carry garbage from one place to another for a few days, and still eventually dispose of it ashore. If this is done, the ecologists will certainly be appreciative. Not all garbage need be carried in this manner. Cans, each with a hole punched in the bottom, can be tossed into deep water, and edible garbage can be dropped overside to feed the fish and the gulls. However, not all food remnants can be regarded as edible. Fruit peelings, for example, should be saved for later disposal, as neither fish nor gulls will eat them, and if thrown into the sea, they may wash up onto someone's beach. Some fancy yachts even have compactors, which reduce garbage into little square cubes that apparently can be kept for a long time.

Once the yacht is truly offshore, disposing of garbage is not much of a problem. Obviously, one can't carry it on board for weeks, so everything must be sent overside, but with a little forethought this can be done in such a manner that pollution is kept to a minimum. Bottles can be broken before being discarded, and tin cans punctured. The plastic bag full of garbage should be upended and emptied of its contents. One occasionally sees people carefully tying bags as one does ashore; these bags, and the garbage within, will drift forever.

Bottle Breaking

Bottle breaking has caused trouble on many boats. Where the bottles have not been broken below the rail cap, glass has ended up back on board, to the great detriment of the crew. The best tool for bottle breaking is a good long ⅜-inch bronze rod. Grab the neck of the bottle, lean overside, and bang the bottle sharply with the rod. The bottom will drop out, and the remainder can then be tossed overside. The bronze rod is also useful for emergency bolt making.

FOOD

STORING FOR EXTENDED CRUISING

Iolaire's seventieth-birthday cruise, in which we sailed twelve thousand miles in seven months without the aid of an engine, included a few long unbroken passages: 15 days, 17 hours, from Halifax to Fastnet Rock, off the coast of Ireland; 14 days from Ireland to Madeira (a really slow passage); and 18½ days from Tenerife to Désirade, off Guadeloupe. During the entire seven months, the crew ate extremely well; we never missed a meal, and the skipper drank warm beer only on the last five days of the transatlantic passage—five days out of seven months! And this on a boat without mechanical refrigeration! For more information, see the discussion of iceboxes in Chapter XV.

With a little extra thought, many of the usual problems relating to food storage can be easily solved.

Food Requiring Refrigeration

When fresh meat is purchased for a long passage, it is worth while to have it frozen solid, like a block of ice. Then, if placed in a good icebox, it will remain frozen for three or four days, and during that time will in effect act like additional ice. Stored in this manner, meat will keep for at least two weeks. Thus there will be only a week or so during which recourse to canned and salted meats will be necessary, since boats are seldom at sea for more than twenty-two or twenty-three days —except when crossing the Pacific. Now that yachts can no longer stop at the Galápagos, the Pacific crossing involves a 4,500-mile jump, taking thirty to fifty days. I'll stick to the Atlantic!

Butter or margarine of course must be kept in the refrigerator, unless purchased in cans, which will preserve it indefinitely.

Lettuce, placed in the icebox in a slightly damp paper bag, will keep for a couple of days even in the tropics. By that time, some of the ice will have melted, and there will be room to set the lettuce, in its paper bag, directly on the ice, which will keep it usable for about six days more.

Food Not Requiring Refrigeration

People often believe the capacity of their icebox or refrigerator to be inadequate when the real problem is that they are continually placing on ice things that do not need refrigeration. There are many types of stores that fall into this category.

For example, even in the tropics, slab bacon will keep, as long as it is hung from the overhead with a piece of line so that air can circulate around it. One simply chops pieces off as needed. Similarly, properly cured ham will keep even in the tropics; one need only cut off a slice and soak it for a day or so before it is to be eaten. Salt fish and smoked fish can be purchased almost anywhere. One can buy a West Indian cookbook and make salt-fish pie, a great break in the diet when the ice has run out. In addition, one can usually find salami, baloney, cheeses, and the like, which will keep without refrigeration; these can provide the basis for excellent lunches.

The availability of canned meats varies drastically from place to place. The best bacon is packed in cans, but in the United States, this is hard to come by, and the canned ham usually sold has to be refrigerated or kept in a cool spot (hence, one is better off with cured ham of the Smithfield type, which requires neither canning nor refrigeration). Canned corned beef is of course to be found, along with meatballs, which can be used in making spaghetti sauce, but that's about it. However, abroad, a number of other types of canned meat are often obtainable, among them canned steak, which makes a great basic ingredient for stew, meat pie, or what-have-you.

Fresh vegetables must be stowed in baskets, burlap sacks, or dry paper bags, so that air can circulate around them. Onions and potatoes which we picked up in Ireland in the last week of October lasted us all the way across the Atlantic. The onions did not run out until mid-December, and the last of the potatoes were finally consumed in mid-January. Needless to say, we were careful to pick over these vegetables every four or five days, throwing out those which had gone bad. Also, these potatoes and onions were straight from a farm and had not been refrigerated. Once refrigerated, potatoes will last only two or three weeks. Peas, beans, carrots, and the like—unwashed—will keep almost indefinitely in a northern climate, especially if stowed in a fairly cool spot, and will keep for many weeks even in the tropics.

Egg storage is considered difficult, and a good deal has been written on the subject. Actually, properly handled, eggs should last at least three weeks, and possibly four, even in the tropics. The eggs should be obtained straight from the farm—unwashed and unrefrigerated—and placed in egg boxes. Every four or five days, they should be turned over, to prevent the shells from drying out. Toward the end of the trip, they should be tested in water before being broken. An egg that floats is rotten, and should be tossed overside. There is no faster way of getting the crew, and especially the cook, seasick than breaking a rotten egg belowdecks.

FREEZE-DRIED FOOD: The freeze-dried peas, beans, carrots, and the like produced by Batchelors and Erin in Ireland (for addresses, see Appendix) taste almost as good as the fresh vegetables, better than most frozen, in my opinion, and infinitely better than the canned. Since they are packed in little plastic bags, they last absolutely forever. We have kept some of these products for twelve months, to test them; just the other day I ate some peas that were a year old, and they tasted almost as if fresh from the garden.

When preparing for a long trip, if these products are not locally available, one might find it worth while to order them directly from Ireland, and to have them shipped by air parcel post. Even huge quantities are feather light, and the price is right. I recently purchased for £7.10 (a little over $12) enough freeze-dried vegetables for thirty dinners for six people—and literally no storage space was required.

CANNED GOODS: As much as possible, canned goods should be avoided, and fresh, freeze-dried, or dried foods used instead. For example, the wide variety of dried soups now available makes it unnecessary to stock up on canned soups, except that for a cruise in the tropics one may wish to carry some canned consommé. Served chilled, this makes a very filling and quick meal that does not require lighting the stove.

Whatever canned goods are carried should be stored in lockers well out of the bilge, since cans do have a tendency to rust.

DRIED FOOD: In Ireland, a wonderful bread mix can be obtained. One just adds milk and water, pounds the dough, pops it into the oven, and presto! fresh bread—which we enjoyed periodically all the way across the Atlantic. Further, once we got into the bread-making routine, we came to the conclusion that the normal yachtsman's practice of sailing from port to port, continually trying to buy bread, is not worth the effort. Given a good oven, a little experimentation, and a cookbook, baking bread, rolls, and the like is not very difficult. The only problem is that the better one gets at baking, the more one has to bake, because consumption by the crew soon outruns production by the cook!

SHIP BISCUIT: Occasionally—in the Canary Islands, for example— one can find really good ship biscuit. This is an excellent munchy, to nibble on watch, since it provides good exercise for the jaw muscles and really fills the stomach. Unfortunately, we did not buy enough for our trip, but finally, one of the crew discovered a recipe for ship biscuit in *The Joy of Cooking,* and proceeded to make some. Ship biscuit is definitely a worth-while addition to the larder for a long voyage.

LOCAL FOOD: At every port a yacht visits, there are local people eating fresh food. It is a good idea to traipse around and find out what is available locally. For instance, in the West Indies visitors discover yams, sweet potatoes, bluggers, plantain (which is related to the banana), christophine—all sorts of excellent vegetables that are inexpensive and will keep well without refrigeration.

So, on arrival in a strange area, and especially one with a strange culture, one should buy a local cookbook, if possible, and then go off to the nearest market, to see what can be found.

LIQUIDS

Especially in the tropics, large quantities of liquid will be consumed, perhaps one gallon per man per day. This can take various forms: water may be drawn directly from the tank and combined with soft-drink concentrates, bouillon cubes, and the like; cans of soft drinks may be piled in lockers; and so on. There are no hard-and-fast rules on this subject, because circumstances are constantly changing. Sometimes, soft drinks are twice as expensive as beer; at other times, the reverse is true. Sometimes, soft drinks are obtainable only in aluminum cans, which if stowed in the bilge would quickly deteriorate; at other times, they are found only in deposit bottles, which cost a fortune.

If beer and soft drinks are carried, and salt water is used in the head and in the galley, it should be possible to keep the total consumption of water drawn from the tank down to two quarts per man per day.

Cold Water

The usual method of getting cold water is to pump out the water, then chip some ice and add it. In warm areas, where the cruising sailor desires cold water very often, this process tends to be a pain in the neck. *Sirocco* has what appears to be the ideal arrangement. A water line goes from a hand pump to the interior of the icebox. There it is connected to a copper tube which is coiled around, and secured to, the side of the box, and which then emerges from a hole through the side and extends to a tap. All one has to do is open the tap and pump, and cold water is instantly available.

COOKING

The subject of cooking is of course the realm of a separate book; however, certain things should be remembered with respect to the galley and the preparation of food.

The safety of a vessel depends upon the fitness of her crew. Crew members who are not fit—who are tired, wet, hungry—are likely to become seasick; crew efficiency can deteriorate to the point where a boat is no longer seaworthy. Correspondingly, the crew with a full belly will hold together through thick and thin.

One of the things in *Iolaire*'s seven-month, twelve-thousand-mile cruise that we are happiest about is the fact that a meal was never missed. A large breakfast and a huge dinner were served; lunch consisted of soup—hot or cold, depending on the weather—and sandwiches. Every night after dinner, coffee, cocoa, and tea were available. It should be remembered that cocoa and hot chocolate are easy to digest and warming, and have tremendous food value. Coffee, on the other hand, is hard to digest, has no food value, and makes one hungry. Tea is easy to digest, and though providing no nourishment in itself, can be given high food value by the addition of honey. Also, drinking hot tea with honey is a great help in averting or overcoming seasickness. In very cold weather, a good hot toddy made with apple cider or apple juice, stick cinnamon, cloves, nutmeg, a big pat of butter per cup, and a shot of rum, is really warming and sticks to the ribs.

Periodically during the night, the stock of beverages was replenished. At times some of the crew did not feel much like eating, but with something always there, eventually they began to take nourishment and then quickly found their sea legs.

Cooking at sea does not have to be fancy, but the food should be plentiful, easily digestible, and appetizing. A crew with a full stomach will find little to complain about.

XII

~~~~~~~~~~~~~~~~~~~~~~~~~~~~

Plumbing

THE BILGE

BILGE PUMPS

The old-fashioned, up-and-down piston bilge pump is, or should be, as dead as the dodo. The only bilge pump to use is the diaphragm pump.

There are many good diaphragm pumps on the market. Diaphragm pumps from most manufacturers have fewer bearing parts than piston pumps, can be taken apart faster, and have intakes and discharges of such large diameter that they will accept just about anything. As a large-capacity pump, the good old Edson diaphragm pump is almost impossible to beat.

This diaphragm pump appears to have only one or two disadvantages. The rocker arm is not quite as robust as it could be. Evidence of this weakness is the fact that by and large, when a diaphragm pump such as the Edson is being used on an old leaky wooden boat, the hole will always be egg-shaped as a result of excessive wear (Drawing 169) —except when the rocker arm has broken off entirely and a new one has just been installed. And indeed, if a boat has this type of pump, a spare rocker arm should always be carried.

Unless the pump is installed belowdecks, a flexible, watertight deck plate is required, to enable one to insert the handle from topside. Edson does build a pump with an offset handle that provides limited remote control; however, the linkages in this type of pump have shown a tendency to fail. If this occurs, one can still get some use out of the pump by converting it into a normal rocker-arm model, which can be done at relatively low cost. With a little luck one may find—as I did—a beautiful old bronze pump with an offset handle for sale cheap because of the broken rocker arm.

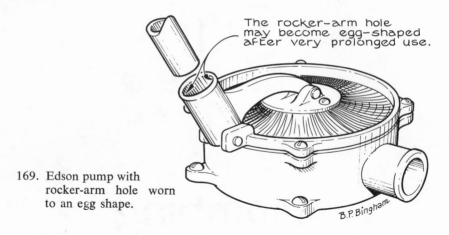

The rocker-arm hole may become egg-shaped after very prolonged use.

169. Edson pump with rocker-arm hole worn to an egg shape.

B.P. Bingham

In any event, let us hope that the small problems with the diaphragm pumps will be corrected in the not-too-distant future, to make these fine products even better. Certainly, were it not for the great capacity and ease of operation of the Edson pump, *Iolaire* would have sunk a dozen times, through the years.

There are of course many very good diaphragm pumps of various sizes on the market, with metal or plastic housings. Whichever one is chosen should be checked carefully and disassembled for cleaning once a year. A supply of necessary spare parts should be kept on hand at all times.

LIMBER HOLES

All boats should have limber holes, so that water coming in will drain down through the entire boat to the pump intake, situated in the lowest part of the bilge. Rod Stephens maintains, justifiably, that a boat owner should be able to throw one bucketful of water into the forwardmost section of the forepeak and another into the aftermost section of the lazaret and a few minutes later pump exactly two bucketfuls of water out of the bilge. All too often, water does not drain in this manner; instead, puddles form here, there, and everywhere, and cause rot on the wooden boat, corrosion on the steel or aluminum boat, or smells on the fiber-glass boat.

On a wooden, steel, or aluminum boat, if limber holes cannot be cut or drilled, the areas where water accumulates should be dried out and cleaned, the hull should then be painted or treated with creosote, and cement should be poured into it up to the level from which water does run aft to the bilge sump.

BILGE SUMPS

Every ocean sailing yacht should have a deep bilge sump—the deeper, the better. All too often, the modern, light-displacement boat has a shallow, canoe-like body with a thin fin keel and no sump. Ten or twelve gallons of water in the bilge will slosh back and forth from rail cap to rail cap, and basically the only way to remove this water will be to go down and sponge it all out, which is not very practical. Hence, in a yacht of this type, the keel should be at least partially hollowed, to form a sump. Once bilge water drains into the sump, it can be pumped out.

On a steel, aluminum, or wooden boat, it is frequently advisable to clean the deepest part of the bilge really well and lay in concrete to create a small, round sump, roughly 50 percent larger than the cross-section area of the bilge-pump suction line. Then a suction pipe can be inserted into the sump, and the bilge can be pumped really dry.

INTERNAL WATER SUPPLY

Water systems vary widely, ranging from the very simple to the extremely complicated. The simplest system of course consists of a ten- or fifteen-gallon header tank on deck which is pumped up by a junior member of the crew every day.

The next most simple is the old PAR pump, a small electric diaphragm pump with a pressure switch which kicks in every time the tap is turned on. This pump is relatively inexpensive and very reliable.

Another system with a pressure switch that has worked well on boats is the helical rotor Oberdorfer pump. This pumps water into a holding tank, its size depending of course on the size of the boat. Within the tank is a rubber diaphragm which is affected by the changes in pressure as water is pumped up into the tank. Because of this diaphragm, once the tank has been filled, 40 or 50 percent of its capacity may be used before the pump is activated. Hence, turning on the tap will only occasionally cause the pump to kick in and make noise. One of the major disadvantages of the system, besides its size and high price, is the fact that if there is a leak, one may not be aware that one's water is being slowly pumped into the bilge, whereas with the PAR pressure system, the continual cycling of the pump is an immediate signal that there is a leak.

PUMPS

In the last fifteen years, pumps for yachts have changed dramatically. Gone are the days of stuffing glands, grease nipples, and the like. Almost invariably, in the piston pump flax packing has been replaced by the O ring, the result being a much cheaper, smaller, and neater pump. However, with every gain there are some losses, and this is especially true with pumps. The idea of the O-ring seal is well-nigh perfect from an engineering standpoint, but from a practical standpoint, it has two grave disadvantages. First, the O ring wears out in time, and a replacement of the correct size may not be available. Second, because the shaft becomes slightly worn, even if an O ring of the correct size is found, it may not make an effective seal no matter how much it is tightened. As a result, one is frequently left with a galley pump, sink pump, or head-discharge pump that sprays water over anything, or anybody, nearby.

Sometimes, a metric O ring can be found that will fit the worn shaft, but that is an outside chance. A much more effective way of ending the difficulty was dreamed up by Ron Smith, of *Daru* (Drawing 170). His method is to take a compression fitting for copper tubing, throw away the olive (compression ring), silver-solder the packing nut to the top of the pump, pass the shaft through the nut, wind on a few strands of greased flax packing (marlin will do in an emergency), place the com-

170. Solution to the problem of a leaky bronze pump on *Daru*.

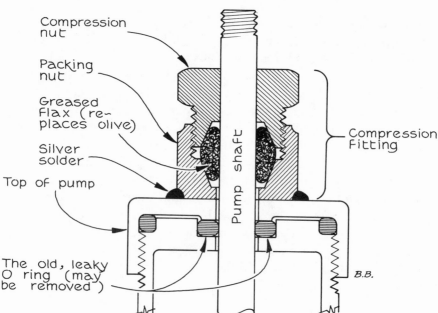

pression nut on top, and tighten. While silver-soldering alone is sufficient for shafts of ⅛ to ⅜ of an inch in diameter, the ½-inch shaft of
a head-discharge pump requires a somewhat different technique: one
should drill the casing that holds the O ring, then bevel and braze.

Even the smallest out-of-the-way machine shop should be able to
perform these operations, and the cost should be low—much less than
it would be to try to locate replacement parts made by an inaccessible
or out-of-business manufacturer.

INTAKES AND DISCHARGES

The salt-water intakes should be carefully placed. They should be
so far down in the bilge that even when the boat is heeled over going to
windward, they do not become air-bound, making it all but impossible
to flush the head, or causing the engine water pump to starve and the
engine to overheat.

Discharges too must be very carefully located. In the old yachting
tradition, the owner and his guests used the starboard side of the boat,
and the crew used the port side. Even today, the boarding ladder is
normally rigged to the starboard side, and swimming is generally done
from the starboard side. In this event, it is well to consider discharging
the head to port, even if doing so requires crossing under the sole. Care
should be taken to keep the head intake well below and forward of the
discharge. All too often, the two are placed close together, and the result is in effect a recirculating head, with the dirty water being drawn
back through the boat. Of course, it is better yet for the head intake
to be on the opposite side of the boat. Similarly, the intake for the salt
water used in the head for washing should be on the opposite side of
the boat from the head discharge.

SEA COCKS

Despite the insistence of many stock-boat manufacturers to the contrary, every hole below or near the waterline should have a good sea
cock, so that it can be closed off. The manufacturers are continually
claiming that holes near the waterline do not need shutoffs. They forget that boats do heel over, through-hulls let go, piping fails, all sorts
of problems exist.

On a popular stock cruising ketch, a large number of discharge lines
came to a great big sea trunk, about three inches in diameter, right at

the waterline, with no sea cock. Plugging this sea trunk if any of the lines had let go would have been a major undertaking. Furthermore, the line was so rigged that in rough weather, on port tack, there was a tendency to siphon back, and the automatic bilge pump was given quite a workout. I hope they have redesigned this installation by now.

When sea cocks are installed, boat manufacturers wishing to save money frequently put in gate valves, even though these are almost universally condemned by really good independent surveyors.

Gate valves are unacceptable for a variety of reasons. If some scrap lodges underneath the gate (Drawing 171), one may think it is closed when actually it is jammed part way open, allowing water to pass. Also, as soon as electrolysis commences, the sharp threads of the screws, nuts, and bolts, as well as the threaded portion of the shaft, begin to deteriorate sight unseen. Once the shaft has lost its threads, closing the valve becomes impossible. Most important, gate valves on yachts are often made of cheap brass instead of true bronze. For the uninitiated, it is most difficult to tell the difference.

In the past, the only acceptable shutoff was the tapered bronze 90-degree sea cock (Drawing 172). However, it turns out that this is not the be-all and end-all, as we discovered on *Iolaire* the hard way when we had a blockage in the 2½-inch sink drain. We turned off the sea cock and pulled off the hose, but water poured in so fast that we thought the sea cock was open rather than closed. I turned the handle 90 degrees, and got blasted across the galley. I quickly turned it another 90 degrees—and still water flooded in. We cleared the sink drain, reconnected it, and scratched our heads.

The next time we hauled the boat, we pulled the sea cock apart, and we discovered that although it was well greased, had looked all right in out-of-the-water checks, and had operated freely through the years (I had installed it myself about sixteen years earlier), it had become wasp-waisted around the holes (Drawing 173). We put on some valve-grinding compound and spent the better part of two days grinding it. At the same time, we checked all the other sea cocks, and we discovered about two-thirds of them in the same state. So here is a warning: do not rely on out-of-the-water checks for sea cocks. Before hauling, shut all the sea cocks, disconnect the lines, and find out how many leak, and how badly.

After this experience was mentioned in an article for *The Telltale Compass,* I learned from a reader that progress was being made. It turned out that the Hatteras Yacht Division for many years had been installing ball-valve sea cocks (similar to the plastic one shown in *OSY*-I, Photo 127) made by the Apollo Ball Valve Division of Con-

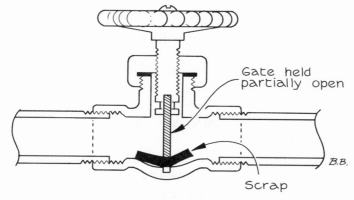

171. Jammed gate valve.

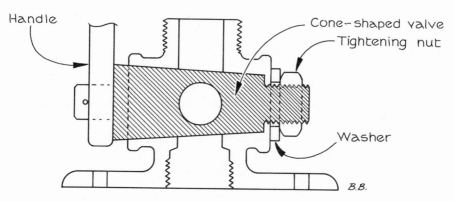

172. An effective marine sea cock, with a cone-shaped valve passing at 90 degrees to the axis of flow.

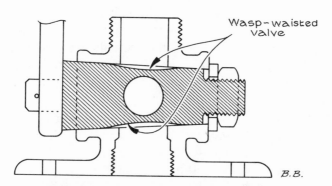

173. Even in the best marine sea cock, the valve may become worn in time, and allow water to flow when in the "closed" position.

solidated Valve Industries (for address, see Appendix). These have Tufnol seals, which should prevent water from passing around the ball to cause corrosion. They are reputedly good for the life of a boat; they are infinitely superior to the tapered, cone type of sea cock, which must be carefully adjusted, disassembled, and greased at each haul; and they are cheaper as well. Another excellent ball-valve sea cock, constructed entirely of reinforced nylon, is produced by Buck-Algonquin (for address, see Appendix).

In summation: every hole near or below the waterline should have a shutoff. The best shutoff appears to be the ball-valve type, like the one made by Consolidated Valve Industries.

WATER TANKS

STAINLESS-STEEL TANKS

The stainless-steel tank, which is being used on more and more boats, is often regarded as the be-all and end-all. Nothing could be further from the truth. Surveyors who work in the tropics report numerous examples of stainless tanks that have lost their bottoms through rusting. As I've said before, caution is required with respect to "stainless." There are many grades, some of them very poor.

INTEGRAL TANKS—FIBER GLASS

There appears to be no reason why the water tank on a fiber-glass boat should not be integral with the hull. This arrangement will maximize water capacity. Also, if the tank is split into two or more sections, each remaining full until its contents must actually be used, the stability of the boat will be enhanced; the free flow of water from side to side, which is always detrimental to stability—and noisy as well—will be eliminated.

Integral tanks must of course have large manholes or at least inspection ports in their tops, so that one can get inside to clean them. Furthermore, if it turns out that the boat needs more ballast, lead pigs can be placed inside the tanks through the manholes, and when the correct amount of weight has been added, they can be permanently fiber-glassed into place.

WATER-TANK REMOVAL

Except for integral tanks, all water tanks should be readily removable. Then the tanks themselves can be checked, and the bilges underneath can be cleaned, chipped, painted, scrubbed, or what-have-you. One reason *Iolaire* has lasted so long is that removing her water tanks is very simple. With few exceptions, the boats designed and built by Fife had tanks which could be removed from the bilge without too much difficulty, though sometimes they fitted together like pieces in a jigsaw puzzle, and one might have a little trouble figuring out the puzzle. However, an amazing number of top-notch designers and builders—among them, on occasion, Sparkman and Stephens, Nevins, Nicholson, and Abeking and Rasmussen—seem to place the tanks in the bilge and build the boat around them. Then the only way to remove the tanks is to disassemble part of the boat, so making repairs and cleaning down in the depths of the bilge is extremely difficult, if not impossible.

HOT WATER

Hot water on a boat may not be necessary in the tropics, but further north, where the water temperature may be down in the 40's or low 50's, washing dishes without hot water can be more than a bit of a chore, especially hard on arthritic hands. Hence, many boats have hot-water systems.

The simplest method of obtaining hot water, of course, is to put a kettle on the stove and heat it. Similarly, if a boat has a coal stove which is always lit, a boiler built into the stove will produce a continuous supply of hot water. A boiler of this type is available as an optional addition to most of the good large coal stoves.

Most commonly, water is heated either by a heat exchanger run off the engine exhaust manifold, or by an electrical element.

Heating water by means of an exchanger run off the exhaust manifold has the advantage of simplicity. The disadvantage with some exchangers is that when the boat is tied up alongside a dock, one must run the engine to get hot water. However, most of the exchangers on the market are offered with optional electric-heating filaments. These may even be added after the exchanger has been installed.

The electrical water-heating system is usually found on the boat with a 110-volt AC generator. When the generator runs, water can be heated electrically. When the boat is tied up alongside a dock, the heating unit can utilize shore power.

Gas heaters are best left at home, since the less gas there is on board the better. Gas is excellent for cooking on a boat, but its use for a hot-water system, or for refrigeration, is not advisable.

Gary Hoyt on the Freedom 40, and Bruce Bingham on his schooner *At Last*, use what is probably the simplest method of obtaining hot water in the tropics. An installation on deck that looks like a skylight is actually a water tank holding about ten gallons and covered with a piece of Lucite. On *At Last*, the tank is enclosed inside a beautiful planked deck box with a wooden top that protects the Lucite when hot water isn't being made. No one would ever guess that it is a water tank. Water gets pumped up into the tank in the morning and is heated by the sun all day. By sunset, one or two people—even three if everyone is very conservative—can get good hot showers.

HOT-WATER TANKS

Heating the water is futile if it is stored in a poorly insulated tank, in which it will rapidly cool down. The tank should be insulated well enough to keep water hot for at least twelve hours; 2-inch Styrofoam can be used for this purpose. Further, the lines from the hot-water tank to the various showers, taps, and so on should be insulated. Otherwise, water consumption is drastically increased, as the lines must be emptied of the cooled-down water they contain before the hot water from the tank can come through. Any refrigeration installer can supply split insulated sleeves of various sizes, to be placed around the lines and secured with hose clamps, tape, or nonrusting wire.

SHOWERS

The simplest shower is made by taking a steel bucket, brazing into the bottom an attachment to fit the hose, filling the bucket with water, hauling it up on the main halyard, putting a spring-loaded nozzle on the end of the hose, and opening it up in the fine-spray position. The result is a shower with plenty of pressure.

The next-simplest shower is the one described in *Sail* magazine by Bruce Bingham in his "Sailor's Sketchbook" for January, 1975, and by Jane Silverman in an article appearing in the same magazine in August, 1976. A 2½-gallon insecticide bottle is filled with water, pressure is built up by the hand pump, and the nozzle is turned to the fine-spray position. This arrangement is cheap, and little effort is required to pump up the pressure. Because of the bottle's limited capacity, and because one can see how much water is used, water consumption is minimized.

Another simple, foolproof shower is the one I saw on the Freedom 40 and on *At Last*, utilizing the water heated by the Lucite-covered tank on deck. Hand diaphragm pumps are employed to pump the water up and to empty the shallow sump into the sink discharge and thus overboard. When one must pump up the water for one's shower and pump out the sump by hand, one is bound to use as little water as possible.

More commonly, the water for showers is drawn from the ship's regular water system, and trouble may arise from the fact that a person taking a shower may use up ten or twenty gallons of water without blinking an eyelash—unless something is done to stop him. One way to minimize water consumption is to have the shower sump designed in such a manner that when two gallons of water have been used, the person finds himself in water up to his ankles, so that he cannot help realizing that he is being wasteful. A second method is to get people to take a submarine-type shower, in which one gets good and wet in the shower, turns off the water, lathers up, and only then turns the shower back on, to rinse off the soap.

When this method is used, water consumption can be further reduced by installation of an on/off valve after the mixing valve. The "telephone"-type shower head with an on/off button seems most popular for this purpose. Then only one adjustment of the water to obtain the correct temperature is necessary during a shower. After one has lathered up, when the shower is turned back on for rinsing, the correct mix of hot and cold is supplied at once, and one does not have to fiddle with the valves, wasting water, in the attempt to get the proper temperature again.

HEADS

SALT WATER IN THE HEAD

On a boat that is to do extensive offshore cruising, a salt-water tap in the head, as well as in the galley, will make possible a considerable saving of fresh water. A person who is good and filthy, from working on the engine, for example, may use a couple of gallons of water in cleaning up. This might just as well be salt water, used either with salt-water soap or with a suitable detergent. Fresh water, in a relatively small amount, can then be used for the final rinse.

HEAD PUMPING SYSTEMS

The arrangement and care of the head are covered in Chapter X, but the choice of a pumping system has yet to be considered. Electric heads may appeal to the lazy man; however, he is likely to find himself becoming the hardworking man, since they tend to break down and need repairs. Furthermore, they are noisy. Hence, most ocean cruising yachts will resort to the old-fashioned hand-pumped head.

I myself prefer the older type with the rocker-arm pump handle because it seems easier to pump than the type with the straight, up-and-down handle. My theory is that if pumping is easy, the user will be encouraged to complete more pump strokes than he would if pumping were more difficult. As I have pointed out, to keep the head from smelling, the discharge pump must be given an absolute *bare minimum* of fifteen strokes after each use, and better twenty or twenty-five. This will not be done unless the pump is easily operated.

HEAD-SINK DRAINS

The head sink should discharge into the head rather than into a sump tank or directly overside. Draining the sink into a sump tank just means that a smelly tank must be emptied periodically. Draining the sink overside requires an extra hole and sea cock, and the arrangement usually works on one tack but not on the other. Draining into the head eliminates these disadvantages, and in addition means that every time the sink is used, the head must be pumped out. As has been mentioned, pumping plenty of water through the discharge system of the head is the best way to prevent the development of smells.

XIII

Electricity

It is still true today that—as was observed in *OSY*-I—although ashore a licensed electrician is required to wire the simplest little house, on a boat any village idiot may, and frequently does, do the wiring. Some of the electrical installations found on boats today must be seen to be believed. It would seem that the builders of stock boats, using a single design for many units, should have the time, money, and energy to provide electrical systems which are properly planned and executed, and utilize the latest available equipment. Yet panels are frequently placed where they are totally inaccessible, and inferior or unsuitable equipment is frequently used even though, if one searches, the right equipment can certainly be found. Despite the obvious advantages of fluorescent lighting on a yacht, where all the electricity must be generated on board, manufacturers still install incandescent lighting below-decks. Worse yet, the wiring often conforms to no known standards.

With a little thought and care, one can avoid pitfalls of this sort. Standards for a yacht's electrical system are obtainable from three sources:

American Boat and Yacht Council   Chief, Office of Boating Safety (G-8)
15 East 26th Street   United States Coast Guard
New York, N.Y. 10010, U.S.A.   Washington, D.C. 20590, U.S.A.

Lloyd's Register of Shipping
Yacht and Small Craft Department
69 Oxford Street
Southampton SO1 1DL, England.

The individual who does the wiring of the boat should be not only a good electrician, but also a good seaman. On all too many boats the work is done by electricians who, though capable in their own field, have not been to sea and do not realize that in a sailboat water inevitably finds its way belowdecks. They fail to take account of the fact that the vessel is likely to be heeled over 20 or 30 degrees, and may be knocked over to 45 or 50 degrees, with water coming out of the bilge and running up the rail cap. Only the electrician who understands these problems can provide a really good electrical system for a yacht.

Admittedly, the presence of salt water increases the difficulty of making a satisfactory installation, and finding equipment specifically designed for the marine environment is not easy. However, a few companies have taken the bull by the horns. In the United States, the Marinetics Corporation (for address, see Appendix) designs whole electrical systems for boats, and can also supply the various bits and pieces needed for making one's own installation. The catalog shows very good equipment designed specifically for low-voltage DC systems. A similar firm in England is Peter Smales (for address, see Appendix). To any others, which we have not mentioned—our apologies. As far as we know, Marinetics and Peter Smales are the only companies that specialize in marine electrical work.

ALTERNATORS AND GENERATORS

Many yachtsmen get very confused as to the difference between a generator and an alternator. Basically, a generator or alternator is a device for transforming mechanical energy (as provided by an engine, for example) into electrical energy. A generator produces direct current at a voltage that varies with its speed. An alternator produces alternating current at a relatively fixed voltage through a wide speed range, but with the alternating cycles varying with the speed.

The small alternators—producing 12, 24, or 32 volts—convert the original alternating current (AC) into direct current (DC) by means of diodes. The large generators—producing 110 volts—are also strictly speaking alternators, but are usually referred to as AC generators. The voltage they produce is stepped down and changed to DC by means of a converter. Formerly, these generators were made with slip rings, but now they are usually brushless and theoretically should run just about forever. Actually, sad to say, they do not.

To produce the correct number of cycles with the large AC generators, the rpm must be kept to a set rate. In an independent generator, this is achieved by means of a governor. When the source of power is the vessel's engine, the belting is arranged so that a four-pole 110-volt AC generator turns 1,800 rpm, and a two-pole generator turns 3,600 rpm, at engine cruising speed. The generator belted off the main engine is usually protected from excessive voltage and erratic cycles by electronic cutoffs.

The great advantage of the small alternators, in which AC is directly converted to DC, is that unlike the large AC generators, they can take wide variations in rpm. They can be set to cut in at very low engine rpm, and yet because of their construction will withstand high engine rpm without flying apart. Their one disadvantage is that the diodes are expensive and easily damaged; a mistake made while one is playing around with the alternator will cause the diodes to blow, and then if there is no spare set on board, one is out of luck. An alternator should never be run on an open circuit. When one is changing from one battery to another, the engine should be shut down. The switch can be made with the engine at dead slow, but doing it that way is playing with danger.

The old generators—now disappearing—that put out straight DC were heavy and relatively indestructible. They were designed not to cut in at low engine rpm, because a generator of this type which did cut in at low rpm would be turning so fast at high rpm that it would destroy itself.

BELT LOADING

If belts are to be expected to last, they should not be heavily loaded. Although it is often believed that 1 h.p. equals 1,000 watts, actually, 1 h.p. equals 746 watts. However, because of inefficiencies in the system, when figuring loading, one should assume that 2 h.p. will be needed to produce 1,000 watts. This figure is not very exact, but seems to work. (Further, watts = amperage $\times$ voltage.) For long belt life, loading should not exceed 2 h.p. per belt.

VOLTAGE

SIX VOLTS DC

The 6-volt system is as dead as a dodo.

TWELVE VOLTS DC

The 12-volt system is standard in the United States for yachts, cars, and trailers. It is discussed in Chapter XIII of *OSY*-I.

TWENTY-FOUR VOLTS DC

The 24-volt system is standard in Europe, where 24-volt equipment is easily obtained. It was popular in the United States right after World War II, when war-surplus aircraft equipment was used on some yachts. After being in abeyance in the United States since the middle 1950's, the system has now begun to make a comeback. Increasingly, 24-volt equipment is being produced in the United States for yachts, and also for trucks, and it appears that the automotive industry will switch to 24 volts in years to come—though we don't know exactly when. Hence we may expect that 24-volt equipment will be readily available and inexpensive, and the 24-volt system will be highly suitable for a yacht. One problem at present is that 24-volt starting motors are still hard to find.

THIRTY-TWO VOLTS DC

The 32-volt system is on its way out. It should be avoided, since it involves needless complications and costs.

110 VOLTS AC

A 110-volt system is necessary far less than most people believe. Electric cooking—which does require 110 volts—is best forgotten on a boat. No one wants to start a 3- or 7.5-kilowatt generator just to make coffee at six in the morning, and the noise would wake up all the neighbors. Cheap household 110-volt equipment does not belong on a boat, since it is grossly inefficient, using up large quantities of power. Formerly, many a boat needed a 110-volt AC system to run the loran and radar, but now, except in the large sizes used on palatial yachts, which are really ships rather than boats, loran, radar, and other navigational equipment can be obtained in 12- or 24-volt versions. Indeed, except on a really large boat, the only reason for having a 110-volt generator may be that it makes possible installation of a 110-volt refrigeration system. This is superior in that it eliminates belt-driven compressors, allowing the use of 110-volt sealed brushless compressor motor units. The 110-volt AC current is stepped down and rectified by a Constavolt to 12 or 24 volts for other uses on board.

If 110-volt AC electricity is absolutely essential on a boat, there must be two sources of supply—either two independent generators, or one generator running off the main engine and one operated by its own motor. A generator always seems to break down at a most inopportune time. Even if it does not, at some point an overhaul will be required, and an alternative power source will be needed during this period.

At any voltage, power leakage can cause electrolysis in a boat, but at 110 volts it can actually destroy the boat or kill somebody. Care should be exerted to make sure that there is no leakage in the original installation, and one should check for leakage at regular intervals thereafter. A useful article on this subject by Conrad Miller can be found in *Motor Boating and Sailing* for September, 1976.

110-Volt Generators Driven by the Main Engine

It is possible to power a 110-volt system from the main engine. There are various methods of doing this.

110-VOLT GENERATORS BELTED OFF THE MAIN ENGINE: The size of generator that can be belted off the engine will depend upon the nature and location of the engine and the amount of space in the engine room. The installation must be carefully designed by a mechanic who understands the engine. The diameters of the sheaves must be such that at normal cruising rpm, the generator turns with the rpm needed to produce the correct voltage and cycles. An electronic cutout should be provided, so that when variations in engine speed would result in excessive or inadequate voltage, the generator disconnects, to protect the 110-volt equipment.

In choosing a generator, one should ask the manufacturer what horsepower will be necessary for the power takeoff. As pointed out earlier in this chapter, approximately 2 h.p. will be required to produce 1,000 watts, and it must be remembered that the horsepower utilized by the generator is not available for the propeller shaft. Accordingly, especially on a boat with a small engine and a big generator, it may be desirable to provide a cutout, so that the generator can be bypassed and full power put on the propeller shaft.

Variable-Speed Clutch Drive   The variable-speed clutch drive, used to produce 110-volt AC current regardless of engine speed, has been widely advertised, and has been employed in the trucking industry for many years, evidently with quite good success. Its reputation among marine users has been mixed. My friend Jon Repke maintains that he has never seen one that works! Probably, as with so many things, the failures can be attributed less to flaws in the basic equipment than to improper installation and use. Auto-Gen (for supplier, see Appendix) seems to be the unit generally adopted for marine purposes.

HYDRAULIC-DRIVE ALTERNATOR: The hydraulic-drive alternator is fairly new in the market. For a time, it was known as the Hydra-Gen; the alternator was produced by Onan, the hydraulic motor and pump by Vickers. At present it is called the Sperry Powerpak, and is produced entirely by Sperry Marine Systems. As the accompanying table indicates, the unit has tremendous possibilities, because it requires considerably less space than does a motor generator. A 6-kilowatt 110-volt Powerpak weighs about 126 pounds, and is 23 inches long, approximately 12 inches high, and 12 inches wide. It can be mounted anywhere in the boat, since it does not have to be near the engine. A fixed-displacement vane pump, which is belted off the engine by at least three belts, drives a hydraulic motor, which in turn drives the 110-volt generator at a constant 60 cycles. The motor and mounts take up a space of approximately 8 by 9 by 9 inches, substantially less than would be occupied by the motor normally used to drive a 6-kilowatt generator. Unfortunately, at this writing the Powerpak is available only in a 6-kilowatt model. It is to be hoped that smaller and larger units will soon be offered. It is sold by Sperry Marine Systems (for address, see Appendix).

Some Dimensions of Generators

	LENGTH, IN INCHES	WIDTH, IN INCHES	HEIGHT, IN INCHES	CUBIC FEET	WEIGHT, IN POUNDS
3-kw independently operating generator	31	26	20	9.32	395
7.5-kw independently operating generator	34	26	20	10.23	560
6-kw hydraulic-drive alternator	23	12	12	1.91	126

Independent Generators

Independent generators are expensive and because they require a fair amount of space, are not practical on yachts less than forty-five feet long. However, on larger yachts, unless there is a twin-engine installation, an independent 110-volt generator may be necessary. A 3-kilowatt 110-volt generator weighs roughly 400 pounds, takes up a space of about 31 by 26 by 20 inches, and costs about $2,204. On a yacht over fifty-five feet long, a 7.5-kilowatt generator may be advisable. This weighs 560 pounds; is 34 inches long, 26 inches wide, and 20 inches high; and costs about $3,400. With respect to maximum generator size on larger yachts, the sky's the limit; the choice will depend upon the equipment on board the boat, and upon space limitations.

Since—despite the manufacturers' claims to the contrary—110-volt generators have a bad habit of giving up the ghost at the most inopportune times, the boat must have an alternative means of obtaining power; this can be a second independent generator, or a 110-volt generator belted off the main engine.

Sometimes an ailing generator can be repaired in place, but frequently the entire generator and engine must be removed from the boat, to be torn apart and rebuilt at a repair shop. When this is necessary, all too often it turns out that because the installation was not properly designed, one cannot simply disconnect the units, lift them out, and take them over to the shop. Instead, the generator and engine may have to be removed part by part and sent out in their bits and pieces. After they have been rebuilt at the shop, and put into working order, they must again be disassembled, to be carted back to the boat in bits and pieces, carried by hand into the engine room, and reassembled. All the disassemblies and reassemblies make the operation very expensive. Also, after having been taken apart four or five times, how can the generator be expected to work?

A good 110-volt-generator installation is one which makes it possible for the average-sized mechanic to complete all normal repairs with the unit still in place. For major repairs, or an overhaul, one should be able to remove the generator through the hatch without excessive difficulty, so that it need not be disassembled to be taken ashore to the shop.

OUTSIDE SILENCING: A generator which will be running when the main engine is not in use must be properly silenced, so that it is barely audible to those on board. Effective measures which can be taken for this purpose are discussed in Chapter XIV.

In addition, attention must be paid to outside silencing. All too often, a generator that has been beautifully silenced so that it does not disturb the people on the boat can be heard by everybody else in the area. Either the exhaust system is not properly designed or the exhaust discharge is in the wrong place. A discharge underneath the long, over-hanging classic yacht transom frequently echoes between the transom and the water, and the echo may carry all the way across the harbor. The best arrangement seems to be an Aqua-Lift exhaust system, as described in Chapter XIV, with a rubber-hose exhaust leading to a discharge at or slightly above the water level.

Consideration for the Neighbors   People who have independent gen-erators, or who run their main engine for generating, should have consideration for their neighbors. The sound of a generator is unpleas-ant. For those who do not have a generator, even the underwater gur-gling is a pain in the neck. Indeed, some marinas flatly refuse to permit generators to be run alongside the dock, insisting that shore power be used instead. In harbors where shore power is not available, the yachts-man who must run his generator incessantly finds himself becoming un-popular in a hurry unless it has been effectively silenced. The yacht with enough AC equipment to need a generator running twenty-four hours a day is large enough to anchor in the far reaches of the harbor, with those on board commuting to and from the shore by launch.

Similarly, those who run the generator one or two hours a day—all that should be necessary if the refrigeration and electrical systems have been correctly designed—should have consideration for their fellow yachtsmen and choose a period during working hours, preferably after 8 A.M. and before noon. Then the noise will not disturb anyone. In the afternoon some people like to take naps, and 5 P.M. is sundowner/cocktail time. Boats which run their generators at that hour should be emphatically informed that they are creating a disturbance.

ELECTRICAL SILENCING: On many boats, as soon as the generator is run, transmitting on the radio is impossible. Having the generator elec-trically silenced is important not only for one's own sake, however, but also in consideration of one's neighbors. All too frequently one sits in English Harbour trying to transmit, either with one's own radio or with Nicholson's shoreside installation, and is totally unable to get out-side the harbor; there are so many boats running generators which are not electrically silenced that the static makes it impossible to break through.

SWITCH PANELS

To fulfill its function most efficiently, the switch panel should be carefully designed and located. It must be accessible—easily reached when equipment is to be turned on or off, or a circuit is to be isolated. It should be so positioned that little or no water is likely to land on the face of the board, but despite this precaution, it must be made of plastic rather than metal, which is more easily shorted out by water.

The panel should be installed in such a manner that a person chasing down shorts (which inevitably occur, even in the best of boats) can examine both sides at the same time. On some boats this is achieved by having a panel that swings out. In other cases, the panel is mounted with the back facing into the engine room, so that a person sitting in the access hatch to the engine room can reach the back with one arm and the front with the other. This is a good arrangement except that all too frequently the back is wide open, with the bare wiring exposed in the engine room. If there is a leak in the water-circulating system and water spurts all over the place, inevitably the whole panel shorts out.

What appears to be a solution to this splash problem can be seen on one Gulfstar model. The back of the panel has a cover—readily removable with five or ten minutes' work—consisting of a piece of ½-inch Lucite mounted on a wooden frame that has a rubber gasket secured to it by a dozen screws. Since the back of the panel is visible at all times, one can see any corrosion, shorts, or what-have-you that may have developed. The panel is not waterproof, but it certainly is splashproof; that should be sufficient.

When a switch panel is installed, room should be left for additional circuits, the number depending of course on the size of the boat. No matter how good the boat's initial design, as time goes by the owner, or some subsequent owner, is bound to install extra equipment. Then, unless new circuits can be put in, it becomes necessary to double up within the panel; this is not particularly safe, and confuses the repairman and frequently the crew.

BATTERIES

CAPACITY

The necessary battery capacity of course will vary from one boat to another. If there is any doubt about how much is needed, the decision should be for more, rather than less. Basically, one should be able to remain at sea on an ocean cruising yacht for three days without having to charge batteries. If one is hove to in a gale or running off before a gale, one does not wish to have to operate the engine.

To determine the battery capacity required, one should ascertain the amperage drawn by each article on board that uses electricity, and multiply this figure by the hours of expected use. For example, the electrical load of the running lights and compass lights should be multiplied by the hours of darkness to be expected during three days. Similar calculations should be made with respect to the main-cabin lights, galley lights, and chart-table lights, and the various pieces of electrical equipment on board. The resulting figure will be an approximation of the total draw for three days; increasing this figure by 50 percent, one obtains a battery capacity sure to be sufficient to take care of the load.

The starting batteries are not included in these calculations, since only in the direst emergency would they be used for any purpose other than starting.

SIZE

Batteries come in all sizes and shapes. It cannot be stressed too strongly that heavy-duty marine batteries from a good manufacturer are by far the best type to install. Twelve-volt batteries appear to weigh roughly ¾ of a pound per ampere; thus a 120-ampere 12-volt battery will weigh approximately 90 pounds. Except in large installations, space is seldom a problem on a yacht, but weight is, and should be carefully considered. For example, *Lone Star* has a high generating capacity and needs approximately 800 amperes at 24 volts, which means a total of approximately 1,200 pounds in battery weight. This is a substantial amount of weight to be added to a fifty-four-foot boat.

For the most efficient space–weight ratio, the batteries should be the largest possible. However, everything is a compromise. When a battery weighs 250 pounds or more, getting it on and off the boat becomes a major operation. Batteries in this size range are acceptable only on the largest boats. On boats of forty to fifty feet, since it may often be desirable to take the batteries ashore for charging, the maximum battery weight should be approximately 90 pounds. On small boats, of forty feet or less, batteries should be in the 40-to-50-pound category.

MOUNTING AND VENTILATION

I must reiterate that, as was stated in *OSY*-I (Ch. XIII), with a modern high-capacity alternator pushing in a quick charge, adequate ventilation of the battery is imperative. Otherwise, the accumulation of hydrogen, which is highly explosive, can cause extensive damage and injury, as has happened more than once. Therefore, though batteries should be covered (so that they will not be damaged if stepped on, and so that a tool dropped on top of them will not cause a spark), they must have plenty of ventilation holes.

Because batteries are heavy, they should of course be mounted as low down as possible. However, they should not be stuck in the bilge, as the combination of salt water, electricity, and copper produces a green gunge and may also cause dead shorts in the batteries.

CHARGE INDICATORS

As has been pointed out by Cap Greene and John Eyre, of the Signal Locker, Antigua, most of the electrical problems on board boats are caused by low batteries. Frequently, the batteries get low because people just do not bother checking them. The best and most accurate way to check batteries is with a hydrometer, but when hove to in a gale—rolling around putting both rails under, with everyone feeling seasick—it is hardly practical to go down to the engine room to check the batteries with the hydrometer. Further, hydrometers are awfully fragile, so there should be available a method for checking the batteries when the hydometer has been broken and a replacement is not at hand.

For these reasons, installation of a charge indicator (voltmeter) is very worth while. It should be set up so that a separate reading is obtained for each battery. Then one can sit at the chart table, flick from one battery to the other, read out the voltage level, and ascertain which batteries need to be charged. A charge indicator is very inexpensive, and is well worth its cost.

CHARGING

There are various methods of charging batteries. Usually, a preset regulator is used. The disadvantage of this procedure is that the charge starts fast but then tapers off, so to charge a battery fully may take many hours. One thing I did learn while serving on a submarine in Uncle Sam's navy is that the lead-acid battery can be charged very rapidly if one is careful and aware of the hazards. As has been pointed out, rapid charging produces hydrogen, and also increases battery temperature. Both of these problems can be minimized by keeping the battery well ventilated. Numerous times when on maneuvers in the old *Sea Leopard* (U.S.S. 483), we would blow to the surface and lie rolling in the swell, with all four engines on the line blasting a massive charge into the batteries, while the electricians reported battery temperatures and hydrogen concentrations every fifteen minutes. The skipper would stand on the bridge chewing his nails, ready to slow down the charge if the hydrogen concentrations or temperatures began to rise dangerously, and to dive instantly if a contact showed up on the radar screen.

A similar method of charging was used on *Iolaire* for many years. Jon Repke installed a large generator belted off our seldom-operated engine, and a big rheostat. I could run the engine for half an hour, belt in 50 or 60 amperes, and then secure before the battery began to overheat. For the person who is willing to monitor his batteries carefully, and knows what he is doing, a manual rheostat in the charging circuit has much to be said for it.

ELECTRONIC-EQUIPMENT POWER SUPPLY

Most of the smaller items of electronic equipment, such as the wind indicator, the Fathometer, and the RDF, can run off self-contained batteries; this arrangement is acceptable in this day and age because, as a result of transistorization and solid-state circuitry, their power drain is low.

However, there is still the possibility of one's special batteries going flat, and if one is off in Timbuktu, where no replacement batteries are available, the equipment then becomes useless. Unfortunately, only a very few manufacturers provide on their equipment a change-over switch, so that power can be obtained either from the special batteries or the ship's 12- or 24-volt supply. If at all possible, equipment installed in the ocean cruising yacht should have this feature, since—it is to be hoped—the vessel will often be cruising in the out-of-the-way places, away from reliable sources of supply.

GROUNDING SYSTEMS

Nowadays, more and more electricity is finding its way into boats. If there are any stray currents wandering around loose as a result of inadvertent grounds on equipment that is wired backward, massive electrolysis results. Hence, it is best to have a negative ground (as almost all boats today do) with everything grounded back to the engine,

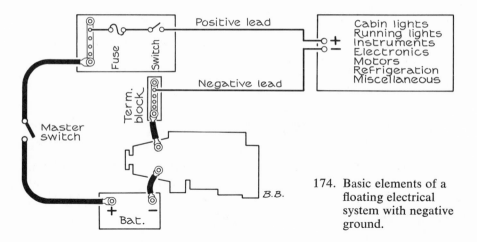

174. Basic elements of a floating electrical system with negative ground.

in a floating system (Drawing 174). If the mountings between the engine and the hull and between the engine and the shaft are of rubber, which is nonconducting, and there is a flexible plastic, nonconducting, salt-water intake line, the only connection to the sea will be through the salt water itself. This arrangement should minimize electrolysis. However, without a really good ground, of the sort which is frequently the cause of massive electrolysis, radios will not transmit decently.

Years ago, everything on *Iolaire* was grounded to the engine, and the shaft was belt-driven from the engine. Hence, there was no electrical contact between the electrical system and the rest of the boat (outside of the salt-water line), and we had little trouble with electrolysis—except where we found Monel screws. Evidently, in 1946 the late Bobby Sommerset had obtained a bucketful of Monel screws (surplus from World War II—they were used to fasten armor plate to the MTB's) and employed them in various places to refasten *Iolaire*. Wherever we ran across a Monel screw below the waterline, we found significant electrolysis problems on any nearby bronze!

If the engine is bolted to the shaft without an insulating flexible coupling, all sorts of troubles may result. A Monel shaft, being inert, may cause the bronze propeller to lose its tips and/or fall off. A stainless-steel shaft, with a bronze propeller, will probably soon be reduced to the consistency of Cheddar cheese unless a sacrificial zinc anode disk is attached to it.

Further, the combination of an iron engine and a copper or bronze heat exchanger has the effect of a good battery.

In an attempt to take care of these problems, sacrificial zinc anode disks are often placed in the engine. These should be regularly checked, and an ample spare supply should be kept on board, so that they can be changed as soon as the zinc is partially deteriorated. This is very important, since the most active part of the zinc goes first, and the degree of protection diminishes rapidly with age.

ELECTROLYSIS

The greatest problem with electrolysis is that it is a subject about which the experts seem unable to agree. One is reminded of an old definition of "expert": *X* is an unknown quantity, and a *spurt* is a drip under pressure. More seriously, electrolysis cannot be completely eliminated from any boat, but it can be kept under control.

It is well known that if there is no electricity on a boat, electrolysis is tremendously reduced. But today almost all of us do have electricity on board, and must face the problem accordingly.

If just one metal were used on board, there would of course be less danger of electrolysis. But this ideal situation is difficult to achieve even on a wooden boat that is bronze-fastened and bronze-strapped. As any experienced surveyor will point out, different bronzes have different electrical potentials, so electrolysis may develop between them. Indeed, this may occur even between bronzes supposedly of the same alloy if they have been manufactured by different companies. The problem is further complicated by the fact that there is disagreement among the experts, as Jay Paris and I discovered when we consulted the galvanic-series tables in five standard engineering manuals, one cold winter's weekend in Brunswick, Maine. We discovered to our horror that there were substantial variations among the tables. If the experts can't agree on which bronzes are compatible, how is the average designer or builder supposed to keep track of them?

In our examination of the various tables, we also learned—to our amazement—that silicon bronze doesn't like lead, and that silicon bronze and aluminum bronze don't like each other. Almost any surveyor will affirm that when Monel alloy is used on a boat, the Monel will be fine, but anything near it will be likely to fall out.

Since even a careful choice of metals cannot be expected to eliminate electrolysis altogether, other precautions must be taken as well. On a wooden boat, all underwater fittings—keel bolts, scarf bolts, and representative plank fastenings—should be periodically pulled and checked.

The situation is exemplified by *Iolaire*. Now in her seventies, she has had so many different metals used in her through the years that I am sure that if I could find enough 1½-volt light bulbs, I could light her forever without ever charging the batteries. Yet, except where there were Monel screws, she has suffered from few electrolysis problems. We have noticed, through the years, as we have pulled and replaced practically every bolt and screw in the boat, that when electrolysis does occur, it is correctable. Instead of the original iron floors, we now have steel floors in the deep part of the boat, installed in such a manner that they can be replaced on a normal haul, with no real trouble. For our wind generator we have a completely floating system, with wires running in a circle to and from the battery, and no ground at all, to minimize the danger of voltage leaks to ground.

On a fiber-glass boat there should be a similar inspection of the stainless-steel bolts. If they are not of the right sort of stainless steel, some kind of corrosion, different on different boats, may result from electrolysis; the nut inside of the hull, and the part of the bolt on the outside, look perfect, but the piece hidden in between may be badly corroded.

A steel hull should be protected by sacrificial zinc anode disks. On an aluminum hull, special sacrificial anodes of a quite different alloy are needed, because aluminum is close to zinc in the galvanic series. Further, an all-metal hull must be watched very carefully; it is a matter of periodically checking the hull thickness electronically, looking for signs of flaking paint on both the outside and the inside of the hull—and hoping. The tightly clutched rabbit's foot is sometimes as effective in preventing electrolysis as good engineering.

Useful discussions of this subject are to be found in two articles, one (previously mentioned) by Conrad Miller, in *Motor Boating and Sailing* for September, 1976, the other by W. S. Amos, in *Yachting World* for March, 1975.

ELECTRICAL SHORTS

The electrical system probably causes more problems than any other part of the boat—more than the sails, rigging, bottom, engines, or what-have-you. As has been pointed out by Larry Pardey, the combination of electricity, copper, and salt water produces (through electrolysis) green gunge, which may result in an inefficient system, or totally nonworking electrical equipment, and in flat batteries as a consequence of discharge to ground. This subject is excellently covered in the articles by Miller and Amos referred to in the preceding section.

To check the electrical system, one needs a multimeter (black box) with which to measure current, voltage, and so on. Unfortunately, this device is very seldom found on yachts, and even when there is one on board, the chances are that no one in the crew is really skillful at operating it. The common belief has been that a multimeter costs a fortune; actually, although a good one is expensive, a model that is adequate for general run-of-the-mill electrical work can be purchased at an electrical or electronic supply store for about thirty dollars. Hence, every yachtsman would be well advised to buy a multimeter and keep it on board, along with copies of the articles by Amos and Miller. The individual who reads the articles carefully, understands them, and checks the electrical system periodically in the light of what he has learned, will probably greatly reduce the number of electrical problems on board his boat.

BONDING TO PREVENT ELECTROLYSIS

The subject of bonding is one of those about which the experts definitely do not agree. Some surveyors insist that all large bodies of metal within the boat—the stem fitting, chain plates, bolts, metal floors, rudderpost, engine, tanks—be bonded together. Others come on board and cut all the bonding straps.

Many of us agree with the latter group, feeling that extensive bonding just means that everything at one end of the galvanic scale will start to deteriorate with alarming rapidity. We would prefer to see all the metals left independent. Everything should then be regularly checked, and if electrolysis is found in a part of the boat, either the metals used should be changed, or—in a minor case—a zinc anode disk should be installed.

I was interested to note, in reading a letter from D. F. Kahan, of the Marinetics Corporation, that he too felt that the various large bodies of metal on the boat should not be bonded together, except of course for lightning protection. It is very pleasing to have an engineering electrical expert agree with the *a posteriori* engineers!

BONDING AND GROUNDING OF FUEL TANKS

Happily, the gasoline engine on the ocean sailing yacht is almost as dead as the dodo. Let us hope that the gasoline engines still remaining will soon be exchanged for diesels. In the meantime, where they are present, it is important that the fuel cap be bonded to the tank and the tank grounded to metal leading out to water, so that no static electricity can build up. Otherwise, there might be a spark between the fuel tank and the fuel-hose nozzle, and the result would be a God-awful explosion.

INDUCED CURRENT TO PREVENT ELECTROLYSIS

The induced-current system appears to work excellently on board metal boats, provided it is correctly installed and carefully monitored by the crew. But if one gets careless . . . ?

BRONZE AND STAINLESS STEEL ABOVE WATER

Theoretically, the difference in electrical potential between bronze turnbuckles and stainless-steel rigging should cause electrolysis, and the combination of stainless wire with a bronze socket having zinc inside would seem to form a perfect battery. Nevertheless, through the years, electrolysis in rigging has been absolutely minimal. Indeed, when it does occur it is normally regarded as a sign that the boat has a massive electrical problem.

ELECTRICAL CONNECTIONS

WIRING

My comments in Chapter XIII of *OSY*-I on the desirability of using tinned copper wire have received support from some of those most familiar with the situation on yachts in the tropics. Jon Repke, who has worked for years with marine electrical, mechanical, and refrigeration systems, feels that tinned copper wire—wire that has been drawn through a bath of solder which protects the copper from breaking down and corroding in the salt-water environment—is well worth the additional expense. Similarly, at Caribbean Sailing Yachts, a firm which has had plenty of experience maintaining boats in the tropics, it has been found that when tinned copper wire is used for rewiring older boats, the reduction in maintenance bills more than compensates for the added expense. Tinned copper wire is now used exclusively in all new boats produced by CSY. Wire of this type is hard to find, but can be obtained from the Michigan Wiring Company (for address, see Appendix).

STUFFING GLANDS

The only stuffing gland normally available in the United States for use in electrical connections is the one mentioned in *OSY*-I—Manhattan Marine's (catalog Fig. 1862), made in one size only, for round wire of ¼ inch OD. As is to be expected, the rubber grommet eventually disintegrates, and the seal is broken. However, the only way to replace the rubber grommet is to buy a whole new unit, which seems rather ridiculous. In the catalog for Peter Smales, in England (for address, see Appendix), stuffing glands are offered in numerous different sizes, but unfortunately spare rubber grommets are not available from this concern either.

JUNCTION BOXES

In *OSY*-I, I recommended a British household junction box (which was shown in Drawing 179) as the best available for marine use. In the years since, no one has written to suggest any other type of junction box as suitable, and I myself did not come across any until the summer of 1976. At that time, I found marine-type plastic junction boxes offered in the catalogs for Peter Smales, in England, and Marinetics, in the United States (for addresses, see Appendix).

TERMINAL BLOCKS

Terminal blocks are, of course, useful throughout the boat. In particular, a terminal block should be provided somewhere near the base of the mast for the wires coming out of the mast and heading back to a switch panel. Otherwise, separating out any one of these wires, when it needs work, will be impractical. Mast boots are not supposed to leak, but they do, so once the wires are connected, and everything has been checked out, the entire terminal block should be covered with silicone seal. Even if this doesn't make the block waterproof, it will make it water-resistant and will reduce corrosion, yet will remain soft enough so that it can be peeled off with a sharp knife when a wire must be disconnected.

LIGHTS

RUNNING LIGHTS

As time passes, the ocean becomes more and more crowded, while the standard of watchkeeping on both yachts and commercial vessels deteriorates. Consequently, the danger of collision has increased immeasurably over the years. The one note of hope is that recently running lights have become available that if properly installed vastly increase the range of visibility of the sailing yacht.

In years gone by, running lights consisted of kerosene lamps mounted on light boards, in the main rigging. The lee rigging of course was slack, so when pounding into a head sea, the light board flopped back and forth. Seldom, if ever, was the lee light anywhere near properly lined up. Further, the lee light was usually obscured by the headsails.

In the course of time, some designers mounted small electric running lights in the bow pulpit. These were a great improvement in that they were not obscured by the sails. However, being in most cases less than waterproof, they tended to short out because of the contact with salt water. To be kept operating, they had to be periodically taken apart, cleaned, and then carefully resealed.

One of the latest ways of mounting running lights, which may look great on the drawing board and on the showroom floor, but is totally impractical and should be totally unacceptable to the yachtsman, is to place them in the bow—mounted in the hull below the sheer. With this arrangement, when the vessel is heeled well down, going to windward, the only being that will ever see the lee-bow light is the friendly porpoise playing under the bow. Further, being built into the side of the hull, in heavy weather these lights will be under water more than above water, and will inevitably short out. How many times have you looked at a running light in the bow of a boat and discovered the lens half full of water? Once shorted out, a light in this location is practically impossible to work on at sea.

Another problem to be considered with respect to running lights is the power drain. Traditionally, three running lights have been used, for port, starboard, and stern. Since each 25-candlepower bulb draws 1 ampere, the total power required for three separate bulbs in ten hours of darkness is 30 amperes—a considerable drain on the batteries.

In Europe, where running lights are especially important, because the North Sea and English Channel are extremely crowded (in fact, crossing the Channel in a sailboat is often compared to jaywalking across Times Square or Piccadilly Circus), a three-way masthead light has been developed (Drawing 175). At present, this light is legal only on boats of 23 meters (about 75 feet) or less LOA. However, I have been informed by the U.S. Coast Guard that an effort is being made to legalize it for sailing yachts of 30 meters (about 98 feet) or less LOA.

The three-way light is available through many manufacturers (ours is the Aqua Signal, obtainable from Channel Marine, and we are ex-

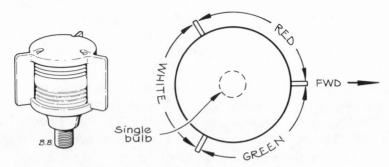

175. Tricolored masthead light reduces consumption of battery power by about 60 percent.

tremely happy with it). This device has tremendous advantages. First of all, since just a single bulb is required, the power drain is only 10 amperes for ten hours, rather than 30 amperes. Further, because the light is set high in the air—twenty-five or thirty feet up even on the smallest boat—it is easily visible from the bridge of a medium-sized ship and can normally be seen from a large ship as well. It is never obscured by sails, and since it lights the masthead fly, a separate masthead light is not needed.

This light is legal only on a boat under sail; once the engine is turned on, one must go back to the normal pattern, with port and starboard bow lights, a stern light, and a steaming light mounted higher than the port and starboard lights. Of course, the four bulbs do draw a considerable amount of power, but when the engine is running, power is also being generated, so this drain is unimportant. Further, the installation of normal running lights in addition to the three-way masthead light is a good safety arrangement, since repairs cannot be made, or a bulb changed, in the masthead light at sea. Incidentally, the steaming light can also be used, among other things, to illuminate the headsails—when one is trying to clear halyards, for example. Spreader lights, shining down, are blinding, but a normal, standard, cast-bronze light, as obtainable from Wilcox-Crittenden and others, with the top off will shine not only forward but up (Drawing 176).

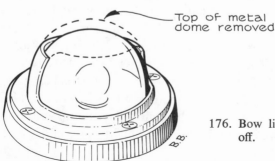

Top of metal dome removed

176. Bow light with top cut off.

Another useful item, available from Channel Marine and others, is a bicolor light, using only one bulb, which can be mounted in the center of the pulpit and therefore has the great advantage over most types of running light of being very easily reached when changing the bulb or making repairs is necessary. The one disadvantage of this center-mounted bow light is that if not carefully installed, it does tend to foul the spinnaker. However, the boathook can be used to keep the spinnaker from drooping over the bow pulpit. One need only secure the inner end of the boathook to a convenient fitting on deck, extend the boathook over the top of the pulpit, and secure it to the pulpit with lashing line.

Fluorescent three-way lights are available, with an absolutely minimal power drain—0.9 of an ampere. They are not universally popular, as some people maintain that the 3-to-5-degree division between the colors is not sufficient. But it can also be said, how many helmsmen on cruising boats steer a really steady course?

Running-Light Circuitry

Each set of running lights should be on its own independent circuit, with its own circuit breaker. That is, there should be one circuit for the three-way masthead light, another for the bow and stern lights, and a third for the steaming light.

SPREADER LIGHTS

Spreader lights of course must be secured firmly to the spreaders, and since they are very prone to damage, plenty of spares must be available. They are great for illumination when one is trying to clear up the spaghetti tangle of lines around the deck, but are totally useless when one must deal with some problem aloft. For that purpose, a steaming light, as previously mentioned, or another light installed facing upward on the forward face of the mast, to light the masthead, is a worthwhile addition.

FLUORESCENT LIGHTS

The fluorescent light is a great boon to the cruising yachtsman: its power drain, normally varying from about 0.4 to 0.9 of an ampere at 12 volts, is much less than that of an incandescent bulb, and it gives off almost no heat. However, in some ways, it has also been a curse. Most fluorescent lights—whether of 6, 12, or 24 volts—are made for the camper market; they are thrown together out of a combination of materials, among them steel, aluminum, and plastic, and are at times very poorly engineered. Some of them blow a transistor if they happen to be hooked up backward. Others are ruined by low or high voltage. Still others produce so much electrical interference that if inadvertently turned on while the navigator is trying to take a DF bearing, the result may be a deaf navigator. Another disadvantage of the fluorescent light is that in almost all cases, it is most difficult to get down for repairs when a part has blown.

To avoid these problems, one should test the lights under various conditions before purchasing them, to make sure that they have been properly designed. Also, a few standard incandescent lights should be installed belowdecks for use when the navigator is listening to the radio, to eliminate any possibility of interference from the fluorescent lights.

An additional precaution is to try to find lights with internal parts that can be readily removed if repairs are necessary. Basically, most fluorescent lights are throwaways, cheaper, in view of the cost of labor in the United States and in England, to replace than to repair. However, the cruising yachtsman often finds himself in areas where he cannot obtain replacements, so he must make repairs.

The "guts" of a fluorescent light are quite small, and there is no reason why they could not take the form of a readily accessible plug-in unit, instead of being soldered in as they are at present. If this were done, one could equip a boat with fluorescent lights, and by taking along three or four spare sets of guts, and some spare switches and bulbs, one would be all set for many years to come.

The little fluorescent light produced by the Guest Corporation (and not advertised, I just stumbled across it on the Freedom 40), is more easily taken apart than most, but still has the guts soldered into the circuit. They could be made readily removable by means of a plug. If in addition the material forming the screws and backing plates were improved—at present it is the cheapest pot metal—this would be a superb light.

COMPASS LIGHTS

The compass light should be carefully placed, so that the helmsman is able to see the compass from all normal steering points. Usually, the compass light is on the forward face of the compass, and on all too many boats, when standing at the helm, one can't see the lubber line.

It would probably be better for the compass light to be mounted on the side of the compass, and to be movable, so that it could always be placed on the side opposite to where the helmsman was sitting.

The compass light is actually used very little, but if it is kept permanently in place, it is exposed to rain, sleet, or snow, and the resulting corrosion may cause it to give out at the most inopportune time. For this reason, it is desirable to install the type of light that can be removed and stored belowdecks when not actually needed.

Also, because the compass light is the most essential light on board —and probably the one that gives the most trouble—it should have its own completely separate circuit. And the vessel should carry not only spare compass-light bulbs but at least one, and better two or three, complete compass lights, so that the whole unit may be easily replaced if necessary.

Emergency Compass Lights

On even the best of boats, one occasionally loses all power; or the compass-light circuit shorts out; or the wires are pinched off by the cables within the steering system. Loss of the light usually produces a major panic, and refitting and rewiring the compass can take a long time. For this reason, some boats carry an emergency compass light consisting of a 12-volt dry-cell battery to which is connected a length of wire with a compass-light bulb in the end. This may be taken up through the hatch, ventilator, or portlight, brought back to the compass, and secured. It is an instantly available compass light good for as much as ten or twelve nights of service, depending on the battery used.

CHART-TABLE LIGHTS

An excellent chart-table light, known as Navigator, with a removable red shield and a built-in rheostat, is made by Bass Products (for address, see Appendix).

RHEOSTATS

Rheostats are hard to find off the shelf. However, according to Jon Repke, they can be obtained in all types, sizes, shapes, and voltages from Allied Radio (for address, see Appendix).

UNCONVENTIONAL METHODS OF GENERATING ELECTRICITY

AIR-DRIVEN GENERATORS

When I first came to the Islands, I heard stories of Kit Kapp and the wind-driven generator, swinging a six-foot blade, which he had mounted on his mast and which gave him plenty of electricity and drove everyone else nuts. I have been intrigued by the possibilities ever since. Ten years ago, upon purchasing a house in Grenada miles from the nearest power line, I mounted a windcharger, a great fabulous heavy wind generator which ever since has provided all the electric power we use at home—more than enough once we switched to fluorescent lighting. With electricity from the wind, water from the roof caught in a cistern, and a bottled-gas stove, we are relatively independent of the rather erratic water and electricity supply found in Grenada.

For many years, I had wanted to use the wind to generate power on board *Iolaire*. I continually asked questions and continually ran up against a blank wall of complete disinterest. My engineer friends either insisted that it couldn't be done or said that it could be done but they didn't have the time to work on the problem. Finally, I ran into Hugh Merewether. In addition to being a sailor—the owner of a Nicholson 38, *Blue Idol,* Hugh Merewether has been a test pilot in the Harrier vertical takeoff and landing fighter program. Being a test pilot, with an inquisitive mind and with access to top-notch aeronautical brains, he had investigated this problem and had come up with a homemade wind generator for *Blue Idol.*

Merewether lent this generator to *Iolaire* for her seventieth-birthday cruise. Although this was a one-off pilot model, it worked extremely well, and we were most happy. Now we have his production model—the Ampair—which except in very unusual circumstances, takes care of all our electricity needs. There can be no doubt about it, for *Iolaire,* with no engine, has no means of charging batteries except the windcharger on the mizzenmast. The results of course depend on the wind velocity (Drawing 177); by and large, the power generated is equivalent to that obtained by running the engine to drive an alternator for thirty to forty-five minutes, or in windy conditions, perhaps an hour, a day. We have fluorescent lighting belowdecks and a single tricolor light at the masthead for running lights, are careful with our electricity, and survive on the Ampair generator. Originally, it produced 0.5 of an ampere at 10 knots, 1.5 amperes at 15 knots, 2.0 amperes at 20 knots,

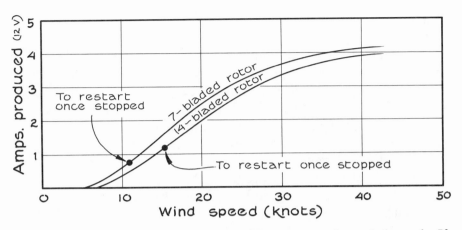

177. Power produced by Ampair wind generators at various wind speeds. If the wind fails, 11–15 knots are required to restart the generators.

but now, with an added box (the nature of which I don't begin to understand) wired into the circuit, it begins to charge at about 5 to 6 knots. In light-air areas, the installation of a larger fan with the same unit would improve its performance, enabling the alternator to start charging at lower wind velocities.

Some people ask why we do not install a larger model, and others ask whether a smaller one could be constructed. Basically, at this time the answer to both questions is no; one is locked in by certain laws of aerodynamics, and also by the limited availability of off-the-shelf fans of suitable size and shape. Indeed, at this writing Hugh is having some difficulty finding a slightly larger fan to be used in light-weather areas.

WATER-DRIVEN GENERATORS

Water-driven generators are nothing new. Back in the late 1940's, *Lang Syne* sailed most of the way around the world, and across the Pacific many times, using electricity obtained by means of a low-rpm generator belted off the propeller shaft. Although the experiment was successful, few have explored the matter any further.

One possibility would be to use the water-driven generator as a supplement to the windcharger. Going to windward and reaching, the wind generator produces a fair amount of current for minimum needs; downwind, it does not operate very satisfactorily, so the water-driven generator could be activated instead. This arrangement is especially attractive because while reaching or running—i.e., just when the efficiency of the wind generator drops off—propeller drag is less important.

Since water is almost a thousand times more dense than air, a relatively small propeller is required. The size actually chosen will be determined by the amount of electricity needed. For the yachtsman who wishes to get large quantities of electricity, the ideal setup seems to be one with a fully feathering adjustable-pitch propeller, a dog clutch enabling him to disengage the shaft to the propeller from the engine, a reverse-thrust bearing to minimize friction, and a generator belt-driven from the propeller shaft. The propeller can be put in pitch and allowed to freewheel, turning the generator. After the batteries are charged, which should take only two or three hours a day, the propeller blades can be directly feathered fore and aft, to minimize drag. Once the propeller really starts turning, the unit with the smallest number of blades will be most efficient; also, a very flat pitch is needed if power is to be obtained from a free-spinning propeller.

How much power is actually available is best determined by experimentation as the power output can be drastically influenced by the type of gearbox used, the tightness of the stern bearing and stuffing box, the flow of water past the propeller, and many other factors.

One method of estimating the power available is to put a sheave around the propeller shaft, obtain sheaves of various sizes for the alternator, go sailing, allow the propeller shaft to freewheel, and keep increasing the diameter of the sheave on the alternator until the alternator cuts in at the speed which you figure is representative for your particular size of boat and type of cruising.

For greater accuracy, one can obtain from John Wilson, of Telcor Instruments (for address, see Appendix), an electronic tachometer which can easily be attached to the shaft. By keeping a log of the shaft rpm of the freewheeling propeller at various sailing speeds, as indicated by the tachometer, one can get an idea of what shaft rpm can be expected. Of course, the torque developed is ??

Another method of estimating the amount of power obtainable from a freewheeling propeller is to use the rule of thumb that the rpm for the freewheeling propeller will be roughly half what they would be for the same propeller pushing the boat in calm water. In other words, to obtain an approximate figure, one can run in calm water under power at 3, 4, 5, 6, and 7 knots, and at each speed check the rpm carefully, taking into account the step-down as determined by the reduction gear. A propeller allowed to freewheel should turn at roughly half the shaft rpm at the various speeds.

We know that on the South African boat *Agwbe,* at a speed of 5 knots, an alternator tied to a three-bladed 18-inch propeller with a 10-inch pitch was able to turn out 30 amperes at 12 volts, more than enough electricity, over a twenty-four hour period, for practically any boat. Indeed, on this basis one can make a case for 12- or 24-volt battery refrigeration. When sailing, the alternator from the shaft would produce enough electricity to run the compressors. Alongside the dock, the compressors could be run from shore power by means of a Consta-volt or similar converter. The only problem would be when anchored out and not sailing every day. In this situation, the engine would have to be run two or possibly three hours a day.

A few cautions must be observed with respect to allowing a propeller to freewheel. First, this should not be done unless one has ascertained from the gearbox manufacturer that the process will not damage the gearbox. Second, one should determine whether there is inside the gearbox a reverse-thrust bearing. A freewheeling propeller is trying to twist itself out of the boat; therefore, to minimize friction and allow free spinning, a bearing to take this thrust is necessary. If such a bearing is not present inside the gearbox, it should be installed externally.

If the gearbox is hydraulic and the manufacturer recommends that lubrication be maintained while the propeller is freewheeling, one can provide lubrication as Stan Young did on *Luna-Quest*—by belting a hydraulic pump off the shaft and running the two lines into the gearbox.

Towed Generators

I have long been intrigued by the idea of a towed generator, so when Hugh Merewether presented us with a production model of the Ampair wind generator, we took apart the old pilot model, and with the bits and pieces built a water-powered generator on the order of the old taffrail log. An 8-inch-diameter outboard propeller was attached to a three-foot shaft of $\frac{9}{16}$-inch steel plus forty feet of $\frac{3}{8}$-inch braided line. We lashed the alternator unit to the pulpit, started sailing, threw propeller and shaft overboard, and lo and behold! the device started registering amperage at approximately 3 knots. At 7–7½ knots it was knocking out 1½ amperes—and this was something just thrown together. Since the propeller lacked adequate weight and skipped on the surface of the water at 7 knots, and the alternator was pivoting only in the horizontal—and not in the vertical—plane, I am sure we were operating at no more than 50 percent efficiency.

Shortly afterward, Hugh Merewether unexpectedly showed up in Grenada with a specially designed propeller. In the meantime, I had

32. Aquair towed generator. HUGH MEREWETHER

collected a variety of Seagull propellers, so we were ready to experiment further. Mr. Blanchard, the owner of *Suivez Moi,* an Allied XL, offered us the use of his boat, and we chugged around the harbor at Prickly Bay, towing the various propellers at various speeds. Some gave better results at the top end of the scale and some at the lower end of the scale; eventually, we made our choice (an 11-inch five-bladed Seagull propeller), and Hugh went back to England and designed a proper taffrail-log unit, called the Aquair (Photo 32), which begins cutting in at about 3.3 knots, and produces 2.5 amperes at 6 knots (Drawing 178). Because the propeller is correctly designed, it yields maximum output with minimum drag; indeed, the drag is only 26 pounds (measured on a spring scale) at 6 knots. Furthermore, when in port, the taffrail generator can be demounted, an air fan secured on the shaft in place of the log line (Photo 33), a fin secured to the generator unit so that it will weathercock, and the whole affair hoisted on a halyard, to continue generating electricity as long as there is wind. This unit seems to provide the best of both worlds. Hamilton Ferris (for address, see Appendix) has also been experimenting with towed generators, and has come up with a unit, using a three-bladed propeller (Photo 34), that cuts in at 4 knots and produces 5 amperes at 6 knots.

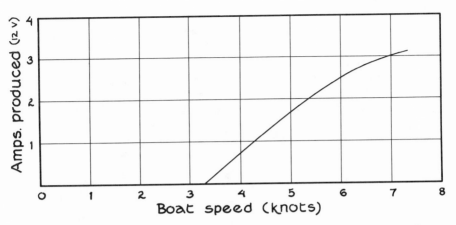

178. Power produced by Aquair towed generator at various boat speeds.

33. *Aquair with air fan in place of log line.* HUGH
MEREWETHER

The towed generator combined with a wind generator certainly seems to be the answer for the cruising yachtsman who has no engine or who wishes to minimize his engine time. Going to windward the wind generator will work; off the wind on long passages, he can throw the towed generator overboard; and in sum, enough power for normal

34. Hamilton Ferris towed generator. HAMILTON FERRIS

needs is likely to be available. From the evidence already at hand, it appears that the average boat cruising in the trades will obtain up to 72 ampere-hours per day—more electricity than one can really use unless one is trying to run a very small 12-volt refrigeration system from the unit.

In addition, the Aquair is now available with an electronic readout that gives amperes and speed, and it functions also as an accumulative log. A price of perhaps five hundred dollars may seem high for a towed generator, but if one is obtaining three instruments in one, the unit certainly becomes economically feasible, attractive to the cruising yachtsman.

SOLAR CELLS

Solar cells obviously do work, as shown by the fact that they supply our various space stations with electricity. However, it must be remembered that money is absolutely no object in the production of the solar cells being used in space; also, they are not subject to the hazards that are encountered on the average sailboat—tons of water running across the deck, people racing back and forth, fog, rain, and so on.

It is all the more interesting, therefore, that two of the Val trimarans in the 1976 OSTAR Race ran their electric autopilots with power produced by solar cells. To be sure, there were problems with the reliability of the solar cells; those installed for the passage eastward across the Atlantic for the start of the race did not work, and had to be thrown overboard. The replacement panels did work perfectly all the way back, but the amount of electricity produced was not very large.

Depending upon who the manufacturer is, 2.25 square feet of solar cells will produce between 16 and 19 ampere-hours per day in times of bright sunlight. Needless to say, when the sun is low on the horizon or obscured by clouds or fog, the amount of electricity produced will drop off, and at night it will go down to zero.

During the summer sailing season, a solar cell on the average (except in very foggy weather), will probably produce as much electricity in the north, where the weather is likely to be overcast or foggy at times, as it will in the deep tropics, where there is usually bright sunlight from dawn to dusk. That is because in the high latitudes around England and to the north, the length of the summer day—eighteen to twenty-two or twenty-three hours, as opposed to twelve hours in the tropics—compensates for the occasional overcast or rainy periods. The average output per hour of daylight will probably be greater in the tropics, but the total output per week will probably be roughly the same.

Solar cells are fragile; they cannot be stepped on. A unit which must be placed on the deck requires a protective Plexiglass or Lexan panel, and this will reduce its efficiency by 10 to 15 percent. Further, the cells are expensive, costing upwards of five hundred dollars per 2.25 square feet.

However, they do have some advantages. In particular, if a unit is well built, once installed it will require no further attention for many years, and as long as the sun shines, it will continue to produce electricity.

Solar cells would appear to be best suited for use on the ends of the hulls of catamarans and the ends of the outer hulls of trimarans, where the crew members seldom walk and there is an abundance of horizontal space that is basically unused.

XIV

~~~~~~~~~~~~~~~~~~~~~~~~~~~~~~

Mechanical Equipment

ENGINES

THE NEED FOR AN ENGINE

It should be apparent by now that in sailing I am a traditionalist and a purist, a little biased against almost anything mechanical. I have never liked engines, and they have never liked me. They have driven me almost to hysteria, but have never managed to drive my boat very well.

Shortly before I purchased *Iolaire,* her previous owners had thrown out the old gasoline engine, and we sailed her happily without one for a year and a half. She was a bit of a bitch to handle in tight quarters, since in those days she had a 660-square-foot mainsail, winches were noticeable by their absence, and there was no mizzen. However, we sailed practically everywhere we wanted to go with no major problems. Then I installed another engine. This was a mistake in my circumstances. It didn't run very well, and we seldom used it—preferring to sail. It was described as the biggest generator and smallest main engine in the Caribbean. After many years of fighting with the beast, my mate Selwyn Nimblette and my wife persuaded me to drop the engine, with shaft, strut, and propeller, into the middle of St. George's harbor, where it now serves as an emergency mooring for *Iolaire* from time to time.

We have never regretted doing so. In the space formerly occupied by the engine, I built a nice (though slightly small) athwartship chart table, which has since served not only as a navigation area, but also as an office. Seated there, I have run my various businesses, and written a number of books and magazine articles. The engine did nothing but use up time, money, and energy, and cause unbelievable frustration; the chart table has produced money instead of consuming it.

Since discarding the engine, I have sailed *Iolaire* tens of thousands of miles without serious incident. However, I like to think that in large part this has been the case because I have a tremendous amount of sailing experience, and *Iolaire* is well (though simply) equipped, well found, and responsive. I make sure that she is manned by the most qualified crews available and that her gear is kept in impeccable working order. So far, the gods have shown their favor, and I do not intend to tempt their wrath by taking any undue risks, sailing into dangerous situations, or wavering in my vigilance.

Furthermore, despite my extensive sailing experience, I have not stopped trying to perfect my skills. Though *Iolaire* is of course a cruising yacht, not a racing machine, I do try to race her every chance I get. I always have a good time, and I profit from the opportunity to practice under pressure the skills required for quick reefing and changing of sails, accurate and sensitive helmsmanship, pinpoint navigation, close-quarters maneuvering, equipment maintenance, and what-have-you.

After a race, most sailors sit at the bar and talk and laugh about their mistakes on the course. This type of post-race critique can provide invaluable instruction for the individual who keeps his ears open. A mistake on the race course may cause the loss of a trophy; a mistake at sea or maneuvering in a harbor may cause the loss of a boat, or a life.

In a word, only the person who has had wide sailing experience, and who takes advantage of every opportunity to hone his skills, should consider himself ready to sail without an engine, enjoying benefits like those we experienced when we dropped *Iolaire*'s engine into the sea.

Iolaire had no aperture and was equipped with an off-center propeller with minimal drag, one of the old South Coast folding propellers. One would think that the removal of the propeller and its appurtenances would not affect the speed and handling of the boat, but nothing could be further from the truth. Although when reaching and running the change in the boat's behavior was minimal, when going to windward there were considerable differences in both helm balance and speed. Before the removal, because of the off-center installation, when the boat heeled on port tack, the propeller became more deeply immersed, and on starboard tack it came closer to the surface; in both cases, the presence of the propeller very definitely affected helm balance. Further, propeller and shaft drag seems to have been considerable. This was demonstrated to us by the fact that in the days when we were dragging a folding propeller, shaft, and strut we always had to keep the main up until the last minute, when maneuvering in tight quarters, to maintain steerageway and make sure we could tack or jibe, but since the removal of the propeller we have been able to sail in restricted waters with nothing but the staysail and mizzen, even in comparatively light airs. The one problem created by this removal is that when we come sailing into a harbor and luff up into the wind, the old girl will carry her way forever, not stopping unless the mizzen is backed to port and starboard as an air brake.

Some people think that only in an area where the trade winds are ever-present can one sail around safely without an engine. However, although offshore the trades do indeed blow almost continually, under the lee of the Islands one encounters very light airs and flat calms. Yet for the last six years we have sailed without the aid of an engine up and down the Islands with no real problems. Of course, this is an area which I know like the back of my hand. We have occasionally been becalmed, but I suspect that the amount of time lost has been less than that lost by some boats as they wait for the shipment of spare parts for their engines.

During *Iolaire*'s seventieth-birthday cruise, we sailed twelve thousand miles in seven months and went to many places some people said would be difficult to reach without an engine. We sailed through the Cape Cod Canal, successfully battled calms on the east coast of the United States and over in Europe, beat to windward all the way up the Thames to St. Katharine's dock, by Tower Bridge, and then had to beat back down to windward, sailed up the Colne and into various harbors in France, and when we were finally completely flat becalmed off Madeira, dropped the dinghy into the water, clapped the two small Seagulls onto its stern, and averaged 3 knots for an hour and a half into the harbor of Funchal.

Ours is not the only boat that has recently succeeded in sailing without the aid of an engine.

Richard Baum, in *Little Dipper,* a beautiful Burgess-designed cutter (which looks somewhat like a little *Iolaire*), not only made two round trips to the Lesser Antilles with no engine but successfully and happily cruised the east coast of the United States and Nova Scotia. He claims that he seldom missed a dinner because of being becalmed, even when sailing in eastern Long Island Sound. One would be well advised to read Chapter XI ("Windjamming") in his wonderful book *By the Wind,* where he beautifully describes the pleasures of sailing without an engine.

Further, one forty-six-foot schooner sailed, without the aid of an engine, not only from the east coast of the United States to the Lesser Antilles and back, but also down the Inland Waterway from Norfolk to Morehead City. This was done even though the boat drew more than seven feet. Since she had been built without an engine, there was no aperture, no shaft, no propeller—nothing to slow her down. On a few long stretches of the Waterway, where she was flat becalmed, the dinghy was dropped overside and strapped alongside, with a Seagull Century Plus outboard with reduction gear on its stern, and happily chugged along at 3 or 4 knots.

Lin and Larry Pardey, in *Seraffyn*, their twenty-four-foot transom-sterned cutter, cruised from California across the Caribbean, up the east coast of the United States, from the Chesapeake across to Europe, and in the North Sea and the Baltic, all without the aid of an engine. Even in the Mediterranean, one of the worst places for a vessel without an engine, they have sailed successfully—all that was necessary was patience, a willingness to work at trimming sails and to hang up all possible canvas, and a readiness to be satisfied with 2½ or 3 knots under sail rather than the 5 or so possible with an engine.

One also thinks again of the individuals mentioned in *OSY*-I—Dr. Gifford Pinchot, who sailed his original *Loon* along the east coast of the United States for twenty years without an engine; and Peter Tange-vald, of *Dorothea,* who threw his engine overboard and subsequently sailed around the world, and unhampered by propeller or aperture drag, turned in some fabulous runs. He visited all sorts of places in the Pacific that reputedly can only be reached by a boat with an engine.

Finally, Gary Hoyt, with his Freedom 40, has really shown that an engine is not essential; when he is becalmed, he rows, though I think I would rather slap an outboard on the dinghy, which would easily push the boat along at 3 to 4 knots in a flat calm.

Gary Hoyt tells the story of how he first began thinking along the lines that led to the Freedom 40. He was out sailing in a friend's new cruising/racing machine, and they were looking for a victim on which to demonstrate their superior speed. The only target in sight was a large old Tortola sloop, crammed with cement bags, vegetables, and children, as well as several goats, and powered by a baggy wreck of a sail—not much of a challenge, but still they wanted to take her apart. Winches were cranked, sheets trimmed, and they were just about ready for the kill—but the damned old Tortola sloop would not come back to them. Finally, after a long chase, they succeeded in passing her, and came up to the cove where they had chosen to anchor. They doused their sail (held up by a halyard that had jammed on their new airfoil head stay), turned on their very expensive engine, bounced off a coral head because they were watching the Fathometer rather than the color of the water (Fathometers frequently register shoal water about ten seconds too late), and at last anchored, only to have the Tortola sloop come sweeping in astern of them and anchor between them and the beach.

The engine was kept running, to provide electric cooking, lights, and hi-fi, and to get the refrigerator cooled down. Unfortunately, a short cropped up just then, and everything came to a slow, grinding halt. There they sat—with half-cooked beef stroganoff on the stove, without water (since the water-pressure system would not work), without lights, and not even able to restart the engine, since the batteries were flat. They finally managed to inflate and launch the "easily" inflated and launched rubber dinghy (try doing that in a hurry), and then had one hell of a job rowing it to the Tortola sloop, since they were hindered by plenty of windage and too-short oars.

At last they arrived alongside the sloop, to find the skipper with a rum in his hand, an old battered kerosene lamp shedding beams of light, and an ancient but workable Primus stove cooking a big pot of excellent fish stew—he had been towing a fishing line instead of watching a steam gauge.

Gary explained their plight, and the Tortola skipper was polite enough to appear more puzzled than amused, but there was not much he could do beyond giving them some water, which he quickly tipped off from a separate barrel on deck, and a charcoal pot and a little charcoal with which to try to resurrect the beef stroganoff. He did, however, pass along some advice, saying, "Man, those conveniences got you all tied up; on the sea you gotta be free." He was so right he even rhymed —and that's where the thinking that led to the Freedom 40 began.

If one looks at the boats that really sail, instead of spending all their time tied up in marinas while their owners talk about their cruises, one finds that a tremendous number of them have no engine and no electricity, or at most minimal electricity. The truly simple boat has little to break down which cannot be fixed right on board, and by and large carries only equipment which is often used. The money not being spent on items that will be employed just a very small percentage of the time, can be spent instead on food, sails, paint, gear, and the like, or can be saved, and the skipper can go sailing instead of having to stay home working to pay for all the fancy equipment.

One reason many people have an engine is that they assume that without it they would have a problem getting home on time—to go to dinner, to be at the office on Monday morning, or to fulfill other commitments. However, this problem really exists mainly in the mind, as Baum makes apparent in Chapter XI of *By the Wind*.

Further, one must remember that if necessary, a dinghy with an outboard can serve as an effective yawl boat. The amount of push needed to propel a boat is negligible until a speed equal to the square root of the waterline length is reached; thereafter, the amount of push required to increase speed does skyrocket. As indicated by the discussion in Chapter IX, and the accompanying chart (Drawing 138), with a speed of $.7\sqrt{\text{LWL}}$, water resistance is approximately 5 pounds per ton, so an engineless boat like the Freedom 40, with a thirty-five-foot waterline length and a displacement of ten tons, can be pushed at a speed of 4 knots or more by an outboard producing 50 pounds of thrust, which is quite minimal. Similarly, the twenty-ton *Iolaire,* with a thirty-five-foot waterline, will do 4 knots with a couple of small Seagull outboards on the dinghy producing 100 pounds of thrust. A little, modern, light-displacement five-ton thirty-five-footer, with a waterline length of twenty-five feet, will do 3½ knots with only 25 pounds of thrust, and will actually get up to 5 knots on a mere 60 pounds of thrust. Of course, at above 5 knots, the resistance curve for a boat this size skyrockets.

A second reason frequently given for having an engine is that it is needed to generate electricity. However, in northern climates the amount of electricity required is minimal, since one can light the boat with kerosene lamps. Electricity really must be supplied only for running lights and a compass light. A couple of good car batteries will provide all the electricity necessary for a running light of the single masthead type and a compass light on a voyage across the Atlantic, but even this arrangement is not necessary now, with the advent of the wind generator and the water-driven generator towed like a taffrail log over the stern.

In the tropics, more electricity is necessary, since the vast majority of boats would be too hot to be comfortable if kerosene lights were used, particularly at sea, where boats are often battened down. However, especially if fluorescent lighting is installed, the needed electricity can still be supplied by a wind generator and/or a water-driven generator. Thus, as noted previously, for more than three years *Iolaire* has depended for electricity entirely on the wind generator (lately aided by the taffrail-type generator) and three not-too-good car batteries of 90 amperes each, except for the times when we have been tied to a dock in some relatively airless place and the wind generator has not been turning over. At that point, we connect up our twenty-dollar Sears, Roebuck trickle charger, and all is well. We usually enter port with our batteries charged up by the wind generator, and have frequently gone for months between charges ashore.

The last reason for having an engine is to obtain enough electric power for the refrigerator and the freezer, without which a tremendous number of people feel they cannot exist. As stated in Chapter XV, if one cannot go a full two weeks on two hundred pounds of ice in the tropics, something is drastically wrong, and with real care, one should be able to manage for three weeks. In northern climates, that amount of ice should be easily adequate for three weeks, and with care, and a properly designed icebox, may even last for four. Hence, power is no more needed for refrigeration than it is for lighting or for moving the boat.

The person who—in view of these arguments—decides to discard his engine, should proceed with caution. As in so many other aspects of sailing, the quickest method is not necessarily the best. He should first honestly review his own qualifications. To sail without an engine on the ocean, along strange coastlines, and into strange harbors, in all kinds of weather, requires the utmost in seamanship and judgment. The engineless sailors mentioned in this chapter are exceptionally qualified and diligent seamen, and even so have had some near escapes from disaster. One way to measure your own particular qualifications, and the capabilities of your boat, is to try sailing for several months under actual cruising conditions with the firm resolve not to use the engine unless absolutely necessary to save life and limb. This experience should indicate where the problems in the boat's responses may lie, and which of your sailing skills most need improvement.

In any event—practice, practice, practice, to attain the highest possible degree of proficiency. Whatever you do, don't take risks or attempt difficult maneuvers simply to show off. Sail conservatively, prepared for the worst. If you allow yourself to become complacent, you'll get into trouble sooner or later. If you ever say, "Donald Street told me to get rid of my engine," remember also that I have given you fair warning.

INBOARD VERSUS OUTBOARD ENGINES

As previously stated, one of the major reasons for having inboard power on the cruising boat of twenty-five to thirty-five feet has been to generate electricity. With the advent of the wind generator and the towed water-driven generator, the yachtsman has an alternative. This hurdle having been crossed, for the smaller boat, outboard power has some significant advantages, as described early in Chapter XIV of *OSY*-I. Not least among these advantages is the fact that it is much easier to take a nonworking outboard to the repair shop than to get the repairman to come down to the boat to work on the inboard.

Until recently, about the only really good outboard for providing auxiliary power on a sailboat was the Seagull Century Plus, with clutch. Although rated at only 5 h.p., it has a high gear ratio and swings a five-bladed propeller 11 inches in diameter, with 10 inches of pitch, so it is a real horse of a pushing engine—no good on a fast, light dinghy, but superb for pushing a heavy sailboat.

Now, various American outboards have appeared on the market which, while they retain the American engine ideas—small pistons, high rpm, and two cylinders, to give smooth operation—have the high rpm stepped down through a reduction gear with a ratio of approximately 3 to 1, and can drive a good, big pushing propeller. Thus, today, the yachtsman who wishes to have outboard power can choose between the Seagull and the modern American high-rpm engine.

The Seagull is rather temperamental and must be understood. But having been designed back in the dark ages, it is fairly simple, so a patient nonmechanic can keep it running. The modern, sophisticated, well-engineered, high-rpm, extremely reliable American outboard is superb until something goes wrong; then, unless one is a good mechanic, it must be sent off to the repair shop. However, both engines, if the model is correctly chosen, provide good pushing power for sailboats.

Though their new outboards may be regarded as a step in the right direction, the American manufacturers, who in general produce excellent engines, have yet to offer a real sailors' model. So far, their efforts in this respect have been singularly discouraging; they really have not put in high-ratio reduction gears. Yet, the amount of thrust picked up by increasing the gear ratio is substantial, as the table on p. 300 indicates. On inboard engines, the objection to a really high reduction gear ratio is that the large propeller causes significant drag. However, this objection does not hold in the case of the outboard, since when sailing, the outboard is either lifted up out of the water or taken on board. Thus there is no reason why the outboard should not have a reduction gear ratio of 4 or 5 to 1, or possibly even higher.

One outboard manufacturer did analyze the situation, and made up a group of trial lower units to be tested on his standard outboards, to ascertain which would give the greatest thrust. However, in the subsequent design of a new production model, the unit which developed the most thrust was not used because its thrust was so great that it broke the mounting. Instead of designing a stronger mounting, the producer chose to install a less efficient unit—with a lower reduction gear ratio than the one yielding maximum thrust, and a propeller of smaller diameter. Well—maybe some day!

GASOLINE ENGINES

With the variety of small diesels now on the marine market, most experienced mechanics who are also seamen feel that for auxiliary power on sailboats, gasoline engines are on their way out, and like the carrier pigeon will in years to come be extinct. Advances in the production of small, lightweight marine diesels in the last five years have been substantial. Stuart Turner no longer builds its old explosion-prone gasoline engine; the firm has now switched to small diesels and *steam* engines, and one wonders about the possibility of mounting a steam engine in a sailboat and exhausting the smoke out through the hollow aluminum mast! Similarly, WaterMota has now switched from gasoline to diesel engines.

Few will lament the demise of the gasoline engine. The individual who is still using one should reread the discussion in *OSY*-I (Ch. XIV) on the safe handling of gasoline engines, and should be extremely careful.

STARTING

The description in *OSY*-I of the various methods of starting motors is still valid, and nothing can be added. However, it should be reiterated not once but probably twenty times that the most essential spare part to be carried for any engine is the starter. On marine engines, starter failure is all too common, and is likely to occur when the nearest source of a replacement is a thousand miles away. Then, if there is not the possibility of hand-starting with the aid of a strong right arm, one is completely foxed. Starters seem to be one of a kind, made to fit only one engine, with practically no interchangeability of parts.

Furthermore, improvising when a replacement is not at hand seems to be just about impossible. Solenoids may be adapted or bypasses rigged, generators or alternators may be adapted and mounted on the engine, other parts tend to come in standard sizes, gaskets can be made, fuel lines made up—practically everything in the engine can be fudged, but not the starter. Hence—and it cannot be stated too emphatically— one should know how to maintain the starter, and every boat should carry a spare, in case it fails nevertheless.

ENGINE MOUNTINGS

Flexible mountings are becoming more and more popular. It cannot be reiterated too often that if they are used, *all* the mountings of the engine must be flexible. Furthermore, there must be flexible connections between the engine and the exhaust pipe, the oil lines, the fuel lines, and the water lines. *Every* line from the engine must have a flexible connection; without it, the line will eventually fatigue and crack. Occasionally, the mechanic who installs an engine overlooks this very important detail.

Flexible mountings and flexible couplings do not last forever. Therefore, it is a good idea to keep spares always on board.

ENGINE SEALS

The rear seal on the engine gearbox is one of those most likely to let go. The seal itself usually costs about a dollar, but changing it may be difficult if engine space is restricted. Sometimes it is necessary to lift the engine off the beds to get at the seal, and this can result in disproportionate expense. Frequently, the reason this seal wears out is that the boat is not used very often and corrosion forms on the hub of the flange, acting like sandpaper and ruining the seal. For this reason, when the engine is out of the boat it is a good idea to remove the flange, polish it, and send it out to have the seal surface (not the face of the flange) chrome plated. In this way, one can minimize the chances of corrosion developing on the flange.

ENGINE ROOMS

DESIGN

Engine rooms are frequently very poorly designed, so it is important to give careful scrutiny to the engine room of a boat under consideration for purchase. On any boat, certain jobs of engine maintenance inevitably have to be done. The answers to the questions on the following checklist will indicate which jobs are difficult or impossible to complete in a particular engine room.

Is the design of the engine drip pan satisfactory?
How long does it take to change the lubricating-oil filter?
How much oil is spilled in the bilge in the process of changing the filter?
How long does it take to change the fuel filters?
How difficult is it to bleed the system once the filters have been changed?

How long does it take to change the starter motor?

How long does it take to change the alternator?

How long does it take to remove and reinstall the water pump or pumps?

How long does it take to remove and reinstall the impeller?

How long does it take to remove and reinstall the fuel-injector pump?

On a gasoline engine, how long does it take to adjust and clean the points?

How long does it take to adjust the tension on the belts for the salt-water pump?

How long does it take to adjust the tension on the belts for the fresh-water pump?

How long does it take to adjust the tension on the belts for the alternator and/or generator?

How long does it take to adjust the tension on the belts for the refrigeration compressor, if there is one?

How long does it take to remove and clean the water strainer?

Is the switch panel made of plastic? (A metal switch panel is unacceptable.)

Is the switch panel waterproof, or at least splashproof?

Is the back of the switch panel readily accessible?

In addition, one should make sure that there is room to wield wrenches, space to move large parts in and out of the area, and decent visibility.

A day spent in the engine room to find out at first hand the answers to these questions, and to ascertain that the tools and spares needed for the various jobs are present, will be time very well spent. Possibly one may discover that special tools are needed. Or one may decide that the engine room is in vast need of redesigning. Or, if the engine room in question is on a boat whose purchase is under consideration, one may conclude that the boat is not suitable and should not be bought. Few experienced yachtsmen would object if a prospective buyer insisted that either he or his surveyor perform the operations specified in the preceding list as part of the purchase survey.

Engine Removal

It goes without saying that an engine in an ocean sailing yacht should be readily removable. On some boats, part of the interior must be dismantled before the engine can be removed, so a relatively simple job like replacing the seals on the gearbox turns into a massive undertaking.

Usually, one can work on an engine without taking it out of the boat. Sometimes it must be lifted up in place, and the pan dropped. The most common method of raising the engine is to attach a chain hoist to the boom, using many wrappings of heavy line. The boom is topped up by means of extra-heavy halyards and the hook of the hoist dropped straight down through a hatch to the engine. On some boats this cannot be conveniently done. For this reason, if at all possible, one should consider securing an eyebolt or a pad eye to the overhead of the engine compartment. A small chain hoist can be hooked to this, and with the hoist hooked onto its top, the engine can be lifted out of the beds by one man rather than two or three.

SOUNDPROOFING

On most yachts, soundproofing of the engine and engine room is not completely possible. Sound, like water, will pass through any hole. Thus, if one wishes to soundproof an engine, one should start underneath it: the selected soundproofing material must be placed below the beds prior to the installation of the drip pan. Accordingly, soundproofing of the engine and engine room should be planned during the early design stages of the boat.

The following systematic consideration of soundproofing for large yachts has been contributed by Lew Bell, a top-notch sound engineer who with his wife and another couple chartered *Iolaire* in 1963, and caught the sailing bug. He has since then become not only a first-rate skipper but also an excellent navigator, sailing in that capacity on *Siren Song*.

NOISE CONTROL ON OCEAN SAILING YACHTS

by Lewis H. Bell

No formal text or design manual exists that deals with noise control on large luxury sailing yachts. A glance at the engine-room construction or bulkhead treatment of recently built boats will reveal a complete lack of understanding of the matter by most designers and builders. In many cases, the noise problem is considered only in the final stages of construction, and the so-called solution often consists of attaching ceiling tile or patches of polyurethane foam to the hatch covers, bulkheads, or any other available bare spot. This superficial procedure, let it be emphasized, provides as much noise reduction as a screen door; in addition, the materials used constitute a serious safety hazard, since they may wick flammable fuels and solvents like a sponge, and may give rise to noxious or poisonous fumes in the presence of heat or fire.

As in any other precise nautical discipline, you get nothing for nothing. Shortcuts and gimmicks do not work. However, on the positive side, it should be noted that there is no mystique involved in solving the noise problem. With the application of a few basic design principles, and with continuous attention to detail throughout construction, most of the unwanted sound can be reduced to a level of little or no annoyance.

Sources of Noise

By far, the major source of noise on sailing yachts is the internal-combustion engine used as an auxiliary or to drive a generator, and the diesel is the worst offender. In quality, the noise is dominantly discrete; it consists of pure tones at the piston-firing frequency, and higher harmonics, and falls in the range of peak annoyance to most ears. Noise generally at a lower level of intensity, but consisting of similarly pure tones, may emanate from gearboxes, hydraulic pumps, superchargers, and the like. Fortunately, these "critters" are almost always located in or near the engine room, so in dealing with the noise problem, attention can be focused on that area.

Noise Paths

Noise may follow one of two paths to reach the ears of the boat owner, his guests, or his crew. First, noise is carried by air, insidiously traveling through small holes or penetrations in the engine-room bulkhead, the engine exhaust ducts, the bilges, and the like. Second, noise is readily carried by the superstructure, bulkheads, or any mechanically continuous route, and reradiated into the salon or staterooms. In addition, complex combinations often exist, paths on which sound is in part airborne and in part structure-borne. With dozens of mazelike routes available, it is obvious that only through great attention to detail during boat design and construction can the noise be contained.

Noise-Control Measures

The basic approaches in noise control are to reduce the noise at its source, and to isolate the source.

Consider first reduction at the source. It is often possible to install a filter/muffler on the air intake of a diesel engine. These combinations, sold by both filter and muffler manufacturers, provide significant noise reduction. Also, engine exhausts should be equipped with high-quality, heavy-duty reactive mufflers. Here again the manufacturer or muffler supplier generally will provide specific recommendations, and will guarantee results. If the mufflers are installed in the engine room, the need for acoustical sealing of the exhaust ducts will be minimized.

Engines and all rotating equipment should be installed on high-quality, vibration isolation mounts. Engine and generator manufacturers usually provide good isolation and specific mounting procedures.

Total enclosure of the diesel engine itself would also be an extremely effective method of reducing noise at the source, but the concomitant problems associated with accessibility, air flow, temperature control, and maintainability are inherent and difficult to solve. Reduction of the noise made by gearboxes, pumps, and other peripheral items is generally obtainable only through major redesign or part replacement, which may involve changes that seriously compromise the durability and integrity of the equipment.

In short, noise reduction at the source is at best difficult, and the results are limited, so *isolation* is left as the most promising avenue to follow.

The engine room can be regarded as a large noise-source enclosure, to which the basic principles of enclosure design apply directly. In particular, to assure effective engine-room isolation, two conditions must be met. First, the enclosure walls must be sufficiently massive (or dense) to serve as a good barrier. Second, the acoustical leaks, such as holes, ducts, penetrations, and lightweight walls, must be taken care of. The importance of fulfilling these two conditions cannot be overemphasized. All others are secondary.

With respect to the walls, from the point of view of noise reduction masonry or brick would be the first choice. However, since space limitations and other considerations make these impractical on a yacht, the following construction guidelines should be observed instead. The surface density of the bulkheads must be at least 8 to 10 pounds per square foot. Construction should be composite in nature, as illustrated in

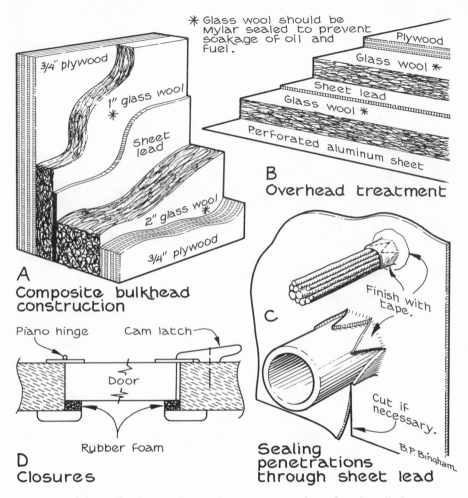

* Glass wool should be Mylar sealed to prevent soakage of oil and fuel.

3/4" plywood

1" glass wool *

Sheet lead

2" glass wool *

3/4" plywood

A
Composite bulkhead construction

Plywood

Glass wool *

Sheet lead

Glass wool *

Perforated aluminum sheet

B
Overhead treatment

Finish with tape.

C

Cut if necessary.

Piano hinge   Cam latch

Door

Rubber foam

D
Closures

Sealing penetrations through sheet lead

B.P. Bingham

179. Highly effective engine-compartment soundproofing installations.

Drawing 179A, for optimum barrier performance. In the drawing, the external material shown is plywood, the likely choice in a wood or fiberglass boat. For an aluminum or steel bulkhead, metal of equal surface density (weight per square foot) may be used. Frequently, the bilges extend into the engine room and provide an airborne path by which noise reaches the adjacent staterooms. Therefore, the bulkhead treatment must extend into the bilges. However, the fiber-glass wool need not be used in the bilges, since it would get soaked and possibly present a problem. The overhead of the engine room should provide some noise absorption, and the recommended treatment is shown in Drawing 179B. Throughout, the fiber-glass wool used should be sealed in 2-mil Mylar or Tedlar or the equivalent (similar to the material used in "baggies" for sandwiches) to prevent it from absorbing any flammable fluids.

To eliminate acoustical leaks, all penetrations by conduit, ducts, pipes, and the like must be sealed. The sheet lead found in the bulk-heads, being quite malleable at 1 pound per square foot, makes an excellent, easy-to-work-with material. Drawing 179C shows a sheet-lead penetration seal. Also, every door should have an overlap with a good rubber seal, and should "dog" in tight, as shown in Drawing 179D.

Finally, it should be emphasized that to render the noise of diesel generators or auxiliaries inaudible on deck or in adjacent staterooms is too ambitious an aim. However, with care, the level of noise can be made low enough so that in no way will it interfere with the pleasant sound of the sea or the tinkle of an ice cube impacting the side of a cocktail glass.

SHAFTS AND DRIVE SYSTEMS

JACKSHAFTS

If much equipment is to be run off the main engine, jackshafts are frequently installed, with V-belts driving the individual units through clutches. This arrangement does make it possible to utilize the main engine for many purposes, but as the engineering adviser Jon Repke points out, all too often the installation is poorly done, and the result is an engine room that is such a mess, with exposed belts and fuzz all over the place, that operation in a seaway becomes rather dangerous. In many cases, a shoreside safety inspector would have a heart attack if he looked in and saw the exposed belting whipping around, trying to ensnare the unwary mechanic who stepped into the engine room at sea. Indeed, just recently exposed belting of this sort cost a crew member four fingers.

If possible, jackshafts and exposed belting should be avoided. If they must be used, one should sit down, study the situation carefully, make a mock-up—try to plan an installation that is as neat and clean as it can be. Guards should be installed to prevent the unwary from becoming ensnared in the belts. Also, it must be remembered that there is a direct relationship between shaft speed and belt size. Therefore, when belting equipment off an engine, one should consult a good engineering manual, to make sure that the installation is done in accordance with correct engineering practice, with belt pulleys and leads of suitable size and in the proper positions for the loads involved. Belts should be kept as short as possible. Long belts tend to flap and whip, slip and wear.

On a boat, the greatest enemy of the belt is the rusty pulley. In addition to wearing out the belt, this throws off a fuzz that makes the front end of the engine look like a mink farm. Another great enemy of the belt is misalignment, which can destroy one in a matter of hours. A further enemy is the practice of bending the belt over a sheave with too small a diameter. The use of two small a sheave is as destructive of belting as of wire halyards.

Since despite all precautions, belting may eventually fail, one should carry lengths of spare adjustable link belting (*OSY*-I, Photo 128), so that replacements can be made without one's having to scour an entire area to find the exact belt to fit the installation.

As mentioned in *OSY*-I (Ch. XIII), engines are sensitive to side loading, which can easily tear out the front-end bearing. Therefore, if a significant amount of horsepower is to be obtained by belting from the front end of the engine, a pillow block should be mounted as shown in *OSY*-I, Drawing 172, to take the side thrust.

On some engines, notably the Farymann diesel, almost full power can be taken from the front end if the jackshaft is properly attached. On others, the crankshaft construction makes this impossible. One must check with the manufacturer to ascertain how much power is available from the front end of any particular engine.

BELT DRIVE

Geared Belt Drive

The commercial development of rubber timing-gear belting (Drawing 180) is most interesting. With correct engineering this type of drive can certainly be employed in yachts for certain applications. Its use means that the engine is lifted out of the bilge and out of a direct line with the shaft, and can be completely flex mounted without having a weak point in the flexible coupling. Further, by regulating the diameter of the geared pulleys, one can vary the reduction as desired. If an ad-

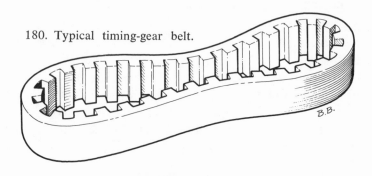

180. Typical timing-gear belt.

B.B.

justable-pitch propeller is being used, the inner end of the drive shaft is accessible, so the adjustable-pitch mechanism is easy to install and to work on.

There are other advantages as well. Fairly small belts will transmit considerable horsepower, and unlike chain drive, the system is quiet. No slippage occurs with this type of belting, and rust in the pulleys, which is practically inevitable on an ocean sailing yacht, does minimal damage to it.

This kind of drive definitely bears investigation. When adopting it, one should of course bear in mind that carrying spare belts is *very* important.

HYDRAULIC DRIVE

Marine applications of hydraulic drive (Drawing 181) are really nothing new; only its use in yachts for propulsion is a novelty. Uncle

181. The elements of hydraulic drive.

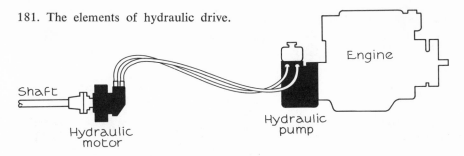

Sam's submarines have employed the swash-plate piston-pump principle since the 1930's. Hydraulic anchor windlasses and capstans have been found on yachts since the 1920's. Indeed, hydraulic pump and motor engineering has a history far deeper and more successful than most sailors imagine. Many still avoid hydraulic installations altogether for little reason except, I suppose, fear of the unknown. I myself have at times been guilty of resisting an advance until the unqualified success of some gimmick or product forced me to recognize it.

I was first impressed with the power and reliability of hydraulic pumps and motors during my duty aboard submarines; bow plane controls, steering, air compressors, heavy-duty pumps of all sorts, and many other systems were operated solely by hydraulics.

Today, hydraulic pump/motor systems are everywhere: moving dirt, digging ditchs, lifting huge loads, motivating vehicles of odd types; they have a wide variety of military and industrial functions, Every time we travel by air we are entrusting ourselves to hydraulics, since the airliners are almost completely hydraulically controlled, even to doors and landing gear. In fact, the worldwide acceptance of hydraulics by industry, which extends even to remote areas, may be one of the great advantages of this type of installation for the boat owner, since it brings with it the availability of parts and of mechanics who know how to work on hydraulic units of all types.

Hydraulic drive on sailing yachts was first introduced about ten years ago, and it was not overly successful; efficiency was poor, and the failure rate high. However, at present most of the difficulties appear to have been eliminated. Hydraulic drive systems are now being marketed by a number of companies. Some of these claim a power transfer of up to 87 percent, essentially equivalent to the power transfer obtained with a conventional gearbox. But although some experts accept this figure, others are less optimistic and put it at 75 percent, while the real pessimists speak of a power transfer of 50 percent. The great variation in these estimates makes the nonengineer wonder about the value of promotional material. I suspect that the higher figures represent results obtained under perfectly controlled conditions, rarely duplicated in actual use.

The reliability of a correctly installed hydraulic system appears to be good. Camper and Nicholsons has put over 150 units into the Nicholson 35's, and both the firm and the individual owners seem happy with them.

It practically goes without saying that if a hydraulic system is installed, the skipper or engineer must understand its workings intimately, and plenty of spares must be carried, including a complete set of seals and a good supply of hydraulic fluid. Also, the design should be such that each individual piece of hydraulic equipment can be disconnected—to allow repair and maintenance, and also to isolate problems, so that, for example, a blown seal on the anchor windlass will not knock out the whole system.

Advantages

The hydraulic drive system offers a great many advantages. First and foremost, the engine can be mounted anywhere on the boat. Similarly, the hydraulic motor is so small that the shaft can be mounted anywhere; indeed, on some of the new ocean racers, motor and shaft are placed down inside the keel (Drawing 182). Since there are fewer difficult shaft-alignment problems, the engine may be truly flex mounted, and since there is no direct connection from the engine to the shaft, only limited engine vibration should be transferred to the hull.

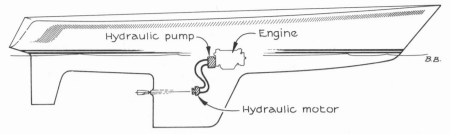

182. Hydraulic drive allows for the most convenient and weight-effective placement of the engine regardless of shaft location.

Another great advantage is that on some units the reduction is infinitely variable; hence, one can choose whatever reduction will produce the best possible combination of engine rpm and shaft rpm for the pitch of the propeller. By contrast, with a conventional gearbox, the reduction is fixed, so if the available combinations are not quite right for the propeller, the only solution is to change the propeller.

This flexibility in the reduction is especially important in twin-engine, single-screw arrangements, since it means that if one engine packs up, the remaining engine can turn the propeller without being overloaded. One merely changes the reduction gear ratio from 2 to 1—for example—to 3 or 4 to 1. This adjustment reduces the shaft rpm, but keeps the propeller operating and protects the working engine.

The combination of two engines and a single shaft (which will be used on *Lone Star*) is not the only one facilitated by the flexibility available with hydraulic drive. On some boats, two engines drive two separate shafts. Normally, the starboard shaft is driven by the starboard engine, but it would be possible to drive the starboard shaft with the port engine in case of emergency. In another variation, Allan Vaitse on his Meadow Larks installs a single engine to drive twin screws. By this means he gives maneuverability to a narrow hull, keeps his propeller diameters small enough to preserve the shoal draft characteristic of the Meadow Lark, and minimizes propeller drag.

A potential advantage of hydraulic drive is the possibility of powering all sorts of equipment off the system. For example, if a manifold is installed, power can be tapped from the engine to drive a generator, an anchor windlass (small ones are available, as indicated in Chapter VIII), a water pump, or a power winch (such as the electrically driven Barient). All sorts of variations may be found. At present, the problems of valving, and of isolating equipment, appear to be formidable, and I can't help wondering if a Pandora's box full of troubles is not also being opened. But this is a new field. Let us hope it will develop rapidly in the years to come.

Disadvantages

As with everything else on a boat, what is gained in one direction is lost in another. There are disadvantages to hydraulic drive: the equipment is expensive, it is noisy, and if one is not careful, leaking hydraulic fluid may make the boat a mess. In addition to a sump and a really good drip pan, with a high lip around it, under the engine, there should be well-designed, well-constructed drip pans under each of the pieces of hydraulic equipment—the hydraulic-drive alternator, the manifold, and the pumps, for example—to catch any fluid leaking from the system.

To minimize the problem of leaks, it is probably best to employ rigid piping for all the long runs, connecting the piping to the pump and to the motor with short lengths of flexible hose, which is then easily accessible. Running long lengths of hose through the bilges, where it is inaccessible and unobservable, would probably be just asking for trouble. Both the rigid piping and the hose end fittings should be nonferrous, and the hose should be of the highest quality. The disadvantage of this arrangement is that some extra joints are added to lines, joints that could leak and cause trouble. Like everything else, this is a compromise.

When hydraulic equipment is being serviced, a terrible mess may result unless great care is taken, and microscopic bits of dirt in the system will stop it cold.

A further disadvantage is that the personnel of the average yacht yard will regard hydraulic equipment as unrepairable. However, all is not lost when repairs are necessary. Since hydraulic drive is used a great deal for earth-moving equipment, the manuals concerning maintenance and repair are explicit, and extremely good. The hydraulic mechanic is used to grabbing his tools and manuals and going out into the middle of the bush to repair a unit on site. After all, who is going to drive a D8 bulldozer for 150 or 200 miles to the nearest mechanic? There are few places in the world where, if one looks hard, one cannot find a mechanic who is accustomed to working on backhoes, bulldozers, forklifts, or the like, all of which use the same basic hydraulic equipment as a boat.

FUEL

FUEL TANKS

Integral tanks are advisable for the water supply but are generally thought to be inadvisable for fuel in a fiber-glass hull because microscopic quantities of salt water tend to work themselves through the hull and get into the tank. A few drops of salt water in the fresh-water supply do not harm the water—they only make it taste better. But a few ounces of salt water in the diesel fuel will do a very good job of fouling up the injectors.

Basically, the observations about fuel tanks made in *OSY*-I (Ch. XIV) still hold true. However, a few words of caution should be added.

First and foremost, all tanks must be really baffled both fore and aft and athwartships. Fuel or water splashing about in a tank not only destroys the stability of the boat but is very noisy. Furthermore, it can sometimes burst the sides of the tank.

In addition to increasing the stability of the boat and reducing noise, dividing the fuel tanks into as many sections as possible contributes to one's peace of mind by making it easier to keep a constant check on how much fuel has been used.

Relying on a fuel gauge to indicate the amount of fuel remaining in the tank is nothing but the height of optimism. Every fuel tank should be capable of having its contents measured directly. Most tanks are not of uniform shape, and one cannot get a really accurate idea of how much is left merely by determining the depth of the fuel. Therefore, the dipstick should be calibrated to show the number of gallons remaining.

It has been pointed out that although—as stated in *OSY*-I—diesel-fuel tanks should not under any circumstances be galvanized on the inside, galvanizing on the outside will increase their longevity appreciably. In most cases, when a diesel-fuel tank rusts through, the rusting begins on the outside rather than the inside of the tank.

Concerning diesel-fuel tanks, one other point should be mentioned. On most diesels not all of the fuel that reaches the engine is used; some is brought back to the tank by means of a return line. Therefore, a double manifold, with one outlet for the suction end of the fuel line and another for the return line, is necessary.

Fuel-Tank Vents

Fuel-tank vents should be of copper pipe of sufficient diameter— at least 25 percent of the cross sectional area of the fill line. All too many boats have vents of ¼-inch ID, which make filling the tanks a drawn-out major operation. The use of *copper* pipe is specified because if fire occurs, pressure will build up in the tanks and fuel will come out through the vent pipes. If these pipes are made of plastic hose below-decks they will burn through, and fuel will be pushed out under pressure. In the case of gasoline the result will be a God-awful explosion; in the case of diesel fuel there will be one hell of a fire, since vaporized diesel fuel under pressure acts like a blowtorch. Once above deck level and well clear of the engine and of any other place where fire is likely, the copper pipe can be joined onto an easily manageable plastic hose. This should be run up the mizzenmast or cabin side for two or three feet and then bent over into a swan neck.

All too frequently, fuel-tank vents are not led high enough above the deck, and salt water gets into the fuel line. No engine will run on salt water. The tank vents mounted on the topsides just below the rail cap which one often sees on modern boats are guaranteed to suck up salt water in heavy weather.

FUEL LINES

Fuel lines must be connected to the engine by flexible hose, but this should not be made of straight plastic or rubber, since in case of fire, either of these materials will ignite almost instantly, causing burning fuel to flow into the engine room. Instead, armored line should be used; although not fireproof, this is fire-resistant, and can be expected to hold up long enough for a fire to be put out with the automatic or hand-held extinguishers.

FILTERING

Filters are among the pieces of equipment most essential for the proper functioning of the engine. The normal diesel will run practically forever if it has clean fuel and clean oil. By the same token, engine failure can in many cases be attributed to inefficient filters. Problems also often arise because too few filters are used; there may be only a single fuel filter, although most engine mechanics advise three—one to separate out the water and then two to take out the dirt.

What one gains in one direction, one loses in the other. If three separate fuel filters are used, there are six connections, all of which may leak air. Second, various types of filter elements need to be provided. And finally, when the filters have been drained, repriming the engine is often very difficult. If there is gravity feed to the engine, the filters can be bled, gravity will refill them, and the engine can be started. However, the gravity feed is seldom found, and in its absence, the fuel must be pumped or sucked through the filters, the air removed from the line, and the diesel engine then started. Diesels are usually provided with a small priming pump, but this is generally so small that trying to send the fuel through the system can leave one very frustrated. Another approach is to install a small pump behind the filters and physically pump the fuel through the filters, driving out the air. Because of the difficulties involved, people tend to avoid changing filters. The result is dirty fuel, followed—all too often—by the loss of a five-hundred-dollar injection pump.

However, attempts are always being made to simplify and improve the fuel filter. Racor Industries (for address, see Appendix) has produced a really good model. In it, three stages of filtering are provided for in one unit, so connections which can leak air are kept to a minimum. In the first stage, heavy solids and liquids are removed by centrifugal action; in the second stage, those contaminating elements which are lighter than the fuel are coalesced out; and in the third stage, the fuel passes up through the center of the filter element to the injection pump. One of the greatest advantages of this product is that water and contaminants, having been filtered down to a very fine degree, can be drained from the filter without the necessity of shutting down the engine or bleeding the system.

PROPELLERS

PROPELLER SIZE

In the discussion of propeller size in *OSY*-I (Ch. XIV), it was pointed out that on a forty-foot boat the average Perkins, Westerbeke, or Mercedes-Benz 40-h.p. diesel with a 2-to-1 reduction gear can usually achieve 7½ knots in calm water, but the speed drops off rapidly when the boat is punching into a head sea.

For this reason, in 1969, when I drew up for a large and well-known Caribbean charter agency (then expanding operations in the southern end of the Caribbean) the specifications for the ideal forty-one-foot keelboat for bareboat charter, I insisted that there be a 3-to-1, or larger, reduction gear. I pointed out that since light airs would seldom be encountered—and then only under the lee of the islands—attaining maximum speed for short distances in calm water was not important. The engine would typically be used when, as a result of bad navigation and strong currents, the boat was set to the lee of the islands late in the afternoon, and those aboard wished to motor sail in, or when they were just fighting their way up from Grenada to Carriacou on a windy day. What was needed was an engine installation that would power them into a big sea and a 15- or 20-knot head wind, and therefore the 3-to-1 or 4-to-1 reduction gear, which would make it possible to swing a really large propeller, was absolutely essential. Those opposing this view contended that with the large propeller the boat would not sail. However, they failed to recognize that when a big wheel is desired, the drag problem can be solved by installation of an adjustable-pitch propeller, an automatically feathering propeller, or a folding propeller, as discussed later in this chapter. On a boat with a separation between the keel and the rudder, a 3-to-1 reduction gear can be installed with a giant two-bladed folding or feathering propeller of the correct pitch. Unfortunately, I could never convince the powers that be of the correctness of my view.

I have never tried to power to windward in the boat as it was finally built, or in others that are comparable, but I have discussed the subject with many knowledgeable and competent yachtsmen who have, and they all say that these boats just will not power decently into a head sea. In this respect, they are typical of almost all the bareboats in the Caribbean, and since the bareboats generally leave much to be desired when trying to sail to windward, this inability to power into a head sea is most discouraging to charterers. One notable exception is a small group of Morgan Out Island 41's, in sailing qualities no better and no worse than the other bareboats available, having a 40-h.p. diesel, with a 3-to-1 reduction, tied in to a big three-bladed propeller. In typical Caribbean weather, a Morgan 41 with this installation can be driven to weather in head seas without any trouble at all.

Thrust Versus Horsepower

Many yachtsmen, and also all too many designers and engine manufacturers, seem to forget that in driving a sailboat, it is not the amount of horsepower in the engine, but rather the amount of thrust produced by the propeller that is important. A high-rpm engine turning a small propeller does produce a great deal of thrust as long as the boat is moving along very rapidly. However, an ocean sailing yacht is likely to have a cruising speed of between 4 knots (for the smallest boat) and 8 knots (for the largest) with a maximum speed of from 6 to 10 knots—and very few boats at the 10-knot end of the scale. Most require maximum propeller efficiency at about 6 to 6½ knots. The accompanying table, by Bob Kress, chief engineer at Michigan Wheel, shows some interesting figures. A little Volvo Penta MD 2B (or another engine of similar size), given a 4-to-1 reduction, can swing a 28-inch propeller with a 17-inch pitch to produce 845 pounds of thrust—

	REDUCTION GEAR RATIO	3-BLADED PROPELLER DIAMETER AND PITCH, IN INCHES	CALCULATED THRUST, IN POUNDS *	% INCREASE IN THRUST
Westerbeke	1.5:1	10 x 7	167	—
6 s.h.p. at 2,800 rpm	2:1	12 x 5	183	10
	2.5:1	14 x 9	197	18
	3:1	16 x 10	207	24
	3.5:1	17.5 x 11	216	29
	4:1	19 x 12	224	34
Volvo Penta MD 2B	1:1	—	—	—
25 s.h.p. at 2,500 rpm	1.5:1	15 x 9	606	—
	2:1	18 x 11	671	11
	2.5:1	22 x 12	728	20
	3:1	24 x 14	776	28
	3.5:1	26 x 16	812	34
	4:1	28 x 17	845	39
	5:1	32 x 20	902	49
Perkins 4-108, or	1:1	12 x 6	638	—
Westerbeke	1.5:1	15 x 8	755	18
35 s.h.p. at 3,000 rpm	2:1	17 x 11	815	28
	2.5:1	20 x 12	890	40
	3:1	22 x 14	938	47
	3.5:1	25 x 15	997	56
	4:1	27 x 16	1,038	63
Perkins 4-154M	2:1	18 x 12	1,115	—
52 s.h.p. at 3,000 rpm	3:1	24 x 15	1,312	18
	4:1	30 x 16	1,455	31
	5:1	34 x 19	1,558	38
Perkins 4-236M	2:1	24 x 13	1,478	—
62 s.h.p. at 2,250 rpm	3:1	32 x 16	1,680	14
	4:1	36 x 22	1,841	25
	5:1	42 x 24	1,971	33

* Thrust calculated at an anticipated hull speed of approximately 5 knots for the first engine listed, and 6–6½ knots for all of the others.
Courtesy of Robert Kress, chief engineer at Michigan Wheel.

which is slightly more than the 815 pounds obtainable from a standard 35-h.p. Perkins 4-108 or Westerbeke, with the usual 2-to-1 reduction, swinging a 17-inch propeller with an 11-inch pitch.

Given a 5-to-1 reduction, the 25-h.p. engine can swing a 32-inch propeller with a 20-inch pitch and yield 902 pounds of thrust, which is 10 percent more than can be produced by the standard Perkins 4-108 or Westerbeke with a 2-to-1 reduction.

In turn, given a 4-to-1 reduction, the 4-108 can swing a 27-inch propeller with a 16-inch pitch to give 1,038 pounds of thrust—only 10 percent less than the thrust produced by the much larger 52-h.p. Perkins 4-154 with a 2-to-1 reduction. And again, the 52-h.p. Perkins with a 5-to-1 reduction produces more thrust than does the 62-h.p. model with the standard 2-to-1 reduction.

It would certainly appear that the proper installation for the ocean sailing yacht is a relatively small engine with a really large reduction and a large but low-drag propeller. This would produce about as much thrust as a larger engine with a smaller reduction, and would leave much more space in the engine room.

The excessive drag caused by a large propeller can be eliminated by use of an adjustable-pitch, folding, or feathering model. If there is a lack of space in the aperture in the boat being designed or repowered, one can choose a propeller of the size the boat would normally use but go to a smaller engine and a larger reduction, thereby obtaining more space in the engine room and saving money and weight in the installation of the engine. In a word, when it is felt that more power is needed, one should think of thrust rather than horsepower; retaining an engine of the original size while adding a larger reduction gear and a larger propeller is likely to be much easier than trying to install a larger engine.

ADJUSTABLE-PITCH PROPELLERS

Adjustable-pitch, or variable-pitch, propellers are widely available in Europe, having been used commercially by fishermen and on trading ketches in northern Europe since the turn of the century. An adjustable-pitch propeller was installed in the cutter *Randihil* about 1915, and was still operating perfectly in 1965, when it was taken apart and examined in St. Thomas.

The adjustable-pitch propeller has tremendous advantages; a good summation of them can be found in a brochure issued by Hundested, the best known of the manufacturers, which has been in business for fifty years. Here follows a presentation of Hundested's views (see also Drawing 183).

First of all, in varying conditions, the sailboat with an adjustable-pitch propeller can obtain propeller thrust anywhere from 18 to 25 percent greater than that obtainable with a fixed-pitch propeller. Also, the full rated engine output can always be efficiently utilized by the propeller—whether the boat is towing, punching into a head sea, or achieving maximum speed in calm water. By contrast, the normal propeller on an auxiliary sailing yacht is designed to give maximum speed

The graph proves these four things:

1. A propeller designed for *speed* cannot develop optimum power when the vessel is heavily laden, or towing or trawling, or under heavy stresses arising from bad weather.

2. A propeller designed for *power* cannot develop optimum speed when it would be desirable, as, for example, when tugs and trawlers are free-running, when cargo vessels are on ballast voyages, or when trawlers are anxious to reach port to catch the market.

3. A propeller designed as a compromise cannot develop either maximum speed or maximum power from engine output.

4. An adjustable-pitch propeller, designed to permit pitch variation, is able to develop maximum speed, or maximum pull, or any combination of speed or power that might be desirable.

(Hundested Motorfabrik—adapted)

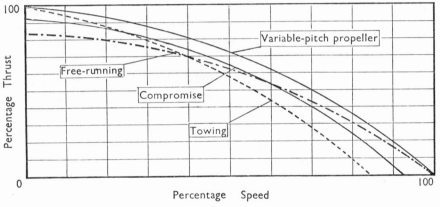

183. Comparative performance of various types of propeller.

in smooth water, or—in some cruising boats—to supply maximum thrust at a set speed, allowing the boat to power into a head sea; then, if sea and wind conditions are not exactly right, efficiency from the propeller falls off.

Another advantage is that because the engine can be run at higher rpm, stalling can be prevented and bad combustion reduced to a minimum. Running slowly for long periods of time, as when powering in a flat calm, need not result in engine overloading because of low rpm; the engine can be run at the rpm ideal for loading and fuel consumption, and the propeller pitch adjusted accordingly to give the best performance.

The adjustable-pitch propeller has fewer moving parts than a fixed-pitch propeller working through a gearbox. In addition, repair costs in the event of propeller damage are likely to be lower because the blades are detachable and interchangeable. One could even carry along a spare blade.

When sails are used in combination with the engine, any pitch requirement can be met. And when sailing, the blades can be adjusted fore and aft to minimize propeller drag.

The adjustable-pitch propeller is superior to the automatically feathering propeller for the same reasons that it is superior to the fixed-pitch propeller. In addition, the automatically feathering propeller does not always feather.

As for the reliability of the adjustable-pitch propeller, which is often questioned, the claim is made in the brochure that the firm's propellers are so strong that none of them has ever suffered any damage to the internal mechanism, although of course many damaged blades have resulted from encounters with fish pots, flotsam and jetsam, and the like. This claim is confirmed by everyday experience. One may ask until hell freezes over before finding a broken fully feathering adjustable-pitch propeller.

By contrast, though no one has the exact failure-rate figures, one can certainly find broken gearboxes without looking too hard. Indeed, there are so many failures in the Lesser Antilles that Power Products, in St. Thomas, finds it profitable to carry standard gearboxes in stock. Further, fully feathering, adjustable-pitch, reversible propellers would hardly have been used as standard on all except light aircraft for the past forty-five years if they were unreliable. A type of propeller that can work on aircraft, where tolerances and weight are critical and rpm extremely high, should surely work on boats, where it is possible to have parts built with extremely large safety factors, and shaft rpm can easily be kept down to 800 or less.

An objection to fully feathering adjustable-pitch propellers that is always raised when a yachtsman asks engine or propeller manufacturers, or naval architects, about their availability is that they are expensive. This view is completely unfounded; people just do not have their facts. As the accompanying table indicates, for the various horsepowers available, the adjustable-pitch installations are *less* expensive than their fixed equivalents. In addition, their superior thrust results in improved fuel efficiency. All of the engines listed in the table are diesels, and the price in each instance is for a complete unit, including engine, shaft, stern tube, propeller, shaft brake (for the fixed models), and so on.

Since the information about the performance of fully feathering adjustable-pitch propellers has been available for the last twenty or thirty years, and much of the equipment has been in existence even

Cost, in Dollars, for Complete Units—Various Types of Propeller

ENGINE	H.P.	ADJUSTABLE-PITCH	FIXED	FOLDING	AUTOMATICALLY FEATHERING
WaterMota *	7	2,165	2,415		
Westerbeke	10		3,016	3,187	3,424
Sabb *	18	2,600			
Westerbeke	20		3,907	4,079	4,417
"	60		5,637	5,837	6,267
Sabb (Ford marine conversion) *	68	4,654			

* For estimated U.S. price, add 25 percent to the figures listed, to cover shipment, duty, and the like.

longer—for about sixty years—one wonders what yacht architects have been thinking about for the past quarter century!

The adjustable-pitch propeller is manufactured in all sizes and combinations. Some companies, such as WaterMota and PNP Marine, specialize in the comparatively small sizes; others, such as Helseth, in Norway, and Hundested, in Denmark, produce the propellers in all sizes, and also make some slow-speed, heavy-duty engines matched to them. (For addresses of the various companies, see Appendix.)

The slow-speed engines are what yachtsmen refer to as "thumpers" —great huge lumps of iron suitable only in a traditional boat that has plenty of room and does not mind a heavy, massive engine. For the average yacht, having bought the propeller, stern tube, shaft, and controlling mechanism from one manufacturer, one is faced with the task of matching these components with the engine; that is, one must provide the suitable bell housing, reduction gear, and the like. However, William Lemieux, of Marine and Industrial (for address, see Appendix), has pointed out that almost all engines are made to fit Borg-Warner gearboxes and therefore have a standard bell housing. The simplest and cheapest installation begins with a mechanical reduction gear (without reverse), which costs much less than the normal reduction gear; this is bolted onto the engine, with the shaft mechanism of the adjustable-pitch propeller then attached directly to the gearbox.

This arrangement does have disadvantages. First and most important is the fact that when the engine is run to charge the batteries, the propeller, in neutral, will always be turning over, and since a spinning propeller cannot be seen in the water, it will be a great danger to the unwary swimmer. Second, unless the engine is relatively small, starting it will be very difficult because of the drag of the propeller, if the batteries are the least bit low.

To eliminate these difficulties, most installations include a thrust bearing and disconnect clutch. The shaft propeller mechanism is disconnected when the engine is being started, and remains disconnected if it is being run merely to charge the batteries. Otherwise, once the engine is running, the propeller is put into neutral, the shaft is connected, and maneuvering is then done by adjusting the pitch as necessary. Another great advantage of this arrangement is that with the clutch present, it is simple to belt an alternator off the shaft and use the propeller to generate electricity, as described in the preceding chapter. The propeller may be feathered for minimal drag when desired, and when sheets are eased and one is not particularly worried about drag, the pitch can be cranked in, the shaft allowed to rotate, and electricity generated. William Lemieux states that suitable clutches are available, and that Maine and Industrial would be most happy to supply the complete unit—engine, reduction gear, clutch mechanism, thrust bearing, and adjustable-pitch propeller.

Complete units are also offered by Sabb, in sizes that could be used on an average ocean sailing yacht. For the 6–18 h.p. range, engines designed and built by the company are used in these units. The 18-h.p. engine, which has two cylinders, weighs only 420 pounds. The larger units have either a four-cylinder standard Ford engine (for which parts can be found world-wide, since it is basically a tractor engine) or a 100 h.p. six-cylinder Ford engine. Above 100 h.p., one is well advised to switch to twin screws, as discussed later in this chapter, for maximum flexibility and minimum propeller drag.

Where there is a hydraulic installation, connecting an adjustable-pitch propeller directly to it is very easy. When this is done, the engine can still be run in neutral without the propeller turning over, but the propeller cannot be allowed to freewheel and generate electricity.

Also, many of the hydraulic drives have an infinitely variable reduction, and when this is present, so many permutations and combinations of engine rpm, shaft rpm, and pitch are possible that one may become very confused and end up not obtaining maximum thrust. Hence, where there is hydraulic drive and also an adjustable-pitch propeller, both an engine tachometer and a shaft tachometer should be utilized, so that one can know exactly how many shaft rpm are being developed, and then adjust the pitch accordingly. Also, in the exhaust manifold should be installed a pyrometer to make sure that the engine is not being overloaded.

The correct size of propeller for a particular installation can be determined by means of the formula shown in Drawing 184. It should be

It is very easy to work out the model of Hundested adjustable-pitch propeller that is most suitable for a given vessel.

Example: A propeller unit is required for an engine which develops 160 SHP at 300 propeller RPM.

$$J = \frac{SHP}{SRPM} = \frac{160}{300} = 0.53 \qquad \frac{HP}{RPM} \geq J$$

Shaft horse power divided by shaft revolution per minute is equal to or less than J.

From the table select the unit whose J factor is nearest above this figure; in this case it will be VP 7 whose factor is 0.55.

Note: This method is for guidance only. It is advisable to consult the manufacturer, or a propulsion engineer, before coming to a final decision.

(Hundested Motorfabrik—adapted)

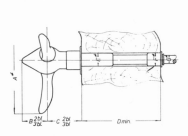

VP size	J	A 2bl. Min	A 2bl. Max	A 3bl. Min	A 3bl. Max	B 2bl	B 3bl	C 2bl	C 3bl	D	E	F	G
1	0027	400	520	380	570	112	110	154	150	240	60	60	38
2	005	580	760	450	660	130	142	200	195	340	76	76	50
3	01	670	1010	620	900	160	178	290	290	390	93	97	65
4	02	770	1215	770	1030	170	180	355	351	450	110	113	75
5	03	890	1300	880	1220	210	215	450	430	470	128	128	89
6	04	1200	1450	825	1260	235	235	500	460	520	140	150	99
7	055	1345	1550	1070	1420	255	235	530	485	580	160	160	108
8	07	1500	1650	1200	1520	270	270	560	525	590	170	170	115
9	10			1345	1660		270		550	590	170	170	115
9½	12			1580	1732		306		550	680	200	190	130
10	17			1600	1900		360		675	750	215	205	145
10	17			1600	1900		360		420	750	215	205	145
10½	25			2000	2130								165
10½	25			2000	2130								165
11	35			2000	2500								197
12	50												

SUBJECT TO MODIFICATION.

184. Main dimensions in millimeters, for Hundested adjustable-pitch propeller units in standard design.

noted that the method is applicable specifically in the choice of a Hundested adjustable-pitch propeller.

Adjustable-pitch propellers are available in both two- and three-bladed models. If the installation is on center, either in the deadwood or hidden behind the keel, obviously the two-bladed model should be used. The propeller shaft should be so marked that the blades can be lined up vertically and fully feathered when stored. Drag will then be absolutely minimal, and the propeller will prevent water from crossing through the aperture from the lee to the windward side of the rudder.

However, for a twin-screw installation, three-bladed propellers are probably best. Their diameter can then be kept to a minimum, so that they may be tucked up under the quarters as high as possible to reduce drag, while yet reaching far enough into the water to provide acceptable efficiency under power.

Basically, there are two types of adjustable-pitch mechanism. In the Sabb unit, a solid shaft slides in and out of the stuffing gland (Drawing 185), and a thrust bearing outside the boat is therefore necessary. In the Hundested and WaterMota models, one shaft slides inside another (Drawing 186).

Each type has advantages and disadvantages. The big advantage of the Sabb arrangement is that the solid shaft can absorb considerable torque; hence, with blades of sufficient size the smaller-sized model of this unit can be used with engines of up to 30 h.p. With the Hundested and WaterMota arrangement of one shaft sliding inside the other, relatively less torque can be absorbed, so one must be very careful to match the propeller to the engine properly—if in doubt, selecting a unit that is oversized.

The disadvantage of the Sabb type is that because the thrust bearing is outside, in an off-center installation an extremely rugged strut must be placed just forward of the propeller. However, this is unnecessary for a propeller mounted in the deadwood or on the after end of the keel.

PROPELLER DRAG

Very few tank tests to determine propeller drag have actually been performed. Indeed, the only ones that come to mind are the tests carried out prior to World War II at the Stevens Institute and reported in *Yachting* in the late 1930's and early 1940's. The figures shown in the accompanying table are drawn from a reading of those articles, supplemented by a few long discussions with naval architects. Drag is presented as a percentage of increase in resistance over that of the same hull with no propeller, shaft, strut, or aperture. The figures in the table are only approximate, since there are various difficulties in drawing any exact conclusions from the tests. First and foremost there is the problem (of which yachtsmen are becoming more and more aware as they follow the testing done in preparation for the America's Cup races) of extrapolating data from tank tests on a comparatively small model, usually $\frac{1}{12}$-sized, to the full-sized boat. Further, it should be remembered that the Stevens Institute tests involved the ocean racing hulls of the late 1930's; also, the propellers used were comparatively small, since at that time the engine and propellers carried by a yacht were likely to be considerably smaller than those found on the modern cruising auxiliary, which is frequently today really a motor sailer.

Furthermore, there are a few variables concerning which little or no testing has been done. To the best of my knowledge, no one has tried to determine experimentally the drag of a hull with no aperture and no propeller as compared to that of a hull with an aperture and no pro-

185. Sabb adjustable-pitch mechanism. (Sabb Motor S.A.)

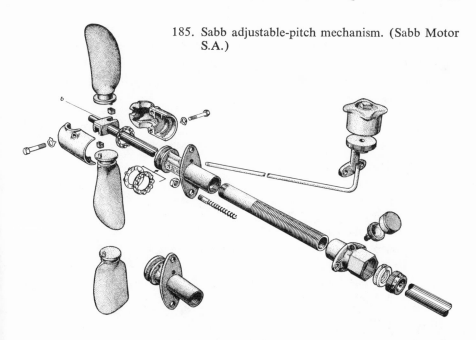

186. WaterMota adjustable-pitch mechanism. (WaterMota Limited)

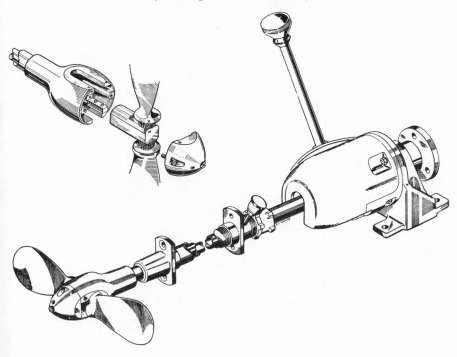

peller. My impression is that on full-sized boats, the aperture alone causes almost as much drag as a propeller; if the propeller is yanked to improve performance, the aperture must be plugged. Also, in the offset mountings, how much of the drag is caused by the propellers, and how much by the strut?

	% Increase in Drag in Alternative Locations	
PROPELLER TYPE	CENTER LINE IN APERTURE	OFFSET
3-bladed solid	21.4	36.0
2-bladed solid	7.5	26.0
3-bladed feathered	3.2	9.0
3-bladed adjustable-pitch, fully feathered	3.2	9.0
2-bladed feathered	probably 2.0	6.0
2-bladed adjustable-pitch, fully feathered	probably 2.0	6.0
2-bladed folding		1.3

It should be noted that the automatically feathering propeller and the adjustable-pitch propeller, in the fully feathered position, have considerably more drag than the folding propeller; this is probably due to the large hub diameter in both the automatically and mechanically feathering models. It is of interest too that the folding propellers of the 1930's had much greater drag when folded than do most modern folding propellers. Finally, it should be noted that the increase in drag shows up drastically at low speeds and going to windward, but is not really significant when a boat is reaching or running at high speed.

Whatever its omissions, the table does make it apparent that our present cruising boats are sailing with sea anchors attached to them. One really begins to wonder about the large yachts that are dragging a three- or even a four-bladed solid wheel. Individuals who have sailed for any period in the incomparably beautiful *America* report that no matter how the four-bladed solid propeller is stopped, at least two blades stick out directly into the slipstream, completely ruining the water flow around the stern and rudder, and causing tremendous drag. This drag is obviously present at all times, but is especially apparent when going to windward or in light airs. Indeed, during the filming of a movie about the *America,* in light airs she had great difficulty in staying ahead of Maine coasters with no propeller and aperture to cause drag—boats one would have expected her to take to the cleaners. Her crew members refer to her as a dog in anything but a blow, for only when it begins to blow hard does the amount of resistance due to the propeller, as compared to the total resistance of the boat, drop off drastically.

Even the three-bladed on-center solid wheel, the standard installation on the average cruising boat, results in resistance substantially higher than that produced by a two-bladed feathering propeller or a two-bladed fully feathering adjustable-pitch propeller—21.4 percent as opposed to about 2.0 percent. Resistance affects boat speed differently on different points of sail. Going to weather in moderate airs, the 21.4-percent resistance produced by the three-bladed solid wheel could reduce the speed of a 29-foot-LWL boat from 5 knots to 4 knots. On a beam reach in the same wind, the speed of the same boat would be reduced from 6 knots to about $5\frac{1}{4}$–$5\frac{1}{2}$ knots. In heavy airs, when a boat reaches its hull speed with little effort, propeller drag has minimal effect on overall performance.

Propeller-Drag Elimination

Fully Feathering Adjustable-Pitch Propellers: So far as I have been able to determine, no one has done any really accurate tests to measure the drag caused by cranking in the pitch and feathering the adjustable-pitch propeller, but some information can be obtained just by casually looking at the steam gauge. The effect of the propeller drag is of course greatest when going to windward and least when going downwind. For example, on the forty-nine-foot Garden-designed *Pixie,* setting the pitch of the propeller appears to reduce speed from $7\frac{1}{4}$ to $6\frac{1}{2}$ knots when going downwind and from $6\frac{3}{4}$ to 6 knots—a proportionately greater reduction—when going to windward.

Val Schaeffer, of *Camelot,* an eighty-five-foot motor sailer, reports that cranking in the pitch probably reduces speed by a little over a knot when *Camelot* is off the wind, but by almost 2 knots when going to windward, to the point where with the pitch cranked in she absolutely will not tack. It was reported in *Yachting* in January, 1977, that on the motor sailer *Wind Seeker,* cranking in the pitch resulted in a drop in speed from $6\frac{1}{2}$–7 knots to $4\frac{1}{2}$–5 knots. In other words, if propeller drag can be minimized by correct adjustment, there may be almost a 40 percent increase in speed.

Hyde Automatically Feathering Propeller: Another method of eliminating drag is to use a Hyde automatically feathering propeller (now built by Paul Luke, for address, see Appendix). The effectiveness of this unit in reducing drag is illustrated by the experience of Bob

Lamson, of *Ventura,* who had a Hyde propeller for many years. At one point he knocked off one blade by hitting a fish pot, and while awaiting the arrival of a new blade, he used a solid wheel. He stated that it felt as if he had thrown a sea anchor off the stern of the boat—she absolutely would not sail.

In the past, the Hyde propeller had a rather bad reputation because it did not always flip when the engine was reversed; you thought you were in reverse when actually you were in ahead, and the result was that many a boat plowed into the dock. One theory is that the cause of this difficulty was lack of maintenance. Owners of this propeller who have had it work well are universal in their view that whenever the boat is hauled, the oil should be drained from the propeller, which should then be well flushed before it is filled with clean oil.

Another way in which improper maintenance can cause trouble was encountered by John Kendall, of *Alaria,* who inherited a Hyde propeller when his father's skipper refused to have it on the boat any longer because it frequently would not reverse, jaming at the most inopportune moments. When Kendall checked out the propeller, he discovered that the wrong grease had been used in it. At the low temperatures common in the Gulf of Maine in the early spring, the grease would congeal, preventing the propeller from feathering and reversing.

FOLDING PROPELLERS: Folding propellers, which have been available for the past forty years, are usually designed to produce minimum drag, but the problem of producing maximum thrust in a unit of this type is not a prime consideration. Their performance in reverse is generally reputed to be inferior, although some modern units, such as the Gori (for address, see Appendix), reportedly have acceptable backing power. The difficulties in reverse arise because of the way a folding propeller operates. While moving ahead, the blades are thrown out by centrifugal force and then held there by the forward thrust of the water pressure, but in reverse the centrifugal force must be sufficient not only to throw the blades out but to hold them in position against the water pressure. Hence, when the engine is put into reverse, it must be revved up to near maximum rpm to build up centrifugal force and get the blades out and into position. Once the propeller is open, speed can be reduced.

It must also be remembered that the shaft should be marked so that the blades are horizontal when the engine is shut down. Otherwise gravity will cause the lower blade to droop and of course cause drag—just what we are trying to avoid.

FREEWHEELING PROPELLERS: The argument about whether drag is better minimized by allowing the propeller to freewheel or by fixing it in place never ends. It is generally agreed that a three-bladed propeller causes less drag when freewheeling than when in the locked position. However, people who are engineers and have thought very fully about the subject tend to accept the conclusion reached by E. G. Martin (one of the founders of the R.O.R.C. and one of the great cruising yachtsmen of the 1920's and 1930's as the owner of *Jolie Brise*) that this is true only if the propeller is completely freewheeling—that is, without friction. In practice, the freewheeling propeller, literally trying to pull itself out of the boat, drags the gearbox, and friction develops in the gearbox and in the stern tube as well. For this reason, Martin recommended that a thrust bearing be installed in the shaft to take the backward thrust of the propeller when it is freewheeling, and thereby minimize the drag.

In addition, it has often happened that under the stress of the free spinning the coupling has vibrated loose, with the result that the propeller suddenly spins completely out of the boat, or spins back and jams the rudder at a most inopportune time. Therefore, on a boat on which the shaft is allowed to spin, the coupling bolts should all be drilled and safety-wired with stainless wire. Also, the coupling set screw should be set into a hole actually drilled ¼ or ⅜ of an inch into the shaft. This coupling set screw too should be safety-wired.

It should also be remembered that if the freewheeling propeller is used to drive the generator, its rotation is slowed and considerable drag results. The fact that the wrong side of the propeller is working when it is being dragged through the water also has the effect of slowing rotation and increasing drag. Therefore, as noted in the preceding chapter, a generator running off the propeller shaft is probably acceptable only during downwind sailing. Going to windward, a wind-powered generator should be used instead for a small to medium-sized boat. Making 5 knots to windward in a 15-knot breeze means about 18 knots across the deck; in these conditions, a small Ampair wind generator yields 1.9 amperes, and will produce in a day as much charge as is obtained by running the average engine for one hour.

Types of Propeller Compared

Solid propeller: can be allowed to freewheel to generate electricity, provided the correct gearbox is chosen, but causes perpetual drag, like a sea anchor.

Folding propeller: cannot be allowed to freewheel to generate electricity, and has poor reversing capabilities, but produces minimum drag, and needs no shaft brake.

Fully feathering adjustable-pitch propeller: can be allowed to freewheel to generate electricity, and can be fully feathered to minimize drag when not generating.

Automatically feathering propeller: cannot be allowed to freewheel to generate electricity, and sometimes fails to reverse, but produces very little drag (though more than the folding propeller), and needs no shaft brake.

APERTURE DRAG

Although apparently no tank tests have ever been performed to measure the drag caused by the aperture alone, its existence and importance is demonstrated by actual experience. Yachtsmen on various boats in various areas of the world come up with versions of the same story: An engine is disabled by a broken shaft, a blown gearbox, or some other mishap, and because the boat is in an out-of-the-way area, prompt repairs are not possible. To minimize drag, a crew member goes overside with a lung, and using a wheel-puller, yanks off the propeller, but sailing performance is only marginally improved. When the boat is hauled, since the engine is still not back in commission, filler blocks to plug the aperture are constructed with plywood and spacers. This is easily done, as shown in Drawing 187A (for an aperture in the deadwood) and in Drawing 187B (for an aperture half in the deadwood and half in the rudder).

The result in all cases is a tremendous improvement in the boat's performance, in some cases to the point where the owners never bother to reinstall the engine at all. Even *Ring Andersen,* a heavy ninety-eight-foot Baltic trader that one would expect to be completely unmanageable without an engine, was temporarily turned into quite a good sailboat after the shaft broke. The propeller and shaft were pulled and the stern tube and aperture were plugged, and John Clegg then sailed her for a number of weeks on charter. Clegg, who obviously knew how she handled, since he had been sailing her for two years, was absolutely amazed at the improvement and at her ability to sail, to tack into restricted waters, and to maneuver in moderately close quarters without help from an engine.

My own experience with *Iolaire* comes to mind in this connection. When I first acquired her, she had no engine, shaft, or propeller, but she did have a fairing block and a big strut. She sailed well. Installa-

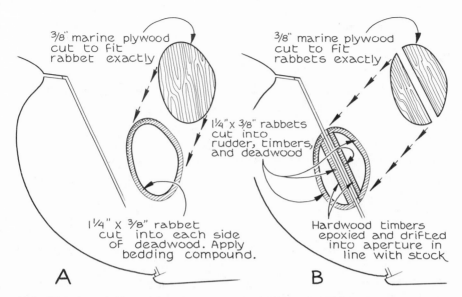

3/8" marine plywood cut to fit rabbet exactly

3/8" marine plywood cut to fit rabbets exactly

1¼"x 3/8" rabbets cut into rudder, timbers, and deadwood

1¼" x 3/8" rabbet cut into each side of deadwood. Apply bedding compound.

Hardwood timbers epoxied and drifted into aperture in line with stock

A

B

187. Plugging the propeller aperture after an engine has been removed will increase sailing performance greatly and improve rudder efficiency: A, aperture fully in deadwood; B, aperture half in deadwood, half in rudder.

tion of an engine, a shaft, and a folding propeller did not appear to make an appreciable difference in her performance. However, after owning her for fourteen years I pulled out the engine, shaft, strut, propeller, and fairing block, giving her a completely smooth underbody. The resulting difference in her handling in light airs was unbelievable.

At this point, I wonder if the fabulous performance Gary Hoyt is turning in racing in the Caribbean with his Freedom 40 is due to his interesting, innovative rig, as described in Chapter III, to his damn-good racing ability and helmsmanship, or to the fact that having no propeller, aperture, strut, or anything else to slow the boat down, the hull is basically that much faster. A great many variables come to mind.

In any event, in view of the apparent drag caused by the aperture alone, one is likely to lean more and more toward the idea of installing twin screws high up under the quarters—either folding or adjustable-pitch fully feathering propellers. This can be done with two separate engines, or with a single engine driving the two screws by means of hydraulic drive.

It is obvious that all sorts of new options are open to those who want a sailboat that will really sail, having auxiliary power with minimal drag—people who do not want the burden of a sea anchor hung out astern.

SHAFT BRAKES

There are many types of shaft brake (propeller lock) on the market, and many homemade devices in use as well. The purely mechanical shaft brake leaves much to be desired. For one thing, starting the engine with the brake on is all too easy. Also, when one tries to apply the shaft brake while sailing fast, the dropping of the spring-loaded ratchet makes one hell of a noise, and all too often this is followed by the *clang, clang, clang,* of bits and pieces rotating around the shaft after the brake has exploded. This has happened to us a number of times while delivering boats.

Hence, there is general agreement that the proper choice for a shaft brake is a fail-safe hydraulic device: when the engine is shut off, the brake closes on the shaft brake disk, slowing down the rotation until the ratchet drops into place, lining the propeller up in the correct position. When the engine is started, the hydraulic pressure immediately opens the brake and lifts the ratchet; therefore, it is impossible to explode the brake by starting the engine in gear. The Hobco brake sold by Wright Britton appears to be one of the best on the market. Wright, who with only his wife as crew has done more offshore sailing in rough weather than almost anyone else alive, recommends it highly.

TWIN-SCREW, TWIN-ENGINE INSTALLATIONS

When twin screws are to be put in and the engine room is under the cockpit, a great many variations in installation are possible, enabling one to choose whatever arrangement is most advantageous. Since two medium-sized engines are shorter in length than one large engine, less space may be taken away from the accommodation. Also, although under the cockpit the engines themselves will be in an area short of headroom, on many large vessels there will be almost full standing headroom outboard of each engine, under the cockpit seats.

Some Dimensions of Engines

	RATED HORSE-POWER	LENGTH, IN INCHES	WIDTH, IN INCHES	HEIGHT, IN INCHES	CUBIC FEET	WEIGHT, IN POUNDS
Perkins 4-236	85	48	25	36	25.00	1026
Perkins 4-154	62	50	23	32	21.29	830
Perkins 4-108	50	44	23	32	18.74	600

From the forward end of each engine a power takeoff can be rigged, as discussed in the section on jackshafts, earlier in this chapter. As noted there, the amount of power that will be available from the front of the engine, even with a pillow block to take the side thrust, varies with different models, so one must get this information from the manufacturer.

When the power takeoff is installed, belts from the jackshaft are run to individual pieces of equipment, which are then driven by means of cone clutches, as found on belt-driven Jabsco pumps. Each piece of equipment will of course draw power away from the drive shaft. Hence, on a really good sailing boat with minimal engine power, if one is a mechanical fiddler and installs whatever available equipment can be fitted in between the engines, one may discover that when all of this auxiliary equipment is in operation, almost no power is available on the shaft. This is really no disadvantage, however, since at the times when full power is needed on the shaft, probably only one or two pieces of auxiliary equipment will be in use.

The approximate horsepower drain for various pieces of equipment is as follows:

	h.p.
2½-inch Jabsco pump	2
50-ampere 12-volt alternator	1
3-kilowatt 110-volt generator	6
5-kilowatt 110-volt generator	10
7-kilowatt 110-volt generator	14
hydraulic pump for small anchor windlass	2
hydraulic pump for large anchor windlass	5
compressor suitable for refrigerator/freezer for forty-foot boat	2
compressor suitable for refrigerator/freezer for sixty-foot boat	4
10-inch-diameter belt-driven engine-room blower	1

In a twin-screw installation, each engine will of course have its own standard alternator, charging its own individual battery. If a good electrician does the wiring, he can arrange matters so that in an emergency, by throwing a few switches, one can use the starboard-engine alternator to charge the port-engine starting battery (and vice versa); and in a good installation it should also be possible to use one of the alternators to charge the ship's 12-volt batteries if the auxiliary generator is not operating.

A twin-screw installation with a proper switching system is especially desirable on the cruising boat of fifty feet or over. In this day and age, once a length of fifty feet it reached, so much electricity is usually required that a normal alternator belted off the engine cannot provide it, and an independent generator must be installed. The engineer then has two engines to maintain, with absolutely no interchangeability of parts. If, on the other hand, a single 60- or 70-h.p. main engine is installed and the 110-volt AC generator is driven from it by means of belts or hydraulic drive, then the engine runs under practically no-load conditions when it is charging. This is not particularly good for the engine, which is subjected to a lot of wear and tear, and runs for relatively long periods, to produce a comparatively small amount of electricity. Furthermore, if this engine breaks down, there is no electricity at all to be had.

However, if instead two smaller engines are installed, each capable of running the big generator, the situation changes. A 6-kilowatt generator running directly from the engine probably absorbs 12 h.p., a decent proportion of the power from the smaller engine, which is therefore not forced to run under no-load conditions. Since both engines can be used for charging, as necessary, an independent generator (which would occupy additional space, as indicated by the table in Chapter XIII) is not required. Furthermore, since the two engines are identical, their parts are interchangeable; the number of spare parts that must be carried is kept down, and in a jam, by cannibalizing, one should always be able to keep at least one engine running.

Some engineers feel that a twin-screw installation is more efficient under power than a single fixed-pitch propeller. If twin fixed propellers are used, sailing drag will be considerable, but this drag is substantially reduced with feathering, folding, or adjustable-pitch propellers in the feathered position.

As the table on p. 446 indicates, the three-bladed on-center solid propeller increases drag under sail by 21 percent, while a pair of two-bladed feathering adjustable-pitch propellers will increase drag by a total of only 12 percent. With no aperture and two small feathering adjustable-pitch propellers, the sailing performance of any boat will be infinitely better than that of her sister ship with a single solid propeller, or possibly even with an adjustable-pitch propeller on center in an aperture.

A twin-screw installation might mean that a boat that would normally have a large 60-h.p. diesel with a 2-to-1 reduction, and an on-center three-bladed fixed-pitch propeller with a pitch of 15 inches and a diameter of 22 inches, would be able to get away with two 20- or 30-h.p. engines driving two adjustable-pitch propellers, their size depending on the reduction gear used. These would have hand-starting capability, another safety factor.

Janeen, a 116-foot staysail schooner which has had various installations over the last eighteen years, is at present equipped with twin adjustable-pitch propellers, and Captain Walter Boudreau reports this to be by far the best arrangement she has had. Among other advantages, it makes possible the use of two small marine engines; these not only provide hand-starting capability but also—since they are true marine engines—have their starters mounted high out of the bilge. Inspection ports make it possible for the engines to be rebuilt in place; and bearings, and even connecting rods, rings, and pistons, can be changed in place. Finally, of course, the number of spare parts that must be carried is cut right in half.

In summary, the advantages of the twin-engine, twin-screw installations are many. With the full-width engine room, a yachtsman can go on installing equipment forever if he enjoys maintaining it himself or has a red-hot engineer to maintain it for him. The chances of being caught in a long calm are very slight, since one way or another, it should be possible to get one engine started. And when sailing with the adjustable-pitch propellers in the fully feathered position, drag will be minimized.

STUFFING BOXES

Stuffing-box leaks are the result of poor or loose packing, and this in turn can be caused either by failure to tighten up the packing gland or by failure to grease the packing often enough. Proper maintenance is frequently made difficult by the fact that the stuffing box is extremely hard to reach. Therefore, a good way to ensure that the packing will be greased regularly is to install a remote stuffing-box greaser (Drawing 188A), obtainable from Tarrow Engineering (for address, see Appendix). If this greaser is placed in some accessible location, it can be given one or two turns each time the engine is started, and the packing will always be well lubricated.

The old-fashioned stuffing box (Drawing 188B) was of solid bronze bolted to the deadwood. A pipe was cast or welded to a flange, flax packing was wound around the shaft, and the whole was set up tight with a compression casting provided with four large cap screws or bolts. There were various problems with the alignment of this type of stuffing box. The modern installation (Drawing 188C) consists of the stern tube bolted to the deadwood or fiber-glassed to the hull, a rubber hose, and then a stuffing box. With this arrangement, a fair degree of mis-

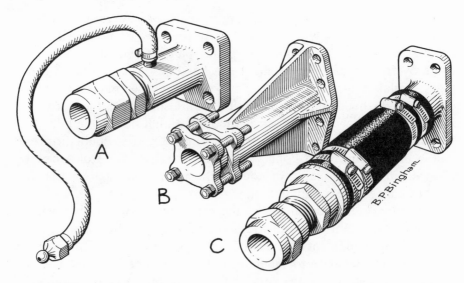

188A. Stuffing box with remote grease fitting. B. Old-fashioned, rigid stuffing box. C. Modern stuffing box with flexible stern tube.

alignment is possible before problems arise, and leakage is less likely; furthermore, the stuffing box is immune to wear caused by vibration, and hence can go a long way before it needs repacking. However, checking at regular intervals is essential.

One difficulty with this type of installation is that the hose clamps may let go and the stuffing box then comes flying forward, leaving a great hole in the bottom of the boat. Unless it is shoved back into place immediately, the boat may flood so badly that a crew not aware of the cause of the flooding, and not realizing how easily it may be stopped, is likely to abandon ship. So it's a good idea to use extra hose clamps just to be sure.

Another problem is that as time goes by the rubber hose deteriorates, and if it is not watched, and replaced as necessary, it may suddenly split. When this happens, stopping the leak is most difficult, since one cannot slip a new hose on the shaft and replace the stuffing gland without pulling the shaft. About the only thing one can do in this case is to allow the shaft to spin free and cut it with a hacksaw, hoping it will drop out without jamming the rudder. Then a wooden bung can be shoved into the hole.

Because of these problems, a yacht classified 100A1 at Lloyd's cannot have this type of installation.

EXHAUST SYSTEMS

Probably more engines die of drowning than of any other cause. Water may be sucked back into the engine by a poorly designed exhaust system, or may run down into the engine when the inner jacket of a double-jacketed system collapses. In this connection it should be remembered that under no circumstances should a diesel engine have a copper exhaust pipe. Because of the sulfuric acid in diesel fumes, copper exhaust pipes are bound to fail within two or three years. These pipes are expensive to install and expensive to reinstall, and repairing an engine that has been full of salt water is even more expensive. Diesel exhaust systems should be made of plain galvanized-iron or steel pipe, and even this should be renewed periodically. One of the great advantages of the Aqua-Lift, as described in *OSY*-I (Ch. XIV), and a little later in this chapter, is that it makes it almost impossible for water to get into an engine, even a diesel.

Exhaust systems should be as short as possible, and hot spots, which must be wrapped in asbestos, should be kept to an absolute minimum. Where asbestos is used, it should be coated, since otherwise segments may break off, filling the engine room with white dust. This is then sucked into the air intake, and the effect is the same as if one poured sand into the intake. A quick method of covering the asbestos is to sew heavy fiber-glass cloth over it, and then coat the cloth with fire-retardant resin. There are also various paints made especially for use over asbestos lagging. These are water soluble and are smeared on as a paste; when solidified, they present a smooth, nonflaking surface.

An exhaust system, whether jacketed, made with a standpipe, or in the form of an Aqua-Lift, must be examined carefully to make sure that water cannot be driven up the exhaust pipe and flood the engine when running downwind in heavy weather, and that water cannot siphon back into the engine. Usually, a siphon break should be installed.

STANDPIPES

As stated in *OSY*-I (Ch. XIV), a cheap exhaust system can easily be made of galvanized-iron piping, available anywhere in the world. One problem with this type of exhaust system that was not mentioned is that it is affected by engine vibration. To minimize this difficulty, the standpipe should be securely bolted to the engine with a number of brackets, so that it will vibrate along with the engine; it should then be connected to the through-hull fitting by means of a flexible rubber exhaust hose. If the standpipe cannot be secured to the engine, it can instead be firmly secured to the boat and connected to the engine by a length of "wrinkle belly" (flexible stainless-steel pipe). This arrangement is not fully satisfactory, however, since eventually the stainless-steel pipe will break, and if there is no spare on board, finding a replacement may be very difficult.

It should be noted that on one- and two-cylinder engines, the vibration is usually so great that the installations described here are not feasible; they are practicable, however, on engines of four cylinders.

AQUA-LIFTS

Yachtsmen who have had plenty of experience with engines seem to agree that about the best exhaust system for a boat is the Aqua-Lift. Onan produces this device in the smaller sizes; in the larger sizes an equivalent can be made to order by any good welding shop. Another possibility is to have a fiber-glass shop mold up a unit of appropriate size and shape to fit the engine, using fire-retardant fiber glass. An Aqua-Lift made of this material will never rust out. In addition, it will absorb sound more and transfer vibration less that would its metal counterpart. A fiber-glass unit designed for the Perkins 4-154 is made by Vernay Products (for address, see Appendix).

Siphon Breaks

Any engine with an Aqua-Lift mounted below the waterline *must* have a siphon break (available as a standard kit from Onan). Otherwise, water will siphon back through the unit, fill it, and slowly flood the entire engine through the valves, causing all sorts of serious problems.

Even if the engine is mounted above the waterline, a siphon break should be installed, since without it, salt water may siphon back through the Aqua-Lift in extremely heavy weather, and flood the engine.

Siphon breaks have a habit of not properly seating under pressure, with the result that salt water is sprayed out—not in large quantities, but just enough to cover the entire engine room with a fine layer of salt, perhaps ruining the electrical system and leaving the place a mess. This situation can be avoided by the installation of a small copper or plastic line leading from the siphon break down into the bilge, so that the salt water will go into the bilge, where it will do no damage, rather than all over the engine room.

ENGINE OIL

DRIP PANS

Today, there are antipollution laws everywhere. Among them is a United States law that requires the display in the engine room of a prominent sign stating that there is a five-hundred-dollar fine for discharging oil into the water. The law is certainly justified, but the boat manufacturers have done little to implement it. On boat after boat the drip pan is absent, and where it is found, it is likely to be ineffective, lacking a proper means for draining the oil and discharging the sludge.

A drip pan should be designed so that even when the boat is heeled over, any oil that has dripped down from the engine will be retained, instead of spilling into the bilge. The pan should be large enough to hold at least a gallon of oil and water without the flywheel picking up the liquid and spraying it all over the engine room. It should have a sump at least three or four inches in diameter and four inches deep, and if possible should be mounted in such a manner that there can be a 90-degree stopcock on a drain line from the sump (or provisions for the easy insertion of a hand pump). The drain line should be connected to a plastic hose through which the contents of the pan can be drained into a plastic jug, to be disposed of in the proper fashion. If the sump is too low to be drained by gravity, a pump should be permanently installed, discharging into a plastic jug.

One last point—the drip pan should be so placed that any stuffing-box leaks will run *under* it and into the bilge. If it catches these leaks, it will soon overflow and fill the bilge with oil and water.

OIL FILTERS

The oil filter is usually located somewhere down under the engine, in about the most inaccessible place known to man, guaranteeing that one must be a contortionist with three hands (to balance mirrors) in order to change it. Furthermore, all the dirty oil in the filter inevitably finds its way into the bilge.

However, there is actually no reason why the oil filter should be mounted directly on the engine; it can instead be placed in an easily reached location, where one can change it readily without spilling any oil. For this arrangement, an adapter plate is made and is bolted to the engine. Two hoses go from the plate to an accessible location on the bulkhead, where the oil filter is installed in a bracket. There should be enough room under the bracket to accommodate a bucket, which can be placed there when the filter is being changed, or a drip pan can be installed, with a drain leading by means of plastic hose into the main engine drip pan.

If the oil filter is mounted in this fashion, readily accessible, it will be changed much more frequently, and the result will be much greater engine reliability and longer engine life.

CHANGING OIL

On most boats changing oil is a time-consuming, dirty job; the mechanic is usually left covered with oil, and usually one or two cans of oil are knocked over somewhere between the engine and the dump— the result is a total mess. This situation is altogether unnecessary. If a boat has a drip pan that can be drained into a plastic jug, with the aid of a pump if need be, as described earlier, changing oil is a simple operation rather than a major project. One can simply drain the oil into the pan and the contents of the pan into the jug. Then one can clean out the drip pan with diesel oil, drain that into the jug, and take the jug ashore and empty it. Another possibility is to have a sump pump built into the engine, with the discharge hose leading into the plastic jug, which can hold the oil until it can be disposed of ashore.

SLUDGE TANKS

Every yacht with an engine should have a sludge tank, a receptacle in which sludge from the drip pan and dirty oil can be stored until there is a chance to dispose of them. Using a bucket for this purpose is really unsatisfactory, since it may be knocked over, especially in the dinghy. In addition, the bucket requires cleaning, which is a messy job. A jerry jug makes a perfect oil-changing receptacle, and can be used repeatedly without cleaning. This should be large enough to hold two oil changes, with a safety margin of 25 percent. Certainly by the time a second oil change has been completed, one should have found a suitable place for disposing of the discarded oil. A rack should be provided in the engine room to hold the jerry jug, so that it cannot fall over, get inadvertently punctured, and dump all the oil into the bilge. The plastic quart Coke bottles with twist-on tops are a good second choice. The oil-filled bottles can be discarded at some appropriate place without making a mess and without having to be emptied out, provided an adequate supply of empties can be kept on hand.

STORING OIL

Every proper cruising yacht should have some provision for the bulk storage of engine oil. In some areas, this oil can be bought in bulk at a considerable saving, and even when it must be purchased in one-quart cans, permanent storage in these cans is not desirable. For one thing, these cans have metal tops, which tend to rust, and trying to pour oil from a rusty can while preventing the rust particles from going into the engine is difficult, if not impossible. Furthermore, metal cans eventually rust through, and those of cardboard composition gradually deteriorate; in both cases, the result is oil running into the bilge. Therefore, oil which is purchased in cans should immediately be drained into plastic storage containers, and the original cans should be discarded. Then good clean lubricating oil will always be available.

ENGINE CONTROLS

VACUUM GEARBOXES

Vacuum gearboxes are improperly described in *OSY*-I (Ch. XIV). Actually, they operate off the intake manifold, *not* off the vacuum side of the exhaust manifold. They are not often seen and should be viewed with suspicion.

MORSE CONTROLS

Morse controls are available on either a single or double lever; the latter type appears to be preferable. Morse controls can be obtained for all sorts of installations. Many units, obviously intended for use on small outboards in fresh water, have parts made very cheaply out of pot metal—aluminum and brass. Others have parts made of stainless steel, bronze, or chrome-plated aluminum. These units are much more expensive, but are correspondingly much more reliable.

If greased well before installation, and then periodically cleaned, oiled, and greased again, good-quality Morse controls will last almost forever. However, if neglected, they can cause great difficulties.

GAUGES AND ALARMS

Even on the best-crewed and best-maintained yacht, mistakes are made, and then one suddenly discovers a loss of oil pressure completely destroying the engine, a flooded bilge ruining the starter motor, or a problem involving any one of the many other things that can go wrong. Hence, few experienced yachtsmen will deny that except on a very small boat, a really good alarm system is well worth the cost.

Many companies make individual bilge alarms, oil-pressure alarms, engine-temperature alarms, gas alarms, and so on. However, one company has attacked the problem as a whole. Security Devices (for address, see Appendix) has come out with a really good system which provides all the above-mentioned alarms in one unit. When the alarm rings it may take a few minutes to figure out whether the problem is in the bilge, the engine, the gas stove, or what-have-you, but at least the crew is alerted.

ATTACHMENT TO THE ENGINE

All too often gauges and alarms are attached to the engine as an afterthought: the fitting on a line leading to the oil-pressure gauge is unscrewed, a tee is installed, and another alarm is tied into it; then another alarm is desired, so another gauge is tied in—and eventually a small tree grows out of the side of the engine. This is very likely to get broken off, and the consequent loss of oil pressure may ruin the en-

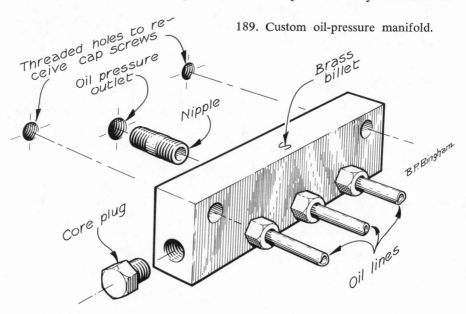

189. Custom oil-pressure manifold.

gine. Therefore, if extra lines are to be brought out of the oil-pressure line, a manifold (Drawing 189) should be made and rigidly secured to the engine. The additional gauges and alarms can then be fastened to the block. Further, it should be noted that rigid copper pipe from the engine to the gauges is sure to fracture at some future date. There must be *flexible line* from the engine to the copper pipe leading to the gauges and alarms.

FIRE-FIGHTING SYSTEMS

The importance of having adequate provisions for dealing with fire is suggested by the fact that Lloyd's of London gives a 5-percent reduction on insurance premiums to any yacht with an automatic fire-fighting system in the engine room. The corresponding reduction granted by American companies varies from nothing to as much as 15 percent.

In years gone by, a large yacht often had an automatic CO_2 fire-fighting system in the engine room. This system was effective, but the equipment was big, cumbersome, and incredibly expensive. Because the pressures in a CO_2 system are considerable, heavy steel bottles were required, and these were difficult to remove, check, or refill.

Recently, as a result of developments in the aircraft and racing-car industries, Halon 1211 and Halon 1301 fire-extinguishing systems, which are extremely sensitive, have become available at very reasonable prices (for supplier, see Appendix). One of the most important features of the Halon-based systems is that the pressures involved are low. The individual units containing the Halon are roughly the size of a large coffee can. Also, the setup is so simple that a really competent yachtsman can buy the components and install his own automatic system in the engine room. In view of the moderate cost and the added safety, most experienced yachtsmen wonder why every yacht does not have a system such as this.

It should of course be remembered that no matter how good the system, there is always the possibility that for one reason or another the automatic sensor will not operate. Hence, a remote pull *outside the engine room* is essential.

XV

Refrigeration

As time goes by, experienced yachtsmen get more and more baffled and disgusted by the almost complete inability of expensive yards and designers to design and install decent iceboxes, refrigerators, and freezers. People lug hundreds of pounds of ice aboard every five or six days, or run their generators three, four, or even five hours a day, in the attempt to obtain suitable box temperatures. Yet if the engine must be run three or four hours at a time to keep things cool, why have a sailboat? One might as well buy a powerboat and listen to the engine all day. Furthermore, running the engine so extensively increases the wear and tear on it; and being reduced from a sailor to a mechanic, changing oil and performing the other routine maintenance jobs that must be done every so many hours of engine operation, is not everyone's cup of tea.

In 1974, at the Newport, Stanford, and Annapolis boat shows, I inspected approximately fifty refrigeration installations, and subsequently, back in the Islands, I discussed with Jon Repke their methods, design, and construction. I would estimate that only three or four boats—at most—had properly designed refrigeration installations. We were more than a little amused to discover that one of the major United States manufacturers, a refrigeration expert, spent almost all his time at the three shows rushing around trying to correct errors in the installation of his units. A small unit was installed in a huge box, or an uninsulated box was used. The yards and designers simply failed to follow his instructions.

Yet only a little common sense and ingenuity are needed to install a refrigerator/freezer that will cool effectively and require an hour or less of engine time a day. If the engine must be run more than one hour, some checking is in order. If running time reaches two hours, the whole system should be torn apart and intelligently rebuilt. Similarly, the yachtsman with an icebox has every right to expect ice to last twelve to fourteen days in the tropics and at least eighteen to twenty-one days farther north. If it does not, some serious re-engineering should be undertaken.

REFRIGERATION METHODS

HEAT REFRIGERATION

Heat refrigeration (using a kerosene or gas flame) is very inefficient when the weather is hot—in the tropics or during the northern summer—but it can work. Or perhaps one should say that it can *almost* work. Well designed and properly installed, a heat refrigerator will cool the wine, and keep the meat from spoiling. However, it will not produce cold beer or—except in ideal circumstances—ice for drinks, and what ice it does produce will be in such small quantities that each cube will be regarded as a block of gold.

For a heat refrigerator on a boat to work, very careful planning, ideal circumstances, and intelligent installation are necessary. First of all, since a heat refrigerator can raise the cabin temperature considerably, which is just what one doesn't want in the tropics, there must be plenty of air space and air flow in the compartment where it is installed, and the refrigerator flue should be vented outboard. Also, the unit should be gimbaled.

A standard shoreside model is usually unsatisfactory because of poor insulation. Indeed, the best results are obtained by removing the guts of a kerosene heat refrigerator and installing them in a specially built box with four inches of poured foam insulation.

Gas heat refrigerators should be avoided at all costs. To be sure, the gas is shut off automatically if the flame blows out, but there is nothing to prevent the flame, mounted close to the cabin floor, from igniting gas from another source—a leak in the stove, for example, or in the supply line to the refrigerator. Therefore, the gas refrigerator should be left ashore, out of the way.

SOLID-STATE REFRIGERATION

Solid-state refrigeration, pioneered for boats by F.Y.A. Engineering (for address, see Appendix), is something new. With its operation based on the Peltier effect—i.e., when dissimilar metals are charged with electricity, one gets cold and the other gets warm—the unit is in effect a heat-transfer pump. The solid-state refrigerator contains two such metals, one coupled to the cold-air fins, the other to the outside warm-air fins.

Models are available for converting iceboxes of up to five cubic feet to electric refrigeration. The advertised advantages are that current drain is low, the noise level during operation is low, and the unit is compact in size, easy to install, and almost maintenance-free.

These claims appear to be true except that the power drain is not really low. According to the figures supplied by the manufacturers, in a temperate climate the five-cubic-foot unit will probably use 50–60 ampere-hours per day, at 12 volts. In hot climates, probably closer to 90–100 ampere-hours per day will be consumed, and even with all this expenditure of power, this type of refrigeration is not particularly effective in the tropics. Obviously, a boat with solid-state refrigeration will require a very large 12-volt alternator belted off the engine, or a fairly large one running off the propeller shaft, as described in Chapter XIII. It's the old story—one doesn't get something for nothing.

One other possibility is in prospect. The smallest solid-state refrigeration unit, cooling a really well insulated box, might be able to operate off a towed generator of the taffrail-log type, as described in Chapter XIII. If electrical needs were not completely taken care of, the engine could be run for an hour or so every third or fourth day. However, this arrangement could be considered only for a well-designed unit, and it is still essentially in the talking stage.

MECHANICAL REFRIGERATION

Holding Plates

Holding plates—eutectic plates—are regarded as the be-all and end-all of refrigeration for boats. With them, it is thought, anyone can have refrigeration. Nothing could be further from the truth. Holding plates work only if they are correctly designed and the box is properly insulated. If the box will not pass the test described in the section on box construction in *OSY*-I (Ch. XV), holding plates will not solve any problems. Similarly, if the box is well insulated, but plates of the wrong size are installed, one will still have an uphill fight against high generating and/or running time. There appears to be no hard-and-fast formula for the relationship between the size of the plates and the cubic content of the box to be kept cold. The rule of thumb which seems to work is that the two largest vertical surfaces of the box should be covered by plates which are about 3 inches thick and weigh about 25 pounds per square foot of area. For instance, an 8-cubic-foot freezer will have two plates of 4 square feet each. For a total of 8 square feet, the weight will be about 200 pounds, which is quite considerable. If the plates are of the correct size, and the insulation is good, the result will be effective refrigeration.

It must be remembered that the colder the box temperatures desired, the more running time will be needed. The exact settings to be used will vary according to the design of the box, being influenced by plate size, box size in relation to plate size, the thickness of the insulation, the effectiveness of the door seal, and so on. As a rough rule of thumb, the plates should be set at ten degrees *below* the desired refrigerator temperature, and at fifteen degrees below the desired freezer temperature. Keeping the freezer down at 0 is unnecessary. Frozen meat stored at, say, under 20 degrees will keep for a tremendously long time. However, when the freezer is being loaded with fresh produce or meat, or with meat carted from the supermarket which has begun to thaw, the box should first be pulled down to 0 degrees.

Compressor, Belt-driven from the Engine

The most common arrangement is to have the compressor belt-driven directly off the engine. This system is by far the simplest, lightest, and cheapest. It can be used on a boat of any size, provided there is an engine.

However, the system does have disadvantages. There are likely to be problems with the end seal and with the magnetic clutches. Also, since the engine must be run to operate the compressor, when the boat is tied up at a dock in the marina for a long period, the engine must be run in a no-load condition for forty-five minutes to an hour a day. This is not necessarily good for the engine, and does not make one overly popular with one's marina neighbors. In addition, there is no way to maintain refrigeration when the boat is secured at a marina where running the engine is not allowed.

Battery Refrigeration

The conventional 12-, 24-, or 32-volt battery-driven unit is similar to the household refrigerator, with cooling coils around an icetray compartment. This system has many disadvantages. As soon as one sails and the boat heels over, any unfrozen water pours out of the icetray and onto the coils, making a mess. Also, since the units are not sealed, there may be trouble with blown shaft seals. DC motors are not overly efficient. With the refrigerator constantly going on and off, the result is a considerable battery drain; hence, a large bank of batteries is normally provided if 12-, 24-, or 32-volt refrigeration is installed. Indeed, with a power drain of 20–25 amperes at 12 volts, the compressor can be used only when power is being generated, either by the engine or by an alternator running off the free-spinning propeller shaft.

To minimize surge loads on the batteries, it is better to install two separate small compressors, and two separate refrigeration systems, instead of one large one.

A further possibility is to install a large Constavolt or similar converter. Then, when the boat is alongside the dock, the compressor can be operated from shore power and it is unnecessary to run the engine.

The biggest advantage of the DC-driven compressor is that if one has a really big alternator to tie to the propeller—*Agwbe* had a 30-ampere alternator running off her free-spinning shaft—one may be able to power 12- or 24-volt battery-driven refrigeration at sea. However, the system will have to be very carefully engineered.

It is possible that in the near future 12-volt refrigeration may become more efficient. At present, DC motors draw essentially the same amperage in both a no-load and a loaded condition, because the field windings require DC voltage from the battery. A 12-volt motor developing ⅓ h.p.—the size necessary for even a small compressor—will draw between 18 and 25 amperes.

However, in recent years it has become possible to build really good, strong permanent magnets; this means that it may be feasible to replace the field windings with a permanent magnet requiring no voltage from the battery. With the load reduced by this method, a ⅓-h.p. motor driving a refrigeration compressor would probably draw only about 6 amperes much of the time. This amount of battery drain would be acceptable even on a comparatively small boat.

Refrigeration units using this type of motor are still in the experimental stage; let us hope that in the near future they will be a reality.

Twelve-Volt Refrigeration with Holding Plates

Battery-driven refrigeration usually consists of cooling coils around icetrays, as in a household refrigerator; the compressor cycles on and off to maintain the box temperature, and the result is a rather large battery drain. On a few boats, *Antilles* for one, the combination of a big compressor and holding plates plus batteries is sometimes seen. This setup at first glance seems redundant, for the plates normally replace batteries (i.e., to cool the plates, the engine is simply run for a short time, whereas without the plates, there is a steady battery drain). However, the combination does serve a purpose. On these boats, a heavy compressor cools holding plates. The power drain of this type of unit is so large that it cannot be run just from batteries—it can operate only when the engine is running and the alternator or generator is putting out plenty of amperes at the same time. But driving a big compressor directly from a 12-volt generator is practically impossible.

This is avoided by including batteries in the system but running the compressor only while the generator is also running, so that the batteries are being continually charged during the period when power is drawn from them for the compressor. If this arrangement is used for cooling down holding plates, the compressor should have to be run only about forty-five minutes a day, usually while the engine is doing its normal charging. And of course installation of a Constavolt or similar converter enables one to take advantage of shore power when at dockside.

Other possibilities are to provide a separate, independent 12-volt motor-driven generator, or a 12-volt generator belted from a freewheeling shaft. Indeed, twelve-volt refrigeration with a compressor cooling holding plates would seem to be the answer for boats that are generating their electricity from a propeller on a free-spinning shaft. Better still, instead of dragging a two- or three-bladed free-spinning propeller, which causes continual noise, drag, and friction, one can belt a large alternator off a fully feathering adjustable-pitch propeller. With this type of installation, the engine can be declutched, the propeller allowed to freewheel, the pitch cranked in to maximize the electrical output, and the compressor turned on. The shaft can be allowed to freewheel for two or three hours a day, as necessary to generate the amperage required to keep the refrigeration system operating. Once sufficient electricity has been generated, the compressor can be turned off and the propeller feathered.

With an installation such as this, a yacht's cruising range would be drastically increased since one would have to run the engine only in calm spells. Whenever there was wind, the freewheeling propeller could generate enough electricity for all needs, including refrigeration.

The more one studies this concept, the more one comes to the conclusion that the fully feathering adjustable-pitch propeller with an alternator belted off it provides the best solution to the electrical, refrigeration, propulsion, and drag problems for the cruising man.

Sealed Units

The method of powering a mechanical refrigeration system must be carefully selected, in the light of the uses to which the boat will be put. On any large boat, of fifty feet or more, the sealed units run by 110-volt AC power are obviously the best. These are the most easily obtained and the most reliable marine refrigeration units. The problem of blown seals, common on belt-driven and battery-driven compressors, is eliminated, and there is little chance of leakage. The units are extremely heavy and rugged, and can cool down holding plates at a great rate. A further advantage is that when the boat is moored alongside a dock, shoreside 110-volt current can be directly used for refrigeration, so neither engine nor generator need be run for this purpose.

The disadvantage is that since a source of 110-volt power must be provided—either an independent generator or one driven by the main engine—the installation is heavy and bulky, as indicated by the figures in the accompanying table for the double system on *Lone Star*.

	SIZE, IN INCHES	WEIGHT, IN POUNDS
Refrigerator/freezer unit (Iceberg Systems, by Power Products)	24 x 18 x 15	260
Two eutectic plates	36 x 24 x 3 (each)	300 total
Two 6-kw hydraulic-drive alternators	23 x 12 x 12 (each)	252 total
12-volt batteries, giving 780 ampere-hours	24 x 55 x 12	500
Two Constavolts	14 x 10 x 19 (each)	148 total

For this type of installation a 6-kilowatt generator is about the smallest that can be used, because of the heavy surge when starting. One advantage of having two ¾-ton compressors instead of one massively huge one is that the surge is reduced. And of course double safety is provided as well.

Compressor and Generator Reliability

It cannot be stressed too frequently that if one wants reliable refrigeration and freezing, two separate systems must be installed: two compressors, condensers, sets of eutectic plates, evaporators. Then if one system breaks down, the other can just be run double time and the food being kept cold will not be lost. Further, as has been mentioned, the starting load on two small compressors is much smaller than the load on one large compressor.

For electrically driven systems, it is absolutely essential to have two separate and totally independent means of generating electricity.

BLOWN SEALS: It has been pointed out by many refrigeration experts that blown seals usually occur when a boat has been laid up for a long time and the compressor is not being run. Hence, they wonder if the problem could be solved, or at least minimized, by the installation of valves, so that one could take the pressure off the compressor when the boat was laid up, without having to discharge the system.

Condenser Cooling

One of the great problems in marine refrigeration is cooling the condenser. Since air-cooled condensers are practically useless in the tropics, a water-cooled model is necessary. The magnetic-drive centrifugal pump would appear to be ideal for circulating water to cool the condenser. However, it has two problems. First of all, it is only obtainable wired for 110 volts AC. Second, the magnet is embedded in a plastic impeller; if the pump inadvertently becomes air-bound, heat builds up, and the plastic impeller dissolves. The problem is aggravated by the fact that many builders don't bother reading the manual. They frequently install the circulating water system for the condenser completely backward. Therefore, an electronically driven pump of suitable voltage for the vessel, with a bronze impeller, is preferable. A bronze impeller may become air-bound, but it will not dissolve. Perhaps, in the future, someone will help matters by manufacturing a magnetic-drive pump in various voltages with a metal impeller.

Another approach to this problem is to eliminate altogether the use of a separate pump to circulate water to cool the condenser. The pump is, after all, another piece of equipment to be maintained, and every time the refrigeration system is started, one must check not only the engine cooling water but also the refrigeration cooling water. If the refrigeration unit is to be used only when the engine and/or generator is running, the simplest arrangement is to run the engine cooling water first through the refrigeration condenser, and then to the engine. Then one only has to check cooling water in one place; and if there is no overheating in the engine and/or generator, the condenser must be getting water.

Everything, of course, is a compromise. The disadvantage of this system is that the refrigeration unit cannot be run off shore power.

Construction Details

FREON: Freon, the gas which is used to cool the refrigeration system, is produced in various types. Most things being equal, Freon 502 will remove heat at twice the rate of Freon 12. Also, Freon 502 appears to be the best gas for the freezer system. However, it cannot be used unless the system has been designed for it.

The yachtsman whose boat has mechanical refrigeration should always carry adequate supplies of spare Freon, and should know exactly how to top up the system. Also, he must make sure that the spare Freon is of the correct type for his particular installation.

LIQUID RECEIVER: In years gone by, one determined the amount of Freon in the system by looking at the sight glass on the dryer. If the indicator turned from blue to pink, a change was necessary. However, sometimes it gave a false reading, so the best policy was to change the dryer when in doubt.

Today, most refrigeration systems have a window in the Freon line. When the Freon is low, one adds more until the line is full. However, one does not know in advance how much will be needed, and the issue is often confused by the presence of air bubbles. The new system offered by Power Products under the name Iceberg Systems is unique in that the window is in the liquid receiver. Since at any time one can see the actual level in the liquid receiver, one can easily ascertain whether more Freon should be added, and if so, how much.

Cost of Mechanical Refrigeration

The estimated cost of mechanical refrigeration in 1977, for boats of various sizes, is shown in the accompanying table.

BOAT SIZE, IN FEET	REFRIGERATOR SIZE, IN CUBIC FEET	FREEZER SIZE, IN CUBIC FEET	COMPRESSOR	COST OF PROFESSIONAL INSTALLATION, IN DOLLARS	COST OF AMATEUR INSTALLATION, IN DOLLARS
35	1	2	¾-ton, driven from the main engine	1,500	500–700
35–50	3	8	¾-ton, driven from the main engine	2,500	1,000
55	5	12	Two ¾-ton, 110-volt AC units, completely independent	3,500	1,800

Installation and Repair of Mechanical Refrigeration

An amateur should not attempt to install a refrigeration system unless he is extremely competent. Even so, he is best advised to go to a marine-refrigeration expert and pay him to design the complete system. The amateur should then assemble the equipment, following the expert's instructions and designs. When everything is ready, he should pay a competent refrigeration mechanic to connect up the system, charge it, and test it, and should have him provide a complete rundown on its operation and adjustment.

With most of us, all this information will go in one ear and 90 percent of it will continue right on out the other, leaving us in a quandary when we must adjust and recharge the system. Therefore, when the refrigeration expert is connecting up and explaining the system, one should record everything on tape. Later, someone can make a typewritten transcript of this material, which can be studied, reorganized, and filed away with the refrigeration manuals, to be consulted six months or a year later, when the inevitable troubles with the refrigeration system develop.

And how does one make sure that an individual presenting himself as a refrigeration expert does indeed know what he is doing? The only way to find out how expert the expert is, is ask him for a list of yachts in which he has installed refrigeration equipment, and then check with the owners to find out how well the installations work.

BOX CONSTRUCTION

An existing box that does not pass the test described in the section on box construction in *OSY*-I (Ch. XV) should be discarded.

On a wooden boat, if at all possible, the refrigeration units should be designed so that they can be removed—not necessarily taken out of the boat altogether, but at least pulled clear of the hull far enough so that when the boat is laid up in the winter or is undergoing a major refit, an overworked and underpaid small boy can crawl down behind the box, clean out the entire area, and paint the hull with wood preservative.

The big icebox we installed on *Iolaire* provided me with eighteen years of good living and cold beer. However, it also necessitated the complete replacement of five frames in 1976: when the box was at last taken out, we found that though the planking behind it was fine, the frames were shot. This situation probably would have been avoided if the box had been designed to be removable, and every year had been pulled clear for a few weeks, cleaned, and aired, while a new coat of wood preservative was applied behind it.

Making a refrigerator/freezer removable necessitates compromises. Solid tubing is least likely to leak, but makes box removal difficult, so some short lengths of hose are necessary. However, Jon Repke insists that the rubber hose and clamp-on fittings used in automotive air conditioning are unacceptable in a yacht, being not only unsightly but very unreliable. Accordingly, to protect oneself from being left with absolutely no refrigeration because the end fittings have blown off the hose a hundred miles offshore, one should select only the best hose with the best possible end fittings, and should keep on board spare fittings and lengths of hose, and the necessary tools.

BOX LOCATION AND DESIGN

After much thought, and discussion with various refrigeration experts, I have concluded that when building a new box one should use at least four inches of insulation—and the more the better, provided the space is available.

At the same time, it should be borne in mind that the process of adding insulation is subject to diminishing returns: going from two to four inches of insulation, one is increasing the thickness of the walls by 100 percent; going from four to six inches (i.e., adding two inches once again), one is increasing the thickness by only 50 percent. Furthermore, doubling the thickness of the insulation in an icebox, as one does when going from two to four inches, will not double the box's holding capacity, since there is a large amount of attrition—ice is chipped off, more food is cooled down, and so on. Instead, going from two to four inches will probably increase the length of time food can be held by 50 percent (or in a mechanical or electric refrigerator halve the running time). Four inches of insulation would have turned *Iolaire*'s twelve-day box into an eighteen-day box. Such a change would have given me cold beer all the way across the Atlantic, but then I probably wouldn't have been in so much of a hurry, and would have taken longer to cross the ocean.

Everyone agrees that almost all stock boats have inadequately built iceboxes and refrigerators. Most of the boxes are poorly insulated on the sides, and even those with decently insulated sides almost universally lack properly insulated tops. The top may have a mere one inch of insulation; there may be voids in the area around a removable top; and in some cases there is absolutely no insulation at all on the top. Yet despite the insistence of many builders to the contrary, experience shows that tops do really need to be well insulated. This is demonstrated by our experience on *Iolaire*. If the icebox-top latches come loose (as they sometimes do) we discover we are buying ice every eight days rather than every ten or eleven days.

Another error frequently made by the stock builders is to place the box in the middle of the cabin, where the sun shines in on the top, through the doghouse windows. How can the box keep its cool?

In choosing the location for the box, besides making sure it is protected from sunlight, one should bear in mind that a unit with a side-opening door must be placed on the athwartship axis. Otherwise, on one tack everything will tend to fall out. In my view, a top-opening box is preferable. Its one disadvantage is that because food gets buried in the bottom, and is very difficult to reach, one spends long periods with the top open, rooting around in an uncomfortable position, barely able to find what one is looking for. In this situation, one way to make food more accessible is to store it in wire, metal, or plastic bins which can be lifted out. Another method used by many people is to have a box with both top and side openings. Then, each day the side door can be opened, and the food for the day can be placed on an upper shelf, where it is easily reached through the top. (A similar procedure—by the way—may be employed with respect to a freezer. One may open it only once or twice a day, with the necessary food then either left out, or stored in the refrigerator. A freezer used in this manner can be placed in a relatively inaccessible corner of the galley, or even down in the engine room.)

The top of the box should fit flush, to provide a smooth working surface. It should be beveled, as shown in Drawing 190. If this beveling is absent (as in *OSY*-I, Drawing 194) the door will not work, because when it opens, the edge opposite the hinge must have room to describe an arc.

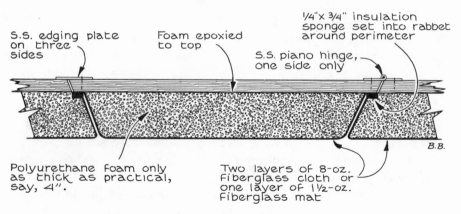

190. Recommended icebox-top construction.

If one has both a refrigerator and a freezer, they are best mounted side by side or one above the other. Then plates are only needed in the freezer. The refrigerator can be cooled by convection currents between it and the freezer. The simplest method of accomplishing this is to install a small sliding door by which—having visually checked the temperature within the refrigerator—one may manually regulate the amount of cold air that passes between the freezer and the refrigerator. Just how much to open the sliding door at any point, one will learn through trial and error. In general, it should be remembered that when the box is loaded with warm food, the door must be opened a considerable distance. Once the refrigerator and the food have been cooled, the door must be closed, since otherwise the contents of the refrigerator will freeze.

A more accurate but slightly more complicated method is to have a small blower tied into a thermostatically controlled switch. The blower will automatically be turned on, and will force cold air into the refrigerator, whenever the temperature reaches above the desired maximum.

BOX MATERIALS

The discussion of box materials in *OSY*-I (Ch. XV) is still largely valid, and should be reviewed.

Lining Materials

The Formica-covered plywood described in *OSY*-I has stood the of time; it is an excellent lining material for refrigerators and freezers. To provide plenty of rigidity and eliminate any danger of delamination, after the box is glued up and the plywood covered with Formica, the part of the plywood that will be against the Styrofoam insulation should be covered with thin fiber glass or Dynel. Two or three layers of Dynel tape placed around all corners, overlapping the edges about two inches, will considerably strengthen the box and guard against any fracturing of the joints and leakage into the foam insulation.

Whether this Formica-covered plywood is also the answer for ice-boxes is debatable, since despite the best intentions of the best crew, all too frequently a fifty-pound block of ice is just dropped into the box. Before too long, the Formica may crack and fracture, allowing water to penetrate the plywood and reach the insulation. If this occurs, repairs will probably be difficult.

For this reason, a lining of fiber-glass-covered plywood may be preferable in an icebox. The repair of broken joints is then relatively easy, involving just grinding down and reglassing. It should be remembered that the taste of newly installed fiber glass can be removed by pouring two or three bucketfuls of boiling water into the box, clamping the lid down tight, and leaving the water there for twenty-four hours. One treatment is usually sufficient. The commercially supplied fiber-glass liners in stock boats are also fine, as they too, if damaged, can be easily ground down and repaired.

Metal liners should be avoided. They are great for conducting cold out of the box, and when damaged are difficult to repair.

MAKING ICE

The vertical icetray made of metal is by far the best for making ice, provided it is correctly designed, but it is expensive. It should be made of fairly heavy metal, and should be tapered. When the tray has been filled with water, a wire with a hook in the end should be inserted. Then, to remove the ice, one can put the tray in a bucket of salt water, and as the ice begins to melt, lift it out by the wire. This method is necessary because a vacuum develops between the ice water and the tapered tray which is difficult to break; the hook embedded in the ice enables one to pull it out against the vacuum.

A method of making ice in plastic ice-cream containers, with nuts and bolts to speed the cooling, is shown in *OSY*-I, Drawing 195. My friend Jon Repke, refrigeration expert and adviser, insists that although he may have kicked the idea around, he never under any circumstances recommended it. He has violent objections to it as being just too

"Mickey Mouse." So I stand corrected. He recommends simply filling the heavy plastic ice-cream containers with water and placing them in the freezer, making sure, of course, that the lids are securely in place. Though the conductivity of plastic leaves much to be desired, the results will be acceptable.

DECK BOXES

Especially when sailing in the tropics, where everyone is likely to stay on deck as much as possible, it is a pain in the neck to have to climb down belowdecks when one wants a beer, a Coke, or a bit of ice. For this reason, about fifteen years ago we installed what we call our ready-ammunition locker—a small wooden icebox (20 by 12 by 15 inches) lined on all four sides plus top and bottom with four-inch-thick Styrofoam. This is just big enough to carry a moderate supply of beer and other drinks and a chunk of ice. Actually, to conserve ice, we normally use instead the water we pump out of the icebox four times a day. Our drinks are not freezing cold, but certainly cool enough.

A deck box is also useful on boats that have a refrigerator/freezer. It is most easily cooled by means of one-gallon plastic bags filled with a solution that freezes at a temperature well below 32 degrees. The number of bags will depend on the size of the deck box. If half the bags are kept in the freezer while the other half are in the box, and they are switched each day, the deck box will remain cold without a complicated system of mechanical cooling, or the mess of making and transferring ice.

AIR CONDITIONING

Air conditioning may be fine on a gin palace permanently tied up at a marina in a hot climate, but it rarely belongs on an ocean cruising yacht. First of all, it is very expensive to put in and to service. The big completely air-conditioned ocean-going luxury vessels that arrive in the Lesser Antilles are loved by the refrigeration experts. Their installations are usually so complicated that a few days' general maintenance work is necessary every time they put into port. A second disadvantage is that no matter how carefully installed, air conditioning inevitably results in condensation, which in the tropics will create havoc on a wooden boat and cause problems on any boat.

In the tropics, a wooden boat is cooler than one made of steel, aluminum, or fiber glass, but a correctly designed boat of any material, with proper ventilation, should not need air conditioning under most circumstances. At sea, with the wind blowing, there should be enough passage of air down below. Similarly, in harbor, with all hatches opened and wind scoops (or galley staysails) rigged, enough air should find its way belowdecks to keep the boat comfortable.

In the two years since we hung a thermometer from the main-cabin overhead on *Iolaire*, the highest temperature we have recorded is 82 degrees; on windy days it is usually 78 or 79 degrees. Our experience exemplifies the results that can be obtained by installing correctly designed hatches, wind scoops, and ventilators, and fans belowdecks to keep the air circulating. All of this can be done for a fraction of the cost of properly air-conditioning a boat.

However, it must be admitted that an ocean sailing yacht does not spend all her time at sea, and some people live in areas where the temperature skyrockets in summer, the wind dies out, and living on board a boat can be all but insufferable. For these people air conditioning may be worth while if the cost can be kept down. However, if a boat is to be air-conditioned, one must make sure that it is properly done, with a carefully selected unit that supplies the correct number of BTU's. Since boats with the same amount of interior space may have very great differences in heat loss and therefore require units of different size, consultation with an air-conditioning expert will be necessary.

Certain considerations other than the capacity of the unit must also be kept in mind. For instance, a wooden boat is the simplest to air-condition in that it is the easiest to keep cool, but one must be extremely careful to have all the cooling lines well insulated, since fresh water dripping into the bilge is guaranteed to cause a massive case of rot.

One system frequently used is the Carrier system. The condenser and cooling unit are both mounted in the engine room; the cooling unit has a blower; and ducts conduct cool air throughout the boat. One great advantage of this system is that if a boat already has a small diesel heater, the ducts from the heater can be transferred to the air-conditioning unit: the same set of ducts can be used for both heating and cooling. This is by far the cheapest and easiest way to air-condition a boat.

The most expensive way, which is probably also the best, is the chilled-water method. The refrigerant cools water which is circulated through the boat by means of cooling coils; behind the coils are very quiet, low-rpm fans. These units are effective and free of noise, but rather expensive and space-consuming.

Both the units described require 110-volt AC power, which they consume at such a rate that it is totally impractical to use them except alongside the dock or possibly for an hour in the evening when the anchor is down. At that time of day, running the generator and the air conditioner for an hour to remove the heat may be sufficient, since if the boat is basically well ventilated, once the sun has set it will be possible to keep her cool.

ICEBOXES

In general, I stand by what was said about iceboxes in *OSY*-I (Ch. XV). Indeed, the theories and ideas presented were proved on *Iolaire*'s seventieth-birthday cruise. During the seven months of the cruise proper, we sailed twelve thousand miles; when all the sailing done between our departure in December, 1974, from Grenada and our final arrival back in Antigua in December, 1975, is counted, it turns out that we covered a total of over fourteen thousand miles in twelve months. In the entire time, we were without ice for only five days—the last five days coming back across the Atlantic. Furthermore, we managed this well despite the fact that, as noted in *OSY*-I, because of *Iolaire*'s shape (her narrow, slack bilge) and the location of the galley forward, her icebox could be given only two inches of foam insulation. If the boat were slightly roomier and the galley were located aft, so that the thickness of the foam could be doubled, the carrying capacity of the installation would certainly increase from twelve days to eighteen days in the tropics and from eighteen or twenty days to almost a month up north. Certainly, wherever one is in the world, one can stumble into an ice supply once a month. Other desirable changes would be to have three separate seventy-five-pound iceboxes instead of the present pair of hundred-pound units, to have an improved drain system (as shown in *OSY*-I, Drawing 196), and to have the ice set on a rack, so that it would remain up out of the water if the box was pumped out regularly. I am sure that with these changes, in a northern climate we would have to load ice only once a month, or perhaps once every five weeks.

In the Caribbean, people are regularly building iceboxes that will keep two hundred pounds of ice two weeks, in a climate where the water temperature is 77 degrees and the daily air temperature runs about 85–88 degrees. We are sure, on the basis of continual cruising, that in a cool climate, with a water temperature of 60–65 degrees and an air temperature in the low 80's, the ice would last three weeks in the same box. If the boat were used only on weekends, one would be able to load two hundred pounds of ice at the beginning of June and not worry about loading ice again until the end of July.

In view of these facts, it astonishes me that year after year the sailing public continues to tolerate obviously inadequate icebox construction in stock boats. As long as the boat owners don't object, I guess I really can't blame the builders for going along their merry way. But shame on the salesmen who sweep the unsuspecting buyers off their feet and send them out to sea with fantasies of wave-swept beaches and native girls—while the food spoils right under their noses. If people would spend more time choosing their boats instead of indulging their dreams, situations of this sort would undoubtedly improve.

Lugging two or three hundred pounds of ice on board every five or six days is clearly unacceptable; the yachtsman is reduced to a coolie, with very poor wages. But lugging ice once every three weeks is actually easier than keeping a refrigeration system working. And when, in addition, one looks at the cost of installing mechanical refrigeration, and thinks of the yearly maintenance bill and the wear and tear on the engine when running the installation, one begins to think that perhaps an efficient icebox is the route to go. I hope something will encourage the modern builders to install boxes that will do more than show the purchaser how big they are inside.

AVAILABILITY OF ICE

Iolaire's cruise included areas where ice was supposedly unobtainable, but we were always able to find it. In some places it was difficult to obtain and expensive; in others, it was easy to locate and cheap; and in still others, it was free! In the Canary Islands, when we asked for two hundred pounds of ice and offered to pay, they roared with laughter, gave us four hundred pounds, and sent us on our way. We filled our belowdecks box and the deck boxes, loaded the cockpit flush to the top with ice, which we covered with canvas, and still had ice left over that we did not know what to do with.

ICEBOX DRAINS

As I pointed out in *OSY*-I, the division of a box into two or three independently insulated units will greatly increase the length of time a given amount of ice will last. Unfortunately, many small or light-

191. Icebox with three individual compartments stepping down one to the other provides superb drainage and excellent stowage of ice and food.

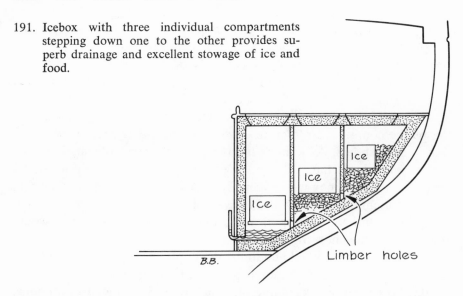

Ice

Ice

Ice

Limber holes

B.B.

displacement boats just can't accommodate this excellent arrangement. But where the present box can hold 150 pounds of ice, dividing it into two separate units is well worth while. If the units are placed, as they should be, stepping down one from the other (Drawing 191), there should be a drain which allows the water from the melting ice to run down to the lowest box. From there it can be pumped out by a small pump or drained into a bucket. In the bulkhead between the units, the drain should be run as shown in *OSY*-I, Drawing 196, to prevent the cold air from dropping from a higher into a lower box.

For years we drained the water from our icebox into a Clorox bottle, which we emptied three times a day. All too frequently, the bottle would spill in the bilge. Our present system, which we much prefer, consists of a Whale piston pump attached to the icebox drain. Now we pump out the icebox three times a day and pour the water down the sink, which drains overside without a pump. If by any chance the icebox drain becomes clogged, we merely disconnect the pump, shove a hose over its discharge end, connect the other end of the hose to the icebox drain hose, place a jug of water under the pump, and start pumping. Hydraulic pressure blows whatever crumbs are in the line back into the box, where they usually disintegrate into particles small enough to be pumped through the drain.

EXTENDING ICE TO ITS LIMIT

There are a number of procedures which will help to extend ice to its limit. First of all, before a box is loaded, some ice should be thrown

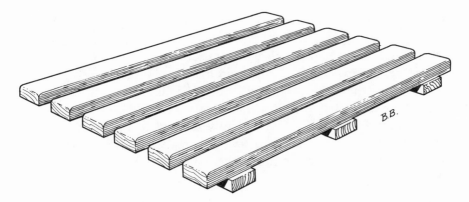

192. Easily built duckboards may be placed at the bottom of the icebox.

into it to cool it down. Then the full amount of ice, preferably in block form, should be placed in it, and all the nooks and crannies around the corners should be chocked down with chipped ice, so that as little air space as possible is left. Further, wherever feasible, the food going into the box should be frozen solid, into blocks; then no ice will be lost cooling it to begin with.

In addition, since the ice will last longer if it does not sit in water, duckboards should be provided (Drawing 192), which will hold the ice two inches above the bottom of the box. The water from the melting ice should be regularly pumped out. This cold water, caught in a bucket, can be used to cool beer, soft drinks, and the like for fifteen minutes before they are placed in the icebox.

If there are two or three separate units stepping down one from the other, the duckboards will be needed only in the lowest. When the ice has been partially used, what remains in the bottom unit can be transferred to the upper ones. Then the duckboards can be removed and beverages can be chilled in the water draining into the bottom unit, while the ice up above will not be sitting in water.

The life of the ice will also be extended by an installation like the one on *Sirocco* (described in Chapter XI), in which water is cooled in a line that is led into the icebox, zigzagged along the side, and then led out again. This arrangement makes it possible to have cold water to drink without opening the icebox door and letting warm air in.

REFRIGERATOR/FREEZER VERSUS ICEBOX

There comes a time when I feel obliged to speak, to make a plea for simplicity, like a voice crying in the wilderness. The simple yacht is infinitely cheaper than the expensive yacht with all the fancy equipment. One can spend a veritable fortune on paraphernalia which may or may not work, and which will surely be expensive to install in the first place and expensive to maintain as the years go by. One may get to the point where one is locked in tight behind a desk, trying to earn enough money to pay for all the accouterments of the dream boat. The boat remains a dream, or stays tightly secured to the dock, while the young executive works so hard trying to make enough money to support the boat that he has no time to go out and sail her.

The refrigeration situation is a case in point. A medium-sized refrigerator/freezer system installed by a very competent amateur is still going to cost $1,000; on a larger boat, the cost will run to $1,800. Think how much ice could be purchased for these sums! On *Iolaire*, in the tropics, our ice consumption is about 100 pounds per week. In St. Thomas, which has almost the most expensive ice in the Caribbean, the cost is $5 for 100 pounds at the factory (and $10 for 100 pounds at the Sheraton Harbour Club, two miles away—transportation must be expensive!) At $5 for 100 pounds, a year's ice costs $260. We can buy ice for *Iolaire* for four years before even approaching the initial investment required for the medium-sized refrigerator/freezer system. Furthermore, repairs and maintenance for the mechanical system will obviously require at least $100 per year. Hence, only after six years will we have drawn even on the costs of the refrigerator/freezer. The contrast in expenses would of course be even greater if a *professionally* installed system were in question. And we have not yet taken into account the costs of wear and tear on the engine!

Another consideration is weight. Our icebox weighs no more than 70 or 80 pounds and holds 30 pounds of food; with 170 pounds of ice, the total weight is about 270 pounds. Were we to have a refrigerator/freezer, the additional weight would be approximately as follows: holding plates (10 square feet at 25 pounds per square foot), 250 pounds; a ¾-ton compressor, 90 pounds; a 110-volt AC generator, 3-kw (as small as possible), 395 pounds; a condenser, 12 pounds; a Constavolt, 74 pounds; additional batteries (the existing bank being too small to absorb the charge), 200 pounds. Thus refrigeration takes up a thousand extra pounds, plus 16 cubic feet of space used for the installation of generator, batteries, compressor, and so on. One would spend a minimum of $2,000 on this type of installation.

If the engine is not large enough to run a 110-volt system, so that one must use the simplest method possible—the compressor belted off the engine—the weight of the equipment, including holding plates, will work out to about 400 pounds. Obviously, from a weight standpoint, the compressor belted off the engine is best. But to install an engine and this refrigeration system will increase costs, over those for a boat without an engine, approximately as shown in the accompanying table, based on figures recently obtained from a representative fiber-glass-boat manufacturer.

DIESEL SIZE, IN H.P.	COST INSTALLED, IN DOLLARS
10	3,500
20	6,000
40	10,000

This cheapest professionally installed refrigeration still ends up costing probably $1,500 more than the installed cost of the engine. And as has been pointed out, this system has very serious disadvantages. When lying alongside the dock, one must run the engine every day to cool the refrigerator. And with this type of compressor one can expect blowing seals, slipping belts, fouled-up magnetic clutches, and the like.

Overall, I think I will continue to buy ice. In some places it is dirt cheap; in others it is actually given away. The money I have not spent on the refrigeration system can be used for food to put into the icebox. Most important, since I don't have to spend time behind a tape recorder or a typewriter earning the money to pay for my installation, *I can go sailing instead!*

As Vic Jorgensen, of *The Telltale Compass,* keeps saying, one should remember the old U.S. Navy engineering motto, and *KEEP IT SIMPLE.*

APPENDICES

GLOSSARY

Aback A sail is aback when so sheeted to windward that it exerts a braking force on the yacht's forward motion, or when the wind comes on what should be its lee side.

Abaft Toward the stern; to the rear of.

Abeam At right angles to the fore-and-aft center line amidships.

Aboard On board or in a vessel.

About A vessel is said to go, come, or put about when she swings her bow through the eye of the wind, i.e., tacks.

Accelerator A chemical (usually put in the resin mix by the manufacturer) which is used in fiber-glass construction and in the preparation for use of polyurethane paint to speed up the rate of curing. It is dangerous to mix the accelerator and the catalyst (*q.v.*) because there may be an explosion. The accelerator should be mixed with the resin, and the catalyst then added.

Accommodation Ladder A ladder or flight of steps enabling one to climb up the topsides from a dinghy to a vessel's deck.

Accommodation Plan A drawing showing the internal arrangements of a vessel.

Acockbill An anchor is said to be acockbill when it is hung in an up-and-down position, ready to be let go. Yards are said to be acockbill when they are topped at an angle with the horizontal.

Aft Toward the stern; behind.

Aground With the keel resting on the bottom; "on the putty" to the British, "parked" to some Americans.

Ahead Toward the bows; in front of.

All Standing To bring up people or things all standing is to bring them to a sudden and unexpected stop.

Aloft Up above; up the mast or in the rigging.

Ambiguous Sector An area where signals from one particular Consolan station give inaccurate and deceptive readings.

Amidships Generally, the middle part of a vessel, between the bow and the stern; sometimes, on the fore-and-aft line (hence, to put the helm amidships is to steer neither to port nor to starboard).

Anemometer An instrument for measuring the strength of the wind.

Apparent Wind   The wind that is felt aboard a moving boat, consisting of a combination of the true wind and the wind caused by the boat's motion. The greater the speed of the boat, the more the apparent wind moves ahead.

Apron   A strengthening piece behind the stem, seldom found in American-designed boats.

Arming   Tallow held in the recess of a sounding lead to bring up a sample of the seabed.

Ashore   Aground, or on land.

Aspect Ratio   The relation of length to width in a sail, a wing, a rudder, a centerboard, or any other object.

Astern   Behind; toward the stern.

Athwart   Across; the opposite of fore and aft.

Awash   Just under, or washed over by, water.

Aweather   To windward; toward the weather side.

Aweigh   An anchor is aweigh when it has broken out of the bottom.

Backbone   The center-line fore-and-aft structure of the boat, consisting of stem, keel, rudderpost, horn timber, and the various knees and aprons that support these timbers.

Baggy Wrinkle   Chafing gear made of old rope ends secured to rigging.

Ballast Keel   The lead or iron bolted onto the wooden structural keel to give a yacht stability.

Ballooner   A light, high-cut genoa which may be used on a reach, sheeted to the end of the main boom.

Bear Away, To;   To put the helm up (to windward) and turn the bow
Bear Off, To   of the boat away from the wind.

Beat, To   To tack to windward, sailing hard on the wind.

Bee Block   British for cheek block (*q.v.*). Also, to the British, a wooden chock on the side of a boom near its after end, to take the standing part of a reef pendant, somewhat similar to a cheek block.

Belay, To   To make fast or secure a rope on a cleat or pin.

Belly   The fullness, or draft, of a sail.

Bend, To   To fasten, as one rope to another or to some other object, a sail to its spars, and so on.

Beneaped   See *Neaped.*

Bermudian Rig   See *Jib-headed Rig; Marconi Rig.*

Bermudian Sail   A triangular fore-and-aft sail without a gaff or yard, set on a boom on the aft side of a mast; also called a "Marconi Sail."

Berth   (1) A sleeping place on board.
(2) The place ashore, in a dock, or at an anchorage, which is occupied by a vessel. To berth a vessel is to put her into such a place.

Bight   (1) A bend or loop in a rope.
(2) An open bay formed by a bend in the coast.

Bilge   (1) The curve of a vessel's bottom where it merges into the side.
(2) The space in a vessel beneath the sole.

Bilge Keel   (1) A rubbing-piece fastened to the outside of the bilge of a dinghy to protect it from chafe when taking the ground or being dragged up a beach.
(2) An actual keel on a larger boat with twin keels; it allows the boat to dry out upright and provides the necessary lateral plane to enable the boat to work to windward.

Bill   A certificate or a written agreement, as in "bill of health," "bill of lading," "bill of exchange."

Binnacle   The case in which a compass is fixed.

Bitt   One of the posts fitted in the foredeck to take the heel of the bowsprit and to which the anchor cable is made fast.

Bitter End   (1) The extreme end.
(2) The inboard length of a ship's cable (from the fact that the cables of ships at anchor used to be belayed to specially fitted center-line bollards called "bitts").

Blade   The flat part of an oar or propeller.

Bleed, To   To drain, usually slowly. To bleed a buoy is to empty it of water. To bleed a fuel system is to loosen a connection and pump until all the air is exhausted from the system. To bleed the monkey is to extract the contents of a rum barrel by boring a small hole in it.

Block   Pulley.

**Block and
  Block;
  Two-Blocked**   The state of a tackle when its standing and moving blocks are hauled close together. Colloquially, the terms can be used to describe the position of any two objects which are close together.

Board	The distance covered in one tack, or leg, when beating to windward.
Boathook	A pole with a hook at one end, used for picking up a mooring buoy, holding onto a dinghy, and the like.
Boatswain's, or Bosun's, Stores	Spare rigging materials carried on board.
Bobstay	A chain, wire, or rod from the stem to the end of the bowsprit, to support it against the upward pull of the jib.
Body Plan	A drawing which shows the shape of the athwartship sections of a vessel.
Boeier	A type of shoal-draft Dutch yacht.
Bollard	(1) A post, usually on a pier or quay, to which mooring or warping lines are made fast. (2) A metal fitting with two heads, on a vessel's deck at the bow or quarter, to which mooring lines are secured.
Boltrope	A rope sewn along the edge of a sail to strengthen it and take the strain off the material.
Bonnet	(1) Any small cover or hood, of canvas or metal, used to close or protect a small fitting or opening. (2) Historically, an extra piece of canvas, laced to the foot of a sail to increase its area.
Boom	A horizontal spar for extending the foot of a sail.
Boot-Top Line	The line just above the load waterline, where the bottom paint joins the topsides paint.
Boot Topping	A strip of specially hard paint around the waterline, which can be scrubbed without damage. It is less used nowadays since hard racing copper antifouling paint can be scrubbed. Boats with high topsides often look better with the boot topping carried up a little way, to reduce the apparent height of the topsides.
Bottle Screw	(1) An adjusting screw fitted at the bottom of a wire stay; "closed-body turnbuckle" to Americans. Bottle screws are solid and internally tapped; they are often used aboard sailing dinghies. (2) Cruising boats usually use open ones, more correctly called "rigging screws," in which the threads can be more easily inspected.

Bottomry	A system of pledging the hull of a ship as security for a loan.
Bouse Down, To	To haul down taut.
Bow, Bows	The entire forepart of a vessel; also the sides of the forepart of a vessel, from the stem to the midship section.
Bow-and-Buttock Line	A line showing the shape of a fore-and-aft vertical section of a vessel. It is seen as a curve on the sheer plan.
Bower	The principal anchor, which is generally used with a chain cable, in England, as opposed to a kedge, which is lighter, and is used with a rope cable; also called a "working anchor."
Bowsprit	A spar on which the jib is set projecting horizontally from the bow.
Brace	A rope by means of which the yard of a square sail is controlled in a horizontal plane.
Brail	A rope which encircles a sail for the purpose of gathering it in to the mast, sprit, or yard.
Brail, To	To take in a sail by the brails.
Breaker	(1) A sea which is breaking, i.e., the water of which is in forward motion. (2) A small barrel for holding fresh water.
Breasthook	A wood or iron knee binding a pair of shelves, stringers, or gunwales to one another and to the stem.
Breast Rope	A rope from bow or stern made fast to the nearest point of a quay, a pier, or another vessel, when lying alongside.
Bridge Deck	Reinforcing beams and bulkheads, decked over, between the cockpit and the cabin. They strengthen a boat a great deal, and help to prevent water from going down the companionway in bad weather, but they restrict access to the cabin.
Brightwork	Woodwork which is kept varnished.
Bring Up, To	To anchor.
Broach, To	To lose control when running downwind and to round up, bringing wind and sea abeam.
Bulkhead	A partition belowdecks separating one part of a vessel from another.

Bulldog Grip	A screw fitting for temporarily clamping two parts of wire rope side by side; also called a "wire rope clamp."
Bull Rope	A rope leading from the bowsprit end to a mooring buoy which is too large to be taken aboard, to keep the buoy from bumping the stem when wind and tide are opposed.
Bull's-eye	A round, hardwood thimble used for altering the lead of a rope.
Bulwarks	The solid protection built around the edges of a deck to prevent people or gear from being washed overboard.
Bumpkin	A spar, projecting horizontally from the stern, to which the mizzen sheet or permanent backstay is attached.
Bunk	A sleeping berth.
Bunk Board	A bulwark of wood to prevent a sleeper from being thrown out of his bunk by the motion of a vessel.
Bunt	The middle part of a sail.
Buntline Hitch	An excellent knot for attaching a dinghy painter made of synthetic line to a ring. It does not tend to come undone as two half hitches would. It is also used to attach a sheet to a sail, and takes up less space than a bowline.
Buoyancy Tank	An airtight tank fitted into a dinghy to maintain buoyancy should she become waterlogged.
Burden Boards	See *Floorboards*.
Burgee	A yacht-club flag.
Burton	A tackle used for lifting the anchor or dinghy aboard.
Butt	The place where two planks or other members touch one another end to end.
Butt End	The larger end of a spar, or any similarly shaped object.
Buttock Line	A line of intersection of a longitudinal vertical plane with the hull of a ship.
By the Lee	Running with the wind on the same side as the boom.
Cable	A chain, or a fiber or wire rope, by means of which a vessel rides to her anchor.
Cable-Laid Rope	Rope made by laying up three complete ropes with a left-handed twist; seldom seen today.

Call Sign	A combination of letters and perhaps numbers identifying a radio operator or station, for use in communication.
Camber	The athwartship curve of the deck; sometimes called the "crown."
Camel	A tank secured to the hull of a ship to provide extra buoyancy, used mainly in salvage work.
Canoe Stern	An overhanging stern with a pointed or rounded end.
Cant, To	To incline from the perpendicular.
Cap	The ring at the top of a lower mast, through which the housing topmast slides.
Capstan	A mechanical appliance with a vertical barrel, used to obtain increased power when hauling on a rope or chain.
Carlin	A fore-and-aft member at the side of a coach roof, hatch, or skylight, to which the ends of the half-beams and the coaming are secured.
Carry Away, To	To break or lose any spar or part of the rigging.
Carvel-built	Constructed with the skin planks lying flush with one another and presenting a smooth surface.
Cast, To	To take a sounding with the lead.
Catalyst	A chemical added to polyester or epoxy resin to start it curing, in fiber-glass construction and in the preparation of polyurethane paint for use. See also *Accelerator*.
Catenary	The curve, or sag, of the cable between a vessel and her anchor.
Cat Rig	A fore-and-aft rig with one mast far forward and only one sail.
Cat the Anchor, To	To secure the anchor for sea.
Caulk, To	To drive strands of cotton or oakum into a seam to make it watertight.
Ceiling	Planking laid fore and aft inside the frames; sometimes installed for appearance's sake, but on commercial and fishing boats, a part of the structure.
Centerboard	A hinged vertical plate or board which can be lowered through a slot in the keel of a shoal-draught yacht or dinghy to provide lateral resistance.

Center of Effort	The geometric center of a sail or sail plan where the lateral force of the wind is theoretically concentrated.
Center of Lateral Resistance	The geometric center of an underwater profile of a vessel's hull—the theoretic point at which one could push the hull sideways without it turning.
Chafe, To	To rub, or damage by rubbing.
Chafing Gear	Anything which is used to prevent chafe.
Chain Plate	A metal strap on the side of a vessel to which the lower end of a shroud or runner is secured.
Channel	One of the ledges sometimes built out from the sides of a vessel to increase the spread of the shrouds.
Chart Datum	The level from which all soundings on a chart are measured. It may vary with the chart, as indicated by the following:

Mean low water (M.L.W.): the average of all low tides; used on charts of the United States Atlantic and Gulf of Mexico coasts.

Mean lower low water (M.L.L.W.): the average of the lower of the two daily tides; used on charts of the United States Pacific coast, Alaska, Hawaii, and the Philippines.

Lowest normal low water (L.N.L.W.): used on Canadian charts.

Mean low water, spring tides (M.L.W.S.); also called *low water, ordinary spring tides* (L.W.O.S.): used on most Admiralty charts.

Lowest astronomical tide (L.A.T.): the lowest tide that can be expected; used on the new British metric charts. This datum can sometimes be considerably below those previously employed.

Check, To	To ease.
Cheek Block	A block bolted to a mast or boom in such a manner that the spar forms its inner face; "bee block" to the British.
Chine	The junction in a deep-bottomed boat between the bottom and the topsides; often it can be a distinct, sharp corner.
Chock	A piece of wood cut to allow an anchor, spinnaker pole, or the like to be lashed firmly in place.
Chopped-Strand Mat	The commonest and most economical reinforcing material in fiber-glass construction. It consists of strands of flexible glass, cut to a uniform length but running

in every direction, which are held together in a mat by a binder that unites with the resin. The mat is made in various weights and thicknesses.

Clamp	A vertical timber bolted underneath the shelf at the junction of the frame and the deck beam.
Clap On, To	To attach one tackle to another or to a rope. "Clap on," is an order to man a fall or a halyard.
Claw Off, To	To beat away from a lee shore.
Clearing Line	See *Danger Bearing*.
Cleat	A fitting to which a rope may be secured.
Clevis Pin	A pin securing rigging to a turnbuckle, mast tang, chain plate, or the like, and secured in place by a cotter pin (split pin) rather than a nut.
Clew	The lower after corner of a fore-and-aft sail.
Clinker-built	See *Lapstrake*.
Clipper Bow	A bow in which the stem has a forward curve and the sides have much flare.
Close, To	A pair of leading marks are said to be closing when a vessel approaches their line, so that they draw closer together. A vessel is said to close with another or with the shore when she is approaching it.
Close-hauled	A vessel is said to be close-hauled when she is sailing as close to the wind as she can with advantage, and her sails are trimmed more nearly fore-and-aft than on any other point of sailing.
Close to the Wind	With the head of the ship directed as nearly as possible to the point from which the wind is blowing.
Clumbungay	A boat old in design and in years, but usually well loved and cared for.
Coach Roof	A part of the deck raised to give increased headroom.
Coaming	The side of a coach roof, hatch, cockpit, or the like extending above deck level.
Combination Rope	Fiber rope which has some wires buried in it.
Companionway	The entry from deck or cockpit to the accommodation area.
Compass Point	A division of the compass card; $\frac{1}{32}$ of a circle, or $11\frac{1}{4}$ degrees.

Compass Rose — A circle, marked like a compass card, which is printed on a chart.

Composite Method — A way of building in which iron framing and a wooden skin are used.

Consolan — A system of obtaining a fix by radio by counting the dots and dashes transmitted by a special station.

Constant Bearing — A constant bearing is said to exist when the bearing with respect to any other vessel remains unchanged, so that if the course is not altered there is risk of collision.

Contline — The spiral space between the strands of a rope.

Cotter Key — A small metal pin used to keep a clevis pin in place or a nut from working loose; also called a "cotter pin"; "split pin" to the British.

Cotter Pin — See *Cotter Key*.

Counter — A stern which extends beyond the rudderstock and terminates in a small transom.

Course — (1) The direction in which a vessel is sailing, measured in degrees or compass points from her meridian. (2) The lowest and largest square sail, above which the topsail, the topgallant sail, and so on may be set.

Covering Board — The outermost deck plank, which covers the heads of the frames or timbers.

Crance Iron — The metal cap or band at the end of the bowsprit to which the shrouds, topmast stay, and bobstay are secured.

Crank — Said of a vessel that is unhandy, easily tipped; the opposite of "stiff."

Cringle — A rope eye formed on the outside of the boltrope of a sail and fitted with a metal thimble.

Crosstree — See *Spreader*.

Crown — (1) The part of an anchor where the arms join the shank. (2) See *Camber*.

Crutch — A wooden or metal fitting into which the boom fits when not in use. A well-designed boom crutch is of great help when reefing, but the often-seen scissors type is almost useless, and has an irritating way of collapsing and even falling overboard when the boom

	is lifted out. A permanent gallows is much more satisfactory.
Cuddy	A small cabin, usually in a day boat.
Cunningham Holes	Heavy grommets sewn in the luff and foot of the sail; they can be pulled, by means of lanyards, toward the tack to adjust the draft of the sail.
Cut Back	See *Rub Back*.
Cutter	A fore-and-aft-rigged vessel with one mast, a mainsail, and two headsails (staysail and jib).
Cutwater	The forepart of the stem of a ship. In sailing vessels with bluff bows it was a false stem.
Danger Bearing	A bearing from a fixed object leading clear of a navigational hazard. For example, "Little Tobago one finger open of Fota clears reef off Palm" means that when one can see Little Tobago open from Fota, one is safe from hitting the reef which is off Palm Island. Also called "clearing line."
Davit	A small crane used for hoisting a boat or large anchor aboard.
Deadeye	(1) A block of hardwood with one or more holes drilled in it to take the ropes of the fall or a simple purchase; the earliest form of block. Now used for standing rigging only.
	(2) A disk of wood with three holes through which a lanyard is rove for setting up the rigging.
Deadlight	A metal cover which can be clamped over the glass of a portlight.
Dead Reckoning (D.R.)	The determination of a vessel's position at sea, as indicated by the records of the course sailed, the distance run, the time spanned, and so on, without the aid of celestial navigation.
Deadwood	The solid wooden part of the fin keel at the aft end, where the rudder is hung.
Decca	A system of navigation widely used in Europe by large vessels. Since it requires heavy equipment, rented from the manufacturer (Kelvin Hughes), it is not usually found in yachts.
Deckhead	The undersurface of the deck.
Deck Light	A piece of glass let flush into a deck.
Deck Log	A small notebook in which all alterations in course,

speed, and weather, and any other relevant matters, are recorded, with the time, so the reckoning can be worked up later by the navigator as desired.

Declination The angle between a celestial body and the equinoctial line (the equator) as measured from the center of the earth.

Deep (1) A depression in the seabed.
(2) One of the fathom points on a lead line which is not marked, as in "deep six."

Depression An area of low atmospheric pressure, bringing rain, wind, and generally bad weather. In the Northern Hemisphere, the wind blows counterclockwise around a depression. The severity of the weather, and particularly of the wind, depends on how low the pressure is.

Derrick A spar rigged with a tackle, for use in lifting something.

Deviation An error of the compass caused by the proximity of iron; it varies with the direction in which the vessel is heading.

DF Radio A radio fitted with a direction finder.

Dip The vertical angle at the eye of the observer between the horizontal and the line of sight to the visible horizon.

Dip, To To lower partially and temporarily; to dip an ensign is to lower and rehoist it as a salute.

Displacement The weight of water displaced by a hull when it floats, which is equal to the actual weight of the hull; also, in England, Thames measurement (*q.v.*).

Dodger Canvas rigged on the lifelines to provide overhead shelter for the cockpit. Also, canvas secured along the lifelines to reduce spray in the cockpit; "weather cloth" to Americans.

Doghouse A structure, usually provided with windows, built on deck over the companionway or cockpit.

Dolphin Striker A strut rigged from the stemhead to the bobstay to give the bobstay a more favorable angle with the stem and the bowsprit end; it performs the same job as the spreader on a mast.

Doubler Plate One of the steel plates welded as reinforcement on top of existing hull plating which has become thin as a result of corrosion.

Douse, To	To lower or slacken suddenly.
Downhaul	A rope used for pulling down a sail.
Down Helm, To	To put the helm to leeward so as to bring the vessel's head toward the wind.
Downwind	To leeward of a particular point.
D.R.	See *Dead Reckoning*.
Draft	The depth of water required to float a vessel.
Drag	The amount by which a long straight keel is off the horizontal.
Drag, To	An anchor is said to drag when it fails to hold the vessel in position.
Draw, To	(1) A sail is said to draw when the wind fills it. To let draw is to let go the weather sheet of a sail and haul in the lee one, so that the sail may drive the vessel ahead. (2) When her draft is specified, a ship is said to draw so many feet.
Draw Ahead, To; Draw Astern, To	A ship is said to draw ahead if her relative position advances, and to draw astern if it drops back.
Dress Ship, To	To run a string of code flags from stem to stern over the mastheads. The flags should terminate in the water at both bow and stern.
Dress the Mast, To	A British expression meaning "to rig the mast"; to put on its standing and running rigging.
Drift	(1) The distance between the blocks of a tackle; the distance forward or aft of the mast that a shroud or stay is attached to its chain plate. (2) Direction of tidal current. (3) See *Drift Pin*.
Drift, To	To move with the tide or wind.
Drift Pin	A long rod, with a head at one end which is usually set down over a heavy washer. The drift pin is driven into a blind hole, with a drive fit, and is used in places where it is difficult or impossible to fit a nut on the end of a bolt. Also called a "drift."
Dunnage	Pieces of wood, matting, old rope, old canvas, and other similar materials when used for raising cargo off the bottom of a hold, for packing it to keep it from shifting, or for covering it to keep it dry.

Earing	A hole in the sail, lined with a bronze ring sewn to the sail, for use in lashing the tack and clew in place while reefing; also called a "reefing cringle."
Ease, To	To slacken.
Echo Sounder	An electronic device that determines the depth of water by measuring the time taken by a sound signal to go to the seabed and return; also known by the trade name Fathometer.
Ensign	A flag displayed by a vessel to indicate her nationality.
Epoxy Resin	A type of resin used in fiber-glass construction and for gluing where exceptional durability, strength, or adhesion is required. It is more expensive than the more commonly used polyester resins.
Eye	(1) A closed loop. (2) The direction from which the wind is blowing.
Eyes	The very forwardmost portion of a boat, right up in the bows.
Fairlead	A bull's-eye or metal fitting through which a rope is passed to alter the direction of its lead or to keep it clear of other gear.
Fake, To; Fake Down, To	To lay out line on deck in successive figure eights, so that it will run out freely without kinking; also called "to flake," "to flake down."
Fall	The hauling part of a rope.
Fall Off, To	A vessel is said to fall off when she shows a tendency to bear away from the wind.
False Keel	An addition to the main keel, its purpose usually being to fill in the space at the after end of the ballast keel.
Fashion Board	See *Splash Board*.
Fathom	A nautical measure of depth; six feet.
Fathometer	See *Echo Sounder*.
Feather, To	(1) To turn the blade of an oar so that it is parallel to the surface of the water, during recovery. (2) To turn the blade of a propeller straight fore and aft, to minimize drag.
Fender	A cushion of cork, rubber, or rope, used to prevent damage when a vessel lies alongside another or at a quay.
Fetch, To	When a vessel is able to reach her objective without tacking, she is said to fetch it.

Fiber Glass

Glass spun into fine threads that are flexible and can be woven or treated like any other thread. In some form it provides the reinforcing in any fiber-glass hull, giving its name to the whole substance, which is correctly described as fiber glass and resin laminate. Fiberglas is the trade name for the product of Owens-Corning, widely used in the United States. "GRP" (for "glass-reinforced plastic") is the term more commonly used in England.

Fid

(1) A large spike of wood.
(2) A short iron bar passing through a hole in the heel of a topmast or bowsprit to hold it in position.

**Fiddle,
    Fiddle Rail**

One of the strips of wood fitted to a table or other surface to prevent crockery from sliding off.

Fiddle Block

A block having two sheaves, one larger and above the other.

Fiddlehead

A clipper bow.

Fife Rail

A rail in which belaying pins are inserted; also called a "pinrail."

Fisherman

A yachtsman anchor, an old-fashioned anchor.

**Fisherman
    Staysail**

A four-sided sail set between the masts of a schooner.

Fit Out, To

To overhaul a vessel after she has been laid up.

Fix, To

To find a vessel's position by making observations of celestial or terrestrial objects.

**Flake, To;
    Flake Down,
    To**

See *Fake, To.*

Flare

The outward curve of a vessel's side.

Flattie

A dinghy with a flat bottom and chines.

Floor

A transverse member of wood or metal binding a pair of frames or timbers to one another and to the keel.

Floorboards

The boards in the bottom of a dinghy which distribute the weight of the load over the timbers; "burden boards" to the British.

Fluke

The pointed section, at the end of the arm of an anchor, which bites into the ground.

Fly

The horizontal length of a flag.

Flying

See *Set Flying.*

Foot

The lower edge of a sail.

Fore	In or toward the front; opposite to "aft."
Fore and aft	In the direction of a line drawn from stem to stern, i.e., parallel to the keel.
Forecastle, Fo'c'sle	That part of the accommodation area which is beneath the foredecks; the forwardmost cabin in the bow, usually the crew's quarters.
Forefoot	That part of the bow which is between the load waterline and the fore end of the keel.
Forepeak	The triangular space belowdecks in the extreme forward part of the bow; now, loosely, the forecastle.
Forereach, To	To make headway when hove to.
Foresail, Fores'l	The fore-and-aft sail set on the aft side of a schooner's foremast. Also, on British cutters sometimes used to mean "staysail," with the result that confusion may occur when a cutter man sails on a schooner.
Foreshore	The beach below the high-water mark.
Forestaysail	See *Staysail*.
Fore-triangle	The area between the head stay, the mast, and the deck.
Foul	(1) Entangled. An anchor is said to be foul when its fluke catches on an obstruction; it is also foul when the cable twists around the arm or the stock. The bottom is said to be foul when there are rocks or chains which might foul the anchor. (2) Encrusted or clogged with a foreign substance. A vessel's bottom is foul when weeds or barnacles have grown on it.
Foul Hawse	An arrangement in which cables from different anchors become crossed or twisted. Compare *Open Hawse*.
Frame	A rib of a vessel.
Frap, To	To bind with lashing; to pass a rope around a sail or over an awning to keep it from breaking loose. Halyards are said to be frapped when they are held in to the mast by spiral turns of one of their number.
Frapping	The bracing together of ropes or lines with crosswise turns, to increase their tension.
Free	Not close-hauled.
Freeboard	The height of a vessel's side above the water.
Freeing Wind	A wind that tends to draw aft, making it possible to ease the sheets.
Freer	See *Lift*.

Front

The boundary between two unlike masses of air; the passage of fronts, usually associated with depressions, is characteristic of weather in temperate climates. A warm front, with warm air pushing colder air in front of it, is likely to result in continuous rain lasting some time; the passage of a cold front can be expected to be accompanied by squalls and followed by a drop in temperature and a dramatic clearing, with blue skies and a fresh northwest wind.

Full and By

Sailing with full sails and sailing by the wind, not by compass or mark.

Full and Change

Full and new moon. See also *H.W.F. & C.*

Furl, To

To fold up or roll up and stop a sail or an awning.

Futtock

One of the several pieces of timber which, overlapped and scarfed together, are used to form a frame which is to be of such size and shape that it cannot be made from a single piece of timber.

Gaff

The spar to which the head of a quadrilateral mainsail, foresail, or mizzen is bent.

Gaff Jaws

The fitting at the inboard end of a gaff which slides on the mast.

Gaff Sail

A quadrilateral sail fitted with a gaff.

Galley

A kitchen on a boat.

Galley Staysail

See *Windsail.*

Gallows, Gallows Frame

A permanent framework on which the end of a boom rests when the sail is lowered.

Galvanize, To

To coat iron or steel with zinc to protect it from corrosion.

Gammon Iron

The ring which holds a bowsprit to the stemhead.

Garboard

The plank which lies next to the keel.

Gasket

(1) A stop used for lashing up a furled sail or awning.
(2) A piece of soft material placed between two metal surfaces to seal the joint.

Gatline

An extra line rigged aloft specifically for hauling a man up in a boatswain's chair, as distinguished from a spare halyard.

Gel Coat

The smooth outer skin of a fiber-glass hull.

Gel Time

The time taken for a resin to start to solidify after the catalyst has been added.

Genamaker	A cross between a spinnaker and genoa; it is set flying like a spinnaker, but is cut more like a ballooner, or reaching jib.
Genoa	A large triangular headsail which alone fills the entire fore-triangle and extends well aft of the shrouds.
Ghosting	A sailing vessel or boat is said to be ghosting, or ghosting along, when she is making good way in a very light breeze.
Gilguy	One of the lanyards tied around halyards and secured to stays to hold the halyards away from the mast when the boat is at anchor. Failure to secure halyards in this manner is what makes aluminum masts so noisy.
Gimbals	An arrangement of concentric rings and pivots for keeping a compass, lamp, stove, table, or other object level regardless of the movements of a vessel at sea.
Glass Fiber	See *Fiber Glass*.
Gnomonic Chart	A type of projection which is useful for plotting routes and calculating distances for long voyages because on it a great circle is represented as a straight line.
Golliwobbler	Technically, the main-topmast balloon staysail, a fisherman that extends from the masthead to the deck, overlapping the mainsail in the same fashion as a genoa. It is generally sheeted to the end of the boom.
Gooseneck	The universal joint which holds the boom to the mast.
Goosewinged	A two-masted vessel is said to be running goosewinged when her mainsail is extended on one side and her mizzen or foresail on the other.
Goosewinged Sail	A sail whose top part has caught on the spreader during jibing and remains on the opposite side of the boat from the boom and the lower part of the sail. The situation, also called a "Chinese jibe," is caused by the boom rising, and can be prevented by a kicking strap. Once it occurs, the only remedy is to jibe back and try again.
Grapnel	A small anchor with four or more arms.
Gripe, To	A vessel is said to gripe when she carries excessive weather helm and shows a strong inclination to round up into the wind.
Grommet	A ring made of rope; an eye made in the edge of a sail inside the boltrope.
GRP	See *Fiber Glass*.

Gudgeon	A metal eye on the after side of a sternpost into which the rudder pintle ships.
Gunter	A fore-and-aft rig used for small craft. Instead of a gaff, the mainsail has a yard which slides vertically on the mast.
Gunwale	The upper edge of a boat's side.
Guy	A steadying rope attached to a spar, holding it in the fore-and-aft plane.
Gybe, To	See *Jibe, To*.
Gypsy	A wheel on a windlass with recesses to hold the links of a chain, such as an anchor chain; also called a "wildcat."
Half-beam	A deck beam which does not extend right across the vessel, but stops short at a carlin.
Half-Breadth Plan	A drawing which shows the shape of the boat's waterlines and level lines.
Half-Tide Rock	A rock which uncovers when the tide is at half ebb.
Halyard	A rope used for hoisting a sail or flag.
Hambroline	Small three-strand rope used for lashings and lacings.
Hand, To	To lower, take in, or stow a sail.
Handsomely	Gradually and steadily.
Handy-billy	A tackle used temporarily to exert extra power on a rope.
Hang Off, To	To hold one rope temporarily with another while something is done with the end or bight of the first rope.
Hank	A clip used to hold the luff of a sail to a stay; a sail which is held to a stay by hanks is said to be hanked on.
Hard	A landing place, usually artificial, where the foreshore is hard.
Harden In, To	To haul in a sheet so as to flatten a sail.
Hardtack	Ship's biscuit, formerly very hard and tough.
Hard Up, Hard Down	The position of the helm—as far as possible to windward or to leeward, respectively.
Hatch	An opening in the deck provided with a cover.
Haul, To	To pull.
Hawsehole	A hole in the bulwarks or topsides through which the anchor cable runs.

Hawsepipe	A tube running diagonally from the deck to the bow slightly above the waterline and used as a fairlead for the anchor cable. Some types of anchor will stow in the hawsepipe.
Head	(1) The bow. (2) The top edge of a sail. (3) A ship's toilet (the "heads" of a sailing man-of-war were platforms on each side of the stem which were used as latrines by the men).
Headboard	A piece of wood or aluminum sewn to the head of a Bermudian sail or a spinnaker to increase the area of the sail slightly, to distribute the load on it, and to prevent it from twisting.
Header	A wind shift that forces one to bear off to keep the sails from luffing.
Headroom	The distance inside a vessel between the sole and the deckhead.
Headsail, Heads'l	A sail set forward of the forwardmost mast on the boat.
Headway	A vessel's movement ahead through the water.
Head Wind	A wind which prevents a vessel from laying the desired course, compelling her to beat.
Heart	A strand in the middle of a rope.
Heave Down, To	To careen.
Heave To, To	To trim the sails and helm in such a manner that the vessel lies almost stationary; heaving to is also called "lying to."
Heaving Line	A light rope, often with a small weight at one end, used for making the initial connection between a vessel and the shore or some other vessel, so that a stronger rope may then be hauled across.
Heel	The after end of a keel; the lower or inboard end of a spar.
Heel, To	To list.
Heeling Error	Deviation of the compass caused by changes in the relative position of nearby iron when a vessel heels.
Helm	The tiller or wheel used for steering.
Highfield Lever	A mechanical appliance used for setting up and letting go a runner or some other part of the rigging.
Hitch	(1) A method of making a rope fast to some object. (2) Sometimes, a short tack.

Hog-Backed	See *Hogged.*
Hogged	Said of a vessel which has been strained so that her sheer is convex instead of concave. Some craft are built with this conformation. "Hog-backed" to the British.
Hoist	The vertical edge or measurement of a sail or flag.
Hoist, To	To haul aloft.
Hold, To	(1) To stop the progress of a boat by holding the blades of the oars steady in the water. (2) An anchor is said to hold when it gets a good grip on the bottom and does not drag.
Holiday	A gap left in a row or line; an unpainted patch in paintwork.
Holystone	One of the blocks of sandstone formerly used for scrubbing decks, so called because their use entailed kneeling down. Medium-sized holystones were called "bibles," and small ones "prayer books."
Hood-end	The end of a plank where it fits into the rabbet cut in the stem or sternpost.
Horn Timber	The fore-and-aft member at the bottom of a counter.
Horse	A bar or rope on which the sheet of a sail may travel athwartships.
Horse Latitudes	One of the two belts, located between the westerlies and the trade winds in the Northern and the Southern Hemispheres, which are characterized by light and variable winds and in which sailing vessels were often becalmed for some time. The name had its origin in the middle of the nineteenth century, when numerous horses which were being transported from Europe to America and the West Indies died from the heat and were thrown overboard. As a result, the belt in the North Atlantic became studded with dead horses.
Hounds	The chocks on a mast on which the eyes of the lower rigging are seated.
Hove Down	A vessel is said to be hove down when she has heeled excessively.
Hull	The body of a vessel exclusive of her masts and gear.
H.W.F. & C.	High water at full and change of the moon, i.e., at the time of the full and of the new moon.
H.W.O.S.	High water, ordinary spring tides.
Initial Stability	The resistance a vessel offers to being heeled, due to

the shape of her hull and not to the effect of her ballast keel.

Inwale	The longitudinal strengthening piece inside the timber heads at the gunwale of a dinghy.
Irons	A vessel is said to be in irons when in attempting to come about she hangs stationary, head to wind, and will not pay off on either tack.
Jackstay	A rope holding the luff of a topsail or fisherman close to the mast.
Jackyard	A short yard used to extend the foot of a topsail beyond the end of the gaff.
Jib	The foremost headsail.
Jibe, Chinese	See *Goosewinged Sail*.
Jibe, To	When running, to bring the wind from one quarter to the other so that the boom swings across. Jibing is the opposite of tacking in that the stern rather than the bow passes through the eye of the wind. Also called "to gybe."
Jib-Headed	Said of any sail the upper part of which terminates in a point.
Jib-Headed Rig	A rig with a mainsail having three sides; also called a "Bermudian rig" or "Marconi rig."
Jib Topsail	A jib set hanked to the topmast stay, with a high clew.
Jig Line	A light line attached to another line to allow for quick adjustment.
Joggle Shackle	A shackle with extra-long arms, used to hold two chains together, and made to fit between the links so that it cannot slip.
Jumper Stay	A stay which runs over a jumper strut; it is used to keep the upper part of a mast straight.
Jumper Strut	A spreader projecting from the forward face of the mast.
Jury Rig	A makeshift or substitute rig, such as may be improvised when the masts or gear have carried away.
Kedge	An anchor smaller than the bower, generally fitted with a line instead of a chain, and used to haul a vessel off when she has gone aground and to prevent her from fouling her bower; also called a "lunch hook."
Kedge, To	To haul forward by means of an anchor.

Kedge Warp   The line attached to a kedge.

Keel   The fore-and-aft member on which the whole structure of a vessel is built.

Ketch   Strictly speaking, a two-masted, fore-and-aft-rigged vessel with the mizzenmast stepped forward of the after end of the waterline; more loosely, a two-masted, fore-and-aft-rigged vessel with the mizzenmast stepped forward of the rudderpost.

Kevel   A type of cleat made by bolting a piece of wood across two bulwark stanchions.

Kicking Strap   See *Vang*.

Killick   A small anchor; hence, a slang term for a Leading Seaman, because the distinguishing badge he wears is an anchor.

King Plank   The center plank of a deck.

Knee   A piece of timber or iron with two arms, used for strengthening certain parts of a vessel. A hanging knee is one arranged in the vertical plane; a lodging knee is in the horizontal plane.

Knock Back   See *Rub Back*.

Knot   A measure of speed; one nautical mile (6,080 feet) per hour.

Laminate   A material built up in layers, such as fiber glass or plywood.

Land   The overlapping part of the planks in a clinker-built boat.

Lanyard   A short rope, especially one used for setting up a shroud or some other part of the rigging.

Lapstrake   Built with the type of construction where the skin planks overlap one another; also called "clinker-built."

Lash, To   To bind or secure with rope.

L.A.T.   See *Chart Datum*.

Latitude   Distance north or south of the equator, expressed in degrees.

Lay   Of a rope, the direction in which the strands are twisted together.

Lay, To   A vessel is said to lay her course when she can sail in the desired direction without tacking.

Lay Up, To   To dismantle a vessel and berth her for the winter.

Lazy Jack	A device, consisting of light lines from the topping lifts to the boom, which keeps sail under control when it is being lowered; usually found in gaff-rigged boats.
LBP	Length between perpendiculars, i.e., from the fore side of the stern to the after side of the sternpost, on deck.
Lead	A weight on a marked line, used for taking soundings.
Leading Edge	The forward part, as in the luff of a sail, or the front of the keel.
Leading Marks	See *Range Marks*.
League, Marine	An obsolete measurement of distance at sea, equivalent to three nautical miles.
Lee	(1) The side opposite to that toward which the wind is blowing. (2) When going dead downwind, the side of the boat that the main boom is on.
Leeboard	One of the boards, rigged outside the hull on each side of a shoal-draught vessel, which can be lowered on the lee side to prevent leeway by providing lateral resistance.
Lee-bow, To	To sail a boat against an adverse tide in such a way that the tide is on the lee bow instead of the weather bow, thereby pushing the boat to windward. If a slight degree of pinching brings the tide on the lee bow instead of the weather bow, it is worth doing.
Lee Canvas	A cloth strip secured to the bottom of a bunk, and overhead, to keep the occupant in the bunk.
Leech	The aftermost part of a sail.
Lee Helm	A vessel is said to carry lee helm when she has a tendency to turn her bow away from the wind, and the helm has to be kept to leeward to prevent her from doing so.
Lee Shore	A shore under a vessel's lee; one toward which the wind tends to drive her.
Leeward	The side away from the wind, i.e., the side of the boat that the main boom is on.
Leeway	The amount of sideways movement made through the water by a vessel, i.e., the difference between the course steered and the course made good, assuming there to be no tidal stream.
Leg	(1) A piece of wood or metal secured to a vessel's

side to keep her upright on a hard when the tide leaves her.

(2) When beating to windward, a tack is sometimes known as a leg.

Leg-o-Mutton Rig

A jib-headed rig with the main boom approximately as long as, or longer than, the mast, as seen in Tortola sloops and other West Indian workboats.

Level Lines

The fore-and-aft sections of a vessel above and parallel to the LWL, shown as curves on the half-breadth plan.

Lie Ahull, To

To heave to in a gale without setting any sail. The angle to the wind may vary considerably, depending upon the design of the boat.

Lie To, To

See *Heave To, To.*

Lifeline

(1) A rope passing through stanchions along the side of a vessel's deck to prevent the crew from falling overboard.

(2) A line secured to a crew member as a safety precaution when he is working on deck in heavy weather.

Lift

A wind shift that allows the boat to head more to windward than previously; also called a "freer."

Lifting

When referring to sails, if someone calls "Lifting," he means the luff of the sail is lifting (i.e., the sail is luffing), and it is time to trim the sails or bear off.

Lignum Vitae

A hardwood of which fairleads, bull's-eyes, parrel balls, and the like, are often made.

Limber Hole

One of the holes in or beneath the floors through which bilge water runs down to the bilge-pump suction.

Line of Position

See *Position Line.*

Lines

The shape of a vessel, as shown in the set of drawings comprising body plan, sheer plan, and half-breadth plan.

L.N.L.W.

See *Chart Datum.*

LOA

Length over all, i.e., the extreme length of the hull.

Locker

A stowage place or cupboard.

Log

An instrument for measuring distance sailed.

Logbook

A record of a voyage.

Log Chip

A float attached to a marked line and tossed overboard, for determining a vessel's speed.

Long in the Jaw

A rope is said to have become long in the jaw when it has stretched considerably and the spiral of the strands is lengthened.

Longitude	Distance east and west of the Greenwich meridian, expressed in degrees.
Longshoreman	A waterman who makes his living near the shore.
Loom	The part of an oar which one grips when rowing. Looms should be left free of paint or varnish, which makes them hard to grip.
LOP	Line of position. See *Position Line*.
Loran	A system of radio navigation utilizing signals emitted by stations of known position; it is becoming increasingly popular because sets are now coming down in size and price, and can be run off a normal 12-volt system (from *lo*ng *r*ange *a*id to *n*avigation).
Lubber Line	The mark on the compass bowl which is aligned with the vessel's head. Also, on some compasses, similar marks set at 45 or 90 degrees from the main lubber line.
Luff	The forward part of a sail.
Luff, To	To put the helm down and bring the vessel's head closer to or into the wind.
Luffing	The flapping of sails which have been incorrectly trimmed.
Luff Rope	The boltrope sewn to the forward edge of a sail.
Lug	A quadrilateral fore-and-aft sail, the head of which is secured to a yard slung on, and projecting a short distance forward of, the mast.
Lunch Hook	See *Kedge*.
LWL	(1) Load waterline. The line on the hull which is reached by the water when a vessel is trimmed to float as the designer intended. (2) Length at waterline.
L.W.O.S.	See *Chart Datum*.
Mainsail, Mains'l	The fore-and-aft sail set on the aft side of the mainmast.
Make Fast, To	To secure a rope.
Making	Tides are said to be "making" during the period between the neap and the spring tide, when their height progressively increases.
Manifest	An official inventory of all cargo carried by a merchant vessel.

Manrope A steadying rope, to provide a handhold for the person climbing up an accommodation ladder.

Marconi Rig At present, generally the jib-headed, or Bermudian, rig, with a mainsail having three sides; historically, the term refers to the rig characteristic of the big cutters just before World War I. They were gaff-rigged, but had an array of diamond struts, stays, and so on, reminiscent of the Marconi radio wireless towers.

Marconi Sail See *Bermudian Sail.*

Marine Glue Not a proper glue, but a soft elastic compound used in deck seams; also called "seam compound."

Marl, To To take turns around some object with small line at frequent intervals, each turn being half-hitched.

Marlin Tarred twine made of two loosely laid-up strands.

Marlinspike A pointed instrument for opening up the strands of a rope and for tightening or loosening the pins of shackles.

Martingale (1) A stay leading from the nose of the jibboom of a sailing vessel to her stem; in some ships it is passed through the head of a dolphin striker to give it a better downward pull on the jibboom.
(2) Any stay which prevents a boom, spar, or strut from topping.

Masthead The top of a mast.

Mast Step The slotted member on the top of the keel or floors into which the lower end of a mast is shipped.

Matthew Walker A stopper knot used on the standing end of a lanyard.

Mercator Projection A method of representing the curved surface of the earth on a flat plane in which the meridians of longitude are shown as parallel, instead of converging. It is used for most charts.

Meridian A true north-and-south line.

Miss Stays, To To fail to go about onto the other tack because conditions of wind or sea stop the boat; it can be embarrassing when one is heading for a nearby shore.

Miter A seam, leading diagonally from the tack to the luff of the sail, on each side of which the weave of the sail's cloth runs in a different direction.

Mizzen The fore-and-aft sail set on the aft side of the mizzenmast.

Mizzenmast	The aftermost mast in a ketch or yawl.
Mizzen Staysail	A triangular sail set from the mizzenmast head to the deck forward of that mast.
M.L.L.W.	See *Chart Datum.*
M.L.W.	See *Chart Datum.*
M.L.W.S.	See *Chart Datum.*
Molding	The dimension of a piece of wood between its vertical surfaces.
Mold Loft	The place in which a vessel's lines are laid down in full scale so that the size and shape of her various parts may be determined prior to cutting.
Moor, To	To make a vessel fast alongside a quay, or between two posts, buoys, or anchors, or to anchor her with two anchors from the bow so that she lies between them, occupying no more space than a circle whose diameter is approximately twice the length of the boat.
Mouse, To	To take turns with twine or marlin around sister hooks to prevent them from opening, or across the open part of a hook so that it cannot become unhooked.
Muzzler	A gale blowing from right ahead.
Navel Pipe	The fitting in the deck through which the anchor chain passes to the chain locker.
Neaped, Be-neaped	A vessel is said to be neaped when she has run aground at high water, and because the tides are taking off, the following tide fails to float her.
Neap Tide	A tide which occurs at the first and third quarters of the moon. It has a smaller-than-average range. Compare *Spring Tide.*
Night Effect	Inaccuracies in radio direction bearings, occurring at sunset and sunrise because the level of the ionosphere (off which radio waves are reflected) changes considerably at these times, and occurring at night because radio waves are reflected off the ionosphere more at night than during the day.
Nip	A sharp bend in a rope, as where it passes over a sheave or through a fairlead.
Nip, To Freshen the	To move a rope or wire, such as a halyard, so that a different part takes the heavy load and wringing effect at a sheave.

Oarlock	A device which supports an oar while it is used for rowing; called "rowlock" by the British, and "spur" by the Irish.
Offing	A position at a distance from the shore.
Offset	One of the measurements supplied by a designer to guide the builder in laying down a vessel's lines in the mold loft.
Off the Wind	Not close-hauled.
Omni	An aid to navigation based upon line-of-sight UHF radio direction bearings. It is used extensively in aircraft because the line of sight to an aircraft gives good range, but it is not very widely used on yachts because it is effective at sea only if the boat is close to an airport; also, the equipment is expensive.
On the Putty	See *Aground*.
On the Wind	Sailing close-hauled.
Open Hawse	An arrangement in which each anchor cable leads from the bow direct to its anchor, without crossing or being twisted up with the other. Compare *Foul Hawse*.
Opening	A pair of leading or clearing marks are said to be opening when, as the vessel leaves their line, they appear to draw farther apart.
Open Up, To	A vessel is said to open up when her planks shrink and her seams are no longer watertight.
Outhaul	The gear used for hauling a sail out along a spar.
Overhang	That part of a vessel at bow or stern which extends beyond her LWL.
Overhaul, To	(1) To overtake. (2) To examine carefully and repair where necessary. (3) To haul the blocks of a tackle apart to the full extent of the fall.
Painter	The rope attached to a dinghy's bow, by which she is made fast.
Palm	(1) A fitting worn on a sailmaker's hand for protection and for use in thrusting the needle through the sailcloth. (2) The flat part of the fluke of an anchor.
Paraffin	Diesel kerosene.
Parbuckle, To	To roll any cylindrical object upward by passing a

rope beneath it, making one end fast, and hauling on the other.

Parcel, To   To bind canvas around a rope in a spiral manner to keep water out.

Parked   See *Aground*.

Parrel Ball   A small wooden ball with a hole for a lanyard.

Parting Agent   A coating of wax sprayed or painted inside the mold in which a fiber-glass hull is to be laid up, so the hull can eventually be removed from the mold; also called the "releasing agent."

Partner   One of the timbers forming the framework or pad which supports the mast where it passes through the deck.

Patent Log   An instrument for recording distance sailed, by means of a rotator in the water attached by a line to a recorder. Also called a "taffrail log."

Pay, To   To run marine glue (seam compound) into a seam after it has been caulked.

Pay Off, To   When the head of a vessel falls to leeward, she is said to pay off.

Pay Out, To   To ease away or slack out.

Peak   (1) The upper after corner of a gaff-headed sail.
(2) The upper end of a gaff.

Pelican Hook   A jointed hook with a pivot pin, held closed by a ring; knocking back the ring causes the hook to release its hold even when it is under great strain. It is found frequently on mizzen backstays and gangway lifelines. "Senhouse slip" to the British.

Pelorus   A compass card without needles, fitted with sighting vanes and used for taking bearings.

Pendant   A hanging rope; for example, the reef pendant, which hangs from the reef cringle on the leech and is used to haul the sail down to the boom.

Pennant   A pointed flag.

Permanent Backstay   A backstay which is cleared by the boom end and therefore does not have to be cast off when tacking or jibing.

Pinch, To   To sail too close to the wind.

Pinrail   See *Fife Rail*.

Pintle	The fitting on a rudder which ships into a gudgeon so as to form a hinge.
Plank-on-edge Cutter	A narrow, deep cutter with a length–beam ratio of 8 or 10 to 1, developed in Europe under the Thames Measurement rule, and popular from the 1880's to the late 1890's.
Polyamide	The plastic from which nylon is made.
Polyester	The plastic from which Dacron, and certain other fibers, are made.
Polyester Resin	The plastic generally used in fiber-glass construction.
Polypropylene	The plastic used for a rope that has the advantage of floating but is not suitable for use on a yacht because it chafes easily, deteriorates in tropical sunlight, and is difficult to knot. Further, the rope from different manufacturers varies widely in quality.
Polythene	A nonrigid but strong plastic much used for waterproof bags, containers, and domestic gear, and also making a good buoyant rope.
Poop, To	An overtaking sea is said to poop a vessel when it breaks aboard over her stern.
Poor Man's Twins	Working headsails set on a head stay and light auxiliary jackstay, and hung out on the main boom and spinnaker pole; used in place of the more expensive specially rigged hanked-on or roller twins.
Port	The left-hand side of a vessel, when one faces forward.
Portlight	A small pane of glass, sometimes made to open, fitted in a topside or coaming.
Port Tack	A boat is on the port tack when the boom is to starboard, and the wind is coming over the port side of the vessel.
Position Line	A bearing, obtained with the compass, sextant angles of shore objects, a DF, or other means, defining a line somewhere along which the vessel lies. Two or more position lines provide a fix. Also called "LOP," or "line of position."
Pram	A dinghy with a transom at the bow and stern.
Preformed Rope	Wire rope of which each strand is set to the linear shape it will assume in the rope before being laid up. Such rope shows no tendency to unlay.
Preventer	(1) Backstay.

(2) Sometimes, fore guy.

(3) Any rope, chain, or fitting backing up or limiting the movement of rigging, spars, cable, and the like.

Profile The shape of a vessel as seen from the side. Compare *Sheer Plan.*

Proud Said of an object projecting from an otherwise flat surface, such as the head of a rivet which is not countersunk; the term is also applied to a wooden shore which is cut slightly longer than the space into which it is to fit, so that it will have to be driven home, and thus jammed into place, when set up.

Pudding A rope fender, cylindrical in shape and sometimes with the ends tapered; generally used on the bows of tugs and harbor launches, also on the griping spar of radial davits.

Puddle Circular ripples made by the blade of an oar as it leaves the water.

Pulpit A structure of tubing in the stem of a boat which provides a secure place where a man can work while changing headsails.

Pump Well The lowest part of the bilge, from which the bilge pump sucks; also called the "well."

Purchase See *Tackle.*

Pushpit See *Stern Pulpit.*

Quadrant A quarter of a circle; usually, a cast-bronze stock, of this shape, by means of which the rudder may be controlled.

Quarter Strictly speaking, the point on each side of a vessel which lies midway between her midship section and her stern; also, frequently, the whole of each side from amidships to astern, just as the bows may be understood as all of the vessel lying forward of amidships.

Rabbet A groove cut in a keel, stem, sternpost, or the like, to receive the edge or end of a plank.

Racking Seizing A seizing made with figure-eight turns.

Radar A method of obtaining ranges and bearings of objects by analyzing very high frequency radio waves reflected from their surfaces (from *ra*dio *d*etection *a*nd *r*anging).

Raffee A triangular sail set in one or two pieces above a square sail.

Rail	A narrow plank fitted to the edge of the deck or top of the bulwarks.
Rake	The fore-and-aft inclination of a mast, sternpost, or the like, out of the perpendicular.
Range	The difference in level between high and low water of a tide. See also *Range Marks*.
Range, To	(1) A vessel is said to range about if she does not lie steadily while at anchor or hove to. (2) To range a cable is to lay it on deck before anchoring.
Range Marks	Objects (buoys, headlands, or whatever) which when correctly lined up give an exact desired bearing, usually used to give a course in or out of a harbor clearing all obstructions; also called "leading marks."
Rating	A lineal number used to figure a yacht's handicap for racing. In American racing, the rating is used in conjunction with tables to determine seconds-per-mile handicapping. In the rest of the world, the rating is used to figure the time correction factor (*TCF*) by formula. Handicaps and results are figured on a time-and-time basis, with elapsed time multiplied by the *TCF* giving corrected time. The formula for converting rating in lineal feet to *TCF* is $$\frac{\text{Rating} + 3}{10} = TCF$$
Ratlines	Horizontal ropes or wooden bars seized to a pair of shrouds to form a ladder in the rigging.
Rat Tail	A reduction of a rope to a fine point, as in the termination of a boltrope.
Reach	A point of sailing at which the wind is abeam or forward of the beam, but not so far forward as to make the vessel close-hauled.
Reef, To	To reduce the area of a sail by tying or rolling down a part of it.
Reefing Cringle	See *Earing*.
Reef Point	A short length of line permanently sewn through the reef eye and used to gather up the bunt of the sail when the sail is being reefed.
Reeve, To	To pass a rope through a block, fairlead, or hole of any kind.
Releasing Agent	See *Parting Agent*.

Releasing Fluid	A liquid that dissolves rust and enables rusted-up parts to be freed. Products much more effective than any oil or kerosene are now available for this purpose, probably the best known being Plus Gas A (in England) and Cabot's Liquid Wrench (in the United States).
Relieving Tackles	Tackles or ropes secured to the tiller of a vessel to assist her steering in a heavy sea.
Render, To	To run or slide freely, said of a rope.
Rhumb Line	A line cutting all the meridians at the same angle, represented on a Mercator chart as a straight line. (For short distances, a straight line between two points.)
Ribband	A flexible piece of wood used in yacht building.
Riding Light	A lantern hung up in the forepart of a vessel at anchor and showing a white light all around.
Rigging	See *Running Rigging; Standing Rigging.*
Rigging Screw	See *Turnbuckle.*
Rise of Tide	The height the water has risen above chart datum (*q.v.*).
Rising	A fore-and-aft member supporting the ends of the thwarts inside a dinghy's timbers.
Roach	The outward curve sometimes given to the leech of a sail.
Road, Roadstead	An exposed or offshore anchorage.
Rocker	The fore-and-aft curvature of a keel.
Roller Reefing	A method of reefing in which the boom is turned in a horizontal axis, rolling the sail around itself much in the fashion of a window shade, when the sail area is to be reduced.
Round Up, To; Round To, To	To bring a vessel head to wind from a run or a reach.
Roving	A bundle of continuous strands of fiber glass. Rovings are sometimes woven into a loose cloth, and are then known as woven rovings.
Rowlock	See *Oarlock.*
Rub Back	The distance between the point of attachment of the tack of the mainsail and the nearest point on a vertical line extending downward from the after face of the sail track; also called a "cut back" or "knock back."

Rudder Box, Rudder Trunk	On older yachts, the housing in the counter through which the large-diameter wooden rudderstock passes. (On newer yachts the metal rudderstock is encased in a stuffing box.) The rudder box or trunk is brought up to deck level. It is large, cumbersome, and prone to damage on the inside by worms, but the arrangement is simple and foolproof.
Rudderstock	The part of a rudder which is closest to the sternpost, and which forms the pivot shaft of the rudder.
Run	The upward sweep of a vessel's bottom from the point of greatest beam to the stern, as shown by the buttock lines on the sheer plan.
Run, To	To sail before the wind.
Run Before It, To	To run dead downwind before a gale or hard squall.
Runner	A movable stay whose purpose is to support the mast from aft against the pull of a headsail or the thrust of the gaff jaws.
Running by the Lee	Running with the wind on the same quarter as the boom.
Running Rigging	Sheets, halyards, topping lifts, and the like, by means of which sails are hoisted, trimmed, and controlled. Compare *Standing Rigging*.
Sag, To	(1) When the luff of a headsail curves to leeward instead of being straight, it is said to sag. (2) A vessel making excessive leeway is said to sag away.
Sail Off, To	To turn away from the wind.
Sail Stop	See *Stop*.
Sail Tie	See *Stop*.
Samson Post	A strong post in the foredeck to which the anchor cable is secured; also, a similar post fitted at the stern or on the quarter for use in mooring fore and aft or in towing. It often receives the inboard end of the bowsprit.
Sawn Frame	A rib which is sawn rather than bent to shape.
Scantling	The dimension of a member used in the construction of a vessel.
Scarf	The diagonal joint between two planks which have been glued or bolted end to end.

Schooner	A fore-and-aft-rigged vessel having two or more masts, the mainmast being as tall as, or taller than, the foremast.
Scope	The length of cable by which a vessel is anchored.
Score	A groove to take a rope, such as is found on the rim of a sheave and on the shell of a rope-stropped block.
Screen	The board to which a sidelight is fixed to prevent it from showing on the opposite bow.
Scull, To	To propel a boat by working one oar from side to side over the stern or by doing likewise with a small-boat rudder.
Sculling Hole	A notch in the transom of a dinghy where an oar can rest, enabling one to scull.
Scupper	A hole in the bulwarks to allow water to drain from the deck.
Sea	A wave.
Sea Anchor	A conical canvas bag or other contrivance for reducing the speed of a vessel to the minimum in heavy weather.
Sea Cock	A valve which prevents sea water from entering a pipe passing through the skin planks.
Seam	(1) Of a sail, the stitching which holds two cloths together. (2) In yacht building, the space between two planks.
Seam Compound	See *Marine Glue*.
Section	Actually, the representation of a vessel as she would appear if cut through by a plane at any angle; unless otherwise defined, the word is assumed to refer to an athwartship section.
Seizing	A binding together of two ropes or of two parts of the same rope.
Senhouse Slip	See *Pelican Hook*.
Sennit	Rope made by plaiting instead of twisting the strands.
Serve, To	To bind tightly with marlin or other small stuff, as a protection.
Set, To	To hoist or make sail.
Set Flying	Said of a sail whose luff is not secured to a mast or hanked to a stay.
Set Up, To	To tighten.

Seven-eighths Rig	A jib-headed rig in which the head stay meets the mast not at the masthead, but at a point located at approximately seven-eighths of the total height of the mast above the deck.
Shackle	(1) A metal U-shaped fitting with an eye in each of its arms through which a pin is screwed or driven. (2) A length of chain, usually fifteen fathoms; also called a "shot."
Shake Out, To	To let out a reef.
Shank	The part of an anchor which joins the arms to the ring.
Sharpie	A vessel with a flat bottom.
Sheave	The wheel, in a block or spar, over which a rope runs.
Sheer	The curve of the gunwale or top strake in the vertical plane.
Sheer, To	(1) To move a vessel at anchor in a tideway to port or starboard of her anchor by putting the helm over. (2) A vessel which does not lie steadily to her anchor, but ranges from side to side, is said to sheer about.
Sheer Plan	A drawing showing the shape of a vessel as viewed from the side; also called a "profile."
Sheer Pole	A rod secured across the lower ends of all the shrouds at one side to prevent them from untwisting.
Sheer Strake	The uppermost plank of the topside.
Sheet	A rope by means of which a sail is trimmed, secured either to the clew of the sail or to the boom.
Shelf	A longitudinal member to which the ends of the deck beams are secured; it is placed with its width in the horizontal plane and its thickness in the vertical plane.
Shell	The outer casing of a block.
Shifting Backstay	A backstay which can be set up or let go according to whether it is to windward or to leeward.
Ship, To	(1) To put a thing in its proper position for working. (2) A vessel is said to ship a sea when a sea invades the deck.
Shot	See *Shackle*.
Shroud	A wire rope giving athwartship support to a mast, bowsprit, or bumpkin.
Sidelight	Running light.
Siding	The dimension of a piece of wood in the horizontal

plane between its flat surfaces when it is in position as a vessel's backbone.

Sight
An observation, by sextant or by compass, that gives a position line.

Sister, To
To double up, e.g., in the case of a frame, to install a duplicate of the frame.

Sister Hooks
Two hooks on a common eye or thimble.

Slab Reefing
The old-fashioned method of reefing the sail, by means of tack and clew earings and reef points.

Slack Water
A short period at the turn of the tide when there is no tidal stream.

Slick
The comparatively smooth patch on the surface of the sea which is left to windward of a boat drifting to leeward.

Slip
A sloping surface of concrete or stone, up which a dinghy may be dragged; also, a hard fitted with rails or skids, used for hauling a vessel out of the water.

Slip, To
(1) To haul a vessel out.
(2) To let go the anchor chain instead of weighing the anchor.

Sloop
A fore-and-aft-rigged vessel similar to a cutter, but having one instead of two headsails.

Slot Effect
The flow of air through the area between two sails into which air is forced, greatly increasing the efficiency of the aftermost sail.

Smoke Head
The chimney for a stove, usually made of metal, and available in various different designs; anything that removes smoke from the belowdecks stove.

Snatch Block
A block with an opening in one side of the shell, so that one can insert a rope by its bight instead of reeving it.

Snub, To
(1) A vessel at anchor is said to snub when her bows lift to a sea and the cable is pulled taut with a jerk.
(2) In line handling, to check slowly.

Snugged Down
Well reefed; under a small or comfortable area of sail.

Soft Eye
An eye made at the end of a rope without a thimble.

Sole
The cabin floor.

Sound, To
To measure the depth of the water with a lead line or by other means.

Sounding
The act of measuring the depth of the water; also, the figure so obtained, as marked on a chart.

Span	A rope, wire, or chain, the ends of which are secured —at some distance apart—to an object, such as a spar or boat, so that it can be lifted or carried.
Spinnaker	A large, light sail set flying on reaches and runs.
Spitfire Jib	A very small jib used in heavy weather.
Splash Board	A plank which can be slid vertically into grooves in a companionway to prevent water from entering, if doors have not been provided; "fashion board" to the British.
Splice, To	To join ropes or form eyes at their ends by interlacing the strands.
Spline	A thin strip of wood fitted into a seam in place of stopping.
Split Pin	See *Cotter Key*.
Spreader	A wooden or metal strut on a mast, which gives the rigging more spread; "crosstree" to the British.
Spring, Spring Line	A rope used to prevent a vessel secured alongside a dock from moving forward or aft.
Spring, To	To burst adrift a plank, or to damage a spar.
Spring Tide	A tide which occurs at the full and the change of the moon. It has a greater-than-average range. Compare *Neap Tide*.
Sprung	A mast or spar is said to be sprung when it is dangerously cracked or split.
Spun Yarn	A coarse kind of marlin.
Spur	See *Oarlock*.
Square Sail	A sail set from a yard slung athwartships on the fore side of a mast.
Stanchion	A support for bulwarks, lifelines, or the like.
Standing Gaff	A gaff that is left aloft (with the sail brailed against it) when not in use, instead of being lowered or hoisted, as necessary.
Standing Part	That part of a rope which is made fast and not hauled upon.
Standing Rigging	Shrouds, stays, and the like which support the mast or some other spar, and are permanently installed and not manipulated in the sailing of the vessel. Compare *Running Rigging*.
Stand Off and On, To	To sail away from and then toward something, usually while waiting.

Starboard	The right-hand side of a vessel, when one faces forward.
Starboard Tack	A vessel is on the starboard tack when the boom is to port, and the wind is coming over the starboard side of the vessel.
Station Pointer	A protractor with movable arms used for taking direct visual bearings of two or more objects. The boat's position is then ascertained by placing the station pointer directly on the chart.
Stay	A wire rope giving fore-and-aft support to a mast.
Stay, To	A vessel is said to stay when she goes about from one tack to the other by turning her head to the wind.
Staysail, Stays'l	A triangular fore-and-aft sail, usually set on a stay; "forestaysail" to the British.
Steerageway	A vessel has steerageway when she is moving through the water with sufficient speed to answer her helm.
Stem	The member to which the plank ends are secured at the fore end of a vessel.
Stern Board	When a vessel that has been in irons moves astern fast enough to answer her helm, so that she can be made to pay off on one tack or the other, she is said to make a stern board.
Sternpost	The member to which the plank ends are secured at the stern and on which the rudder is hung.
Stern Pulpit	A structure of tubing, similar to a pulpit but located in the stern of a boat, whose purpose is to prevent people from falling overboard; "pushpit" to the British.
Stern Sheets	The part of an open boat which lies abaft the aftermost rowing thwart.
Sternway	A boat is making sternway when she is going backward.
Stiff	A vessel is said to be stiff when she does not heel readily; the opposite of "crank" and "tender."
Stock	The bar of an anchor which passes through a hole in the shank and lies on a plane at right angles to the arms.
Stop	(1) One of the weak bindings of easily broken cotton put around a sail which is to be hoisted but not broken out immediately. At the proper time, one need only give a stout pull on the sheet to break the stops and put the sail into use. Also called a "sail stop."

(2) One of the strips of flat canvas, nylon, or Dacron used to secure furled sails to the spars; "sail tie" or "tier" to the British.

Stopper Knot A knot worked on the end of a rope to prevent it from unreeving through an eye, block, cringle, or the like.

Stopping Putty worked into a seam after caulking.

Stopwater A soft pine plug inserted in a hole drilled at a right angle through a scarf joint. The stopwater swells up and prevents water from passing along the joint.

Strake One of the skin planks of the hull of a vessel.

Strand One of the lengths of wire or yarn twisted together in rope making.

Stranded A rope is said to be stranded when one of its strands is broken.

Stretcher A crossbar in the bottom of a dinghy against which the oarsman braces his feet.

Strike Over, To To move a vessel off the cradle or slip on which she has been hauled up.

Stringer A longitudinal strengthening member secured on the inner side of the frames or timbers of a vessel.

Strip Planking A method of construction in which one plank is secured to another by vertical fastening and gluing. The resulting structure is strong and requires few frames, but has the disadvantage of being difficult to repair.

Strop An iron or rope band used for securing rigging or a block to a mast or spar.

Strum Box To the British, a kind of strainer on the end of a bilge-pump suction, used to prevent foreign matter from choking the pump.

Stud-Link Chain Chain in which each link has a crossbar to prevent the sides from pulling together.

Surge The lateral movement of a stationary vessel caused by a swell or by the wash of a passing ship.

Swashway A channel across or between shoals or spits.

Sweat Up, To To give an extra hard pull on a rope so as to eliminate every vestige of slack in it.

Sweep A long oar, of the kind used to propel lighters, barges, and small sailing vessels.

Sweep, To	To drag the bight of a wire or chain along the bottom to locate or recover a sunken object.
Swell	Long, easy waves, the crests of which do not break.
Swig, To	To tighten a rope by holding its fall around a cleat or pin while the standing part is hauled away from the mast, the slack then being taken up around the cleat or pin.
Swing, To	(1) To turn the head of a vessel to the points of the compass, one by one, when checking or adjusting the compass. (2) A vessel at anchor is said to swing when she turns at the change of the tide or the wind.
Tabernacle	The housing on deck for the heel and pivot of a lowering mast.
Tabling	A doubling of cloth on the three edges of a sail.
Tack	(1) The lower forward corner of a fore-and-aft sail. (2) A point of sailing as close to the wind as a vessel will go with advantage.
Tack, To	To beat or work to windward in a zigzag manner, close-hauled first on one tack, then on the other, putting the bow of the boat through the eye of the wind.
Tackle	A device consisting of two blocks with line reeved through each, used to increase mechanical advantage; also called a "purchase."
Tack Tackle	A purchase applied to the tack of a fore-and-aft sail to get its luff taut.
Taffrail	The rail across or around the stern.
Taffrail Log	See *Patent Log*.
Tail	A short rope attached to a block so that it can be temporarily secured to something.
Tail On, To	To clap on to a rope.
Tail Up, To	To pull on a line.
Take Charge, To	An inanimate object, such as a rope or a cable, is said to take charge when it gets out of control and runs out by its own momentum.
Take In, To	To lower, take in, or stow a sail.
Taken Aback	Surprised; a sailing vessel is said to be taken aback when the wind strikes her sails on the wrong side.

Take Off, To	The tides are said to be taking off when they decrease progressively, between the spring tide and the neap tide.
Take Up, To	(1) To make taut, as when one takes up the slack of a rope or nut. (2) To absorb, to swell; thus, when a dry boat is placed in the water her planking will gradually take up and become tight. (3) To buy, or acquire (in reference to supplies).
Tang	One of the metal fittings, screwed or bolted to a mast or spar, to which a vessel's rigging is attached.
Taut	Stretched tight.
Tender	(1) Easily heeled, somewhat crank; the opposite of "stiff." (2) Sometimes, a yacht's dinghy.
Terylene	The British equivalent of Dacron.
Thames Measurement	A "tonnage" formula, in general use in Great Britain. The formula is $\dfrac{(L - B) \times \frac{1}{2}B^2}{94}$, where B equals the extreme beam, and L equals the length between posts, i.e., the length between the stem and the sternpost at deck level. It is used by Lloyd's Underwriters in figuring premiums, to the great disadvantage of American boats, which usually are beamier than the British, as the Underwriters charge a certain amount of money per unit of Thames Measurement. Two boats can have the same displacement, i.e., weight, yet have a vastly different Thames tonnage measurement.
Thimble	A round or heart-shaped metal eye or ring, concave on its outer surface so that a rope may be taken around it and spliced or seized; the thimble protects the rope from chafe.
Throat	The upper forward corner of a gaff sail.
Thumb Cleat	A triangular piece of wood secured to a spar or spreader to keep some part of the rigging in place.
Thwart	An athwartship seat in a dinghy.
Tier	See *Stop*.
Tie Rod	A rod with a thread and nut, used, for example, to bind the carlin of a coach roof to the shelf so that the side deck cannot open and leak.
Tiller	A wooden or metal bar, secured to the rudderhead, by means of which a vessel is steered.

Timber	A rib which has been bent to shape instead of being sawn.
Toggle	A short piece of wood which can be passed through the eye in the end of a rope to hold it without making a bend and in such a way that it can be cast off quickly.
Tonnage	Gross tonnage and net tonnage have nothing to do with the actual weight of a boat—they are custom-house figures; compare *Displacement, Thames Measurement.*
Top, To; **Top Up, To**	To lift a boom into or above its normal sailing position.
Top Off, To	To fill to capacity; i.e., water or fuel tanks.
Topmast	The upper part of a mast; sometimes, a separate spar.
Topping Lift, **Top 'n' Lift**	A rope or wire used to support the after or outboard end of a boom while the sail is being set or doused, or to take the weight of the boom in a seaway.
Topsail, Tops'l	(1) A triangular fore-and-aft sail set above a gaff-headed sail. (2) A square sail set above a course.
Topsides	Those parts of a vessel's sides which are above water when she is afloat but not heeled.
Track Chart	A small-scale chart on which a vessel's positions are plotted during a long passage.
Transom	A type of stern consisting of planks bolted athwartships on the sternpost to receive the after ends of the skin planks.
Traveler	A span across the deck which allows a block or carriage to slide from side to side; it may be made of wire, rope, or flat, heavy sail track, and is now available in the form of an X-shaped track with roller-bearing slides.
Treenail	A wooden peg split and wedged in place, formerly used instead of a rivet, nail, or screw; also called a "trunnel."
Trestletree	One of the pieces of wood on a mast which serve to support the heel of a topmast.
Triatic Stay	A wire rope connecting the mastheads of a schooner or a ketch.
Trim	The angle made with the water by the fore-and-aft line of a vessel, when she is afloat.

Trim, To	To adjust the helm, centerboard, leeboards, or sails; to sheet a sail so that it draws to the best advantage.
Trim Tab	A small adjustable portion of the trailing edge of either the rudder or the keel. When located on the rudder, it makes possible control of the total movement of the rudder with very little effort. When located on the keel, it serves mainly to give lift to the keel and to increase windward performance, but it may also be used to minimize weather helm.
Trough	A valley between two seas.
Truck	A wooden cap at the masthead or topmast head which has holes or a sheave for the burgee halyard.
Trunnel	See *Treenail.*
Trysail, Trys'l	A small sail of heavy Dacron sometimes set in place of the mainsail in heavy weather.
Tufnol	A material consisting of plastic reinforced with linen or paper, often preferred for blocks intended for nautical use; it has the great advantage of being lubricated by water.
Tumble Home	The inward curve that the sides of some vessels have above the load waterline.
Turnbuckle	A fitting with threaded ends screwing into a common body, used for setting up the rigging; "rigging screw" to the British.
Turn to Windward, To	To beat, tack, or work to windward, steering a zigzag course.
Turn Up, To	To make fast a rope on a cleat or pin.
Unbend, To	To remove a sail from its spars and other gear.
Under Bare Poles	Under way, but with no sail set.
Underrun, To	To weigh a kedge by hauling the dinghy along the warp (which slides in the sculling hole) until the dinghy is directly over the kedge.
Under Way	A vessel is said to be under way when she is moving over the ground or through the water.
Unreeve, To	To pull a rope out of a block, sheave, eye, or the like.
Unship, To	To remove something from its proper working position.
Up and Down	An anchor cable is said to be up and down when it has been hauled in until it is vertical and any further hauling will break out the anchor.

Up Helm, To	To put the helm to windward so as to make a vessel bear away.
Vang	A rope generally used to flatten a sail; with it, the main boom is hauled down and forward to take the twist out of the mainsail, or down and aft from the gaff end to take the twist out of the mainsail with respect to the gaff sail. To the British, the boom vang is a "kicking strap."
Variation	The difference between true and magnetic north at a particular place.
Veer, To	(1) To pay out anchor cable. (2) The wind is said to veer when it changes its direction in the same way as the sun moves—clockwise.
Wake	The path of disturbed water left astern of a moving vessel.
Warp	A strong rope attached to an anchor or dock. See also *Kedge Warp.*
Warp, To	To move a boat by hauling on a long line secured to a fixed object, such as an anchor or dock.
Waterline	One of the horizontal sections of a vessel's hull at and below the load waterline, seen as curves on the half-breadth plan.
Way	The movement of a vessel through the water.
Wear, To	The act of putting a vessel about onto the other tack by turning her away from the wind and jibing instead of staying.
Weather, To	A vessel is said to weather something when she is able to pass to windward of it without tacking.
Weather Cloth	See *Dodger.*
Weather Helm	A vessel is said to have a weather helm when she has a tendency to turn her bow into the wind, and the helm has to be kept to windward to prevent her from doing so.
Weatherly	Said of a vessel which is capable of sailing close to the wind.
Weather Shore	A shore to windward of a vessel; therefore, one which offers shelter.
Weather Side	See *Windward.*
Weigh, To	To raise the anchor from the bottom.
Well	See *Pump Well.*

Whip	A purchase in which only one block is used.
Whip, To	To bind the end of a rope with twine to prevent it from unlaying.
Whisker	One of the struts from the bows, which spread the bowsprit shrouds.
Whisker Stay	One of the stays supporting the bowsprit in the horizontal plane.
Wildcat	See *Gypsy*.
Winch	A mechanical appliance consisting of a drum on an axle, a pawl, and a crank handle with or without gearing, used to obtain increased power when hauling on a rope.
Windlass	A type of winch which has a horizontal drum and is fitted with a gypsy, for handling chain cable.
Windsail, Wind Scoop	A ventilation trunk of canvas slung from aloft with its mouth set to catch the wind and its foot led below to the space to be ventilated; also called a "galley staysail."
Windward, Windward Side	The side of the boat closest to the wind, i.e., always the opposite side of the boat from the main boom; also called "weather side."
Wire Rope Clamp	See *Bulldog Grip*.
Wishbone	A spar in two halves like a wishbone, between which a sail is hoisted, its clew sheeted to the outer end of the wishbone.
Working Anchor	See *Bower*.
Working Sails	Sails normally used when cruising, in contrast to racing or light sails, such as the genoa.
Worm, To	To fill in the contlines of a rope with small line or yarn before parceling and serving.
Yankee, Yankee Jib	To the British, a large, high-cut triangular headsail, used in light or moderate winds and set on the topmast stay, overlapping the mast only slightly. Unlike a genoa, it does not fill the whole fore-triangle, but is set in combination with the working or reaching staysail. Also, on a modern boat, a masthead jib, cut high in the clew, usually hoisted over a large overlapping staysail; referred to by most Americans as the No. 1 jib topsail.
Yard	A spar to which a topsail or square sail is bent.

Yarn

Fibers which are twisted together to form a strand of a rope.

Yaw, To

To wobble about on either side of the intended course. A good helmsman will prevent unnecessary yawing with minimum movement of the helm in good time, instead of waiting until the yaw has developed and heavy movement of the helm becomes necessary.

Yawl

A two-masted boat with the mizzenmast aft of the after end of the waterline (the position of the helm is irrelevant).

Yawl Boat

A small boat with an engine, used to propel a larger vessel which has no power of her own.

TOOLS AND SPARES

First of all, it is absolutely essential that the boat carry the manual for every piece of equipment on board. These manuals should be carefully filed away, so that when an item needs to be repaired the manual can be found readily and the repairs carried out correctly.

TOOLS

Hull

A small vise is essential; a large vise is very useful. The large vise should be bolted to a piece of one-inch plywood long enough to reach across the companionway hatch; then the whole unit can be clamped into place with wood clamps when heavy work is to be done.

Claw hammer; ball peen hammer; tack hammer.

Crosscut saw; small backsaw; hacksaw; keyhole saw with various blades.

Mallet.

Chisels, four sizes.

Six-foot tape.

Small plane; large plane.

Small square, with adjustable bevel.

Whetstone.

Brace.

Four sizes of screwdriver bits; wood bits in ¼″, 5⁄16″, 3⁄8″, 7⁄16″, ½″, 5⁄8″, 1″ sizes; expansion bit.

High-speed drills in 1⁄16″ through 3⁄8″ sizes; flat high-speed wood bits in ¼″ through 1″ sizes.

Small eggbeater drill; large two-speed eggbeater drill.

Set of all-in-one countersinks for wood screws.

Plug cutters in 3⁄8″, ½″, 5⁄8″, ¾″ sizes.

End cutters.

Screwdrivers, short, long, fine, stubby, and so on.

Caulking irons, three sizes.

Wood rasps, flat, round, and oval.

Grinding stones, small hand-powered on most boats, electric on larger boats.

Electric drill. The standard ¼″ drill is generally too small. The 3⁄8″ drill, though it costs a little more, is preferable, as it is much more powerful. The ½″ drill is good for some uses but too large and cumbersome for most; hence it is valuable as a backup for the smaller drill, but should not be selected as the only one. A 12-volt drill which can be powered from the ship's supply is excellent; it is available by mail from Foulkes, in England. A cordless drill too is excellent, but expensive; also, it is difficult to charge from the ship's supply, and impossible to charge in areas using 220-volt single-phase current, which is found extensively outside the United States. A 110-volt drill is cheap, and on a ship with a 12-volt system, the power can be stepped up by means of an inverter. However, the capacity of the inverter should be checked against the amperage needed by the drill under load. Further, if going abroad, one should be sure to purchase a transformer capable of converting from other voltages to 110. European 220-volt equipment needs a transformer if it is to be used with United States 110-volt equipment.

Saber saw. A small saber saw is useful; the comments about choice of an electric drill, above, apply to the saber saw as well.

Rigging

Special tools, as needed, to dismantle the winches.

For rigging wire up to 5⁄16″, Nicopress. The small tool sold by S and F Tool Company is satisfactory. Or if it is not too expensive, one of the bolt-cutter types can be carried; these can sometimes be found with jaws for three or four different sizes of Nicopress. Also available are Nicopress jaws to be used with a standard bolt cutter.

For rigging wire above 5⁄16″, hot sockets or Norseman or Sta-Lok fittings.

Splicing vise. For 7 by 19 wire up to ¼″ in diameter, the best splicing vise I know of is the one made by Herman Melin, formerly head rigger at Ratsey and Lapthorn. For 1 by 19 wire, the best splicing vise available is made by Durko Marine (formerly Durkee).

Hollow fid, small, for tail splices.

Again the best I know of is the one made by Herman Melin and available through Ratsey and Lapthorn.

Wire spikes (marlinspikes). There is a lot more than meets the eye to a spike. The flat-tipped spike is much better than the round type, as once it is spliced between the strands of wire it may be rotated ninety degrees, allowing room for wire to be passed through alongside the vertical spike. Excellent flat-tipped spikes of various sizes can be obtained from Topping Brothers. Herman Melin also makes special spikes for splicing small wire.

Block of lead, for smoothing wire splices.

Serving mallet. If a hole is drilled diagonally through the handle and the ball of marlin is placed over the handle, the marlin can be fed through the hole from the center of the ball; thus one person can serve, without needing a second person to pass the ball of marlin.

A cold chisel and a piece of bronze, for cutting wire. (Cutting the wire on a piece of bronze protects the edge of the chisel.)

Cable cutters of adequate size. These should be tested in advance on the largest-diameter wire to be carried aboard, since the manufacturers' estimates of their capacity tend to be optimistic.

Sails

Palms, the number depending on the size of the boat. Two kinds, seaming palms and roping palms, should be carried. Normally, all palms are right-handed, though once in a while a left-handed one can be found. Most smart left-handed people carry their own palms.

Needles, various sizes, from the smallest (No. 21) up through the large ones. The exact sizes and quantities desirable will depend on the size of the boat; in any event, large supplies of small needles should be carried, as they are easily broken. A good method of stowing needles is to place them in a baby-food jar with coffee grounds; the coffee grounds absorb the dampness and keep the needles shining.

Bench hook.

Wooden fid, big enough to make the largest cringle on board the yacht. Making a cringle without a big fid is almost impossible. A small wooden fid is also useful.

Hollow fids, small, for line ½″ or less in diameter; large, for line above ½″ in diameter, up to the largest anchor rode carried.

Hollow tube for splicing braided line. This can be made from aluminum tubing, with a removable wooden plug at one end.

Sewing machine. A hand-powered machine will go through two layers of 8-ounce Dacron. It can be stowed in the ballast box of a gimbaled table. A boat 50 feet LOA, or longer, should carry a regular heavy-duty sewing machine on any long cruise. The machine and its table may be disassembled and packed in a box.

Plumbing

Tubing cutters.
Flaring tools.
Pipe wrenches, various sizes.

Electricity

Wire cutters.
Wire strippers.
Small screwdrivers.
Meter for checking out the electrical system.
Soldering attachment for the gas torch, or 12-volt electric soldering iron that will work off the electrical system (see Sources of Supply).

Mechanical Equipment

The largest set of mechanic's tools that one can afford should be purchased. Sometimes they can be obtained on sale at a place like Sears, Roebuck or Montgomery Ward.

Files, round, flat, square, rattail.
A set of taps and dies in sizes to ½″.
Impact wrench.
A set of "easy outs."
Adjustable open-end wrench, large enough to fit on stern gland and rudder-post stuffing box. On some boats, two may be necessary.
Pipe wrenches, one small, one 8″.
Slip-joint pliers; vise-grip pliers.

Bottled-gas torch with various tips; the type that can be attached to a cooking-gas bottle is preferable.

GASOLINE ENGINE

A check should be made as to whether any special tools are needed for the particular engine. For example, the boat with a valve-in-head engine should carry a valve lifter, since this tool is difficult to locate now that the overhead-valve engine has become popular.

Tappet wrenches, as many as are needed to adjust the valves. Some engines require the use of three tappet wrenches at the same time.

Ignition wrenches, to adjust the points.

Small wrenches and screwdrivers to dismantle the carburetor.

Feeler gauge.

Valve-grinding tool and compound.

DIESEL ENGINE

Wrenches to dismantle the fuel system. Spares should be carried as well, since all too often a wrench slips and is lost in the bilge, and it is then impossible to bleed the system.

Large magnet to retrieve tools dropped in the bilge.

SPARES

Hull

WOOD

Sheets of plywood, cut to fit under the bunks.

Two-by-fours and one-by-sixes, stowed wherever possible.

Lead sheeting and bedding compound. Lead sheeting is hard to find, but very useful on a wooden boat, since it can be cut up into strips, placed over the bedding compound, and nailed down, to seal a leaking seam. Without the aid of an aqualung, his breathing assisted only by a snorkel, Jim Crawford repaired *Dirigo II* in this fashion, and she was then able to sail from the Galápagos to Tahiti in record time.

Underwater epoxy patching compound.

ALUMINUM AND STEEL

For the hull itself nothing much can be carried in the way of spares. Most repairs will have to be done with quick-drying cement, epoxy, fiber glass, or the like; underwater epoxy is especially useful.

For aluminum hulls, a large supply of the correct type of welding rod.

FIBER GLASS

Mat.

Cloth.

Resin.

Underwater epoxy.

GENERAL REPAIRS

All boats should carry as generous a supply as possible of the following items:

Tapered wooden bungs, preferably with a coarse spiral thread, in various sizes to fit all through-hull fittings.

Bolts.

Bronze rods.

Nuts of various sizes.

Wood screws.

Self-tapping metal screws.

Galvanized nails, not very pretty but sometimes very useful in an emergency.

Rigging

Turnbuckles.

Toggles.

Thimbles.

Split pins; clevis pins.

Serving wire.

Shackles; snap shackles.

Blocks.

Spreader, usable as either upper or lower spreader if the boat is double-spreader-rigged.

Wire. At least one length of wire longer than the longest stay, with a fitting already in place at one end, and a spare Norseman fitting for the lower end. The boat's rigging book should give the exact length of each stay, so that the replacement can be made up on deck as necessary and then sent aloft.

End fittings of the type being used, along with the materials and tools necessary to install them.

Halyard, made up ready to go.

Plenty of line. For a long cruise, six-hundred-foot coils of various sizes of line should be bought from one of the discount houses, such as Defender Industries. Coiled down carefully, an amazing amount of line can be carried on a boat.

Winch springs; bronze wire for making springs.

Ratchets and pawls for all winches.

Roller-reefing handles; winch handles.

Steel tape, fifty or a hundred feet, depending on the size of the boat.

Sails

Rip-stop tape.

Cloth of various weights, the quantity depending upon the size of the boat and length of the cruise.

Leather—rawhide, elk, or the like—for chafing patches for the sails.

Sail twine; big balls of waxed nylon and Dacron; Dacron thread for the sewing machine.

Sailcloth, various weights.

Jib snaps.

Sail slides; shackles to secure slides to sails; plastic chafing patches to place between the shackles and the sails.

Toothed grommets (No. 3, standard); grommet tool.

Cringles of stainless steel or bronze, various sizes; Italian hemp, for making cringles.

Thimbles and the like, as needed for the boat's particular sails; the Howe and Bainbridge catalog should prove useful.

Commonsense fasteners, and tool for placing fasteners in dodgers.

Deck

Emergency shutters, or material to make shutters, for use if the cabin or doghouse windows are damaged, should be carried by all boats, no matter what material they are made of.

Plumbing

Complete parts for all pumps and heads.

Hoses, various sizes.

Hose clamps—stainless steel, not cadmium-plated.

Nipples.

Adapters.

Reducers.

Pipe fittings, various sizes.

Valves and/or stopcocks.

Tufnol tape.

Permatex.

Electricity

Wire.

Fuses.

Circuit breakers.

Junction boxes.

Bulbs; running-light glasses.

Gaskets, or material for making gaskets.

Electrical tape.

Silicone sealant.

Solder.

Rosin.

Fine sandpaper and emery paper for cleaning contacts.

Crimp-on fittings and tools.

Battery lugs.

Hydrometer.

Distilled water.

Brushes for starter motor and generator.

Diodes for alternator.

Complete starter, essential.

Complete generator, if possible.

Voltage regulator.

Mechanical Equipment

GASOLINE ENGINE

Complete gasket set.

Half set of valves.

Set of rods.

Set of main bearings.

Carburetor rebuilding kit.

Points.

Distributor cap and rotor.

High-tension leads.

Coil.

Condenser.

Water pump and spare belts.

Filters.

Gasket cement; O rings of various sizes.

Penetrating oil; light oil; engine oil; grease; CRC or equivalent.

Spray to protect the electrical system.

Spark plugs.

Set of piston rings.

Starter motor, complete.

DIESEL ENGINE

Gasket set.

Set of valves.

Set of rods.
Set of main bearings.
Set of piston rings.
At least two injectors.
Set of injector lines, if the engine is not absolutely new.
Fuel injector pump, if it can be afforded.
Filters.
Belts.
Water-pump impellers.

Gasket cement; O rings.
Penetrating oil; grease; CRC or equivalent.
Starter motor, complete.

AUXILIARY GENERATOR

Same as above, along with the necessary electrical parts—brushes, diodes, bearings, and so on, as advised by a good mechanic.

SOURCES OF SUPPLY

Publications

GENERAL INFORMATION

Boat Owners Buyers Guide
Yachting Publishing Corp.
50 W. 44th St.
New York, N.Y. 10036
    (*issued annually*)

The Mariner's Catalog
International Marine Publishing Co.
21 Elm St.
Camden, Me. 04843
    (*a listing of available books—among them practical manuals—on marine subjects*)

Sailboat and Equipment Directory
38 Commercial Wharf
Boston, Mass. 02110
    (*issued annually*)

PERIODICALS

Boating (Dick Rath)
1 Park Ave.
New York, N.Y. 10016

Cruising World (Murray Davis)
Thames St.
Newport, R.I. 20840
    (*a cruising man's magazine*)

Gear Test
Kenneth Mason Publications
13–14 Homewell
Havant
Hants PO9 1EF, England

Motor Boating and Sailing (Jeff Hammond)
224 W. 57th St.
New York, N.Y. 10019

National Fisherman
21 Elm St.
Camden, Me. 04843

Sail (Keith Taylor)
38 Commercial Wharf
Boston, Mass. 02110
    (*a sailors' magazine, with no space wasted discussing powerboats or fishing*)

The Telltale Compass (Victor Jorgensen)
18418 South Old River Dr.
Lake Oswego, Oreg. 97034
    (*newsletter, with no advertising—the only publication that can "tell it as it is"; a must for the serious yachtsman; publishes many of my articles that all other yachting magazines feel are too hot to handle*)

WoodenBoat (Jonathan Wilson)
P.O. Box 78
Brooklin, Me. 04616
    (*an absolute must for the yachtsman who likes wooden boats*)

Yachting (William Robinson)
50 W. 44th St.
New York, N.Y. 10036

Yachting Monthly (Des Sleightholme)
Kings Reach Tower
Stamford St.
London S.E.1 9LX, England
    (*a real cruising man's magazine*)

Yachting World (Bernard Hayman)
Dorset House
Stamford St.
London S.W.1, England

Marine Equipment (General)

Alexander-Roberts Co.
1851 Langley Ave.
Irvine, Calif. 92714

Brookstone Co.
127 Vose Farm Rd.
Peterborough, N.H. 03458
(603) 924-7181
(hard-to-find tools)

Camper and Nicholsons
Southampton, England
(discount house)

M. S. Gibbs
Warsash
Southampton 503 6ZG, England

Lewmar Marine
Southmoor Lane
Havant
Hants PO9 1JJ, England

London Yachting Centre
9 Devonshire Row
London E.C.2M 4RL, England

Manhattan Marine and Electric Co.
116 Chambers St.
New York, N.Y. 10007

Merriman Holbrook
301 Olive St.
Grand River, Ohio 44045

Nicro/Fico
2065 West Ave. 140th
San Leandro, Calif. 94577

Schaefer Marine Products
2 Industrial Park
New Bedford, Mass. 02745

Seaboard and Star Hardware
New Whitfield St.
Guilford, Conn. 06437

Seaway Supply Co.
4201 Redwood Ave.
Los Angeles, Calif. 90066

Simpson Lawrence
St. Andrews Square
Glasgow, Scotland

South Western Marine Factors
43 Pottery Rd.
Poole
Dorset, England

Taselaar B.V.
Lindtsedijk 76
Zwijndrecht, Holland

Wilcox-Crittenden
699 Middle St.
Middletown, Conn. 06457
(203) 347-9441

Yacht Tests
22 High St.
Burnham on Crouch
Essex, England

MAIL-ORDER SUPPLY

James Bliss Marine
Rte. 128
Dedham, Mass. 02026

Defender Industries
255 Main St.
New Rochelle, N.Y. 10801
(discount house)

Thomas Foulkes
Lansdowne Rd.
Leytonstone
London E.11 3HB, England
(ships anywhere in the world;
American yachtsmen can realize un-
believable savings on British equip-
ment ordered direct from Foulkes)

Goldbergs' Marine Distributors
202 Market St.
Philadelphia, Pa. 19106

Jay Stuart Haft
8925 N. Tennyson Dr.
Milwaukee, Wis. 53217
(414) 352-7551

Manhattan Marine and Electric Co.
116 Chambers St.
New York, N.Y. 10007

Oyster Bay Boat Shop
2 South St.
Oyster Bay, N.Y. 11771

Hull Construction and Maintenance

TOOLS

Brookstone Co.
127 Vose Farm Rd.
Peterborough, N.H. 03458
(603) 924-7181

John Stortz and Son
210 Vine St.
Philadelphia, Pa. 19106

Woodcraft Supply Corp.
313 Montvale Ave.
Woburn, Mass. 01801

FASTENINGS

Clendenin Brothers
4309 Erdman Ave.
Baltimore, Md. 21213
  (*copper nails and burs*)

T. E. Conklin Brass and Copper Co.
324 W. 23rd St.
New York, N.Y. 10011
  (*one of the largest suppliers of brass
  and bronze in the marine industry*)

Termont Nail Co.
P.O. Box 111
Wareham, Mass. 02571

EPOXY GLUE

Canadian Multihull Services
Hangar 2
Toronto Island Airport
Toronto, M5U 1A1
Ontario, Canada

Chem-Tech
4481 Greenwold Rd.
Cleveland, Ohio 44121

Gougeon Brothers
706 Martin St.
Bay City, Mich. 48706

UNDERWATER PATCHING COMPOUND

Berger Paint Co.
Port of Spain
Trinidad, W.I.
  (*Navicoat*)

Pettit Paint Co.
36 Pine St.
Rockaway, N.J. 07866
(201) 625-3100

KEEL-BOLT X-RAYING

X-Ray Marine Ltd.
175 Piccadilly
London, England
01-496-5786

Steering Systems

Don Allen Inc.
1427 S. Pacific Ave.
San Pedro, Calif. 90731

Canpa Yacht Equipment
Mumby Rd.
Gosport
Hants, England

Edson
473 Industrial Park Rd.
New Bedford, Mass. 02745

Yacht Specialties Co.
1555 E. St. Gertrude Pl.
Santa Ana, Calif. 92705

Spars

WOODEN SPARS

I Brasker
Masten Makerij
Langeraar, Holland
01 722 2425

Van der Nuit
Alphew 91 DR IN
Energigweg, Holland
01 720 95951

  (*Both of the preceding make wooden
  spars unbelievably cheaply and
  quickly, in all sizes up to 160 feet
  long.*)

ALUMINUM SPARS

Famet Marine
745 2nd Ave.
Redwood City, Calif. 94063

Hood Yacht Systems
Shetland Pk.
Salem, Mass. 01970

Palmer Johnson
61 Michigan St.
Sturgeon Bay, Wis. 54235

LeFiell Marine Products
13700 Firestone Blvd.
Santa Fe Springs, Calif. 90670
  (*do-it-yourself kits; one of the few
  makers to supply bits and pieces,
  allowing the competent yachtsman
  to assemble his own spar, at a considerable saving*)

Metalmast Marine
137 Providence St.
Putnam, Conn. 06260
(203) 928-2776

Ian Proctor Metal Masts
Duncan Rd.
Swanwick
Southampton, England

Schaefer Marine Products
2 Industrial Park
New Bedford, Mass. 02745

Sheerline Spars
Alexander-Roberts Co.
1851 Langley Ave.
Irvine, Calif. 92714
  (*Sheerline—a new concept, spars
  built of interlocking components,
  without welding; an Australian
  development*)

Sound Spars
29 Sagamore Hill Dr.
Port Washington, N.Y. 11050
(516) 883-3550

Sparcraft
P.O. Box 925
Costa Mesa, Calif. 92627

Sparlight
Southbourne near Emsworth
Hants PO1 08PG, England

Super Spar
15678 Graham St.
Huntington Beach, Calif. 92649

Zephyr Products
Wareham, Mass. 02571

Fiber-Glass Spars

Ocean Boats Ltd.
HAVSBATAR AB
Tulkavagen 76
S-763 00 Hallstavik, Sweden

Rigging

Riggers

MacDonald Yacht Rigging
Yacht Haven West
Stamford, Conn. 06902
  (*for many years justifiably referred
  to as "Riggers to the 12's"*)

Oyster Bay Boat Shop
2 South St.
Oyster Bay, N.Y. 11771

St. Margaret's Rigging
Wilmington, Del.
  (*specialists in old-fashioned classic
  rigging, but also do modern rigging*)

Spencer Rigging
Cowes
Isle of Wight, England
  (*justifiably referred to as "Rigger to
  the World"*)

Rigging Materials

Bridon Caribbean
G.P.O. Box 1093
San Juan, Puerto Rico 00936

Hackensack Cable
110 Orchard St.
Hackensack, N.J. 07602

C. Sherman Johnson
Norwich Rd., Rte. 82
East Haddam, Conn. 06423
(203) 873-8697
  (*Castlok terminals*)

Leeward Rigging
Bentley
Ipswich 1P9 2LT, England
  (*Sta-Lok—similar to Norseman but
  easier to use*)

Loos and Co.
370 Cable Rd.
Pomfret, Conn. 06258
  (*wire, terminal fittings, and cable
  cutters*)

Macwhyte Wire Rope
2906 14th Ave.
Kenosha, Wis. 53140
(414) 654-5381

Norseman Ropes
Bridge Rd.
Sarisbury Green
Southampton SO3 7EH, England
  (*Norseman terminal fittings*)

S and F Tool Co.
Box 1546
Costa Mesa, Calif. 92626
  (*Nicopress sleeves and tools*)

Testing Liquid

Magnaflux Corp.
7300 W. Lawrence Ave.
Chicago, Ill. 60656
  (*Spotcheck Type SK 3*)

Wooden Blocks

A. Dauphine and Sons
Lunenburg, Nova Scotia

Sailors Art
1313 East Pacific Coast Highway
Wilmington, Calif. 90744

Traditional Yacht Hardware
Box 233
Brunswick, Me. 04011

Troy Brothers Marine Gear
P.O. Box 71
239 Seal Beach Blvd.
Seal Beach, Calif. 90740

Shackles (see also *Marine
Equipment, General*)

Wichard France
BP 139
Thiers 63300
France
(73) 80 1623
(*drop-forged captive pin shackle*)

TOOLS

Beaver Tool and Machine Co.
P.O. Box 94717
540 S.E. 29th St.
Oklahoma City, Okla. 73109
(405) 634-4148
(*splicing vise*)

Durko Marine (formerly Durkee)
610 Commercial Ave.
Garden City, N.Y. 11530
(*splicing vises*)

Ratsey and Lapthorn
E. Schofield St.
City Island
Bronx, N.Y. 10464
fids)
(*small splicing vises, small hollow*

Topping Brothers
4405 S. Clinton Ave.
Plainfield, N.J. 07080
(*marlinspikes*)

WINCHES

Abeking and Rasmussen
Lemwerder, Germany

Barient Co.
936 Bransten Rd.
San Carlos, Calif. 94070

Barlow
102 Seymour Pl.
London W.1H 5DG, England

Camper and Nicholsons
Southampton, England

Enkes
P.O. Box 328, 7 Hawkes St.
Marblehead, Mass. 01945

M. S. Gibbs
Warsash
Southampton 503 6ZG, England

Lewmar Marine
Southmoor Lane
Havant
Hants PO9 1JJ, England

Paul E. Luke
East Boothbay, Me. 04544
(207) 633-4971

Merriman Holbrook
301 Olive St.
Grand River, Ohio 44045

Taselaar B.V.
Lindtsedijk 76
Zwijndrecht, Holland

Sail-Making Materials

Adix Manufacturing Co.
381 Park Ave. S.
New York, N.Y. 10016
(*Vivatex*)

Aquino Sailcloth
225 Fordham St.
City Island
Bronx, N.Y. 10464

The Astrup Co.
2937 W. 25th St.
Cleveland, Ohio 44113
(216) 696-2800

Howe and Bainbridge
220 Commercial St.
Boston, Mass. 02109
(*all sail-making supplies: sailcloth, battens, cringles, grommets, zippers, and so on*)

SEA-GOING SEWING MACHINE

J. J. & J. Read
327 Shirley Rd.
Southampton, England

Deck Layout

HERRESHOFF CLEATS (see also *Marine Equipment, General*)

Wilcox-Crittenden
699 Middle St.
Middletown, Conn. 06457
(203) 347-9441

YS Fittings
Queens St., Industrial Estate
Queens Drive, Charlestown
Walsall W77 8QF, England

BOARDING LADDERS

Detroit Marine Engineering
2001 W. Alexandrine
Detroit, Mich. 48208
(*boarding ladder that folds up like an accordion in minimum space*)

Anchors and Anchoring

ANCHORS

C. E. Beckman Co.
35 Commercial St.

New Bedford, Mass. 02741
(*Herreshoff type*)

Danforth Division, The Eastern Co.
500 Riverside Industrial Pkwy.
Portland, Me. 04103

Jay Stuart Haft
8925 N. Tennyson Dr.
Milwaukee, Wis. 53217
(414) 352-7551
(*U.S. distributor for Simpson
Lawrence*)

Paul E. Luke
East Boothbay, Me. 04544
(207) 633-4971
(*Herreshoff three-piece, true copy;
the best anchor in the world*)

WINDLASSES

Jay Stuart Haft
8925 N. Tennyson Dr.
Milwaukee, Wis. 53217
(414) 352-7551
(*U.S. distributor for Simpson
Lawrence*)

Ideal Windlass Co.
5810 Post Rd.
East Greenwich, R.I. 02818
(*electric windlass*)

Lunenburg Foundry
Lunenburg, Nova Scotia

PNP Marine
Burnham on Crouch
Essex, England
(*small hydraulic windlass, suitable
for forty-foot boat*)

Seagull Marine
1851 McGaw Ave.
Irvine, Calif. 92714
(*Simpson Lawrence large hydraulic
windlass, suitable for boats of sixty-
five feet and over*)

Dinghies

BUILDERS

The Anchorage
61 Miller St.
Warren, R.I. 02885
(401) 245-3300
(*Dyer Dhow, the yachtsman's old
favorite*)

Graves Yacht Yard
Marblehead, Mass. 01945
(*10-foot fiber-glass pulling boat*)

Jarvis Newman
Southwest Harbor, Me. 04679
(*fiber-glass 11-foot 9-inch pulling
boat*)

Parker River Marine
Rte. 1A at Parker River
Newbury, Mass. 01950
(*fiber-glass Whitehall-type pulling
boat*)

Salt Marine
931 S.W. 22nd St.
Fort Lauderdale, Fla. 33315
(*lapstrake 14-foot Whitehall boat*)

Note: Good wooden lapstrake dinghies
can still be built to order, at a cost—
at this writing—of about $30–$35 per
foot in England and Ireland, and about
$75–$100 per foot in the United States.
The names of builders in England and
Ireland can be obtained from the
author (who can be reached at
Glandore, County Cork, Ireland), and
the names of builders in the United
States can be obtained from *Wooden-
Boat* (P.O. Box 78, Brooklin, Me.
04616).

TWO-PIECE DINGHIES

Beacon Boats
P.O. Box 15
Alton
Hampshire, England
(*United Kingdom agent for the
Yacht Werf Zuidersee twin dory
listed below*)

Paul Johnson
Yacht *Venus*
St. Georges, Bermuda
(*16-foot 6-inch double-ended sailing
dinghy, of fiber glass and foam plank,
that separates into two sections*)

Yacht Werf Zuidersee D.V.
Julianaweg 145
Volendam, Holland
(*V-bottomed sailing/rowing dory
which comes apart, in two pieces;
very favorably reviewed by Brian
Cooper in* Yachting World)

CLIP-ON SAIL

Outboard Sail
P.O. Box 1064, Station Q
Toronto, Ontario, Canada
(*Sail and rudder clamp on transom*

like an outboard; even Jack Knights says it works.)

Accommodation

ANTI-NIGHT-BLINDNESS LIGHT

REC Specialties
15155 Stagg St.
Van Nuys, Calif. 91405
(213) 782-1203

VENTILATORS

Abeking and Rasmussen
Lemwerder, Germany

Manhattan Marine and Electric Co.
116 Chambers St.
New York, N.Y. 10007

Moyle Marine Products
Afco Works
73 Walton Rd.
Woking
Surrey, England

Nicro/Fico
2065 West Ave. 140th
San Leandro, Calif. 94577

HATCHES

Goiot
809 Aquidneck Ave.
Middletown, R.I. 02840
(401) 846-5442
(*the only hatch on the market which can be opened either fore or aft from belowdecks*)

PORTLIGHTS

Alexander-Roberts Co.
1851 Langley Ave.
Irvine, Calif. 92714

W. H. Denouden Inc.
Box 8712
Baltimore, Md. 21240

Gray Enterprises
P.O. Box 8236
Tampa, Fla. 33604
(813) 885-2182
(*Rainguard, can be left open in the rain*)

PYHI
25028 S. Vermont Ave.
Harbor City, Calif. 90710

Wilcox-Crittenden
699 Middle St.
Middletown, Conn. 06457
(203) 347-9441

KEROSENE LAMPS (ALADDIN)

Faire Harbour Boats
44 Captain Pierce Rd.
Scituate, Mass. 02066

Jay Stuart Haft
8925 N. Tennyson Dr.
Milwaukee, Wis. 53217
(414) 352-7551

Washington Stove Works
P.O. Box 687
Everett, Wash. 98201

Galley

STOVES

Fatsco
251 N. Fair Ave.
Benton Harbor, Mich. 49022

Kenyon Marine
P.O. Box 308
Guilford, Conn. 06437

Paul E. Luke
East Boothbay, Me. 04544
(207) 633-4971
(*among the best gas and alcohol stoves in the world*)

Shipmate Stove Division
Richmond Ring Co.
Richmond Rd.
Souderton, Pa. 18964

Taylor's Para-Fin
East-West Moorings
Fullbridge
Maldon, Essex CM9 7XH, England
(*among the best kerosene stoves in the world*)

GAS BOTTLES

Worthington Cylinders
P.O. Box 29008
Columbus, Ohio 43229
(*aluminum cylinders*)

GAS-BOTTLE SHUTOFF VALVE

Marinetics Corp.
P.O. Box 2676
Newport Beach, Calif. 92663
(714) 646-8889

GAS DETECTOR

D. A. E. Holbrook
28 The Spain
Petersfield
Hants, England

TABLEWARE

Yachting Tableware Co.
P.O. Box 546
Wilmington, Del. 19899
(*nonskid plates, cups, and bowls—
considered essential on any yacht*)

FREEZE-DRIED VEGETABLES

Batchelors Foods
Cabra W7
Dublin, Republic of Ireland

Erin Foods
Earlsfort Terrace 2
Dublin, Republic of Ireland

(*The vegetables supplied by both of
the preceding are cheap, last indefinitely, and taste better than frozen.*)

Plumbing

HEADS, VALVES, SEA COCKS

Apollo Ball Valve Division
Consolidated Valve Industries
P.O. Box 125
Pageland, S.C. 29728
(*flanged ball cock, vastly superior to
cove stopcock or gate valve*)

Blake and Sons
Park Rd.
Gosport
Hants, England

Buck-Algonquin
Second St. and Columbus Ave.
Philadelphia, Pa. 19122

Gross Mechanical Labs
1530 Russell St.
Baltimore, Md. 21230

Wilcox-Crittenden
699 Middle St.
Middletown, Conn. 06457
(203) 347-9441

PUMPS

Dart Union Co., Marine Division
134 Thurbers Ave.
Providence, R.I. 02905
(*Guzzler pump*)

Edson
473 Industrial Park Rd.
New Bedford, Mass. 02745
(*diaphragm pump, one of the best
big pumps in the world*)

Henderson Pumps and Equipment
38 Medina Rd.

Cowes
Isle of Wight, England

Jack Holt
The Embankment
Putney
London S.W.15, England
(*rubber hose pump, Wykeham
Martin type*)

ITT Jabsco Products
1485 Dale Way
Costa Mesa, Calif. 92626
(*PAR water systems*)

Munster Simms Engineering
Imperial House
Donegall Sq. E.
Belfast, N. Ireland
(*Whale diaphragm pump*)

RUBBER DRINKING-WATER TANKS

Taselaar B.V.
Lindtsedijk 76
Zwijndrecht, Holland

Electricity

ALTERNATORS AND GENERATORS

Mercantile Manufacturing Co.
Box 895
Minden, La. 71055
(*Auto-Gen 110-volt generators*)

C. E. Niehoff and Co.
4925 W. Lawrence St.
Chicago, Ill. 60603
(*alternators*)

Onan
1400 73rd Ave. N.E.
Minneapolis, Minn. 55432
(*generators*)

Sperry Marine Systems
Great Neck, N.Y. 11020
(*Sperry Powerpak—a hydraulic-
drive alternator*)

JUNCTION BOXES AND SWITCH PANELS

Crouch Engineering Co.
Kings Rd.
Burnham on Crouch
Essex, England

C.W.C. Equipment
Maidenhead
Berks, England

Marinetics Corp.
P.O. Box 2676
Newport Beach, Calif. 92663
(714) 646-8889

Peter Smales
2 Bramble Rd.
Southsea
Hants PO4 ODT, England

ELECTRICAL WIRE AND TERMINAL ENDS

Belden Corporation, Electrical
    Division
Suite 300
2200 Kensington Ct.
Oak Brook, Ill. 60521

Michigan Wiring Co.
1934 Heide St.
Troy, Mich. 48084
(313) 362-1680
    (*electrical wire*)

Thomas and Betts Co.
520 Westfield Ave.
Elizabeth, N.J. 07208

Weller Division of Cooper Industries
100 Wellco Rd.
Easton, Pa.
    (*12-volt electric soldering iron*)

RHEOSTATS

Allied Radio
12311 Industry St.
Garden Grove, Calif. 92641

LIGHTS

Bass Products
P.O. Box 901
Marblehead, Mass. 01945
(617) 744-7003
    (*chart-table light*)

Channel Marine
49 Harbour Parade
Ramsgate
Kent CT11 8LL, England
    (*Aqua Signal—tricolored running
    light mounted at masthead, one light
    does the job of three*)

REC Specialties
15155 Stagg St.
Van Nuys, Calif. 91405
(213) 782-1203
    (*anti-night-blindness light, fluores-
    cent white and red*)

WIND GENERATORS

Ampair Products (Hugh Merewether)
Aston House
Blackheath, Guildford
Surrey GU4 8RD, England

GENERATORS BELTED OFF THE SHAFT

Marine and Industrial (William
    Lemieux)
Granite St.
Dorchester, Mass.

TOWED GENERATORS

Ampair Products (Hugh Merewether)
Aston House
Blackheath, Guildford
Surrey GU4 8RD, England

Hamilton Ferris
P.O. Box 1165
Santa Cruz, Calif. 95061

SOLAR POWER

Edmunds Scientific Co.
International Operations Department
8880 Edscorp Building
Barrington, N.J. 08007
    (*solar cells*)

Solar Power Corp.
5 Executive Park Dr.
North Billerica, Mass. 01862
(617) 667-8376
    (*solar battery charger*)

TACHOMETERS

Telcor Instruments (John Wilson)
17785 Sky Park Circle
Irvine, Calif. 92714

Mechanical Equipment

ENGINE ACCESSORIES

Huber Industries
4960 Hillside Ave.
Cincinnati, Ohio 45233
    (*oil sump pump working off electric
    drill*)

Racor Industries
1137 Barium Rd.
Modesto, Calif. 95351
    (*three-stage fuel filter, with an ex-
    cellent reputation*)

Research Enterprises
P.O. Box 232
Nutley, N.J. 07110
    (*automatic fuel shutoff*)

SEAGULL MANUAL

Clymer Publications
222 N. Virgil Ave.
Los Angeles, Calif. 90004

PROPELLERS, STANDARD AND FOLDING

Alexander-Roberts Co.
1851 Langley Ave.
Irvine, Calif. 92714
(714) 540-2141

Columbian Hydrosonics
216 N. Main St.
Freeport, N.Y. 11520

Elica A Bandiera
Pizza Castello 5
Milan, Italy
(*a new automatically feathering propeller, very popular with I.O.R. racing boats; hub smaller than the Hyde's*)

Gori
Fynsuev 109
DK 6000 Kocding, Denmark
(*folding propellers*)

Lehman Manufacturing Co.
800 E. Elizabeth Ave.
Linden, N.J. 07036
(201) 486-5700

Little Harbor Boatyard
Little Harbor Way
Marblehead, Mass. 01945

Paul E. Luke
E. Boothbay, Me. 04544
(207) 633-4971
(*the old Hyde automatically feathering propeller*)

Martec
2257 Gaylord St.
Long Beach, Calif. 90813

Michigan Wheel
1501 Buchanan Ave. S.W.
Grand Rapids, Mich. 49507

PROPELLERS, ADJUSTABLE PITCH

Helseth Motorverksted
6400 Molde, Norway
(*propeller and gearbox with various reductions*)

A/S Hundested Motorfabrik
Skansevej 1–9
DK3390 Hundested, Denmark
(*all sizes*)

Marine and Industrial (William Lemieux)
Granite St.
Dorchester, Mass.

(*reduction gear, clutch, propeller; alternator belted from freewheeling propeller*)

PNP Marine
Burnham on Crouch
Essex, England

Sabb
Box 2626
Bergen, Norway
(*6 to 100 h.p., including Sabb 2-cyl. 18 h.p. and Ford 4-cyl. 68 h.p. or 6-cyl. 100 h.p.; whole units, including engine—no components*)

Verheys
Bedriven Bv.
4–10 Opdijk
Holland
(*large models only*)

WaterMota
Abbotskerswell
Newton Abbot
South Devon TQ12 5NF, England
(*maximum 12-h.p. motor and 12-inch-diameter propeller*)

PROPELLER ACCESSORIES

Bird Engineering Products Co.
41 Upland Drive
Greenwich, Conn. 06830
(*cable and hydraulic propeller locks*)

Britton of Southport
W. Southport, Me. 04576
(207) 633-3169
(*hydraulic propeller lock*)

Tarrow Engineering
Plymouth
Devon, England
6 0752 62884
(*remote stuffing-box lubricator*)

EXHAUST SYSTEMS

Onan
1400 73rd Ave. N.E.
Minneapolis, Minn. 55432
(*Aqua-Lift*)

Vernay Products
77 S. College St.
Yellow Springs, Ohio 45387
(*fiber-glass exhaust system, Aqua-Lift type*)

SECURITY DEVICES

Security Devices Ltd.
Thames House

Thames St.
Sunbury on Thames
Middlesex, England
(*single alarm unit for oil pressure,
engine temperature, gas, bilge fire*)

FIRE EXTINGUISHERS

American La France
P.O. Box 430
Ranson, W.V. 25438

Anchorline Products
35 S. State St.
Newton, Pa. 18940
(215) 957-9600
(*Fiquench*)

The Ansul Co.
1 Stanton St.
Marinette, Wis. 54143

Fike Metal Products
704 S. 10th St.
Blue Springs, Mo. 64015
(*Fiquench*)

Graviner
1121 Bristol Rd.
Mountainside, N.J. 07092
(201) 654-6800
(*automatic Halon*)

Intercontinental Equipment Corp.
Chobham Rd.
Camberley, Surrey, England
(*Noxfire Freon extinquishers*)

Refrigeration

EQUIPMENT AND DESIGN

Adler and Barbour Yacht Services
43 Lawton St.
New Rochelle, N.Y. 10801

F.Y.A. Engineering
Berth 44 Outer Harbor
San Pedro, Calif. 90731
(213) 547-0860
(*solid-state refrigeration, not particularly effective in the tropics*)

Grunert
195 Drum Point Rd.
Osbornville, N.J. 08723

Power Products (Jon Repke)
6 Long Bay Road
St. Thomas, U.S. Virgin Islands 00801
(*Repke probably has more experience at installing refrigeration units
on boats in the deep tropics than
anyone else.*)

PARTS AND MATERIALS

Carlsen Kolevognsfabrik
Humlebaek, Denmark
(*holding plates*)

March Manufacturing Co.
1819 Pickwick Ave.
Glenview, Ill. 60025
(*magnetic-drive pumps*)

Reichhold Chemicals
523 N. Broadway
White Plains, N.Y. 10602
(*Freon II foam insulation*)

Virginia Chemicals
Portsmouth, Va.
(*dryer*)

HOSE ENDINGS

Aeroquip
300 S. East Ave.
Jackson, Mich. 49203

Navigation

Channel Marine
49 Harbour Parade
Ramsgate
Kent CT11 8LL, England
(*Young's Course Corrector; Young's
Tidal Estimator*)

Coast Navigation School
418 E. Canon Perdido
Santa Barbara, Calif. 93102
(*navigational equipment*)

Danforth Division, The Eastern Co.
500 Riverside Industrial Pkwy.
Portland, Me. 04103
(*circular nautical slide rule*)

Kelvin Hughes
St. Clare House
Minories
London E.C.3, England
(*charts and navigational equipment*)

M. Low
110 Hudson St.
New York, N.Y. 10013
(*charts and navigational equipment;
small taffrail log, good but a little
expensive*)

The Navigator's Corner
1 Fulham Ct.
Silver Spring, Md. 20902
(*Mercator Matic, navigational
plotter–parallel rule, the handiest I
have ever used*)

New York Nautical Instrument and
  Service Corp.
140 W. Broadway
New York, N.Y. 10013
  (*largest chart supplier in the western
  hemisphere, and one of the most
  helpful in the world*)

Offshore Instruments
47 Upper Grosvenor St.
London W.1, England
  (*small hand-bearing compass; compass inside binoculars*)

Weems and Plath
222 Severn Ave.
Annapolis, Md. 21403
  (*Weems star finder, similar to HO
  2102-D*)

Self Steering

WIND-VANE SELF-STEERING GEAR

Automate Products
Pitts Lane
Binstead, Ryde
Isle of Wight, England

Bingley, Son, and Follit
50 Minerva Rd.
Cowes
Isle of Wight, England

Chris Bock Instruments
2321 Washington Blvd.
Marina Del Rey, Calif. 90291
(213) 821-5811

Gibb Yachting Equipment
415 Tamal Plaza
Corte Madera, Calif. 94925
(415) 924-7283
  (*Aries—regarded as one of the best*)

M. S. Gibbs
Warsash
Southampton 503 6ZG, England

W. L. Green and Co.
2417 Dorrington
Houston, Texas 77025
(713) 668-5634
  (*Aries—regarded as one of the best*)

M. F. Gunning
Little Hawstead Steep
Petersfield
Hants, England

Quadrant
250 Kennington Lane
London S.E.11, England

Quantock Marine Enterprises
82 Durleigh Rd.
Bridgewater
Somerset, England

AUTOPILOTS

Autohelm Nautech
Asser House
Airport Services Rd.
Portsmouth
Hampshire PO3 5QF, England
0705 694551/2
  (*very low drain, will work off either
  compass or wind indicator, waterproof—tested by Des Sleightholme,
  among others, and highly regarded
  everywhere*)

Hepplewhite America
2 St. James Pl.
Rowayton, Conn. 06853
(203) 838-6863

Isotack Co.
1409 Mimosa Lane
Silver Spring, Md. 20904
  (*wind-sensing tiller type*)

Safe Flight Instrument Corp.
Box 550
White Plains, N.Y. 10602
  (*reading off wind indicator*)

Sharp and Co.
Richborough Hall
Sandwich
Kent, England
  (*hydraulic, electric, and reading off
  wind indicator or compass*)

Signet Scientific
129 E. Tujunga Ave.
Burbank, Calif. 91503

Tiller Master
P.O. Box 1901
Newport Beach, Calif. 92663
  (*tiller type*)

Safety

SAFETY EQUIPMENT (GENERAL)

Camper and Nicholsons
Southampton, England

Canpa Yacht Equipment
Mumby Road
Gosport
Hants, England

Frank Moore
Northam
Southampton, England

Nordby Supply Co.
Salmon Bay Terminal
Seattle, Wash. 98119

Revere Survival Products
605 W. 29th St.
New York, N.Y. 10001
(212) 565-2660

Signal Products
East Alton, Ill. 62024
(618) 258-2000

Smith and Wesson
2100 Roosevelt Ave.
Springfield, Mass. 01101

Survival and Safety Designs
1 Fifth Ave.
Oakland, Calif. 94606
(*G. Sigler, of this firm, has tested his equipment and theories by sailing a rubber raft from California to Hawaii with only survival equipment on board.*)

Vec/Trak Research and Development
Corp.
186 E. Main St.
Elmsford, N.Y. 10523

CLOTHING

Fulton Supply Co.
23 Fulton St.
New York, N.Y. 10007

LIFE RAFTS

Avon Rubber Co.
Dafen, Llanelli
Carms, Wales

Beaufort Equipment
Beaufort Rd.
Birkenhead, England

Survival and Safety Designs
1 Fifth Ave.
Oakland, Calif. 94606
(*As previously noted, the rubber raft offered by this firm has been tested by sailing from California to Hawaii.*)

The Winslow Co.
P.O. Box 578
Osprey, Fla. 33559

STROBE LIGHTS

Chromalloy American Corp.
ARC Electronics Division
160 Fifth Ave.
New York, N.Y. 10010

Derritron
Marine Division
24 Upper Brook St.
London W.1, England

Hoskins
Symbolic Displays
1188 Batavia
Orange, Calif. 92667
(*large strobe lights*)

DISTRESS ROCKETS

Channel Marine
49 Harbour Parade
Ramsgate
Kent CT11 8LL, England
(*Schermuly rockets available here rise 1,300 feet into the air; Very flares rise only 300 feet.*)

EMERGENCY RADIOS

Channel Marine
49 Harbour Parade
Ramsgate
Kent CT11 8LL, England

Derritron
Marine Division
24 Upper Brook St.
London W.1, England

Direction Corp.
P.O. Box 5800
Grand Central Station
New York, N.Y. 10017
(*small emergency radios*)

IRW Electronics
Forehammer Industrial Estate
Cumbran, Mon., Wales

Nordby Supply Co.
Salmon Bay Terminal
Seattle, Wash. 98119

SAIL SPECIFICATIONS

The main reason many sails do not give satisfactory service is that, all too often, the owner or sailmaker has paid insufficient attention to the details necessary in making up a really good set of sails. Many things must be kept in mind when ordering; it is not sufficient simply to give the dimensions of the three sides of each sail.

First and foremost, sails should be ordered from a sail plan, but not from this alone. The actual spar should be measured and the dimensions checked against the sail plan, and then and *only* then should the sail be drawn out on the sail plan and ordered.

The following are some basic specifications for sails, such as I draw up when sending an order to Cheong Lee, my Hong Kong sailmaker. For each type of sail, a section of Comments is to be found following the specifications. A raised number after an item indicates that it is discussed in this section. The Comments for the first few sails listed should be read with special attention, since many of the observations apply also to the corresponding items in the specifications for other sails.

Marconi Mains and Mizzens

DIMENSIONS

LUFF	LEECH	FOOT	AREA	MATERIAL [1]	RUB BACK [8]	JAWS		DEPTH	WIDTH
$x'\,x''$	$x'\,x''$	$x'\,x''$	x sq. ft.	x-oz. U.S.	x''	outhaul (*clew*) gooseneck (*tack*)		[in inches and fractions of an inch]	

DETAILS

Head, tack, and clew to be heavily reinforced, as per attached sketch. One reef, x' deeper at clew than at tack, x' above boom at tack; reefing-clew cringle to be, if anything, heavier and stronger than main clew cringle. Clew cringles to be supported by Dacron tape, as per attached sketch; tape to be not only sewn to sail but also hand stitched through the entire clew patch with heavy waxed Dacron twine.[2]

Chafe patches and chafing strips to be installed as per attached sketches.[3]

SLIDES [4]

TYPE	NUMBER	SPACING	METHOD OF ATTACHMENT
	x	x''	Dacron tape

CUNNINGHAM HOLES [5]

To be provided x'' up from tack, x'' aft of tack.

BATTEN POCKETS

Four battens to be provided. Batten pockets to fit standard Howe and Bainbridge battens. Each pocket to be sewn onto a piece of Dacron, the entire piece of Dacron then being sewn onto the sail in the *middle* of a panel rather than over a seam. Bottom batten to be parallel to main boom. Pockets to be hand stitched as well as machine stitched to sail.

JACK LINE [6]

To be installed on the bottom 6′ of sail.

ROLL REEF [7]

x' deep at clew with two reefing eyes outer half of boom.

REEFING [8]

STITCHING

Triple stitching with heaviest Dacron thread available.

HEAT SEALING [9]

To be used on all cut edges of panels and reinforcement patches.

MARKINGS [10]

Actual stretched dimensions to be marked on luff, leech, and foot. Head, tack, and clew to be identified by markings. Name of boat and year of sail manufacture to be marked on tack.

COMMENTS—MARCONI MAINS AND MIZZENS

1. One way of ascertaining what weight of Dacron should be used for a mainsail is to check the standard sail specifications for a racing boat of similar size and then order the sail one weight heavier. The one exception to this rule is that for ketches of fifty-five feet and above, the sail should be of the same weight as that specified for the racing main; indeed, on really large boats it should be one weight lighter. The use of lighter-weight cloth will help minimize the trouble in furling the mainsail which may be encountered on larger boats, and is all the more acceptable because in heavy weather a storm trysail should always be used in preference to the double-reefed main. See also, in the Appendix, Table XXIV ("Weights of Cloth for Various Sails, and Equivalents in American, British, and Continental Measures").

2. Sketches of tack and clew fittings should be sent with the order, as there is nothing more aggravating when bending on a new sail than to discover that the clew cringle will not fit inside the jaws of the outhaul fitting. The types of reinforcement desired should also be indicated by sketches (see Drawings 84–86, in Chapter VI). In some circumstances it may be feasible to refer the sailmaker directly to the relevant drawings in Chapter VI.

3. Chafe patches or chafing strips are sometimes placed at the points where the sail chafes on spreader tips and upper shrouds when broad off. The patches should be kept as small as possible. Sketches can be supplied to show the placement and nature of these patches, or the old sail can be taken to the sailmaker so he can pick off the chafe marks.

4. A sample of the sail slide desired should be supplied, if possible. Better yet, when ordering a new main or mizzen, or a foresail for a schooner, one should retain the old sail slides. If they have been in use for several years, the burrs will have worn off and they will slide freely in the existing track, whereas new slides inevitably bind slightly for the first few months.

This point was brought home to me when, in September, 1973, *Iolaire*'s mainsail and mizzen were stolen. I had to order new sails and install new slides, and for the next twelve months the main and mizzen did not run freely, and did not drop instantly when the halyards were cast off. These difficulties were most discouraging, as the old slides, which had been in use for seven years, were perfectly worn in.

One method of getting sail slides to run freely is to put a few drops of light 3-in-One Oil on them when they are stacked up just before the sail is raised; then the process of hoisting spreads the oil very evenly up and down the track. Another method is to carefully spray the entire track with Teflon, which will make the slides operate with ease. If the problem arises with plastic slides which are not made to close tolerances, one should trim them with a sharp knife until they run freely.

The actual number of sail slides desired on luff and foot should be specified.

5. Cunningham holes, originated by the racing yachtsman, are well worth while on cruising boats, as was indicated in *OSY*-I (Ch. IV). Many experienced seamen feel that except on mizzens on yawls and ketches and on mainsails on schooners which have overhanging booms, where a standard outhaul is necessary for ease in bending on a sail, a fixed outhaul with a Cunningham hole in the foot is preferable. It is more easily adjustable, and one can save a great deal of expense by putting a light tackle on the inner end of the sail, leading to a small winch, instead of indulging in the very expensive outhaul fittings which are presently installed on many large cruising yachts.

6. With roller reefing a jack line is essential; with straight slab reefing, though not essential it is still desirable, since it still makes furling the sail easier and relieves the diagonal strains along the foot when the sail is furled along the boom without the outhaul being slacked.

7. Especially on an older cruising boat with a fairly long boom, a roll reef (as shown in *OSY*-I, Drawing 84) is desirable to prevent the boom from dipping while reaching or running in heavy weather. The roll reef should be 12–18 inches deep for every 10 feet of boom length. One should check the sail plan, or better yet, check on board the boat, to make sure that when the boom is topped up for the roll reef, it can still pass inside the permanent backstay. This is not a problem on modern boats, but on older boats there may be some difficulty.

8. When roller reefing is specified, the rub-back dimension must be supplied; also, one set of reefing cringles should always be provided, for use in case the roller reefing does not work. When slab reefing is chosen, the specifications must indicate the method to be used—reef points, continuous line, or jiffy reefing with a wire sewn into the sail.

If there is roller reefing and also the possibility of tying in a reef, the best way to double-reef and still preserve the shape of the sail is to tie in the single reef and roll down the necessary amount above the tied-in reef. If this is done for only two or three turns, the sail will reef evenly; one will not have the problem of the leech crawling forward and becoming over-strained, while causing a drooping boom and a baggy sail.

9. It is essential that the sailmaker carefully heat-seal all cut edges of panels and reinforcement patches; otherwise these edges will fray with great rapidity.

10. If the actual stretched dimensions are marked on the sail, they can

be checked against the original specifications. The name of the boat should be placed on the tack, because in out-of-the-way areas all too often yachtsmen "borrow" each other's sails, but well-marked sails are seldom taken.

Gaff Sails

DIMENSIONS

LUFF	LEECH	FOOT	HEAD	DIAGONAL [1]	AREA	MATERIAL
$x'\,x''$	$x'\,x''$	$x'\,x''$	$x'\,x''$	$x'\,x''$	x sq. ft.	x-oz. U.S. Dacron

DETAILS

Head, tack, peak, and clew to be heavily reinforced, as per attached sketch. One reef, x' deeper at clew than at tack, x' above boom at tack; reefing-clew cringle to be, if anything, heavier and stronger than main clew cringle. Clew cringles to be supported by Dacron tape, as per attached sketch; tape to be not only sewn to sail but also hand stitched through the entire clew patch with heavy waxed Dacron twine. Chafe patches to be installed as per attached sketches.

SLIDES

TYPE	NUMBER	SPACING	METHOD OF ATTACHMENT
	x	x''	Dacron tape

HOOPS [2]

NUMBER	METHOD OF ATTACHMENT
x	

CUNNINGHAM HOLES

To be provided x'' up from tack, x'' aft of tack.

BATTEN POCKETS

Four battens to be provided. Batten pockets to fit standard Howe and Bainbridge battens. Each pocket to be sewn onto a piece of Dacron, the entire piece of Dacron then being sewn onto the sail in the *middle* of a panel rather than over a seam. Bottom batten to be parallel to main boom. Pockets to be hand stitched as well as machine stitched to sail.

JACK LINE

To be installed on the bottom 6' of sail.

ROLL REEF

x' deep at clew with two reefing eyes outer half of boom.

REEFING [3]

STITCHING

Triple stitching with heaviest Dacron thread available.

HEAT SEALING

To be used on all cut edges of panels and reinforcement patches.

MARKINGS

[As for mainsail.]

COMMENTS—GAFF SAILS

1. For all four-sided sails, gaff or sprit, the diagonal measurement—either tack to peak or clew to throat—must be given.

2. The number of hoops should be specified, and the method of attachment described in detail.

3. When roller reefing is specified, the rub-back dimension must be supplied; also, one set of reefing cringles should always be provided, for use in case the roller reefing does not work. When slab reefing is chosen, the specifications must indicate the method to be used—reef points, continuous line, or jiffy reefing with a wire sewn into the sail.

If there is roller reefing and also the possibility of tying in a reef, the best way to double-reef and still preserve the shape of the sail is to tie in the single reef and roll down the necessary amount above the tied-in reef. If this is done for only two or three turns, the sail will reef evenly; one will not have the problem of the leech crawling forward and becoming overstrained, while causing a drooping boom and a baggy sail.

Headsails

DIMENSIONS

LUFF	LEECH	FOOT	AREA	MATERIAL
$x'\,x''$	$x'\,x''$	$x'\,x''$	x sq. ft.	x-oz. U.S. Dacron

DETAILS

Head, tack, and clew to be heavily reinforced, as per attached sketch. Clew cringle to be supported by Dacron tape, as shown in sketch, which is both machine and hand stitched to the sail. Clew cringle inside diameter to be x''.[1] Head and tack thimbles must be either solid or welded across the throat, as per attached sketch, to enable them to be securely lashed to the tensioning eye in the sail.[2]

Chafe patches and chafing strips to be installed as per attached sketches.

Luff wire to be of x''-diameter 7 by 19, and to be plastic covered, or insulated from the Dacron sail with tape. Wire to be loose inside the luff of the sail, external eyes to be secured as shown in sketch.[3]

LEECH LINE [4]

To be installed.

HEAD PENDANT [5]

Length $x'\,x''$. Snaps to be secured at top, middle, and bottom.

TACK PENDANT [6]

Length $x'\,x''$.

JACK LINE [7]

To be installed on the bottom x' of the luff of the sail (if it is to be set on a boom).

CUNNINGHAM HOLES [8]

To be installed on genoas only.

HANKS

NUMBER	DISTANCE (OF FIRST HANK) FROM TACK [9]	SPACING	TYPE
x	x''	x''	

STITCHING

Triple stitching with heaviest Dacron thread available.

HEAT SEALING

To be used on all cut edges of panels and reinforcement patches.

MARKINGS

[As for mainsail.]

COMMENTS—HEADSAILS

1. The inside diameter of the clew cringle should be large enough to permit three sheets to be knotted through it at the same time. The exact design of the clew cringle will of course vary according to the size of the sail.

2. A sketch showing the thimble welded across the throat, as in Drawing 86B, should be included.

3. The attachment of external eyes is shown in Drawing 86A. Adjusting the tension between the luff wire and the sail, if it should become necessary, is much easier if the eyes have been secured by the method shown here.

4. On a low-cut sail, the leech line should be adjustable at the clew by means of a small cam cleat or leather buttons. On a high-cut jib, the leech line cannot be reached at the clew, and all too frequently it fouls on the staysail stay as it passes around it when tacking; therefore, it should be adjustable at the head. Needless to say, one can adjust it only when the sail is down, but that is better than being unable to make adjustments at all.

5. The head pendant should be of such a length that the halyard splice always reaches the winch. A snap should be secured just below the top to prevent the halyard shackle from wrapping the halyard around the head stay in rough weather.

6. On a headsail a tack pendant may be desirable to bring the sail clear of the bow pulpit.

7. The jack line, as discussed in the section on club jack lines in Chapter IV, and shown in Drawing 98, can be used on a staysail only if it is boomed.

8. For genoas, a Cunningham hole is recommended. A line may be secured alongside the sail and run up through the Cunningham hole, down through a small snatch block, and back to the anchor windlass, winch, or what-have-you. It is much easier to adjust the draft in the sail by hauling down on the Cunningham hole than by hauling up on a halyard.

9. The first hank must be far enough from the tack to clear the jaw opening of the lower turnbuckle.

Roller-Furling Headsails

DIMENSIONS

LUFF	LEECH	FOOT	AREA	MATERIAL [1]	LUFF WIRE [2]
$x'\,x''$	$x'\,x''$	$x'\,x''$	x sq. ft.	x-oz. U.S. Dacron	x''-diameter 1 by 19

DETAILS

Head, tack, and clew to be more heavily reinforced than in standard headsail. Clew cringles and head and tack eyes as per attached sketches.[3]

Luff wire to be plastic covered, or insulated with tape. Sail to be securely seized to the luff wire.

LEECH LINE

To be installed.

HEAD PENDANT

Length x' x''. Snaps to be secured at top, middle, and bottom.

TACK PENDANT

Length x' x''.

SACRIFICIAL STRIP [4]

A layer of 3-oz. or 4-oz. Dacron to be sewn on the starboard side of the sail for 18 inches along the leech and foot.

STITCHING

Triple stitching with heaviest Dacron thread available.

HEAT SEALING

To be used on all cut edges of panels and reinforcement patches.

MARKINGS

[As for mainsail.]

COMMENTS—ROLLER-FURLING HEADSAILS

1. Because a roller-furling headsail is secured only at three corners, it needs to be one weight heavier than one would normally expect for the corresponding hanked-on headsail—e.g., a 320-square-foot No. 1 high-cut jib on a forty-five-foot boat should be made of 8-ounce U.S. Dacron.

2. On a roller-furling headsail, the luff wire should be similar in size and construction to the head stay (i.e., 1 by 19 should be used). A properly rigged roller-furling headsail will take the entire load; no load should fall on the head stay. Further, an accurate drawing of the roller-furling end fittings must be sent, to make sure that the end fittings on the wire fit into the jaws on the roller-furling gear.

3. Exact specifications, to be shown in the sketches, will depend on the dimensions of the roller-furling gear to be used.

4. To minimize the sunburn damage that occurs when the sail is left aloft between trips, on the starboard side of the sail, for 18 inches along the leech and foot, a sacrificial layer of 3-ounce or 4-ounce Dacron should be sewn. This will absorb the ultraviolet light, protecting the sail. Since this sacrificial layer can be renewed when necessary, it can be lighter than the other reinforcements.

Mizzen Staysails

DIMENSIONS

LUFF	LEECH	FOOT	AREA	MATERIAL [1]
x' x''	x' x''	x' x''	x sq. ft.	x-oz. U.S. Dacron

DETAILS [2]

Luff wire to be of x''-diameter 7 by 19, and to be plastic covered, or insulated from the Dacron sail with tape. Wire to be loose inside the luff of the sail, external eyes to be secured as shown in sketch.

HANKS

NUMBER [3]	DISTANCE (OF FIRST HANK) FROM TACK	SPACING	TYPE
x	x''	x''	

MARKINGS

[As for mainsail.]

COMMENTS—MIZZEN STAYSAILS

1. A mizzen staysail is usually made of 1.5-ounce nylon. On the cruising boat, where it will have much more use than on a racing boat, and may be left up for weeks on end, heavier material could be used.

2. On a cruising boat of more than forty-five feet, the corners of the sail should be more heavily reinforced than usual, and leather chafing strips should be sewn onto the luff wire where it crosses the main backstay.

3. On a cruising boat of more than forty-five feet, the mizzen staysail may have three to five luff hanks. These enable one to hoist it on a light jackstay, making it easy to douse even in heavy weather.

Storm Trysails

DIMENSIONS

LUFF	LEECH	FOOT	AREA [1]	MATERIAL [2]
$x'\,x''$	$x'\,x''$	$x'\,x''$	x sq. ft.	x-oz. U.S. Dacron

CUT [3]

Scotch cut. Leech to be cut with slight hollow, no battens.

DETAILS

Head, tack, and clew to be more heavily reinforced than usual, as per attached sketch. One reef, x' from tack, with heavily reinforced clew and tack cringles. Clew and tack cringles to be supported by Dacron tape, as per attached sketch; tape to be not only sewn to sail but also hand stitched through the entire clew patch with heavy waxed Dacron twine. Clew cringle inside diameter to be x''.[4] Tack ring inside diameter to be x''.

Reinforcement patches to be thicker and longer than those used on mainsail.

HEAD PENDANT [5]

Length $x'\,x''$.

TACK PENDANT [6]

Length $x'\,x''$.

SLIDES

TYPE	NUMBER	SPACING	METHOD OF ATTACHMENT
	x	$\frac{2}{3}$ that of mainsail	Dacron tape

STITCHING

Triple stitching with heaviest Dacron thread available.

HEAT SEALING

To be used on all cut edges of panels and reinforcement patches.

MARKINGS

[As for mainsail.]

COMMENTS—STORM TRYSAILS

1. As noted in the text, the storm trysail should be the same size as a double-reefed main; a set of reef points, with extra tack and clew cringles, make it possible to reef the storm trysail to minimum size.

2. Because of the strength of Dacron, the reduced sail area, and the extra reinforcements, the cloth used for the storm trysail need be no heavier than for the mainsail.

3. The leech should be cut with a slight hollow so no battens are needed. If extensive sailing in heavy weather with a trysail is anticipated, it may be desirable to have the sail of Scotch cut (*OSY*-I, Drawing 91), with seams running parallel to the leech and foot. Then the sail will not split luff to leech if a seam begins to open.

4. The clew cringle should be of such diameter that both sheet tackles (which should be secured with screw shackles, *not* snap shackles), along with the reefing-clew line, can fit through it easily at the same time.

5. If the boat does not have a reel self-stowing wire halyard, but instead has a halyard with a tail splice, a pendant with a slide secured just below its top should be placed at the head of the trysail, so that the halyard shackle will not swing free when the trysail is being hoisted. The pendant should be of such length that the wire–rope splice is on the winch drum when the trysail is fully hoisted.

6. The tack pendant should be a length of line that can be hooked under a cleat or cheek block, passed back up through the tack cringle, and then led to a winch or second cleat. With this arrangement, one can use the tack pendant rather than the halyard to adjust the height of the trysail and the luff tension—an advantage because hauling down is easier than hauling up.

Storm Headsails

DIMENSIONS

LUFF	LEECH	FOOT	AREA	MATERIAL [1]
$x'\,x''$	$x'\,x''$	$x'\,x''$	x sq. ft.	x-oz. U.S. Dacron

CUT [2]

Scotch cut.

DETAILS

Head, tack, and clew to be more heavily reinforced than usual, as per attached sketch. Clew cringle to be supported by Dacron tape, as shown in sketch, which is both machine and hand stitched to the sail. Clew cringle inside diameter to be x''. Head and tack thimbles must be either solid or welded across the throat, as per attached sketch, to enable them to be securely lashed to the tensioning eye in the sail.

Chafe patches and chafing strips to be installed as per attached sketches.

Luff wire to be of x''-diameter 7 by 19, and to be plastic covered, or insulated from the Dacron sail with tape. Wire to be loose inside the luff of the sail, external eyes to be secured as shown in sketch.

LEECH LINE [3]

None.

HEAD PENDANT

Length x' x''. Snaps to be secured at top, middle, and bottom.

TACK PENDANT

Length x' x''.

JACK LINE

To be installed on the bottom x' of the luff of the sail (if it is to be set on a boom).

HANKS [4]

NUMBER	DISTANCE (OF FIRST HANK) FROM TACK	SPACING	TYPE
x	x''	x''	

STITCHING

Triple stitching with heaviest Dacron thread available.

HEAT SEALING

To be used on all cut edges of panels and reinforcement patches.

MARKINGS [5]

[As for mainsail.]

COMMENTS—STORM HEADSAILS

1. Though general specifications are the same as for a normal headsail, the storm headsail should be the same weight as the mainsail.

2. With Scotch cut, the shape will not be as good as with normal cut, but there is less likelihood of splitting a seam luff to leech.

3. The leech line should be dispensed with because it is just one more thing to foul up in heavy weather.

4. The hanks should be more closely spaced than on the standard headsail, and should be either Merriman or Abeking and Rasmussen snaps (*OSY*-I, Photos 55 and 56). There is nothing worse in heavy weather than having the sail flog, and the snaps come open, so that one is suddenly left with the storm headsail flying free, secured only at head, tack, and clew!

5. Markings to identify the head, tack, and clew are especially important on storm sails, as there is nothing worse than hoisting a seldom-used sail in heavy weather and suddenly discovering that it is upside down.

TABLES

Table I. Weights of Boat-Building Materials

Material	Lbs. per Cubic Foot	Material	Lbs. per Cubic Foot
Styrofoam	1.3	Spanish cedar	37
Cork	16	Cypress	40
White cedar	23	Elm	40
White pine	26	Walnut	40
Spruce	27	Mexican mahogany	41
Redwood	28	Ash	41
Port Oxford cedar	30	Longleaf yellow	
Alaskan yellow		pine (pitch pine)	41
cedar	31	Teak at least	45
Douglas fir		(depending on age and dryness)	
(Oregon pine)	32	Black locust	49
African mahogany	32	Hickory	53
Honduras mahogany	35	White oak	53
Butternut	35	Greenheart (won't float)	66
Philippine mahogany	36	Fiber glass (70 percent glass,	
Fir plywood	36	30 percent resin)	96

Table II. Screw Sizes for Various Planking Thicknesses

Planking Thickness, in Inches	Screw Gauge Number
5/16	5
3/8	6
7/16	7
1/2	8
5/8	9
3/4	10
7/8	12
1	14
1¼	16
1½	18
1¾	20
2	24

Table III. Weights of Commonly Used Materials

Material	Pounds per Cubic Foot	Material	Pounds per Cubic Foot
Aluminum, cast	165	Zinc	440
sheet	168	Gasoline (6.19 pounds per gallon)	46.3
Brass	534		
Bronze, 7.9–14% tin	509	Kerosene (paraffin) (6.8 pounds per gallon)	50.9
aluminum	481		
phospor	537	Oil, diesel (7.13 pounds per gallon)	53.3
Copper	556		
Iron, cast	450	bunker fuel (8.09 pounds per gallon)	60.6
wrought	485		
Lead, scrap	700	lube (7.69 pounds per gallon)	57.5
virgin	712	Water, fresh	62.4
Mercury	849	sea	64
Monel	556		
Steel, stainless	492–510		
structural	490		

Table IV. Weights and Dimensions of Stores

Potatoes	40 lbs. per cubic ft.; 60 lbs. per bushel
Liquor	3 lbs. per quart
Beer, by the case, 9½-ounce cans	20 lbs.; 11¾″ x 4½″ x 16″
10-ounce bottles	34 lbs.; 10¼″ x 6½″ x 15″
Soda, by the case, cans	approximately the same as beer
6½-ounce bottles	38 lbs.; 11¾″ x 8½″ x 18″
Milk, by the 48-can case, 14½-ounce cans	54 lbs.; 12″ x 8″ x 18″
Consumable stores	5½ lbs. per man per day
Sea kit, temperate or cool climate	75–100 lbs.
warm climate	25 lbs.
Coal	47–58 lbs. per cubic foot
Charcoal	10–12 lbs. per cubic foot
Ice, 50-lb. block	approx. 1500 cubic inches
50 lbs. of cubes	approx. 1600 cubic inches

Gas bottles	Dimensions	Weight, Empty, in Pounds	Weight, Full, in Pounds
United States			
horizontal, steel	10″ x 20″	20	40
horizontal, aluminum*	13″ x 19⅜″	9	29
vertical, aluminum	10⅜″ x 14½″	4.5	12.5
British			
vertical, steel	12″ x 21″	20	40
Well-equipped engine toolbox, with tools			60
Well-equipped woodworking toolbox, with tools, including electric drill, saber saw, and so on			80

*New sizes of aluminum cylinders are continually coming on the market. The latest information can be obtained by checking the Worthington Cylinders catalog (for address see Sources of Supply).

Table V. Nomograph for Determining Pounds per Inch of Immersion in Salt Water

Design Waterline in Feet

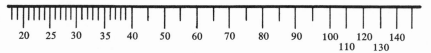

Pounds per Inch of Immersion

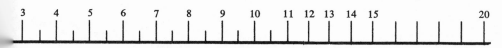

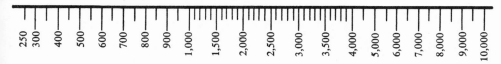

Beam on Design Waterline in Feet

If the points on the top and bottom lines are connected by a straight line, its point of intersection with the middle line gives the increase in displacement per inch of immersion.

Beam is measured at the waterline, not at the deck; the difference between these two dimensions is sometimes sizable.

Long-ended boats will have considerably different waterline lengths at 2, 4, and 6 inches of immersion; for these boats, interpolation is necessary to obtain an accurate answer.

From *Skene's Elements of Yacht Design*,
Revised by Francis S. Kinney, New York, Dodd, Mead, 1962.

Table VI. Comparative Strength, Rigging Materials

Manila		Polypropylene		Filament Dacron		Nylon		Samson Braid		CHAIN		WIRE 1 x 19 Stainless	
Diameter, in Inches	Strength, in Pounds										Test		
1/4	690												
						3/16	850			3/16	966		
5/16	1,200	1/4	1,250	1/4	1,200	1/4	1,100					3/32	1,200
3/8	1,600									1/4	1,680		
7/16	1,930	5/16	1,900	5/16	1,800	5/16	1,800						
								1/4	2,100			1/8	2,100
				3/8	2,600	3/8	2,600			5/16	2,500		
1/2	2,900	3/8	2,700					5/16	2,700				
								3/8	3,000			5/32	3,300
										3/8	3,640		
		1/2	4,500	1/2	4,500								
5/8	4,800					1/2	5,000	7/16	4,900	7/16	4,950	3/16	4,700
3/4	5,900	5/8	6,600	9/16	6,800	9/16	6,400			1/2	6,600	7/32	6,300
7/8	7,700	3/4	8,000			5/8	8,000	1/2	7,500	9/16	8,250	1/4	8,000
1	9,000			5/8	9,300	3/4	10,500			5/8	10,120	9/32	10,300
								5/8	11,000				
				3/4	12,600							5/16	12,500
						7/8	14,000						
				1	16,000	1	16,000	3/4	16,500				
												3/8	17,600
								7/8	22,000			7/16	23,400
												1/2	29,700
												9/16	37,000
												5/8	46,000

These figures are from manufacturers' catalogs.

Table VII. Comparative Weights, Wire and Line

STAINLESS-STEEL WIRE

Diameter, in Fractions of an Inch	Construction	Weight per 100 Feet, in Pounds	Diameter, in Fractions of an Inch	Construction	Weight per 100 Feet, in Pounds
1/8	1 x 19	3.6		7 x 7	
3/16		8.0		*Approximately the same as 1 x 19.*	
1/4		14.5		7 x 19	
5/16		22.2	1/8		2.9
3/8		31.8	3/16		6.5
7/16		44.0	1/4		11.0
1/2		58.0	5/16		17.3
9/16		73.0	3/8		24.3
5/8		90.0			

WIRE					TURNBUCKLES				SHACKLES				CLEVIS PINS	
7 x 7 Stainless	7 x 19 Stainless		7 x 19 Galvanized		Merriman		Lewmar Superston		Bronze		Stainless		Bronze (Shear Load)	
									3⁄16	1,200				
1,700	1⁄8	1,900	1⁄8	1,800										
2,600	5⁄32	2,600	5⁄32	2,500	1⁄4	2,300								
											1⁄4	2,800		
3,700	3⁄16	3,900	3⁄16	3,800	5⁄16	3,600					3⁄16	3,500		
											1⁄4	4,200		
4,800	7⁄32	5,200	7⁄32	5,100	3⁄8	5,600	5⁄16	5,500						
6,100	1⁄4	6,600	1⁄4	6,500					3⁄8	6,000	5⁄16	6,600	3⁄8	6,300
	9⁄32	7,800	9⁄32	8,000	7⁄16	7,500			7⁄16	8,500				
9,100	5⁄16	9,000	5⁄16	9,800	1⁄2	10,500	3⁄8	9,300			3⁄8	10,000	1⁄2	10,300
									1⁄2	11,000				
12,600	3⁄8	12,000												
			3⁄8	14,300										
	7⁄16	16,300					7⁄16	15,300						
							1⁄2	16,100			1⁄2	16,000		
					5⁄8	17,500							5⁄8	17,500
1,300							5⁄8	23,000						
	1⁄2	23,800			3⁄4	25,000								
					7⁄8	34,000					5⁄8	31,000		
							3⁄4	39,000						
					1	45,000								

DACRON OR NYLON

Diameter, in Fractions of an Inch	Approx. Weight per 600 Feet, in Pounds
3⁄8	20
1⁄2	40
5⁄8	67
3⁄4	90

Table VIII. Chain Weights and Volumes

Diameter, in Inches	*Weight per Shot (15 Fathoms, or 90 Feet), in Pounds*	*Space to Stow One Shot in Self-Stowing Locker, in Cubic Feet*
¼	70	0.9
5/16	102	1.3
⅜	148	1.8
7/16	202	2.4
½	257	3.1

Table IX. Comparative Stretch, K-Kore and *Iolaire* 1 by 19 Wire

K-Kore, 5/16-Inch Diameter			Old 1 by 19, 5/16-Inch Diameter		
Original Length	*Load, in Pounds*	*Stretch, in Inches*	*Original Length*	*Load, in Pounds*	*Stretch, in Inches*
19′ ¾″	—	—	19′ 5″	—	—
	1,000	½		1,000	¼
	2,000	⅞		2,000	¼
	3,000	1¼		3,000	½
	4,000	1½		4,000	¾
	5,000	2⅛		5,000	13/16
	6,000	2¼		6,000	1⅛
	7,000	2½		7,000	1⅜
	8,000	3		8,000	1¾
	10,000	3¾		10,000	1 7/16

Table X. Stretch of ¼-Inch 7 by 19 Stainless-Steel Wire

Load, in Pounds	*Stretch per 50 Feet, in Inches*
300	0.841
500	1.261
1,000	2.161
1,500	2.971
2,000	3.811
2,500	4.501

Table XI. Dimensions of Norseman Fittings

EYE

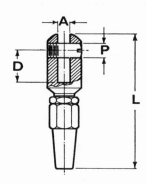

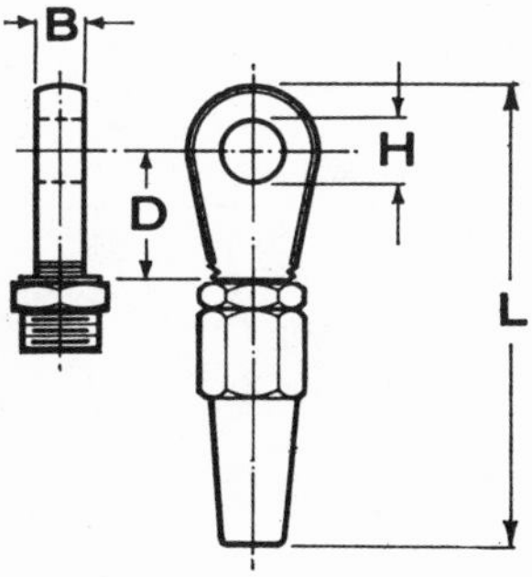

Terminal size (Wire dia.)		H		D		B		L	
mm.	in.	mm.	in.	mm.	in.	mm.	in.	mm.	in.
3	⅛	5.6	.219	12.7	.50	4.7	.187	48	1.88
4	5/32	6.4	.250	16.0	.63	6.4	.250	54	2.13
5	3/16	8.0	.313	17.5	.69	7.9	.312	62	2.44
6	¼	11.1	.437	23.9	.94	9.5	.375	92	3.63
7	9/32	12.7	.500	23.9	.94	9.5	.375	92	3.63
8	5/16	14.3	.563	25.4	1.00	11.1	.437	95	3.75
9	⅜	15.9	.625	26.9	1.06	12.7	.500	121	4.75
10	13/32	15.9	.625	26.9	1.06	12.7	.500	121	4.75
12	½	19.1	.750	36.5	1.43	18.8	.740	140	5.50
14	9/16	22.2	.875	38.1	1.50	21.3	.840	165	6.50
16	⅝	25.4	1.00	50.8	2.00	24.6	.968	165	6.50

FORK

Terminal size (Wire dia.)		P		D		A		L	
mm.	in.	mm.	in.	mm.	in.	mm.	in.	mm.	in.
3	⅛	4.7	.187	12.7	.50	4.8	.189	56	2.19
4	5/32	6.1	.240	14.7	.58	6.9	.270	64	2.50
5	3/16	7.9	.312	16.3	.64	8.1	.317	73	2.88
6	¼	9.5	.375	21.3	.84	9.7	.380	98	3.88
7	9/32	9.5	.375	21.3	.84	9.7	.380	98	3.88
8	5/16	11.1	.437	22.2	.88	11.7	.460	102	4.00
9	⅜	12.7	.500	25.4	1.00	12.8	.505	130	5.13
10	13/32	12.7	.500	25.4	1.00	12.8	.505	130	5.13
12	½	18.8	.750	34.9	1.38	19.1	.750	147	5.75
14	9/16	22.2	.875	38.1	1.50	23.5	.925	178	7.00
16	⅝	25.4	1.00	44.5	1.75	25.7	1.010	190	7.50

STUD

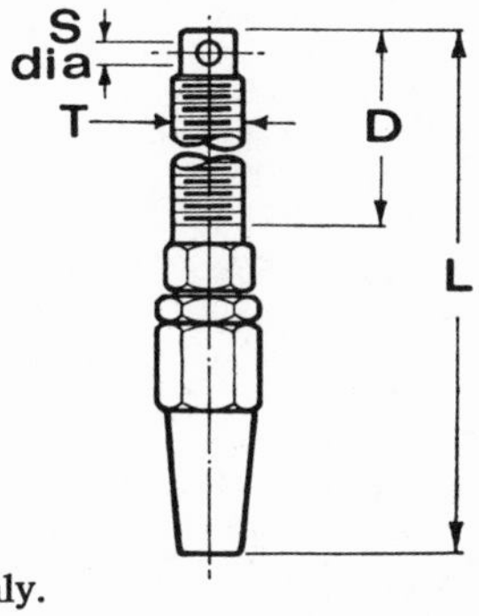

Terminal size (Wire dia.)		T	D		S		L	
mm.	in.	U.N.F.	mm.	in.	mm.	in.	mm.	in.
3	⅛	¼	48	1.88	2.4	.094	83	3.25
4	5/32	5/16	52	2.06	2.8	.109	95	3.75
5	3/16	⅜	64	2.50	3.2	.125	102	4.00
6	¼	7/16	73	2.88	4.0	.156	143	5.63
7	9/32	½	79	3.13	4.0	.156	147	5.75
8	5/16	½	79	3.13	4.0	.156	152	6.00
9	⅜	⅝	95	3.75	4.0	.156	187	7.38
10	13/32	⅝	95	3.75	4.0	.156	187	7.38

The above tables apply to the Mk. III stainless-steel versions only.

Courtesy of Norseman Ropes Ltd.

Table XII. Dimensions of Sta-Lok Fittings

Courtesy of Sta-Lok.

cable				EYE type				
dia mm	b/l * kgf	DE	LE	SE	RE	T	H †	wt kg
3	720	11.1	47.0	18.0	8.7	5.0	6.5	.032
4	1280	14.2	54.0	21.4	11.9	5.5	8.0	.050
5	2000	17.4	64.3	27.0	12.8	7.5	10.0	.080
6	2880	22.2	81.7	35.7	20.8	9.5	13.0	.185
7	3550	25.4	84.9	35.7	20.8	10.5	13.0	.195
8	4640	28.5	96.8	44.5	26.2	12.0	16.0	.320
9	5870	28.5	100.0	44.5	26.2	13.0	16.0	.350
10	7270	31.7	109.6	47.6	29.4	13.0	16.0	.500
11	9450	38.1	138.9	59.0	35.4	19.0	20.0	.910
12	10400	38.1	138.9	59.0	35.4	19.0	20.0	.910
14	14200	50.8	159.6	74.6	41.6	22.0	23.0	1.361
16	18600	57.1	169.8	74.6	44.8	22.0	23.0	1.672

				FORK type				
dia mm	b/l * kgf	DF	LF	SF	RF	W †	P †	wt kg
3	720	14.2	49.6	19.0	11.3	6.5	6.0	.045
4	1280	17.4	56.3	23.0	13.5	8.0	7.0	.060
5	2000	20.6	66.6	28.0	16.5	10.0	9.0	.110
6	2880	27.0	85.0	39.0	21.5	13.0	12.0	.245
7	3550	28.5	88.0	39.0	21.5	13.0	12.0	.265
8	4640	33.3	102.4	46.2	26.4	16.0	15.0	.450
9	5870	34.9	107.9	46.2	26.4	16.0	15.0	.460
10	7270	38.1	113.4	49.5	26.4	16.0	15.0	.800
11	9450	47.6	140.0	59.5	32.4	20.0	19.0	1.250
12	10400	47.6	140.0	59.5	32.4	20.0	19.0	1.250
14	14200	57.1	162.6	73.0	41.2	23.0	22.0	1.956
16	18600	63.5	169.9	79.3	41.2	23.0	22.0	2.382

				STUD type				
dia mm	b/l * kgf	DS	LS	RS	TS	HS	wt kg
4	1280	14.0	91.2	54.0	5/16"	2.8	.057
5	2000	16.0	102.4	63.5	3/8"	2.8	.086
6	2880	20.5	130.2	76.2	7/16"	3.2	.185
7	3550	24.0	141.2	95.2	1/2"	3.2	.197
8	4640	25.4	144.5	95.2	1/2"	3.2	.260
9	5870	27.0	168.4	98.5	5/8"	4.0	.351
10	7270	28.8	173.0	98.5	5/8"	4.0	.467

* British Standard   † British Standard for rigging connecting parts
TS—overall diameter of thread—right hand UNF (SAE)

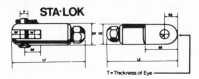

STA·LOK

T = Thickness of Eye

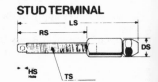

STUD TERMINAL

Wire Size (Diameter, in Inches)	7 x 19 A INCHES	B INCHES
1/16	1⅛	.039
3/32	1½	.056
1/8	2¼	.075
5/32	2¾	.091
3/16	3½	.108
7/32	4	.124
1/4	4½	.142
9/32	5	.160

Table XIII. Dimensions of Standard U.S. End Fittings, and Recommended Sheave Dimensions

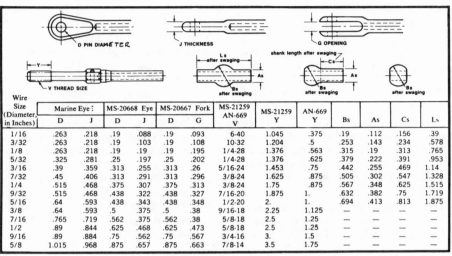

Wire Size (Diameter, in Inches)	Marine Eye D	J	MS-20668 Eye D	J	MS-20667 Fork D	G	MS-21259 AN-669 V	MS-21259 Y	AN-669 Y	Bs	As	Cs	Ls
1/16	.263	.218	.19	.088	.19	.093	6-40	1.045	.375	.19	.112	.156	.39
3/32	.263	.218	.19	.103	.19	.108	10-32	1.204	.5	.253	.143	.234	.578
1/8	.263	.218	.19	.19	.19	.195	1/4-28	1.376	.563	.315	.19	.313	.765
5/32	.325	.281	.25	.197	.25	.202	1/4-28	1.376	.625	.379	.222	.391	.953
3/16	.39	.359	.313	.255	.313	.26	5/16-24	1.453	.75	.442	.255	.469	1.14
7/32	.45	.406	.313	.291	.313	.296	3/8-24	1.625	.875	.505	.302	.547	1.328
1/4	.515	.468	.375	.307	.375	.313	3/8-24	1.75	.875	.567	.348	.625	1.515
9/32	.515	.468	.438	.322	.438	.327	7/16-20	1.875	1.	.632	.382	.75	1.719
5/16	.64	.593	.438	.343	.438	.348	1/2-20	2.	1.	.694	.413	.813	1.875
3/8	.64	.593	.5	.375	.5	.38	9/16-18	2.25	1.125	—	—	—	—
7/16	.765	.719	.562	.375	.562	.38	5/8-18	2.5	1.25	—	—	—	—
1/2	.89	.844	.625	.468	.625	.473	5/8-18	2.5	1.25	—	—	—	—
9/16	.89	.884	.75	.562	.75	.567	3/4-16	3.	1.5	—	—	—	—
5/8	1.015	.968	.875	.657	.875	.663	7/8-14	3.5	1.75	—	—	—	—

By permission of Merriman Holbrook, Inc., Grand River, Ohio.

Table XIV. Properties of Commonly Used Marine Alloys

Nickel Aluminum Bronze. A very high strength corrosion-resistant bronze, used for cast snap shackles, turnbuckles, and furling gear, that has a tensile strength of 115,000 lbs. per sq. inch. Yield 75,000 psi.

Everdur Bronze. A bronze widely used in forgings, such as turnbuckles, snap shackles, and toggles. Everdur provides an excellent combination of strength, corrosion resistance, and ductility, and has a tensile strength of 90,000 lbs. per sq. inch. Yield 55,000 psi.

Manganese Bronze. A high-strength corrosion-resistant bronze widely used where strength is important, in fittings such as large winches, winch handles, genoa and spinnaker slides, pad eyes, headboard shackles, turning blocks, and tiller fittings. Tensile strength is 80,000 lbs. per sq. inch. Yield 40,000 psi.

Navy Bronze. A very ductile, corrosion-resistant bronze used where great strength is not as important as lack of brittleness. Navy bronze is used for tee track, sail track, small winches, cleats, shackles, and some block sheaves. Tensile strength is 40,000 lbs. per sq. inch. Yield 18,000 psi.

Beryllium Copper. A super-strength copper alloy used in castings and forgings where 180,000 lbs. per sq. inch strength is needed. Yield 150,000 psi.

40-E Aluminum. A very strong and corrosion-resistant alloy used for cleats, spinnaker-pole fittings, track end stops, and all other aluminum castings. Tensile strength is 40,000 lbs. per sq. inch. Yield 31,000 psi.

6061 T-6 Aluminum. A wrought-aluminum alloy with excellent corrosion resistance and strength, used for tee track, block sheaves, and spinnaker poles, and in aluminum castings. Tensile strength is 45,000 lbs. per sq. inch. Yield 40,000 psi.

303 Stainless Steel. A free machining stainless steel with good corrosion resistance, used for shafts, axles, and pins. Strength is 90,000 lbs. per sq. inch. Yield 35,000 psi.

303 SE Stainless Steel. Very similar to standard 303 except that the addition of selenium makes it suitable for swage fittings. Strength is 90,000 lbs. per sq. inch. Yield 35,000 psi.

302/304 Stainless Steel. Very similar to 303 but used in the form of flat bar, strip, and sheet for block straps, clevis pins, pins and cotter pins, also in forgings for block swivels and life-rail eyes. Strength is 90,000 lbs. per sq. inch. Yield 35,000 psi.

316 Stainless Steel. Similar but more corrosion resistant than 303, used for precision castings such as headboard shackles, genoa cars, and spinnaker slides. Strength is 90,000 lbs. per sq. inch. Yield 35,000 psi.

22-13-5 Stainless Steel. A very high-strength corrosion-resistant alloy used for rod rigging and pins. This alloy is resistant to stress corrosion cracking and intergranular corrosion, and has a tensile strength of 170,000 lbs. Yield 135,000 psi.

17-4 Stainless Steel. A super-strength stainless steel gives up some corrosion resistance for its tensile strength of 180,000 psi. It is used for precision castings of winch pawls, gears, snap shackles, and pins. Yield 170,000 psi.

Monel Metal. An extremely stiff and corrosion-resistant nickel alloy used for plunger pins in snap shackles, has a tensile strength of 100,000 psi. Yield 80,000 psi.

MP-35-N Alloy. A very expensive alloy of nickel, cobalt, chromium, and molybdenum that is unequaled for strength and corrosion resistance. It is absolutely inert to corrosion by seawater and has a tensile strength of 300,000 psi. It is used for rod rigging and pins. Yield 290,000 psi.

By permission of Merriman Holbrook, Inc., Grand River, Ohio.

Table XV. Galvanic Series in Sea Water

Corroded End (Least Noble)

Magnesium
Magnesium alloys

Aluminum CB75 (anode alloy)
Aluminum B605 (anode alloy)
Zinc
Galvanized steel

Aluminum 7072
Aluminum 5456
Aluminum 5086
Aluminum 5052
Aluminum 3003, 1100, 6061, 356
Aluminum 6053
Alclad

Cadmium

Aluminum 2024
Aluminum 2117 (rivet alloy)

Mild steel
Wrought iron
Cast iron
Hi-resist irons

13% Cr stainless steel Type 410 (active)
50-50 Lead-tin solder

18-8 Stainless steel Type 304 (active)
18-8-3 Stainless steel Type 316 (active)

Incoloy alloy 825 (active)
Inconel alloy 718 (active)

Lead
Tin

Muntz metal
Manganese bronze

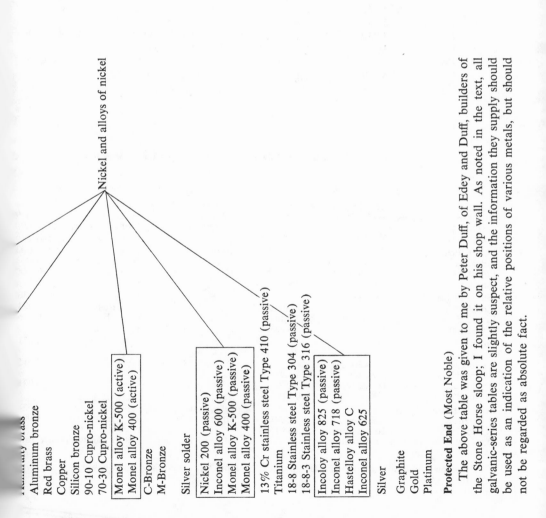

Admiralty brass
Aluminum bronze
Red brass
Copper
Silicon bronze
90-10 Cupro-nickel
70-30 Cupro-nickel

Monel alloy K-500 (active)
Monel alloy 400 (active)

C-Bronze
M-Bronze

Silver solder

Nickel 200 (passive)
Inconel alloy 600 (passive)
Monel alloy K-500 (passive)
Monel alloy 400 (passive)

13% Cr stainless steel Type 410 (passive)
Titanium
18-8 Stainless steel Type 304 (passive)
18-8-3 Stainless steel Type 316 (passive)

Incoloy alloy 825 (passive)
Inconel alloy 718 (passive)
Hastelloy alloy C
Inconel alloy 625

Silver

Graphite
Gold
Platinum

Nickel and alloys of nickel

Protected End (Most Noble)

The above table was given to me by Peter Duff, of Edey and Duff, builders of the Stone Horse sloop; I found it on his shop wall. As noted in the text, all galvanic-series tables are slightly suspect, and the information they supply should be used as an indication of the relative positions of various metals, but should not be regarded as absolute fact.

Table XVI. Diameter–Circumference Equivalents

Diam., in Ins.	Circum., in Ins.	Nearest Frac. Circumference, in Ins.		Diam., in Ins.	Circum. Ins.	Nearest Frac. Circumference, in Ins.	
¼	0·785	¾	−	1½	4·712	4¾	+
⁵⁄₁₆	0·981	1	+	1⁹⁄₁₆	4·908	5	+
⅜	1·178	1¼	+	1⅝	5·105	5⅛	+
⁷⁄₁₆	1·374	1⅜	=	1¹¹⁄₁₆	5·301	5⅜	+
½	1·570	1½	−	1¾	5·497	5½	=
⁹⁄₁₆	1·767	1¾	−	1¹³⁄₁₆	5·694	5¾	+
⅝	1·963	2	+	1⅞	5·890	5⅞	−
¹¹⁄₁₆	2·159	2³⁄₁₆	+	1¹⁵⁄₁₆	6·086	6	−
¾	2·356	2⅜	+	2	6·283	6¼	−
¹³⁄₁₆	2·552	2½	−	2⅛	6·675	6⅝	−
⅞	2·748	2¾	=	2¼	7·068	7	−
¹⁵⁄₁₆	2·945	3	+	2⅜	7·461	7½	+
1	3·141	3⅛	−	2½	7·853	7⅞	+
1⅛	3·534	3½	−				
1³⁄₁₆	3·730	3¾	+				
1¼	3·926	4	+				
1⁵⁄₁₆	4·123	4⅛	=				
1⅜	4·319	4⅜	+				
1⁷⁄₁₆	4·516	4½	−				

To convert diameter into circumference, multiply by 3·14159.

To convert circumference into diameter, multiply by 0·3183.

Courtesy of Norseman Ropes Ltd.

Table XVII. Conversion to and from Metric Measures

English Measures to Metric Measures			*Metric Measures to English Measures*		
Pounds	To Kilograms	× 0·45357	Kilograms (Kilos)	To Pounds	× 2·204
Long Hundredweights (Cwts.) *	To Kilograms	× 50·80	Kilograms	To Long Cwts.	× 0·019
			Kilograms	To Long Tons	× 0·000
Long Tons *	To Kilograms	× 1016·00	Millimeters	To Inches	× 0·039
Lineal Inches	To Millimeters	× 25·3999	Millimeters	To Feet	× 0·003
Lineal Feet	To Millimeters	× 304·7997	Millimeters	To Yards	× 0·001
Lineal Yards	To Millimeters	× 914·3992	Millimeters	To Fathoms	× 0·000
Lineal Fathoms	To Millimeters	× 1828·7984	Meters	To Inches	× 39·37
Lineal Inches	To Meters	× 0·0254	Meters	To Feet	× 3·280
Lineal Feet	To Meters	× 0·3048	Meters	To Yards	× 1·093
Lineal Yards	To Meters	× 0·9144	Meters	To Fathoms	× 0·546
Lineal Fathoms	To Meters	× 1·8288	Kilos per Lineal Meter	To Pounds per Foot	× 0·671
Pounds per Lineal Foot	To Kilos per Meter	× 1·4881	Kilos per Lineal Meter	To Pounds per Yard	× 2·015
Pounds per Lineal Yard	To Kilos per Meter	× 0·4960	Kilos per Lineal Meter	To Pounds per Fathom	× 4·031
Pounds per Lineal Fathom	To Kilos per Meter	× 0·2480	Kilos per Sq. mm.	To Long Tons per Sq. Inch	× 0·63
Long Tons per Sq. Inch	To Kilos per Sq. mm.	× 1·5748	Sq. mm.	To Square Inch	× 0·00
Square Inch	To Sq. mm.	× 645·1549			

One-eighth of an inch of Circumference = One mm. of Diameter.

Mm. of Diameter ÷ 8 = Circumference in inches.

*A long hundredweight equals 112 pounds; a long ton equals 20 hundredweights or 2,240 pounds.

Fractions of an Inch to Decimals of an Inch and to Millimeters

Inches	Inches	Millimeters	Inches	Inches	Millimeters
1/64	0·015625	0·3969	33/64	0·515625	13·0969
1/32	0·03125	0·7938	17/32	0·53125	13·4938
3/64	0·046875	1·1906	35/64	0·546875	13·8906
1/16	0·0625	1·5875	9/16	0·5625	14·2875
5/64	0·078125	1·9844	37/64	0·578125	14·6844
3/32	0·09375	2·3812	19/32	0·59375	15·0812
7/64	0·109375	2·7781	39/64	0·609375	15·4781
1/8	0·125	3·175	5/8	0·625	15·875
9/64	0·140625	3·5719	41/64	0·640625	16·2719
5/32	0·15625	3·9688	21/32	0·65625	16·6688
11/64	0·171875	4·3656	43/64	0·671875	17·0656
3/16	0·1875	4·7625	11/16	0·6875	17·4625
13/64	0·203125	5·1594	45/64	0·703125	17·8594
7/32	0·21875	5·5562	23/32	0·71875	18·2562
15/64	0·234375	5·9531	47/64	0·734375	18·6531
1/4	0·25	6·35	3/4	0·75	19·05
17/64	0·265625	6·7469	49/64	0·765625	19·4469
9/32	0·28125	7·1438	25/32	0·78125	19·8438
19/64	0·296875	7·5406	51/64	0·796875	20·2406
5/16	0·3125	7·9375	13/16	0·8125	20·6375
21/64	0·328125	8·3344	53/64	0·828125	21·0344
11/32	0·34375	8·7312	27/32	0·84375	21·4312
23/64	0·359375	9·1281	55/64	0·859375	21·8281
3/8	0·375	9·525	7/8	0·875	22·225
25/64	0·390625	9·9219	57/64	0·890625	22·6219
13/32	0·40625	10·3188	29/32	0·90625	23·0188
27/64	0·421875	10·7156	59/64	0·921875	23·4156
7/16	0·4375	11·1125	15/16	0·9375	23·8125
29/64	0·453125	11·5094	61/64	0·953125	24·2094
15/32	0·46875	11·9062	31/32	0·96875	24·6062
31/64	0·484375	12·3031	63/64	0·984375	25·0031
1/2	0·5	12·7	1	1	25·4

Feet and Fathoms to Meters

Feet	6	12	18	24	30	36	42	48	54	60
Fathoms	1	2	3	4	5	6	7	8	9	10
Meters	1.8	3.6	5.5	7.3	9.1	10.9	12.8	14.6	16.4	18.3
1	0.3	2.1	3.9	5.8	7.6	9.4	11.3	13.1	14.9	16.7	18.6
2	0.6	2.4	4.2	6.1	7.9	9.7	11.6	13.4	15.2	17.0	18.9
3	0.9	2.7	4.5	6.4	8.2	10.0	11.9	13.7	15.5	17.3	19.2
4	1.2	3.0	4.9	6.7	8.5	10.3	12.2	14.0	15.8	17.7	19.5
5	1.5	3.3	5.2	7.0	8.8	10.6	12.5	14.3	16.1	18.0	19.8

Square Measure, Metric Equivalents

1 square inch	6.451 square centimeters
1 square foot	0.093 square meters
1 square yard	0.836 square meters
100 square feet	9.29 square meters

Liquid Measure, Metric Equivalents

United States		*Imperial*	
1 quart	0.946 liters	1 quart	1.136 liters
1 gallon	3.785 liters	1 gallon	4.545 liters

Courtesy of Norseman Ropes Ltd.

Table XVIII. Periods and Lengths of Sea Waves

Velocity, in Knots	Length, in Feet	Velocity, in Knots	Length, in Feet
1	.56	16	142.4
2	2.23	17	160.8
3	5.01	18	180.2
4	8.90	19	200.8
5	13.90	20	222.5
6	20.0	21	245.3
7	27.2	22	269.2
8	35.6	23	294.3
9	45.0	24	320.4
10	55.6	25	347.7
11	67.3	26	376.1
12	80.1	27	405.5
13	94.0	28	436.2
14	109.0	29	467.8
15	125.2	30	500.6

Courtesy of *Practical Boat Owner*, Tower House, London.

Table XIX. Maximum Wave Size for Given Fetch, Wind Velocity, and Time Duration

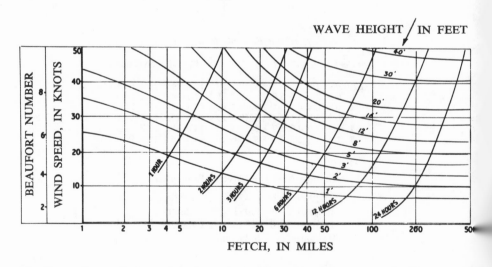

To READ: *Enter wind speed and go along sideways until you meet the line corresponding to the duration of the storm or the fetch, stopping at whichever comes first. At this point the wave heights can be read off.*

Courtesy of *Practical Boat Owner*, Tower House, London.

Table XX. Simplified Laterals of Departure

Δ, in Degrees	A	
1	0.17	Δ is course right or left of the rhumb line.
5	0.87	A is distance from the rhumb line after
10	1.73	ten miles of sailing. A quick rule of
15	2.58	thumb is that this distance is .17 miles
20	3.42	(340 yards) in ten miles, per degree of
25	4.22	divergence from the rhumb line.
30	5.00	Courtesy of H. Marvin Berning, Virgin Islands Engineering and Surveying.

Table XXI. Tacking Downwind

A (in degrees)	B	C (in percents)	
0	–	–	A gives course relative to true wind, in degrees.
5	(Infinitesimal)	(Any increase in speed makes course alteration worth while.)	B gives extra distance traveled by tacking downwind, in miles per mile of direct course. C gives minimum percentage of increase in speed over direct downwind speed required to justify change in course.
10	0.015	1.5	Courtesy of H. Marvin Berning, Virgin Islands Engineering and Surveying.
15	0.035	3.5	
20	0.064	6.4	
25	0.103	10.3	
30	0.154	15.4	
35	0.221	22.1	
40	0.305	30.5	
45	0.414	41.4	
50	0.556	55.6	
55	0.743	74.3	
60	1.000	100.0	

Table XXII. Optimum Course to Steer When Beating to Windward

If your original tacking angle to TRUE wind is:	And you alter the tacking angle to:	You must increase your boat speed at least this percentage to make an improvement in your position to windward:	You may decrease your speed up to this percentage to make an improvement in your position to windward:
40°	30°	—	11.5%
	35°	—	6.5%
	45°	8.3%	—
	50°	19.2%	—
	55°	33.6%	—
	60°	53.2%	—
	65°	81.3%	—
45°	30°	—	18.4%
	35°	—	13.7%
	40°	—	7.7%
	50°	10.0%	—
	55°	23.3%	—
	60°	41.4%	—
	65°	67.3%	—
50°	30°	—	25.8%
	35°	—	21.5%
	40°	—	16.1%
	45°	—	9.1%
	55°	12.1%	—
	60°	28.6%	—
	65°	52.1%	—
	70°	87.9%	—
	75°	148.3%	—
55°	35°	—	30.0%
	40°	—	25.1%
	45°	—	18.9%
	50°	—	10.8%
	60°	14.7%	—
	65°	35.7%	—
	70°	67.7%	—
	75°	121.6%	—
60°	35°	—	39.0%
	40°	—	34.7%
	45°	—	29.3%
	50°	—	22.2%
	55°	—	12.8%
	65°	18.3%	—
	70°	46.2%	—
	75°	93.2%	—
65°	40°	—	44.8%
	45°	—	40.2%
	50°	—	34.3%
	55°	—	26.3%
	60°	—	15.5%
	70°	23.6%	—
	75°	63.3%	—
	80°	143.3%	—

Table XXIII. Total Distance to Be Traveled When Beating to Windward at Various Tacking Angles and Various Wind Directions, and Percentage of Time Spent on Each Tack

Tacking Angle		90°	100°	110°	120°	130°	140°
Ship's Course Relative to the True Wind* Δ, in Degrees		45°	50°	55°	60°	65°	70°
0	A	1.41	1.56	1.74	2.00	2.37	2.92
	B	50	50	50	50	50	50
	C	50	50	50	50	50	50
5	A	1.41	1.55	1.74	1.99	2.36	2.91
	B	54	54	53	53	52	51
	C	46	46	47	47	48	49
10	A	1.39	1.53	1.72	1.97	2.33	2.88
	B	59	57	56	55	54	53
	C	41	43	44	45	46	47
15	A	1.37	1.50	1.68	1.93	2.29	2.80
	B	63	61	59	58	56	55
	C	37	39	41	42	44	45
20	A	1.33	1.46	1.60	1.88	2.22	2.74
	B	68	65	63	61	58	57
	C	32	35	37	39	42	43
25	A	1.28	1.41	1.58	1.81	2.14	2.64
	B	73	70	66	63	60	58
	C	27	30	34	37	40	42
30	A	1.22	1.35	1.51	1.73	2.04	2.53
	B	79	74	71	67	63	61
	C	21	26	29	33	37	39
35	A	1.16	1.27	1.43	1.64	1.93	2.39
	B	85	79	75	70	66	63
	C	15	21	25	30	34	37
40	A	1.08	1.19	1.34	1.53	1.81	2.23
	B	92	85	79	74	70	65
	C	8	15	21	26	30	35
45	A	1.00	1.10	1.23	1.41	1.67	2.06
	B	100	92	85	79	73	68
	C	0	8	15	21	27	32
50	A		1.00	1.12	1.28	1.52	1.87
	B		100	91	84	78	72
	C		0	9	16	22	28
55	A			1.00	1.15	1.36	1.67
	B			100	91	83	76
	C			0	9	17	24
60	A				1.00	1.18	1.46
	B				100	90	82
	C				0	10	18
65	A					1.00	1.23
	B					100	89
	C					0	11

(key on following page)

Table XXIII, Key

A is total distance to be traveled in relation to one mile on the rhumb-line course.

B is percentage of time to be spent on the long tack to end up on the rhumb line.

C is percentage of time to be spent on the short tack to end up on the rhumb line.

Δ is wind direction in degrees right or left of the rhumb-line course.

* Ship's course relative to true wind is considered to be one-half the tacking angle and assumes no wind change and consistent sea conditions on each tack.

Courtesy of H. Marvin Berning, Virgin Islands Engineering and Surveying.

Table XXIV. Weights of Cloth for Various Sails, and Equivalents in American, British, and Continental Measures

MAINSAILS

The rule of thumb of Sol Lamport (American Dacron manufacturer) is

$$\frac{\text{LOA} + \text{mainsail hoist in feet}}{10} = \text{weight, American measure.}$$

The rule of thumb of Howard-Williams (Ratsey and Lapthorn, England) is

$$\frac{\text{Main hoist}}{4} = \text{weight, British measure}$$

Very large mainsails, of over 550 square feet, can be slightly below weight to reduce the difficulty of furling. The amount below weight will be minimal on sloops and cutters (unless they have a very large trysail carried on switch track), as the main is used in heavy weather. On yawls the mainsail weight can be reduced, as in heavy weather they should be able to sail on headsails and mizzen, or on headsails, trysail, and mizzen. On big ketches, the mainsail weight can be substantially reduced, as the mainsail is seldom used in heavy weather.

MIZZENS

On yawls, the mizzen should be just one weight less than the main; despite its small size, this sail needs heavy cloth as it will be used in heavy weather. Similarly, on ketches the mizzen should be the same weight as the main.

WORKING HEADSAILS

The staysail, working jib, and large Yankee, should be the same weight as the mainsail; since the large Yankee is the sail that makes a boat go, the main should be reefed first, and the Yankee may remain up until the wind reaches 18 to 20 knots.

STORM SAILS

Storm sails should be the same weight as working mainsail; if heavier, they become too hard to handle and to stow. The storm trysail on large boats (of at least 60 feet LOA) can be lighter than the main to facilitate ease of handling. The necessary strength can be achieved by Scotch cut, large head, tack, and clew patches, and roping all around.

THREE-QUARTERS WORKING GENOA

This most useful sail should be the same weight as the main; it will frequently be used in conjunction with a reefed main or no main. Since it is only used when the wind is at 10 knots or over, this weight does not create problems.

LIGHT GENOA OR REACHING JIB

On cruising boats this sail can be half the weight of the main, since it will be taken off early in the game when going to windward. On reaches, comparatively light Dacron will hold its shape with a hatful of wind. On cruising boats the light genoa or reacher must be light and easily stowed by a small crew, since space and man-power are limited.

GENOA STAYSAIL

This sail should be one weight below the main. In heavy weather a working stay-sail the same weight as the main will be used instead.

REACHING GENOA STAYSAIL

This sail is set under a high-clewed reaching jib (ballooner) or under a spinnaker. Since it is seldom used going to windward, it can be of very light cloth to facilitate stowage.

Equivalent Sailcloth Weights

sh measure *ces per* *re yard)*	0	1	2	3	4	5	6	7	8	9	10	11	12	13	14	15	16	17	18	19	20
rican measure *ces per run-* *yard—28½* *'s wide)*		1	2	3	4	5	6	7	8	9	10	11	12	13	14						
inental measure *ns per square* *r)*	0	50	100	150	200	250	300	350	400	450	500	550	600								

Table XXV. Identification of Label-less Cans

Campbell, V-8, Franco-American, and Swanson products can be identified by means of the code stamped on the can end. Where there are three rows of characters, the code is given in the top row; where there are two rows, the code is shown as the last two characters in the bottom row.

01
CEXN3
810

CR C7
BY933

Tomato	01	Cream of Celery	16
Vegetable	02	Onion	17
Cream of chicken	03	Beef Broth (Cond.)	18
Consomme	04	Green Pea	19
Chicken w/Rice	05	Cream of Asparagus	20
Chicken Vegetable	07	Beef Noodle	22
Chicken Gumbo	08	Vegetable Beef	23
Black Bean	10	Turkey Noodle	24
Beef	11	Chicken Noodle	25
Clam Chowder (Man.)	12	Cream of Mushroom	26
Pepper Pot	13	Scotch Broth	28
Minestrone	14	Bean w/Bacon	29
Vegetarian Vegetable	15	Turkey Vegetable	31

(continued)

Table XXV. Identification of Label-less Cans (Continued)

Vegetable Bean	32	Chicken Giblet Gravy	J6
V-8 Vegetable Juice	33	Cream of Shrimp	J7
Tomato Juice	36	Macaroni & Cheese	J8
Chili Bean	37	Macaroni & Beef	L1
Tomato Rice	43	Chunky Beef	L2
Split Pea w/Ham	46	Chunky Sirloin Burger	L8
Cheddar Cheese	47	Golden Mushroom	M3
Beef Gravy	50	Beef Stew	M5
Spaghetti	51	Chicken Stew	M6
Spaghetti w/Meatballs	54	Brown Gravy w/Onions	M9
Pork & Beans	55	Beans & Franks	N6
Chicken Gravy	57	Barbecue Beans	N8
Spaghetti w/Gr. Beef	59	Beans & Beef	N9
Mushroom Gravy	60	SpaghettiOs	R0
Chili Con Carne	61	Cream of Potato	R4
		Stockpot	R6
Clam Chowder (N.E.)	A0	Tomato Bisque	T9
Oyster Stew	A9	Home-style Pork & Beans	U1
Noodles w/Ground Beef	B6	SpaghettiOs w/Meatballs	U5
Chicken Dumplings	C9	Chicken Noodle-Os	U6
Old-Fashioned Vegetable	E1	Tomato Beef Noodle-Os	W6
Chicken & Stars	F3	Chunky Vegetable	W7
SpaghettiOs w/Franks	F7	Chunky Chicken	W9
Hot-Dog Bean	F9	Rice Pudding	X3
Boned Chicken w/Broth	G7	Golden Veg. Noodle-Os	X7
Boned Turkey w/Broth	G8	Chunky Turkey	X8
Chicken Spread	H1	Curly Noodle	Y2
Beef Broth	H2	Chunky Clam Chowder	Y3
Chicken Broth	H3		

From *Meals Ahoy!*, Campbell Soup Company.

BIBLIOGRAPHY

Design

Baader, Juan, *The Sailing Yacht,* New York, Norton, 1965.
Beiser, Arthur, *The Proper Yacht,* New York, Macmillan, 1966.
Birt, Douglas H. C., *Sailing Yacht Design,* Southampton, Robert Ross & Co., 1951.
Chapelle, Howard I., *Yacht Designing and Planning,* revised, New York, Norton, 1971.
Fox, Uffa, *According to Uffa,* New York, St. Martin's, 1961.
—— *Crest of the Wave,* London, Peter Davis, 1939.
—— *Racing and Cruising Design,* New York, Scribner's, 1938.
—— *Sail and Power,* New York, Scribner's, 1937.
—— *Sailing Boats,* New York, St. Martin's, 1960.
—— *Sailing, Steamship and Yacht Construction,* New York, Scribner's, 1934.
—— *Thoughts on Yachts and Yachting,* New York, Scribner's, 1939.
—— *Uffa Fox's Second Book,* New York, Scribner's, 1935.
Herreshoff, L. Francis. *The Common Sense of Yacht Design,* New York. Rudder Publishing Co., 1946.
Illingworth, John, *Further Offshore,* Chicago, Quadrangle Books, 1969.
Marchaj. C. A., *Sailing Theory and Practice,* New York, Dodd, Mead, 1964.
Skene's Elements of Yacht Design, revised by Francis S. Kinney, New York, Dodd, Mead, 1962.

Construction

Bell, Charles, *How to Build Fiberglass Boats,* New York, Coward-McCann, 1957.
Chapelle, Howard I., *Boatbuilding,* New York, Norton, 1941.
Cobb, Boughton, *Fiberglass Boats, Construction and Maintenance,* Third Edition, New York, Yachting Publishing Corp., 1969.
Gibbs and Cox, Staff of, *Fiberglass Marine Design,* New York, McGraw-Hill, 1960.
—— *Marine Survey Manual,* Tuckahoe, John de Graff, 1962.
Smith, Hervey Garrett, *Boat Carpentry,* Princeton, Van Nostrand, 1955.

Navigation

The American Practical Navigator, originally by Nathaniel Bowditch (issued by the U. S. Naval Oceanographic Office), Washington. U.S. Government Printing Office, periodically revised.
Blewitt, Mary, *Celestial Navigation for Yachtsmen,* Tuckahoe, John de Graff, 1967.
Chapman, Charles F., *Piloting, Seamanship and Small Boat Handling,* New York, Motor Boating, periodically revised.
Devereux, Frederick L., Jr., *Practical Navigation for the Yachtsman,* New York, Norton, 1972.
Mixter, George W., *Primer of Navigation,* Third Edition, edited by Donald McClench, Princeton, Van Nostrand, 1967.
—— and Williams, Ramon, *Navigation Problems and Solutions,* Princeton, Van Nostrand, 1951.

Sails and Their Care

Bowker, R. M. and Budd, S. A., *Make Your Own Sails,* New York, Macmillan, 1960.
Gray, Alan, *Sailmaking Simplified,* New York, Rudder Publishing Co., 1932.
Howard-Williams, Jeremy, *The Care and Repair of Sails,* New York, Norton, 1976.
—— *Sails,* Third Edition, Tuckahoe, John de Graff, 1972.
Ratsey, Ernest A. and de Fontaine, W. H., *Yacht Sails, Their Care and Handling,* New York, Norton, 1948.

Passage Making

Bruce, Errol, *Deep Sea Sailing,* New York, D. Van Nostrand Comp. Inc., 1953.
Coles, K. Adlard, *Heavy Weather Sailing,* Tuckahoe, John de Graff, 1968.

Hiscock, Eric, *Cruising Under Sail,* London, Oxford University Press, 1967.
—— *Voyaging Under Sail, London,* Oxford University Press, 1959.
Worth, Claud, *Yacht Cruising,* New York, Yachting Inc., 1926.
—— *Yacht Navigation and Voyaging,* New York, Yachting Publishing Corp., 1927.

See also the list of publications at the beginning of Sources of Supply.

INDEX

The Author

DONALD M. STREET, Jr., basically lives wherever *Iolaire*'s anchor happens to be down; he winters in the eastern Caribbean and summers in Glandore, Ireland. He is the major Lloyd's insurance broker in the eastern Caribbean, serves as a design consultant on new construction and on the redesign of older boats, is agent for Cheong Lee sails, and in order to keep in touch with the latest developments in cruising yachts, delivers boats from the United States to the Islands. Besides the two volumes of *The Ocean Sailing Yacht,* he has written *Cruising Guide to the Lesser Antilles* and *Yachting Guide to the Grenadines,* and his articles have appeared in *Yachting, Sail, Boating, WoodenBoat, Yachting Monthly,* and *The Telltale Compass.*

The Illustrator

BRUCE BINGHAM is a boatbuilder, designer, surveyor, and marine illustrator and writer. He regularly illustrates marine catalogs, and produces detailed perspective drawings for boatbuilders, riggers, and sailing-instruction programs; his "Sailor's Sketchbook" is in its fifth year in *Sail* magazine. He has produced a book on yacht construction and has illustrated several books. Bingham lives aboard his schooner, *At Last.*